MODERN ADVANCED ACCOUNTING

MODERN ADVANCED ACCOUNTING

Second Edition

WALTER B. MEIGS, Ph.D., C.P.A.
Emeritus Professor of Accounting
University of Southern California

A. N. MOSICH, Ph.D., C.P.A.
William C. Hallett Professor of Accounting
University of Southern California

E. JOHN LARSEN, D.B.A., C.P.A.
Associate Professor of Accounting
University of Southern California

McGraw-Hill Book Company

New York   St. Louis   San Francisco   Auckland   Bogotá   Düsseldorf   Johannesburg
London   Madrid   Mexico   Montreal   New Delhi   Panama   Paris
São Paulo   Singapore   Sydney   Tokyo   Toronto

Library of Congress Cataloging in Publication Data

Meigs, Walter B
    Modern advanced accounting.

    Includes bibliographical references and index.
    I. Accounting. I. Mosich, A. N., joint author.
II. Larsen, E. John, joint author. III. Title.
HF5635.M494 1979   657'.046   78-12040
ISBN 0-07-041201-4

This book was set in Vega by Monotype Composition Company, Inc.
The editors were Donald E. Chatham, Jr., Marjorie Singer, and Edwin Hanson;
the cover was designed by Charles A. Carson;
the production supervisor was Dennis J. Conroy.
Fairfield Graphics was printer and binder.

Material from the Uniform CPA Examinations and Unofficial Answers,
copyright © 1963, 1964, 1965, 1966, 1967, 1968, 1969, 1970, 1971, 1972, 1973,
1974, 1975, 1976, 1977, and 1978, by the American Institute of Certified Public
Accountants, Inc., is reprinted (or adapted) with permission.

CONTENTS

PREFACE   XV

CHAPTER 1   PARTNERSHIP ORGANIZATION AND OPERATION   1

Organization   2

   Characteristics of the partnership   2
   Deciding between a partnership and a corporation   2
   Is the partnership a separate entity?   3
   The partnership contract   4
   Owners' equity accounts for partners   5
   Loans to and from partners   6
   Valuation of investments by partners   6

Income-sharing arrangements   7

   Partners' equity in assets versus share in earnings   7
   Division of net income or loss   7
   Income statement presentation   16
   Statement of partners' capitals   17
   Adjustment of net income of prior years   17

Changes in personnel   19

   Accounting for changes in partnership personnel   19
   Accounting and managerial issues   19
   Admission of a new partner   20
   Purchase of an interest by direct payment to one or more
      partners   21
   Acquisition of an interest by investment   22
   Bonus or goodwill allowed to old partners   23
   Bonus or goodwill allowed to new partner   26
   Retirement of a partner   28

CHAPTER 2   PARTNERSHIP LIQUIDATION; JOINT VENTURES   46

Liquidation of a partnership   46

   The meaning of liquidation   46
   Distribution of loss or gain   47
   Distribution of cash   48
   Determining the settlement with each partner   48
   Division of losses and gains during liquidation   49
   Equity of each partner sufficient to absorb loss from
      liquidation   49

Equity of one partner not sufficient to absorb that partner's share of loss from liquidation 51
Equities of two partners not sufficient to absorb their shares of loss from liquidation 53
Partnership insolvent but partners personally solvent 55
Partnership insolvent and partners personally insolvent 57

Installment payments to partners 60

General principles guiding installment payment procedures 61
Advance planning for installment payments to partners 62
Withholding of cash for unpaid liabilities and liquidation expenses 67

Incorporation of a partnership 69

Joint ventures 70

Present-day ventures 70
Accounting for a joint venture 71
Appendix: Financial Statements for a CPA partnership 88

CHAPTER 3 INSTALLMENT SALES AND CONSIGNMENTS 95

Installment sales 95

Special characteristics of installment sales 96
Methods for recognition of profits on installment sales 97
The installment method of accounting 99
Illustration 1: Single sale of real estate on the installment plan 100
Illustration 2: Sales of merchandise on the installment plan by a dealer 102
Defaults and repossessions 107
Other accounting issues relating to installment sales 108
Financial statement presentation of accounts for installment sales 112

Consignments 114

The meaning of consignments 114
Distinguishing between a consignment and a sale 115
Rights and duties of the consignee 115
The account sales 116
Accounting methods for consignee 117
Accounting methods for consignor 120
Should gross profits on consignments be determined separately? 120
Illustration of accounting methods for consignor 121

Accounting for partial sale of consigned goods 121
Return of unsold merchandise by consignee 124
Advances from consignees 125
Nature of the Consignment Out account 125

CHAPTER 4 ACCOUNTING FOR BRANCHES; COMBINED
FINANCIAL STATEMENTS 142

Branches and divisions 142
Sales agency contrasted with branch 143
Accounting system for a sales agency 143
Accounting system for a branch 145
Reciprocal accounts 145
Expenses incurred by home office and charged to branches 146
Alternative methods of billing merchandise shipments to branch 146
Separate financial statements for branch and home office 147
Combined financial statements for home office and branch 148
Working paper for combined financial statements 151
Billing of merchandise to branches at prices above cost 155
Working paper when billings to branches are made at prices above
cost 159
Treatment of beginning inventories priced above cost 159
Reconciliation of reciprocal accounts 165
Transactions between branches 170
Start-up costs of opening new branches 172

CHAPTER 5 BUSINESS COMBINATIONS 187

Business combinations: why and how? 188

Antitrust considerations 188
Methods for arranging business combinations 189
Establishing the price for a business combination 190

Methods of accounting for business combinations 191

Purchase accounting 191
Determination of cost of a combinee 191
Allocation of cost of a combinee 192
Pooling-of-interests accounting 195
Popularity of pooling accounting 196
Abuses of pooling accounting 200
The Westec Corporation scandal 202
Abuses of purchase accounting 202
Action by the AICPA 203

Conditions requiring pooling accounting   203
Presentation of business combinations in financial statements   206
Disclosure of business combinations in financial statements   208

Appraisal of accounting standards for business combinations   209

Criticism of purchase accounting   209
Criticism of pooling accounting   210
FASB study of accounting for business combinations   210

Appendix: Specified conditions for pooling-of-interests accounting   212

CHAPTER 6   CONSOLIDATED FINANCIAL STATEMENTS: AT DATE OF PURCHASE BUSINESS COMBINATION   233

Nature of consolidated financial statements   233
Should all subsidiaries be consolidated?   234
The meaning of "controlling financial interest"   235
Criticism of traditional concept of control   235
Unconsolidated subsidiaries in consolidated financial statements   235

Consolidation of wholly owned purchased subsidiary at date of business combination   236

Consolidation of partially owned purchased subsidiary at date of business combination   244

Footnote disclosure of consolidation policy   253
Advantages and shortcomings of consolidated financial statements   254

CHAPTER 7   CONSOLIDATED FINANCIAL STATEMENTS: AT DATE OF POOLING BUSINESS COMBINATION   266

Consolidation of wholly owned pooled subsidiary at date of business combination   267

Consolidation of partially owned pooled subsidiary at date of business combination   273

Nature of minority interest   278

CHAPTER 8 CONSOLIDATED FINANCIAL STATEMENTS: SUBSEQUENT TO DATE OF PURCHASE BUSINESS COMBINATION 291

Accounting for operating results of wholly owned purchased subsidiaries 291

Equity method 292
Cost method 292
Choosing between equity method and cost method 292
Illustration of equity method for wholly owned purchased subsidiary 293
Cost method of accounting for wholly owned purchased subsidiary 301

Accounting for operating results of partially owned purchased subsidiary 301

Illustration of equity method of accounting for partially owned purchased subsidiary 301
Illustration of cost method for partially owned purchased subsidiary 309
Concluding comments on equity and cost methods 314

CHAPTER 9 CONSOLIDATED FINANCIAL STATEMENTS: SUBSEQUENT TO DATE OF POOLING BUSINESS COMBINATION 325

Illustration of equity method of accounting for wholly owned pooled subsidiary 325
Illustration of equity method of accounting for partially owned pooled subsidiary 330

Accounting for intercompany transactions not involving profit or loss 334

Loans on notes or open account 335
Leases of real or personal property 338
Rendering of services 339
Income taxes applicable to intercompany transactions 339
Summary: Intercompany transactions and balances 339

CHAPTER 10 CONSOLIDATED FINANCIAL STATEMENTS: INTERCOMPANY PROFITS AND LOSSES 347

Importance of eliminating or including intercompany profits and losses 347

Intercompany sales of merchandise (inventories)   348

    Intercompany sales of merchandise at cost   348
    Intercompany profit in ending inventories   350
    Intercompany profit in beginning and ending inventories   354
    Intercompany profit in inventories and minority interest   355
    Elimination of net profit versus elimination of gross profit   356

Intercompany sales of plant assets and intangible assets   356

    Intercompany profit on sale of land   357
    Intercompany profit on sale of depreciable plant asset   359
    Intercompany profit on sale of intangible asset   364

Purchases of affiliate's bonds   364

    Illustration of purchase of affiliate's bonds   364
    Accounting for gain in subsequent years   368
    Reissuance of intercompany debentures   373

Comprehensive illustration of consolidating financial statements working papers   373

    Concluding comments   383

CHAPTER 11   CONSOLIDATED FINANCIAL STATEMENTS: SPECIAL PROBLEMS   398

    Installment acquisition of parent company's controlling interest in a subsidiary   398
    Changes in parent company's ownership interest in a subsidiary   404
    Subsidiary with preferred stock   409
    Stock dividends distributed by a subsidiary   414
    Treasury stock transactions of a subsidiary   415
    Indirect shareholdings and parent company's stock owned by a subsidiary   416
    Accounting for income taxes for a consolidated entity   418
    Statement of changes in financial position for a consolidated entity   427
    Concluding comments   432

CHAPTER 12   SEGMENT REPORTING; INTERIM STATEMENTS; FINANCIAL FORECASTS   458

Segment reporting   458

    Background of segment reporting   459
    Major issues in segment reporting   459

Specification of segments   460
Segment operating results to be reported   462
Presentation of segment information   467
SEC requirements for segment information   467
Reporting the effects of disposal of a segment of a business   467

Interim financial statements   468

Problems in interim financial statements   469
Misleading interim financial statements   469
APB Opinion No. 28   470
Reporting accounting changes in interim periods   475
Conclusions on interim financial statements   476

Financial forecasts   477

Arguments in support of published financial forecasts   477
Arguments in opposition to published financial forecasts   477
The SEC's position on financial forecasts   478
AICPA pronouncement on financial forecasts   478
Importance of assumptions in forecasting   479
Illustration of financial forecast   479
Conclusion   480
Appendix: Examples of segment reporting   481

**CHAPTER 13   FINANCIAL REPORTING BY MULTINATIONAL
                COMPANIES**   500

Variations in international accounting standards   500

Actions to narrow differences in international accounting and
   auditing standards   501

Accounting for transactions involving foreign currencies   502

FASB Statement No. 8   504
Transactions involving foreign currencies   504
Exchange gains and losses   505
Forward exchange contracts   507

**Consolidated or combined financial statements for foreign
subsidiaries or branches**   515

Current/noncurrent method   517
Monetary/nonmonetary method   517
Current rate method   517

Standards for translation established by the FASB 518
Illustration of translation of foreign currency financial statements 520
Translation of financial statements of foreign subsidiaries 524
Forward exchange contracts for foreign currency exposed positions 524
Financial statement disclosures of foreign currency matters 524
Criticism of *FASB Statement No. 8* 525

CHAPTER 14   BANKRUPTCY AND CORPORATE
             REORGANIZATION   543

Bankruptcy   544

The Bankruptcy Act   544
Ordinary bankruptcy   545
Role of court in ordinary bankruptcy   547
Role of accountant in ordinary bankruptcy   549
Financial condition of debtor company: Statement of affairs   549
Accounting and reporting for receiver or trustee   554
Concluding comment on ordinary bankruptcy   556

Arrangements   556

Petition for arrangement   557
Appointment of receiver or control by debtor   557
Role of creditors   557
Confirmation of arrangement   558
Accounting for an arrangement   558
Disclosure of arrangements   560

Corporate reorganization   561

Petition for reorganization   561
Plan of reorganization   562
Accounting for a corporate reorganization   562
Footnote disclosure of corporate reorganizations   563
Reorganization compared to an arrangement   564
Proposed change in bankruptcy law   564
Concluding comments   565

CHAPTER 15   ACCOUNTING FOR ESTATES AND TRUSTS   580

Legal and accounting aspects of estates   580

Provisions of Uniform Probate Code governing estates   581
Provisions of Revised Uniform Principal and Income Act governing
  estates   584
Illustration of accounting for an estate   585
Concluding comments on accounting for estates   597

Legal and accounting aspects of trusts   597

    Provisions of Uniform Probate Code affecting trusts   597
    Provisions of Revised Uniform Principal and Income Act governing
      trusts   598
    Illustration of accounting for a trust   598

**CHAPTER 16   GOVERNMENT ENTITIES: FUNDS AND
                PROGRAMS**   613

Nature of government entities   613

Theory of accounting for government entities   614

    The governmental accounting entity   615
    The modified accrual basis of accounting   616
    Recording of expenditures rather than expenses   617
    Recording of purchase orders for merchandise and services   617
    Recording the budget   618

Illustrations of accounting for government entities   621

    Accounting for the general fund   622
    Accounting for special revenue funds   630
    Accounting for capital projects funds   630
    Accounting for debt service funds   633
    Accounting for special assessment funds   635
    Accounting for enterprise funds   636
    Accounting for internal (or intragovernmental) service funds   638
    Accounting for trust and agency funds   639
    General fixed assets and general long-term debt groups of accounts   640
    Combined financial statements for governmental units   641
    Checklist of accounting for government entities   641
    Criticism of accounting for government entities   641
    Prototype consolidated financial statements of United States
      Government   643
    Appendix: Prototype Consolidated Financial Statements of United
      States Government   645

**CHAPTER 17   ACCOUNTING FOR NONPROFIT
                ORGANIZATIONS**   669

Characteristics of nonprofit organizations   671

Accounting for nonprofit organizations   672

    Unrestricted fund   672
    Restricted fund   679

Endowment fund   680
Agency fund   681
Annuity and life income funds   681
Loan fund   682
Plant fund   683
Financial statements for nonprofit organizations   684
FASB interest in accounting for nonprofit organizations   684
Appendix: Financial Statements and Notes of Financial
 Accounting Foundation   686

CHAPTER 18 ACCOUNTING AND REPORTING FOR THE SEC   702

Organization and scope of the SEC   703
Role of the SEC in establishment of accounting principles   703
Role of the SEC in initial offerings of securities   711
Reporting to the SEC by publicly owned companies   716
Rules for proxies and tender offers   717
Recent developments in accounting and reporting for the SEC   718

APPENDIX: COMPOUND INTEREST TABLES   725

INDEX   739

PREFACE

This edition of **Modern Advanced Accounting** represents a major revision of the popular first edition. The number of chapters devoted to the discussion of business combinations and consolidated financial statements has been expanded from five to seven, and the chapter on present value concepts and applications in the first edition has been replaced by a new chapter, "Accounting and Reporting for the SEC." The number of chapters has been held to eighteen in recognition of the fact that the time allotted to the advanced accounting course is now seldom more than one semester or two quarters.

Highlights of the second edition

New and challenging topics characterize this edition of **Modern Advanced Accounting** despite its relatively compact size. The coverage includes many of the current controversial topics which have stirred the accounting profession and the financial community in recent years. Considerable attention is given to issues dealing with the pooling-of-interests concept of accounting for business combinations (including the **FASB Discussion Memorandum** on this subject), interim statements, financial forecasts, reporting for segments of a business enterprise, financial reporting by multinational companies (including a discussion of **FASB Statement No. 8**), accounting for nonprofit organizations, and accounting and reporting requirements of the Securities and Exchange Commission.

The traditional topics of advanced accounting are presented in concise fashion. Thus, partnerships and joint ventures are covered in the first two chapters which carry the student from the basic concepts often summarized in introductory accounting to the CPA examination level, with its more complex problems of profit-sharing, realignment of ownership equities, and liquidation. Chapter 3, "Installment Sales and Consignments," has been updated and placed in the first section of the book. Chapter 4, "Accounting for Branches; Combined Financial Statements," provides a logical stepping-stone to the important area of business combinations in Chapter 5. Chapter 4 also sets the stage for the discussions and illustrations of consolidated financial statements, which comprise a major portion of the book and are presented in a carefully coordinated and realistic format in Chapters 6 through 11.

The chapter in the first edition dealing with consolidated financial statements at the date of a business combination has been expanded into two chapters, one devoted to purchase combinations and one devoted to pooling combinations. Similarly, the chapter in the first edition dealing with consolidated financial statements subsequent to the date of a business combination has been expanded into two separate chapters addressed to purchase combinations and to pooling combinations.

The remainder of the book includes individual streamlined chapters on the following topics: Segment reporting, interim statements, and financial forecasts; financial reporting by multinational companies; bankruptcy and corporate reorganization; accounting for estates and trusts; government entities; nonprofit organizations; and accounting and reporting for the Securities and Exchange Commission. In earlier advanced accounting textbooks some of these topics either were not covered or were covered in more than one chapter.

Carefully selected financial statements, or portions thereof, recently published by a large CPA firm, by the United States government, by a nonprofit organization, and by leading corporations are presented in appendices at the end of appropriate chapters so that many of the theoretical concepts in the text may be traced to real-world situations. Compound interest tables are presented in an appendix at the end of the book.

The authoritative pronouncements of the Financial Accounting Standards Board, the AICPA, the SEC, and the now-defunct Accounting Principles Board are interwoven into the discussion and in problem material throughout the book. However, we believe that an accounting textbook should encourage students to participate in a critical evaluation of accounting principles and should make students aware of the conflicts and shortcomings that exist within the traditional structure of accounting theory. We have therefore tried to provide students with an analytical basis for making this evaluation, to help them see that most of the controversial areas of accounting ultimately center on underlying issues and questions to which there are no neat and simple answers.

Review questions, exercises, short cases for analysis and decision, and problems

In providing four levels of problem material at the end of each chapter, this book goes well beyond the conventional range of textbooks in advanced accounting.

The *review questions* are intended for use by students as a self-testing and review device to measure their comprehension of key points in each chapter. Many of the questions are provocative, which makes them suitable for written assignments and leads to lively class discussion.

The *exercises* typically cover a specific important point or topic and generally do not require extensive computations. Many instructors may wish to use the exercises to supplement problem assignments, for class discussion, and for examination purposes.

The *short cases for analysis and decision* generally require some analytical reasoning but involve little or no computational effort by students. In these short cases students are called upon to analyze business situations, to apply generally accepted accounting principles, and to propose a course of action. However, students are not required to prepare lengthy working papers or otherwise to manipulate accounting data on an extensive scale. The short cases have been class-tested and have proven to be an effective means of encouraging students to take clear-cut positions in the argument of controversial accounting issues. A number of the cases have been adapted from recent Uniform CPA Examinations, and are especially recommended if the instructor wishes students to develop skill in communicating accounting concepts and to weigh the merits of opposing arguments.

The **problems** range in difficulty from simple to complex and in the length of time required for solution—from 15 minutes to more than an hour. Some of the problems also are adapted from recent Uniform CPA Examinations, and many have been designed especially to demonstrate the concepts presented in the theoretical discussion. Probably no more than a third of the short cases and problems would be used in a single offering of a course in advanced accounting; consequently, ample opportunity exists to design homework assignments for different sections and from semester to semester.

The *Study Guide*

An important supplement accompanying this edition is a *Study Guide* prepared by the authors of the textbook and designed to help students measure their progress by immediate feedback. The *Study Guide* contains for each chapter an outline of the most important points in the textbook, plus a variety of objective questions and short exercises. Answers to the questions and exercises appear in the back of the *Study Guide* to help students in a prompt self-evaluation of their understanding of significant subject matter included in each chapter. Experience indicates that the use of the *Study Guide* increases student understanding of the subject matter with a minimum of additional effort.

Partially filled-in working papers (accounting work sheets)

A set of partially filled-in working papers for all problems is published separately for use by students. On these working papers the company names, the problem numbers, numerous headings, and some preliminary data (such as trial balances) have been entered to save students time and to facilitate rapid review by the instructor.

Teaching aids

A full complement of teaching aids is available for instructors who adopt *Modern Advanced Accounting*. In addition to a complete solutions manual the publisher has prepared a book of examination questions, a set of transparencies for problem solutions, and a checklist of key figures for problems.

The **solutions manual** contains complete answers to all questions, exercises, short cases, and problems. A brief description, time estimate, and a difficulty rating are given in the solutions manual for each case and problem.

One of the new supplements accompanying this edition is a bound book of **Examination Questions** with test material arranged chapter by chapter for the entire text. Numerous true or false questions, completion statements, multiple-choice questions, and short problems are included for each chapter. This book of examination questions should be a most useful source for instructors who prefer to assemble their own examinations to emphasize certain chapters or topics. The increased use of objective questions on the Uniform CPA Examinations has provided an extensive source of this type of test material. The use of these questions should aid students preparing for the Accounting Theory and Accounting Practice sections of the Uniform CPA Examination, as well as providing comprehensive testing over the subject matter covered in each chapter.

Another new feature is a set of **transparencies** for instructors who wish to display in the classroom complete solutions for problems assigned for homework. These transparencies are considered by many instructors to be an effective means of showing good solutions format for the more complex problems. The checklist of key figures for problems is available at no cost and in quantity to instructors who wish to distribute it to students. The purpose of the checklist of key figures is to aid students in verifying solutions for problems assigned as homework.

Contributions by others

The many instructors and students who used the first edition of **Modern Advanced Accounting** have contributed immeasurably to the improvement of this edition. Their suggestions for modification of certain problems and expansion or contraction of numerous sections of the text material have been most useful. Especially helpful was the advice received from Professors Howard L. Godfrey, University of North Carolina, Charlotte; Russell D. Langer, California State University, San Francisco; Richard A. Scott, Virginia Commonwealth University; Peter A. Budwitz, Central Connecticut State College; Charles F. Louie, The University of Santa Clara; James Graham, University of Wisconsin, Superior; Arthur A. Hiltner, The University of North Dakota, Grand Forks; Orville Keister, University of Akron, Akron; James Adler, University of Illinois, Chicago Circle; Hein F. Redelinghuys, The University of Texas at Dallas; Russell J. Petersen, University of Illinois; Robert W. Hill, California Polytechnic University, San Luis Obispo; Richard L. Strayer, California State University, Northridge; Stewart Berkshire, California State University, Long Beach; Philip Fu, The Chinese University of Hong Kong; Jon G. Norem,

University of Northern Iowa; and William R. Smith and Douglas A. Hester, University of Southern California.

We are especially indebted to Professor Joseph F. Guy of Georgia State University for his thorough review of end-of-chapter problem material for accuracy and clarity; to the following students at the University of Southern California—George Saunders, James Costello, John Antoci, Randall Nishiyama, and David White; and to Dorothy Mosich, Kathleen Larsen, and Judi Takagaki for typing and proofreading the manuscript.

We acknowledge with appreciation permission from the American Institute of Certified Public Accountants to quote from many of its pronouncements and to utilize materials adapted from the Uniform CPA Examinations, and from the Financial Accounting Standards Board which granted us permission to quote from FASB Statements, Discussion Memoranda, Interpretations, and Exposure Drafts. All quotations used are copyrighted © by the Financial Accounting Standards Board, High Ridge Park, Stamford, Connecticut 06905, U.S.A., and are reprinted with permission. Copies of the complete documents are available from the FASB.

A. N. Mosich
E. John Larsen

1
PARTNERSHIP ORGANIZATION AND OPERATION

Much of our discussion of partnerships will be based on the Uniform Partnership Act which has been adopted by many of the states. This Act defines a *partnership* (often referred to as a *firm*) as "an association of two or more persons to carry on, as co-owners, a business for profit." Although the word *persons* suggests living individuals, a partnership can also include other partnerships among its members; in some states a corporation can become a partner. The creation of a partnership requires no approval by the state; in fact, a partnership may be formed without a written contract, although a carefully formulated written contract is highly desirable.

Partnerships traditionally are associated with the practice of law, medicine, public accounting, and other professions, and also with small businesses. In some states the licensed professional person such as the CPA is forbidden to incorporate on grounds that the creation of a corporate entity might weaken the personal relationship between the practitioner and the client. However, a number of states have approved legislation designed to permit *professional corporations.* A few large industrial and merchandising businesses also operate as partnerships.

ORGANIZATION

Characteristics of the partnership

The basic characteristics of a partnership are briefly summarized below:

Ease of Formation In contrast to a corporation, a partnership may be created by an oral or written contract between two or more persons or may be implied by their conduct. This advantage of convenience and minimum expense in the formation of a partnership in some cases may be offset by certain difficulties inherent in such an informal organizational structure.

Limited Life A partnership may be ended by the death, retirement, bankruptcy, or incapacity of a partner. The admission of a new member to the partnership legally ends the former partnership and establishes a new one.

Mutual Agency Each partner has the authority to act for the partnership and to enter into contracts binding upon it. However, acts beyond the normal scope of business operations, such as the borrowing of funds by a partner, generally do not bind the partnership unless specific authority has been given to the partner to enter into such transactions.

Unlimited Liability The term *general partnership* refers to a firm in which all the partners are personally responsible for debts of the firm and all have authority to act for the firm. Each partner in a general partnership is personally responsible for the liabilities of the firm. Creditors who are having difficulty in collecting from the partnership will be likely to turn to those individual members of the firm who have other financial resources. In a *limited partnership* one (or more) of the partners has no personal liability for debts of the partnership. The activities of limited partners are somewhat restricted, and they must maintain an agreed investment in the partnership. Statutes providing for limited partnerships require that the firm identify itself publicly as a limited partnership and that at least one member of the firm be a general partner.

Co-ownership of Partnership Property and Earnings When individuals invest assets in a partnership, they retain no claim to those specific assets but merely acquire an *equity in all assets* of the partnership. Every member of a partnership has an ownership interest in earnings; in fact, participation in earnings and losses is one of the tests of the existence of a partnership.

Deciding between a partnership and a corporation

One of the most important considerations in choosing between a partnership and the corporate form of business organization is the income tax status of the business and of its owners. A partnership pays no income tax but is required to file an information return showing its revenue and expenses, the amount of its net income, and the division of the net income among the partners. The partners include their respective shares of the **ordinary net income** from the partnership and such items as dividends, capital gains and losses, and charitable contributions on their individual income tax returns, regardless of whether they received more or less than this amount of cash from the partnership during the year.

The corporation is a separate legal entity subject to a corporate income tax. The net income, when and if distributed to stockholders in the form of dividends, is also taxable income to stockholders. Certain corporations with not more than ten stockholders can elect not to be taxed as corporations, provided their income or loss is fully assumed by their stockholders. These "tax-option corporations" file information returns as do partnerships, and their stockholders report on individual tax returns their respective shares of the year's profit or loss. Thus, a partnership can incorporate as a Subchapter S Corporation to gain the advantages of limited liability but at the same time elect to be taxed as a partnership. Income tax rates and regulations are subject to frequent change, and new interpretations of the rules often arise. The tax status of the owners is also likely to change from year to year. For all these reasons, management should regularly review the tax implications of the partnership and corporate forms of organization so that the business entity may adapt most successfully to the tax environment.

The burden of taxation is not the only factor in making a choice between the partnership and the corporate form of organization. Perhaps the factor which most often tips the scales in favor of incorporation is the opportunity for obtaining larger amounts of capital when ownership can be divided into shares of stock, readily transferable, and offering the advantages inherent in the separation of ownership and management.

Is the partnership a separate entity?

In accounting literature, the legal aspects of partnerships have generally received more emphasis than the managerial and financial issues. It has been common practice to distinguish a partnership from a corporation by saying that the former was an association of persons and the latter a separate entity. Such a distinction unfortunately stresses the legal form rather than the economic substance of the business organization. In terms of managerial policy and business objectives, many partnerships are as truly business entities as are corporations. Such parnerships typically are guided by long-range plans not likely to be affected by the admission or withdrawal of a single member. In these firms the accounting policies logically should carry out the concept of the partnership as an entity apart from its owners.

Viewing the partnership as a business entity often will aid in developing financial statements that provide the most meaningful picture of financial position and results of operations. Among the accounting policies to be stressed is continuity in asset valuation, despite changes in the ratio of profit sharing and changes in personnel. Another helpful step may be recognition in expense accounts of the value of personal services rendered by partners who also hold managerial positions. In theoretical discussions considerable support is found for viewing every business as an entity, apart from its owners, regardless of the form of legal organization. A managing partner under this view plays two roles: one as an employee of the entity, and the other as an owner. The value of the personal services rendered by the partner is an expense of managing the business entity.

The inclusion of partners' salaries among expenses has been opposed by some accountants on grounds that partners' salaries may be set at unrealistic levels unrelated to the value of the services and that the partnership is an association of individuals who are owners and not employees of the partnership.

A partnership has the characteristics of a separate entity in that it may hold title to property in its own name, may enter into contracts, and in some states may sue or be sued as an entity. In practice many accountants are accustomed to viewing partnerships as separate entities with continuity of accounting policies and asset valuations not broken by changes in partnership personnel. However, much work must yet be done before generally accepted accounting principles are adequate to guide accountants in recording the admission of a partner to the partnership and the withdrawal of a partner from the partnership.

The partnership contract

Although a partnership may exist on the basis of an oral agreement or be implied by the actions of its members, good business practice demands that the partnership contract be clearly stated in writing. Among the more important points to be covered by the partnership contract are:

1 The date of formation of the partnership, the duration of the contract, the names of the partners, and the name and nature of the partnership.
2 The assets to be invested by each partner, the procedure for valuing noncash investments, and the penalties for failure to invest and maintain the agreed amount of capital.
3 The authority to be vested in each partner and the rights and duties of each.
4 The accounting period to be used, the nature of accounting records, financial statements, and audits by certified public accountants.
5 The plan for sharing net income or loss, including the frequency of income measurement and the distribution of the net income or loss to the partners.
6 The salaries and drawings allowed to partners and the penalties, if any, for excessive withdrawals.
7 Insurance on the lives of partners, with the partnership or surviving partners named as beneficiaries.

8 Provision for the arbitration of disputes and the liquidation of the partnership at the end of the specified term of the contract or at the death or withdrawal of a partner. Especially important in avoiding disputes is agreement upon procedures of valuation of the business and the method of settlement with the estate of a deceased partner.

One advantage of developing an adequate partnership contract with the aid of attorneys and accountants is that the process of reaching agreement on specific issues will develop a better understanding among the partners on many issues which might be highly controversial if not settled at the outset. Of course, it is seldom possible to cover specifically in a partnership contract every issue which may later arise. Revision of the partnership contract generally requires the approval of all partners.

Disputes arising among partners which cannot be resolved by reference to the partnership contract may be settled by arbitration or in courts of law. The partner who is not satisfied with the handling of disputed issues always has the right to withdraw from the partnership.

Owners' equity accounts for partners

Accounting for a partnership differs from accounting for a single proprietorship or a corporation with respect to the sharing of net income and losses and the maintenance of the owners' equity accounts. Although it would be possible to operate a set of partnership accounting records with only one equity account for each partner, the usual practice is to maintain three types of accounts. These equity accounts consist of (1) *capital* accounts, (2) *drawing* or *personal* accounts, and (3) accounts for *loans* to and from partners.

The original investment by each partner in the firm is recorded by debiting the assets invested, crediting any liabilities being assumed by the firm, and crediting the partner's capital account with the current fair value of net assets invested. Subsequent to the original investment, the partner's equity may be *increased* by additional investment of cash or other property and by a share of the partnership net income. The partner's equity in the firm may be *decreased* by withdrawal of cash or other assets and by a share of net losses incurred by the firm.

Another possible source of increase or decrease in partners' equity arises from changes in partnership personnel, as discussed on pages 19–30.

The original investment of assets by partners is recorded by credits to the capital accounts; drawings by partners in anticipation of profits or drawings which are considered salary are recorded by debits to the drawing accounts. However, a large withdrawal which is viewed as a permanent reduction in the ownership equity of a partner should be debited directly to the partner's capital account.

At the end of the accounting period the net income or net loss in the Income Summary account is transferred to the partners' capital accounts in accordance with the partnership contract. The debit balances in the drawing accounts at the end of the year are also closed into the partners' capital accounts. Since the accounting procedures for partners' equity accounts are not subject to state regulations as in the case of capital stock and other stockholders' equity accounts of a corporation, many deviations from the procedures described here are possible.

Loans to and from partners

Occasionally a partner may withdraw a substantial sum from the partnership with the intention of repaying this amount. Such a transaction may be debited to the Notes Receivable from Partners account rather than to the partner's drawing account.

On the other hand, a partner may make an advance to the partnership which is viewed as a loan rather than an increase in the capital account. This type of transaction is recorded by a credit to Loans Payable to Partners and generally is accompanied by the issuance of a note payable. Amounts due from partners may be reflected as assets in the balance sheet and amounts owing to partners shown as liabilities. The classification of these items as current or long-term generally would depend upon the maturity date, although these *related party transactions* may result in noncurrent classification of the partners' loans, regardless of maturity dates.

If a substantial unsecured loan has been made by a partnership to one of the partners and repayment appears doubtful, the better financial statement presentation may be to offset the receivable against the partner's capital account. If this is not done, assets and the owners' equity may be inflated to the point of being misleading. In any event, adequate disclosure calls for separate listing of any receivables from partners.

Valuation of investments by partners

The investment in the firm by a partner often includes assets other than cash. It is imperative that the partners agree upon the current fair value of assets at the time of their investment and that the assets be recorded at current fair values. Any gain or loss resulting from the disposal of such assets during the operation of the partnership or at the time of liquidation will be divided according to the plan for sharing net income and net losses. Equitable treatment of the individual partners, therefore, requires a starting point of current fair values recorded for all assets invested in the firm. It will then follow that partnership gains or losses upon disposal of noncash assets invested by the partners will be limited to the difference between the disposal price and the current fair value of the assets when invested by the partners, adjusted for depreciation or amortization to the date of disposal.

INCOME-SHARING ARRANGEMENTS

Partners' equity in assets versus share in earnings

The equity of a partner in the net assets of the partnership should be distinguished from a partner's share in earnings. Thus, to say that X is a one-third partner is not a clear statement. X may have a one-third equity in the net assets but have a larger or smaller share in the earnings of the firm. Such a statement might also be interpreted to mean that X was entitled to one-third of the earnings, although X's capital account represented much more or much less than one-third of the total ownership equity. To state the matter concisely, partners may agree upon any type of *income-sharing plan* (or *profit and loss ratio*) regardless of the amount of their respective capital accounts. The Uniform Partnership Act states that *if partners fail to specify a plan for sharing net income and net loss, it shall be assumed that they intended to share equally.* Because income sharing is of such great importance, it is extremely rare to find a situation in which the partnership contract is silent on this point.

Division of net income or loss

The many possible arrangements for sharing of net income or loss among partners may be summarized into the following four categories:

1 Equally or in some other ratio
2 In the ratio of partners' capitals as of a particular date, or in the ratio of average capitals during the year
3 Allowing salaries to partners and dividing the remaining net income or loss in a specified ratio
4 Allowing salaries to partners, allowing interest on capitals, and dividing the remaining net income or loss in a specified ratio

These variations in income-sharing arrangements emphasize that the value of personal services rendered by individual partners may vary widely, as may the amounts of capital invested by each. The amount and quality of managerial services rendered and the amount of capital invested are important factors in the success or failure of the partnership. Therefore, it is often logical to provide for salaries to partners and interest on their respective capitals as a preliminary step in the division of net income or loss of the business. Any remaining net income or loss then may be divided equally.

Another factor affecting the success of a partnership may be that one of the partners has very large personal financial resources, which cause the partnership to have a high credit rating. Similarly, partners with names widely known in a professional field or industry may contribute importantly to the success of the partnership even though they may not actively participate in the activities of the partnership. These two factors may be taken into account in devising the income-sharing plan by judicious selection of the ratio in which any remaining net income or loss is divided.

We shall now illustrate how each of the methods of dividing net income or loss may be applied. This series of illustrations is based on data for A & B Partnership, which is assumed to earn net income of $30,000 during the first year of operation. The partnership contract provides that each partner may withdraw $500 on the last day of each month. These drawings are not a factor in dividing net income; they are recorded by debits to the partners' drawing accounts and are not to be regarded as salaries. All other withdrawals, investments, and net income or loss will be entered in the partner's capital accounts.

Partner A originally invested $40,000 on January 1, Year 1, and invested an additional $10,000 on April 1. Partner B invested $80,000 on January 1 and withdrew $5,000 on July 1. These transactions are illustrated in the following capital and drawing accounts for the two partners and the Income Summary account showing a net income of $30,000 to be divided.

General ledger accounts for Year 1

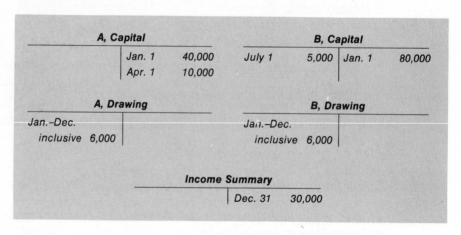

Equal Division of Earnings or in Some Other Ratio Many partnership contracts provide that net income or loss will be divided equally. Also, if the partners have made no specific agreement for sharing earnings, the Uniform Partnership Act provides that an intent of equal division will be assumed. The net income of $30,000 for the A & B Partnership therefore will be transferred from the Income Summary account to the partners' capital accounts by the following journal entry:

Closing the Income Summary account

Income Summary	30,000	
A, Capital		15,000
B, Capital		15,000
To divide the net income equally between A and B.		

The drawing accounts will now be closed to the partners' capital accounts so that each partner's capital account at the end of the year will show the equity resulting from combining the positive factors of beginning capital, subsequent investments, and share of net income with the negative factors of monthly drawings and any other withdrawals of capital.

If the A & B Partnership had reported a net loss of, say, $20,000 during the first year, the Income Summary account would show a debit balance of $20,000. This loss would be transferred to the capital accounts by a debit to each capital account for $10,000 and a credit to the Income Summary account for $20,000.

Assuming that A and B agreed to share earnings in the ratio of 60% to A and 40% to B and that net income amounted to $30,000, the net income would be divided $18,000 to A and $12,000 to B. The agreement that A should receive 60% of the net income (perhaps because of greater experience and personal contacts) would cause Partner A to suffer a larger share of the net loss if the business operated unprofitably. Some partnership contracts provide that a net income is to be divided in a certain ratio such as 60% to A and 40% to B, but that a net loss is to be divided equally or in some other ratio. Another variation intended to compensate for unequal contributions by the partners provides that the agreed ratio (60% and 40% in our example) shall be applicable to a given amount of income but that additional income shall be shared in some other ratio. A profit-sharing plan of this type places extreme importance on the *timing* of partnership income. Close decisions are often necessary in determining whether a given expenditure shall be treated as expense immediately or as a prepayment. Similar decisions may be necessary in deciding whether certain revenue items belong in the current year or in the following year.

Division of Earnings in the Ratio of Partners' Capitals   Division of partnership earnings in proportion to the capital provided by each partner is most likely to be found in partnerships in which substantial investment is the principal ingredient for success. For example, a partnership engaged in purchasing land and holding it for higher prices might select this method of dividing net income. To avoid controversy, it is essential that the partnership contract specify whether the income-sharing ratio is based on the original capital investments, the capitals at the beginning of each year, the capitals at the end of each year (before the distribution of net income or loss), or the average capitals during each year.

Continuing our illustration for the A & B Partnership, assume that the partnership contract calls for division of net income in the ratio of *original capitals.* The first year's net income would be divided as follows:

A: $30,000 × $40,000/$120,000 = $10,000
B: $30,000 × $80,000/$120,000 = $20,000

The journal entry to close the Income Summary account would be similar to the journal entry illustrated on page 8.

Assuming that the net income is divided in the ratio of capitals at the *end of the year* (before drawings and the distribution of net income), the net income for the first year would be divided as follows:

A: $30,000 × $50,000/$125,000 = $12,000
B: $30,000 × $75,000/$125,000 = $18,000

Dividing net income on the basis of (1) original capitals, (2) yearly beginning capitals, or (3) yearly ending capitals may prove inequitable if there are significant changes in capital during the year because of withdrawals or added investments by partners. Use of average capitals as a basis is preferable in that it reflects the capital actually available for use by the partnership during the year.

If the partnership contract provides for sharing net income in the ratio of average capitals during the year, it also should state the amount of drawings each partner may make without affecting the capital account. In our continuing example for the A & B Partnership, the partners are entitled to withdraw $500 monthly, and these drawings are recorded in the drawing accounts. Any additional withdrawals and any investments are entered in the partners' capital accounts and therefore influence the computation of the average capital ratio. The partnership contract also should state whether capital balances are to be computed in terms of dollar-months, dollar-weeks, or dollar-days.

In our example, ratio of average capitals in dollar-months for A and B and division of net income are computed at the top of page 11.

In making these calculations we could have computed the average capital for each partner by dividing each partner's dollar-months by 12. Thus, average capital for A was $570,000 ÷ 12, or $47,500; and average capital for B was $930,000 ÷ 12, or $77,500. The ratio between these average capitals is the same as the ratio of dollar-months in the working paper on page 11.

It is worth repeating that partners may divide earnings in any manner they wish.

A & B PARTNERSHIP
Computation of Average Capitals
For Year 1

Partner	Date	Decrease in capital	Increase in capital	Capital balance	Months unchanged	Dollar-months
A	Jan. 1		$40,000	$40,000	3	$ 120,000
	Apr. 1		10,000	50,000	9	450,000
					12	$ 570,000
B	Jan. 1		80,000	80,000	6	$ 480,000
	July 1	$5,000		75,000	6	450,000
					12	$ 930,000

Total dollar-months for A and B combined $1,500,000

Division of net income:

To A: $30,000 × $570,000/$1,500,000 .... $ 11,400

To B: $30,000 × $930,000/$1,500,000 18,600

Total net income... $ 30,000

Interest on Partners' Capitals with Remaining Net Income or Loss Divided in a Specified Ratio   In the preceding section the plan for dividing the entire net income in the ratio of partners' capital was based on the assumption that invested capital was the dominant factor in profitable operation of the partnership. However, in most cases the amount of invested capital is only one of several factors which are significant in achieving profitable operation. Consequently, many partnerships choose to divide only a portion of net income in the capital ratio, and to divide the remainder equally or in some other ratio.

To allow interest on capitals at an agreed rate of, say, 6% is the same as dividing a *limited portion* of net income in the ratio of partners' capitals. If the partners agree to allow interest on capital as a first step in dividing net income, they should specify the interest rate to be used and also state whether the calculation is to be based on capital accounts at specific dates or on average capitals during the year.

Let us use again our basic illustration for the A & B Partnership with a net income of $30,000 during the first year and capital accounts as shown on page 8. Assume that the partnership contract allows interest on partners' average capitals at 6% with any remaining net income or loss to be divided equally. The net income of $30,000 would be divided as follows:

Division of net income		A	B	Combined
Interest on average capitals:				
A: 6% of $47,500		$ 2,850		$ 2,850
B: 6% of $77,500			$ 4,650	4,650
Subtotal				$ 7,500
Balance ($30,000 − $7,500) divided equally		11,250	11,250	22,500
Totals		$14,100	$15,900	$30,000

The journal entry to close the Income Summary account follows:

Closing the Income Summary account		
Income Summary 30,000		
A, Capital		14,100
B, Capital		15,900
To divide the net income for the year.		

As a separate case, assume that the A & B Partnership was unsuccessful in its first year and sustained a net loss of $1,000. If the partnership contract provides for allowing interest on capitals, this provision **must be enforced regardless of whether operations are profitable or unprofitable.** The only justification for omitting the allowance of interest on partners' capitals during a loss year would be in the case of a partnership contract containing a specific clause requiring such omission. Note in the following analysis that the $1,000 debit balance in the Income Summary account resulting from the operating loss is increased by the allowance of interest to a debit total of $8,500, which is then divided equally between A and B.

Division of net loss		A	B	Combined
Interest on average capitals:				
A: 6% of $47,500		$ 2,850		$ 2,850
B: 6% of $77,500			$ 4,650	4,650
Subtotal				$ 7,500
Resulting deficiency ($1,000 + $7,500) divided equally		(4,250)	(4,250)	(8,500)
Totals		$(1,400)	$ 400	$(1,000)

The journal entry to close the Income Summary account is shown below:

Closing the
Income
Summary
account
with a
debit
balance

A, Capital	1,400	
Income Summary		1,000
B, Capital		400
To divide the net loss for the year.		

At first thought, the idea of a net loss of $1,000 causing one partner's capital to increase and the other partner's capital to decrease may appear unreasonable, but there is sound logic to support this result. Partner B invested substantially more capital in the firm than did A; this capital was used to carry on operations, and the fact that a net loss was incurred in the first year is no reason to deny recognition of B's larger capital investment.

A significant contrast between two of the income-sharing plans we have discussed (the capital-ratio plan and the interest-on-capitals plan) is apparent if we consider the case of a partnership operating at a loss. Under the capital-ratio plan, the partner who has invested more capital will be required to bear a larger share of the net loss. This result may be considered unreasonable, because the investment of capital is presumably not the cause of a net loss. Under the interest-on-capitals plan of sharing earnings, the partner who has invested more capital will receive credit for this factor and thereby will be charged with a lesser share of the net loss or may even end up with a net credit.

We have thus far considered interest allowances on partners' capitals as a technique for sharing partnership earnings equitably but as having no effect on determining the net income or loss of the partnership. Interest on partners' capitals is not an expense of the partnership, but interest on loans from partners is regarded as expense and a factor in determining net income or loss for the period. Similarly, interest earned on loans to partners represents an element of revenue. This treatment is consistent with the point made earlier that loans to and from partners are assets and liabilities of the partnership.

Another item of expense arising from dealings between a partnership and one of its partners is commonly encountered when the partnership rents property from a landlord who is also a partner. Rent expense and a liability for rent payable should be recognized in such situations. The landlord, although a partner, is also a creditor of the partnership.

Salary Allowances with Remaining Net Income or Loss Divided in a Specified Ratio In discussing salaries to partners, we must distinguish clearly between salaries and drawings. Because the word *salary* has a connotation of weekly or monthly cash payments for personal services, the accountant should be quite specific in suggesting and defining the terminology used in accounting for a partnership. We have used the term *drawings* in only one sense: a withdrawal of assets which reduces the partner's equity but plays no part in the division of net income. We shall limit the word *salaries* in partnership accounting to mean a device for sharing net income. When *salaries* is used with this meaning, the division of net income is the same regardless of whether salaries have been paid in cash or accrued in a year-end computation.

A partnership contract which permits partners to make regular withdrawals of specific amounts should clearly state whether such withdrawals are intended to be a factor in the division of earnings. Assume, for example, that the contract states that Partner A may make drawings of $300 monthly and Partner B $800. If the intent is not clearly stated to include or exclude these drawings as an element in the division of net income, controversy is probable because one interpretation will favor A and the opposing interpretation will favor B.

Assuming that Partner A has more experience and ability than Partner B and also devotes more time to the partnership, it seems reasonable that the partners will want to recognize the more valuable contribution of personal services by A in choosing a plan for division of net income. One approach to this objective would be to adopt an unequal ratio: for example, 70% of net income to A and 30% to B. Use of such a ratio usually is not a satisfactory solution, however, for the same two reasons mentioned in criticizing the capital ratio as a profit-sharing plan. A ratio based only on personal services may not reflect the fact that other factors apart from personal services of partners are important in determining the profitability of the partnership. A second significant point is that if the partnership sustains a net loss, the partner rendering the most personal services will absorb the largest portion of that net loss.

A simple solution to the problem of recognizing unequal personal services by partners is to provide in the partnership contract for varying salary allowances to partners, with the remaining net income or loss divided equally or in some other ratio. Let us apply this reasoning to our continuing illustration for the A & B Partnership, and assume that the partnership contract provides for an annual salary of $10,000 to A and $6,000 to B with any remaining net income or loss to be divided equally. The salaries are not actually paid during the year. The first year's net income of $30,000 would be divided as follows:

Division of net income		A	B	Combined
Salaries		$10,000	$ 6,000	$16,000
Balance ($30,000 − $16,000) divided				
equally		7,000	7,000	14,000
Totals		$17,000	$13,000	$30,000

If partners choose to take their monthly salaries in cash, these payments should be debited to the partners' drawing accounts.

Bonus to Managing Partner Based on Income   A partner serving as a manager of the business may be entitled by contract to receive a bonus equal to a given percentage of income. The partnership contract should state whether the basis of the bonus is income before deduction of the bonus or income minus the bonus. For example, assume that the A & B Partnership provides for a bonus to B, the managing partner, of 25% of income *before* deduction of the bonus and that the remaining income is to be divided equally. As in the preceding examples, the income before the bonus is assumed to be $30,000. After the bonus of $7,500 to B, the remaining $22,500 of income would be divided $11,250 to A and $11,250 to B. Thus A would receive $11,250 of the income and B would receive $18,750.

On the other hand, if the partnership contract provides that the basis of the bonus is income *after* a 25% bonus, the bonus would be computed as follows:

Bonus + income after the bonus = $30,000
   Let X = income after the bonus
   .25X = bonus
Then 1.25X = $30,000 income before bonus
      X = $30,000 ÷ 1.25
      X = $24,000
   .25X = $6,000 bonus to B[1]

The net income of $30,000 in this case would be divided as follows: A, $12,000; B, $18,000.

[1] An alternative computation consists of converting the bonus percentage to a fraction. The bonus then can be computed by adding the numerator to the denominator and applying the resulting fraction to the income before the bonus. In the preceding example, 25% is converted to ¼, and by adding the numerator to the denominator, the ¼ becomes ⅕. One-fifth of $30,000 equals $6,000.

The concept of a bonus is not applicable to a net loss; in other words, if a partnership operates at a loss, the bonus provision becomes non-operative. The partnership contract may also specify that extraordinary items or other unusual gains and losses are to be excluded from the basis for the computation of the bonus.

Salaries to Partners with Interest on Capitals   Many partnerships find it reasonable to divide net income by allowing salaries to partners and also interest on their respective capital accounts. Any remaining net income or loss is divided equally or in some other ratio. Such plans have the merit of recognizing that the value of personal services rendered by different partners may vary greatly, and that differences in amounts of invested capital also warrant recognition in devising an equitable plan for sharing net income or loss. The procedures for carrying out this type of plan are the same as illustrated in earlier sections.

Income statement presentation

Explanations of the division of net income between partners may be included in the income statement or in a note accompanying the income statement. This information is sometimes referred to as the *distribution section* of the income statement. The following illustration for the A & B Partnership shows, in a highly condensed income statement for Year 1, the division of net income between the partners:

A & B PARTNERSHIP
Income Statement
For Year 1

Sales	$300,000
Cost of goods sold	180,000
Gross profit on sales	$120,000
Operating expenses	90,000
Net income	$ 30,000
Distribution of net income:	
Partner A	$14,100
Partner B	15,900
Total	$30,000

If salaries paid to partners are included in operating expenses, the amount of such salaries should be disclosed.

Internal reports for use by management in appraising the performance of individual *profit centers* may call for different accounting concepts and classifications from those generally used for the financial statements prepared for outsiders. To develop the most meaningful cost data for internal use, the accountant may treat partners' salaries as expenses rather than as a device for dividing net income. This approach is particularly appropriate if one profit center (for example, a branch) has a partner as active manager and another profit center is managed by a salaried employee. In large organizations with a number of partners of whom only one or two are active in the management of the business, partners' salaries should be viewed as operating expenses similar to payments to employees. This approach follows the view that the partnership is an accounting entity and that all expenses must be deducted from revenue to measure the net income of the entity.

Statement of partners' capitals

Partners generally want a complete explanation of the changes in their capital accounts each year. To meet this need, a *statement of partners' capitals* is prepared as a basic financial statement. The following illustrative statement of partners' capitals for Year 1 is based on the accounts presented on page 8 and also uses the division of net income illustrated on page 16 for the A & B Partnership:

A & B PARTNERSHIP Statement of Partners' Capitals For Year 1			
	A	B	Combined
Partners' capitals, Jan. 1	$40,000	$80,000	$120,000
Additional investment (or withdrawal) of capital	10,000	(5,000)	5,000
Balances before net income and drawings .	$50,000	$75,000	$125,000
Net income	14,100	15,900	30,000
Subtotal	$64,100	$90,900	$155,000
Less: Drawings	6,000	6,000	12,000
Partners' capitals, Dec. 31	$58,100	$84,900	$143,000

A complete set of financial statements for a CPA partnership is presented on pages 88–94.

The combined capital of $143,000 is reported as ownership equity in the balance sheet of the partnership.

Adjustment of net income of prior years

Any business enterprise, whether it be organized as a single proprietorship, partnership, or corporation, will from time to time discover errors made in the measurement of net income in prior years. Examples include errors in the computation of depreciation, errors in inventory valuation, and omission of accruals of revenue or expenses. When such errors come to light, the question arises as to whether the corrections should be treated as part of the determination of net income for the current period or as **prior period adjustments** and entered directly to partners' capitals.

The correction of prior years' net income becomes particularly important when the profit-sharing ratio has been changed. For example, assume that in Year 1 the net income for A & B Partnership was $50,000 and that the partners shared net income equally, but in Year 2 they changed the ratio to 60% for A and 40% for B. During Year 2, it was discovered that the ending inventory for Year 1 had been overstated by $10,000 because of a clerical error. The $10,000 reduction in the net income for Year 1 should be divided $5,000 to each partner, in accordance with the income-sharing ratio which prevailed in the **year in which the error occurred.**

Somewhat related to the correction of errors of prior years is the treatment of nonoperating gains and losses. When the income-sharing ratio of a partnership is changed, the partners should consider the differences which exist between the carrying amount of assets and their current fair values. As a somewhat extreme example, assume that the A & B Partnership owns securities acquired for $20,000 which have risen in value to $50,000 at the date when the income-sharing ratio is changed from 50% for each partner to 60% for A and 40% for B. If the securities were sold for $50,000 just prior to the change in the income-sharing ratio, the $30,000 gain would cause each partner's capital account to increase by $15,000. If the securities were sold for $50,000 immediately after establishment of the 60:40 income-sharing ratio, the $30,000 gain would be divided $18,000 to A and only $12,000 to B.

A solution sometimes suggested for such partnership problems is to revalue the assets to current fair value when the income-sharing ratio is changed or when a new partner is added or an old one retires. In most cases the revaluation of assets may be justified, but in general the continuity of cost valuations in a partnership is desirable, for the same reasons that support the use of the cost principle in a corporation. A secondary objection to revaluation of assets is that, with a few exceptions such as marketable securities, satisfactory evidence of current fair value is seldom available. The best solution to the problem of change in the ratio of income sharing usually may be achieved by making appropriate adjustments among partners' capitals rather than by restating asset values.

When accountants act in the role of management consultants to a partnership, they should bring to the attention of the partners any significant differences between carrying accounts and current fair values of assets, and make the partners aware of the implications of a change in the income-sharing ratio.

CHANGES IN PERSONNEL

Accounting for changes in partnership personnel

Most changes in partnership personnel are accomplished without interrupting the regular operation of the partnership business. For example, when a large and well-established partnership promotes one of its employees to partnership status, there is usually no significant change in the financial condition, the accounting policies, or the operating routines of the business. However, from a legal viewpoint a partnership is dissolved by the retirement or death of a partner or by the admission of a new partner to the partnership.

Dissolution of a partnership may also result from such causes as the bankruptcy of the firm or of any partner, the expiration of a time period stated in the partnership contract, or the mutual agreement of the partners to end their association.[2]

Before trying to summarize accounting principles applicable to dissolution of a partnership, we must consider the wide range of business events to which the term *dissolution* may be applied. These events include, on the one hand, a minor change of ownership interest not affecting operation of the business; on the other hand, a joint decision of all members of a firm to end entirely their business relationship. In the one type of event the going-concern principle, which is so fundamental to accounting policies, is left undisturbed; in the more serious example of dissolution, the going-concern principle must be abandoned. Consequently, it is difficult to formulate a single set of accounting principles to be applied universally to all changes in partnership personnel.

Accountants are concerned with the economic substance of a transaction rather than with its legal form. Therefore, they must evaluate all the circumstances of the individual case in determining how a change in a partnership can be reflected most effectively in the accounting records and in the financial statements. In the remaining pages of this chapter, we shall consider the principal kinds of changes in partnership personnel and illustrate one or more acceptable accounting treatments for each type of change.

Accounting and managerial issues

Although a partnership association is ended in a legal sense when a partner withdraws or a new partner is added, the partnership as a going concern often continues with little outward evidence of change. In cur-

---

[2] The *dissolution* of a partnership is defined by the Uniform Partnership Act as "the change in the relation of the partners caused by any partner ceasing to be associated in the carrying on as distinguished from the winding up of the business."

rent accounting practice, a partner's interest is often viewed as a share in a continuing business which may be transferred, much as shares of stock are transferred between stockholders, without disturbing the continuity of the entity. For example, in a successful firm of certified public accountants, if a partner wishes to retire or a new partner enters the firm, the contract for the change in ownership is usually carefully planned to avoid disturbing client relationships. In a very large CPA firm with hundreds of partners scattered throughout the country, the decision to promote an employee to the rank of partner often may be made by a committee rather than by the action of all partners.

Changes in partnership personnel in any line of business raise a number of complex accounting and managerial issues on which the professional accountant can serve as consultant. Among these issues are the setting of terms for admission of a new partner, the possible revaluation of assets, the development of a new basis for the division of net income, and the determination of the amount to be paid to a retiring partner.

Admission of a new partner

When a new partner is admitted to a small firm of perhaps two or three partners, it is particularly appropriate to consider the fairness and adequacy of past accounting policies and the need for correction of errors in prior years' accounting data. The terms of admission of a new partner often are influenced by the level and trend of past earnings, because they may be indicative of future earnings. Sometimes specific accounting policies, such as the completed-contract method of recognizing profits on long-term construction contracts, may cause the accounting records to convey a misleading impression of operating results in the periods preceding the admission of a new partner.

Adjustments of the accounting records may be necessary to provide an equitable statement of partners' capitals and other elements of financial position before the change in membership of the firm is carried out. Carrying amounts and current fair values of assets often are far apart.

As an alternative to revaluation of the assets, it may be preferable to evaluate the dollar significance of any discrepancies between the accounts and current fair values and to make appropriate adjustment in the terms set for admission of the new partner. In other words, the amounts invested or price paid by the incoming partner can be set at a level which reflects the current fair value of the business even though the carrying amounts of assets remain unchanged in the accounting records. Consideration must be given to the fact that if assets have appreciated in value but such appreciation is ignored, the subsequent disposal of the assets after admission of a new partner will cause the new partner to share in net income which accrued before the new partner joined the firm.

The admission of a new partner to a firm may occur in one of two ways: (1) through the *purchase* of all or part of the interest of one or more of the existing partners, or (2) through the *investment* of assets in the firm by the new partner, with a resultant increase in the net assets of the partnership.

Purchase of an interest by direct payment to one or more partners

If the incoming partner purchases an interest from one or more of the existing partners, the transaction is recorded by opening a capital account for the new partner and decreasing the capital accounts of the selling partners by the same amount. No assets are received by the partnership; the transfer of assets is between two or more individuals.

As a very simple illustration of this situation, assume that L and M are partners sharing earnings equally and each having a capital account balance of $60,000. Partner N (with the consent of M) purchases one-half of L's interest in the partnership. The journal entry to record this change in ownership is:

N buys one-half of L's interest in partnership

L, Capital	30,000	
N, Capital		30,000
To record the transfer of one-half of L's capital to N.		

The price paid by N in buying half of L's interest may have been the carrying amount of $30,000 or it may have been more or less than the carrying amount. Possibly no price was established; L may have made a gift to N of the equity in the partnership, or perhaps N won it in a poker game. Regardless of the terms of the transaction between L and N, the journal entry illustrated above is all that is required in the partnership's accounting records. No change has occurred in the assets, the liabilities, or the total of the owners' equity.

To explore further some of the implications involved in the purchase of an interest by an incoming partner, assume that N paid $40,000 to L for one-half of L's $60,000 equity in the business. Some accountants have suggested that the willingness of the new partner to pay $10,000 in excess of carrying amount for a one-fourth interest in the total capital of the partnership indicates that the total capital should be valued at $40,000 more than presently shown in the accounting records. From this assumption they reason that the assets of the old firm should be written up by $40,000, or goodwill of $40,000 should be recorded as an asset with offsetting credits of $20,000 each to the capital accounts of the old partners, L and M. However, most accountants take the position that the payment by N to L is a personal transaction between them and that the partnership, which has neither received nor distributed any assets, should make no journal entry except to transfer one-half of L's capital to N, the new partner.

What are the arguments for these two opposing views of the purchase of an interest by a new partner? Those who advocate a write-up of assets stress the legal concept of dissolution of the old partnership and formation of a new partnership. This change in identity of owners, it is argued, justifies departure from the going-concern principle and the revaluation of assets to current fair values to achieve an accurate measurement of the capital invested by each member of the new partnership.

The opposing argument, that the purchase of an interest by an incoming partner requires only a transfer from the capital account of the selling partner to the capital account of the new partner, is based on several points. First, the partnership as an entity did not participate in negotiating the price paid by N to L. Many factors other than the valuation of assets may have been involved in the negotiations between the two individuals. Perhaps N paid more than carrying amount because N was allowed very generous credit terms or received more than a one-fourth share in earnings as part of the purchase contract. Perhaps the new partner was very anxious to join the firm because of the personal abilities of L and M or because of the anticipated growth in the particular industry.

Based on these and other similar reasons, we may conclude that the purchase price of an interest transferred from an existing partner to a new partner is not dependable or objectively verifiable evidence to support extensive changes in the carrying amounts of the partnership's assets. This conclusion is equally applicable whether the new partner pays less than carrying amount or more than carrying amount for an interest in the assets of the partnership.

Acquisition of an interest by investment

An incoming partner may gain admission to the firm by investing assets directly in the partnership. The assets which the incoming partner invests are recorded in the firm's accounting records, and consequently the total assets of the firm and its total partners' equity are increased.

As an example, assume that X and Y are partners operating an automobile rental business. They share earnings equally and each has a capital account of $60,000. Assume also that the carrying amounts of the partnership assets are approximately equal to current fair values. Adjacent to the business is a tract of land owned by Z which could be used for expansion of operations. X and Y agree to admit Z to the partnership upon investment of the land; earnings of the new firm are to be shared equally. Cost of the land to Z was $50,000, but the current appraisal indicates it is now worth $80,000.

The admission of Z to the partnership is recorded by the following journal entry:

New partner invests land

Land	80,000	
Z, Capital		80,000
To record admission of Z.		

Z has a capital account $20,000 larger than the capitals of X and Y. In other words Z owns a 40% (or $80,000/$200,000) interest in the firm. The fact that the three partners share earnings equally does not require that their capital accounts be equal.

Bonus or goodwill allowed to old partners

In a profitable, well-established firm, the partners may insist that a portion of the investment by a new member be allowed to them as a bonus or that goodwill be recognized and credited to the original partners. The incoming partner may agree to such terms because of the benefits to be gained by becoming a member of a firm with high earning power.

Bonus to Old Partners   Assume that A and B are partners who share earnings equally and have capital accounts of $45,000 each. The carrying amounts of the partnership assets are assumed to approximate current fair value. The partners agree to admit C to a one-third interest in capital and a one-third share in earnings upon investment of $60,000. The total assets of the new firm will therefore amount to $150,000 (or $45,000 + $45,000 + $60,000). The following journal entry will give C the agreed one-third interest in capital and will divide the $10,000 bonus equally between A and B in accordance with their prior contract to share earnings equally.

Recording bonus to old partners

Cash	60,000	
A, Capital		5,000
B, Capital		5,000
C, Capital		50,000
To record investment by C for a one-third interest in capital, with bonus of $10,000 divided equally between A and B.		

Recognition of Goodwill   In the preceding illustration, C invested $60,000 but received a capital account of only $50,000, representing a one-third interest in the firm. C might prefer that the full amount invested, $60,000, be credited to C's capital. This could be done while still allotting C a one-third interest if goodwill is recorded in the accounts with the offsetting credit divided equally between the two original partners. If C is to be given a one-third interest represented by a capital account of $60,000, the total indicated capital is $180,000, and the capitals of A and B together must total $120,000. Since their present combined capitals amount to $90,000, a write-up of $30,000 in net assets would be recorded as follows:

Cash	60,000	
Goodwill	30,000	
A, Capital		15,000
B, Capital		15,000
C, Capital		60,000

To record investment by C for a one-third interest in capital, with goodwill of $30,000 divided equally between A and B.

Evaluation of Bonus and Goodwill Methods   When the incoming partner invests an amount larger than the carrying amount of the interest acquired, the transaction usually should be handled by allowing a bonus to the old partners. The bonus method has the advantage of adhering to the cost principle of asset valuation and is in accord with the concept of a partnership as a continuing business entity. The alternative method of recording the goodwill *implied* by the purchase price is not considered acceptable by the authors. Use of the goodwill method signifies the substitution of estimated current fair value of an asset rather than valuation on a cost basis. The goodwill of $30,000 shown in the preceding example was not purchased. Its existence is implied by the price the incoming partner paid for a one-third interest in the firm. As previously pointed out, the price paid by the incoming partner may have been influenced by many factors, some of which may be personal rather than economic in nature. To attribute the excess of the purchase price over carrying amount of net assets to goodwill is an assumption which may be difficult to support with objective evidence.

Apart from the questionable theoretical basis for such recognition of goodwill, there are other practical difficulties. The presence of goodwill created in this manner is likely to evoke criticism of the firm's financial statements, and such criticism may lead the partnership to amortize or to write off the goodwill.[3] Also, if the business should be liquidated, the

[3] According to *APB Opinion No. 17*, "Intangible Assets," issued by the AICPA in 1970, only purchased goodwill should be recorded in the accounting records, and it must be amortized over a period of 40 years or less.

goodwill probably would have to be written off as a loss. Will the recording of goodwill and its subsequent write-off injure one partner and benefit another? The net results to the individual partners will be the same under the bonus and goodwill methods only if two specific conditions are met: (1) the new partner's share of earnings must be equal to the percentage equity in net assets the new partner receives at the time of admission, and (2) the original partners must continue to share earnings between themselves in the same ratio as in the original partnership. Both these conditions were met in our example; that is, the new partner, C, received a one-third interest in the net assets and a one-third share of earnings. Secondly, the original partners shared earnings equally both before and after the admission of C.

Assume, however, that the three partners agreed on an income-sharing ratio of A 40%, B 40%, and C 20%; the goodwill method would then benefit C and injure A and B as compared with the bonus method. This is demonstrated below:

Comparison of bonus and goodwill methods

	A	B	C	Combined
Capitals if bonus method is used	$50,000	$50,000	$50,000	$150,000
Capitals if goodwill method is used	$60,000	$60,000	$60,000	$180,000
Write-off of goodwill (40%, 40%, 20%) ...	(12,000)	(12,000)	(6,000)	(30,000)
Capitals after write-off of goodwill	$48,000	$48,000	$54,000	$150,000

The first of the two necessary conditions for equivalent results from the bonus method and goodwill method is no longer met. Partner C's share of earnings is not equal to C's share of assets. C is now assumed to have a 20% share of earnings, although as in the preceding example C has a one-third share of assets. The use of the goodwill method in admitting C and the subsequent write-off of the goodwill would cause a $4,000 shift of capital from Partners A and B to Partner C. The preceding discussion may be summarized concisely as follows: When an incoming partner's share of earnings exceeds the partner's share of assets, the incoming partner will benefit from the use of the bonus method.

Fairness of Asset Valuation In the preceding examples of bonus or goodwill allowed to the original partners, it was assumed that the carrying amounts of assets in the accounting records of the original partnership approximated current fair values. If such assets as land and buildings have been owned by the partnership for many years, it is probable that carrying amounts and current fair values are quite far apart. Inventories priced on the lifo basis also may differ substantially from current replacement costs.

To bring this problem into focus, let us assume that the assets of the A & B Partnership, carried at $90,000, were estimated to have a current fair value of $120,000 at the time of admission of C as a partner. Our previous example called for C to receive a one-third interest upon investment of $60,000. Why not write up the assets from $90,000 to $120,000, with a corresponding increase in the capitals of the original partners? Neither a bonus nor the recognition of goodwill then would be necessary to record the admission of C to a one-third interest upon investment of $60,000 because this investment is equal to one-third of the total owners' equity.

Such restatement of asset values would not be acceptable practice in a corporation merely because the corporation's stock had risen in price. If we assume the existence of certain conditions in a partnership, then adherence to cost as a basis for asset valuation is as appropriate a policy as for a corporation. These specific conditions are that the ratio for sharing net income or loss should correspond to the share of equity held by each partner, and that the income-sharing ratio should continue unchanged. When these conditions do not exist, a restatement of assets from carrying amount to current fair value may be the most convenient method of achieving equity among the partners.

Bonus or goodwill allowed to new partner

An existing partnership may be very anxious to bring a new member into the firm, because the business is desperately in need of cash or because the prospective new member has unusual ability or valuable business contacts. To ensure the admission of the new partner, the present firm may offer the new partner a capital account larger than the amount invested.

Bonus to New Partner   Assume that F and G, who have capital accounts of $35,000 each and share earnings equally, offer to admit H to a one-third interest in assets and a one-third share of income upon an investment of $20,000. Their offer is based on a need for more cash and upon the conviction that H's personal abilities and business contacts will be of great value to the business. The investment of $20,000 cash in the firm by H, when added to the existing capital of $70,000, gives a total capital of $90,000, of which H is entitled to one-third, or $30,000. The excess of H's capital account over the amount invested represents a $10,000 bonus allowed to H by F and G. Because F and G share earnings equally, the $10,000 bonus will be deducted from their capital accounts in equal amounts, as shown by the following journal entry to record admission of H:

<table>
<tr><td rowspan="5">Recording
bonus to
new partner</td></tr>
</table>

Recording bonus to new partner	*Cash* 20,000	
	F, Capital 5,000	
	G, Capital 5,000	
	H, Capital ....*	30,000
	To record admission of H, with bonus of $10,000 from F and G.	

In outlining this method of accounting for the admission of H, we have assumed that the assets of the old partnership were valued properly. If the admission of the new partner to a one-third interest upon investment of $20,000 was based upon recognition that the assets owned by the old partnership were worth only $40,000, consideration should be given to writing down assets by $30,000. Such write-downs would be proper if accounts receivable, for example, included doubtful accounts or if inventories were obsolete.

Goodwill to New Partner Assume that the new partner H is the owner of a successful business which H invests in the partnership rather than making an investment in cash. Using the same data as in the preceding example, assume that F and G with capital accounts of $35,000 each give H a one-third interest in assets and earnings. The identifiable tangible and intangible assets comprising the business owned by H are worth $20,000, but, because of its superior earnings record, a current fair value for this going business is agreed to be $35,000. The admission of H as a partner is then recorded as follows:

New partner invests goodwill	*Identifiable Tangible and Intangible Assets* 20,000	
	Goodwill 15,000	
	H, Capital ....*	35,000
	To record admission of H; goodwill is assigned to going business invested by H.	

The point to be stressed here is that generally goodwill is recognized as part of the investment of a new partner only when the new partner invests a going business of superior earning power. If H is admitted by reason of a cash investment and is credited with a capital larger than the cash invested, the proper accounting for the transaction is to subtract this differential from the capitals of the old partners or to write down any overvalued assets. Goodwill should be recognized in the accounting records only when substantiated by objective evidence; it should not be recorded in the accounting records to avoid recognition of a loss or as a convenient balancing device.

Retirement of a partner

A partner retiring from a partnership usually receives cash or other assets directly from the partnership. It is also possible that a retiring partner might arrange for the sale of a partnership interest to one or more of the continuing partners or to an outsider. Since we have already considered the accounting principles applicable to the purchase of an interest by an incoming or continuing partner, our discussion of the retirement of a partner is limited to the situation in which the partner receives settlement from the assets of the partnership.

An assumption underlying this discussion is that the partner has a right to withdraw under the terms of the partnership contract. A partner always has the *power* to withdraw, as distinguished from the *right* to withdraw. A partner who withdraws in violation of the terms agreed upon in the partnership contract, and without the consent of the other partners, may be liable for damages.

Computing the Settlement Price   What is a fair measurement of the equity of a retiring partner? A first indication is the amount of the retiring partner's capital account, but this amount may require various adjustments before it represents an equitable settlement. These adjustments may include the correction of errors in accounting data and the recognition of differences between carrying amounts of assets and current fair values. In approaching these adjustments, the accountant will first refer to the partnership contract, which may contain specific provisions for computing the amount to be paid a retiring partner. These instructions, for example, might provide for the appraisal of assets, might call for an audit by certified public accountants, and might prescribe a formula to be used in determining goodwill. If the business has not maintained accurate accounting records or has not been regularly audited, it is possible that the capital accounts are misstated because of improper depreciation charges, failure to provide for doubtful accounts expense, and other accounting deficiencies.

If the partnership contract does not contain provisions for computing the equity of a retiring partner, the accountant may be able to obtain joint authorization from the partners to follow a specific approach to determining an equitable settlement amount.

In most cases the equity of the retiring partner is computed on the basis of current fair values for all assets. The gain or loss indicated by the difference between the carrying amounts of assets and their current fair values is divided in the income-sharing ratio. After the equity of the retiring partner has been computed in terms of current fair values for assets, the partners may agree to settle by payment of this amount or they may agree upon a higher or lower amount. The computation of an estimated current fair value for the partner's equity is a necessary step in reaching a settlement; an independent decision should be made as to whether the current fair values and the related changes in partners' capitals should be recorded in the accounting records.

Payment of Bonus to Retiring Partner   The partnership contract may provide for recognition of goodwill at the time of a partner's retirement and may specify the methods of computing it. Usually the amount of the computed goodwill will be attributable to the partners in the income-sharing ratio. For example, assume that C is to retire from the partnership of A, B, and C. Each partner has a capital account of $60,000 and earnings are shared equally. The partnership contract states that a retiring partner is entitled to receive the balance in the retiring partner's capital account plus a share of any goodwill. At the time of C's retirement, goodwill in the amount of $30,000 is computed to the mutual satisfaction of the partners. In the opinion of the authors this goodwill should not be entered in the accounting records of the partnership.

Serious objections exist to recording goodwill as determined in this fashion. Because only $10,000 of the goodwill is included in the payment for C's equity, the remaining $20,000 of goodwill **has not** been purchased by the continuing partnership. Its inclusion in the balance sheet of the partnership is not supported by the cost principle nor by any verifiable evidence. The fact that the partners "voted" for $30,000 of goodwill does not meet our need for objective evidence of asset value. As an alternative, it would be possible to record only $10,000 of goodwill and credit C's capital for the same amount, since this amount was "paid for" by the continuing partnership in acquiring C's interest. This method is perhaps more justifiable, but objective evidence is still lacking that goodwill exists. The most satisfactory method of accounting for the retirement of partner C is to treat the amount paid to C for goodwill as a $10,000 bonus. Since the settlement with C is for the amount of C's capital ($60,000) plus estimated goodwill of $10,000, the following journal entry could be made to record the amount paid to C:

Bonus paid	C, Capital	*60,000*	
to a retiring	A, Capital	*5,000*	
partner	B, Capital	*5,000*	
	Cash		*70,000*
	To record payment to retiring partner C, including a bonus of		
	$10,000.		

The bonus method illustrated here is appropriate whenever the settlement with the retiring partner exceeds the carrying amount of that partner's capital. The agreement for settlement may or may not use the term **goodwill;** the essence of the matter is determining the amount to be paid to the retiring partner.

Settlement with Retiring Partner for Less than Carrying Amount Partners may be so anxious to escape from unsatisfactory business situations that they surrender their equity for less than carrying amount. In other cases, willingness by the retiring partners to accept a settlement below carrying amount may reflect personal problems entirely apart from the business. Another possible explanation is that retiring partners consider the assets overvalued, or that they anticipate declining earnings or even losses in future years.

In brief, there are many factors which may induce partners to accept less than carrying amount upon withdrawal from a partnership. Because a settlement below carrying amount is seldom supported by objective evidence of overvaluation of assets, the preferred accounting treatment is to leave asset valuations undisturbed unless a large amount of goodwill is carried in the accounting records. The difference between the retiring partner's capital account and the amount paid in settlement should be credited as a bonus to the continuing partners in the income-sharing ratio.

For example, assume that in the partnership of A, B, and C with capital accounts of $60,000 each, partner B retires upon payment of $50,000. Assuming that earnings are shared equally, the journal entry is:

Bonus to continuing partners	B, Capital 60,000	
	Cash	50,000
	A, Capital	5,000
	C, Capital	5,000
	To record the retirement of partner B for an amount below the carrying amount of B's equity.	

The final settlement with a retiring partner is often deferred for some time after withdrawal to permit the accumulation of cash, the determination of earnings to date of withdrawal, the obtaining of bank loans, or other steps needed to complete the transaction. The retirement of a partner does not terminate the retiring partner's personal responsibility for partnership debts existing at the date of retirement.

Death of a Partner The partnership contract often provides that partners shall purchase life insurance policies on each others' lives so that funds will be available for settlement with the estate of a deceased partner. A buy-and-sell agreement may be formed by the partners, with a trustee appointed to carry out the plan. Under a buy-and-sell agreement, the partners commit their estates to sell their equities in the business and the surviving partners to buy such equities. Another form of such an agreement gives the surviving partners an option to buy or "first refusal," rather than imposing an obligation to buy.

REVIEW QUESTIONS

1 In the formation of a partnership, partners often invest in the firm such assets as land, buildings, and machinery as well as cash. Should these noncash assets be recorded by the partnership at current fair value, at cost to the partners, or at some other amount? Give reasons for your answer.

2 Some CPA firms have thousands of staff members, and hundreds of partners, and operate on a national or international basis. Would not the corporate form of organization be more appropriate than the partnership form for such large organizations? Explain.

3 Explain the proper presentation in the balance sheet of loans to and from partners, and the treatment of interest on such loans.

4 Explain how partners' salaries should be shown in the income statement, if at all.

5 List at least six items that should be covered in a partnership contract.

6 List at least five methods by which partnership earnings may be divided.

7 The partnership of Ainsley and Burton offered to admit Paul Craig to a one-third interest in the firm upon his investment of $50,000. Does this offer mean that Craig would be entitled to one-third of the partnership earnings?

8 Duncan and Eastwick are negotiating a partnership contract, with Duncan investing $60,000 and Eastwick $20,000. Duncan suggests that interest be allowed on average capitals at 8% and that any remaining earnings be divided in the ratio of average capitals. Eastwick prefers that the entire earnings be divided in the ratio of average capitals. Comment on these proposals.

9 The partnership contract of Fay and Garr is very brief on the subject of sharing earnings. It says: "Earnings are to be divided 70% to Fay and 30% to Garr, and each partner is entitled to draw $800 a month." What difficulties do you see in carrying out this contract? Illustrate possible difficulties under the assumption that the partnership earned $40,000 in the first year.

10 Muir and Miller operated a partnership for several years, sharing earnings equally. On January 1 of the current year, they agreed to revise the income-sharing ratio to 70% for Muir and 30% for Miller because of Miller's desire for semiretirement. On March 1 the partnership received $10,000 in settlement of a disputed error on a contract completed last year. Since the outcome of the dispute had been considered highly uncertain, no receivable had ever been entered in the accounts. Explain the accounting treatment you would recommend for the $10,000 cash receipt.

11 Should the valuation of assets as shown by the accounting records of a partnership be changed to correspond to current fair value whenever a partner withdraws or a new partner is admitted to the firm? Explain fully and give specific examples.

12 A new partner admitted to an established firm is often required to invest an amount larger than the carrying amount of the interest in net assets the new partner acquires. In what ways can such a transaction be recorded? What is the principal argument for each method?

13 Bono, Claire, and Drummond have operated a partnership business for many years and have shared earnings equally. The partners now agree that Gray, a key employee of the firm who is an able manager but has limited financial resources, should become a partner with a one-sixth interest in capital. It is further agreed that the four partners will share earnings equally in the future. Bono suggests that the assets in the accounting records of the old partnership should be restated to current fair value at the time Gray is admitted, but Claire and Drummond advocate that the accounts be left undisturbed in order to have a consistent accounting record. What is the argument for restating assets at the time of Gray's admission? What alternative, if any, would you suggest for such restatement of asset values?

14 The partnership of Ed Loeser, Peter Wylie, and Herman Martin has operated successfully for many years, but Martin has now reached retirement age. In discussions of the settlement to be made with Martin, the point was made that the inventories of the firm had consistently been valued on a lifo basis for many years. Martin suggested that the current replacement value of the inventories be determined and the excess of this sum over the carrying amount be regarded as a gain to be shared equally. Loeser objected to this suggestion on the grounds that any method of inventory valuation would give reasonably accurate results provided it were followed consistently and that a departure from the long-established method used by the partnership would produce an erroneous picture of the earnings realized over the life of the partnership. Evaluate the objections raised by Loeser.

15 George Lewis and Anna Marlin are partners who share earnings equally. They offer to admit Betty Naylor to a one-third interest in assets and in earnings upon her investment of $50,000 cash. The total capital of the partnership prior to Naylor's admission was $110,000. Naylor makes a counteroffer of $40,000, explaining that her investigation of the business indicates that many receivables are past due and that a significant amount of obsolescence exists in the inventories. Lewis and Marlin deny both these points. They contend that inventories are valued in accordance with generally accepted accounting principles and that the receivables are fully collectible. However, after prolonged negotiation, the admission price of $40,000 proposed by Naylor is agreed upon. Explain two ways in which the admission of Naylor could be recorded and indicate which method is more justifiable. Comment on the possibility of recording goodwill.

16 Two partners each invested capital of $200 to form a partnership for the construction of a shopping center. The partnership obtained several loans to finance construction, but no payments on these loans were due for two years. Each partner withdrew excess cash of $50,000 from the partnership out of the proceeds of the loans. How should the investment of $400 and the $100,000 of withdrawals be presented in the balance sheet of the partnership?

17 A partnership contract provided that in the computation of net income, a provision for income taxes is to be made, and the amount of the provision will be considered an expense of the partnership. In the income statement for the partnership, would the net income (after the provision for income taxes) be considered as having been determined in conformity with generally accepted accounting principles?

18 An auditor was asked to give an opinion on the financial statements of a limited partnership. Should the financial statements of the limited partnership and the auditor's report thereon include the financial statements of the corporate general partner?

EXERCISES

Ex. 1-1 Monte Whipple, a partner in the Deep Venture Partnership, has a 30% participation in net income. Whipple's capital account had a net decrease of $60,000 during Year 4. During Year 4, Whipple withdrew $130,000 (charged against his capital account) and invested property with a current fair value of $25,000 in the partnership.

Compute the net income of the Deep Venture Partnership for Year 4.

Ex. 1-2 In the firm of Dunin, Lum, and Beers, the partnership contract provided that Dunin as managing partner should receive a bonus equal to 20% of earnings and that the remaining earnings should be divided 40% each to Dunin and Lum and 20% to Beers. Earnings for the first year (before the bonus) amounted to $63,600.

Explain two alternative ways in which the bonus provision could be interpreted. Compute the division of the year's earnings under each interpretation.

Ex. 1-3 Emma Neal and Sally Drew are partners sharing earnings equally; each has a capital account of $100,000. Drew (with the consent of Neal) sold one-fifth of her interest to her daughter Paula for $25,000, with payment to be made in five annual installments without any interest charge.

Give the journal entry to record the change in ownership, and explain why you would or would not recommend a change in the valuation of assets in the accounting records of the partnership.

Ex. 1-4 L and M are partners with capital accounts of $70,000 each who share earnings equally. The partners agree to admit N to a one-third interest in net assets and a one-third share in earnings upon N's investment in the firm of $100,000. Assume that the assets are fairly valued and that N's admission is recorded by allowing a bonus to the old partners.

Prepare a journal entry to record the admission of N to the firm.

Ex. 1-5 Assume that A and B are partners in a successful business, sharing earnings in a 60:40 ratio. Their capital accounts are A, $60,000 and B, $40,000. They agree to admit C to a 30% interest in net assets and a 20% interest in earnings upon C's investment of $50,000. The new income-sharing ratio is to be 48:32:20 for A, B, and C, respectively. The partners are discussing whether to record the admission of C by a bonus to A and B or by recording goodwill.

What would be the amount of the bonus to A and B, respectively? What would be the total goodwill implied by C's investment? Would the goodwill method be more advantageous to C if we assume the goodwill were written off in full two years later? What would be the dollar amount of the advantage or disadvantage to C from use of the goodwill method?

Ex. 1-6 The partnership of Farley and Grammas was formed on March 1. At that date the following assets were invested:

	Farley	Grammas
Cash	$ 25,000	$35,000
Inventories	-0-	55,000
Land	-0-	25,000
Building	-0-	75,000
Furniture and equipment	115,000	-0-

The building is subject to a mortgage loan of $30,000, which is to be assumed by the partnership. The partnership contract provides that Farley and Grammas share earnings 40% and 60%, respectively.

a Compute the amount of Grammas' capital account at March 1, assuming that each partner is credited for the full amount of net assets invested.

b If the partnership contract provides that the partners initially should have an equal interest in partnership capital with no contribution of intangible assets, what would be the balance in Farley's capital account at March 1?

Ex. 1-7 Lewis and Mason have capitals at the beginning of the year of $40,000 and $45,000, respectively. They share earnings as follows: (1) 8% interest on beginning capitals, (2) salary allowance of $15,000 to Lewis and $7,500 to Mason, and (3) balance in 3:2 ratio. The partnership earned only $10,000 during the current year before interest and salary allowances to partners.

a Show how the net income of $10,000 should be divided between Lewis and Mason.

b Assuming that Lewis and Mason simply agree to share earnings in a 3:2 ratio with a minimum of $12,000 guaranteed to Mason, show how the net income of $10,000 should be divided.

Ex. 1-8 Activity in the capital accounts for Pando and Pavich for Year 10 follows:

	Pando	Pavich
Balances at Jan. 1	$20,000	$40,000
Investment on Mar. 1	10,000	
Withdrawal on Nov. 30		20,000

Net income for the year amounted to $24,000 before interest or salary allowances.

Determine the division of the net income under each of the following assumptions:

a The partnership contract is silent as to sharing of earnings.

b Earnings are divided on the basis of the weighted-average capitals (not including the net income or loss for the current year).

c Earnings are divided on the basis of beginning capitals.

d Earnings are divided on the basis of ending capitals (not including the net income for the current year).

Ex. 1-9 Floyd Austin and Samuel Bradford are partners who share earnings equally and have equal capital accounts. The net assets of the partnership have a carrying amount of $40,000. Jason Crane is admitted to the partnership with a one-third interest in earnings and net assets. To acquire this interest, Crane pays $18,000 cash to the partnership.

Prepare journal entries to show three possible methods of recording the admission of Crane in the accounting records of the partnership. State the conditions (if any) under which each method would be appropriate.

Ex. 1-10 A and B have capital accounts of $15,000 and $10,000, respectively. They share earnings in a 3:1 ratio. What journal entries would be made to record the admission of C to the partnership under each of the following conditions?

a C invests $15,000 for a one-fourth interest in net assets; the total capital after C's admission is to be $40,000.

b C invests $15,000, of which $5,000 is considered a bonus to A and B. In conjunction with the admission of C, the carrying amount of the inventories is increased by $8,000. C's capital is recorded at $10,000.

Ex. 1-11 Paul and Quinn formed a partnership on January 2, Year 4, and agreed to share earnings 90% and 10%, respectively. Paul invested cash of $25,000. Quinn invested no assets but has a specialized expertise and manages the firm full time. There were no withdrawals during the year. The partnership contract provides for the following:

(1) Capital accounts are to be credited annually with interest at 5% of beginning capital.

(2) Quinn is to be paid a salary of $1,000 a month.

(3) Quinn is to receive a bonus of 20% of income calculated before deduction of salary and interest on capital accounts.

(4) Bonus, interest, and Quinn's salary are to be considered partnership expenses.

The Year 4 income statement for the partnership includes the following:

Revenue	$96,450
Expenses (including salary, interest, and bonus)	49,700
Net income	$46,750

Compute Quinn's bonus for Year 4.

Ex. 1-12 The balance sheet for the partnership of Louie, Moore, and Newman at April 30, Year 5, is shown below. The partners share earnings in the ratio of 2:2:6, respectively.

Assets, at carrying amount	$100,000
Louie, loan	$ 9,000
Louie, capital	15,000
Moore, capital	31,000
Newman, capital	45,000
Total	$100,000

Louie is retiring from the partnership. By mutual agreement, the assets are to be adjusted to their current fair value of $130,000 at April 30, Year 5. Moore and Newman agree that the partnership will pay $37,000 cash for Louie's partnership interest, exclusive of the loan, which is to be paid in full. No goodwill is to be recorded. Compute the balance of Newman's capital account after Louie's retirement.

SHORT CASES FOR ANALYSIS AND DECISION

Case 1-1 When asked how the organizers of a business might choose between a partnership and a corporation in order to minimize the burden of taxation, an accounting student made the following statement:

"The choice is very simple. Organization as a partnership will result in only one income tax, that is, the tax on individual income. If the business is incorporated, it must pay the corporation income tax, and in addition the owners must pay individual income taxes as the net income of the corporation is distributed to them. Consequently, the partnership form of organization always provides a lesser burden of taxation."

Instructions Do you agree with the student? Explain.

Case 1-2 X, Y, and Z, partners who share earnings equally, reported operating income of $30,000 for the first year of business. However, near the end of the year, they learned of two unfavorable developments: (a) the bankruptcy of Sasha, maker of a two-year promissory note for $20,000 which had been transferred to the partnership by Partner X at face amount as X's original investment; and (b) the appearance on the market of new competing patented devices which rendered worthless a patent transferred to the partnership by Partner Y at a valuation of $10,000 as part of Y's original investment.

The partnership had retained the promissory note with the expectation of discounting it when cash was needed for operating purposes. Quarterly interest payments had been received regularly prior to the bankruptcy of Sasha, but present prospects were for no further collections of either interest or principal.

Partner Z states that the $30,000 operating income should be divided $10,000 to each partner, with the $20,000 loss on the note debited to the capital account of Partner X and the $10,000 loss on the patent debited to the capital account of Partner Y.

Instructions Do you agree with Partner Z? Should the apparent losses on the note and the patent be handled in the same manner? Explain.

Case 1-3 Sally Decker and Jane Evanson have been partners for many years and have shared earnings equally. They own and operate a resort hotel which includes a golf course and other recreational facilities. Decker has maintained a larger capital investment than Evanson, but Evanson has devoted much more time to the management of the partnership.

The business is located in one of the fastest-growing areas in the country and has been expanding rapidly. To help meet the problems of this expansion, the partners decide to admit Laura Fane as a partner with a one-third interest in the partnership and a one-third share in earnings. Fane is known as an excellent administrator and has ample cash to invest for her share in the partnership. You are retained by the partnership to give advice upon any accounting issues created by the admission of Fane as a partner.

Instructions List the factors that you believe deserve consideration and prepare a set of recommendations to guide the partners in dealing with these issues.

Case 1-4 Dan Doyle and Wally Williams formed a partnership on January 1, Doyle investing cash of $50,000 and Williams investing cash of $20,000 and marketable securities with a current fair value of $80,000. A portion of the securities was sold at carrying amount in January to provide funds for business operations.

The partnership contract stated that earnings were to be divided in the capital ratio and that each partner was entitled to withdraw $1,000 monthly. Doyle withdrew $1,000 on the last day of each month, but Williams made no withdrawals until July 1, when he withdrew all the securities which had not been sold by the partnership. The securities which Williams took had a current fair value of $46,000 when invested in the partnership on January 1 and a current fair value of $62,000 on July 1 when withdrawn. Williams instructed the accountant for the partnership to record the transaction by reducing his capital account by $46,000, which was done. Income from operations for the first year amounted to $24,000. Income tax issues may be ignored.

Instructions You are asked to determine the proper division of net income for the first year. If the income-sharing provision of the partnership contract is unsatisfactory in any respect, state the assumptions you would make in order to arrive at an equitable interpretation of the partners' intentions. Also indicate what adjustments, if any, you believe should be made in the accounting records of the partnership.

PROBLEMS

1-5 The partnership of Saul, Teel, and Upman was formed on January 1, Year 1. The original cash investments were as follows:

Saul	$ 96,000
Teel	144,000
Upman	216,000

    According to the partnership contract, net income or loss will be divided among the respective partners as follows:
(1) Salaries of $14,400 for Saul, $12,000 for Teel, and $9,600 for Upman
(2) Interest of 8% on the average capital balances during the year
(3) Remainder divided equally
    Net income of the partnership for the year ended December 31, Year 1, was $84,000. Saul invested an additional $24,000 in the partnership on July 1, Year 1; Upman withdrew $36,000 from the partnership on October 1, Year 1; and Saul, Teel, and Upman made regular drawings of $12,000 each against their shares of net income during Year 1.

Instructions
a Prepare a summary showing the division of net income among the three partners. Show supporting computations in good form.
b Prepare a statement of partners' capital for Year 1.

1-6 Adams and Becker formed a partnership at the beginning of Year 6. Their capital accounts show the following changes during Year 6:

	Adams	*Becker*
Original investment, Jan. 7, Year 6	$120,000	$180,000
Investments: May 1	15,000	
July 1		15,000
Withdrawals: Nov. 1	(30,000)	(75,000)
Capital accounts, Dec. 31, Year 6	$105,000	$120,000
	125,000	175,000

    The net income, before allowances for salaries or interest, was $69,600. The net income included an extraordinary gain of $12,000.

Instructions Determine each partner's share of net income to the nearest dollar, assuming the following alternative income-sharing arrangements:
a The partnership contract is silent as to division of net income.
b Income before extraordinary items is shared equally after allowance of 8% interest on average capitals (computed to the nearest month) and after allowance of $20,000 to Adams and $30,000 to Becker as salaries. Extraordinary items are shared in the ratio of original investments.
c Income before extraordinary items is shared on the basis of average capitals, and extraordinary items are shared on the basis of original investments.
d Income before extraordinary items is shared equally between Adams and Becker after allowance of a 25% bonus to Becker based on income before extraordinary items after the bonus. Extraordinary items are shared on the basis of original investments.

1-7 Cameron and Duncan wish to purchase the partnership interest of their partner Eddy at June 30, Year 5. Partnership assets are to be used to purchase Eddy's partnership interest. The balance sheet for the partnership on this date shows the following:

CAMERON, DUNCAN, AND EDDY PARTNERSHIP
Balance Sheet
June 30, Year 5

Assets		Liabilities & Partners' Capital	
Cash	$ 54,000	Liabilities	$ 45,000
Receivables (net)	36,000	Cameron, capital	120,000
Equipment (net)	135,000	Duncan, capital	60,000
Goodwill	30,000	Eddy, capital	30,000
Total	$255,000	Total	$255,000

The partners share earnings in the ratio of 3:2:1.

Instructions Record the withdrawal of Eddy under each of the following four assumptions:

a Eddy is paid $33,000 and the excess paid over the amount in Eddy's capital account is viewed as a bonus to Eddy.

b Eddy is paid $27,000 and the difference is viewed as a bonus to Cameron and Duncan.

c Eddy is paid $27,000 and goodwill currently in the accounting records of the partnership is reduced by the total amount implicit in the transaction.

d Eddy accepts cash of $19,500 and equipment with a current fair value of $12,000. The equipment cost $30,000 and was 90% depreciated, with no residual value.

1-8 Moore, Nolan, and Olson are partners sharing earnings in a 3:2:1 ratio. The business has been successful, as indicated by the following data concerning the partners' capital accounts:

	Original investments	Retained earnings	Present balances
Moore, capital	$38,000	$42,000	$ 80,000
Nolan, capital	21,300	28,000	49,300
Olson, capital	11,500	12,500	24,000
Totals	$70,800	$82,500	$153,300

At this time Olson becomes ill and retires from the partnership, receiving $30,000 in cash. Moore and Nolan decide to continue in partnership and to share earnings equally. However, as a condition of this change in the income-sharing ratio, Nolan agrees to invest an additional $12,000 cash in the firm. The investment is made, but the partners have difficulty in agreeing on the method to be used in recording Olson's withdrawal from the firm. Moore wants to record the entire goodwill of the partnership as implied by the amount paid for Olson's interest. Nolan argues that the amount of goodwill to be recorded should not be larger than the amount paid for Olson's share of the partnership goodwill. The accountant for the firm points out that the income-sharing ratio is being changed and suggests that this is a reason for recognizing the goodwill of the business prior to Olson's withdrawal. Olson suggests that the entire controversy over goodwill can be avoided by treating any amount paid to a withdrawing partner in excess of that partner's capital account as a bonus from the other partners.

Instructions

a Give the journal entries in the accounts of the partnership required by the recommendation of each of the three partners (three independent sets of journal entries).

b Assume that the business is sold for $171,300 in cash shortly after the withdrawal of Olson, with the buyer assuming the liabilities. Prepare analyses showing how the cash would be divided between Moore and Nolan under each of the three alternative methods for handling the withdrawal of Olson as previously described.

c For this portion of the problem, assume the same data as to original investments and retained earnings by Moore, Nolan, and Olson. However, rather than having Olson withdraw from the partnership, assume that the three partners agree to admit Newsome as a fourth partner for an investment of $45,100 cash in the firm. Newsome is given a 25% interest in the partnership net assets and a 25% share in earnings. Moore, Nolan, and Olson will share the remaining 75% of partnership earnings in the same original ratio existing among them prior to admission of Newsome to the firm. Moore, Nolan, and Olson each withdraws $10,000 cash from the business. Prepare the journal entries needed to record the withdrawals of cash and the admission of Newsome into the partnership using (1) the goodwill method and (2) the bonus method.

d Assume the same facts presented in c above, and further that the business is sold for $176,400 shortly after the admission of Newsome to the firm. The buyer assumes the liabilities. Prepare an analysis showing how the cash would be distributed among the four partners if the admission of Newsome had been recorded by using (1) the goodwill method and (2) the bonus method.

1-9 Polo and Queen started a partnership in Year 1, each investing $12,000 cash and agreeing to share earnings equally. At the beginning of Year 3, Remy was admitted to the partnership upon an investment of $14,500. Remy's admission to the partnership was recorded by a debit to Cash and a credit to Remy, Capital for $14,500. The income-sharing ratio for the new partnership was set at 3:2:1 for Polo, Queen, and Remy, respectively.

Additional information is given below for each of the first four years ending at December 31:

	Year 1	Year 2	Year 3	Year 4	Total
Net income as reported.....	$18,000	$27,500	$36,000	$44,700	$126,200
Drawings (equal amounts for each partner)..........	15,000	22,000	27,000	15,600	79,600
Accounts receivable not recorded at year-end......	5,000	8,000	15,000	18,000	46,000
Inventories not counted at year-end	3,000	4,500	6,600	11,300	25,400
Accounts payable not recorded at year-end......	6,000	4,000	10,000	17,500	37,500
Capital balances:					
Polo	13,500	16,250	25,250	42,400	
Queen	13,500	16,250	19,250	28,950	
Remy			11,500	13,750	

Each year the income statement was prepared on the cash basis of accounting, that is, accounts receivable were not recorded and payments for merchandise were treated as cost of goods sold. All accounts receivable are considered collectible.

Instructions

a Prepare a statement of partners' capitals covering the four-year period based on the accrual basis of accounting. Combine net income and drawings for Years 1 and 2 and for Years 3 and 4. Prepare a supporting analysis to restate net income from the cash to the accrual basis of accounting for the first two-year period (Years 1 and 2) and for the second two-year period (Years 3 and 4).

b Prepare a balance sheet for the partnership at December 31, Year 4. Prepare a separate schedule to determine the cash figure appearing in the balance sheet. Assume that the only assets and liabilities are: cash, accounts receivable, inventories, and accounts payable.

c Using the information given in the problem and the partners' capital balances at December 31, Year 4, determined in part **a**, prepare a journal entry to restate the accounts of the partnership from the cash basis to the accrual basis of accounting.

1-10 The partnership of Seel and Tabor has maintained accounting records on the accrual basis, except for the method of handling credit losses. Doubtful accounts expense has been recognized by a direct charge-off to expense at the time individual accounts receivable were determined to be uncollectible.

The partners are anticipating the admission of a third member, Tom Unger, to the firm, and they retain you to review the accounting records before this action is taken. You suggest that the firm change retroactively to the allowance method of accounting for doubtful accounts so that the planning for admission of Unger to the partnership can be based upon a full accrual basis of accounting. The following information is available:

Year accounts receivable originated	Year accounts were written off			Additional estimated expense
	2	3	4	
1	$1,200	$ 200		
2	1,500	1,300	$ 600	$ 450
3		1,800	1,400	1,250
4			2,200	4,800
Totals	$2,700	$3,300	$4,200	$6,500

The partners shared earnings equally until Year 4. In Year 4 the income-sharing plan was changed as follows: salaries of $8,000 and $6,000 to be allowed Seel and Tabor, respectively; any balance to be divided 60% to Seel and 40% to Tabor. Net income of the partnership for Year 4, according to the accounting records, was $28,000.

Instructions

a Prepare a journal entry giving effect to the change in accounting method for doubtful accounts expense. Support your entry with a summary showing changes in net income for the year.

b Assume that after you prepared the journal entry in **a** above, Seel's capital is reported at $48,000 and Tabor's capital is reported at $22,000. If Tom Unger invested $30,000 for a 20% interest in total net assets of the partnership and a 25% share in net income, illustrate by journal entries two methods that may be used to record Unger's admission to the partnership. Any increase in the capital of old partners is to be divided 60% and 40%. Which method would be more advantageous to Unger if the goodwill is later substantiated through a sale of the business at a gain? Which method would be more advantageous to Unger if we assume that the goodwill is written off in the year following his admission to the firm?

1-11 The retail business operated as a partnership by D, E, and F was completely destroyed by fire on December 31, Year 2. The only assets remaining were the bank account with a balance of $26,765 and a claim against the insurance company which was settled for $220,000 early in Year 3. All accounting records were destroyed in the fire. The company had only a few creditors, and all of these have presented their claims, which amounted in total to $32,000 at December 31, Year 2.

The present partnership was formed on January 1, Year 1. Prior to that time D and E had been partners for several years and had shared earnings equally. No written partnership contract was prepared for the new firm, and a dispute has now arisen as to the terms of the partners' oral contract for sharing earnings. The business had not utilized the services of certified public accountants, except for some assistance with the information return required for income tax purposes at December 31, Year 1.

You are retained by the partnership to determine the income-sharing plan which was followed for Year 1 and to apply this same plan to the events of Year 2, thus determining the present equity of each partner. The partners agree in writing that the income-sharing plan used in Year 1 was correct and should be applied in an identical manner to the net income or loss for Year 2. The information available to you consists of the following: a copy of the information tax return of the partnership for Year 1, and a statement of the withdrawals made by the partners during Year 2. This latter statement has been agreed to in writing by all three partners and appears as follows:

	D	E	F	Combined
Inventories	$ 1,500	$850	$2,300	$ 4,650
Salaries	8,000		6,000	14,000
Other cash withdrawals	750			750
Totals	$10,250	$850	$8,300	$19,400

Partner D explains to you that the $750 in "other cash withdrawals" resulted from the accidental payment by the firm of a personal debt when the invoice was sent to the partnership address.

From the partnership tax return for the preceding year, you obtain the following information.

	D	E	F	Combined
Capitals, Jan. 1, Year 1	$40,000	$50,000	$92,500	$182,500
Capitals, Dec. 31, Year 1	$51,000	$61,000	$85,300	$197,300
Division of net income for Year 1:				
Salaries	$12,000	$15,000	$ 6,000	$ 33,000
Interest on capitals	2,000	2,500	4,625	9,125
Remainder (15%:30%:55%)	6,821	13,643	25,011	45,475
Totals	$20,821	$31,143	$35,636	$ 87,600

Instructions

a Prepare a statement of partners' capitals for Year 2, supported by a summary showing the computation of net income or loss for Year 2 and the division of the net income or loss among the partners in accordance with the income-sharing plan followed in the preceding year. Round computations to the nearest dollar.

b How much cash will each partner receive if the partnership is terminated early in Year 3?

1-12 The partnership of Kim, Gerson, and Flamson engaged you to adjust its accounting records and convert them to the accrual basis of accounting in anticipation of the admission of Ward as a new partner. Some accounts are on the accrual basis and others are on the cash basis. The partnership's accounts were closed at December 31, Year 5, by the accountant for the partnership, who prepared the following general ledger trial balance:

KIM, GERSON, AND FLAMSON PARTNERSHIP
Trial Balance
December 31, Year 5

Cash	$ 16,250	
Accounts receivable	40,000	
Inventories	26,000	
Land	9,000	
Buildings	50,000	
Accumulated depreciation: buildings		$ 2,000
Equipment	56,000	
Accumulated depreciation: equipment		8,250
Goodwill	5,000	
Accounts payable		59,000
Reserve for future inventory losses		3,000
Kim, capital		40,000
Gerson, capital		60,000
Flamson, capital		30,000
Totals	$202,250	$202,250

Your inquiries disclosed the following:

(1) The partnership was organized on January 1, Year 4, with no provision in the partnership contract for the distribution of earnings. During Year 4 earnings were distributed equally among the partners. The partnership contract was amended effective January 1, Year 5, to provide for the following income-sharing ratio: Kim, 50%; Gerson, 30%; and Flamson, 20%. The amended partnership contract also stated that the accounting records were to be maintained on the accrual basis and that any adjustments necessary for Year 5 should be allocated according to the Year 5 distribution of earnings.

(2) The following amounts were not recorded as prepayments or accruals:

	December 31, Year 5	Year 4
Unexpired insurance	$700	$ 650
Advances from customers	200	1,100
Accrued interest payable		450

The advances from customers were recorded as sales in the year the cash was received.

(3) In Year 5 a provision of $3,000 was recorded (by a debit to expense) for anticipated declines in inventory prices. You convinced the partners that the provision was unnecessary and should be removed from the accounts.

(4) Equipment purchased for $4,400 on January 3, Year 5, was debited to expense. This equipment has an estimated economic life of 10 years and an estimated residual value of $400. The partnership depreciates its equipment under the declining-balance method at twice the straight-line rate.

(5) The partners agreed to establish an allowance for doubtful accounts at 2% of current accounts receivable and 5% of past-due accounts. At December 31, Year 4, the partnership had $54,000 of accounts receivable, of which only $4,000 was past due. At December 31, Year 5, 15% of accounts receivable was past due, of which $4,000 represented sales made in Year 4, and was considered collectible. The partnership had written off uncollectible accounts in the year the accounts became worthless as follows:

	Year 5	Year 4
Year 5 accounts	$ 800	
Year 4 accounts	1,000	$250

(6) Goodwill was recorded improperly in Year 5 and credited to the partners' capital accounts in the income-sharing ratio in recognition of an increase in the value of the business resulting from improved sales volume. The partners agreed to write off the goodwill before Ward was admitted to the partnership.

Instructions

a Prepare an adjusted trial balance for the partnership on the accrual basis of accounting at December 31, Year 5. All adjustments affecting income should be made directly to partners' capital accounts. Number your adjustments. Supporting computations should be in good form. (Do not prepare formal financial statements or formal journal entries. The working paper should have pairs of columns for Unadjusted Trial Balance, Adjustments, and Adjusted Trial Balance.)

b Without prejudice to your solution to **a** above, assume that the assets of the partnership were properly valued, that the adjusted total of the partners' capital account balances at December 31, Year 5, was $140,000, and that Ward invested $60,000 in the partnership. Compute the amount of goodwill that might be recorded in the partnership accounting records under each of the following alternative agreements and allocate the goodwill to the partners:

(1) Ward is to be granted a one-fourth interest in the partnership. The other partners will retain their 50:30:20 income-sharing ratio for the remaining three-fourths interest in earnings.

(2) The partnership has been earning, and expects to continue to earn, an annual return of 18% on invested capital. The normal rate of return for comparable partnerships is 15%. The superior earnings (expected earnings of the new partnership in excess of the normal rate of return) are to be capitalized as goodwill at the rate of 20%. The partners are to share earnings (including any goodwill) in the following ratio: Kim, 40%; Gerson, 30%; Flamson, 10%; Ward, 20%.

1-13 The law firm of L, M, and N was organized on January 1, Year 1, when the three attorneys decided to combine their individual law practices. The partners reached agreement on the following matters:

(1) All partners would invest in the firm the assets and liabilities of their indi-

vidual practices and would be credited with capital accounts equal to the net assets taken over by the partnership. The partners personally guaranteed that the receivables invested were collectible. The assets and liabilities acquired by the partnership in this manner were as follows:

	L	M	N
Cash	$10,000	$10,000	$10,000
Accounts receivable	28,000	12,000	32,000
Law library and furniture	8,600	5,000	12,400
Accumulated depreciation	(4,800)	(3,000)	(9,400)
Total assets	$41,800	$24,000	$45,000
Less: Accounts payable	1,600	3,800	4,400
Net assets (capital invested)	$40,200	$20,200	$40,600

(2) The partners decided to occupy N's office space until the lease expired on June 30, Year 1. The monthly rental was $1,200, but the partners agreed that this was an excessive rate for the space provided and that $900 monthly would be reasonable. They therefore agreed that the excess rent would be charged to N at the end of the year. When the lease expired on June 30, Year 1, the partners moved to a new office with a monthly rental of $1,000.

(3) The income-sharing agreement did not provide for salaries to the partners but specified that individual partners should receive 20% of the gross fees billed to their respective clients during the first year of the partnership. The balance of the fees after deduction of operating expenses was to be credited to the partners' capital accounts as follows: L, 40%; M, 40%; N, 20%.

A new partner, O, was admitted to the partnership on April 1, Year 1; O was to receive 20% of the fees from new business obtained after April 1 after deduction of expenses applicable to that new business. Expenses were to be apportioned to the new business in the same ratio that total expenses, other than doubtful accounts expense, bore to total gross fees.

(4) Fees were billed during Year 1 as follows:

L's clients	$ 44,000
M's clients	24,000
N's clients	22,000
New clients acquired after Jan. 1, Year 1:	
Prior to April 1	6,000
After April 1	24,000
Total	$120,000

(5) Total expenses for Year 1 were $38,700, excluding depreciation and doubtful accounts expense but including the total amount paid for rent. Depreciation was to be computed at the rate of 10% on original cost to individual partners. Depreciable assets purchased during Year 1, on which one-half year's depreciation was to be taken, totaled $10,000.

(6) Cash withdrawals debited to the partners' drawing accounts during Year 1 were as follows:

L	$10,400
M	8,800
N	11,600
O	5,000
Total	$35,800

(7) Accounts receivable acquired from L in the amount of $2,400 and from M in the amount of $900 proved to be uncollectible. Also, a new client billed in March for $3,000 had been adjudged bankrupt and a settlement of 40 cents on the dollar was made.

Instructions Prepare a statement of partners' capitals for the year ended December 31, Year 1. All supporting computations should be carefully organized and presented in good form. Disregard income taxes.

2

PARTNERSHIP LIQUIDATION; JOINT VENTURES

LIQUIDATION OF A PARTNERSHIP

The meaning of liquidation

The liquidation of a partnership means winding up the business, usually by selling the assets, paying the liabilities, and distributing the remaining cash to the partners. In some cases, the business may be sold as a unit, with the purchaser assuming the liabilities; in other cases, the assets may be sold in installments and most or all of the cash received must be used to pay creditors. A business which has ended normal operations and is in the process of converting its assets into cash and making settlement with its creditors is said to be *in liquidation* or in the process of being liquidated. This process of liquidation may be completed quickly or it may require several months or years.

The term *liquidation* is also used in a narrower sense to mean the payment of liabilities; however, in this chapter we shall use it only in the broader sense of bringing to a close the business of a partnership. Another term commonly used by a business in process of liquidation is *realization,* which means the conversion of assets into cash.

When the decision is made to liquidate a partnership, the accounting records should be adjusted and closed, and the net income or net loss for the final period of operations entered in the capital accounts of the partners.

The liquidation process usually begins with the sale (realization) of assets. The gains or losses from realization of assets should be divided among the partners in the income-sharing ratio and entered in their capital accounts. The amounts shown as their respective equities at this point are the basis for settlement. However, before any payment to partners, all outside creditors must be paid in full. If the cash obtained through realization of assets is insufficient to pay liabilities in full, any unpaid creditor may act to enforce collection from the personal assets of any partner, regardless of whether that partner has a positive or negative capital account balance. As pointed out in the preceding chapter, a partnership is viewed as an entity for many purposes such as changes in partnership personnel, but it cannot use the shield of a separate entity to protect partners personally against the claims of partnership creditors.

Distribution of loss or gain

The underlying theme in accounting for the liquidation of a partnership may be stated as follows: *Distribute the loss or gain from the realization of assets before distributing the cash.* As assets are sold, any loss or gain is apportioned among the partners' capital accounts in the income-sharing ratio. The amount of cash, if any, which a partner is entitled to receive in liquidation cannot be determined until partners' capital accounts have been adjusted for any loss or gain on the realization of the assets. Strictly interpreted, this reasoning might indicate that no cash can be distributed to a partner until after all the assets have been sold, because the net loss or gain will not be known until the sale of all assets has been completed. In this chapter we shall illustrate a series of liquidations in which the realization of assets is completed before any payments are made to partners. Also, we shall consider liquidation in installments; that is, payments to partners after some of the assets have been sold and the liabilities paid, but with the final loss or gain from sale of the remaining assets not yet known. The installment payments to partners are computed by a method which provides a safeguard against overpayment.

An important service by accountants to a partnership in liquidation is to determine proper distribution of cash or other assets to individual partners after the liabilities have been paid. The partners may choose to receive certain assets, such as automobiles or furniture, *in kind* rather than to convert such property into cash. Regardless of whether cash or other assets are being distributed to partners, it is imperative to follow the basic rule that no distribution of assets may be made to partners until after all possible losses and liquidation expenses have been taken into account. Failure to follow this basic rule may result in overpayment of a partner. If the partner is unable to return the excess payment, the person who authorized the improper distribution may become personally liable for any losses sustained by the other partners.

Distribution of cash

The Uniform Partnership Act lists the order for distribution of cash as (1) payment of creditors in full, (2) payment of partners' loan accounts, and (3) payment of partners' capital accounts. The indicated priority of partners' loans over partners' capitals appears to be a legal fiction. This rule is nullified for all practical purposes by an established legal doctrine called the **right of offset.** If a partner has a debit balance in his or her capital account (or even a potential debit balance depending on possible future losses), any credit balance in a partner's loan account must be offset against the deficiency (or potential deficiency) in the capital account. Because of the right of offset, the total amount of cash received by a partner during the liquidation process always will be the same as if loans to the partnership had been recorded in the capital account. Furthermore, the existence of a partner's loan account will not advance the time of payment to any partner during the liquidation. Consequently, in preparing a statement of realization and liquidation, the accountant may prefer to reduce the number of columns and simplify the statement by combining the amount of a partner's loan with the amount shown in the partner's capital account. The statement of realization and liquidation then will include only one column for each partner; the top figure in the column will be the total equity (including any loans) of the partner at the beginning of liquidation.

Combining the capital and loan accounts of a partner in the statement of realization and liquidation does not imply merging these accounts in the ledger. Separate ledger accounts for capital and for loans should be maintained to provide a clear record of the terms under which funds were invested by the partners.

Determining the settlement with each partner

The amount which each partner receives from the liquidation of a partnership will be equal to (1) the capital invested in the business, whether recorded in a capital account or in a loan account; (2) a share of operating net income or loss minus the drawings; and (3) a share of loss or gain from the realization of assets in the course of liquidation. In other words, each partner will receive in the settlement the amount of his or her equity in the partnership. The amount of a partner's equity is increased by the positive factors of investing capital and sharing in net income; it is decreased by the negative factors of drawings and sharing in net losses. If the negative factors are larger, the partner will have a capital deficiency (a debit balance in a capital account), and the partner must pay to the partnership the amount of such deficiency. Failure to make good a capital deficiency by payment to the partnership would mean that the partner had not lived up to the partnership contract for sharing net income or loss. This would cause the other partners to bear more than their contractual share of losses, or, stated conversely, to receive less in settlement than their equities in the business.

Division of losses and gains during liquidation

The income-sharing ratio used during the operation of the partnership is also applicable to the losses and gains during liquidation, unless the partners have a different agreement. A partnership contract is not super-seded because of the decision to cease operations; the agreement for division of earnings therefore continues in force.

Accountants generally agree that the annual or quarterly determina-tions of net income or loss are approximations because of the estimates involved on such matters as the economic life of plant assets and the collectibility of accounts receivable. Errors in these estimates affect the periodic net income or loss allocated to the partners. Consequently, the net loss or gain resulting from the liquidation of a partnership should be divided among the partners in the same ratio used in dividing net income or loss from normal operations.

When the net loss or gain from liquidation is divided among the part-ners, the final balances in the partners' capital and loan accounts will be equal to the cash available for distribution to them. *Payments are then made in the amounts of the partners' respective equities in the business.*

Equity of each partner sufficient to absorb loss from liquidation

Assume that A and B, who share earnings equally, decide to liquidate their partnership. A condensed balance sheet at June 30, Year 5, just prior to liquidation, is as follows:

A & B PARTNERSHIP
Balance Sheet
June 30, Year 5

Assets		Liabilities & Partners' Capitals	
Cash	$10,000	Liabilities	$20,000
Other assets	75,000	B, loan	20,000
		A, capital	40,000
		B, capital	5,000
Total	$85,000	Total	$85,000

As a first step in the liquidation, the noncash assets with a carrying amount of $75,000 are sold for cash of $35,000, with a resultant loss of $40,000 to be shared equally by A and B. Since B's capital account is only $5,000, it will be necessary for the accountant to exercise the right of offset by transferring $15,000 from the loan account to the capital account. The following statement of realization and liquidation, covering the period July 1–15, Year 5, shows the division of the loss between the partners, the payment of creditors, and the distribution of the remaining cash to the partners. (The income-sharing ratio appears next to each partner's name.)

A & B PARTNERSHIP
Statement of Realization and Liquidation
July 1–15, Year 5

	Assets				Partners' capitals	
	Cash	Other	Liabilities	B, loan	A(50%)	B(50%)
Balances before liquidation	$10,000	$75,000	$20,000	$20,000	$40,000	$ 5,000
Sale of assets at a loss of $40,000	35,000	(75,000)			(20,000)	(20,000)
Balances	$45,000		$20,000	$20,000	$20,000	$(15,000)
Payment to creditors	(20,000)		(20,000)			
Balances	$25,000			$20,000	$20,000	$(15,000)
Offset B's capital deficit against loan account				(15,000)		15,000
Balances	$25,000			$ 5,000	$20,000	
Payment to partners	(25,000)			(5,000)	(20,000)	

In the statement of realization and liquidation, B's loan account of $20,000 and capital account of $5,000 may be combined into a single equity figure of $25,000 for B. As stated earlier, such a procedure would be appropriate because the statutory priority of a partner's loan account has no significance in determining either the total amount of cash paid to a partner or the timing of the payments during liquidation.

In the preceding illustration, partner A received a settlement of $20,000 and partner B a settlement of $5,000. Neither partner received payment until after creditors had been paid in full. Because assets consist entirely of cash of $25,000 at this point, it is reasonable to assume that checks to A and B for $20,000 and $5,000, respectively, were written and delivered to the partners at the same time. It is apparent that a partner's loan account has no special significance in the liquidation process. Therefore, in succeeding illustrations we shall not show a partner's loan account in a separate column of the statement of realization and liquidation. Whenever a partner's loan account is encountered, it may be combined with the partner's capital account in the statement of realization and liquidation.

Equity of one partner not sufficient to absorb that partner's share of loss from liquidation

In this case, the loss on realization of assets when distributed in the income-sharing ratio results in a debit balance in the capital account of one of the partners. It may be assumed that the partner with a debit balance has no loan account, or that the total of the partner's capital account and loan account combined is less than the partner's share of the loss on realization. To fulfill an agreement to share a given percentage of partnership earnings, the partner must pay to the partnership sufficient cash to eliminate any capital deficiency. If the partner is unable to do so, the deficiency must be absorbed by the other partners as an additional loss to be shared in the same proportion as they have previously shared earnings among themselves. Assume the following balance sheet for D, E, and F just prior to liquidation.

D, E, & F PARTNERSHIP
Balance Sheet
May 20, Year 10

Assets		Liabilities & Partners' Capitals	
Cash	$ 20,000	Liabilities	$ 30,000
Other assets	80,000	D, capital	40,000
		E, capital	21,000
		F, capital	9,000
Total	$100,000	Total	$100,000

The income-sharing ratio is D 20%, E 40%, and F 40%. The other assets with a carrying amount of $80,000 are sold for $50,000 cash, resulting in a loss of $30,000 to be divided among the partners. Partner F is charged with 40% of this loss, or $12,000, which creates a debit balance of $3,000 in F's capital account. In the following statement of realization and liquidation, it is assumed that F pays the $3,000 to the partnership:

D, E, & F PARTNERSHIP
Statement of Realization and Liquidation
May 21–31, Year 10

	Assets			Partners' capitals		
	Cash	Other	Liabilities	D(20%)	E(40%)	F(40%)
Balances before liquidation	$20,000	$80,000	$30,000	$40,000	$21,000	$ 9,000
Sale of assets at a loss of $30,000	50,000	(80,000)		(6,000)	(12,000)	(12,000)
Balances	$70,000		$30,000	$34,000	$ 9,000	$ (3,000)
Payment to creditors	(30,000)		(30,000)			
Balances	$40,000			$34,000	$ 9,000	$ (3,000)
Cash paid in by F	3,000					3,000
Balances	$43,000			$34,000	$ 9,000	
Payments to partners	(43,000)			(34,000)	(9,000)	

Illustration of completed liquidation

Next, let us change one condition of the preceding illustration by assuming that partner F was not able to pay the $3,000 debt to the partnership. If the cash on hand after payment of creditors is to be distributed to D and E without a delay to determine the collectibility of the $3,000 claim against F, the statement of realization and liquidation will appear as follows:

Illustration of incomplete liquidation

D, E, & F PARTNERSHIP
Statement of Realization and Liquidation
May 21–31, Year 10

	Assets			Partners' capitals		
	Cash	Other	Liabilities	D(20%)	E(40%)	F(40%)
Balances before liquidation	$20,000	$80,000	$30,000	$40,000	$21,000	$ 9,000
Sale of assets at a loss of $30,000	50,000	(80,000)		(6,000)	(12,000)	(12,000)
Balances	$70,000		$30,000	$34,000	$ 9,000	$ (3,000)
Payment to creditors	(30,000)		(30,000)			
Balances	$40,000			$34,000	$ 9,000	$ (3,000)
Payment to partners	(40,000)			(33,000)	(7,000)	
Balances				$ 1,000	$ 2,000	$ (3,000)

The cash payments of $33,000 to D and $7,000 to E leave them with a sufficient credit balance to absorb their share of the additional loss if F fails to make good the capital account debit balance of $3,000. The income-sharing ratio is 20% for D and 40% for E; consequently, the possible additional loss of $3,000 would be charged to them in the proportion of $2/6$ or $1,000 to D, and $4/6$ or $2,000 to E. The payment of the $40,000 cash available to partners therefore is divided between them in a manner that pays D down to a capital account balance of $1,000 and pays E down to a balance of $2,000.

If F later pays in the $3,000 owed to the partnership, this amount will be divided $1,000 to D and $2,000 to E. The preceding statement of realization and liquidation then could be completed as follows:

Completion of liquidation: deficiency paid in by Partner F

	Cash	D(20%)	E(40%)	F(40%)
Balance from bottom of page 52 .		$1,000	$2,000	$(3,000)
Cash paid in by F	$3,000			3,000
Payments to partners	(3,000)	(1,000)	(2,000)	

On the other hand, if the $3,000 due from F is determined to be uncollectible, the statement of realization and liquidation would be completed with the write-off of F's debit balance shown as an additional loss borne by D and E as follows:

Completion of liquidation: Partner F unable to pay deficiency

	Cash	D(20%)	E(40%)	F(40%)
Balances from bottom of page 52		$1,000	$2,000	$(3,000)
Additional loss from inability to collect deficiency from F		(1,000)	(2,000)	3,000

Equities of two partners not sufficient to absorb their shares of loss from liquidation

We have already observed that inability of a partner to make good a deficiency in a capital account causes an additional loss to the other partners. A partner may have sufficient capital or combination of capital and loan accounts to absorb any direct share of loss on the realization of assets, but not a sufficient equity to absorb additional actual or potential losses caused by inability of the partnership to collect the deficiency in another partner's capital account. In brief, one capital deficiency, if not collectible, may cause a second capital deficiency, which may or may not be collectible.

Assume that J, K, L, and M are partners sharing earnings in the ratio of 10%, 20%, 30%, and 40%. Their capital accounts for the period August 1–15, Year 4, are as shown in the statement of realization and liquidation on page 56. The assets are realized at a loss of $80,000, and creditors are paid in full. Cash of $20,000 is available for distribution to the partners. In this distribution, the guiding principle is to pay each partner an amount equal to the excess of a partner's capital account over any additional possible losses which may be charged against the partner. In other words, pay a partner's capital account down to the level necessary to absorb any additional losses which may be charged against one partner because of the uncollectibility of deficiencies owed by other partners.

The statement of realization and liquidation on page 56, along with Schedule A below, show that the $20,000 of available cash can be distributed $16,000 to J and $4,000 to K. If the $24,000 deficiency in M's capital proves uncollectible, the additional loss to be divided among the other three partners will cause L's capital account to change from a $6,000 credit balance to a $6,000 debit balance (deficiency). L is therefore not eligible to receive a cash payment. If this deficiency in L's account proves uncollectible, the balances remaining in the capital accounts of J and K, after the cash payment indicated above, will be equal to the amounts needed to absorb the additional loss shifted from L's account.

J, K, L, & M PARTNERSHIP
Schedule A: Computation of Cash Payments to Partners
August 15, Year 4

	Partners' capitals			
	J(10%)	K(20%)	L(30%)	M(40%)
Capital balance before distribution of cash to partners	$22,000	$16,000	$ 6,000	$(24,000)
Additional loss to J, K, and L if M's deficiency is uncollectible (ratio of 10:20:30)	(4,000)	(8,000)	(12,000)	24,000
Balances	$18,000	$ 8,000	$ (6,000)	
Additional loss to J and K if L's deficiency is uncollectible (ratio of 10:20)	(2,000)	(4,000)	6,000	
Amounts which may be paid to partners	$16,000	$ 4,000		

Partnership insolvent but partners personally solvent

If a partnership is insolvent, at least one and perhaps all of the partners will have deficiencies in their capital accounts. In any event, the total amount of the deficiencies will exceed the total of the credit balances. If the partner or partners with a capital deficiency pay in the required amount, the partnership will have cash to pay its liabilities in full. However, the creditors may demand payment from **any** partner individually, regardless of whether a partner's capital account shows a deficiency or a credit balance. In terms of relationships with creditors, the partnership is not a separate entity. A partner who personally makes payment to partnership creditors receives a credit to the capital account. As an illustration of an insolvent partnership with partners personally solvent, assume that N, O, and P, who share earnings equally, present the following condensed balance sheet just prior to liquidation (May 10, Year 8):

N, O, & P PARTNERSHIP
Balance Sheet
May 10, Year 8

Assets		Liabilities & Partners' Capitals	
Cash	$ 15,000	Liabilities	$ 65,000
Other assets	85,000	N, capital	18,000
		O, capital	10,000
		P, capital	7,000
Total	$100,000	Total	$100,000

The other assets with a carrying amount of $85,000 are sold on May 12, Year 8, for $40,000 cash, which causes a loss of $45,000 to be divided equally among the partners. The total cash of $55,000 is paid to the creditors, which leaves unpaid liabilities of $10,000. Partner N has a credit balance of $3,000 after absorbing one-third of the loss. Partners O and P owe the partnership $5,000 and $8,000, respectively. If O and P pay in the amounts of their deficiencies, the partnership will use $10,000 of the $13,000 to pay the remaining liabilities and will distribute $3,000 to N on May 30, Year 8. These events are portrayed in the statement of realization and liquidation at the top of page 57.

J, K, L, & M PARTNERSHIP
Statement of Realization and Liquidation
August 1–15, Year 4

	Assets			Partners' capitals			
	Cash	Other	Liabilities	J(10%)	K(20%)	L(30%)	M(40%)
Balances before liquidation	$ 20,000	$200,000	$120,000	$30,000	$32,000	$30,000	$ 8,000
Sales of assets at a loss of $80,000	120,000	(200,000)		(8,000)	(16,000)	(24,000)	(32,000)
Balances	$140,000		$120,000	$22,000	$16,000	$ 6,000	$(24,000)
Payment to creditors	(120,000)		(120,000)				
Balances	$ 20,000			$22,000	$16,000	$ 6,000	$(24,000)
Payment to partners (Schedule A on page 54)	(20,000)			(16,000)	(4,000)		
Balances				$ 6,000	$12,000	$ 6,000	$(24,000)

N, O, & P PARTNERSHIP
Statement of Realization and Liquidation
May 10–30, Year 8

	Assets			Partners' capitals		
	Cash	Other	Liabilities	N(⅓)	O(⅓)	P(⅓)
Balance before liquidation ..	$15,000	$85,000	$65,000	$18,000	$10,000	$ 7,000
Sale of assets at a loss of						
$45,000	40,000	(85,000)		(15,000)	(15,000)	(15,000)
Balances	$55,000		$65,000	$ 3,000	$ (5,000)	$ (8,000)
Partial payment to creditors .	(55,000)		(55,000)			
Balances	$ -0-		$10,000	$ 3,000	$ (5,000)	$ (8,000)
Cash paid in by O and P ..	13,000				5,000	8,000
Balances	$13,000		$10,000	$ 3,000		
Final payment to creditors ..	(10,000)		(10,000)			
Balances	$ 3,000			$ 3,000		
Payment to N	(3,000)			(3,000)		

Assume that there was some delay in collecting the deficiencies from O and P, and during this period the creditors demanded and received payment of their $10,000 in claims from partner N. This payment by N would cause N's equity to increase from $3,000 to $13,000. When O and P paid in their deficiencies totaling $13,000, this amount of cash then would be paid to N by the partnership.

Another alternative is that creditors might collect the final $10,000 due them directly from O or P. Payments by these partners to creditors would increase their equities and eliminate or reduce their indebtedness to the firm. As long as we assume that the partners with deficiencies make payment to the partnership or directly to partnership creditors, the results are the same. Creditors will be paid in full and partners will share losses on liquidation as provided in the partnership contract.

Partnership insolvent and partners personally insolvent

In the preceding illustration of an insolvent partnership, we assumed that the partners were personally solvent and therefore able to pay in their capital deficiencies. We shall now consider an insolvent partnership in which one or more of the partners are personally insolvent. This situation raises a question as to the relative rights of two groups of creditors: (1) those persons who extended credit to the partnership, and (2) those persons who extended credit to the partners as individuals. The relative rights of these two groups of creditors are governed by the legal rules of *marshaling of assets.* These legal rules provide that assets of the partnership are first available to creditors of the partnership, and that assets owned individually by the partners are first available to their personal creditors. After the debts of the partnership have been paid in full, if any assets remain in the partnership, the creditors of an individual partner have a claim against the assets of the partnership to the extent of that partner's equity in the partnership.

After the personal creditors of a partner have been paid in full from the personal assets of the partner, any remaining personal assets are available to partnership creditors, regardless of whether the partner's capital account shows a credit or debit balance. Such claims by creditors of the partnership are permitted only when these creditors are unable to obtain payment from the partnership.

To illustrate the relative rights of creditors of an insolvent partnership and personal creditors of an insolvent partner, assume that R, S, and T, who share earnings equally, have the following balance sheet just prior to liquidation on November 30, Year 10:

R, S, & T PARTNERSHIP
Balance Sheet
November 30, Year 10

Assets		Liabilities & Partners' Capitals	
Cash	$ 10,000	Liabilities	$ 60,000
Other assets	100,000	R, capital	5,000
		S, capital	15,000
		T, capital	30,000
Total	$110,000	Total	$110,000

Assume also that on November 30, Year 10, the partners as individuals have the following personal assets and liabilities apart from the equities they have in the partnership:

Partner	Personal assets	Personal liabilities
R	$100,000	$25,000
S	50,000	50,000
T	5,000	60,000

List of personal assets and liabilities

The realization of partnership assets results in a loss of $60,000, as shown in the statement of realization and liquidation at the top of page 59 for the period December 1–12, Year 10.

R, S, & T PARTNERSHIP
Statement of Realization and Liquidation
December 1–12, Year 10

	Assets			Partners' capitals		
	Cash	Other	Liabilities	R(⅓)	S(⅓)	T(⅓)
Balances before liquidation	$10,000	$100,000	$60,000	$ 5,000	$15,000	$30,000
Sale of assets at a loss of $60,000	40,000	(100,000)		(20,000)	(20,000)	(20,000)
Balances	$50,000		$60,000	$(15,000)	$(5,000)	$10,000
Payment to creditors..	(50,000)		(50,000)			
Balances			$10,000	$(15,000)	$ (5,000)	$10,000

Liquidation not completed   The creditors of the partnership have received all the assets of the partnership and still have unpaid claims of $10,000. They cannot collect from S or T personally because the personal assets of these two partners are just sufficient or are insufficient to meet their personal liabilities. However, the partnership creditors can collect the $10,000 in full from R, who is personally solvent. By chance, R has a capital deficiency of $15,000, but this is of no concern to the creditors. Creditors could collect in full from any partner who had sufficient personal assets, regardless of whether that partner's capital account showed a debit or a credit balance. The statement of realization and liquidation shown above is now continued to show the payment by R personally of the final $10,000 due to partnership creditors. Since our assumptions about R's personal finances showed that R had $100,000 of assets and only $25,000 in liabilities, R is also able to pay into the firm the additional $5,000 needed to offset the capital deficiency. This $5,000 of cash is paid to partner T, the only partner with a positive capital balance.

Continuation of statement of realization and liquidation

			Partners' capitals		
	Cash	Liabilities	R(⅓)	S(⅓)	T(⅓)
Balances as above		$10,000	$(15,000)	$(5,000)	$10,000
Payment by R to partnership creditors		(10,000)	10,000		
Balances			$ (5,000)	$(5,000)	$10,000
Additional investment by R	$5,000		5,000		
Balances	$5,000			$(5,000)	$10,000
Payment to T (or to T's creditors)	(5,000)				(5,000)
Balances				$(5,000)	$ 5,000

The continued statement of realization and liquidation now shows that S owes $5,000 to the firm; however, S's personal assets of $50,000 are exactly equal to S's personal liabilities of $50,000. Under the Uniform Partnership Act, all the personal assets of S will go to personal creditors; therefore the $5,000 deficiency in S's capital account represents an additional loss to be shared equally by R and T. To conclude the liquidation, R, who is personally solvent, will be required to pay $2,500 to the partnership, and the amount will go to T or to T's personal creditors, because T is insolvent. These payments are shown below to complete the statement of realization and liquidation.

Completion of liquidation

| | Cash | Partners' capitals | | |
		R(⅓)	S(⅓)	T(⅓)
Balances carried forward			$(5,000)	$5,000
Write off S's deficiency as uncollectible .		$(2,500)	5,000	(2,500)
Balances		$(2,500)		$2,500
Cash paid in by R	$2,500	2,500		
Balances	$2,500			$2,500
Payment to T (or to T's creditors)	(2,500)			(2,500)

The final results of the liquidation show that the partnership creditors received payment in full because of the personal financial strength of partner R. Since R was personally solvent, the personal creditors of R could also collect in full. The personal creditors of S were paid in full, thereby exhausting S's personal assets; however, because S failed to make good the $5,000 capital deficiency, an additional loss of $5,000 was shifted to R and T. The personal creditors of T received all of T's personal assets of $5,000 and also $7,500 from the partnership, representing T's equity in the firm. However, T's personal creditors were able to collect a total of only $12,500 on their claims of $60,000.

INSTALLMENT PAYMENTS TO PARTNERS

In the illustrations of partnership liquidation in the preceding sections, all the assets were sold and the total loss from liquidation was divided among the partners before any payments were made to them. However, the liquidation of some partnerships may extend over several months; in these extended liquidations the partners usually will want to receive cash as it becomes available rather than waiting until all assets have been converted into cash. Installment payments to partners are quite proper if the necessary safeguards are used to ensure that all creditors are paid in full and that no partners are paid more than the amount to which they would be entitled after all losses on realization of assets have become known.

Liquidation in installments may be regarded as a process of selling some of the assets, paying creditors, paying the remaining available cash to partners, selling additional assets, and making further payments to partners. The liquidation continues until all assets have been sold and all cash has been distributed to creditors and partners.

The circumstances of installment liquidation are likely to vary; consequently, our approach is to emphasize the general principles guiding liquidation in installments rather than to provide illustrative models of all possible liquidation situations. Among the variables which cause partnership liquidations to differ are the sufficiency of each partner's capital to absorb that partner's share of the possible losses remaining after each installment, the shifting of losses from one partner to another because of inability to collect a capital deficiency, the offsetting of loan accounts against capital deficiencies, and the possible need for setting aside cash to meet future liquidation expenses or unpaid liabilities.

General principles guiding installment payment procedures

The critical element in installment liquidations is that the liquidator authorizes cash payments to partners before losses that may be incurred on the liquidation are known. If payments are made to partners and later losses cause deficiencies to develop in the capital accounts, the liquidator will have to ask for the return of the payments. If the payments cannot be recovered, the liquidator may be personally liable to the other partners for the loss caused them by the improper distribution of cash. Because of this danger, the only safe policy for determining installment cash payments to partners is summarized as follows:

1 Assume a total loss on all remaining assets and provide for all possible losses, including potential liquidation expenses.
2 Assume that any partner with a potential capital deficiency will be unable to pay anything to the firm; in other words, distribute each installment of cash as if no more cash would be forthcoming, either from sale of assets or from collection of deficiencies from partners.

Under these assumptions the liquidator will authorize a payment to a partner only if that partner has a credit balance in the capital account (or in the capital and loan accounts combined) in excess of the amount required to absorb a portion of the maximum possible loss which may be incurred on liquidation. A partner's "share of the maximum possible loss" would include any loss that may result from the inability of partners to make good any capital deficiencies which may arise in their capital accounts.

When installment payments are made according to these rules, the effect will be to bring the equities of the partners into the income-sharing ratio as quickly as possible. *When installment payments have pro-*

ceeded to the point that the partners' capitals correspond to the income-sharing ratio, all subsequent payments can be made in that ratio, because each partner's capital will be sufficient to absorb an appropriate share of the maximum possible remaining loss.

Advance planning for installment payments to partners

The amounts of cash which could be distributed safely to the partners each month (or at any other point in time) may be determined by calculating the impact on partners' equities (capital and loan balances) of the maximum possible remaining loss. Although this method is sound, it is somewhat cumbersome. Furthermore, it does not show at the beginning of the liquidation how cash will be divided among the partners as it may become available. For these reasons, it is more efficient to prepare a complete cash distribution program in advance to show how cash will be divided in the course of liquidation. If such a program of cash distribution is prepared, any amounts of cash received from disposal of partnership assets can be paid immediately to the partners as specified in this program.

Assume that X, Y, and Z, who share earnings in a 4:3:2 ratio, decide to liquidate their business and want a complete cash distribution program prepared in advance. The balance sheet for the X, Y, & Z Partnership just prior to liquidation on July 5, Year 1, is as follows:

X, Y, & Z PARTNERSHIP
Balance Sheet
July 5, Year 1

Assets		Liabilities & Partners' Capitals	
Cash	$ 8,000	Liabilities	$ 61,000
Other assets	192,000	X, capital	40,000
		Y, capital	45,000
		Z, capital	54,000
Total	$200,000	Total	$200,000

The first $61,000 of available cash must, of course, be paid to creditors; any additional amount can be paid to partners. The amount of cash to be paid to partners during liquidation may be developed as illustrated on pages 63 and 64.

The procedures followed in the development of the cash distribution program are explained below:

1 The net capital balances before liquidation represent the **equities** of the partners in the partnership, that is, the balance in a partner's capital account,

plus or minus the balance (if any) of a loan made by a partner to the partnership or a loan made by the partnership to a partner.

2 The net capital balance before liquidation for each partner is divided by each partner's income-sharing ratio to determine the amount of net capital per unit of income sharing for each partner. This step is critical because it (**a**) identifies the partner with the largest net capital per unit of income sharing who therefore will be the first to receive cash, (**b**) facilitates the ranking of partners in the order in which they will be entitled to receive cash, and (**c**) provides the basis for determining the amount of cash each partner should receive at various stages of the liquidation. Because Z's net capital per unit of income sharing is largest, Z will be the first to receive cash, followed by Y, and finally by X.

X, Y, & Z PARTNERSHIP
Cash Distributions to Partners during Liquidation
July 5, Year 1

	X	Y	Z
Net capital balances before liquidation	$40,000	$45,000	$54,000
Income-sharing ratio	4	3	2
Divide net capital balances before liquidation by income-sharing ratio to obtain net capital per unit of income sharing for each partner ..	$10,000	$15,000	$27,000
Required reduction in capital per unit of income sharing for Z to bring Z's balance down to the next highest balance (for partner Y). This is the amount of the first cash distribution to a partner **per unit** of the partner's income sharing. Because Z has 2 units of income sharing, Z will receive the first $24,000 ($12,000 × 2 = $24,000)			(12,000)
Balances per unit of income sharing	$10,000	$15,000	$15,000
Required reduction in capital per unit of income sharing for Y and Z to bring their balances down to X's balance, which is the lowest capital per unit of income sharing. The required reduction is multiplied by each partner's income-sharing ratio to determine the amount of cash to be paid. Thus Y receives $15,000 ($5,000 × 3 = $15,000), and Z receives $10,000 ($5,000 × 2 = $10,000)		(5,000)	(5,000)
Balances per unit of income sharing after payment of $15,000 to Y and $34,000 to Z. **Remaining cash now can be distributed in the income-sharing ratio**	$10,000	$10,000	$10,000

(continued)

X, Y, & Z PARTNERSHIP

Cash Distributions to Partners during Liquidation (continued)

July 5, Year 1

Summary of cash distribution program:

	Total	X	Y	Z
To creditors before partners receive anything	$ 61,000			
To partners:				
1 First distribution to Z:				
$12,000 × 2	24,000			$24,000
2 Second distribution to Y and Z in 3:2 ratio:				
Y—$5,000 × 3 .... $15,000				
Z—$5,000 × 2 10,000	25,000		$15,000	10,000
	$110,000			
3 Any amount in excess of $110,000 to X, Y, and Z in income-sharing ratio		$4/9$	$3/9$	$2/9$

3 Z receives enough cash to bring Z's net capital balance of $27,000 per unit of income sharing down to $15,000 so that it will be equal to the balance for Y, the second ranking partner. To accomplish this, Z's balance must be reduced by $12,000 per unit of income sharing, and because Z has 2 units of income sharing, Z must receive $24,000 ($12,000 × 2 = $24,000) before Y receives any cash.

4 At this point the net capital balances per unit of income sharing for Y and Z are equal at $15,000, indicating that they are entitled to receive cash until their balances are reduced by $5,000 to bring them down to the $10,000 balance for X, the lowest ranking partner. Because Y has 3 units and Z has 2 units of income sharing, Y receives $15,000 ($5,000 × 3 = $15,000) and Z receives $10,000 ($5,000 × 2 = $10,000) before X receives any cash. After Z receives $24,000, Y and Z would share any amount of cash available up to a maximum amount of $25,000 in a 3:2 ratio.

5 After Y has received $15,000 and Z has received $34,000 ($24,000 + $10,000 = $34,000), the net capital balances per unit of income sharing are $10,000 for each of the three partners, and any additional cash is paid to the partners in the income-sharing ratio (4:3:2) because their capitals have been brought down to the income-sharing ratio. This is illustrated below:

	X($4/9$)	Y($3/9$)	Z($2/9$)
Net capital balances before liquidation	$40,000	$45,000	$54,000
First payment of cash to Z			(24,000)
Second payment of cash to Y and Z in 3:2 ratio......................................		(15,000)	(10,000)
Net capital balances (in income-sharing ratio of 4:3:2) after payment of $49,000 to Y and Z.....................................	$40,000	$30,000	$20,000

Only when installment payments reach the point at which partners' net capital balances correspond to the income-sharing ratio can subsequent payments be made in that ratio.[1]

We should point out that a cash distribution program, such as the one developed above, should also be used to ascertain an equitable distribution of noncash assets to the partners. The current fair value of noncash assets such as securities, inventories, or equipment distributed to partners should be treated as equivalent to cash payments. If a distribution of noncash assets departs from the cash distribution program by giving one of the partners a larger distribution than that partner is entitled to receive, subsequent distributions should be adjusted to allow the remaining partners to "make up" the distribution prematurely made to one of the partners. In such cases it would be desirable to prepare a **revised cash distribution program,** because the original relationship between the partners' capital accounts has been disrupted. To be on the safe side, the liquidator may also choose to require a bond from the partner receiving the premature distribution or may arrange for such noncash assets to be placed in trust until the liquidation has been completed.

To illustrate how the cash distribution program can be used, assume that the realization of assets by the partnership of X, Y, and Z from July 5 to September 30, Year 1, is as follows:

	X, Y, & Z PARTNERSHIP Realization of Assets July 5–September 30, Year 1		
Month	Carrying amount of assets sold	Loss on sale	Cash received by partnership
July	$ 62,000	$13,500	$ 48,500
August	66,000	36,000	30,000
September	64,000	31,500	32,500
Totals	$192,000	$81,000	$111,000

The cash available each month should be paid to creditors and partners according to the summary of cash distribution program on page 64 as follows:

---

[1] The procedure for preparing a cash distribution program illustrated above can be used regardless of the number of partners involved and the complexity of the income-sharing ratio. For example, assume that partners share earnings as follows: A 41.2%, B 32.3%, C 26.5%. We can view the income-sharing ratio as 412 for A, 323 for B, and 265 for C and apply the same technique illustrated in this section.

X, Y, & Z PARTNERSHIP
Distribution of Cash to Creditors and Partners
July 5–September 30, Year 1

Month	Cash	Liabilities	Partners' capitals		
			X($4/9$)	Y($3/9$)	Z($2/9$)
July (including $8,000 on hand at July 5)	$ 56,500	$56,500			
August	30,000	4,500			$24,000 ⎫
				$ 900	600 ⎬
September	32,500			14,100	9,400 ⎫
			$4,000	3,000	2,000 ⎬
Totals	$119,000	$61,000	$4,000	$18,000	$36,000

The entire cash balance of $56,500 available in July is paid to creditors, leaving $4,500 in unpaid liabilities. When $30,000 becomes available in August, $4,500 should be paid to creditors, thus leaving $25,500 to be paid to the partners according to the cash distribution program developed earlier. The program calls for Z to receive the first $24,000 available for distribution to partners and for Y and Z to share the next $25,000 in a 3:2 ratio. In August only $1,500 ($30,000 − $4,500 − $24,000 = $1,500) is available for payment to Y and Z; thus Y and Z receive $900 and $600, respectively. Of the $32,500 available in September, the first $23,500 is paid to Y and Z in a 3:2 ratio, or $14,100 and $9,400, respectively, in order to complete the distribution of $25,000 to Y and Z before X participates; this leaves $9,000 ($32,500 − $23,500 = $9,000) to be distributed to X, Y, and Z in the 4:3:2 income-sharing ratio.

A complete statement of realization and liquidation for X, Y, & Z Partnership is presented below:

X, Y, & Z PARTNERSHIP
Statement of Realization and Liquidation
July 5–September 30, Year 1

	Assets			Partners' capitals		
	Cash	Other	Liabilities	X(4)	Y(3)	Z(2)
Balances before liquidation	$ 8,000	$192,000	$61,000	$40,000	$45,000	$54,000
July installment:						
Sale of assets at a loss of $13,500	48,500	(62,000)		(6,000)	(4,500)	(3,000)
Balances	$56,500	$130,000	$61,000	$34,000	$40,500	$51,000
Payment to creditors ...	(56,500)		(56,500)			
Balances	$ -0-	$130,000	$ 4,500	$34,000	$40,500	$51,000

(continued)

X, Y, & Z PARTNERSHIP
Statement of Realization and Liquidation (continued)
July 5 to September 30, Year 1

	Assets			Partners' capitals		
	Cash	Other	Liabilities	X(4)	Y(3)	Z(2)
August installment:						
Sale of assets at a loss						
of $36,000	30,000	(66,000)		(16,000)	(12,000)	(8,000)
Balances	$30,000	$ 64,000	$ 4,500	$18,000	$28,500	$43,000
Payment to creditors ...	(4,500)		(4,500)			
Balances before any						
payment to partners ..	$25,500	$ 64,000		$18,000	$28,500	$43,000
Payment to partners ...	(25,500)				(900)	(24,600)
Balances	$ -0-	$ 64,000		$18,000	$27,600	$18,400
September installment:						
Sale of assets at a loss						
of $31,500	32,500	(64,000)		(14,000)	(10,500)	(7,000)
Balances	$32,500			$ 4,000	$17,100	$11,400
Payment to partners ...	(32,500)			(4,000)	(17,100)	(11,400)

The summary journal entries required to record the realization of assets and to complete the liquidation of the X, Y, & Z Partnership appear on page 68.

Withholding of cash for unpaid liabilities and liquidation expenses

As previously emphasized, creditors are entitled to payment in full before anything is paid to partners. However, in some cases the liquidator may find it more convenient to set aside in a separate fund the cash required to pay certain liabilities, and to distribute the remaining cash to the partners. The withholding of cash for payment of recorded liabilities is appropriate when for any reason it is not practicable or advisable (as when the amount of the claim is in dispute) to pay an obligation before cash is distributed to partners. An amount of cash equal to recorded unpaid liabilities which is set aside in a fund is not a factor in computing possible future losses; the possible future loss is measured by the amount of noncash assets, any *unrecorded* liabilities, and any potential liquidation expenses which may be incurred.

Any expenses incurred during the liquidation should be deducted to determine the cash available for distribution to partners. Expenses of liquidation thereby are treated as part of the total loss from liquidation. However, in some cases, the liquidator may wish to withhold cash in anticipation of future liquidation expenses. The amount of cash withheld

X, Y, & Z PARTNERSHIP
Journal Entries to Record Liquidation
July 5–September 30, Year 1

July	Cash	48,500	
	X, Capital	6,000	
	Y, Capital	4,500	
	Z, Capital	3,000	
	Other Assets		62,000
	To record sale of assets and division of loss of $13,500 among partners.		
	Liabilities	56,500	
	Cash		56,500
	Partial payment to creditors.		
Aug.	Cash	30,000	
	X, Capital	16,000	
	Y, Capital	12,000	
	Z, Capital	8,000	
	Other Assets		66,000
	To record sale of assets and division of loss of $36,000 among partners.		
	Liabilities	4,500	
	Y, Capital	900	
	Z, Capital	24,600	
	Cash		30,000
	Paid balance due to creditors and first installment to partners.		
Sept.	Cash	32,500	
	X, Capital	14,000	
	Y, Capital	10,500	
	Z, Capital	7,000	
	Other Assets		64,000
	To record sale of remaining assets and division of loss of $31,500 among partners.		
	X, Capital	4,000	
	Y, Capital	17,100	
	Z, Capital	11,400	
	Cash		32,500
	Paid final installment to partners to complete liquidation.		

or set aside for future liquidation expenses or for payment of liabilities not recorded in the accounts should be combined with the noncash assets in the computation of the maximum possible loss that may be incurred in completion of the liquidation of the partnership.

INCORPORATION OF A PARTNERSHIP

Most successful partnerships give consideration at times to the possible advantages to be gained by incorporating. Among the advantages are limited liability, ease of attracting outside capital without loss of control, and possible income tax savings.

A new corporation formed to take over the assets and liabilities of a partnership usually will sell capital stock to outsiders for cash, either at the time of incorporation or at a later date. To assure that the former partners receive an equitable portion of the total capital stock, the assets of the partnership must be adjusted to current fair value before being transferred to the corporation. Any identifiable intangible assets or goodwill developed by the partnership should be included among the assets transferred.

The accounting records of a partnership may be modified and continued in use when the firm changes to the corporate form. As an alternative, the partnership accounts may be closed and a new set of accounting records established for the corporation. The latter alternative generally is followed and is illustrated in the *Intermediate Accounting* text of this series.

If new accounting records are to be opened for the corporation, journal entries first should be made in the partnership accounts for revaluation of assets, liabilities, and partners' capitals. The next step is to transfer the assets and liabilities to the corporation, setting up a special receivable for the net amount due. This receivable is collected through receipt by the partnership of capital stock. The final journal entry to close the partnership accounts is based on distribution of the shares of capital stock to the partners by debits to their capital accounts and credits to the asset account representing capital stock of the new corporation held by the partnership.

The journal entries in the accounting records of the corporation consist of recording the net assets acquired from the partnership at the adjusted valuations, with an offsetting liability for the amount owed to the partnership. This liability is discharged by the issuance of shares of capital stock to the partnership, accompanied by credits to the Capital Stock and Paid-in Capital in Excess of Par accounts.

JOINT VENTURES

A *joint venture* differs from a partnership in that it is limited to carrying out a single project, such as the sale of a lot of merchandise or construction of a building. Historically, joint ventures were used to finance the sale or exchange of a cargo of merchandise in a foreign country. In an era when marine transportation and foreign trade involved many hazards, individuals would band together to undertake a venture of this type. The capital required usually was larger than one person could provide, and the risks were too great to be borne alone. Because of the risks involved and the relatively short duration of the project, no net income was recognized until the venture had been completed. At the end of the voyage, the net income was divided among the participants and their association was ended. A joint venture therefore may be regarded as a type of partnership which comes to an end with the attainment of a specific business objective.

In its traditional form, the accounting for a joint venture did not follow the accrual concept. The assumption of continuity was not appropriate; instead of the determination of net income at regular intervals, the measurement and reporting of net income or loss awaited the completion of the venture.

Present-day ventures

In today's business community, joint ventures are less common but still are employed for many projects such as (1) the purchase, development, and sale of a specific tract of real estate; (2) the sale of agricultural products; (3) exploration for oil and gas; or (4) the construction of a bridge, building, or dam. Since these associations are formed to carry out a specific project, they may be called joint ventures.

The term *corporate joint venture* also is used at present by many large American corporations to describe overseas operations by a company whose ownership is divided between the American corporation and a foreign company. Many examples of jointly owned companies also are found in some domestic industries. A corporate joint venture and the accounting for such a venture are described in *APB Opinion No. 18* as follows:

> "Corporate joint venture" refers to a corporation owned and operated by a small group of businesses (the "joint venturers") as a separate and specific business or project for the mutual benefit of the members of the group. A government may also be a member of the group. The purpose of a corporate joint venture frequently is to share risks and rewards in developing a new market, product or technology; to combine complementary technological knowledge; or to pool resources in developing production or other facilities. A corporate joint venture also usually provides an arrangement under which each joint venturer may participate, directly or indirectly, in the overall management of the joint venture. Joint venturers thus have an interest or relationship other than as passive investors. An entity which is a subsidiary of

one of the "joint venturers" is not a corporate joint venture. The ownership of a corporate joint venture seldom changes, and its stock is usually not traded publicly. A minority public ownership, however, does not preclude a corporation from being a corporate joint venture.[2]

. . . .

The Board concludes that the equity method best enables investors in corporate joint ventures to reflect the underlying nature of their investment in those ventures. Therefore, investors should account for investments in common stock of corporate joint ventures by the equity method, both in consolidated financial statements and in parent-company financial statements prepared for issuance to stockholders as the financial statements of the primary reporting entity.[3]

. . . .

When investments in common stock of corporate joint ventures or other investments of 50% or less accounted for under the equity method are, in the aggregate, material in relation to the financial position or results of operations of an investor, it may be necessary for summarized information as to assets, liabilities, and results of operations of the investees to be presented in the notes or in separate statements, either individually or in groups, as appropriate.[4]

Our use of the term *joint venture* in this chapter is in the traditional meaning of a partnership limited to carrying out a single project.

Accounting for a joint venture

The key issue in accounting for a joint venture is whether to establish a separate set of accounting records for the venture. If a separate set of accounting records is not established, two alternative methods are commonly used. One method calls for the recording of all transactions of the venture in the personal accounting records of each partner (participant). Each participant opens a Joint Venture account and also a receivable or payable for every other participant. The other method calls for recording in the accounting records of each participant only those venture transactions in which each is involved directly.

Separate Set of Accounting Records   The complexity of modern business, the emphasis upon good organization and strong internal control, the importance of income taxes, the extent of government regulation, and the need for preparation and retention of adequate accounting records are strong arguments for establishing a complete separate set of accounting records for every joint venture of large size and long duration. This approach views the joint venture as a separate accounting entity. Each participant is credited for the amount of cash or for the current fair value of noncash assets invested by each. The fiscal year of the joint venture may or may not coincide with the fiscal years of the participants,

[2] *APB Opinion No. 18,* "The Equity Method of Accounting for Investments in Common Stock," AICPA (New York: 1971), pp. 348–349.

[3] Ibid., p. 355.

[4] Ibid., p. 361.

but the use of the accrual method of accounting and periodic financial statements for the venture permit regular reporting of the share of net income or loss allocable to each participant.

The accounting records of such a joint venture will include all usual accounts for assets, liabilities, owners' equity, revenue, and expenses. The entire accounting process will conform to generally accepted accounting principles customarily followed in a partnership or a corporation, from the recording of transactions to the preparation of financial statements.

Each participant in the venture will open an Investment in Joint Venture account. This account is debited for assets invested in the venture, for any services billed to the venture, and for the proper share of any venture net income. The Investment in Joint Venture account is credited for any amounts received from the venture and for a proper share of any venture net loss. The Investment in Joint Venture account normally will have a debit balance, representing the participant's net investment in the venture. A participant does not record any journal entries for transactions between the venture and the other participants. The Investment in Joint Venture account will appear in the balance sheet as an asset, either current or noncurrent, depending upon the expected completion date for the venture.

No Separate Set of Accounting Records If a separate set of accounting records is not maintained by the venture as an accounting entity, there are, as previously explained, two common alternative methods available. Each participant may record all transactions entered into by the venture, or each participant may record only those transactions in which that participant is involved directly. Let us assume the first method is in use. Thus, if Jack Flamson invests merchandise in a venture, he debits Joint Venture and credits inventories. Each of the other participants makes an entry debiting Joint Venture and crediting an account with Flamson. When a sale is made, the participant handling the transaction debits Cash or Accounts Receivable and credits Joint Venture. The other participants debit the participant who executed the sale and credit Joint Venture. In brief, each participant maintains a complete record of all transactions by the joint venture and of the equities of the other participants in the joint venture.

Upon completion of the joint venture, the net income or loss is shown by the balance in the Joint Venture account. Assuming that a net income has been realized, the journal entry to divide the net income and to close the Joint Venture account will be to debit Joint Venture for the balance, credit each other participant for an appropriate share of the net income, and credit Income Summary for the participant's own share. Each participant will then have an account balance with each of the other participants in the venture; the final step is to make payment or collection of these balances.

If a joint venture has not been completed at the date one of the participants prepares a balance sheet, only the equity of that participant should be presented as an asset. Because the ledger account Joint Venture shows the total investment by all participants, the balance of this account less the equities of the other participants should be listed as an asset in the balance sheet.

The operation of a joint venture without a separate set of accounting records is appropriate only when the venture is expected to be of short duration and does not involve complex or numerous transactions. If prompt communication among participants in the venture is not practicable, convenience may dictate that individual participants record only transactions of the venture in which each is directly involved.

REVIEW QUESTIONS

1 Agasse and Bowman, partners, have capital accounts of $60,000 and $80,000, respectively. In addition, Agasse has made a non-interest-bearing loan of $20,000 to the firm. Agasse and Bowman now decide to liquidate their partnership. What priority or advantage, if any, will Agasse enjoy in the liquidation with respect to the loan account?

2 State briefly the procedure to be followed in a partnership liquidation when a debit balance arises in the capital account of one of the partners.

3 In the liquidation of the partnership of Camm, Dehn, and Ellerman, the sale of the assets resulted in a loss which produced the following balances in the capital accounts: Camm, $25,000 credit; Dehn, $12,500 credit; and Ellerman, $5,000 debit. The partners shared earnings in a 5:3:2 ratio. All liabilities have been paid, and $32,500 of cash is available for distribution to partners. However, it is not possible to determine at present whether Ellerman, who is ill, will be able to make good the $5,000 capital deficiency. Can the cash on hand be distributed without a delay to determine the collectibility of the amount due from Ellerman? Explain.

4 After disposing of all assets and distributing all available cash to creditors, the partnership of A, B, and C still had accounts payable of $12,000. The capital account of Partner A showed a credit balance of $16,000 and that of B a credit balance of $2,000. Creditors of the partnership demanded payment from A, who replied that the three partners shared earnings equally and had begun operations with equal capital investments. A, therefore, offered to pay the creditors one-third of their claims and no more. What is your opinion of the position taken by A? What is the balance in C's capital account? What journal entry, if any, should be made in the partnership accounting records for a payment by A personally to the partnership creditors?

5 In the partnership of Avery, Blum, and Chee, Avery serves as general manager. The partnership contract provides that Avery is entitled to an annual salary of $12,000, payable in 12 equal monthly installments, and that remaining earnings shall be divided equally. On June 30, the partnership suspended operations and began liquidation. Because of a shortage of working capital, Avery had not drawn any salary for the last two months of operation. How should Avery's claim for $2,000 of "unpaid wages" be handled in the liquidation of the partnership?

6 M and N are partners and have agreed to share earnings equally. State your reasons in support of dividing losses incurred in liquidation equally or in the ratio of capital balances.

7 State briefly the basic rule or principle to be observed in the distribution of cash to partners when the liquidation of a partnership extends over several months.

8 During the installment liquidation of a partnership, it is necessary to determine the possible future loss from sale of the remaining assets. What journal entries, if any, should be made to reflect in the partners' capital accounts their respective shares of the maximum possible loss which may be incurred during the remaining stages of liquidation?

9 The XYZ Partnership is liquidated over a period of eleven months with several distributions of cash to the partners. Will the total amount of cash received by each partner under these circumstances be more, less, or the same amount as if the liquidator had retained all cash until all assets had been sold and had then made a single payment to the partners?

10 Under what circumstances, if any, is it sound practice for a partnership undergoing installment liquidation to distribute cash to partners in the income-sharing ratio?

11 Judd, Klein, and Lund, partners who share earnings equally, have capital balances of $30,000, $25,000, and $21,000, respectively, when the partnership begins the process of liquidation. Among the assets is a note receivable from Klein in the amount of $7,000. All liabilities have been paid. The first assets sold during the liquidation are marketable securities carried in the accounts at $15,000; cash of $18,000 is received from the sale of marketable securities. How should this $18,000 of cash be divided among the partners?

12 When the partnership of R, S, and T began the process of liquidation, the capital accounts were R $38,000, S $35,000, and T $32,000. When the liquidation was complete, R had received less cash than either of the other two partners. List several factors which might explain why the partner with the largest capital account might receive the smallest amount of cash in liquidation.

13 Explain how a *joint venture* differs from a partnership.

14 When the concept of the joint venture is considered from a historical viewpoint, how has the process of net income determination differed from that of a partnership or corporation? Does this difference prevail in present practice?

15 What are *corporate joint ventures?* What accounting procedures for such ventures were recommended in *APB Opinion No. 18?*

EXERCISES

Ex. 2-1 Pullias and Mautner share earnings in a 60:40 ratio. They have decided to liquidate their partnership. A portion of the assets has been sold but other assets with a carrying amount of $42,000 still must be realized. All liabilities have been paid, and cash of $20,000 is available for distribution to partners. The capital accounts show balances of $40,000 for Pullias and $22,000 for Mautner. How should the cash be divided?

Ex. 2-2 Nicosia and Odmark started a partnership some years ago and managed to operate profitably for several years. Recently, however, they lost a substantial legal suit and incurred unexpected losses on accounts receivable and inventories. As a result, they decided to liquidate. They sold all assets, and only $18,000 was available to pay liabilities, which amounted to $33,000. Their capital balances before the start of liquidation and their income-sharing ratios are shown below:

	Capital balances	Income-sharing ratios
Nicosia..............................	$23,000	60%
Odmark	13,500	40%

a Compute the total loss incurred on the liquidation of the partnership.
b Show how the final settlement should be made between the partners, after Nicosia pays $15,000 to creditors. Nicosia is personally insolvent after paying the creditors, but Odmark has personal net assets in excess of $100,000.

Ex. 2-3 The balance sheet of the A & B Partnership immediately prior to liquidation follows:

Assets		Liabilities & Partners' Capitals	
Cash	$ 5,000	Liabilities	$ 25,000
Investments	20,000	A, capital	72,000
Other assets	100,000	B, capital	28,000
Total	$125,000	Total	$125,000

Partners A and B share operating income in a 2:1 ratio and capital gains and losses in a 3:1 ratio.

Partner A takes over the portfolio of investments at an agreed current fair value of $45,000; the rest of the assets (except cash) and the trade name are sold to Gleason Company for $200,000 face amount of bonds having a current fair value of $180,000. (Assume that any gain or loss on this transaction is treated as a capital gain or loss.)

Prepare appropriate journal entries in the accounts of the partnership to record the liquidation. Assume that (1) Partner A takes $100,000 face amount of bonds, (2) Partner B takes $60,000 face amount of bonds, (3) the remaining bonds are sold for $35,600 net of commissions, (4) all liabilities are paid, and (5) any available cash is distributed to the partners.

Ex. 2-4 After sale of a portion of the assets of the XYZ Partnership, which is being liquidated, the capital accounts are X $33,000; Y $40,000; and Z $42,000. Cash of $42,000 and other assets with a carrying amount of $78,000 are on hand. Creditors' claims total $5,000. X, Y, and Z share earnings equally. What cash payments can be made to the partners at this time?

Ex. 2-5 When Ledwith and Melody, partners who shared earnings equally, were incapacitated in an airplane accident, a liquidator was appointed to wind up their business. The accounts showed cash, $35,000; other assets, $110,000; liabilities, $20,000; Ledwith's capital, $71,000; and Melody's capital, $54,000. Because of the highly specialized nature of the noncash assets, the liquidator anticipated that considerable time would be required to dispose of them. The expenses of liquidating the business (advertising, rent, travel, etc.) are estimated at $10,000. How much cash can be distributed safely to each partner at this point?

Ex. 2-6 The following balance sheet was prepared for the partnership of Pardee, Quon, and Ramsey:

Assets		Liabilities & Partners' Capitals	
Cash	$ 25,000	Liabilities	$ 52,000
Other assets	180,000	Pardee, capital (40%)	40,000
		Quon, capital (40%)	65,000
		Ramsey, capital (20%)	48,000
Total	$205,000	Total	$205,000

Figures shown parenthetically reflect the income-sharing ratio.

a The partnership is being liquidated by the sale of assets in installments. The first sale of noncash assets having a carrying amount of $90,000 realizes $50,000, and all cash available after settlement with creditors is distributed to partners. Compute the amount of cash each partner should receive in the first installment.

b If the facts are as in **a** above except that $3,000 cash is withheld for possible liquidation expenses, how much cash should each partner receive?

c As a separate case, assume that each partner properly received some cash in the distribution after the second sale of assets. The cash to be distributed amounts to $14,000 from the third sale of assets, and unsold assets with a $6,000 carrying amount remain. How should the $14,000 be distributed to partners?

Ex. 2-7 D, E, and F have capital balances of $20,000, $25,000, and $9,000, respectively, and share earnings in a ratio of 4:2:1.

a Prepare a cash distribution program for liquidation of the partnership in installments.

b How much will be paid to all partners if D receives only $4,000 upon liquidation?

c If D received a $13,000 share of the cash paid pursuant to liquidation, how much did F receive?

d If E received only $11,000 as a result of the liquidation, how much did the partnership lose on the sale of assets? (No partner invested any additional amounts in the partnership.)

Ex. 2-8 The balance sheet for P & Q Partnership at June 1 of Year 10 follows:

Assets		Liabilities & Partners' Capitals	
Cash	$ 5,000	Liabilities	$20,000
Other assets	55,000	P, capital	22,500
		Q, capital	17,500
Total	$60,000	Total	$60,000

Partners share earnings as follows: P 60%; Q 40%. In June, assets with a carrying amount of $22,000 are sold for $18,000, creditors are paid in full, and $2,000 is paid to partners in such a way as to reduce their capital account balances closer to the income-sharing ratio. In July, assets with a carrying amount of $10,000 are sold for $12,000, liquidation expenses of $500 are paid, and cash of $12,500 is distributed to partners. In August, the remaining assets are sold for $22,500, and final settlement is made between the partners.

Compute the amount of cash each partner should receive in June, in July, and in August.

Ex. 2-9 The net equities and income-sharing ratios for A, B, C, and D before liquidation are as follows:

	A (6)	B (4)	C (2)	D (1)
Net equity in partnership	$36,000	$32,400	$8,000	$(500)

Assets will be sold for cash significantly in excess of carrying amounts.

Prepare a program showing how cash should be distributed as it becomes available in the course of liquidation.

Ex. 2-10 McKee and Nelson enter into a contract to speculate on the stock market, each using approximately $5,000 of personal cash. The earnings are to be divided equally, and settlement is to be made at the end of the year after all securities have been sold. A summary of the monthly brokerage statements for the year follows:

	McKee	Nelson
Total of all purchase confirmations	$45,000	$18,000
Total of all sales confirmations	48,700	16,800
Interest charged on margin accounts	80	50
Dividends credited to accounts	40	100

How should settlement be made between McKee and Nelson at the end of the year?

SHORT CASES FOR ANALYSIS AND DECISION

Case 2-1 The partnership of Capata, Dreyer, and Ernst is insolvent and in process of liquidation under the Uniform Partnership Act. After the assets were converted into cash and the resultant liquidation loss was distributed equally among the three partners, their positions are as follows:

	Equity in partnership	Personal financial position other than equity in partnership	
		Assets	Liabilities
Gary Capata	$20,000	$110,000	$45,000
Michael Dreyer	(21,000)	20,000	40,000
Oscar Ernst	(55,000)	55,000	35,000

Instructions Explain the prospects for collection by
a The creditors of the partnership.
b The personal creditors of each partner.

c Partner Capata from the copartners. Assuming that Capata has a $20,000 equity in the partnership, what is the amount of loss he should sustain?

Case 2-2 On November 15, in beginning the liquidation of the X, Y, & Z Partnership, the liquidator found that an 8% note payable for $100,000 issued by the partnership had six months remaining until maturity on May 15 of next year. Interest had been paid to November 15. Terms of the note provided that interest at 8% to the maturity date must be paid in full in the event the note is paid prior to maturity. The liquidator had paid all other liabilities and had on hand cash of $150,000. The remaining noncash assets had a carrying amount of $200,000. The liquidator believed that six months would be required to dispose of them and that the realization of the noncash assets over this period would produce cash at least 25% in excess of the carrying amount of the assets.

Partner X made the following statement to the liquidator: "I realize you can't pay the partners until creditors have been paid in full, but I need cash for another business I'm starting. So I'd like for you to pay off the note immediately and interest to May 15 of next year and distribute the remaining available cash to the partners." Partner Y objected to this proposal for immediate cash payments on the ground that it would entail a loss of $4,000. Y argued that if such action were taken, the interest cost of $4,000 should be charged entirely against X's capital account. Partner Z had no particular concern in the matter, but as a convenience agreed to assume the note liability in return for $102,000 cash payment from the liquidator. To insure the noteholder against loss, Z would deposit collateral of $104,000 in government bonds. The noteholder expressed willingness to accept this arrangement. Partner Z specified that the proposed payment of $102,000 would be in Z's new role as a creditor and that it would not affect Z's right to receive any cash distributions in the course of liquidation.

Instructions   Evaluate the proposal by each partner. What action should be taken by the liquidator? Would your answer differ if the assumptions were changed to indicate a probable loss on the realization of the remaining noncash assets?

Case 2-3 Lois Allen and Barbara Brett formed a partnership and share earnings equally. Although the partners began business with equal capitals, Allen made more frequent withdrawals than Brett, with the result that her capital account became the smaller of the two. The partners have now decided to liquidate their business at June 30; on that date the accounts were closed and financial statements prepared. The balance sheet showed a capital account for Allen of $40,000 and Brett's capital as $60,000. In addition, the balance sheet showed that Brett had made a $10,000 loan to the partnership.

The liquidation of the partnership was managed by Allen because Brett was hospitalized by an auto accident on July 1, the day after regular operations were suspended. The procedures followed by Allen were as follows: First, to sell all the assets at the best prices obtainable; second, to pay the creditors in full; third to pay Brett's loan account; and fourth, to divide all remaining cash between Brett and herself in the 40:60 ratio represented by their capital account balances.

When Brett was released from the hospital on July 5, Allen met her and informed her that through good luck and hard work, she had been able to find buyers for the assets and complete the liquidation during the five days of Brett's hospitalization. As the first step in the liquidation, Allen delivered two cashier's checks to Brett at the moment of her release from the hospital. One check was for $10,000 in payment of the loan account; the other was in settlement of Brett's capital account.

Instructions
a Do you approve the procedures followed in the liquidation? Explain fully.
b Assume that the liquidation procedures followed resulted in the payment of

$24,000 to Brett in addition to the payment of her loan account in full. What was the amount of gain or loss on the liquidation? If you believe that other methods should have been followed in the liquidation, explain how much more or less Brett would have received under the procedure you recommend.

Case 2-4 In reply to a question as to how settlement with partners should be made during liquidation of a partnership, Student J made the following statement:

"Accounting records are usually based on cost and reflect the going-concern principle. When a business is broken up, it is often necessary to sell the assets for a fraction of their carrying amount. Consequently, a partner usually receives in liquidation a settlement far below the amount of his or her equity in the business."

Student K offered the following comment:

"I agree fully with what J has said, but she might have gone further and added that no payment should ever be made to any partner until all the assets of the partnership have been sold and all creditors have been paid in full. Until these steps have been completed, the residual amount available for distribution to partners is unknown, and therefore any earlier payment to a partner might have to be returned. If the partner were unable to return such amount, the person who authorized the payment might be held personally responsible."

Student L made the following statement:

"In the liquidation of a partnership, each partner receives the amount of his or her equity in the business; no more and no less. As to timing of payments, it is often helpful to a partner to receive a partial payment before the assets are sold and creditors are paid in full. If proper precautions are taken, such early partial payments are quite satisfactory."

Instructions Evaluate the statement made by each student.

PROBLEMS

2-5 The partnership accounts of Axel, Brown, and Collins, who share earnings in a 5:3:2 ratio, are as follows on December 31, Year 5:

Axel, drawing (debit balance)	$(16,000)
Collins, drawing (debit balance)	(6,000)
Brown, loan	20,000
Axel, capital	82,000
Brown, capital	67,000
Collins, capital	72,000

Total assets amount to $319,000, including $35,000 cash, and liabilities total $100,000. The partnership was liquidated on December 31, Year 5, and Collins received $55,500 cash pursuant to the liquidation.

Instructions
a Compute the total loss from the liquidation of the partnership.
b Prepare a statement of realization and liquidation.
c Prepare journal entries for the accounting records of the partnership to account for the liquidation.

2-6 Following is the balance sheet for the partnership of Donner, Epperly, and Farrington prior to liquidation:

DONNER, EPPERLY, AND FARRINGTON
Balance Sheet
June 15, Year 1

Assets		Liabilities & Partners' Capitals	
Cash	$ 3,000	Liabilities	$17,000
Other assets	94,000	Epperly, loan	4,000
		Donner, capital	27,000
		Epperly, capital	39,000
		Farrington, capital	10,000
Total	$97,000	Total	$97,000

The partners share earnings as follows: Donner 40%; Epperly 40%; Farrington 20%. On June 15, Year 1, other assets were sold for $30,700, and $17,500 had to be paid to liquidate the liabilities because of unrecorded claims amounting to $500. Donner and Epperly are personally solvent, but Farrington's personal liabilities exceed personal assets by $8,000.

Instructions
a Prepare a statement of realization and liquidation. Combine Epperly's loan and capital accounts.
b Prepare journal entries required to record the liquidation.
c How much cash would other assets have to realize upon liquidation in order that Farrington would take enough out of the partnership to pay personal creditors? Assume that $17,500 is required to liquidate the partnership liabilities.

2-7 Gorman, Harris, and Imke present the following balance sheet on April 30, Year 3, just prior to liquidation of the partnership.

GORMAN, HARRIS, AND IMKE
Balance Sheet
April 30, Year 3

Assets		Liabilities & Partners' Capitals	
Cash	$ 20,000	Liabilities	$ 80,000
Other assets	280,000	Gorman, capital	60,000
		Harris, capital	70,000
		Imke, capital	90,000
Total	$300,000	Total	$300,000

During May, assets with a carrying amount of $105,000 were sold for $75,000 cash, and all liabilities were paid. During June, assets with a carrying amount of $61,000 were sold for $25,000 cash, and in July the remaining assets with a carrying amount of $114,000 were sold for $90,000 cash. The cash available at the end of each month was distributed promptly. The partners shared net income and losses equally.

Instructions

a Prepare a statement of realization and liquidation covering the entire period of liquidation, and a supporting schedule showing the computation of installment payments to partners as cash becomes available.

b At what point in the liquidation did the partners' capital accounts have balances corresponding to the income-sharing ratio? Of what significance is this relationship with respect to subsequent cash distributions to partners?

2-8 Jenner, Kline, and Lowe decide to form a partnership on January 10, Year 6. Their capital investments and income-sharing ratio are listed below:

Jenner: $45,000—50%

Kline: $30,000—30%, with a salary allowance of $18,000 per year or a proportionate amount for a period less than a year

Lowe: $24,000—20%

During the first six months of Year 6, the partners were not particularly concerned over the poor volume of business and the net loss of $42,000 reported by their accountant, because they had been told that it would take at least six months to establish their business and to achieve profitable operations. Business during the second half of the year did not improve and the partners decided to go out of business before additional losses were incurred. The decision to liquidate was hastened when two major customers filed bankruptcy petitions.

The sale of assets was completed during October and all available cash was paid to creditors. Suppliers' invoices of $5,400 remained unpaid at this time. The personal financial status of each partner on October 31, Year 6, was as follows:

	Personal assets	Personal liabilities
Jenner	$30,000	$25,500
Kline	60,000	15,000
Lowe	75,000	42,000

The partners had made no cash withdrawals during Year 6; however, in August Lowe had withdrawn merchandise with a cost of $1,200 and Kline had taken title to equipment at a current fair value of $750.

The partners have decided to end the partnership immediately and to arrive at a settlement among themselves in accordance with the provisions of the Uniform Partnership Act.

Instructions Prepare a four-column statement of partners' capitals (including liquidation) for the period January 10, Year 6, to October 31, Year 6. You need not show the changes in liabilities, cash, or noncash assets; however, the changes in the total capital and individual capitals of the three partners should be shown.

2-9 Partners M, N, and O share earnings in a ratio of 5:3:2. At the end of a very unprofitable year, they decided to liquidate the firm. The partners' capital account balances at this date were as follows: M, $22,000; N, $27,900; O, $14,000. The liabilities shown in the balance sheet amounted to $32,000, including a loan of $8,000 from M. The cash balance was $6,000.

The partners plan to sell the noncash assets on a piecemeal basis and to distribute cash as rapidly as it becomes available. All three partners are personally solvent.

Instructions Answer each of the following questions and show how you reached your conclusions. (Each question is independent of the others. An advance program for cash distributions to partners would be helpful.)

a If N received $6,000 from the first distribution of cash, how much did M and O each receive at that time?

b If M received a total of $25,000 as a result of the liquidation, what was the total amount realized by the partnership on the sale of the noncash assets?

c If O received $4,400 on the first distribution of cash, how much did M receive at that time?

2-10 Parker and Queenan were attorneys and automobile fanciers who became acquainted because of their interest in imported automobiles. They decided to form a partnership, and persuaded a third attorney, Rey, to join with them. The partnership maintained only meager accounting records, but a secretary in the firm did maintain a careful daily record of cash receipts, which were almost entirely in the form of checks received through the mail. The only other systematically maintained record was the checkbook used for all disbursements by the partnership. Some miscellaneous working papers were on file relating to income tax returns of prior years.

Early in Year 7 the partners quarreled over the use of partnership funds to buy expensive automobiles; this quarrel led to a decision to liquidate the firm as of June 30, Year 7. You were retained to assemble the financial data needed for an equitable distribution of assets. You learn that the partnership was formed four years ago with equal capital investments and agreement to share net income and losses equally. By inspection of the income tax return for the calendar year ended December 31, Year 6, you determine that the amounts of depreciable assets and accumulated depreciation were as follows at December 31, Year 6:

	Depreciable assets (cost)	Accumulated depreciation, Dec. 31, Year 6
Office equipment	$ 7,500	$ 2,250
Library of reference books	4,500	900
Automobiles:		
Bentley—assigned to Parker	10,000	3,000
Buick—assigned to Queenan	5,000	1,000
Rolls-Royce—assigned to Rey	15,000	3,000
Totals	$42,000	$10,150

By reference to the cash records, you find that cash receipts for the first six months of Year 7 amounted to $310,000. The cash payments were summarized as follows:

Automobile and miscellaneous expenses	$ 9,490
Entertainment expense	30,000
Wages and salaries expense	80,510
Rent expense	7,000
Drawings: Parker	45,000
Drawings: Queenan	50,000
Drawings: Rey	60,000
Total cash payments	$282,000

The automobiles were depreciated on a straight-line basis over a five-year economic life with no residual value and depreciation was treated as a charge against partnership revenue. A 10-year economic life was used for depreciation of office equipment and the library. As one step in the liquidation, the partners agree that the automobiles which were purchased from partnership funds should be retained by the partners to whom assigned. They also agree upon equal distribution of the office equipment among them in kind. The entire library will be distributed to Parker. All assets distributed are assigned a current fair value equal to carrying amounts.

Cash on hand and in bank at June 30, Year 7, amounted to $70,010. **The capital account balances of the partners were equal at December 31, Year 6.** Assume that the partnership had no other assets or liabilities, either at the beginning or the end of the six-month period ended June 30, Year 7.

Instructions Prepare a statement of partners' capitals for the period January 1 to June 30, Year 7, including the final distribution of cash and other assets to partners. To support this statement, prepare an income statement for the six months ended June 30, Year 7.

2-11 On August 19, Year 4, Sumser, Terry, and Underwood entered into a partnership contract to acquire a speculative second mortgage on undeveloped real estate. They invested $55,000, $32,500, and $12,500, respectively. They agreed on an income-sharing ratio of 4:2:1, respectively.

On September 1, Year 4, the partnership purchased for $100,000 a mortgage note with an unpaid balance of $122,200. The amount paid included interest accrued from June 30, Year 4. The note principal matures at the rate of $2,000 each quarter. Interest at the annual rate of 8% on the unpaid balance is also due quarterly.

Regular interest and principal payments were received on September 30 and December 31, Year 4. A petty cash fund of $50 was established, and collection expenses of $138 were paid in December.

In addition to the regular payment on September 30, the mortgagor made a principal reduction payment of $10,000 plus a penalty of 2% (on $10,000) for early repayment.

Because of the speculative nature of the note, the partners agree to defer recognition of the discount until their cost has been fully recovered.

Instructions
a Assuming that no cash distributions were made to the partners, prepare a working paper computing the cash balance available for distribution to the partners on December 31, Year 4.
b After payment of collection expenses, the partners wish to distribute the cash as soon as possible so that they individually can reinvest it. Prepare a working paper showing how any available cash should be distributed to the partners by installments as it becomes available.
c Show how the cash on hand at December 31, Year 4, as computed in **a**, should be distributed to the partners.

2-12 A partnership doing business as Newmark's was formed on January 2, Year 5, by equal investment from Don New and Jerome Mark. New, who was in the toy business, invested $22,500 of inventories for a 50% interest and Mark, who was in the appliance business, invested inventories with a current fair value of $16,000 plus $6,500 in cash for a 50% interest. The partners share earnings equally.

The operation of Newmark's did not prove profitable, and after the Christmas shopping season of Year 5, New and Mark decided to dissolve the partnership. They retained you at this time to assist in the termination of the business. Your investigation reveals the following information:
(1) The part-time accountant employed by Newmark's was also the accountant for Mark's other businesses. The condition of the accounting records indicated a lack of competence. The accountant had discarded all cash register tapes and invoices for expenses and purchases of merchandise.

(2) The partners assure you in writing that the only liabilities are to entities which they own as single proprietorships. The amounts are $19,480 owing to New Toys and $10,520 owing to Mark's Appliances.
(3) Through an analysis of bank statements and paid checks, you are able to construct the following summary of cash transactions for Year 5:

NEWMARK'S
Summary of Cash Transactions
For Year 5

Balance, Jan. 2, Year 5		$ 6,500
Receipts:		
Sales...	$150,500	
Liquidation of inventories	14,000	164,500
Subtotal		$171,000
Disbursements:		
Purchases of merchandise	$ 72,000	
Operating expenses.......................................	52,000	
Leasehold improvements (five-year lease)	12,000	
Liquidation expenses	8,500	144,500
Balance, Dec. 31, Year 5		$ 26,500

(4) Payments of $13,250 were made to each of the partners on December 31, Year 5, pending a final accounting for the liquidation.
(5) You are informed by the partners that the dollar amounts of regular sales during the year were divided approximately equally between toys and appliances and that the dollar amounts of liquidation sales of toys and appliances were also approximately equal. The markup was uniformly 40% of cost on toys and 25% of cost on appliances. All sales were for cash. The ending inventories of shopworn merchandise were liquidated on December 31, Year 5, for 50% of the retail sales price. The partners believe that some appliances may have been returned to Mark's Appliances, but the accountant failed to enter any such returns in the accounting records of either organization.

Instructions
a Prepare a working paper showing the computation of unrecorded returns of merchandise by Newmark's. Assume that no theft of merchandise had occurred.
b Prepare an income statement for Newmark's for the period January 2 to December 31, Year 5.
c Prepare a statement of partners' capitals for the year ended December 31, Year 5.

2-13 D, E, & F Partnership has called upon you to assist in winding up the affairs of the partnership. You are able to gather the following information:
(1) The trial balance of the partnership at March 1, Year 3, is as follows:

D, E, & F PARTNERSHIP
Trial Balance
March 1, Year 3

Cash	$ 10,000	
Accounts receivable (net)	22,000	
Inventories	14,000	
Plant assets (net)	99,000	
D, loan receivable	12,000	
F, loan receivable	7,500	
Accounts payable		$ 21,000
D, capital..		67,000
E, capital		45,000
F, capital		31,500
Totals	$164,500	$164,500

(2) The partners share earnings as follows: D 50%; E 30%; and F 20%.

(3) The partners are considering an offer of $104,000 for the accounts receivable, inventories, and plant assets at March 1, Year 3. The $104,000 would be paid to the partners in installments, the number of installments and amounts of which are to be negotiated.

Instructions

a Prepare a cash distribution program as of March 1, Year 3, showing how the total available cash of $114,000 ($10,000 + $104,000 = $114,000) would be distributed as it becomes available.

b Assume the same facts as in *a,* except that the partners have decided to liquidate their partnership instead of accepting the offer of $104,000. Cash is distributed to the partners at the end of each month.

A summary of the liquidation transactions follows:

March: $16,500 collected on accounts receivable, balance is uncollectible.

$10,000 received for all inventories.

$1,000 liquidation expenses paid.

$8,000 cash was retained in the business.

April: $1,500 liquidation expenses paid.

As part payment of Partner F's capital account balance, F accepted equipment that had a carrying amount of $4,000. The partners agreed that a current fair value of $10,000 was appropriate for the equipment for liquidation purposes.

$2,500 cash was retained in the business.

May: $92,000 received on sale of remaining plant assets.

$1,000 liquidation expenses paid.

No cash was retained in the business.

Prepare a summary of cash payments for the three months ended May 31, Year 3, showing how the cash was distributed.

2-14 A, B, C, and D have decided to liquidate their partnership. They plan to sell the assets gradually in order to minimize losses. They share earnings as follows: A 40%; B 35%; C 15%; and D 10%. Presented below is the partnership's trial balance as of October 1, Year 8, the date on which liquidation begins.

A, B, C, & D PARTNERSHIP

Trial Balance

October 1, Year 8

Cash	$ 12,400	
Receivables (net)	51,800	
Inventories, Oct. 1, Year 8	85,200	
Equipment (net)	39,600	
Accounts payable		$ 18,000
A, loan		12,000
B, loan		20,000
A, capital		40,000
B, capital		43,000
C, capital		36,000
D, capital		20,000
Totals	$189,000	$189,000

Instructions

a Prepare a working paper as of October 1, Year 8, showing how cash will be distributed among partners by installments as it becomes available. To simplify computations, restate the income-sharing ratio to 8:7:3:2.

b On October 31, Year 8, cash of $49,400 became available to creditors and partners. How should the $49,400 be distributed?

c If, instead of being liquidated, the partnership continued operations and earned $52,500 for the year ended September 30, Year 9, how should this income be distributed if, in addition to the aforementioned income-sharing arrangement, it was provided that D receive a bonus of 5% of the income after treating the bonus as an expense? The income of $52,500 is before deduction of the bonus to D.

2-15 A joint venture was formed by Q, R, and S when they agreed to sell hot dogs on July 3 and 4 of Year 1. Q agreed to construct a stand on the front lawn of S and charge the construction costs to operations as an expense. S agreed, but asked $25 for the cost of sod replacement and cleaning the lawn after July 4. Q, R, and S decided that net income, if any, would be distributed first by the $25 payment to S and then by a 40% commission on sales made by each participant. The balance of net income would be distributed 75% to Q and 25% to R. They agreed that a cash box would only complicate matters and that all purchase and sales transactions would be out-of-pocket and the responsibility of each participant. All sales were made at 100% markup on cost and the ending inventory of supplies might be purchased from the joint venture by Q, R, or S at 50% of cost.

The activity of the venture for the period July 2 to 5, Year 1, is summarized below:

July 2 Q constructed a stand on front lawn of S at a cost of $100.

July 3 Q paid $1,000 for supplies (rolls, weiners, mustard, etc.). S paid $50 for a city permit to operate the concession.

July 4   Q purchased additional supplies for $1,500. Sales for the day were as follows: Q, $1,700; R, $2,600; and S, $600.

July 5   S paid $90 for fire extinguishers; these were distributed equally among Q, R, and S for their personal use. S agreed to pay $50 for the stand. The balance of the inventory of supplies was taken by Q at 50% of cost.

Instructions   Prepare a working-paper analysis of the transactions which will give Q, R, and S the following information: (1) net income or loss from operation of the joint venture, (2) distribution of net income or loss to Q, R, and S, and (3) the final cash settlement among the participants.

The following headings are suggested for the working paper: Transactions; Inventory Reconciliation (at cost); Net Income or Loss; Q, Capital; R, Capital; S, Capital.

APPENDIX: Financial Statements for a CPA partnership

Arthur Andersen Worldwide Organization

Combined Statements of Financial Position

   August 31, 1977 and 1976 (not audited in 1976)

	1977	1976
ASSETS	*(in thousands)*	*(in thousands)*
Current Assets:		
Cash	$ 24,410	$ 23,549
Short-term cash investments, at cost (approximates market)	4,508	13,880
Receivables from clients, less allowances of $2,998 in 1977 and $3,393 in 1976 for uncollectible accounts	62,762	55,998
Unbilled services, at estimated billable amounts	53,426	47,268
Other current assets	14,756	10,587
Total current assets	$159,862	$151,282
Property and Equipment, at cost (Notes 1, 2, and 7):		
Center for Professional Development—		
Land, buildings, and equipment	$ 11,868	$ 11,610
Less—Accumulated depreciation	3,521	2,859
	$ 8,347	$ 8,751
Offices—		
Land and buildings	$ 6,643	$ 6,720
Leasehold improvements	23,242	18,538
Furniture and equipment	36,847	30,917
	$ 66,732	$ 56,175
Less—Accumulated depreciation and amortization	23,167	18,569
	$ 43,565	$ 37,606
Net property and equipment	$ 51,912	$ 46,357
	$211,774	$197,639
LIABILITIES AND PARTNERS' CAPITAL		
Current Liabilities:		
Notes payable to banks (Note 2)	$ 3,756	$ 2,102
Current portion of long-term debt	153	111
Accounts payable	7,303	7,132
Accrued payroll, withholdings, and fringe benefits	28,184	23,726
Accrued taxes (Note 1)	4,427	4,193
Other accrued liabilities (Note 8)	5,022	6,603
Total current liabilities	$ 48,845	$ 43,867
Long-term Debt (Note 2)	$ 43,018	$ 43,160
Partners' Capital (Notes 1, 3, and 8):		
Paid-in capital	$ 55,923	$ 50,461
Pro forma capital	62,155	54,039
Undistributed cash earnings	1,833	6,112
Total partners' capital	$119,911	$110,612
	$211,774	$197,639

The accompanying notes are an integral part of these statements.

Arthur Andersen Worldwide Organization

Combined Statements of Earnings

for the Years Ended August 31, 1977 and 1976 (not audited in 1976)

	1977	1976
	(in thousands)	*(in thousands)*
Fees for Professional Services	$471,470	$424,654
Expenses (not including partner compensation):		
Employee compensation and fringe benefits (managers, professional staff, and office support personnel)	$245,744	$224,510
Other expenses—		
Occupancy (including depreciation and amortization)	$ 30,297	$ 26,216
Training, research, and quality control (including depreciation on Center for Professional Development)	19,525	17,552
Personnel recruiting, transfers, and expatriate allowances	10,536	9,219
Professional indemnity insurance and litigation, net	5,780	6,351
Communications and supplies, net	6,046	6,145
Contributions and civic activities	3,595	3,071
Foreign exchange losses, net (including $1,523 of translation losses in 1977 and $1,811 in 1976)	1,621	1,479
Interest, net	3,108	1,899
Entity income and business taxes (Note 1)	3,743	3,547
Other	27,375	23,542
	$111,626	$ 99,021
Total expenses	$357,370	$323,531
Earnings for the Year (Note 1)	$114,100	$101,123
Allocation of Earnings (Notes 3 and 5):		
To partners active during the year—		
Resigned, retired, and deceased partners	$ 8,914	$ 3,308
Partners active at year end	97,691	90,568
To retired partners and estates of deceased partners—retirement and death payments	3,629	3,538
Not allocated to partners—retained for specific partnership purposes	3,866	3,709
	$114,100	$101,123
Number of partners active at year end	961	921
Average earnings per partner	$101,656	$ 98,337

The accompanying notes are an integral part of these statements.

Arthur Andersen Worldwide Organization

Combined Statements of Changes in Partners' Capital
for the Years Ended August 31, 1977 and 1976 (not audited in 1976)

	1977	1976
	(in thousands)	*(in thousands)*
Paid-in Capital (Note 3):		
Balance, beginning of year	$ 50,461	$ 42,197
Capital paid in by partners	8,731	9,536
Repayment of paid-in capital to resigned and retired partners and estates of deceased partners	(3,269)	(1,272)
Balance, end of year	$ 55,923	$ 50,461
Pro Forma Capital (Note 3):		
Balance, beginning of year	$ 54,039	$ 54,535
Cash earnings for the year	$106,234	$101,725
Memorandum adjustments to reflect accrual basis of accounting, net (Note 1).	7,866	(602)
Earnings for the year	$114,100	$101,123
Cash earnings for the year transferred to undistributed cash earnings	(106,234)	(101,725)
Other	250	106
Balance, end of year	$ 62,155	$ 54,039
Undistributed Cash Earnings (Note 3):		
Balance, beginning of year	$ 6,112	$ 3,881
Cash earnings for the year	106,234	101,725
Distribution of cash earnings	(110,513)	(99,494)
Balance, end of year (paid subsequent to fiscal year end)	$ 1,833	$ 6,112

Combined Statements of Changes in Financial Position
for the Years Ended August 31, 1977 and 1976 (not audited in 1976)

	1977	1976
	(in thousands)	*(in thousands)*
Source of Working Capital:		
Earnings for the year	$114,100	$101,123
Depreciation and amortization—not requiring an outlay of working capital	7,632	6,503
Total from operations	$121,732	$107,626
Capital paid in by partners (Note 3)	8,731	9,536
Additional long-term debt	—	40,280
Other	250	106
Total	$130,713	$157,548
Disposition of Working Capital:		
Distribution of cash earnings	$110,513	$ 99,494
Repayment of paid-in capital to resigned and retired partners and estates of deceased partners	3,269	1,272
Net additions to property and equipment	13,187	16,138
Reduction of long-term debt	142	22,093
Total	$127,111	$138,997
Increase in Working Capital (Note 6)	$ 3,602	$ 18,551
Working Capital—Beginning of Year	107,415	88,864
Working Capital—End of Year	$111,017	$107,415

The accompanying notes are an integral part of these statements.

Arthur Andersen Worldwide Organization
Notes to Combined Financial Statements
August 31, 1977 and 1976 (not audited in 1976)

---

(1) Summary of Significant Accounting Policies:

Basis for Presentation of Financial Statements—

The accompanying financial statements include the combined accounts of the worldwide organization of Arthur Andersen (the firm) which includes Arthur Andersen & Co. (an Illinois partnership), separate legal entities with the Arthur Andersen name, and organizations with which Arthur Andersen & Co. has exclusive representation agreements, all of which are authorized under the laws of the countries in which such operations are located. Within this worldwide organization, there are partners, participating principals, non-United States principals, and overseas representatives (collectively referred to herein as "partners").

Except as required by the laws of certain countries or by established precedent, the Illinois partnership and related worldwide organization entities maintain books and records and file income tax returns on the cash basis of accounting. Cash distributions to partners are determined on the cash basis of accounting. The accompanying combined financial statements have been prepared in accordance with generally accepted accounting principles on the accrual basis of accounting by combining cash-basis accounting records with memorandum adjustments to include receivables for billed and unbilled services, accounts payable, accrued liabilities, etc.

Earnings for the Year—

Earnings for the year are not comparable to the net income of a corporation and are not profit to the partners. Rather, they represent the amount available to cover the partners' executive compensation equivalent; resignation, retirement, and death payments; and return on capital at risk. Each partner must personally pay for retirement and payroll-type fringe benefits.

Income Taxes—

Since partnerships in most countries are not taxable as entities, substantially all taxes on earnings are paid by the partners on the basis of their individual income tax returns.

The accompanying combined statement of earnings includes provisions of $2,678,000 in 1977 and $2,667,000

in 1976 for income taxes on certain non-U.S. entities which are taxed as entities. Earnings of certain such non-U.S. entities are required to be reported on a basis different for tax purposes than for accounting purposes. Deferred non-U.S. entity income taxes (not material in amount) have been provided to reflect the tax effect of such timing differences.

Revenue Recognition—

Fees for professional services in the accompanying financial statements are recognized at the time such services are rendered, at estimated billable amounts.

Training, Research, and Quality Control—

All training, research, and quality control costs are charged to expense as incurred.

Property and Equipment, Depreciation, and

Amortization—

Generally, depreciation on property and equipment and amortization of leasehold improvements are computed by use of the following methods and lives:

	Method	Life in Years
Land improvements	Declining balance	10
Buildings	Straight line	19 to 37
Furniture and equipment	Double declining balance	6 to 12
Leasehold improvements	Straight line	Term of lease

Maintenance and repairs are charged to expense as incurred; major replacements and improvements are capitalized. The cost and accumulated depreciation of items sold, retired, or fully depreciated are removed from the property accounts and any resultant gain or loss is recorded currently in earnings.

The firm has purchased a 22⅛% interest in a partnership which owns the Chicago office building in which the firm leases approximately 50% of the floor space. The building is subject to a nonrecourse mortgage. As of August 31, 1977, the balance of $1,700,437 related to this investment was classified in land and buildings.

(2) Financing Arrangements:

Long-term debt as of August 31, 1977 and 1976, consisted of the following:

	1977	1976
	(in thousands)	
Unsecured note payable to a nonclient insurance company, payable $4,000,000 annually from 1982 to 1991, with interest at 8.95% payable semiannually....	$40,000	$40,000
Purchase mortgage note, payable $406,000 annually to 1990, including interest at 10% (secured by Center for Professional Development)...............	2,884	2,991
Other mortgage debt...........	287	280
	$43,171	$43,271
Less—Current portion..........	153	111
Long-term debt..........	$43,018	$43,160

The insurance company has committed to lend, and the firm has agreed to borrow, an additional $5,000,000 in August, 1979, and $5,000,000 more in August, 1980, with the same principal maturity dates and interest rate as the note payable for $40,000,000. The insurance company notes may not be prepaid prior to September 2, 1981, and then only upon certain conditions, and at decreasing prepayment penalties to 1990.

The loan agreement provides that, subject to certain conditions, the firm may incur additional unsecured long-term debt of up to $10,000,000 annually for ten successive years commencing on September 1, 1981 (up to $100,000,000 in the aggregate), provided that the total of all outstanding long-term debt does not exceed the net book value of the firm's property and equipment (excluding its investment in the Chicago office building). The firm may also incur secured debt (in addition to the mortgage debt outstanding as of August 31, 1976) not to exceed 10% of its net assets, provided that the total of all long-term debt does not exceed the net book value of the firm's property and equipment plus, until August 31, 1978, $5,000,000.

The loan agreement also provides, among other things, that the firm may not incur any long-term debt in addition to the $40,000,000 borrowed in June, 1976, or enter into any lease with an initial term of more than two years unless certain ratios have been met.

The maturities of outstanding long-term debt as of August 31, 1977, through fiscal 1982 are as follows (in thousands):

1978...........	$ 153
1979...........	167
1980...........	183
1981...........	200
1982...........	4,219

A $15,000,000 line of credit at the prime interest rate has been arranged with a nonclient bank to cover temporarily unforeseen conditions and to allow time to effect a rearrangement of the firm's capital structure. Borrowings under this line of credit must be eliminated for a period of not less than thirty days each year. This line requires the firm to maintain an average deposit balance of 10% of the line or 20% of outstanding loans thereunder, whichever is greater. There were no borrowings under this line of credit during 1977 or 1976.

A $10,000,000 multicurrency line of credit at the best local interest rate has also been arranged with the same bank for use in countries outside the United States, primarily to hedge foreign currency needs. This line requires no compensating balances or commitment fees, and borrowings are subject to the availability of funds. The firm has additional lines of credit of approximately $6,850,000 in countries outside the United States (principally overdraft arrangements) which have been established with several nonclient banks for the same purpose. Borrowings under these lines of credit averaged $2,860,000 in 1977 and $1,707,000 in 1976 at average interest rates of 12.9% and 12.1%, respectively. Maximum borrowings under these lines were $4,266,000 in 1977 and $2,356,000 in 1976.

(3) Partners' Capital:

Partners' capital as of August 31, 1977 and 1976, consisted of the following:

Paid-in Capital (in thousands)—

	1977	1976
Paid-in capital...............	$55,923	$50,461

In August, 1977 and 1976, existing partners contributed $4,337,000 and $4,345,000, respectively, of additional paid-in capital pursuant to a plan to increase paid-in capital from $500 per unit of participation to $750 per unit at the rate of $50 per unit annually for each of the five years ending September 1, 1980.

On September 1, 1977, 82 new partners were admitted; 104 were admitted on September 1, 1976. Paid-in capital as of August 31, 1977, includes $1,389,000 paid in by new partners admitted to the firm on September 1, 1977, and by existing partners for additional units of participation awarded effective September 1, 1977. Additional paid-in capital of $4,586,000, receivable from partners as of September 1, 1977, was not recorded as of August 31, 1977.

Paid-in capital is repayable within sixty days following a partner's resignation, retirement, or death. No amounts are paid in or returned to partners for goodwill or appreciation of assets; thus, partners do not realize any appreciation on their paid-in capital.

Pro Forma Capital (in thousands)—

	1977	1976
Allocated to partners	$43,453	$39,203
Not allocated to partners—retained for specific partnership purposes (partner retirement [Note 5] and uninsured risks [Note 8])	18,702	14,836
	$62,155	$54,039

Pro forma capital represents uncollected receivables and unbilled services, less accounts payable, accrued liabilities, etc. Pro forma capital allocated to partners is payable at various dates after resignation, retirement, or death.

Undistributed Cash Earnings (in thousands)—

	1977	1976
Undistributed cash earnings (paid subsequent to fiscal year end) . .	$1,833	$6,112

(4) Employee Profit Sharing and Retirement Plans:

The firm has a trusteed profit sharing plan which provides deferred compensation benefits for employees in the United States and Puerto Rico and a noncontributory retirement plan for office support, administration, and certain other employees in the United States and Puerto Rico, both of which were amended in 1976 to conform with the provisions of the United States Employee Retirement Income Security Act of 1974.

The annual contribution to the profit sharing plan is determined by the Board of Directors. The contribution to the profit sharing trust was $4,500,000 in 1977 and $3,539,000 in 1976, which was approximately 5% of members' compensation.

The provision for retirement plan expense was $1,244,000 in 1977 and $1,058,000 in 1976, which includes the amortization of unfunded past-service costs over a 30-year period. As of July 1, 1977 (date of actuarial valuation), the unfunded past-service liability was $6,946,000, and the actuarially computed vested benefits in excess of retirement plan fund assets were $4,427,000. This compares with $4,874,000 and $4,461,000, respectively, in 1976.

The firm also has profit sharing and/or retirement plans or participates in similar government-sponsored plans for employees in a number of other countries. It is generally the firm's policy to fund profit sharing and retirement costs.

(5) Partner Resignation, Retirement, and Death Payments:

All eligible partners are required to participate in the United States Partners' Profit Sharing Plan (Keogh plan)

or equivalent plans outside the United States. Such plans are administered by a committee of partners, and benefits are paid by the trusts.

Basic retirement payments are made by the firm to retired partners and the estates of deceased partners. Such payments were made at the rate of $12,600 annually in 1977 and $12,000 in 1976, commencing at mandatory retirement age (62) for life or for ten years certain in case of death. Such payments may begin at an earlier age at reduced amounts. The amounts payable are subject to annual adjustment, based upon a price index. Such payments aggregated $1,161,000 in 1977 and $953,000 in 1976. An actuarial determination of retirement amounts payable to partners as of August 31, 1977 (being amortized over 30 years), was approximately $19,440,000, of which approximately $9,962,000 was applicable to partners already retired. These basic retirement payments may be rescinded at any time by a two-thirds vote of the partners.

Supplementary retirement benefits are payable upon resignation, retirement, or death to partners with more than one year of service as a partner as of July 1, 1974. As of August 31, 1977, the aggregate amount payable was $36,912,000, including interest to that date, which is being allocated from annual earnings over a ten-year period ending in 1984. Payments of $5,441,000 were made in 1977 and $3,968,000 in 1976.

Payments and allocations of earnings for partner retirement aggregated $9,400,000 in 1977 and $8,500,000 in 1976.

(6) Changes in Working Capital:

Changes in current assets and current liabilities which increased working capital to $111,017,000 and $107,415,000 as of August 31, 1977 and 1976, respectively, were as follows (in thousands):

	1977	1976
Current assets—		
Cash and cash investments	$ (8,511)	$16,798
Receivables from clients, net . . .	6,764	3,841
Unbilled services	6,158	1,663
Other current assets	4,169	4,565
	$ 8,580	$26,867
Current liabilities—		
Notes payable to banks and current portion of long-term debt .	$ 1,696	$ (594)
Accounts payable	171	1,729
Accrued payroll, withholdings, and fringe benefits	4,458	3,027
Other	(1,347)	4,154
	$ 4,978	$ 8,316
Increase in working capital	$ 3,602	$18,551

(7) Lease Commitments:

The firm has various lease agreements, principally for office space. Rental expense (net of sublease income) was $22,288,000 in 1977 and $18,853,000 in 1976. In most cases, such rentals include insurance, normal maintenance, etc. As of August 31, 1977, commitments under leases, excluding expense escalation provisions, aggregated $180,733,000 which is payable as follows (in thousands):

1978	$21,095
1979	18,624
1980	17,416
1981	16,136
1982	14,512
1983–1987	50,358
1988–1992	24,561
1993–1997	12,455
1998–2009	5,576

The present value of these rental commitments at 8.95% (the interest rate on the firm's principal long-term debt) is approximately $112,172,000.

(8) Litigation:

The firm has been named a defendant in a number of lawsuits and certain claims are pending. Based upon the opinions of legal counsel and other relevant data, estimated liabilities for uninsured risks with respect to such lawsuits and claims were accrued as of August 31, 1977 and 1976.

In order to provide equity among partners for lawsuits which may be filed in the future with respect to professional services rendered in the past, a portion of pro forma capital has been allocated to cover such uninsured risks.

(9) Segment Information:

The only line of business of the firm is rendering professional services to clients. Fiscal 1977 fees, earnings, and total assets at August 31, 1977, for the United States and all other countries are as follows (in millions):

	Total		United States		All Other Countries	
	1977	1976	1977	1976	1977	1976
Fees	$471.5	$424.7	$351.2	$319.4	$120.3	$105.3
	100%	100%	74%	75%	26%	25%
Earnings	$114.1	$101.1	$101.3	$ 89.2	$ 12.8	$ 11.9
	100%	100%	89%	88%	11%	12%
Total Assets	$211.8	$197.6	$154.5	$151.3	$ 57.3	$ 46.3
	100%	100%	73%	77%	27%	23%

Report of Independent Auditors

To the Partners of the Arthur Andersen Worldwide Organization:

We have examined the combined statement of financial position of the Arthur Andersen Worldwide Organization as of August 31, 1977 and the related combined statements of earnings, changes in partners' capital, and changes in financial position for the year then ended. Our examination was made in accordance with generally accepted auditing standards and, accordingly, included such tests of the accounting records and such other auditing procedures as we considered necessary in the circumstances.

In our opinion, the aforementioned combined financial statements present fairly the financial position of the Arthur Andersen Worldwide Organization at August 31, 1977 and the results of its operations, changes in partners' capital, and changes in financial position for the year then ended, in conformity with generally accepted accounting principles applied on a basis consistent with that of the preceding year.

The combined financial statements of the Arthur Andersen Worldwide Organization for the year ended August 31, 1976 were not audited by us and, accordingly, we do not express an opinion on them.

Harkins & Sells

Chicago, Illinois

October 7, 1977

3

INSTALLMENT SALES AND CONSIGNMENTS

INSTALLMENT SALES

Although the concept of the installment sale was first developed in the field of real estate and for high-priced durable goods such as automobiles, it has spread through nearly every sector of the economy.[1] Almost all single-family residences are sold on the installment plan, with monthly payments extending as long as 25 to 30 years. Installment sales also are widely used by dealers in home furnishings and appliances and in farm equipment. For these products the installment payments usually are made monthly for periods of from 6 to 36 months.

For many types of business, the technique of installment sales has been a key factor in achieving large-scale operations. The automobile industry, for example, could not have developed to anything like its present size without the use of installment sales. The huge volume of output achieved by the auto industry has made possible economies in tooling, production, and distribution which could not have been achieved on a small scale of operation. Credit losses often are increased when a business sells goods on the installment plan, but this disadvantage generally is more than offset by the expanded sales volume.

Installment sales pose some challenging problems for accountants. The most basic of these problems is the matching of costs and revenue.

[1] Early in 1978, the installment debt of consumers in the United States was in excess of $215 billion, including $80 billion owed on installment purchases of automobiles. In contrast, the total installment debt of consumers 30 years earlier was only $9 billion.

Should the gross profit from an installment sale be treated as realized in the period the sale occurs, or should it be spread over the life of the installment contract? What should be done with costs which occur in periods subsequent to the sale? How should defaults, trade-ins, and repossessions be handled?

Regardless of the accounting issues raised by installment sales, we can assume that installment contracts will continue to be a major force in our economy. The accountant, therefore, must examine the issues and develop the most effective techniques possible for measuring, controlling, and reporting installment sales. As we progress through this chapter, it will be apparent that installment sales are one of the many thorny problems confronting the accounting profession as it searches for a consistent body of accounting principles.

Special characteristics of installment sales

An installment sale is a sale of real or personal property or services which provides for a series of payments over a period of months or years. A down payment usually, but not always, is required. Since the seller must wait a considerable period of time to collect the full sales price, it is customary to provide for interest on the unpaid balance, and to add carrying charges to the listed selling price.

The risk of noncollection to the seller is increased greatly when sales are made on the installment plan. Customers generally are in weaker financial condition than those who buy on open account; furthermore, the credit rating of the customers and their ability to pay may change significantly during the period covered by an installment contract. To protect themselves against this greater risk of noncollection, sellers of real or personal property usually select a form of contract called a *security agreement* which enables them to repossess the property if the buyer fails to make payments.

The sellers' right to protect their *security interest* (uncollected balance of a sales contract) and to repossess the property varies by type of industry, the form of the contractual arrangement, and the statutes relating to repossessions. For the service-type business, repossession obviously is not available as a safeguard against the failure to collect. In reality, for many types of personal property as well, the sellers' right to repossess may be more of a threat than a real assurance against loss. The product sold may have been damaged or may have depreciated to a point that it is worth less than the balance due on the installment contract. A basic rule designed to minimize losses from nonpayment of installment contracts is to require a sufficient down payment to cover the loss of value when property moves out of the "new merchandise" category. A corollary rule is that the payment schedule should not be outstripped by the projected decline in value of the property sold. For example, if a customer buying an automobile on the installment plan finds after a year or so that the car is currently worth less than the balance still owed on the contract, the customer's motivation to continue the payments may be reduced.

Competitive pressures within an industry often will not permit a business to adhere to these standards. Furthermore, repossession may be a difficult and expensive process, especially if the customer is noncooperative or has disappeared. Reconditioning and repair may be necessary to make the merchandise salable, and the resale of such merchandise may be difficult. For these reasons, doubtful accounts expense is likely to be significantly higher on installment sales than on regular credit sales.

A related problem is the increased collection expense when payments are spread over an extended period. Accounting expenses also are multiplied by the use of installment sales, and large amounts of working capital are tied up in installment receivables. In recognition of these problems, many business executives have concluded that the handling of installment receivables is a separate business, and they therefore sell their installment receivables to finance companies which specialize in credit and collection activities.

Methods for recognition of profits on installment sales

The determination of net income on installment sales is complicated by the fact that the amounts of revenue and related costs and expenses are seldom known in the period when the sale is made. Substantial expenses (as for collection, accounting, repairs, and repossession) are likely to be incurred in subsequent periods. In some businesses, *the risk of noncollection may be so great as to raise doubts as to the recognition of any revenue or profit at the point of sale.*

The first objective in the development of accounting policies for installment sales should be a reasonable matching of costs and revenue. However, in recognition of the diverse business conditions under which installment sales are made, accountants have used three approaches to the problem: (1) Recognition of gross profit at the time of sale; (2) cost recovery method; and (3) recognition of gross profit through the use of the installment method of accounting.

Recognition of Gross Profit at Time of Sale To recognize the entire gross profit at the time of an installment sale is to say in effect that installment sales should be treated like regular sales on credit. The merchandise has been delivered to the customer and an enforceable receivable of definite amount has been acquired. The excess of the receivable contract over the cost of merchandise delivered is *realized* gross profit in the traditional meaning of the term. The journal entry consists of a debit to Installment Contracts Receivable and a credit to Installment Sales. If a perpetual inventory system is maintained, another journal entry is needed to transfer the cost of the merchandise from the Inventories account to the Cost of Installment Sales account. No recognition is given to the seller's retention of title to the merchandise because the normal expectation is completion of the contract through collection of the receivable. Implicit in this recognition of gross profit at the time of sale is the assumption that all expenses relating to the sale will be recognized in the same period so that the determination of net income consists of matching realized revenue with expired costs.

The expenses associated with the sale include collection and doubtful accounts expenses. Recognition of these expenses in the period of sale requires an estimate of the customer's performance over the entire term of the installment contract. Such an estimate may be considerably more difficult to make than the normal provision made for doubtful accounts from regular sales, which generally involve credit extension for 30 to 60 days. However, with careful analysis of experience in the industry and in the particular business, reasonably satisfactory estimates can be made in most situations. The journal entries to record such expenses would consist of debits to expense accounts and credits to asset valuation accounts such as Allowance for Doubtful Accounts and Allowance for Collection Costs. The allowance accounts would be debited in later periods as uncollectible installment contracts become known and as collection costs are incurred.

Cost Recovery Method In some cases accounts receivable may be collectible over a long period of time. In addition, the terms of sale may not be definite, and the financial position of customers may be extremely unpredictable, thus making it virtually impossible to find a reasonable basis for estimating the degree of collectibility of the receivables. In such cases, either the installment method or the cost recovery method of accounting may be used for installment sales. Under the *cost recovery method,* no profit is recognized until all costs of the item sold have been fully recovered. After all costs have been recovered, additional collections on the installment receivables would be recognized as revenue, and only current collection expenses would be charged to such revenue. The cost recovery method of accounting is rarely used; therefore it will not be illustrated in this chapter.

Recognition of Gross Profit through the Use of the Installment Method of Accounting The third approach to the measurement of income from installment sales is to recognize gross profit in installments over the term of the contract on the basis of cash collections. Emphasis is shifted from the acquisition of receivables to the collection of the receivables as the basis for realization of gross profit; in other words, *a modified cash basis of accounting is substituted for the accrual basis.* This modified cash basis of accounting is known as the *installment method of accounting.*

The installment method of accounting

Under the installment method of accounting, each cash collection on the contract is regarded as including both a return of cost and a realization of gross profit in the ratio in which these two elements were included in the selling price.

For example, assume that Marianne McDermott, a farm equipment dealer, sells for $10,000 a machine which cost her $7,000. The $3,000 excess of the sales price over cost is regarded as **deferred gross profit.** Since cost and gross profit constituted 70% and 30%, respectively, of the sales price, this 70:30 ratio is used to divide each collection under the contract between the recovery of cost and the realization of gross profit. If $1,000 is received as a down pahment, then $300 of the deferred gross profit has been realized and is taken into income of the current period. At the end of each accounting period, the Deferred Gross Profit account will equal 30% of the installment receivable remaining uncollected. The Realized Gross Profit on Installment Sales account will show for each period an amount equal to 30% of the collections during that period. In this example the question of interest and carrying charges is omitted; it is considered later in the chapter.

The method described is acceptable under income tax regulations. In fact, the opportunity to postpone the recognition of taxable income has been responsible for the popularity of the installment method of accounting for income tax purposes. Although the income tax advantages are readily apparent, the theoretical support for the installment method of accounting is less impressive.

Many years ago the Committee on Concepts and Standards Underlying Corporate Financial Statements of the American Accounting Association stated:[2]

> There is no sound accounting reason for the use of the installment method for financial statement purposes in the case of closed transactions in which collection is dependent upon lapse of time and the probabilities of realization are properly evaluated. In the opinion of the Committee, such income has accrued and should be recognized in the financial statements, . . .

Accounting Research Study No. 3 stated that revenue should be recognized in the accounting period in which the major economic activity necessary for the production and disposition of goods is performed. **ARS No. 3** rejected the use of the installment method of accounting in published financial statements:[3]

> Collectibility of receivables is not necessarily less predictable because collections are scheduled in installments. The postponement of recognition of

[2] *Accounting and Reporting Standards for Corporate Financial Statements and Preceding Statements and Supplements,* "Supplementary Statement No. 4," dated Aug. 1, 1952, American Accounting Association (Sarasota: 1957), p. 33.

[3] Robert T. Sprouse and Maurice Moonitz, *Accounting Research Study No. 3,* "A Tentative Set of Broad Accounting Principles for Business Enterprises," AICPA (New York: 1962), p. 48.

revenues until they can be measured by actual cash receipt is not in accordance with the concept of an accrual accounting. Any uncertainty as to collectibility should be expressed by a separately calculated and separately disclosed estimate of uncollectibles rather than by a postponement of the recognition of revenue.

APB Opinion No. 10 virtually removed the installment method of accounting from the body of generally accepted accounting principles because it reaffirmed the general concept that income is realized when a sale is made, unless the circumstances are such that the collection of the selling price is not reasonably assured. *APB Opinion No. 10* stated:[4]

> Revenues should ordinarily be accounted for at the time a transaction is completed, with appropriate provision for uncollectible accounts. Accordingly, ... in the absence of the circumstances referred to above, the installment method of recognizing revenue is not acceptable.

The "circumstances" in which the use of the installment method of accounting was permitted were: (1) Collection of installment receivables is not reasonably assured; (2) receivables are collectible over an extended period of time; and (3) there is no reasonable basis for estimating the degree of collectibility. In such situations, either the installment method or the cost recovery method of accounting may be used.

Because the installment method still may be used for financial accounting purposes in some cases and because *it is widely used for income tax purposes,* we shall illustrate its use in the following pages, first for a single sale of real estate and then for sales of merchandise by a dealer.

Illustration 1: Single sale of real estate on the installment plan

The owner of real estate which has appreciated greatly in value often is willing to sell only on the installment plan so that the gain can be spread over several years for income tax purposes. Federal income tax regulations presently permit the use of the installment method for the sale of real estate if the payment received during the year of the sale does not exceed 30% of the sales price.

Let us assume that on November 1, Year 1, John Kane, who maintains accounting records on a calendar-year basis, sold for $110,000 a parcel of land acquired for $40,000. Commission and other expenses pertaining to the sale were $10,000. Because Kane was not in the real estate business, these expenses were treated as deductions in determining the gross profit on the sale rather than as charges to specific expense accounts. The net amount receivable from the sale was therefore $100,000, of which 40% represented the return of the investment in land and 60% represented deferred gain. All collections from the buyer, including the down payment, were regarded as consisting of 40% cost recovery and 60% realization of gain.

---

[4] *APB Opinion No. 10*, "Omnibus Opinion—1966," AICPA (New York: 1966), p. 149.

The contract of sale called for a down payment of $20,000 and a promissory note, with payments every six months in the amount of $7,500 plus interest at the annual rate of 8% on the unpaid balance. One-half of the down payment was applied in the escrow statement to pay commissions and other expenses of sale. The journal entries below and on page 102 show the sale of the land on November 1, Year 1, the interest accrual at the end of Year 1, the collections on the note during Year 2, and the realization of a portion of the deferred gain in Years 1 and 2. Because this transaction was an isolated sale by a non-dealer, there was no need to use an Installment Sales account; the deferred gain on sale of land was recorded at the time of sale.

JOHN KANE

Journal Entries to Record Sale of Land on Installment Plan

For Year 1 and Year 2

Year 1

Nov. 1   Cash 10,000

          Notes Receivable 90,000

                Land 40,000

                Deferred Gain on Sale of Land 60,000

          Sold land on installment plan, receiving note calling for payments of $7,500 every six months plus 8% annual interest on the unpaid balance. Broker's commissions and other expenses of $10,000 were deducted in the computation of the net cash received and the deferred gain.

Dec. 31   Deferred Gain on Sale of Land 6,000

                Realized Gain on Sale of Land 6,000

          Realized gain computed at 60% of cash collected on the contract during Year 1.

    31   Interest Receivable 1,200

                Interest Revenue......................... 1,200

          To accrue interest for two months at 8% on note receivable of $90,000.

Year 2

May 1   Cash 11,100

                Interest Receivable 1,200

                Interest Revenue......................... 2,400

                Notes Receivable 7,500

          Collected semiannual installment on note receivable plus interest for six months at 8% on $90,000.

JOHN KANE

Journal Entries to Record Sale of Land on Installment Plan

For Year 1 and Year 2 (Continued)

Year 2			
Nov. 1	Cash	10,800	
	Interest Revenue		3,300
	Notes Receivable		7,500
	Collected semiannual installment on note receivable plus interest for six months at 8% on unpaid balance of $82,500 ($90,000 − $7,500 = $82,500).		
Dec. 31	Deferred Gain on Sale of Land	9,000	
	Realized Gain on Sale of Land		9,000
	Realized gain computed at 60% of amount collected on principal of note during Year 2 ($15,000 × 60% = $9,000).		
31	Interest Receivable	1,000	
	Interest Revenue		1,000
	To accrue interest for two months at 8% on $75,000 unpaid balance of note receivable ($90,000 − $15,000 = $75,000).		

Journal entries for the remaining life of the note would follow the same pattern illustrated for Year 1 and Year 2, assuming that the buyer makes all payments as required by contract.

This example brings out the contrast between the timing of gross profits on ordinary sales and on sales accounted for by the installment method. If the land sold by John Kane had been recorded as an ordinary sale, a gross profit of $60,000 would have been reported in the year of sale. Use of the installment method of accounting resulted in the recognition of only $6,000 gross profit in the year of sale, followed by a profit of $9,000 ($15,000 × 60% = $9,000) in each of the next six years. If a sale on the installment plan results in a loss, **the entire loss must be recognized in the year of the sale.**

Illustration 2: Sales of merchandise on the installment plan by a dealer

In the preceding example we dealt with a single sale of real estate on the installment plan by a nondealer. Now we shall consider a large volume of installment sales of merchandise by a retailing company which uses the installment method of accounting because the collectibility of the receivables cannot be estimated.

A first requirement is to keep separate all sales made on the installment plan as distinguished from ordinary sales. The accounting records for installment receivables usually are maintained by contract rather than by customer; if several articles are sold on the installment plan to one customer, it is convenient to account for each contract separately. However, it is not necessary to compute the rate of gross profit on each individual installment sale or to apply a different rate to collections on each individual contract. The average rate of gross profit on all installment sales during a given year generally is computed and applied to all collections received (net of interest and carrying charges) on installment receivables originating in that year.

Data for Illustration   To illustrate the procedures of accounting for merchandise sales on the installment plan, assume that Longview Company sells merchandise on the installment plan as well as on regular terms (cash or 30-day open accounts) and uses a perpetual inventory system. For an installment sale the customer's account is debited for the full amount of the selling price, including interest and carrying charges, and is credited for the amount of the down payment. The installment contract receivable thus provides a complete record of the transaction. Doubtful accounts expense is recognized at the time the accounts are **known to be uncollectible.** Assume that at the beginning of Year 5, Longview Company's ledger included the following accounts:

Account balances, Jan. 1, Year 5	*Installment contracts receivable—Year 3* .... *$20,000 debit*
	Installment contracts receivable—Year 4 .... *85,000 debit*
	Deferred interest and carrying charges on installment sales ...... *17,500 credit*
	Deferred gross profit—Year 3 installment sales .... *4,500 credit*
	Deferred gross profit—Year 4 installment sales .... *19,460 credit*

The gross profit rate on installment sales (excluding interest and carrying charges) was 25% in Year 3 and 28% in Year 4.

During Year 5, the following transactions relating to installment sales were completed by Longview Company:

(1) Installment sales, cost of installment sales, and deferred gross profit for Year 5 are listed below:

Sales and cost of sales for Year 5	*Installment sales (not including $30,000 deferred interest and carrying charges)* *$200,000*
	Cost of installment sales *138,000*
	Deferred gross profit—Year 5 installment sales *62,000*
	Rate of gross profit on installment sales *31%*

(2) Cash collections on installment contracts during Year 5 are summarized below:

	Sales price	Interest and carrying charges	Total cash collected
Installment contracts receivable—			
Year 5...............................	$ 80,000	$10,000	$ 90,000
Installment contracts receivable—			
Year 4...............................	44,500	12,500	57,000
Installment contracts receivable—			
Year 3...............................	17,000	1,850	18,850
Total	$141,500	$24,350	$165,850

(3) Customers who purchased merchandise in Year 3 were unable to pay the balance of their contracts, $1,150. The contracts consisted of $1,000 sales price and $150 in interest and carrying charges, and included $250 ($1,000 × 25% = $250) of deferred gross profit. The current fair (net realizable) value of the merchandise repossessed was $650.

(4) Deferred gross profit realized in Year 5 is determined as follows:

Relating to Year 5 sales, $80,000 × 31%	$24,800
Relating to Year 4 sales, $44,500 × 28%	12,460
Relating to Year 3 sales, $17,000 × 25%	4,250

Recording Transactions The journal entries to record the transactions for Longview Company relating to installment sales for Year 5 are given below:

LONGVIEW COMPANY
General Journal

Installment Contracts Receivable—Year 5	230,000	
Installment Sales		200,000
Deferred Interest and Carrying Charges on Installment		
Sales		30,000
To record installment sales during Year 5.		
Cost of Installment Sales	138,000	
Inventories		138,000
To record cost of installment sales.		

LONGVIEW COMPANY
General Journal

Cash	165,850	
Installment Contracts Receivable—Year 5		90,000
Installment Contracts Receivable—Year 4		57,000
Installment Contracts Receivable—Year 3		18,850
To record collections on installment accounts during Year 5.		
Inventories (repossessed merchandise)	650	
Deferred Gross Profit—Year 3 Installment Sales	250	
Deferred Interest and Carrying Charges on Installment Sales .	150	
Doubtful Accounts Expense	100	
Installment Contracts Receivable—Year 3		1,150
To record default on installment contracts originating in Year 3 and repossession of merchandise.		

Adjusting Entries   The adjusting journal entries for Longview Company at December 31, Year 5, are as follows:

<table>
<tr><td rowspan="19">Adjusting entries at end of Year 5</td></tr>
</table>

Installment Sales	200,000	
Cost of Installment Sales		138,000
Deferred Gross Profit—Year 5 Installment Sales		62,000
To record deferred gross profit on Year 5 installment sales.		
Deferred Gross Profit—Year 5 Installment Sales	24,800	
Deferred Gross Profit—Year 4 Installment Sales	12,460	
Deferred Gross Profit—Year 3 Installment Sales	4,250	
Realized Gross Profit on Installment Sales		41,510
To record realized gross profit as computed below:		

Year 5: $80,000 × 31%	$24,800	
Year 4: $44,500 × 28%	12,460	
Year 3: $17,000 × 25%	4,250	
Total	$41,510	

Deferred Interest and Carrying Charges on Installment Sales .	24,350	
Revenue from Interest and Carrying Charges		24,350
To record interest and carrying charges earned during Year 5, consisting of following:		

On Year 5 accounts	$10,000	
On Year 4 accounts	12,500	
On Year 3 accounts	1,850	
Total	$24,350	

The Realized Gross Profit on Installment Sales and the Revenue from Interest and Carrying Charges accounts would be closed to the Income Summary account at the end of Year 5. The accounts relating to installment sales appear in the general ledger at the end of Year 5 as follows:

Account balances at end of Year 5	Installment contracts receivable—Year 4	$ 28,000 debit
	Installment contracts receivable—Year 5	140,000 debit
	Deferred interest and carrying charges on installment sales	23,000 credit
	Deferred gross profit—Year 4 installment sales	7,000 credit
	Deferred gross profit—Year 5 installment sales	37,200 credit

These amounts may be rearranged in slightly different form to test the accuracy of the deferred gross profit on installment contracts at the end of Year 5:

LONGVIEW COMPANY
Proof of Deferred Gross Profit
December 31, Year 5

	Contracts receivable	Deferred interest and carrying charges	Net contracts receivable	Gross profit, %	Deferred gross profit
Year 4 accounts ..	$ 28,000	$ 3,000	$ 25,000	28	$ 7,000
Year 5 accounts ..	140,000	20,000	120,000	31	37,200
Totals	$168,000	$23,000	$145,000		$44,200

Instead of segregating the collections applicable to the sales price and to the interest and carrying charges, it would be possible to determine the gross profit rate by inclusion of the interest and carrying charges in the selling price in the computation of the gross profit rate. The resulting *larger* gross profit rate then would be applied to the total amount collected each period in the determination of the realized gross profit. Applying this approach to the Longview Company example above, the gross profit rate for Year 5 would be determined as follows:

Gross profit rate	Sales, including interest and carrying charges of $30,000	$230,000
	Gross profit on installment sales ($230,000 − $138,000 cost of installment sales)	92,000
	Gross profit rate on installment sales ($92,000 ÷ $230,000)	40%

The 40% gross profit rate thus determined would be applied to the total collections each year to compute the realized gross profit. Under this approach, the realized gross profit on Year 5 sales would have been $36,000 ($90,000 × 40% = $36,000).[5]

The use of the installment method of accounting requires installment contracts and collections to be segregated by year of origin. In addition, the gross profit rate must be computed separately for each year. However, a single controlling account for installment contracts receivable may be used if the accounting records are computerized or if the accounts are analyzed at the end of each year to ascertain uncollected balances by year of origin.

The journal entry on page 105 to record the default on installment contracts originating in Year 3 and the repossession of merchandise by Longview Company is explained below.

Defaults and repossessions

If a customer defaults on an installment contract for services and no further collection can be made, we have an example of default without the possibility of repossession. A similar situation exists for certain types of merchandise which have no significant resale value. The journal entry required in such cases is to write off the uncollectible installment contract receivable, cancel the deferred gross profit related to the receivable, and debit Doubtful Accounts Expense for the difference. In other words, the doubtful accounts expense is equal to the *unrecovered cost* contained in the installment contract receivable.

However, in most cases a default by a customer leads to repossession of merchandise. The doubtful accounts expense is reduced by the current fair value of the property repossessed, and it is possible, though not likely, for the repossession to result in a gain.

The principal difficulty in accounting for defaults followed by repossession is estimation of the *current fair value* of the merchandise at the time of repossession. In setting a current fair value, the objective is to choose an amount that will allow for any necessary reconditioning costs and provide a normal gross profit on resale. As reconditioning costs are incurred, they should be added to the Inventories account, provided this does not become unreasonable in relation to the expected selling price. In other words, the carrying amount of the repossessed merchandise for financial accounting purposes should not exceed its *net realizable value.*

The journal entry on page 105 to record the default and repossession by Longview Company accomplished the following: (1) It eliminated the defaulted installment contracts receivable of $1,150; (2) it canceled the deferred gross profit of $250 ($1,000 × 25% = $250) and the deferred interest and carrying charges of $150 applicable to the defaulted con-

[5] This procedure must be used for income tax purposes by dealers in personal property who compute taxable income on the installment basis [Sec. 453 (a) of Internal Revenue Code].

tracts receivable; (3) it recognized an asset equal to the $650 current fair value of the repossessed merchandise; and (4) it recognized doubtful accounts expense of $100, the difference between the unrecovered cost in the defaulted contracts receivable ($750) and the current fair value of the repossessed merchandise ($650). When the installment method of accounting is used, no loss or expense is recognized with respect to the deferred gross profit and interest and carrying charges contained in the defaulted installment contracts, because these amounts had not been recognized previously as realized revenue.

Other accounting issues relating to installment sales

Special accounting issues arise in connection with (1) acceptance of used property as a trade-in, (2) computation of interest on installment contracts receivable, (3) the use of the installment method of accounting solely for income tax purposes, and (4) retail land sales. These issues are discussed in the following sections.

Trade-ins　The automobile business is a familiar example of the use of trade-ins; that is, the acceptance by the dealer of a used automobile as partial payment for a new car. An accounting problem is raised only if the dealer grants an *overallowance* on the used car taken in trade. An overallowance is the excess of the trade-in allowance over the current fair value of the used automobile in terms of the dealer's ability to resell it at a price which will recover all direct costs and result in a normal gross profit. A rough approximation of the current fair value of the used automobile to the dealer may be the currently quoted wholesale price for used cars of the particular make and model.

An overallowance on trade-ins is significant because it actually represents a reduction in the stated selling price of the new merchandise. *The stated selling price must be reduced by the amount of the overallowance* to arrive at a valid amount for the net selling price for the new merchandise. This net selling price less cost gives the gross profit on the sale of the new merchandise.

As an illustration, assume that an article with a cost of $2,400 is sold on an installment contract for $3,300. Used merchandise is accepted as a trade-in at a "value" of $1,100, but the dealer expects to spend $50 in reconditioning the used merchandise before reselling it for only $1,000. Assume that the customary gross profit rate on used merchandise of this type is 15%, which will cover the selling costs, various overhead costs, and also provide a reasonable gross profit on the resale of the used merchandise. The current fair value of the trade-in and the amount of the overallowance is computed as follows:

<table>
<tr><td>Computation
of over-
allowance</td><td>Trade-in allowance given to customer $1,100
Deduct current fair value of trade-in:
   Estimated resale value of article traded in $1,000
    Less: Reconditioning cost expected to be incurred $ 50
       Gross profit margin ($1,000 × 15%) 150   200
   Current fair value of article traded in 800
Overallowance on trade-in .... $ 300</td></tr>
</table>

Assuming that a perpetual inventory system is used, the journal entry to record the installment sale and the merchandise traded in follows:

<table>
<tr><td>Installment
sale
involving
trade-in</td><td>Inventories (trade-ins) 800
Installment Contracts Receivable ($3,300 − $1,100) 2,200
Cost of Installment Sales 2,400
   Installment Sales ($3,300 − $300) 3,000
   Inventories (new) 2,400
To record sale of merchandise for $3,000, consisting of gross sales
price of $3,300 minus an overallowance of $300 given on the
trade-in.</td></tr>
</table>

Cost of the new article was $2,400; therefore the deferred gross profit on the installment sale of $3,000 amounts to $600. The gross profit rate is 20% ($600 ÷ $3,000). This rate will be applied in the computation of realized gross profit on the basis of cash collections. The current fair value of the merchandise accepted as a trade-in, $800, is viewed as the equivalent of a cash collection for this purpose.

Interest on Installment Contracts Receivable Installment contracts usually provide for interest and other so-called "carrying charges" to be paid concurrently with each installment payment. Such *deferred payment charges,* regardless of the label placed on them, represent a cost of borrowing to the buyer and logically may be referred to as "interest." Only that portion of the payment which is applied to reduce the principal of the contract is considered in the measurement of realized gross profit under the installment method of accounting.

The arrangement for adding interest to installment contracts may follow one of the following plans:

1 Equal periodic payments, with a portion of each payment representing interest on the uncollected balance of the principal and the remainder of the payment representing a reduction in the principal

2 Interest computed on each individual installment payment from the beginning date of the contract to the date each payment is received

3 Interest computed each month on the balance of the principal outstanding during the month

4 Interest computed throughout the entire contract period on the original amount of the sale minus any down payment

The first plan is probably the most widely used. Contracts with customers usually state how payments are to be allocated between principal and interest. Regardless of the plan used by dealers for adding interest to installment contracts, interest revenue for financial accounting purposes should be computed periodically by application of the *effective interest rate* to the unpaid balance of the installment contracts receivable.

Installment Method for Income Tax Purposes Only The popularity of the installment method for income tax purposes is explained by its capacity for postponing the recognition of taxable income and the payment of income taxes. For example, assume that Costello Company uses the accrual basis of accounting for financial accounting purposes as required by generally accepted accounting principles. The pre-tax accounting income for Year 10 is $200,000, as indicated by the following condensed partial income statement:

COSTELLO COMPANY	
Condensed Partial Income Statement (accrual basis)	
For Year 10	
Sales	$800,000
Cost of goods sold	500,000
Gross profit on sales	$300,000
Operating expenses	100,000
Income before income taxes	$200,000

Assume that the deferred gross profit on installment sales was $55,000 at the beginning of Year 10 and $105,000 at the end of Year 10. To take advantage of the installment method of accounting for income tax purposes, the taxable income would be determined for Year 10 as follows:

Taxable income	Pre-tax accounting income for Year 10 (accrual basis) ...		$200,000
	Less: Deferred gross profit on installment sales at the end of Year 10	$105,000	
	Add: Deferred gross profit on installment sales at the beginning of Year 10	55,000	50,000
	Taxable income for Year 10 under installment method of accounting		$150,000

Income taxes for Year 10 would be recorded as follows, assuming that the income tax rate for Costello Company is 45% of taxable income:

<table>
<tr><td rowspan="6">Journal
entry to
record
income
taxes</td><td>Income Taxes Expense ....</td><td>90,000</td><td></td></tr>
<tr><td>Income Taxes Payable ....</td><td></td><td>67,500</td></tr>
<tr><td>Deferred Income Tax Liability ....</td><td></td><td>22,500</td></tr>
<tr><td colspan="3">To record income taxes for Year 10, determined as follows:</td></tr>
<tr><td colspan="3">Income taxes expense: $200,000 × 45% = $90,000.</td></tr>
<tr><td colspan="3">Income taxes payable: $150,000 × 45% = $67,500.
Deferred income tax liability: $50,000 × 45% = $22,500.</td></tr>
</table>

For a thorough discussion of the problem of income tax allocation, the reader should refer to the **Intermediate Accounting** text of this series.

Accounting for Retail Land Sales   In 1973, the AICPA published an **Industry Accounting Guide,** "Accounting for Retail Land Sales," which called for the use of the accrual basis of accounting for land development projects in which collections on contracts are reasonably assured and **all** the following conditions are present:[6]

1 The properties clearly will be useful for residential or recreational purposes at the end of the normal payment period.

2 The project's improvements have progressed beyond preliminary stages, and there is evidence that the project will be completed according to plan.

3 The receivable is not subject to subordination to new loans on the property (except for home construction purposes).

4 Collection experience for the project indicates that collectibility of receivables is reasonably predictable and that 90% of the contracts in force six months **after sales are recorded** will be collected in full.

Unless all four of these conditions for the use of the accrual basis of accounting are met for the entire project, the installment method of accounting should be used for all recorded sales of land. If all four conditions subsequently are satisfied, a change to the accrual basis of accounting should be adopted for the entire project and accounted for as a change in accounting estimate.[7]

The **Industry Accounting Guide** suggested that the procedures to be applied under the installment method of accounting for retail land sales should include the following:[8]

1 The entire contract price applicable to the installment sale, without reduction for cancellations or discounts, should be reported as revenue in the income statement of the year the sale is recorded.

[6] An AICPA Industry Accounting Guide, "Accounting for Retail Land Sales," AICPA (New York: 1973), pp. 7–8.
[7] Ibid., pp. 8–9.
[8] Ibid., pp. 15–16.

2 Cost of sales (including provision for future improvement costs) and nonde-ferable operating expenses (except to the extent deferred in **3** below) should be charged to income of the current period.

3 Gross profit less selling costs directly associated with the project should be deferred and recognized in income as payments of principal are received on the sales contracts receivable.

4 Interest at the stated contract rate should be recorded as revenue when received, and the unamortized deferred profit **should be deducted from related contracts receivable** in the balance sheet.

5 Disclosure should be made of the portion of sales and receivables applicable to the installment method.

Financial statement presentation of accounts for installment sales

The presentation of accounts relating to installment sales in the financial statements raises some interesting theoretical issues, regardless of whether the accrual basis or the installment method of accounting is used.

Income Statement A partial income statement for Year 5 for Longview Company, which uses the installment method of accounting, is presented below. This statement is based on the installment sales information illustrated on pages 103 to 106, plus additional assumed data for regular sales.

LONGVIEW COMPANY
Partial Income Statement
For Year Ended December 31, Year 5

	Installment sales	Regular sales	Combined
Sales	$200,000	$300,000	$500,000
Cost of goods sold	138,000	222,000	360,000
Gross profit on sales	$ 62,000	$ 78,000	$140,000
Less: Deferred gross profit on Year 5 installment sales	37,200		37,200
Realized gross profit on Year 5 sales ...	$ 24,800	$ 78,000	$102,800
Add: Realized gross profit on prior years' installment sales (see page 104)			16,710
Total realized gross profit			$119,510

If the accrual basis of accounting were used for all sales, a gross profit of $140,000 would be reported in Year 5. The three-column form illustrated above, while useful for internal purposes, generally would not be used to report the results of operations to outsiders. In a single-step income statement, revenue from interest and carrying charges on installment contracts may be added to sales to arrive at total revenue; in a classified income statement, such revenue generally is reported as Other Revenue.

Balance Sheet Installment contracts receivable, net of deferred interest and carrying charges, are classified as current assets, although the collection period often extends more than a year beyond the balance sheet date. This rule is applicable whether the accrual basis or the installment method of accounting is used. The definition of current assets specifically includes installment accounts and notes receivable if they conform generally to normal trade practices and terms within the industry. This classification is supported by the concept that current assets include all resources expected to be realized in cash or sold or consumed during the normal operating cycle of the business.

A recent balance sheet for General Motors Acceptance Corporation included the following (in millions of dollars):

Finance receivables (including installments maturing after one year, $6,690.9; less unearned income, $1,256.3; and allowance for financing losses, $164.5) *$18,696.4*

The listing of installment contracts receivable in the current asset section may be made most informative by separation of the amounts maturing each year or by disclosure of this information in notes accompanying the financial statements.

The classification of deferred gross profit on installment sales in the balance sheet **when the installment method of accounting is used for financial accounting purposes** has long troubled accountants. A common practice for many years was to classify it as a deferred credit at the end of the liability section. Critics of this treatment pointed out that no obligation to an outsider existed and that the liability classification was improper.

The existence of a deferred gross profit account is based on the argument that the profit element of an installment sale has not yet been realized. Acceptance of this view suggests that the related installment receivable will be overstated unless the deferred gross profit account is shown as a deduction from installment contracts receivable. This classification as an asset valuation account seems theoretically preferable and was recommended in the **AICPA Industry Accounting Guide,** "Accounting for Retail Land Sales."[9]

Efforts to find an acceptable compromise for these conflicting views have brought forth the suggestion that deferred gross profit be sub-

[9] Ibid., p. 16.

divided into three parts: (1) an allowance for collection costs and doubt-ful accounts which would be deducted from installment receivables; (2) a liability representing future income taxes on the gross profit not yet realized; and (3) a residual income element. The residual income ele-ment would be classified by some accountants as a separate item in the stockholders' equity section and by others in an undefined section between liabilities and stockholders' equity. Such a detailed classifica-tion of deferred gross profit in the balance sheet seldom is encountered in the business world.

The lack of agreement on the proper classification of deferred gross profit in the balance sheet is evidence of the inherent contradiction between the installment method of accounting and the assumptions of accrual-basis accounting. Because the chief reason for the use of the installment method is the income tax advantage it affords, the most satisfactory solution in most cases is to recognize gross profits on installment sales on the accrual basis for financial accounting purposes and to defer recognition of gross profits for income tax purposes until installment contracts are collected.

CONSIGNMENTS

The meaning of consignments

The term *consignment* means a transfer of possession of merchandise from the owner to another person who acts as the sales agent of the owner. Title to the merchandise remains with the owner, who is called a *consignor;* the sales agent who has possession of the merchandise is called a *consignee* or a *commission merchant.*

From a legal viewpoint a consignment represents a *bailment.*[10] The relationship between the consignor and consignee is that of principal and agent, and the law of agency controls the determination of the obli-gations and rights of the two parties.

Consignees are responsible to consignors for the merchandise placed in their custody until the merchandise is sold or returned. Since consignees do not acquire title to the merchandise, they neither in-clude it in inventories nor record an account payable or other liability. The only obligation of consignees is to give reasonable care to the con-signed merchandise and to account for it to consignors. When the mer-chandise is sold by a consignee, the resulting account receivable is the property of the consignor. At this point the consignor recognizes the passage of title to the purchaser and also recognizes any gross profit or loss on the sale.

The shipment of merchandise on consignment may be referred to by

[10] A *bailment* is a contract for the delivery or transfer of possession of money or personal property for a particular purpose such as for safekeeping, repairs, or sale.

the consignor as a **consignment out,** and by the consignee as a **consignment in.**

Distinguishing between a consignment and a sale

Although both a sale and a consignment involve the shipment of merchandise, a clear distinction between the two is necessary for the proper measurement of income. Because title does not pass when merchandise is shipped on consignment, the consignor continues to carry the consigned merchandise as part of inventories. No profit should be recognized at the time of the consignment shipment because there is no change in ownership of merchandise. If the consignee's business should fail, the consignor would not be in the position of a creditor; instead, the consignor would have the right to take possession of any unsold consigned merchandise.

Why should a producer or wholesaler prefer to consign merchandise rather than to make outright sales? One possible reason, especially with new products, is that the consignor may be able to persuade dealers to stock the items on consignment, whereas they would not be willing to purchase the merchandise outright. Secondly, the consignor avoids the risk inherent in selling on credit to dealers of questionable financial strength.

From the viewpoint of a consignee, the acquisition of a stock of merchandise on consignment rather than by purchase has the obvious advantage of requiring less capital investment. The consignee also avoids the risk of loss if the merchandise cannot be sold because of style obsolescence and physical deterioration.

Rights and duties of the consignee

When merchandise is shipped on consignment, a formal written contract is needed on such points as credit terms to be granted to customers by the consignee, expenses of the consignee to be reimbursed by the consignor, commissions allowable to the consignee, frequency of reporting and payment by the consignee, and handling and care of the consigned merchandise. In addition to the explicit contractual arrangements, the general rights and duties of the consignee may be summarized as follows:

Rights of Consignee

1 To receive **compensation** for merchandise sold for the account of consignor.

2 To receive **reimbursement** for expenditures (such as freight and insurance) made in connection with the consignment.

Duties of Consignee

1 To give **care and protection** reasonable in relation to the nature of the consigned merchandise.

2 To keep the consigned merchandise **separate from other inventories** or be able to identify the consigned merchandise. Similarly, the con-

signee must *identify* and *segregate the consignment receivables* from other receivables.

3 To sell consigned merchandise on *credit* if the consignor has not forbidden credit sales.

3 To use care *in extending credit* on the sale of consigned merchandise and to be diligent in *setting prices* on consigned merchandise and in collecting consignment receivables.

4 To make the usual *warranties* as to the quality of the consigned merchandise and to bind the consignor to honor such warranties.

4 To *render complete reports* of sales of consigned merchandise and to make appropriate and timely payments to the consignor.

In granting credit, as in caring for the consigned merchandise, the consignee is obliged to act prudently and to protect the interests of the consignor. Because the receivables from the sale of consigned merchandise are the property of the consignor, the consignor bears any credit losses, providing the consignee has exercised due care in granting credit and making collections. However, the consignee may guarantee the collection of receivables; under this type of consignment contract, the consignee is said to be a *del credere agent.*

The consignee must also follow any special instructions by the consignor as to care of the merchandise. If the consignee acts prudently in providing appropriate care and protection, the consignee is not liable for any damage to the merchandise which may occur. Although the consignee is not usually obligated to maintain a separate bank account for cash from consignment sales, a strict legal view of the relationship between consignor and consignee requires separate identification of all property belonging to the consignor.

The account sales

The report rendered by the consignee is called an *account sales;* it shows the merchandise received, merchandise sold, expenses incurred, advances made, and amounts owed or remitted. Payments may be scheduled as agreed portions of the shipment are sold or may not be required until the consigned merchandise either has been sold or has been returned to the consignor.

Assume that Lane Company ships on consignment to Ralph & Co. 10 television sets to be sold at $400 each. The consignee is to be reimbursed for freight costs of $135 and is to receive a commission of 20% of the authorized selling price. After selling all the consigned merchandise, Ralph & Co. sends the consignor an account sales similar to the one on page 117, accompanied by a check for the amount due.

Ralph & Co.
Beverly Hills, California
ACCOUNT SALES

August 31 , 19___

Sales for account and risk of:

Lane Company

Dallas, Texas

Sales: 10 TV sets @ $400		$4,000
Charges:		
Freight	$135	
Commission (20% of $4,000)	800	935
Balance (check enclosed)		$3,065
Consigned TV sets on hand		none

Accounting methods for consignee

The receipt of the consignment shipment of 10 television sets by Ralph & Co. could be recorded in any of several ways. The objective is to create a memorandum record of the consigned merchandise; no purchase has been made and no liability exists. The receipt of the consignment could be recorded by a memorandum notation in the general journal, or by an entry in a separate ledger of consignment shipments, or by a memorandum entry in a general ledger account entitled Consignment In—Lane Company. In this illustration, the latter method is used and the ledger account would appear as follows:

Consignee receives merchandise on consignment

Consignment In—Lane Company

Received 10 TV sets to be
  sold for $400 each at a
  20% commission.

The journal entries by Ralph & Co. to record the payment of freight charges on the shipment and the sale of the television sets would be as follows:

<table>
<tr><td>Consignee
records
freight
charges
and sale of
consigned TV
sets</td><td>Consignment In—Lane Company 135
     Cash 135
Paid freight charges on shipment from consignor.

Cash 4,000
     Consignment In—Lane Company 4,000
Sold 10 TV sets at $400 each.</td></tr>
</table>

The journal entry to record the 20% commission earned by the consignee consists of a debit to the Consignment In account and a credit to a revenue account, as follows:

<table>
<tr><td>Commission
revenue
recorded by
consignee</td><td>Consignment In—Lane Company 800
     Commission Revenue—Consignment Sales 800
Commission of 20% earned on TV sets sold.</td></tr>
</table>

The payment by the consignee of the full amount owed will be recorded by a debit to the Consignment In account and will result in closing that account. The journal entry is:

<table>
<tr><td>To record
payment to
consignor</td><td>Consignment In—Lane Company 3,065
     Cash 3,065
Payment in full to consignor.</td></tr>
</table>

After the posting of this journal entry, the ledger account for the consignment will appear as follows in the consignee's accounting records:

<table>
<tr><td rowspan="2">Summary of
Consignment
In account</td><td colspan="2" align="center">Consignment In—Lane Company</td></tr>
<tr><td>Received 10 TV sets to be
  sold for $400 each at a
  20% commission.
Freight   135
Commission earned   800
Payment to consignor 3,065
                  4,000</td><td>Sales—10 sets @ $400 each   4,000

                              4,000</td></tr>
</table>

Several variations from the pattern of journal entries illustrated might be mentioned. If the policy of Ralph & Co. is to charge inbound freight on both consignment shipments and purchases of merchandise to a Freight In account, the portion applicable to the Lane Company consignment later should be reclassified by a debit to Consignment In— Lane Company and a credit to Freight In. If an advance is made by the consignee to the consignor, it is recorded as a debit to the Consignment In account, and the final payment is reduced by the amount of the advance. If merchandise is received on consignment from several consignors, a controlling account entitled Consignments In may be established in the general ledger, and a supporting account for each consignment set up in a subsidiary consignments ledger.

If the consignee, Ralph & Co., does not wish to determine profits from consignment sales separately from regular sales, the sale of the consigned goods may be credited to the regular Sales account. Concurrently, a journal entry should be made debiting Cost of Goods Sold (or Purchases) and crediting the Consignment In account for the amount payable to the consignor for each unit sold (sales price minus the commission). Costs chargeable to the consignor would be recorded by debits to the Consignment In account and credits to Cash or expense accounts, if the costs previously were recorded in expense accounts. No journal entry would be made for commissions earned, because the profit element would be represented by the difference between the amount credited to Sales and the amount debited to Cost of Goods Sold (or Purchases). The Consignment In account would be closed by a debit for the payment made to the consignor in settlement for the consigned merchandise. This method usually is less desirable, because information on the profits earned on consignment sales as compared with other sales usually is needed by the consignee as a basis for sound business decisions.

At the end of the accounting period when financial statements are prepared, some Consignment In accounts in the subsidiary consignments ledger may have debit balances and others credit balances. A debit balance will exist in a Consignment In account if the total of expenditures, commissions, and advances to the consignor is larger than the proceeds of sales of that particular lot of consigned merchandise. A credit balance will exist if the proceeds of sales are in excess of the expenditures, commissions, and advances to the consignor. The total of the Consignment In accounts with debit balances should be included among the current assets in the balance sheet; the total of the Consignment In accounts with credit balances should be classified as a current liability. Any commissions earned but not recorded should be entered in the accounts before financial statements are prepared. The balance of the Consignments In controlling account represents the difference between the Consignment In accounts with debit balances and those with credit balances. This net figure should not be presented in the balance sheet, because it would violate the accounting principle which prohibits the offsetting of asset and liability accounts.

Accounting methods for consignor

When the consignor ships merchandise to consignees, it is essential to have a record of the location of this portion of inventories. Therefore, the consignor may establish in the general ledger a Consignment Out account for every consignee (or every shipment on consignment). If consignment shipments are numerous, the consignor may prefer to use a controlling account for subsidiary consignment out accounts. If the inventory records are computerized, special coding may be used to identify inventories in the hands of consignees. The Consignment Out account should not be intermingled with accounts receivable, because it represents a special category of inventories rather than receivables.

Should gross profits on consignments be determined separately?

First, let us distinguish between a separate determination of *net income* on consignment sales and a separate determination of *gross profits* on consignment sales. Another possibility to consider is a separate determination of consignment revenue apart from other sales revenue.

Naturally, it would be useful to have very detailed information on the relative profitability of selling through consignees as compared with selling through other channels of distribution. However, our inclination to develop such information must be influenced by several practical considerations. First, the determination of a separate net income from consignment sales seldom is feasible, because this would require allocations of many operating expenses on a rather arbitrary basis. The work required would be extensive, and the resulting data would be no better than the arbitrary expense allocations. In general, therefore, the determination of *net income* from consignment sales cannot be justified.

The determination of gross profits from consignment sales as distinguished from gross profits on other sales is much simpler, because it is based on the identification of *direct costs* associated with the consignments. However, the compilation of these direct costs can be an expensive process, especially if the gross profit is computed by individual consignments or consignees. Management should weigh the cost of this extra work against the need for information on consignment gross profits. A separate determination of gross profits on consignments becomes more desirable if consignment transactions are substantial in relation to other sales.

A separation of consignment sales from other sales is usually a minimum step to develop information needed by management if consignment sales are an important part of total sales volume. On the other hand, no separation of consignment sales from other sales may be justified if only an occasional sale is made on a consignment basis.

Illustration of accounting methods for consignor

The choice of accounting methods by the consignor depends upon whether (1) consignment gross profits are to be determined separately from gross profits on regular sales or (2) sales on consignment are to be merged with regular sales without any effort to measure gross profits separately for the two types of transactions.

The journal entries required under these alternative methods of accounting for consignment shipments now will be illustrated, first under the assumption that gross profits on consignment sales are to be determined separately and second under the assumption that consignment sales are to be merged with regular sales without a separate determination of gross profits. The assumed transactions for these illustrations already have been described from the consignee's viewpoint but now are restated to include the cost data available to the consignor. In all remaining illustrations, we shall assume that the consignor uses a perpetual inventory system.

Lane Company shipped on consignment to Ralph & Co. 10 television sets which cost $250 each. Authorized selling price was $400 each. The cost of packing the merchandise for shipment was $30; all costs incurred in the packing department are debited to the Packing Expense account. Freight charges of $135 by an independent truck line to deliver the shipment to Ralph & Co. were paid by the consignee. All 10 sets were sold by the consignee for $400 each. After deducting the commission of 20% and the freight charges of $135, Ralph & Co. sent Lane Company a check for $3,065 and the account sales illustrated on page 117.

The journal entries for the consignor, assuming that gross profits on consignment sales are determined separately and gross profits on consignment sales are not determined separately, are summarized on pages 122 and 123 for a completed consignment.

If the consigned merchandise is sold on credit, the consignee may send the consignor an account sales but no check. In this case the debit would be to Accounts Receivable rather than to the Cash account. When sales are reported by the consignee and gross profits are not determined separately, the account credited is Sales rather than Consignment Sales, because there is no intent to separate regular sales from consignment sales. Similarly, commissions paid to consignees are merged with other commissions expense, and freight applicable to the consignment shipment is combined with other freight expense.

Accounting for partial sale of consigned goods

In the preceding examples, we have assumed that the consignor received an account sales showing that the entire consignment had been

LANE COMPANY (consignor)

Journal Entries, Ledger Account, and Income Statement Presentation for a Completed Consignment

Explanations	Gross profits determined separately	Gross profits not determined separately

(1) Shipment of merchandise costing $2,500 on consignment; consigned merchandise is transferred to a separate inventories account. Consignor uses a perpetual inventory system.	Consignment Out— Ralph & Co. 2,500
	  Inventories 2,500
		Consignment Out— Ralph & Co. 2,500
		  Inventories 2,500

(2) Packing expense of $30 allocated to consigned merchandise; this expense previously was recorded in the Packing Expense account.	Consignment Out— Ralph & Co. .... 30 Packing Expense 30	No journal entry required; total packing expense is reported among operating expenses.

(3) Consignment sales of $4,000 reported by consignee and payment of $3,065 received. Charges by consignee: freight, $135; commission, $800.	Cash 3,065
	Consignment Out— Ralph & Co. 135
	Commission Expense— Consignment Sales 800
	  Consignment Sales .. 4,000
		Cash 3,065
		Freight Expense 135
		Commission Expense 800
		  Sales 4,000

(4) Cost of consignment sales recorded, $2,665 ($2,500 + $30 + $135 = $2,665).	Cost of Consignment Sales 2,665
	  Consignment Out— Ralph & Co. 2,665
		Cost of Goods Sold 2,500
		  Consignment Out— Ralph & Co. 2,500

(5) *Summary of Consignment Out account.*

Consignment Out—Ralph & Co.

2,500	2,665
30	
135	
2,665	2,665

Consignment Out—Ralph & Co.

2,500	2,500

(6) *Presentation in income statement.*

Consignment sales		$4,000	*Included in total sales $4,000*
Less: Cost of consignment			*Included in cost of all merchandise*
sales	$2,665		*sold 2,500*
Commission	800		*Included in total packing expense .. 30*
		3,465	*Included in total freight expense ... 135*
Gross profit on consignment			*Included in total commission*
sales		$ 535	*expense 800*

sold by the consignee. The account sales was accompanied by remittance in full, and the consignor's journal entries were designed to record the gross profit from the completed consignment.

Let us now change our conditions by assuming that only four of the ten TV sets consigned by Lane Company to Ralph & Co. had been sold by the end of the accounting period. To prepare financial statements, the consignor must determine the amount of gross profit realized on the four units sold and the inventory value of the six unsold units. The account sales received by Lane Company at the end of the current period includes the following information:

RALPH & CO.
Account Sales to Lane Company

Sales: 4 TV sets at $400		$1,600
Charges: Freight	$135	
Commission ($1,600 × 20%)	320	455
Balance payable to consignor		$1,145
Check enclosed	$500	
Balance due to consignor	645	$1,145
Consigned merchandise on hand		6 TV sets

The journal entries for the consignor to account for this uncompleted consignment are presented on pages 126 and 127.

In the illustration of a partial consignment sale, we have employed the familiar accounting principle of carrying forward as part of inventories a pro rata portion of those costs incurred to place the inventories in a location and condition necessary for sale. The selling commission allowed to the consignee for the units sold is an operating expense of the current period.

Return of unsold merchandise by consignee

We have stressed that the costs of packing and shipping merchandise to a consignee, whether paid directly by the consignor or by the consignee, properly are included in inventories. However, if the consignee for any reason returns merchandise to the consignor, the packing and freight costs incurred on the original outbound shipment should be written off as expense of the current period. The place utility originally created by these costs is lost when the merchandise is returned. Any charges borne by the consignor on the return shipment also should be treated as expense, along with any repair expenditures necessary to place the merchandise in salable condition.

Finally, a clear distinction should be made between freight costs on consignment shipments and outbound freight on regular sales. The latter is a current expense, because the revenue from sale of the merchandise is recognized in the current period. The freight costs create an increment in value of the merchandise which is still the property of the consignor. This increment, along with the cost of acquiring or producing the merchandise, is to be offset against revenue in a future period when the consigned merchandise is sold.

Advances from consignees

Although cash advances from a consignee sometimes are credited to the Consignment Out account, a better practice is to credit a liability account, Advances from Consignees. The Consignment Out account will then continue to show the carrying amount of the merchandise on consignment rather than being shown net of a liability to the consignee.

Nature of the Consignment Out account

When accounting students encounter for the first time a ledger account such as Consignment Out, they may gain a clear understanding of its function more quickly by considering where it belongs in the basic five types of accounts: assets, liabilities, owners' equity, revenue, and expenses. Classification of the Consignment Out account within this structure will depend upon the methods employed by a particular company in accounting for consignments.

Whether or not a company uses a system of determining gross profits on consignment sales separately from regular sales, the Consignment Out account belongs in the asset category. The account is debited for the cost of merchandise shipped to a consignee; when the consignee reports sale of all or a portion of the merchandise, the cost is transferred from Consignment Out to Cost of Consignment Sales. To be even more specific, Consignment Out is a current asset, one of the inventories group to be listed on the balance sheet as Inventories on Consignment, or perhaps combined with other inventories if the amount is not material. As stated earlier, the costs of packing and transporting consigned merchandise constitute costs of inventories, and these costs should be debited to the Consignment Out account.

Another concept of the Consignment Out account *not* illustrated in this chapter but used by some companies is summarized briefly as follows: The Consignment Out account may be debited for the cost of merchandise shipped to the consignee and credited for the sales proceeds remitted by the consignee. This normally will result in a credit balance in the Consignment Out account when the entire shipment has been sold. This credit balance represents the profit earned by the consignor. The account is closed by a debit to Consignment Out and a credit to an account such as Profit on Consignment Sales. No separate

LANE COMPANY (consignor)

Journal Entries, Ledger Account, and Income Statement Presentation for a Partial Sale of Consigned Merchandise

Explanations	Gross profits determined separately	Gross profits not determined separately
(1) Shipment of merchandise costing $2,500 on consignment; consigned merchandise is transferred to a separate Inventories account. Consignor uses a perpetual inventory system.	Consignment Out— Ralph & Co. .... 2,500 Inventories 2,500	Consignment Out— Ralph & Co. .... 2,500 Inventories 2,500
(2) Packing expense of $30 allocated to consigned merchandise; this expense previously was recorded in the Packing Expense account.	Consignment Out— Ralph & Co. .... 30 Packing Expense 30	No journal entry required; total packing expense is reported among operating expenses.
(3) Consignment sales of $1,600 reported by consignee and payment of $500 received. Charges by consignee: freight, $135; commissions, $320.	Cash .... 500 Accounts Receivable ...... 645 Consignment Out— Ralph & Co. .... 135 Commission Expense— Consignment Sales ...... 320 Consignment Sales .. 1,600	Cash .... 500 Accounts Receivable ...... 645 Freight Expense ...... 135 Commission Expense— ...... 320 Sales 1,600
(4) Cost of consignment sales recorded: $4 \times (\$250 + \$3 + \$13.50) = \$1,066$ $4 \times \$250 = \$1,000$	Cost of Consignment Sales .... 1,066 Consignment Out— Ralph & Co. 1,066	Cost of Goods Sold ...... 1,000 Consignment Out— Ralph & Co. 1,000

(5) Direct costs relating to unsold merchandise in hands of consignee deferred when profits are not determined separately:

Packing costs, 6 × $3 .... $18
Freight costs, 6 × $13.50 81
Total $99

No journal entry required.

Consignment Out—
Ralph & Co. 99
 Packing Expense 18
 Freight Expense 81

(6) Summary of Consignment Out account.

Consignment Out—Ralph & Co.

2,500			1,066
30		Balance	1,599
135			
2,665			2,665
Balance	1,599		

Consignment Out—Ralph & Co.

2,500			1,000
99		Balance	1,599
2,599			2,599
Balance	1,599		

(7) Presentation in balance sheet.

Current assets:
 Inventories on consignment $1,599

Current assets:
 Inventories on consignment $1,599

account is used for Consignment Sales, and the income statement does not show the amount of sales made through consignees. Under this system, the Consignment Out account does not fit into any of the five basic classes of accounts. It is a mixture of asset elements and revenue and must be closed or reduced to its asset element (cost of unsold consigned merchandise) before financial statements are prepared at the end of an accounting period.

The methods we have illustrated in accounting for consignments are widely used, but many variations from these methods are possible.

REVIEW QUESTIONS

1 What do you consider to be the most important characteristics that distinguish an installment sale from an ordinary sale on 30-day credit?

2 In a discussion of the theoretical support for the installment method of accounting, a student stated: "If a business is going to sell personal property over a period as long as 36 months, no one can predict how difficult or costly collections may be. To recognize the gross profit as earned at the time of sale would violate well-established accounting principles such as conservatism and the 'completed-transaction' concept." What opposing arguments can you offer?

3 What position did **APB Opinion No. 10** establish for the use of the installment method of accounting for financial accounting purposes?

4 On December 1, Ann Haggard agreed to sell for $150,000 a tract of land which she had acquired several years ago at a cost of $60,000. The buyer offered to pay $50,000 down and the balance in 20 semiannual installments plus 6% interest on the unpaid balance. Haggard agreed to these terms, except that she insisted that the down payment be only $44,000 and the semiannual payments be increased accordingly. The buyer quickly agreed and the deal was completed. Why did Haggard insist on reducing the down payment? Assume that Haggard (who is not a dealer in real estate) computes net income on a calendar-year basis and chooses to use the installment method of accounting. How much gross profit did Haggard realize in the year of sale on this transaction?

5 The following journal entry appears in the accounting records of a real estate company using the installment method of accounting:

Inventories (repossessed land)	1,750	
Deferred Gross Profit on Installment Sales—Year 10	1,505	
Doubtful Accounts Expense	1,045	
Installment Contracts Receivable		4,300

What was the rate of gross profit on the original sale? What was the probable source of the $1,750 debit to the Inventories account?

6 How should the **current fair value** of merchandise traded in be determined? What accounting treatment would you recommend for any **overallowance** granted to customers on merchandise accepted as a trade-in?

7 What conditions generally must be present before the accrual basis of ac-

counting can be used to account for the sale of land on the installment plan?

8 Discuss the balance sheet classification of deferred gross profit on the installment sales of real estate, touching on both current practice and theoretical considerations in your answer.

9 How does a **consignment** of merchandise differ from a **sale** of merchandise?

10 Majors Corporation sells merchandise outright for cash and on 30-day credit; it also makes sales through consignees. Explain how the two methods of marketing differ with respect to the time when income is recognized. What relationship, if any, exists between the recognition of profit and the receipt of cash by Majors Corporation?

11 Give reasons why the use of consignments may be advantageous from the viewpoint of both the consignor and the consignee.

12 On December 31, HP Motor Company received a report from one of its consignees that 40 motors out of a consignment of 100 had been sold. No check was enclosed, but the report indicated that payment would be made later. HP Motor Company keeps its accounting records on a calendar-year basis and maintains perpetual inventory records. It determines profits on consignment sales separately from profits on regular sales. What accounting action, if any, should be taken by HP Motor Company at December 31 with respect to the consignee's report?

13 A Denver manufacturer of outboard motors accumulates production costs on job cost sheets. On March 20, Lot No. K-37, consisting of 100 identical motors, was completed at a cost of $14,000. Twenty-five of the motors were shipped on consignment to a dealer in Florida, and another 25 were sent to a consignee in California. The remaining 50 motors were still in the manufacturer's stockroom at March 31, the end of the fiscal year. Neither of the consignees submitted an account sales for March. Explain the quantity and valuation of motors in the manufacturer's balance sheet at March 31.

14 Identify each of the following accounts by indicating whether it belongs in the ledger of the consignor or the consignee; whether it normally has a debit or credit balance; and how the account would be classified in the financial statements.
   a Cost of Consignment Sales
   b Consignment Out
   c Consignment Sales
   d Consignment In

15 What difference, if any, do you see between outbound freight expense on regular sales and outbound freight costs on consignment shipments?

16 Ohio Outboard Company makes a number of shipments on consignment, although most of its output is sold on 30-day credit. Consignment shipments are recorded on sales invoices which are posted as debits to Accounts Receivable and credits to Sales. Ohio Outboard Company has never before been audited by independent public accountants, but at the suggestion of the company's bank you are retained to make an audit for the current year.
   Would you as an independent auditor take exception to the company's method of accounting for consignments? Explain. What adjusting journal entries, if any, would be needed at year-end?

EXERCISES

Ex. 3-1 On September 30, Year 1, Basin Land Corporation sold for $50,000 (net of selling costs) a tract of land which had a cost of $30,000. The company received a down payment of $8,000, the balance to be received at the rate of $3,000 every three months starting December 31, Year 1. In addition, the buyer agreed to pay interest at the rate of 2% per quarter on the unpaid balance. Because collection of the installments was highly uncertain. Basin Land Corporation elected to report the gain on the installment basis, both for financial accounting and for income tax purposes.

Prepare journal entries (*a*) to record the sale of the land, (*b*) to record the receipt of the first installment on December 31, and (*c*) to recognize at December 31 the portion of gain realized in Year 1 under the installment method of accounting.

Ex. 3-2 Early in Year 1, Vargo Company sold a parcel of land with a carrying amount of $40,000 for a net selling price of $100,000. The buyer paid $10,000 down and agreed to pay the balance plus interest in three equal annual installments starting on December 31, Year 1.

Assuming that collections are made as agreed, prepare a working paper showing the gross profit that Vargo Company would recognize each year using (*a*) the accrual basis of accounting, (*b*) the installment method of accounting, and (*c*) the cost recovery method of accounting.

Ex. 3-3 Gross profits for Sunset Home Products, Inc., were 35%, 33%, and 30% of sales price for Year 1, Year 2, and Year 3, respectively. The following account balances are available at the end of Year 3:

Sales	Installment contracts receivable	Deferred gross profit (before adjustment)
Year 1	$ 6,000	$ 7,230
Year 2	61,500	60,750
Year 3	195,000	120,150

The installment contracts receivable and the deferred gross profit include interest and carrying charges.

Prepare a journal entry as of the end of Year 3 to recognize the realized gross profit on installment sales.

Ex. 3-4 Merchandise was sold for $1,600 in Year 5 at a gross profit of 25% on cost. In Year 5 a total of $600 was collected on this contract; in Year 6 no collections were made on this contract and the merchandise was repossessed. The current fair value of the merchandise was $655; however, the accountant recorded the repossession as follows:

Allowance for Doubtful Accounts 1,000
    Installment Contracts Receivable—Year 5 1,000
To write off balance of defaulted installment contract.

Prepare a journal entry to correct the accounts, assuming that the accounts are still open for Year 6 and that an allowance for doubtful installment contracts receivable is used. Ignore interest and carrying charges. The company records installment sales on the accrual basis.

Ex. 3-5 Avalon Corporation sold a new automobile for a list price of $6,600. Cash of $300 was received on the sale, together with an old-model automobile accepted at a trade-in allowance of $1,500. The balance of $4,800 was due in 24 monthly installments. Cost of the new automobile was $5,100. The company anticipated reconditioning cost on the trade-in of $200 and a resale price of $1,300. Used automobiles normally are sold at a gross profit of 25% of selling price.

Prepare journal entries to record (**a**) the sale of the new automobile, (**b**) reconditioning costs of $200 on the automobile acquired as a trade-in, and (**c**) the sale of the used automobile for cash at a "sacrifice" price of $1,250. Ignore interest and carrying charges.

Ex. 3-6 Coronado Island Corporation sells merchandise on three-year installment sales contracts. At February 28, Year 5, the end of its first fiscal year, the results of operations prior to provision for income taxes are summarized below:

Sales	$1,000,000
Cost of goods sold	700,000
Operating expenses	80,000

The balance at February 28, Year 5, in the Installment Contracts Receivable account was $600,000. No allowance for doubtful contracts receivable was required.

Prepare a journal entry to record federal and state income taxes at February 28, Year 5, assuming that Coronado Island Corporation accounts for sales on the accrual basis for financial accounting purposes and on the installment basis for income tax purposes. Assume a combined state and federal income tax rate of 55%.

Ex. 3-7 For financial accounting purposes, Hollis Company uses the accrual basis of accounting for installment sales; for income tax purposes it uses the installment method of accounting. Hollis Company has no other differences between pre-tax accounting income and taxable income. For the fiscal year ended November 30, Year 2, Hollis Company's pre-tax accounting income was $500,000; its combined federal and state income tax rates totaled 60%. The income tax accounting records show total deferred gross profit on installment sales at November 30, Year 1, of $80,000 and at November 30, Year 2, of $120,000.

Prepare the journal entry or entries to record Hollis Company's income taxes expense for the year ended November 30, Year 2.

Ex. 3-8 The Consignment Out account in the accounting records of Oregon Wood Products Company for Year 1 appears below:

Consignment Out—Bend Sales Co.

Shipped 20 units	3,200	Sales price 12 units	
Freight out paid by consignor	260	(per account sales)	3,500
Charges by consignee:			
Unpacking	100		
Commission on sale of 12			
units	350		

The company debited the Consignment Out account for all costs relating to the consignment and credited the account for the full sales price of units sold.

   a Prepare a journal entry in the accounting records of the consignor to correct the Consignments Out account at the end of Year 1, assuming that consignment profits are determined separately. (Show computations.)

   b Give the journal entries that would appear in the accounting records of the consignee, assuming that consignment profits are determined separately. The consignee sold the units for cash and made remittance in full at the end of Year 1.

Ex. 3-9 Carl Warren consigns radios to retailers, debiting Accounts Receivable for the retail sales price of the radios consigned and crediting Sales. All costs relating to consigned radios are debited to expenses of the current period. Net remittances from consignees are credited to Accounts Receivable.

In December, 500 radios costing $60 per unit and retailing for $100 per unit were sent to The Sunset Shop. Freight costs of $1,100 were debited to Freight Expense by the consignor. On December 31, The Sunset Shop remitted $35,550 to Carl Warren in full settlement to date; Accounts Receivable was credited for this amount. The consignee deducted a commission of $10 on each radio sold and $450 for delivering the radios sold.

a Compute the number of radios sold by The Sunset Shop.

b Give a single correcting journal entry required in the accounting records of the consignor at December 31, assuming that the accounts are still open, that perpetual inventories are maintained, and that profits on consignments are determined separately by use of separate revenue and expense accounts. Prepare a schedule allocating costs between radios sold and radios on hand in support of the correcting journal entry.

Ex. 3-10 Information relating to regular sales and consignment sales of Oceanside Flowers for Year 1 is shown below:

	Regular sales	Consignment sales	Total
Sales	$120,000	$30,000	$150,000
Cost of goods sold	84,000	26,000	110,000
Operating expenses	?	1,760	16,910

Income taxes expense is 20% of pre-tax accounting income.

You ascertain that an inventory of $6,500 is in the possession of consignees and is included in cost of consignment merchandise sold. Operating expenses of $15,150 (more than half of which are fixed) are to be allocated to regular sales and consignment sales on the basis of volume. The $1,760 of operating expenses relating to consignment sales includes a commission of 5% and $260 of costs incurred by consignees relating to the entire shipment costing $26,000.

Prepare a three-column income statement showing the net income on regular sales, consignment sales, and total sales. Advise management whether the company should continue to sell on a consignment basis.

SHORT CASES FOR ANALYSIS AND DECISION

Case 3-1 The firm of Clark and Dickson, certified public accountants, is attempting to develop the management advisory services area of its practice. One of the firm's income tax clients, Pula Corporation, affords an opportunity for work along this line. Pula Corporation, a manufacturer of machinery, in the past has sold its products through wholesalers and also directly to some large retail outlets.

During a telephone conversation on income tax matters between the president of Pula Corporation and Paul Clark, the president posed the following question: "We are considering making sales of our products on a consignment basis as well as through our present outlets; would it be feasible to establish accounting procedures that would show separately the net income we earned on the consignment transactions? I don't have time to discuss it now, but write me a memo and let me have your reactions."

Instructions Write the memo that Paul Clark might write to the president of Pula Corporation, making any assumptions you consider necessary and summarizing the issues involved and the alternatives available.

Case 3-2 Sound Delight Music Co., which maintains its accounts on a calendar-year basis. sold a stereo set to Liz Butler on October 1, Year 1. Cost of the set was $800, and the sales price was $1,200. A down payment of $300 was received along with a contract calling for the payment of $50 on the first day of each month for the next 18 months. No interest or carrying charge was added to the contract.

Liz Butler paid the monthly installments promptly on November 1 and December 1, Year 1. She also made seven payments in Year 2 but then defaulted on the contract. Sound Delight Music Co. repossessed the set on November 1, Year 2.

Instructions
a State three different amounts which **might** be reported as realized income from this transaction for Year 1, and indicate the circumstances under which each of the three amounts might be acceptable.
b Without regard to income tax considerations, which of the three amounts do you believe has the strongest support from a theoretical standpoint? Which has the weakest support? Explain.
c If the stereo set repossessed on November 1, Year 2, has a wholesale value of $200 and a retail value of $300, prepare a journal entry to record the repossession under the installment method of accounting. Explain fully the reasoning applicable to the journal entry. Assume that an allowance for doubtful accounts is used.

Case 3-3 Southampton Sales Company sells furniture on the installment plan. For its income tax returns, it reports gross profit from sales using the installment method of accounting. For its financial statements, it considers the entire gross profit to be earned in the year of sale.

Instructions
a Discuss the relative merits of the two methods of reporting gross profit.
b Explain the installment method of accounting as used for income tax purposes.
c Discuss the effects of the concurrent use of these two bases of accounting by Southampton Sales Company on its reported annual income. What recommendation would you make to the company to produce an income statement in accordance with generally accepted accounting principles?

Case 3-4 Quick Food Services, Inc., sells franchises to independent operators. The contract with the franchisee includes the following provisions:
(1) The franchisee is charged an initial fee of $30,000. Of this amount $5,000 is payable when the agreement is signed and a $5,000 non-interest-bearing note is payable at the end of each of the five subsequent years.
(2) All the initial franchise fee collected by the franchisor is to be refunded and the remaining obligation canceled if, for any reason, the franchisee fails to open the franchise.
(3) In return for the initial franchise fee, the franchisor agrees to (1) assist the franchisee in selecting the location for the business, (2) negotiate the lease for the land, (3) obtain financing and assist with building design, (4) supervise construction, (5) establish accounting and income tax records, and (6) provide advice over a five-year period relating to such matters as employee and management training, quality control, and product promotion.
(4) In addition to the initial franchise fee, the franchisee is required to pay to Quick Food Services, Inc., a monthly fee of 2% of sales for menu planning, recipe innovations, and the privilege of purchasing ingredients from Quick Food Services, Inc., at or below prevailing market prices.

Management of Quick Foods Services, Inc., estimates that the value of the services rendered to the franchisee at the time the contract is signed amounts to at least $5,000. All franchisees to date have opened their locations at the scheduled time and none has defaulted on any of the notes receivable.

The credit ratings of all franchisees would entitle them to borrow at the current interest rate of 10%. The present value of an ordinary annuity of five annual receipts of $5,000 each discounted at 10% is $18,954.

Instructions

a Discuss the alternatives that Quick Food Services, Inc., might use to account for the initial franchise fee, evaluate each by applying generally accepted accounting principles to this situation, and give illustrative journal entries for each alternative. Assume that a Discount on Notes Receivable account is used.

b Given the nature of the contract with franchisees, when should revenue be recognized by Quick Food Services, Inc.? Discuss the question of revenue realization for both the initial franchise fee and the additional monthly fee of 2% of sales and give illustrative journal entries for both types of revenue.

c Assume that Quick Food Services, Inc., sells some franchises for $40,000 which includes a charge of $10,000 for the rental of equipment for its economic life of ten years, that $15,000 of the fee is payable immediately and the balance on non-interest-bearing notes at $5,000 per year, that no portion of the $10,000 rental payment is refundable in case the franchisee goes out of business, and that title to the equipment remains with the franchisor. What would be the preferable method of accounting for the rental portion of the initial franchise fee? Explain.

PROBLEMS

3-5 Belair Digital Sciences, Inc., sells computers. On January 1, Year 5, Belair entered into an installment sale contract with Trousdale Company for a seven-year period expiring December 31, Year 11. Equal annual payments under the installment sale are $1,000,000 and are due on January 1. The first payment was made on January 1, Year 5.

Additional information is as follows:

(1) The cash selling price of the computer, that is, the amount that would be realized on an outright sale, was $5,355,000.

(2) The cost of the computer was $4,284,000.

(3) The finance charges relating to the installment period were $1,645,000, based on a stated (and appropriate) interest rate of 10%. For income tax purposes, Belair uses the accrual basis of accounting for recording finance charges as revenue.

(4) Circumstances are such that the collection of the installment receivable is reasonably assured.

(5) The installment sale qualified for the installment method of reporting for income tax purposes.

(6) The effective income tax rate for Belair is 40%.

Instructions

a Compute the pre-tax accounting income (loss) that Belair should record for financial accounting purposes as a result of this transaction for the year ended December 31, Year 5. Show supporting computations in good form.

b Compute the provision for deferred income taxes, if any, that Belair should record for financial accounting purposes as a result of this transaction for the year ended December 31, Year 5. Show supporting computations in good form.

c Prepare a journal entry to record income taxes expense at December 31,

Year 5, as a result of this transaction. Ignore any expenses other than cost of goods sold.

3-6 Prlain Corporation accounts for its retail sales of land using the installment method of accounting because the collection of contracts *is not reasonably assured.* The balances in the accounts for installment contracts receivable at the beginning and end of Year 10 were:

	January 1, Year 10	December 31, Year 10
Installment contracts receivable—Year 8 (sales and cost of sales for Year 8 were $600,000 and $480,000, respectively)	$ 45,000	$ 3,000
Installment contracts receivable—Year 9 (sales and cost of sales for Year 9 were $675,000 and $526,500, respectively)	324,000	90,500
Installment contracts receivable—Year 10 (sales and cost of sales for Year 10 were $900,000 and $675,000, respectively)		600,000

An allowance for doubtful contracts is not used. Interest and carrying charges are included in the selling price and in the computation of the yearly gross profit rates.

Upon default in payment by customers in Year 10, the company repossessed land which had a current fair value of $4,000; in recording the repossession, the company debited Inventories and credited Installment Contracts Receivable—Year 9 for $4,000. The sale of the land had been made in Year 9 for $10,000 and $4,400 had been collected prior to the default. The $3,000 in installment contracts receivable at December 31, Year 10, from sales made in Year 8 are considered uncollectible.

Instructions
a Prepare a journal entry to record realized gross profits at the end of Year 10.
b Prepare a journal entry to write off the uncollectible installment contracts receivable originating in Year 8.
c Prepare any correcting journal entries required as a result of the incorrect treatment of the repossession of land in Year 10.

3-7 Mission Bay Sales, Inc., started business in Year 1. It sells merchandise on the installment plan and on regular 30-day open accounts. Activities for Year 1 are summarized below:

Regular sales	$350,000
Installment sales, including $90,000 deferred interest and carrying charges	690,000
Cost of regular sales	203,000
Cost of installment sales	360,000
Operating expenses	150,000
Collections on regular sales	310,000
Collections on installment sales, including $30,000 interest and carrying charges	250,000

The company uses a perpetual inventory system and does not include interest and carrying charges in the computation of gross profit on installment sales. Income taxes are levied at 45% of taxable income. Accrued interest and carrying charges at the end of Year 1 may be ignored.

Instructions

a Prepare journal entries to record all transactions and adjustments for Year 1, using only the information given in the problem. Assume that the accrual basis of accounting is used for financial accounting purposes, and the installment method is used for income tax purposes. Closing entries are not required.

b Prepare journal entries to record all transactions for Year 1 (including the setting up of deferred gross profit and adjusting entries), using only the information given in the problem. Assume that the installment method of accounting is used for both financial accounting and income tax purposes. Closing entries are not required.

3-8 Parthian Jade Products Co. derives a major part of its revenue from sales made through numerous consignees throughout the United States. The company determines profits on consignment sales by the use of separate sales, cost of goods sold, and expense accounts. Under the perpetual inventory system designed by the company's accountant, all costs relating to consigned merchandise initially are recorded in the Inventory on Consignment account. During the last quarter of Year 1, the following transactions were completed with Larry Revsine, a new consignee in Chicago:

Oct. 2   Consigned 25 lathes costing $12,000 and paid $500 shipping costs.

Dec. 28   Sent a mechanic to Chicago to install safety devices on 10 lathes which have not been sold. The costs of this alteration were: parts from inventories, $60; cash expenditure, $40.

Dec. 31   Received an account sales as follows:

Sales: 20 lathes @ $900		$18,000
Charges: Commission (15% of $18,000)	$2,700	
Advertising	75	
Delivery and installation costs on 20 lathes sold . .	140	2,915
Balance (check no. 1269 enclosed)		$15,085

Instructions

a Prepare a working paper for Parthian Jade Products Co. showing the allocation of costs to lathes sold by Revsine and to the consignment inventories at the end of Year 1.

b Prepare journal entries for Parthian Jade Products Co. to record the transactions with Revsine, including a journal entry to recognize the cost of consignment sales at December 31, Year 1.

3-9 Alma Mae King sells pianos for Paderewski Music Co. on a consignment basis. The ledger account on page 137 for Alma Mae King summarizes consignment activities for the month of November.

Consignment In—Paderewski Music Co.

Memo: Received 10 pianos		Sale of 6 pianos	14,544
Paid freight and insurance	360		
Delivery of 6 pianos to customers	240		
Commissions earned	2,169		
Storage fees on 4 unsold pianos			
(as agreed)	72		
Remittance	6,390		

The cost of the pianos to Paderewski Music Co. was $1,440 each. The accounting policies of Paderewski Music Co. provide for a separate determination of profits on consigned pianos as distinguished from profits on direct sales. The company maintains perpetual inventory records and also maintains a separate Consignment Out account for each consignee. All costs applicable to a consignment of pianos are debited to the Consignment Out account. When sales are reported by a consignee, the gross sales price is credited to Consignment Sales. The Consignment Out account then is relieved of the cost of the units sold and this amount is transferred to a Cost of Consignment Sales account.

Instructions

a Prepare all journal entries required in the accounts of the consignor, Paderewski Music Co., during November.

b Construct the Consignment Out ledger account for Paderewski Music Co. relating to the transactions with Alma Mae King, showing all journal entries during November.

c How should the month-end balances in the Consignment Out and Consignment In accounts appear in the financial statements of the consignor (Paderewski Music Co.) and the consignee (Alma Mae King) at November 30?

3-10 Green Isle Land Corporation sold a parcel of undeveloped land on December 31, Year 1, for "a consideration of $318,611," net of commissions and all other expenses of sale. The land had a carrying amount of $179,997 in the accounting records of Green Isle Land Corporation. The consideration received consisted of the following:

Cash down payment on Dec. 31, Year 1	$ 51,310
Three notes of $100,000 each with payments starting Dec. 31, Year 2, including interest at an annual rate of 6% (present value of an ordinary annuity of three rents of $1 at 6% = $2.673012)	267,301
Total	$318,611

You conclude that 10% is a more reasonable rate of interest and that the current fair value of the three notes should be computed as follows:

Annual payments due on three notes	$100,000
Present value of ordinary annuity of three rents of $1 discounted at 10%.	×2.486852
Current fair value of notes	$248,685

The notes are recorded by Green Isle Land Corporation at current fair value on a 10%-yield basis without the use of a Discount on Notes Receivable account. The gain realized each year on this transaction should be recorded net of a 30% income tax rate applicable to long-term capital gains.

Instructions

a Assuming that the installment method is used to account for this transaction, both for financial accounting and income tax purposes, prepare journal entries to record all transactions through Year 4. Round all computations to nearest dollar.

b Assuming that the installment method is used to report the gain for income tax purposes and that the accrual basis is used for financial accounting purposes, prepare journal entries to record all transactions through Year 4.

3-11 On January 2, Year 5, Somerset Products Company entered into a contract with a manufacturing company to purchase room-size air conditioners and to sell the units on an installment plan with collections over 30 months, with no separately identified interest or carrying charge.

For income tax purposes, Somerset Products Company elected to report income from its sales of air conditioners under the installment method of accounting.

Purchases and sales of new units were as follows:

	Units purchased		Units sold	
	Quantity	Price (each)	Quantity	Price (each)
Year 5	4,800	$100	4,000	$150
Year 6	7,200	90	8,000	140
Year 7	3,200	105	2,800	143

Collections on installment contracts receivable were as follows:

	Collections received		
	Year 5	Year 6	Year 7
Year 5 sales	$120,000	$240,000	$240,000
Year 6 sales		280,000	460,000
Year 7 sales			84,000

In Year 7, 160 units from the Year 6 sales were repossessed and sold for $72.50 each on the installment plan. At the time of repossession, $4,800 had been collected from the original purchasers, and the units had a current fair value of $10,080.

General and administrative expenses for Year 7 were $200,000. No charge has been made against current income for the applicable insurance expense under a three-year policy expiring June 30, Year 8, costing $9,600, and for an advance payment of $40,000 on a new contract to purchase air conditioners beginning January 2, Year 8.

Instructions Assuming that the weighted-average method is used for determining the cost of inventories, including repossessed merchandise, prepare working papers computing the following:

a (1) The cost of goods sold on the installment plan for each year
   (2) The weighted-average unit cost of goods sold on the installment plan for each year
b The gross profit percentages for each year
c The gain or loss on repossessions in Year 7
d The taxable income from installment sales for Year 7

3-12 Glendora Corporation sells a limited number of its products through agents on a consignment basis. In the spring of Year 1, the company arranged to sell outboard motors through a consignee, Marina Mecca. The motors were to be sold by the consignee at a price of $300 each, and the consignee was allowed a 15% commission on gross sales price. The consignee agreed to guarantee the accounts receivable and to remit all collections less the commission on accounts collected. The consignee also was allowed to deduct certain reimbursable costs; these costs were chargeable to the consignor as incurred. Both companies maintain perpetual inventory records.

Transactions relating to the consignment during the first six months of Year 1 were as follows:

Consignor's (Glendora Corporation's) transactions:

Apr. 10	*Sent 90 motors to consignee, cost of each motor $180.*
	Total packing costs paid for shipment $360.
June 30	*Received account sales from consignee and check for $12,765.*

Consignee's (Marina Mecca's) transactions:

Apr. 15	*Received 90 motors and paid freight charges, $450.*
May 1–June 23	*Sold 60 motors and collected $15,600.*
June 2	*Paid $45 for minor repairs on six motors sold.*
June 30	*Sent account sales to consignor with a check for $12,765, enclosed.*

Instructions

a Prepare all journal entries in the accounts of Glendora Corporation and in the accounts of Marina Mecca, assuming that both companies wish to report profits on consignment sales separately. Closing journal entries are not required.

b Prepare all journal entries in the accounts of Glendora Corporation and in the accounts of Marina Mecca, assuming that consignment sales are combined with regular sales. Closing journal entries are not required.

c Would the balance of the Consignment In account maintained by Marina Mecca be the same amount at June 30 under the differing assumptions in **a** and **b** above? What is the balance in the Consignment In account and how should it be shown in the balance sheet of Marina Mecca at June 30?

3-13 Hawaiian Furniture Company began business on January 1, Year 1. All sales of new merchandise are made on installment contracts. Because of the risks of noncollection, the company recognizes income from the sale of new merchandise under the installment method and employs the periodic inventory system. The following information was taken from the company's accounting records at December 31 for the years indicated:

	Year 2	Year 1
Installment contracts receivable:		
Year 1 sales	$ 17,300	$ 40,000
Year 2 sales	56,000	
Cash sales of trade-ins	20,500	
Installment sales	310,000	221,000
Purchases	176,700	170,180
Inventories of new merchandise—Jan. 1	42,000	
Operating expenses	59,556	53,718
Loss on defaulted contracts	9,850	

Your audit as of December 31, Year 2, disclosed the following:

(1) The inventories of new and repossessed merchandise on hand at December 31, Year 2, were $36,432 and $4,650, respectively.

(2) When a customer defaults on a contract, the repossessed merchandise is recorded at its approximate wholesale market value in a separate inventory account. Differences between the unpaid balance on the contract and the wholesale market value are debited to the Loss on Defaulted Contracts account. Repossessed merchandise is sold on the installment plan.

(3) The wholesale market value of repossessed merchandise is determined as follows:

(a) Merchandise repossessed during year of sale is valued at 45% of original selling price.

(b) Merchandise repossessed subsequent to the year of sale is valued at 20% of original selling price.

(4) There were no defaulted contracts during Year 1. An analysis of contracts defaulted and written off during Year 2 follows:

	Original selling price	Unpaid contract balance
Year 1 contracts................................	$19,500	$10,500
Year 2 contracts................................	11,000	8,200

(5) On January 1, Year 2, the company began granting allowances on merchandise traded in as part payment on new sales. During Year 2 the company granted trade-in allowances of $22,600. The wholesale market value of traded-in merchandise was $15,800. All merchandise traded in during the year was sold for cash.

(6) The company uses the installment method of reporting income on merchandise sold on the installment basis for both financial accounting and income tax purposes. Assume that the income tax rate is 20%.

Instructions

a Prepare a working paper for deferred gross profit at December 31, Year 2 and Year 1, from installment sales. Include a supporting schedule calculating the gross profit percentage on installment sales for each year.

b Compute the adjustment (if any) that you would recommend be made in the Loss on Defaulted Contracts account.

c Prepare an income statement (showing cash sales, installment sales, and total sales) for the year ended December 31, Year 2. A total of 5,000 shares of capital stock is outstanding. The following supporting schedules should be prepared in good form:

(1) Unrealized gross profit on Year 2 installment sales

(2) Realized gross profit on Year 1 installment sales

(3) Realized gross profit on sales of traded-in merchandise

3-14 You are examining the December 31, Year 7, financial statements of Lilly Award Company, a new client. The company was organized on January 2, Year 6, and is a distributor of air-conditioning units. The company's income statements for Year 6 and Year 7 are as follows:

LILLY AWARD COMPANY
Income Statements
For Years Ended December 31, Year 7 and Year 6

	Year 7	Year 6
Sales...	$1,287,500	$1,075,000
Cost of goods sold..	669,500	559,000
Gross profit on sales.....................................	$ 618,000	$ 516,000
Selling and administrative expenses	403,500	330,000
Income before income taxes	$ 214,500	$ 186,000
Income taxes, 50%..	107,250	93,000
Net income..	$ 107,250	$ 93,000
Earnings per share..	$ 2.15	$ 1.86

Your examination disclosed the following:
(1) Some sales were made on open account; other sales were made through dealers to whom units were shipped on a consignment basis. Both sales methods were in effect in Year 6 and Year 7. However, in both years the company recorded all shipments as outright sales.
(2) The sales price and cost of the units were the same in Year 6 and Year 7. Each unit had a cost of $130 and was uniformly invoiced at $250 to open-account customers and to consignees.
(3) During Year 7, the amount of cash received from consignees in payment for units sold was $706,500. Consignees paid for the units as soon as they were sold. Account sales received from consignees showed that they had a total of 23 unsold units on hand at December 31, Year 7. Consignees were unable to confirm the unsold units on hand at December 31, Year 6.
(4) The cost of goods sold for Year 7 was determined by the client as follows:

		Units
Units on hand in warehouses, Dec. 31, Year 6............		1,510
Purchases		4,454
Available for sale		5,964
Units on hand in warehouses, Dec. 31, Year 7............		814
Shipments to: Open-account customers	3,008	
Consignees.......................	2,142	5,150 @ $130 = $669,500

Instructions
a Compute the total amount of Lilly Award Company's inventories at December 31, Year 7, and December 31, Year 6.
b Prepare the auditor's working paper adjustments to correct the financial statements for the year ending December 31, Year 6.
c Prepare the formal adjusting journal entries to correct the accounts at December 31, Year 7. Record corrections to Year 6 net income in a Prior Period Adjustment (or Retained Earnings) account. (The accounts have not been closed. Do not prepare closing entries.)

4

ACCOUNTING FOR BRANCHES; COMBINED FINANCIAL STATEMENTS

Branches and divisions

As a business enterprise grows it often establishes branches to market its products over a larger territory. The term **branch** has been used to describe a company unit located at some distance from the home office which carries inventories of merchandise, makes sales in its local area, approves customers' credit, and makes collection of its own receivables.

A branch may obtain merchandise solely from the home office or a portion may be purchased from outside suppliers. The cash receipts of the branch often are deposited in a bank account belonging to the home office; the expenses then are paid from an imprest fund provided by the home office. As the imprest fund is depleted, the branch submits a list of disbursements supported by vouchers and receives a check from the home office to replenish the fund.

The use of an imprest fund gives the home office strong control over the cash receipts and disbursements of the branch. However, it is common practice for a larger branch to maintain its own bank accounts; that is, to deposit its cash receipts and issue its own checks. The extent of independence and responsibility given to a branch will vary in different companies and even among different branches within the same company.

A segment of a business may also be operated as a **division.** The accounting procedures for a division which is not organized as a separate corporation (**subsidiary company**) are similar to those used to account for branch operations. When a segment of a business is operated as a separate corporate entity, consolidated financial statements would generally be required. Consolidated financial statements are described in detail in Chapters 6 through 11; accounting and reporting problems for segments of a business entity are included in Chapter 12.

Sales agency contrasted with branch

The term **sales agency** sometimes is applied to a company unit which performs only a small portion of the functions traditionally associated with a branch. For example, a sales agency usually carries samples of products but does not have an inventory of merchandise. Orders are taken from customers and transmitted to the home office, which approves the customers' credit and ships the merchandise directly to customers. The agency's accounts receivable are maintained at the home office, which also performs the collection function. An imprest fund generally is maintained at the sales agency to permit payment of its operating expenses.

Accounting system for a sales agency

A sales agency which does not carry an inventory of merchandise, maintain receivables, or make collections has no need for a complete set of accounting records. All that is needed is a record of sales to customers and a listing of cash payments supported by vouchers.

If the home office wants to measure the profitability of each sales agency separately, it will establish in the general ledger separate revenue and expense accounts in the name of the agency, for example, Sales: Lakeview Agency; Rent Expense: Lakeview Agency. The cost of goods sold by each agency also must be determined. When a perpetual inventory system is in use, shipments to customers of the Lakeview Agency are debited to Cost of Goods Sold: Lakeview Agency and credited to Inventories.

If a periodic inventory system is in use, a shipment of goods sold by an agency may be recorded by a debit to Cost of Goods Sold: Lakeview Agency and a credit to Shipments to Agencies. This journal entry is recorded only at the end of the accounting period if a memorandum record is maintained during the period listing the cost of goods shipped to fill sales orders received from agencies. At the end of the period the Shipments to Agencies account will be offset against the total of beginning inventories and purchases to determine the cost of goods available for sale by the home office in its own operations.

Office furniture or other assets located at a sales agency may be carried in a separate account in the general ledger of the home office, or control over such assets may be achieved by use of a subsidiary ledger with a detail record for each item showing cost, location, and other data.

Illustrative Journal Entries for Operation of a Sales Agency   The journal entries required for the home office in connection with the operation of a sales agency are illustrated below, assuming that a perpetual inventory system is used:

Journal entries to record agency activities

Home Office General Journal

Inventory of Samples: Lakeview Agency	1,500	
Inventories		1,500
Shipped merchandise to agency for use as samples.		
Imprest Fund: Lakeview Agency	1,000	
Cash		1,000
To establish agency imprest fund.		
Accounts Receivable	50,000	
Sales: Lakeview Agency		50,000
To record sales made through Lakeview Agency.		
Cost of Goods Sold: Lakeview Agency	35,000	
Inventories		35,000
To record cost of goods sold through Lakeview Agency.		
Various Expense Accounts: Lakeview Agency	10,000	
Cash		10,000
To replenish imprest fund. (This entry represents several checks sent to the agency during the period.)		
Sales: Lakeview Agency	50,000	
Cost of Goods Sold: Lakeview Agency		35,000
Various Expense Accounts: Lakeview Agency		10,000
Income Summary: Lakeview Agency		5,000
To close revenue and expense accounts to a separate Income Summary account for sales agency.		
Income Summary: Lakeview Agency	5,000	
Income Summary		5,000
To close agency net income to Income Summary account.		

Accounting system for a branch

The extent of the accounting activity at a branch depends upon company policy. The policies of one company may provide for a complete set of accounting records at each branch; policies of another company may call for concentration of all accounting records in the home office. In some of the drug and grocery chain stores, for example, the branches submit daily reports and documents to the home office, which enters all transactions by branches in computerized accounting records kept in a central location. The home office may not even conduct operations on its own but merely serve as an accounting and control center for the branches.

In many fields of business the branch maintains a complete set of accounting records consisting of journals, ledgers, and a chart of accounts similar to those of an independent business. Financial statements are prepared at regular intervals by the branch and forwarded to the home office. The number and types of accounts, the internal control system, the form and content of financial statements, and the accounting policies generally are prescribed by the home office. Internal auditors may perform examinations to determine whether branch personnel carry out these policies and procedures.

In the remainder of this chapter we shall be concerned with a branch operation that includes a complete set of accounting records. The range of transactions to be accounted for by the branch ordinarily should include all controllable expenses and revenue for which the branch manager is held responsible. If the manager has responsibility over all branch assets and all expenditures, then the branch accounts should reflect this responsibility. More commonly, expenses such as depreciation are regarded as not subject to control by the branch manager, and both plant assets and related depreciation accounts are maintained by the home office.

Reciprocal accounts

The accounting records maintained by the branch will include a Home Office account which will be credited for all merchandise, cash, or other resources provided by the home office; it will be debited for all cash, merchandise, or other resources sent by the branch to the home office or to other branches. The Home Office account is an ownership equity account which shows the net investment in the branch. At the end of the accounting period when the branch closes its accounts, the Income Summary account is closed to the Home Office account. A net income increases the credit balance in the Home Office account; a net loss decrease this balance.

In the home office accounting records, a reciprocal account with a title such as Investment in Branch is maintained. This account is debited for the cash, merchandise, and services provided to the branch, and for net income earned by the branch. It is credited for the cash or other assets received from the branch, and for any net loss incurred by the branch. A separate investment account generally is maintained by the home office for each branch. If there is only one branch, the account title is likely to be Investment in Branch; if there are numerous branches, each account title will include a name or number to identify the individual branch.

Expenses incurred by home office and charged to branches

Some companies follow a policy of notifying branches of expenses incurred by the home office in the branches' behalf. As previously mentioned, plant assets located at branches generally are carried in the home office accounting records. This practice facilitates the use of standard depreciation procedures throughout the company. If an asset is purchased by the home office for the branch, the journal entry for the acquisition is a debit to an asset account and credit to Cash or Accounts Payable. If the branch acquires a plant asset, it will debit the Home Office account and credit Cash or Accounts Payable. The home office debits an asset account, such as Equipment: Branch Z, and credits the reciprocal account Investment in Branch Z.

The home office also usually purchases insurance, pays property and other taxes, and arranges for advertising which benefits all branches. Clearly such expenses as depreciation, taxes, insurance, and advertising must be considered in determining the profitability of a branch. A policy decision must be made as to whether these expense data are to be retained at the home office or are to be reported to the branches so that the income statement prepared by each branch will give a complete picture of operations.

If the home office does not make sales itself but functions only as a control center, most or all of its expenses may be allocated to the branches. To facilitate comparison of the operating results of the various branches, the home office may charge each branch interest on the capital invested in that branch. Such interest expense recorded by the branches would be offset by interest revenue to the home office and would not appear in the combined income statement of the company as a whole.

In some companies the expenses incurred by the home office relating to branch operations are not transmitted to the branches but are used in the home office to restate and analyze the financial statements prepared by the branches.

Alternative methods of billing merchandise shipments to branch

Three alternative methods are available to the home office for pricing merchandise shipped to a branch. The merchandise shipped may be billed (1) at cost, (2) at cost plus an appropriate percentage, or (3) at retail selling price.[1] Of course the shipment of merchandise to a branch does not constitute a sale because ownership of the merchandise does not change.

Billing *at cost* is the simplest procedure and is widely used. It avoids the complication of unrealized gross profit in inventories and permits the financial statements of the branch to give a meaningful picture of operations. However, billing merchandise to branches at cost attributes all gross profits of the organization to the branches, even though some of the merchandise may be manufactured by the home office. Under these circumstances cost may not be the most realistic basis for pricing shipments to branches.

Billing shipments to the branch *at a percentage above cost* (such as 110% of cost) may be intended to allocate a reasonable gross profit to home office operations or may be used to prevent branch personnel from knowing the full net income earned by the branch. The latter reason is a dubious one because a competent branch manager will be well aware of the cost of merchandise. When merchandise is billed to the branch at a price above cost, the net income reported by the branch will be understated and the ending inventories will be overstated. Adjustments must be made by the home office to compensate for the excess of inventory pricing above cost before completion of the combined financial statements for the home office and the branch.

Billing shipments to a branch *at retail selling price* may be based on a desire to conceal profit information from branch personnel and also to strengthen internal control over inventories. The Inventories account of the branch shows the merchandise received at retail selling prices and shows units sold at the same prices. Consequently, the account will show the ending inventories which *should be* on hand priced at retail. The home office record of shipments to a branch, when considered along with sales reported by the branch, provides a perpetual inventory stated at selling price. If the physical inventories taken periodically at the branch do not agree with the amounts thus determined, some type of error or theft would be indicated and should be investigated promptly.

Separate financial statements for branch and home office

A separate income statement and balance sheet should be prepared by the branch so that management may review the operating results and financial position of the branch. The income statement has no unusual features if merchandise is billed to the branch at cost. However, if merchandise is billed to the branch at retail selling price, the income statement will show a net loss approximating the amount of operating expenses. The only unusual aspect of the balance sheet for a branch is

[1] Billing of merchandise to branches at a price above cost is illustrated on pages 155 to 165.

the use of the Home Office account in lieu of the ownership equity accounts used by a separate business entity. The separate financial statements prepared by a branch may be revised at the home office to include expenses incurred by the home office allocable to the branch, and to show branch operations after elimination of any intracompany profits.

Separate financial statements also may be prepared for the home office so that management will be able to appraise the results of its operations and its financial position. However, it is important to emphasize that separate financial statements of the home office and of the branch are prepared for internal use only; they do not meet the needs of investors, bankers, or other external users of financial statements.

Combined financial statements for home office and branch

A balance sheet for distribution to bankers, creditors, stockholders, and government agencies must show the financial position of the business enterprise as a *single unit.* A convenient starting point in the preparation of a combined balance sheet consists of the adjusted trial balances of the home office and of the branch. A working paper for the combination of these trial balances is illustrated on pages 152 and 153.

The assets and liabilities of the branch are substituted for the Investment in Branch account shown in the home office trial balance. Similar accounts are combined to produce one amount for the total cash of the business, one amount for accounts receivable, and similarly for other assets and liabilities.

In the preparation of a combined balance sheet, reciprocal accounts are eliminated because they lose all significance when the branch and home office are viewed as a single entity. The Home Office account is offset against the Investment in Branch account; also any receivables and payables between branches or between the home office and a branch are eliminated.

The operating results of the entire business enterprise are shown by an income statement in which the revenue and expenses of the branch are combined with corresponding revenue and expense accounts for the home office. Any intracompany profits or losses must be eliminated.

Illustrative Journal Entries for Operation of a Branch   Assume that Rex Pen Company bills merchandise to Branch X at cost, and that the branch maintains complete accounting records and prepares monthly financial statements. *Both the home office and the branch use the perpetual inventory system.* Equipment used at the branch is carried in the home office accounting records. Certain expenses, such as advertising and insurance, are incurred by the home office on behalf of the branch and are billed to the branch. Transactions during the first year (Year 1) of operation of the branch are summarized on page 149.

Transactions for Year 1:

(1) Cash of $1,000 was sent to the branch
(2) Merchandise with a cost of $60,000 was shipped to the branch
(3) Equipment was purchased by the branch for $500, to be carried in home office accounting records (Other assets for the branch normally are purchased by the home office)
(4) Sales by the branch on credit amounted to $80,000; the cost of the merchandise sold was $45,000
(5) Collections of accounts receivable by the branch amounted to $62,000
(6) Payments for operating expenses by the branch totaled $20,000
(7) Cash of $37,500 was remitted by the branch to the home office
(8) Operating expenses incurred by the home office and charged to the branch totaled $3,000

These transactions are recorded by the home office and by the branch as illustrated below and on page 150.

Typical home office and branch transactions (perpetual inventory system)	Home Office Accounting Records		Branch Accounting Records	
	(1) Investment in		Cash 1,000	
	Branch X 1,000		Home Office	1,000
	Cash	1,000		
	(2) Investment in		Inventories 60,000	
	Branch X 60,000		Home Office	60,000
	Inventories	60,000		
	(3) Equipment:		Home Office 500	
	Branch X 500		Cash	500
	Investment in			
	Branch X	500		
	(4) None		Accounts Receivable .. 80,000	
			Cost of Goods Sold ... 45,000	
			Sales	80,000
			Inventories	45,000
	(5) None		Cash 62,000	
			Accounts	
			Receivable	62,000
	(6) None		Operating Expenses ... 20,000	
			Cash	20,000

Home Office Accounting Records		Branch Accounting Records	
(7) Cash 37,500		Home Office 37,500	
Investment in		Cash	37,500
Branch X	37,500		
(8) Investment in		Operating Expenses ... 3,000	
Branch X 3,000		Home Office	3,000
Operating			
Expenses	3,000		

When the branch acquires merchandise from outsiders as well as from the home office, the merchandise acquired from the home office should be recorded in a separate account such as Inventories from Home Office.

In the home office accounting records, the Investment in Branch X account has a debit balance of $26,000 *before* the accounts are closed and the branch net income of $12,000 is transferred to the Investment in Branch X account illustrated below:

Reciprocal account in home office ledger

Investment in Branch X			
Explanation of transactions	Debit	Credit	Balance
Cash sent to branch	1,000		1,000 dr
Merchandise billed to branch at cost	60,000		61,000 dr
Equipment purchased by branch, recorded in home office accounts		500	60,500 dr
Cash received from branch		37,500	23,000 dr
Operating expenses billed to branch	3,000		26,000 dr

In the branch accounting records, the Home Office account has a credit balance of $26,000 *before* the accounts are closed and the net income of $12,000 is transferred to the Home Office account illustrated below:

Reciprocal account in branch ledger

Home Office			
Explanation of transactions	Debit	Credit	Balance
Cash received from home office		1,000	1,000 cr
Merchandise received from home office		60,000	61,000 cr
Equipment purchased by branch	500		60,500 cr
Cash sent to home office	37,500		23,000 cr
Operating expenses billed by home office		3,000	26,000 cr

Assume that the perpetual inventories of $15,000 at the end of Year 1 for Branch X had been verified by a physical count. The adjusting and closing entries relating to the branch are given below:

Adjusting and closing entries (perpetual inventory system)	Home Office Accounting Records		Branch Accounting Records	
	None		Sales 80,000	
			Cost of Goods	
			Sold	45,000
			Operating	
			Expenses	23,000
			Income Summary	12,000
	Investment in Branch X . 12,000		Income Summary 12,000	
	Income: Branch X	12,000	Home Office	12,000
	Income: Branch X 12,000		None	
	Income Summary	12,000		

Working paper for combined financial statements

A working paper for combined financial statements has three purposes: (1) to combine accounts for like assets and like liabilities, (2) to eliminate any intracompany profits or losses, and (3) to eliminate the reciprocal accounts. The working paper on pages 152 and 153 for Rex Pen Company is based on the branch transactions illustrated on pages 149 and 150 and additional assumed data for the home office trial balance. All the routine year-end adjusting entries are assumed to have been made and the working paper is begun with the adjusted trial balances of the home office and the branch. Income taxes are ignored in this illustration.

Note that the $26,000 debit balance in the Investment in Branch X account and the $26,000 credit balance in the Home Office account are the balances before the accounts are closed, that is, before the $12,000 net income of the branch is entered in these two reciprocal accounts. In the Combination Elimination columns, elimination (a) offsets the Investment in Branch X account against the Home Office account. This elimination appears in the working paper only; it is not recorded in the accounts of either the home office or the branch, because its only purpose is to aid in the preparation of combined financial statements.

REX PEN COMPANY

Working Paper for Combined Financial Statements of Home Office and Branch X

For Year Ended December 31, Year 1

(Perpetual Inventory System: Billings at cost)

	Adjusted trial balances				Combination elimination		Home office and branch combined	
	Home office		Branch					
	Debit	Credit	Debit	Credit	Debit	Credit	Debit	Credit
Income statement								
Sales		400,000		80,000				480,000
Cost of goods sold	235,000		45,000				280,000	
Operating expenses	90,000		23,000				113,000	
Subtotals	325,000	400,000	68,000	80,000			393,000	480,000
Net income (to statement of retained earnings below)	75,000		12,000				87,000	
Totals	400,000	400,000	80,000	80,000			480,000	480,000
Statement of retained earnings								
Retained earnings, Jan. 1, Year 1		70,000						70,000
Net income (from above)		75,000		12,000				87,000
Dividends	40,000						40,000	
Retained earnings, Dec. 31, Year 1 (to balance sheet below)							117,000	
Totals							157,000	157,000

Balance sheet

	Home Office	Branch	Eliminations Dr	Eliminations Cr	Combined
Cash	24,000	5,000			29,000
Accounts receivable (net)	40,000	18,000			58,000
Inventories	45,000	15,000			60,000
Investment in Branch X	26,000			(a) 26,000	
Equipment	150,000				150,000
Accumulated depreciation	10,000				10,000
Accounts payable	20,000				20,000
Home office		26,000	(a) 26,000		
Capital stock, $10 par	150,000				150,000
Retained earnings (from above)	105,000	12,000			117,000
Totals	285,000	38,000	26,000	26,000	297,000

(a) To eliminate reciprocal accounts.

Combined Financial Statements Illustrated   The working paper on pages 152–153 provides the information for the combined financial statements of Rex Pen Company given below:

REX PEN COMPANY
Income Statement
For Year Ended December 31, Year 1

Sales	$480,000
Cost of goods sold	280,000
Gross profit on sales	$200,000
Operating expenses	113,000
Net income	$ 87,000
Earnings per share	$ 5.80

REX PEN COMPANY
Statement of Retained Earnings
For Year Ended December 31, Year 1

Retained earnings, Jan. 1, Year 1	$ 70,000
Net income	87,000
Subtotal	$157,000
Less: Dividends	40,000
Retained earnings, Dec. 31, Year 1	$117,000

REX PEN COMPANY
Balance Sheet
December 31, Year 1
Assets

Cash		$ 29,000
Accounts receivable (net)		58,000
Inventories		60,000
Equipment	$150,000	
Less: Accumulated depreciation	10,000	140,000
Total assets		$287,000

(continued)

Liabilities & Stockholders' Equity

Liabilities:		
Accounts payable		$ 20,000
Stockholders' equity:		
Capital stock, $10 par	$150,000	
Retained earnings	117,000	267,000
Total liabilities & stockholders' equity		$287,000

Billing of merchandise to branches at a price above cost

As explained earlier, some companies prefer to bill merchandise to branches at cost plus a markup percentage, or at retail selling price. Since both these methods involve similar modifications of accounting procedures, a single example will illustrate the key points involved. We shall now repeat the illustration for Rex Pen Company, with one changed assumption: the home office bills merchandise to the branch at 50% above cost.

Under this assumption the journal entries for the first year's transactions by the home office and the branch will be the same as those previously presented on pages 149–150, except for the journal entries showing shipments from the home office to the branch. These shipments ($60,000 + 50% markup = $90,000) are recorded under a perpetual inventory system as follows:

Shipment to branch at a price above cost (perpetual inventory system)	Home Office Accounting Records		Branch Accounting Records	
	(2) Investment in		Inventories 90,000	
	Branch X 90,000		Home Office	90,000
	Inventories	60,000		
	Allowance for			
	Overvaluation of			
	Inventories:			
	Branch X	30,000		

In the home office accounting records the Investment in Branch X account now has a debit balance of $56,000 before the accounts are closed and the branch net income or loss is entered in the Investment in Branch X account. This amount is $30,000 higher than the $26,000 balance in the prior illustration; the increase represents the 50% markup over cost of the merchandise shipped to Branch X. The Investment in Branch X account is illustrated on page 156.

Reciprocal
account in
home office
ledger

Investment in Branch X			
Explanation of transactions	Debit	Credit	Balance
Cash sent to branch	1,000		1,000 dr
Merchandise billed to branch at 50% above cost	90,000		91,000 dr
Equipment purchased by branch, recorded in home office accounts		500	90,500 dr
Cash received from branch		37,500	53,000 dr
Operating expenses billed to branch	3,000		56,000 dr

In the branch accounting records the Home Office account now has a credit balance of $56,000 before the accounts are closed and the branch net income or loss is transferred to the Home Office account:

Reciprocal
account in
branch ledger

Home Office			
Explanation of transactions	Debit	Credit	Balance
Cash received from home office		1,000	1,000 cr
Merchandise received from home office		90,000	91,000 cr
Equipment purchased by branch	500		90,500 cr
Cash sent to home office	37,500		53,000 cr
Operating expenses billed by home office		3,000	56,000 cr

The branch recorded the merchandise received from the home office at the invoiced amount of $90,000. The $90,000 debit balance in the Inventories account in the accounting records of the branch represents, in the accounting records of the home office, a reduction in the Inventories account of $60,000 and an Allowance for Overvaluation of Inventories: Branch X account with a credit balance of $30,000.

The use of the allowance account enables the home office to maintain a record of the **cost** of merchandise shipped to the branch, as well as the amount of the unrealized "write-up" on the shipments.

At the end of the period the branch will report its inventories (based on invoice prices) at $22,500. The cost of these inventories is $15,000 (computed as follows: $22,500 ÷ 1.50 = $15,000). In the home office accounting records the required balance in the Allowance for Overvaluation of Inventories: Branch X account is $7,500; thus this account must be reduced from its present balance of $30,000 to $7,500. The reason for this reduction is that the 50% write-up of merchandise over cost has become realized gross profit with respect to the merchandise sold by the branch. Consequently, at the end of the year the home office should reduce its allowance for overvaluation of the branch inventories to the $7,500 excess valuation contained in the ending inventories. The adjustment of $22,500 in the allowance account is transferred as a credit to the Income: Branch X account, because it represents additional gross profit on branch operations over that reported by the branch. (An alternative interpretation under certain circumstances would be to regard the $22,500 portion of the year's combined net income as realized gross profit attributable to the operations of the home office.)

Of course the actual net income earned through operation of the branch will be the same amount of $12,000 as shown in the prior illustration, in which merchandise was billed to the branch at cost. Under the present assumption, however, the branch will **report** a net loss of $10,500. This amount will be recorded by the home office and adjusted to a net income of $12,000, as shown by the following journal entries at the end of Year 1 relating to branch operations:

End-of-period journal entries

Home Office Accounting Records

Income: Branch X 10,500
    Investment in Branch X   10,500
To record net loss reported by branch.

Allowance for Overvaluation of Inventories: Branch X 22,500
    Income: Branch X   22,500
To reduce allowance to amount by which ending inventories
exceed cost.

Income: Branch X 12,000
    Income Summary   12,000
To close branch net income (as adjusted) to Income Summary.

After these journal entries have been posted, the accounts in the home office ledger used to portray branch operations appear as shown below:

End-of-period balances in home office accounting records

Investment in Branch X

Explanation of transactions	Debit	Credit	Balance
Cash sent to branch	1,000		1,000 dr
Merchandise billed to branch at 50% above cost	90,000		91,000 dr
Equipment purchased by branch, recorded in home office accounts		500	90,500 dr
Cash received from branch		37,500	53,000 dr
Operating expenses billed to branch	3,000		56,000 dr
Net loss for Year 1 reported by branch		10,500	45,500 dr

Allowance for Overvaluation of Inventories: Branch X

Explanation of transactions	Debit	Credit	Balance
Write-up of merchandise shipped to branch during Year 1 (50% of cost)		30,000	30,000 cr
Realization of 50% write-up on merchandise sold by branch during Year 1	22,500		7,500 cr

Income: Branch X

Explanation of transactions	Debit	Credit	Balance
Net loss reported for Year 1 by branch	10,500		10,500 dr
Realization of 50% write-up on merchandise sold by branch		22,500	12,000 cr
Net income of branch (as adjusted) closed to Income Summary	12,000		-0-

A separate balance sheet prepared for the home office alone would show the $7,500 credit balance in the Allowance for Overvaluation of Inventories: Branch X account as a deduction from the $45,500 debit balance in the Investment in Branch X account. As an alternative the net amount of $38,000 could be reported as Investment in Branch X.

The closing entries for the branch at the end of Year 1 are as follows:

Closing entries for branch (perpetual inventory system)

Branch Accounting Records

Sales	80,000	
Income Summary	10,500	
Cost of Goods Sold		67,500
Operating Expenses		23,000
To close the nominal accounts.		
Home Office	10,500	
Income Summary		10,500
To close the net loss in the Income Summary account to the Home Office account.		

After these closing entries have been posted by the branch, the Home Office account in the branch accounting records (on page 159) will have a credit balance of $45,500, the same as the debit balance in the Investment in Branch X account in the accounting records of the home office.

Compare this
account with
Investment in
Branch X
account on
page 157

Home Office			
Explanation of transactions	Debit	Credit	Balance
Cash received from home office		1,000	1,000 cr
Merchandise received from home office		90,000	91,000 cr
Equipment purchased by branch	500		90,500 cr
Cash sent to home office	37,500		53,000 cr
Operating expenses billed by home office		3,000	56,000 cr
Net loss for Year 1	10,500		45,500 cr

Working paper when billings to branches are made at prices above cost

The working paper for combined financial statements when billings to the branch are made at prices above cost is shown on pages 160–161. It differs from the previously illustrated working paper by the inclusion of a combination elimination to restate the ending inventories of the branch to a cost basis. Also the net loss reported by the branch is adjusted by the $22,500 of merchandise "write-up" which was realized as a result of sales by the branch. Bear in mind that the amounts in the Combination Eliminations columns appear only in the working paper. The amounts represent a mechanical step to aid in the preparation of combined financial statements and are not entered in the accounting records of either the home office or the branch.

Note that the amounts in the Home Office and Branch Combined columns of this working paper are exactly the same as in the working paper prepared when the merchandise shipments to the branch were billed at cost. Consequently, the financial statements would be identical with those presented on pages 154–155.

Treatment of beginning inventories priced above cost

The working paper on pages 160 and 161 shows how the ending inventory and the related allowance for overvaluation of inventories were handled. However, because this was the first year of operation for the branch, no beginning inventories were involved.

Perpetual Inventory System   Under the perpetual inventory system, no special problems arise when the beginning inventories of the branch include an element of unrealized intracompany profit. The working paper combination eliminations would be similar to those illustrated on pages 160 and 161.

REX PEN COMPANY
Working Paper for Combined Financial Statements of Home Office and Branch X
For Year Ended December 31, Year 1
(Perpetual inventory system: Billings above cost)

	Adjusted trial balances				Combination eliminations		Home office and branch combined	
	Home office		Branch					
	Debit	Credit	Debit	Credit	Debit	Credit	Debit	Credit
Income statement								
Sales		400,000		80,000				480,000
Cost of goods sold	235,000		67,500			(a) 22,500	280,000	
Operating expenses	90,000		23,000				113,000	
Subtotals	325,000	400,000	90,500	80,000			393,000	480,000
Net income (to statement of retained earnings below)	75,000			10,500	(b) 22,500		87,000	
Totals	400,000	400,000	90,500	90,500			480,000	480,000
Statement of retained earnings								
Retained earnings, Jan. 1, Year 1		70,000						70,000
Net income (from above)		75,000	10,500			(b) 22,500		87,000
Dividends	40,000						40,000	
Retained earnings, Dec. 31, Year 1 (to balance sheet below)				10,500			117,000	
Totals							157,000	157,000

Balance sheet

	Home Office Dr	Home Office Cr	Branch Dr	Branch Cr	Eliminations Dr	Eliminations Cr	Combined Dr	Combined Cr
Cash	24,000		5,000				29,000	
Accounts receivable (net)	40,000		18,000				58,000	
Inventories	45,000		22,500			(a) 7,500	60,000	
Allowance for overvaluation of inventories: Branch X		30,000			(a) 30,000			
Investment in Branch X	56,000					(c) 56,000		
Equipment	150,000						150,000	
Accumulated depreciation		10,000						10,000
Accounts payable		20,000						20,000
Home office				56,000	(c) 56,000			
Capital stock, $10 par		150,000						150,000
Retained earnings (from above)								117,000
Totals	355,000	355,000	56,000	56,000	108,500	108,500	297,000	297,000

(a) To reduce ending inventories and cost of goods sold of branch to a cost basis and to eliminate balance in Allowance for Overvaluation of Inventories: Branch X.

(b) To increase reported net income of branch by the portion of merchandise write-up which was realized.

(c) To eliminate reciprocal accounts.

Periodic Inventory System We shall continue the illustration for Rex Pen Company into a second year of operations (Year 2) to demonstrate the handling of beginning inventories carried by the branch at an amount above cost. However, we shall assume that both the home office and Branch X adopted the periodic inventory system in Year 2. When the periodic inventory system is used, the home office credits the Shipments to Branch account for the *cost* of merchandise shipped and the Allowance for Overvaluation of Inventories account for the *markup* over cost. The branch debits the Shipments from Home Office account for the billed price of merchandise.

The beginning inventories for Year 2 were carried by Branch X at $22,500, or 150% of the cost of $15,000. Assume that during Year 2 the home office shipped to Branch X merchandise which cost $80,000 and was billed at $120,000, and that Branch X sold merchandise which was billed at $112,500 for $150,000. The journal entries to record the shipments and sales under a periodic inventory system would be as follows:

Shipments to branch at a price above cost (periodic inventory system)	**Home Office Accounting Records**		**Branch Accounting Records**	
	Investment in		Shipments from	
	Branch X 120,000		Home Office ... 120,000	
	Shipments to		Home Office	120,000
	Branch X	80,000		
	Allowance			
	for Over-			
	valuation			
	of Inventories:			
	Branch X	40,000		
	None		Cash (or Accounts	
			Receivable) 150,000	
			Sales	150,000

The branch inventories at the end of Year 2 amounted to $30,000 at billed price, representing cost of $20,000 plus a 50% markup by the home office at time of shipment to the branch. The flow of merchandise for Branch X during Year 2 is summarized at the top of page 163.

REX PEN COMPANY
Flow of Merchandise for Branch X
During Year 2

	Cost	Markup	Billed price
Beginning inventories	$15,000	$ 7,500	$ 22,500
Add: Shipments from home office	80,000	40,000	120,000
Available for sale	$95,000	$47,500	$142,500
Less: Ending inventories	(20,000)	(10,000)	(30,000)
Merchandise sold	$75,000	$37,500	$112,500

The activities of the branch during Year 2, as shown by the home office accounting records, are reflected in the ledger accounts below:

End-of-period balances in home office accounting records

Investment in Branch X

Explanation of transactions	Debit	Credit	Balance
Balance, Dec. 31, Year 1			45,500 dr
Merchandise billed to branch at 50% above cost	120,000		165,500 dr
Cash received from branch		113,000	52,500 dr
Operating expenses billed to branch	4,500		57,000 dr
Net income for Year 2 reported by branch	10,000		67,000 dr

Allowance for Overvaluation of Inventories: Branch X

Explanation of transactions	Debit	Credit	Balance
Balance, Dec. 31, Year 1 (see page 158)			7,500 cr
Write-up of merchandise shipped to branch during Year 2 (50% of cost)		40,000	47,500 cr .
Realization of 50% write-up on merchandise sold by branch during Year 2	37,500		10,000 cr

Income: Branch X

Explanation of transactions	Debit	Credit	Balance
Net income reported for Year 2 by branch		10,000	10,000 cr
Realization of 50% write-up on merchandise sold by branch during Year 2		37,500	47,500 cr
Net income of branch (as adjusted) closed to Income Summary account	47,500		-0-

In the home office accounting records at the end of Year 2, the balance required in the Allowance for Overvaluation of Inventories: Branch X account is $10,000, that is, the billed price of $30,000 less cost of $20,000 for merchandise in the ending inventories. The allowance account should therefore be reduced from its present balance of $47,500 to $10,000. This reduction of $37,500 represents the 50% write-up of merchandise above cost which was realized by the branch during Year 2 and is credited to the Income: Branch X account.

In the branch accounting records the Home Office account shows the following activity for Year 2:

<table>
<tr><td rowspan="2" style="text-align:right">Reciprocal account in branch ledger</td><td colspan="4">Home Office</td></tr>
</table>

	Explanation of transactions	**Debit**	**Credit**	**Balance**
	Balance, Dec. 31, Year 1			45,500 cr
	Merchandise received from home office		120,000	165,500 cr
	Cash sent to home office	113,000		52,500 cr
	Operating expenses billed by home office		4,500	57,000 cr
	Net income for Year 2		10,000	67,000 cr

The working paper for combined financial statements under the periodic inventory system appears on pages 166 and 167.

Closing Entries   In the branch accounting records, the closing entries at the end of Year 2 are as follows:

<table>
<tr><td rowspan="2" style="text-align:right">Closing entries for branch (periodic inventory system)</td><td colspan="2">Branch Accounting Records</td></tr>
</table>

Inventories, Dec. 31, Year 2	30,000	
Sales	150,000	
Inventories, Dec. 31, Year 1		22,500
Shipments from Home Office		120,000
Operating Expenses		27,500
Income Summary....................................		10,000
To record ending inventories and to close beginning inventories and nominal accounts.		
Income Summary..	10,000	
Home Office		10,000
To close Income Summary account.		

In the home office accounting records, the closing entries at the end of Year 2 will be as illustrated below:

Closing
entries for
home office
(periodic
inventory
system)

Home Office Accounting Records

Investment in Branch X	10,000	
Income: Branch X		10,000
To record the net income reported by the branch.		
Allowance for Overvaluation of Inventories: Branch X	37,500	
Income: Branch X		37,500
To recognize as realized income the write-up of merchandise applicable to goods sold by the branch during Year 2.		
Income: Branch X	47,500	
Income Summary		47,500
To close branch income to Income Summary account.		
Inventories, Dec. 31, Year 2	70,000	
Sales	500,000	
Shipments to Branch X	80,000	
Inventories, Dec. 31, Year 1		45,000
Purchases		400,000
Operating Expenses		120,000
Income Summary		85,000
To record ending inventories and to close beginning inventories and nominal accounts.		
Income Summary	132,500	
Retained Earnings		132,500
To close Income Summary account.		
Retained Earnings	60,000	
Dividends		60,000
To close Dividends account.		

Reconciliation of reciprocal accounts

At the end of an accounting period, the Investment in Branch account in the home office accounting records may not agree with the Home Office account in the branch accounting records, because certain transactions may have been recorded by one office but not by the other. The situation is comparable to that of reconciling the ledger account for Cash in Bank with the balance shown by the bank statement. The lack

REX PEN COMPANY

Working Paper for Combined Financial Statements of Home Office and Branch X

For Year Ended December 31, Year 2

(Periodic Inventory System: Billings above cost)

	Adjusted trial balances				Combination eliminations		Home office and branch combined	
	Home office		Branch					
	Debit	Credit	Debit	Credit	Debit	Credit	Debit	Credit
Income statement								
Sales		500,000		150,000				650,000
Inventories, Dec. 31, Year 1	45,000		22,500			(b) 7,500	60,000	
Purchases	400,000						400,000	
Shipments to Branch X		80,000			(a) 80,000			
Shipments from Home Office			120,000			(a) 120,000		
Inventories, Dec. 31, Year 2		70,000		30,000	(c) 10,000			90,000
Operating expenses	120,000		27,500				147,500	
Subtotal	565,000	650,000	170,000	180,000			607,500	740,000
Net income (to statement of retained earnings below)	85,000		10,000		(d) 37,500		132,500	
Totals	650,000	650,000	180,000	180,000			740,000	740,000
Statement of retained earnings								
Retained earnings, Dec. 31, Year 1		117,000						117,000
Net income (from above)		85,000		10,000		(d) 37,500		132,500
Dividends	60,000			10,000			60,000	
Retained earnings, Dec. 31, Year 2 (to balance sheet below)							189,500	
Totals							249,500	249,500

Balance sheet

	Home Office	Branch X	Eliminations (Dr)	Eliminations (Cr)	Combined
Cash	30,000	9,000			39,000
Accounts receivable (net)	64,000	28,000			92,000
Inventories, Dec. 31, Year 2	70,000	30,000		(c) 10,000	90,000
Allowance for overvaluation of inventories: Branch X	47,500		(a) 40,000 (b) 7,500		
Investment in Branch X	57,000			(e) 57,000	
Equipment	158,000				158,000
Accumulated depreciation	15,000				15,000
Accounts payable	24,500				24,500
Home office		57,000	(e) 57,000		
Capital stock, $10 par	150,000				150,000
Retained earnings (from above)			57,000	57,000	189,500
Totals	439,000	67,000	232,000	232,000	379,000

(a) To eliminate reciprocal accounts for merchandise shipments.
(b) To reduce beginning inventories of branch to a cost basis.
(c) To reduce ending inventories of branch to a cost basis.
(d) To increase reported net income of branch by portion of merchandise write-up which was realized.
(e) To eliminate reciprocal accounts.

of agreement between the reciprocal accounts causes no difficulty during the accounting period, but at the end of the accounting period the reciprocal accounts must be brought into agreement before combined financial statements are prepared.

As an illustration of the procedure for reconciling reciprocal accounts at the year-end, assume that the home office and branch accounting records of Mercer Co. contain the following data at December 31, Year 10:

Reciprocal accounts before adjustments

Investment in Branch A (in accounting records of Home Office)

Date	Explanation of transactions	Debit	Credit	Balance
Nov. 30	Balance			62,000 dr
Dec. 10	Cash received from branch		20,000	42,500 dr
Dec. 27	Collection of branch account receivable		1,000	41,500 dr
Dec. 29	Merchandise shipped to branch	8,000		49,500 dr

Home Office (in accounting records of Branch A)

Date	Explanation of transactions	Debit	Credit	Balance
Nov. 30	Balance			62,500 cr
Dec. 7	Cash sent to home office	20,000		42,500 cr
Dec. 28	Purchased office equipment	3,000		39,500 cr
Dec. 30	Collection of home office account receivable		2,000	41,500 cr

Comparison of the two reciprocal accounts shows the existence of four reconciling items described below:

1 A debit of $8,000 in the Investment in Branch A account without a related credit in the Home Office account.

On December 29 the home office shipped merchandise to the branch in the amount of $8,000. The home office normally will debit its account with the branch on the date merchandise is shipped, but the branch will not credit its account with the home office until the merchandise is received, perhaps several days later. The required adjustment at year-end for this type of reconciling item, assuming use of the perpetual inventory system, is a journal entry in the branch accounting records as follows:

Inventories	8,000	
Home Office		8,000

In determining its ending inventories, the branch must add to the inventories on hand the $8,000 of merchandise in transit. This merchandise will appear in the branch balance sheet and also as part of the total inventories in the combined financial statements.

2 A credit of $1,000 in the Investment in Branch A account without a related debit in the Home Office account.

On December 27 an account receivable of the branch was collected by the home office. The collection was recorded by the home office by a debit to Cash and a credit to Investment in Branch A. No journal entry has been made by the branch; therefore, the following entry is needed in the branch accounting records:

Home Office	1,000	
Accounts Receivable		1,000

3 A debit of $3,000 in the Home Office account without a related credit in the Investment in Branch A account.

On December 28 the branch purchased equipment at a cost of $3,000. Because the assets in use at the branch are carried in the home office accounting records, the journal entry made by the branch was a debit to Home Office and a credit to Cash. No journal entry has yet been made by the home office; therefore, the following entry is made at December 31 in the home office accounting records:

Equipment: Branch A	3,000	
Investment in Branch A		3,000

4 A credit of $2,000 in the Home Office account without a related debit in the Investment in Branch A account.

On December 30 an account receivable of the home office was collected by the branch. The collection was recorded by the branch by a debit to Cash and a credit to Home Office. No journal entry has been made by the home office; therefore, the following entry is needed in the home office accounting records:

Investment in Branch A	2,000	
Accounts Receivable		2,000

The effect of these four end-of-period journal entries is to bring the reciprocal accounts into agreement, as shown by the reconciliation on page 170.

MERCER COMPANY
HOME OFFICE AND BRANCH A
Reconciliation of Reciprocal Accounts
December 31, Year 10

	Investment in Branch A account (In home office accounting records)	Home Office account (In branch accounting records)
Balances prior to adjustment	$49,500 dr	$41,500 cr
Add:		
(1) Merchandise shipped to branch		8,000
(4) Home office account receivable collected by branch	2,000	
Less:		
(2) Branch account receivable collected by home office . . .		(1,000)
(3) Equipment purchased by branch	(3,000)	
Adjusted balances	$48,500 dr	$48,500 cr

Transactions between branches

Efficient operations may on occasion require that merchandise or equipment be transferred from one branch to another. Normally a branch does not carry an account with another branch but records the transfer through its account with the home office. For example, if Branch A ships merchandise to Branch B, Branch A will debit Home Office and credit Inventories (assuming that the perpetual inventory system is used). Upon receipt of the merchandise, Branch B will debit Inventories and credit Home Office. The home office will record the transfer between branches by a debit to Investment in Branch B and a credit to Investment in Branch A.

The transfer of merchandise from one branch to another does not justify increasing the carrying amount of inventories by the freight costs incurred because of the indirect routing. The amount of freight costs properly included in inventories at a branch is limited to the cost of shipping the merchandise directly from the home office to its present location. Excess freight costs should be treated as an operating expense of the home office for the current period.

To illustrate the accounting for excess freight costs on interbranch transfers of merchandise, assume the following data. The home office shipped merchandise costing $6,000 to Branch D and paid freight of $400. Subsequently, the home office instructed Branch D to transfer this merchandise to Branch E. Freight cost of $300 was paid by Branch D to carry out this order. If the merchandise had been shipped directly from the home office to Branch E, the freight cost would have been $500. The journal entries to be made in the three sets of accounting records (assuming that the perpetual inventory system is used) are as follows:

In Accounting Records of Home Office:

Investment in Branch D	6,400	
Inventories		6,000
Cash		400
To record shipment of merchandise and payment of freight cost.		
Investment in Branch E	6,500	
Excess Freight Expense—Interbranch Transfers	200	
Investment in Branch D		6,700
To record transfer of merchandise from Branch D to Branch E.		
Interbranch freight of $300 paid by Branch D caused total freight		
cost on this merchandise to exceed direct shipment costs by		
$200 ($400 + $300 − $500 = $200).		

In Accounting Records of Branch D:

Inventories	6,000	
Freight In	400	
Home Office		6,400
Received merchandise from home office with freight cost paid in		
advance by the home office.		
Home Office	6,700	
Inventories		6,000
Freight In		400
Cash		300
Transferred merchandise to Branch E at instruction of home		
office; paid freight cost of $300.		

In Accounting Records of Branch E:

Inventories	6,000	
Freight In	500	
Home Office		6,500

Received merchandise from Branch D transferred by order of
home office; recorded normal freight cost billed by home office.

The practice of treating excess freight cost on merchandise transferred from one branch to another as an expense of the current period
is a specific example of the accounting principle that losses should be
given prompt recognition rather than being concealed by inflation of the
carrying amounts of assets. The excess freight cost from such shipments is in most cases the result of inefficient planning of original shipments. The expense arising from such inefficiencies does not add to the
utility of the merchandise and should not be included in the cost of
merchandise.

In treating excess freight cost of interbranch transfers as an expense
attributable to the home office, we have assumed that the home office
makes the decisions directing all shipments. If branch managers are
given authority to order shipments, then the excess freight cost should
be borne by the branches.

Start-up costs of opening new branches

The establishment of a new branch often requires the incurring of considerable cost before a significant flow of revenue can be generated.
Operating losses in the first few months are very likely. Some companies
would prefer to capitalize these start-up losses on the grounds that such
losses are a necessary prelude to successful operation at a new location.
However, most companies recognize start-up costs in connection with
the opening of a new branch as an expense of the period in which the
costs are incurred.

The decision should be based on the principle that net income is
measured by matching costs against realized revenue. If a given cost
can be shown to benefit future periods, it should be deferred and allocated to those periods. Seldom is there positive assurance that a new
branch will achieve a profitable level of operations in later years.

REVIEW QUESTIONS

1 Explain the usual distinctions between a *sales agency* and a *branch.*

2 Palmer Company has several sales agencies and wishes to determine the

profitability of each. Describe the principal accounting procedures that you would recommend be performed by the home office and by the individual sales agencies to achieve this goal.

3 Some branches maintain complete accounting records and prepare financial statements in much the same way as an autonomous business. Other branches perform only limited accounting functions, with most accounting activity concentrated in the home office. Assuming that a branch has a fairly complete set of accounting records, what criterion or principle would you suggest be used in deciding whether various types of expenses applicable to the branch should be recorded by the home office or by the branch?

4 Explain the use of **reciprocal accounts** in home office and branch accounting systems in conjunction with a periodic inventory system.

5 The branch and home office reciprocal accounts of Hok Company are out of balance at the year-end by a substantial amount. What factors might have caused this lack of agreement?

6 Kapnick Company operates a number of branches but centralizes its accounting records in the home office and maintains rigorous control of branch operations. The home office finds that Branch D has ample inventories of a certain item of merchandise but that Branch E is almost out of this item. The home office therefore instructs Branch D to ship merchandise with a cost of $5,000 to Branch E. What journal entry should Branch D make, and what principle should guide the treatment of freight costs? (Assume that Branch D uses the perpetual inventory system.)

7 The president of Steele Company informs you that a branch store is being opened and requests your advice in the following words: "I have been told that we can bill merchandise shipped to the branch at cost, at selling price, or anywhere in between. Do you as an independent certified public accountant really have that much latitude in your definition of generally accepted accounting principles?"

8 The policies of Biegler Company provide that equipment in use by its branches shall be carried in the accounting records of the home office. The purchase of new equipment may be carried out either by the home office or by a branch with the approval of the home office. Branch X, with the approval of the home office, purchases new equipment at a cost of $8,000. Prepare the journal entries for the branch and for the home office to record the purchase of this equipment.

9 Hanson Company operates ten branches in addition to its main store, and bills merchandise to the branches at 10% above cost. The plant assets for the entire company are carried in the home office accounting records. The home office also conducts a regular advertising program which benefits all branches. Each branch maintains its own accounting records and prepares separate financial statements. In the home office, the accounting department prepares (a) financial statements for the main store; (b) revised financial statements for each branch; and (c) combined financial statements for the company as a whole.

Explain the purpose of the financial statements prepared by the branches, the home office financial statements, the revised financial statements for the branches, and the combined financial statements.

EXERCISES

Ex. 4-1 Prepare journal entries in the accounting records of the home office and in the accounting records of Branch P for each of the following transactions (omit explanations):

a Home office transferred cash of $5,000 and merchandise (at cost) of $10,000 to Branch P. Both the home office and the branch use a perpetual inventory system.

b Home office allocated operating expenses of $1,500 to Branch P.

c Branch P informed the home office that it had collected $416 on a note payable to the home office. Principal amount of the note was $400.

d Branch P made sales of $12,500, terms 2/10, n/30, and incurred operating expenses of $2,500. The cost of goods sold was $8,000, and the operating expenses were paid in cash.

e Branch P reported a net income of $500. (Debit Income Summary in branch accounting records.)

Ex. 4-2 Majestic Textile Company has a single branch in Toledo. On March 1, Year 1, the accounting records of the company contain an account entitled Allowance for Overvaluation of Branch Inventories with a balance of $32,000. During March, merchandise costing $36,000 was shipped to the Toledo branch and billed at a price representing a 40% markup on the billed price. At March 31, the branch prepared an income statement indicating a loss of $11,500 for March, with ending inventories at billed price of $25,000.

a What was the cost of the branch inventories on March 1, assuming a uniform markup on all shipments to the branch?

b Prepare the journal entry to adjust the Allowance for Overvaluation of Branch Inventories account at March 31 in the accounting records of the home office.

c What was the correct net income or net loss for the Toledo Branch for the month of March as reflected by the above information?

Ex. 4-3 A home office bills the Orleans Branch at 25% above cost for all merchandise shipped to the branch. Both the home office and the Orleans Branch use the periodic inventory system. During Year 5, the home office shipped merchandise to the Orleans Branch at a billed price of $30,000. Branch inventories for Year 5 were as follows:

	Jan. 1	Dec. 31
Acquired from home office (at billed price)	$15,000	$19,500
Acquired from outsiders	6,800	8,670

a Prepare the journal entries (including adjusting entries) that should appear in the accounting records of the home office for Year 5 to reflect the foregoing information.

b Assuming that the home office holds merchandise costing $29,500, including $2,500 held on consignment from Texarkana Corporation, show how the inventories should be reported in a combined balance sheet for the home office and the Orleans Branch at the end of Year 5.

Ex. 4-4 Purdy Company bills its only branch for merchandise at 30% above cost. The branch sells the merchandise at 10% above billed price. Shortly after the close of business on January 28, some of the branch merchandise was destroyed by fire. The following additional information is available:

Inventories, Jan. 1 (at billed price from home office) $19,500

Inventories, Jan. 28 of merchandise not destroyed (at selling price) 7,150

Shipments from home office from Jan. 1 to Jan. 28 (at billed price)........... 71,500

Sales from Jan. 1 to Jan. 28 51,840

Sales returns from Jan. 1 to Jan. 28 (merchandise actually returned) 3,220

Sales allowances from Jan. 1 to Jan. 28 (price adjustments) 300

a Compute the estimated cost (to the home office) of the merchandise destroyed by fire.

b Prepare the journal entry in the accounting records of the branch to recognize the fire loss.

Ex. 4-5 The following accounts appear in the accounting records of Baker Branch on December 31:

Home Office

Cash remitted directly to home office	8,100	Balance, Jan. 1	22,180
Merchandise returned to home office	630	Merchandise received from home office	18,300
Purchase of fixtures	3,000	Supplies received from home office	610

Income Summary		Home Office Notes Collected	
Expenses	19,040	Revenue	21,900

Income Summary			Home Office Notes Collected		
Expenses	19,040	Revenue	21,900	Cash deposited in home office bank account 1,550	Balance, Jan. 1 1,350 Notes collected 800

The branch collects non-interest-bearing notes receivable as an accommodation to the home office and periodically deposits the proceeds in a home office bank account.

a Reproduce the Investment in Baker Branch account in the home office accounting records, assuming that all intracompany transactions are recorded in a single reciprocal account by the home office.

b Prepare the journal entries required to bring the branch accounting records up to date, assuming that the branch also uses a single reciprocal account to record intracompany transactions.

SHORT CASES FOR ANALYSIS AND DECISION

Case 4-1 You are engaged in the audit of Aurbach Corporation, which opened its first branch office in Year 10. During the audit the president, George Aurbach, raises the question of the accounting treatment of the branch office operating loss for its first year, which is material in amount.

Aurbach proposes to capitalize the operating loss as a start-up cost to be amortized over a five-year period, stating that branch offices of other companies engaged in the same field generally suffer a first-year operating loss which is invariably capitalized, and you are aware of this practice. Therefore, according to Aurbach, the loss should be capitalized so that the accounting will be conservative; further, the accounting must be consistent with established industry practice.

Instructions
a Discuss Aurbach's use of the words **conservative** and **consistent** from the standpoint of accounting terminology. Discuss the accounting treatment you would recommend.

b What disclosure, if any, would be required in the financial statements of Aurbach Corporation?

Case 4-2 Santana Company operates a number of branches as well as a main store. Each branch carries in stock a complete line of merchandise which is obtained almost entirely from the home office. The branches also handle their own billing, approve customer credit, and make collections. Each branch has its own bank account and each maintains complete accounting records. All noncurrent assets at the branches, consisting chiefly of furniture and office equipment, are carried in the home office accounting records and depreciated by the straight-line method at 10% a year.

On July 1, Year 1, the Denver Branch bought office equipment on the orders of the newly appointed branch manager. The equipment had a list price of $2,400 but was acquired on the installment payment plan with no down payment and 24 monthly payments of $110 beginning August 1, Year 1. No journal entry was made for this transaction by the branch until August 1, when the first monthly payment was recorded by a debit to Miscellaneous Expense. The same journal entry was made for the next four monthly payments made during Year 1. On December 2 the branch manager became aware, during a meeting at the home office, that equipment could be purchased by the branches only with prior approval by the home office. Regardless of whether the home office or the branches purchased assets, such assets were to be carried in the home office accounting records. To avoid criticism, the Denver Branch manager immediately disposed of the office equipment acquired July 1 by sale for $1,500 cash to an independent store in a nearby town. The manager then paid off the balance due on the installment contract using a personal check and the $1,500 check received from sale of the equipment. In consideration of the advance payment of the remaining installments on December 3, the equipment dealer agreed to a $100 reduction in the total balance of the contract. No journal entry was made for the disposal of the equipment or the settlement of the liability.

Assume that you are a CPA engaged to perform a year-end audit of Santana Company. During your visit to the Denver Branch you analyze the Miscellaneous Expense account and investigate the five monthly debits of $110. This investigation discloses the acquisition and subsequent disposal of the office equipment. After some hesitation the branch manager gives you a full account of the events.

Instructions
a Would you, as an independent auditor, take any action on this matter? Indicate the major issues involved rather than the accounting details. Give reasons for your answers.
b Prepare the journal entries which should have been made for the entire series of events in the accounting records of the branch. Assume that Santana Company accepts responsibility for the branch manager's actions.
c Prepare the journal entries which should have been made on the home office accounting records for the entire series of events, assuming that the home office was informed of each event and accepts responsibility for all actions by the branch manager.
d As an independent situation from *b* and *c,* draft the journal entries to be made at the time of your audit to correct the accounts with a minimum of work. One compound journal entry in each set of accounting records is suggested. Assume that interest expense belongs in the branch accounting records. Also assume that the company wishes to show in the branch accounting records a liability to the branch manager for personal "loans," if any, and will consider later any disciplinary action to be taken. The accounts have not been closed for Year 1.

PROBLEMS

4-3 Pratt Company bills shipments of merchandise to Branch Z at 140% of cost. During the first year after Branch Z was established, the following were among the transactions completed:
(1) The home office shipped merchandise with a cost of $100,000 to Branch Z.
(2) Branch Z sold for $80,000 cash merchandise which was billed by the home office at $70,000 and incurred operating expenses of $15,000 (all paid in cash).
(3) The physical inventories taken by Branch Z at the end of the first year were $68,600 at billed price.

Instructions
a Assuming that a perpetual inventory system is used both by the home office and by Branch Z, prepare for the first year:
(1) All journal entries, including closing entries, in the accounting records of Branch Z.
(2) All journal entries, including the adjustment of the inventories overvaluation account, in the accounting records of the home office.
b Assuming that a periodic inventory system is used both by the home office and by Branch Z, prepare for the first year:
(1) All journal entries, including the closing entry, in the accounting records of Branch Z.
(2) All journal entries, including the adjustment of the inventories overvaluation account, in the accounting records of the home office.

4-4 Gilles Sales Company, which uses the periodic inventory system, established the Carolina Branch on January 1, Year 3. During the first year of operation, Gilles Sales Company shipped to the branch merchandise which cost $200,000. Billings were made at prices 20% above cost. Freight charges amounting to $7,000 were paid by the home office. Sales by the branch were $300,000 and operating expenses were $64,000, all on the cash basis. At December 31, Year 3, the branch took a physical inventory which showed merchandise on hand of $48,000 at billed price.

Instructions Prepare journal entries to record (in the home office and branch accounts) the shipment of merchandise, payment of freight charges, setting up of the ending inventories, and other related adjustments at December 31, Year 3. (Allocate a proportional amount of freight charges to the ending inventories of the branch.)

4-5 Big Valley Equipment Corporation operates a branch in King City to which it bills merchandise at prices 30% above cost. The branch obtains merchandise only from the home office and sells it at prices averaging 15% above the prices billed by the home office. Both the home office and the branch maintain perpetual inventory records and both close their accounts on December 31.

On March 10, Year 1, a fire at the branch destroyed a part of the inventories. Immediately after the fire, a physical inventory taken of the stock of merchandise on hand and not damaged showed it to have a selling price of $5,980. On January 1, Year 1, the inventories of the branch at billed price had been $15,600. Shipments from the home office during the period January 1 to March 10 were billed to the King City branch in the amount of $57,200. The branch accounting records show that sales during this period were $41,472, before sales returns of $808.

Instructions Prepare the journal entries necessary to record the fire loss in the (1) branch accounting records and (2) home office accounting records. Show how all amounts were determined. You need not prepare closing entries.

4-6 On December 31, Year 5, the Investment in Kathy Branch account in the ledger of the home office of Rancho Products Company shows a debit balance of $31,960. You ascertain the following facts in analyzing this account:

(1) On December 31 merchandise billed at $5,800 was in transit from the home office to the branch. Assume that a periodic inventory system is used by both the home office and the branch.

(2) The branch collected a home office account receivable for $275; the home office was not notified.

(3) On December 29, the home office mailed a check for $2,000 to the branch, but the accountant for the home office recorded the check as a debit in the Charitable Contributions account; the branch had not received the check as of December 31.

(4) Branch net income for December was recorded erroneously by the home office at $840 instead of $480. The credit was entered by the home office in the Income: Kathy Branch account.

(5) The branch returned supplies costing $220 to the home office; the home office had not recorded the receipt of the supplies. The home office records acquisitions of supplies in the Inventory of Supplies account.

Instructions

a Assuming that all other transactions have been recorded properly, prepare a working paper to determine the *unadjusted* balance of the Home Office account in the ledger of the branch at December 31, Year 5.

b Prepare the journal entries for the home office to bring its accounting records up to date. Closing entries have not been made.

c Prepare the journal entries for the Kathy Branch to bring its accounting records up to date.

d Prepare a reconciliation at December 31, Year 5, of the Investment in Kathy Branch account in the accounting records of the home office and the Home Office account in the accounting records of the Kathy Branch. Use a single column for each account and start with the unadjusted balances.

4-7 On January 1 of Year 5, Nishiyama Camera Company opened its first branch with instructions to Wilson Gates, the branch manager, to perform the functions of granting credit, billing customers, accounting for receivables, and making collections. The branch paid its operating expenses by checks drawn on its bank account. The branch obtained merchandise solely from the home office; billings for these shipments were on the basis of cost to the home office. The trial balances for the home office and for the branch on December 31, Year 5, were as follows:

NISHIYAMA CAMERA COMPANY
Trial Balances
December 31, Year 5

	Home office		Branch office	
	Debit	Credit	Debit	Credit
Cash	$ 42,000		$ 14,600	
Notes receivable	7,000			
Accounts receivable (net)	120,400		37,300	
Inventories, Dec. 31, Year 5	95,800		24,200	
Furniture and equipment (net)	48,100			
Investment in branch	82,700			
Accounts payable		$ 41,000		
Capital stock, $2 par		200,000		
Home office				$ 82,700
Retained earnings, Dec. 31, Year 4		25,000		
Sales....................................		400,000		101,100
Cost of goods sold......................	200,500		85,800	
Operating expenses	69,500		21,900	
Totals	$666,000	$666,000	$183,800	$183,800

The physical inventories taken on December 31, Year 5, were in agreement with the perpetual records in the accounts of the home office and the branch.

Instructions

a Prepare the closing entries needed at December 31, Year 5, in the accounting records of the branch.

b In the home office accounting records, prepare the adjusting entries pertaining to the branch and also all closing entries for the home office.

c Prepare an eight-column working paper for combined financial statements of the home office and branch.

4-8 You are engaged to make an audit for the year ended December 31, Year 1, of Mount Sierra Distributing Co., which carries on merchandising operations at both a home office and a branch location. The trial balances of the home office and of the branch are given below:

MOUNT SIERRA DISTRIBUTING CO.
Trial Balances
December 31, Year 1

	Home office Dr (Cr)	Branch office Dr (Cr)
Cash	$ 20,000	$ 7,950
Inventories: home office, Jan. 1, Year 1	23,000	
Inventories: branch, Jan. 1, Year 1		11,550
Miscellaneous assets	200,000	48,450
Investment in branch	60,000	

(continued)

MOUNT SIERRA DISTRIBUTION CO.
Trial Balances (continued)
December 31, Year 1

	Home office Dr (Cr)	Branch office Dr (Cr)
Allowance for overvaluation of branch inventories,		
Jan. 1, Year 1	(1,000)	
Purchases	190,000	
Purchases from home office		105,000
Freight in from home office		5,250
Miscellaneous expenses	42,000	24,300
Current liabilities	(35,000)	(8,500)
Home office		(51,500)
Sales	(155,000)	(142,500)
Sales to branch	(110,000)	
Capital stock, $2.50 par	(200,000)	
Retained earnings	(34,000)	
Totals	$ -0-	$ -0-

The audit at December 31, Year 1, disclosed the following:
(1) The branch office deposits all cash receipts in a local bank for the account of the home office. The audit working papers for the cash cutoff revealed the following:

Amount	Date deposited by branch	Date recorded by home office
$1,050	Dec. 27, Year 1	Dec. 31, Year 1
1,100	Dec. 30, Year 1	Jan. 2, Year 2
600	Dec. 31, Year 1	Jan. 3, Year 2
300	Jan. 2, Year 2	Jan. 6, Year 2

(2) The branch office pays expenses incurred locally from an imprest bank account that is maintained with a balance of $2,000. Checks are drawn once a week on this imprest account, and the home office is notified of the amount needed to replenish the account. At December 31, Year 1, an $1,800 reimbursement check was mailed to the branch office.
(3) The branch office receives all its merchandise from the home office. The home office bills the merchandise at cost plus a markup of 10% of cost. At December 31, Year 1, a shipment with a billed price of $5,000 was in transit to the branch. Freight costs typically are 5% of billed price. Freight costs are considered to be inventoriable costs. Both the home office and the branch use the periodic inventory system.
(4) Beginning inventories in the trial balance are shown at the respective costs to the home office and to the branch office. The inventories at December 31, Year 1, excluding the shipment in transit, are:

Home office, at cost $30,000
Branch office, at billing value 10,400

Instructions Prepare a working paper for Mount Sierra Distributing Co. and its branch with columns for Trial Balances (one column for the home office and one for the branch). Combination Adjustments and Eliminations, Home Office Income Statement, Branch Income Statement, and Combined Balance Sheet. The adjustment should include the determination of cost of goods sold for both the branch and the home office. The branch income statement should be prepared on the basis of home office cost. Disregard income taxes. (Formal journal entries are not required. Supporting computations must be in good form.) Number the combination adjustments and eliminations.

4-9 The following reciprocal accounts are found in the accounting records of the home office and the Pico Branch of Masingale Mattress Company:

Investment in Pico Branch

Feb. 1	Balance	124,630	Mar. 31	Cash received		2,000
Feb. 6	Shipment of merchandise,		Apr. 2	Merchandise returned		450
	160 cases @ $49	7,840	Apr. 29	Corrected loss on disposal of		
Feb. 17	Note receivable collected by			branch equipment from $780		
	branch	2,500		to $250		530
Apr. 26	Loss on disposal of branch					
	equipment	780				
Apr. 28	Operating expenses					
	chargeable to branch	1,200				

Home Office

Mar. 30	Deposited cash in bank		Feb. 1	Balance	124,630
	account of home office	2,000	Feb. 8	Merchandise from home	
Mar. 31	Returned merchandise	450		office, 160 cases	7,480
Apr. 29	Paid a repair bill for the home		Feb. 14	Received shipment directly	
	office	375		from supplier, invoice to be	
Apr. 30	Excess merchandise returned			paid by home office	2,750
	to home office (billed at cost)	4,100	Feb. 15	Note receivable collected	
				for home office	2,500
			Apr. 30	Net income for quarter	
				(tentative)	9,210

You have been retained by the company to assist it with some accounting work preliminary to the preparation of financial statements for the quarter ended April 30, Year 2. Your first task is to prepare a reconciliation of the reciprocal accounts. Additional information available to you follows:

(1) Branch equipment is carried in the accounting records of the home office; the home office notifies the branch periodically as to the amount of depreciation applicable to equipment used by the branch. Gains or losses on disposal of branch equipment are reported to the branch and included in the branch income statement.

(2) Because of the error in recording the shipment from the home office on February 8, Year 2, the sale of this merchandise has been charged improperly to cost of goods sold at $46.75 per case.

(3) The branch frequently makes collections of home office accounts receivable and the home office also collects receivables belonging to the branch. On April 30, Year 2, the branch collected a receivable of $350 belonging to the

home office but the branch employee who recorded the collection mistakenly treated the receivable as belonging to the branch.

(4) The branch recorded the tentative net income of $9,210 by a debit to Income Summary and a credit to Home Office, although the revenue and expense accounts had not been closed.

Instructions

a Reconcile the reciprocal accounts to the correct balances at April 30, Year 2. Use a four-column working paper (debit and credit columns for the Investment in Branch account in the home office accounting records and debit and credit columns for the Home Office account in the branch accounting records). Start with the unadjusted balances at April 30, Year 2, and work to corrected balances, inserting full explanations of all adjusting or correcting items.

b Prepare individual journal entries for the branch to bring its accounting records up to date, assuming that corrections still can be made to revenue and expense accounts. The branch uses a perpetual inventory system.

c Prepare required journal entries in the accounting records of the home office. The home office uses a perpetual inventory system.

4-10 The preclosing general ledger trial balances at December 31, Year 3, for Great Plains Company and its San Antonio Branch are shown below.

GREAT PLAINS COMPANY
Trial Balances
December 31, Year 3

	Home office Dr (Cr)	San Antonia Branch Dr (Cr)
Cash	$ 25,000	$ 8,000
Accounts receivable (net)	35,000	12,000
Inventories, Jan. 1, Year 3	70,000	15,000
Equipment (net)	90,000	
Investment in San Antonio Branch	20,000	
Accounts payable	(36,000)	(13,500)
Accrued liabilities	(14,000)	(2,500)
Home office		(9,000)
Capital stock, $10 par	(50,000)	
Retained earnings, Jan. 1, Year 3	(45,000)	
Sales	(429,000)	(95,000)
Purchases	290,000	24,000
Purchases from home office		45,000
Operating expenses	44,000	16,000
Totals	$ -0-	$ -0-

Your audit disclosed the following:

(1) On December 23, Year 3, the branch manager purchased $4,000 of equipment but failed to notify the home office. The branch accountant, knowing that equipment is carried in the home office accounts, recorded the proper journal entry in the branch accounting records. It is the company's policy not to take any depreciation on equipment acquired in the last half of a year.

(2) On December 27, Year 3, Wylie Co., a branch customer, erroneously paid its

account of $2,000 to the home office. The accountant made the correct journal entry in the home office accounts but did not notify the branch.

(3) On December 30, Year 3, the branch remitted cash of $5,000, which was received by the home office in January, Year 4.

(4) On December 31, Year 3, the branch erroneously recorded the December allocated expenses from the home office as $500 instead of $1,500.

(5) On December 31, Year 3, the home office shipped merchandise billed at $3,000 to the branch, which was received in January, Year 4.

(6) All the merchandise in the beginning inventories of the branch had been purchased from the home office. Home office Year 3 shipments to the branch were purchased by the home office in Year 3. The physical inventories at December 31, Year 3, excluding the shipment in transit, are home office—$55,000 (at cost); branch—$20,000 (comprising $18,000 from home office and $2,000 from outside vendors). Both the home office and the branch use the periodic inventory system.

(7) The home office consistently bills shipments to the branch at 20% above cost. The Sales account is credited for the invoice price.

Instructions Prepare a working paper with two columns each for Trial Balances (one column for the home office and one column for the branch), Combination Adjustments and Eliminations, Home Office Income Statement, Branch Income Statement, and Combined Balance Sheet. The branch income data should be on the basis of home office cost. Number the combination adjustments and eliminations. The adjustments should include the determination of cost of goods sold for both the branch and the home office. (Formal journal entries are not required. Supporting computations, including the computation of the ending inventories, should be in good form. Disregard income taxes.)

4-11 Sans Amoros, Inc., is a merchandising business which makes sales at its home office location and also through a branch located a few hundred miles away. The home office bills goods to the branch at 125% of cost, and is the only supplier of merchandise to the branch. The shipment of merchandise to the branch is recorded improperly by a credit to the Sales account for the invoice price. Both the home office and the branch use the perpetual inventory system.

The company engages you to conduct an audit for the year ended December 31, Year 1. This is the first time the company has utilized the services of independent certified public accountants. You are provided with the following trial balances:

SANS AMOROS, INC.

Trial Balances

December 31, Year 1

	Home office Dr (Cr)	Branch office Dr (Cr)
Cash	$ 15,000	$ 2,000
Accounts receivable (net)	20,000	17,000
Inventories, Dec. 31, Year 1	30,000	8,000
Equipment (net)	150,000	
Investment in branch	44,000	
Accounts payable	(23,000)	
Accrued liabilities		(2,000)
Mortgage note payable	(50,000)	

(continued)

SANS AMOROS, INC.
Trial Balances (continued)
December 31, Year 1

	Home office Dr (Cr)	Branch office Dr (Cr)
Capital stock, $10 par	(100,000)	
Home office		(9,000)
Retained earnings, Jan. 1, Year 1	(26,000)	
Sales	(350,000)	(150,000)
Cost of goods sold	220,000	93,000
Operating expenses	70,000	41,000
Totals	$ -0-	$ -0-

Additional information disclosed by your examination includes the following:
(1) On January 1, Year 1, inventories of the home office amounted to $25,000. Inventories at this date in the branch accounts were $6,000. During Year 1, the branch was billed for $105,000 for shipments from the home office.
(2) At December 31, Year 1, the home office billed the branch for $12,000, representing the branch's share of operating expenses paid by the home office. This billing has not been recorded by the branch.
(3) All cash collections made by the branch are deposited in a local bank to the account of the home office. Deposits of this nature included the following:

Amount	Date deposited by branch	Date recorded by home office
$5,000	Dec. 28, Year 1	Dec. 31, Year 1
3,000	Dec. 30, Year 1	Jan. 2, Year 2
7,000	Dec. 31, Year 1	Jan. 3, Year 2
2,000	Jan. 2, Year 2	Jan. 5, Year 2

(4) Operating expenses incurred locally by the branch are paid from an imprest bank account which is reimbursed periodically by the home office. Just prior to the end of Year 1, the home office forwarded a reimbursement check in the amount of $3,000, which was not received by the branch office until January, Year 2.

Instructions
a Prepare a working paper for the company and its branch with columns for Trial Balances, Combination Adjustments and Eliminations, Branch Income Statement, Home Office Income Statement, and Combined Balance Sheet. Complete the working paper and key and explain all combination adjustments and eliminations.
b Prepare a reconciliation of branch office and home office reciprocal accounts showing the corrected balances, ignoring income tax considerations.

4-12 Comparative balance sheets for the home office of Carmella Corporation follow:

CARMELLA CORPORATION—HOME OFFICE
Balance Sheets

Assets	Dec. 31, Year 5	Dec. 31, Year 4
Cash	$ 38,000	$ 25,600
Accounts receivable	85,000	80,000
Allowance for doubtful accounts	(3,000)	(2,400)
Inventories	100,000	112,000
Equipment (net)...	200,000	180,000
Investment in Junior Avon Branch	120,000	
Investment in Junior Avon, Inc. (100%)		80,000
Total assets..	$540,000	$475,200

Liabilities & Stockholders' Equity

Accounts payable	$ 88,000	$ 95,300
Accrued liabilities	3,500	2,700
Capital stock, $5 par	200,000	200,000
Retained earnings..	248,500	177,200
Total liabilities & stockholders' equity	$540,000	$475,200

The home office purchased equipment for $50,000 in Year 5, and equipment with a carrying amount of $10,000 was sold at a loss of $3,000. The loss was debited to the Retained Earnings account by mistake. Dividends of $12,000 were paid during Year 5 and net income for Year 5 was $86,300, including $40,000 earned by the branch. The branch remitted $10,000 to the home office during the year; the remittance was credited in error to the Accounts Receivable account

Comparative balance sheets for the Junior Avon Branch are

CARMELLA CORPORATION—JUNIOR AVON BRANCH
Balance Sheets

Assets	Dec. 31, Year 5	Dec. 31, Year 4
Cash	$ 28,000	$ 15,000
Accounts receivable (no allowance)	25,000	20,000
Inventories	70,500	65,000
Short-term prepayments	1,500	2,000
Total assets	$125,000	$102,000

Liabilities & Stockholders' Equity

Accounts payable	$ 15,000	$ 22,000
Capital stock, no par		10,000
Retained earnings		70,000
Home office	110,000	
Total liabilities & stockholders' equity	$125,000	$102,000

The branch was operated as a wholly owned subsidiary corporation (Junior Avon, Inc.) until January 1, Year 5, at which time the corporation was liquidated and the branch was formed.

Instructions

a Prepare comparative combined (or consolidated) balance sheets for Carmella Corporation on December 31, Year 4, and on December 31, Year 5.

b Prepare a statement of changes in financial position for Carmella Corporation on a working capital basis for Year 5, assuming that the accounts of Junior Avon, Inc., were consolidated with the accounts of Carmella Corporation at December 31, Year 4. In the consolidation of the financial statements of the two corporations, the investment in Junior Avon, Inc., (in Carmella Corporation's accounting records) is eliminated against the stockholders' equity accounts of Junior Avon, Inc. Do not include the composition of working capital in the statement of changes in financial position.

c Prepare a statement of changes in financial position for Carmella Corporation on a cash basis for Year 5, assuming that the accounts of Junior Avon, Inc., were consolidated with the accounts of Carmella Corporation at December 31, Year 4. Do not include the composition of working capital in the statement of changes in financial position.

5

BUSINESS COMBINATIONS

Business combinations—events or transactions in which two or more business enterprises, or their net assets, are brought under common control and into one accounting entity[1]—have been consummated in substantial numbers in recent years. Statistics issued by W. T. Grimm & Co., a financial consulting firm which compiles data on business combinations, show that as many as 4,000 or more business combinations have been completed in some recent years.

The Financial Accounting Standards Board has suggested the following definitions for terms commonly used in discussions of business combinations:

Combined enterprise. The accounting entity that results from a business combination

Constituent companies. The business enterprises that enter into a combination

Combinor. A constituent company entering into a combination whose owners as a group end up with control of the ownership interests in the combined enterprise

Combinee. A constituent company other than the combinor in a business combination[2]

In the first section of this chapter we shall discuss reasons for the popularity of business combinations and methods of arranging them. Then, the two presently accepted methods of accounting for business

---

[1] *FASB Discussion Memorandum,* "An Analysis of Issues Related to Accounting for Business Combinations and Purchased Intangibles," FASB (Stamford: 1976), p. 2.

[2] Ibid., p. 3.

combinations—*purchase* and *pooling of interests*—will be explained and illustrated. Finally, we shall appraise purchase accounting and pooling-of-interests accounting.

BUSINESS COMBINATIONS: WHY AND HOW?

Why do business enterprises enter into a business combination? Although a number of reasons have been cited, probably the overriding one in recent years has been *growth.* Business enterprises should have—and do have—major operating objectives other than growth, but that goal increasingly has motivated enterprise managements to undertake business combinations. Advocates of this *external* method of achieving growth point out that it is much more rapid than growth through *internal* means. There is no question that expansion and diversification of product lines, or enlarging the market share for current products, is achieved readily through a business combination with another enterprise. However, the disappointing experiences of many enterprises engaging in business combinations suggest that much can be said in favor of more gradual and reasoned growth through internal means, using available management and financial resources.

Other reasons often advanced in support of business combinations are obtaining new management strength or better use of existing management, and achieving manufacturing or other operating economies. In addition, a business combination may be undertaken for the income tax advantages available to one or more parties to the combination.

Antitrust considerations

One danger faced by large corporations which undertake business combinations is the possibility of antitrust litigation. The U.S. government often has expressed opposition to unwarranted concentration of economic power in very large business enterprises. Consequently, business combinations frequently have been attacked by the Federal Trade Commission or the Antitrust Division of the Department of Justice, under the provisions of Section 7 of the Clayton Act, which reads in part as follows:

> . . . no corporation engaged in commerce shall acquire, directly or indirectly, the whole or any part of the stock or other share capital and no corporation subject to the jurisdiction of the Federal Trade Commission shall acquire the whole or any part of the assets of another corporation engaged also in commerce, where in any line of commerce in any section of the country the effect of such acquisition may be substantially to lessen competition or to tend to create a monopoly.

The breadth of the preceding legislation has led to federal antitrust action against all types of business combinations: *horizontal* (combinations involving enterprises in the same industry), *vertical* (combinations between an enterprise and its customers or suppliers), and *conglomerate* (combinations between enterprises in unrelated industries or markets).

Methods for arranging business combinations

The four most common methods for carrying out a business combination are statutory merger, statutory consolidation, acquisition of capital stock, and acquisition of assets.

Statutory Merger As its name implies, a statutory merger is executed under provisions of applicable state laws. In a statutory merger, the boards of directors of the two or more corporations involved approve a plan for the exchange of voting stock (and perhaps some preferred stock, cash, or debt) of one of the corporations (the "survivor") for all the voting stock of the other corporations. Shareholders of all involved corporations must approve the terms of the merger; some states require approval of a two-thirds majority of shareholders. The surviving corporation issues its stock for the stock owned by the shareholders of the other corporations, thus acquiring those companies' assets and liabilities. The other corporations then cease to exist as separate legal entities. The business operations of the defunct corporations often are continued as *divisions* of the survivor.

Statutory Consolidation Like a statutory merger, a statutory consolidation is consummated in accordance with state law. However, in a consolidation a *new* corporation is formed to issue its stock for the stock of two or more existing corporations, which then go out of existence. The new corporation thus acquires the assets and liabilities of the defunct corporations, whose business operations may be continued as divisions of the new corporation.

Acquisition of Capital Stock One corporation (the *investor*) may issue capital stock, cash, debt, or a combination thereof to acquire all or part of the voting stock of another corporation (the *investee*). This stock acquisition program may function through direct purchase in the stock market, through negotiations with the principal shareholders of a closely held company, or through a *tender offer.* A tender offer is a publicly announced intent by the offering corporation to acquire, for a stated amount of cash or stock per share, a maximum number of shares "tendered" by holders thereof to an agent, such as a commercial bank. The price per share stated in the tender offer usually is well above the prevailing market price. If more than 50% of a corporation's voting stock is acquired, that corporation becomes *affiliated* with the acquiring corporation as a *subsidiary* but remains a separate legal entity. Business combinations arranged through stock acquisitions require authorization by the acquiring corporation's board of directors, and ratification by the acquirer's shareholders is sometimes required. Accounting for business combinations involving the acquisition of stock is discussed in Chapters 6 and 7.

Acquisition of Assets   One enterprise may buy all or most of the assets of another enterprise for cash, debt, the combinor's capital stock, or a combination thereof. The transaction must be approved by the boards of directors and stockholders of the constituent companies. The selling enterprise continues its existence as a separate entity or it may be liquidated; it does not become an *affiliate* of the combinor.

Establishing the price for a business combination

An important early step in planning a business combination is deciding upon an appropriate price to pay. The amount of cash or debt securities, or the number of shares of capital stock, to be issued in a business combination usually is determined by one or both of the following methods:

1 Capitalization of expected average annual earnings of the acquired enterprise at a desired rate of return
2 Determination of current fair value of the acquired enterprise's tangible and intangible assets (including goodwill) less liabilities

   The price for a business combination consummated for cash or debt is usually expressed in terms of the aggregate dollar amount of the consideration issued. When capital stock is issued in exchange for shares of the combinee, the price is expressed as a ratio of the number of shares of the combinor's capital stock to be exchanged for each share of the combinee's capital stock.

Illustration of Exchange Ratio   The negotiating officers of Palmer Corporation have agreed with Ronald Simpson, sole shareholder of Simpson Company, to acquire all 20,000 outstanding shares of Simpson Company stock for an aggregate price of $1,800,000. Palmer Corporation's common stock is presently trading on a national stock exchange at $65 per share. Ronald Simpson agrees to accept 30,000 shares of Palmer Corporation's common stock at a value of $60 per share in exchange for his stock in Simpson Company. The exchange ratio is expressed as 1½ shares of Palmer Corporation common stock for each share of Simpson Company stock, in accordance with the following computation at the top of page 191.

Number of Palmer Corporation shares to be issued	*30,000*
Number of Simpson Company shares to be exchanged	*20,000*
Exchange ratio: 30,000 ÷ 20,000	*1½:1*

METHODS OF ACCOUNTING FOR BUSINESS COMBINATIONS

Purchase accounting

Since the majority of business combinations involve an identified combinor and one or more combinees, many accountants consider it logical to account for business combinations, regardless of how consummated, as the acquisition of assets. Thus, assets (including goodwill) acquired in a business combination for cash would be recorded at the amount of cash paid, and assets acquired in a business combination involving the issuance of capital stock would be recorded at the current fair values of the assets or of the capital stock, whichever was more readily determinable. This approach is known as **purchase accounting** for business combinations, and was widely used prior to the increase in popularity of pooling-of-interests accounting.

APB Opinion No. 16, "Business Combinations," set forth the concept of purchase accounting as follows:[3]

> Accounting for a business combination by the purchase method follows principles normally applicable under historical-cost accounting to record acquisitions of assets and issuances of stock and to accounting for assets and liabilities after acquisition.

Determination of cost of a combinee

The cost of a combinee in a business combination accounted for by the purchase method is the total of the consideration paid by the combinor, the combinor's **direct** "out-of-pocket" costs of the combination, and any **contingent consideration** which is determinable at the date of combination.

Amount of Consideration   This is the aggregate of the amount of cash paid, the current fair value of other assets distributed, the discounted present value of debt securities issued, and the current fair value of equity securities issued by the combinor.

Out-of-Pocket Costs   Included in this category are legal fees and "finder's fees." Costs of registering and issuing equity securities are a reduction in the current fair value of the securities, not direct costs of the busi-

---

[3] *APB Opinion No. 16,* "Business Combinations," AICPA (New York: 1970), p. 311.

ness combination. Indirect and general expenses of the combination are expensed as incurred by the constituent companies.

Contingent Consideration   Contingent consideration is additional cash, other assets, or securities which may be issuable in the future, contingent upon future events, such as a specified level of earnings or a designated market price for a security issued to carry out the business combination. Contingent consideration which is *determinable* at the consummation date of a business combination is recorded as part of the cost of the combination. Contingent consideration *not determinable* at the date of the business combination should be recorded as an additional cost of the combination when the contingency is resolved and the additional consideration is paid or issued (or becomes payable or issuable).

Allocation of cost of a combinee

APB Opinion No. 16 provided the following principles for allocating cost of a combinee in a business combination accounted for as a purchase:[4]

> First, all identifiable assets acquired . . . and liabilities assumed in a business combination . . . should be assigned a portion of the cost of the acquired company, normally equal to their fair values at date of acquisition.

> Second, the excess of the cost of the acquired company over the sum of the amounts assigned to identifiable assets acquired less liabilities assumed should be recorded as goodwill.

The recognition of goodwill is quite common in business combinations, because the total price paid tends to exceed the current fair value of identifiable assets acquired. However, in some business combinations (known as *bargain purchases*), the current fair values assigned to the assets acquired exceed the total cost of the combinee. A bargain purchase is most likely to occur for a combinee with a history of net losses or when stock prices are extremely low. The excess of the current fair values over total cost is applied pro rata to reduce the amounts initially assigned to noncurrent assets other than long-term investments in corporate securities. In assigning current fair values to assets acquired, the accountant must not overstate the worth of the assets in terms of their ability to generate earnings for the combined enterprise.

"Negative Goodwill"   If the proration described in the preceding paragraph does not extinguish the bargain-purchase excess, a deferred credit, sometimes termed *negative goodwill,* is established. Negative goodwill means an excess of current fair value of assets acquired over their cost to the combinor. It is amortized over the period benefited, not to exceed 40 years.

---

[4] Ibid., p. 318.

Illustration of Purchase Accounting   On April 30, Year 6, Mason Company merged with Saxon Corporation. Both companies used the same accounting principles for assets, liabilities, revenue, and expenses. Saxon Corporation exchanged 150,000 shares of its $10 par common stock (current fair value $25 per share) for all 100,000 issued and outstanding shares of Mason Company's no par, $10 stated value capital stock. In addition, Saxon Corporation incurred the following out-of-pocket costs associated with the business combination:

Out-of-pocket costs of business combination with Mason Company

CPA audit fees for SEC registration statement	$ 60,000
Legal fees:	
For the business combination	10,000
For SEC registration statement	50,000
Finder's fee	56,250
Printer's charges for printing securities and SEC registration statement	23,000
SEC registration statement fee	750
Total out-of-pocket costs of business combination	$200,000

Immediately prior to the merger, Mason Company's condensed balance sheet was as follows:

MASON COMPANY
Balance Sheet
April 30, Year 6

Assets

Current assets	$1,000,000
Plant assets (net)	3,000,000
Other assets	600,000
Total assets	$4,600,000

Liabilities & Stockholders' Equity

Current liabilities	$ 500,000
Long-term debt	1,000,000
Capital stock, $10 stated value	1,000,000
Paid-in capital in excess of stated value	700,000
Retained earnings	1,400,000
Total liabilities & stockholders' equity	$4,600,000

The board of directors of Saxon Corporation adjudged the current fair values of Mason Company's identifiable assets and liabilities to be current assets—$1,150,000; plant assets—$3,400,000; other assets—$600,000; current liabilities—$500,000; long-term debt (discounted present value)—$950,000.

The following condensed journal entries would be made in the accounting records of Saxon Corporation (the combinor) to record the merger with Mason Company on April 30, Year 6, as a purchase:

Purchase

Investment in Mason Company (150,000 shares × $25)...	3,750,000	
Common Stock		1,500,000
Paid-in Capital in Excess of Par		2,250,000

To record merger with Mason Company as a purchase.

Investment in Mason Company ($10,000 + $56,250)......	66,250	
Paid-in Capital in Excess of Par ($200,000 − $66,250).....	133,750	
Cash		200,000

To record payment of costs incurred in merger with Mason Company. Legal and finder's fees in connection with the merger are recorded as an acquisition cost; other out-of-pocket costs are recorded as a reduction in the proceeds received from issuance of common stock.

Current Assets.......................................	1,150,000	
Plant Assets (net)	3,400,000	
Other Assets..	600,000	
Goodwill	116,250	
Discount on Long-Term Debt	50,000	
Current Liabilities		500,000
Long-Term Debt		1,000,000
Investment in Mason Company		3,816,250

To allocate cost of Mason Company acquisition to identifiable assets and liabilities, with the remainder to goodwill. (Income tax effects are disregarded.)

Accounting for the income tax effects of business combinations is considered in Chapter 11.

Mason Company (the combinee) would prepare the following condensed journal entry to record the liquidation of the company at April 30, Year 6:

Current Liabilities	500,000	
Long-Term Debt	1,000,000	
Capital Stock	1,000,000	
Paid-in Capital in Excess of Stated Value	700,000	
Retained Earnings	1,400,000	
Current Assets		1,000,000
Plant Assets (net)		3,000,000
Other Assets		600,000

To record liquidation of company in conjunction with merger with Saxon Corporation.

Pooling-of-interests accounting

In the late 1940s, the pooling-of-interests method of accounting for business combinations received increasing attention from business executives and accountants. The major premise of this method was that certain business combinations involving the issuance of capital stock were more in the nature of a *combining of stockholder interests* than an *acquisition of assets.* Combining of stockholder interests was evidenced by combinations involving common stock exchanges between corporations of approximately equal size. The shareholders and managements of these enterprises continued their relative interests and activities in the combined enterprise as they previously did in the separate corporations. Since neither of the like-size constituent companies could be considered the *combinor,* the pooling-of-interests method of accounting provided for carrying forward the combined assets, liabilities, and retained earnings of the constituent companies at their *carrying amounts* in the accounting records of the constituent companies. The current fair value of the capital stock issued to effect the business combination and the current fair value of the combinee's net assets were disregarded.

Illustration of Pooling-of-Interests Accounting The Saxon Corporation—Mason Company business combination described on page 193 would be accounted for as a pooling of interests by the condensed journal entries on page 196 in Saxon Corporation's accounting records at April 30, Year 6.

The expenses of business combination are not deductible for income tax purposes; thus Saxon Corporation should not adjust its income taxes expense and liability accounts.

Mason Company's journal entry at April 30, Year 6, to record the liquidation of the company would be identical to the journal entry illustrated at the top of the page.

Pooling of Interests

Current Assets	1,000,000	
Plant Assets (net)	3,000,000	
Other Assets	600,000	
Current Liabilities		500,000
Long-Term Debt		1,000,000
Common Stock		1,500,000
Paid-in Capital in Excess of Par		200,000
Retained Earnings		1,400,000

To record merger with Mason Company as a pooling of
interests.

Expenses of Business Combination	200,000	
Cash		200,000

To record payment of out-of-pocket costs incurred in
merger with Mason Company.

In the first of the preceding journal entries, Mason's assets, liabilities, and retained earnings are assigned their carrying amounts in Mason's premerger balance sheet (see page 193). Since the common stock issued by Saxon Corporation must be recorded at *par* (150,000 shares × $10 = $1,500,000), the $200,000 credit to paid-in capital in excess of par is a *balancing figure* for the journal entry. It can be verified as follows:

Computation
of credit to
paid-in
capital in
excess of par

Total paid-in capital of Mason Company prior to merger	$1,700,000
Par of Saxon Corporation common stock issued in merger	1,500,000
Amount credited to Saxon Corporation's paid-in capital in excess of par	$ 200,000

If the par value of common stock issued by Saxon Corporation had **exceeded** the total paid-in capital of Mason Company, Saxon's Paid-in Capital in Excess of Par account would have been **debited** in the illustrated journal entry. If the balance of Saxon's Paid-in Capital in Excess of Par account were insufficient to absorb the debit, the Retained Earnings account would be reduced.

Popularity of pooling accounting

The pooling method of accounting for business combinations was sanctioned initially by the AICPA in *Accounting Research Bulletin No. 40,* "Business Combinations," issued in 1950. However, **ARB No. 40** provided very few criteria for identifying those business combinations which qualified for pooling accounting, and was therefore unsatisfactory as a guide for this accounting method. Consequently, in 1957 **ARB No. 48,** "Business Combinations," superseded the previous pronouncement with an expanded discussion of the pooling concept. **ARB No. 48** continued to permit pooling accounting for most business combinations involving an exchange of equity securities. However, **ARB No. 48** also failed to provide definitive guidelines for identifying those business combinations which qualified for pooling accounting. As a result, a substantial number of business combinations arranged during the 1950s and 1960s were accounted for as poolings, despite the fact that the "combining of stockholder interests" aspect was often absent.

Why had pooling accounting become so popular? Some of the reasons are apparent from the following comparison of the combined Saxon Corporation journal entries illustrated previously for the merger with Mason Company.

Comparison of combinor's journal entries —purchase and pooling	**Purchase accounting**		**Pooling accounting**	
Current Assets	1,150,000		1,000,000	
Plant Assets (net)	3,400,000		3,000,000	
Other Assets	600,000		600,000	
Goodwill	116,250		-0-	
Discount on Long-Term Debt	50,000		-0-	
Expenses of Business Combination	-0-		200,000	
Current Liabilities		500,000		500,000
Long-Term Debt		1,000,000		1,000,000
Common Stock		1,500,000		1,500,000
Paid-in Capital in Excess of Par		2,116,250		200,000
Retained Earnings		-0-		1,400,000
Cash		200,000		200,000
To record merger with Mason Company.				

Differences in Net Assets   The first difference to consider in comparing the preceding journal entries is that the net assets recorded by the purchase method ($3,616,250) exceed the pooling-method net assets ($2,900,000) by $716,250. The composition of the $716,250 is summarized as follows:

Composition of difference in net assets— purchase versus pooling

Excess of purchase asset values over pooling asset values:

Current assets	$150,000
Plant assets	400,000
Goodwill	116,250

Excess of pooling liability values over purchase liability values:

Long-term debt	50,000
Excess of purchase net asset values over pooling net asset values	$716,250

If we assume that the $400,000 difference in plant assets is attributable to depreciable assets rather than to land, total expenses of Saxon Corporation years subsequent to April 30, Year 6, will be $716,250 larger under purchase accounting than would be the case in pooling accounting. Assume, for example, that the $150,000 difference in current assets is attributable to inventories which will be allocated to cost of goods sold on a fifo basis; the average economic life of plant assets is 10 years; the goodwill is to be amortized over the maximum 40-year period; and the long-term debt has a remaining five-year term to maturity.[5] Saxon Corporation's **pre-tax income** for the year ending April 30, Year 7, would be nearly $203,000 less in purchase accounting than in pooling accounting, attributable to the following larger expenses in purchase accounting:

Difference in pre-tax income— purchase versus pooling

Cost of goods sold	$150,000
Depreciation ($400,000 × $1/10$)	40,000
Amortization of goodwill ($116,250 × $1/40$)	2,906
Interest expense ($50,000 × $1/5$)	10,000
Excess of Year 7 pre-tax income using pooling accounting rather than purchase accounting	$202,906

It is true that pre-tax income for the year ended April 30, Year 6 (the year of the merger) is reduced $200,000 in pooling accounting, because the pooling method included the immediate **expensing** of the out-of-pocket costs of the business combination. However, this situation tends to be obscured by the fact that the income statements of Saxon Corporation and Mason Company would be combined in pooling accounting for the **entire** year ended April 30, Year 6 (as described in a subsequent section of this chapter).

In summary, the favorable effect of pooling accounting on post-combination earnings has been a popular feature of this accounting method.

[5] For the sake of simplicity, the discount on long-term debt is amortized by the straight-line method. Theoretically, and in actual practice, the *effective interest* method described in *Intermediate Accounting* of this series should be used.

Differences in Total Paid-in Capital The increase in Saxon Corporation's total paid-in capital is $1,916,250 less ($3,616,250 − $1,700,000 = $1,916,250) in pooling accounting than in purchase accounting. Of this difference, $1,200,000 ($1,400,000 − $200,000 = $1,200,000) is attributable to a net increase in Saxon Corporation's retained earnings in the pooling accounting method. If state laws make this $1,200,000 available as a basis for dividend declaration, one advantage of the pooling method of accounting is readily apparent.

Impact of Divergent Price-Earnings Ratios Even more dramatic than the preceding advantages inherent in pooling accounting is the potential impact on the market price of Saxon Corporation's common stock if the price-earnings ratios for Saxon's and Mason's stock differed significantly prior to the merger. Suppose, for example, that Saxon Corporation and Mason Company had the following financial measurements prior to the business combination:

		Saxon Corporation	*Mason Company*
Selected financial measurements prior to business combination	*Year ended Apr. 30, Year 6:*		
	Net income	$500,000*	$375,000
	Earnings per share	$0.50	$3.75
	At Apr. 30, Year 6:		
	Number of shares outstanding	1,000,000†	100,000†
	Market price per share	$25	$30
	Price-earnings ratio	50	8

* Net of $200,000 expenses of business combination
† Outstanding during entire year

After consummation of the business combination as a pooling, Saxon Corporation's income statement for the year ended April 30, Year 6, would report the combined corporation's net income as $875,000—the total of the separate net incomes of the two merged companies. "Pooled" earnings per share for Saxon Corporation would thus be increased to approximately $0.76. This increased amount of earnings per share is computed by dividing combined earnings of $875,000 by 1,150,000 (1,000,000 + 150,000 = 1,150,000), the **effective** number of Saxon Corporation shares outstanding during the year ended April 30, Year 6. If the price-earnings ratio for Saxon's common stock continued unchanged, the stock's market price would increase after the merger to $38 per share ($0.76 × 50)—a 52% increase. Saxon Corporation probably would attain the reputation of an "exciting growth company" in investing circles; and Saxon's directors likely would seek out another merger prospect like Mason Company.

Less spectacular advantages attributed to the pooling method of accounting for business combinations result from the fact that the carrying amounts of assets are not restated. Pooling accounting thus parallels income tax accounting if the business combination qualifies as a "tax-free corporate reorganization." Further, goodwill amortization (not deductible in computing taxable income) is not required in the pooling method.

Abuses of pooling accounting

The attractive features of pooling accounting described in the preceding section, together with the absence of firm guidelines for poolings in *ARB No. 48,* led to a number of serious abuses of the method during the 1960s. Among these abuses were *retroactive poolings; retrospective poolings; part-pooling, part-purchase accounting; treasury stock issuances; issuances of unusual securities; creation of "instant earnings"; contingent payouts;* and *"burying" the costs of pooling combinations.*

Retroactive Poolings   After *ARB No. 48* was issued in 1957, some accountants interpreted its provisions as permitting pooling accounting for many business combinations which already had been accounted for as *purchases* under *ARB No. 40.* Accordingly, a significant number of business combinations treated as purchases in the late 1950s and early 1960s were *restated retroactively* as poolings in subsequent years.[6] The obvious question was: When is the accounting for business transactions *finalized?*

Retrospective Poolings   The theory that the constituent companies in a pooling business combination were *effectively combined* in accounting periods preceding the actual business combination led to the practice of *retrospective poolings.* This technique involved the consummation of pooling business combinations shortly after the close of a combinor's fiscal year but prior to the issuance of its annual financial statements. The income statement which ultimately was issued included the operating results of the subsequently pooled combinee on a retrospective basis. Thus, a desired earnings per share figure might have been attained simply by a working paper adjustment.

Part-Pooling, Part-Purchase Accounting   Some business combinations involving the issuance of common stock as well as cash and debt were accounted for as *poolings* to the extent of the stock issuance, and as

---

[6] A. N. Mosich "Retroactive Poolings in Corporate Mergers," *The Journal of Business,* July 1968, pp. 352–362.

purchases for the remainder of the consideration. This hybrid method seemed inconsistent with any orderly structure of accounting theory.

Treasury Stock Issuances Pooling accounting required the exchange of common stock between the constituent companies. One method devised to avoid the potential dilution of earnings per share resulting from common stock issuances was the cash acquisition of treasury stock, and its subsequent reissuance in a pooling business combination. If substance is emphasized over form, such a combination is effected for *cash,* not for *previously unissued stock.*

Issuances of Unusual Securities As another means of minimizing the dilutive effects of common stock issuances in poolings, many unusual securities were devised to consummate business combinations. These securities, usually in the form of either preferred stock or a second or third class of common stock, were in most cases convertible into the combinor corporation's regular common stock. In substance, therefore, these unusual securities may not have been equivalent to voting common stock, yet the business combinations involving these securities frequently were treated as poolings.

Creation of "Instant Earnings" The discussion on pages 197 to 200, comparing the purchase and pooling journal entries for Saxon Corporation, pointed out how pooling accounting could *instantly increase earnings per share* for the year of a business combination. Another technique for creating instant earnings was the sale of a combinee's assets shortly after the pooling combination. Because the sales price generally exceeded the carrying amounts of the assets, a one-time gain was created. Yet the sales price usually paralleled the current fair value of the combinor's capital stock issued in the business combination; thus in substance the instant earnings were fictitious. The gain in effect represented proceeds from issuance of capital stock.

Contingent Payouts If the "combining of stockholder interests" feature of a pooling combination were genuine, there would be no unresolved contingencies with respect to the number of shares to be issued in the combination. Nevertheless, a large number of business combinations involving contingent issuances of additional shares were accounted for as poolings.

"Burying" the Costs of Pooling Combinations The out-of-pocket costs of most pooling business combinations effected before 1970 were charged to paid-in capital in excess of par rather than to expenses of the combined enterprise. This accounting method violated the basic assumption that a pooling is not in substance an *acquisition* of one company by another or an *obtaining of new capital.*

The Westec Corporation scandal

Perhaps the most spectacular example of pooling accounting abuse was revealed in the Westec Corporation scandal. Westec was a rapidly growing, diversified company whose stock increased from a market price low of $2 per share in 1964 to more than $67 per share early in 1966. Thereafter, the market price of the stock began to decline. In August 1966, trading in the stock was suspended when it was learned that approximately 160,000 shares of Westec common stock, purchased by or on behalf of the president of the company, had not been paid for.

The trend in Westec's reported earnings had been as follows:

	Period	Net income	Earnings per share
An example of growth through poolings	Year ended Dec. 31,		
	1963	$ 270,000	*(not available)*
	1964	1,332,000	$0.43
	1965	4,869,000	1.10
	Six months ended June 30, 1966 (unaudited)	5,346,000	1.15

The 1965 net income included the operating results of five companies acquired in pooling business combinations **early in 1966.** The amount of the retrospectively pooled income was not disclosed but was variously estimated at $1.5 million to $2.5 million.

Westec subsequently entered into bankruptcy proceedings, and audited financial statements for the eight months ended August 31, 1966, showed a **net loss** of $2,576,000. The former president of Westec pleaded guilty to charges of stock price manipulation and issuance of false earnings statements, and the former board chairman was convicted of the same charges as well as of mail fraud.

Abuses of purchase accounting

Purchase accounting was not free of improprieties during the 1950s and 1960s. The principal abuse of purchase accounting was the failure to allocate the cost of an acquired company to the identifiable assets acquired and to goodwill. Instead, an "Excess of Cost over Book Value of Purchased Company" account was created and presented in the post-combination balance sheet as an intangible asset—usually not subject to amortization. Consequently, reported earnings subsequent to these purchase combinations were the same as though pooling accounting had been used. Also, as in pooling business combinations, "instant earnings" often were created by the sale of understated identifiable assets shortly after the purchase business combination.

Action by the AICPA

In 1970 the AICPA's Accounting Principles Board reacted to the abuses of pooling accounting and purchase accounting by tightening the rules permitting pooling to be used and by limiting drastically the range of situations in which pooling would be allowed. The Board's action is summarized in the following paragraph of *APB Opinion No. 16*, "Business Combinations":[7]

> The Board concludes that the purchase method and the pooling of interests method are both acceptable in accounting for business combinations, although not as alternatives in accounting for the same business combination. A business combination which meets specified conditions requires accounting by the pooling of interests method. A new basis of accounting is not permitted for a combination that meets the specified conditions, and the assets and liabilities of the combining companies are combined at their recorded amounts. All other business combinations should be accounted for as an acquisition of one or more companies by a corporation. The cost to an acquiring corporation of an entire acquired company should be determined by the principles of accounting for the acquisition of an asset. That cost should then be allocated to the identifiable individual assets acquired and liabilities assumed based on their fair values; the unallocated cost should be recorded as goodwill.

By this action the Accounting Principles Board effectively eliminated many of the abuses of pooling accounting and purchase accounting described on pages 200 to 202. Retrospective poolings and part-pooling, part-purchase accounting were expressly prohibited. Substantial restrictions were placed upon the use of treasury stock and unusual securities to consummate pooling combinations. Pooling accounting was forbidden for a business combination containing any contingent payout provisions or plans shortly to dispose of assets acquired in the combination. Out-of-pocket costs of pooling-type business combinations were required to be expensed, even though these costs were not deductible for income tax purposes.

Conditions requiring pooling accounting

The APB provided a number of specified conditions for business combinations that were to be accounted for as poolings. The conditions, *all* of which were to be satisfied for pooling to be appropriate, were divided into three groups as follows:

1 *Attributes of the combining companies.* The conditions in this group were designed to assure that the pooling combination was truly a combining of two or more enterprises whose common stockholder interests were previously independent of each other.

2 *Manner of combining interests.* The conditions in this group supported the requirement for pooling accounting that an exchange of stock to combine existing voting common stock interests actually took place, in substance as well as in form.

[7] *APB Opinion No. 16*, p. 283.

3 *Absence of planned transactions.* The planned transactions prohibited by this group of conditions were those which would be inconsistent with the combining of entire existing interests of common stockholders.

The appendix on page 212 includes the specified conditions outlined by the Accounting Principles Board for pooling accounting. Many of the conditions are self-explanatory. However, four of them warrant brief explanation.

Independence of Constituent Companies   At the dates of initiation and consummation of a business combination, no constituent company may have more than a 10% ownership of the outstanding voting common stock of another constituent company. Otherwise, the companies could not be considered independent of each other.

Substantially All Voting Common Stock   This condition requires that at least 90% of the combinee's outstanding voting common stock be exchanged for the combinor's majority voting common stock. The following are excluded from the computation of the number of shares exchanged:

1 Shares acquired before the date the business combination is initiated and held by the combinor or its subsidiaries at that date

2 Shares acquired by the combinor or its subsidiaries after the business combination is initiated, other than in exchange for the combinor's voting common stock

3 Shares of the combinee still outstanding at the date the business combination is consummated

In addition, any voting common stock of the combinor owned or acquired by the combinee before the business combination is effected must be considered. These combinor shares are converted into equivalent shares of the combinee for the 90% test.

To illustrate, assume that on March 13, Year 2, Patton Corporation and Sherman Company initiated a plan of business combination. Under the plan, 1½ shares of Patton Corporation voting common stock (1,000,000 shares issued at March 13, Year 2) were to be exchanged for each outstanding share of Sherman Company capital stock (100,000 shares issued at March 13, Year 2).

At this time, Patton Corporation owned 7,500 shares of Sherman Company capital stock, and Sherman Company owned 6,000 shares of Patton Corporation voting common stock; in addition, 500 shares of Sherman Company stock were in Sherman's treasury. On March 26, Year 2, Patton Corporation purchased in the stock market for cash 1,000 shares of Sherman Company capital stock; and on June 30, Year 2, Patton Corporation issued 136,500 shares of its voting common stock in exchange for 91,000 outstanding shares of Sherman Company capital stock to complete the business combination.

Computation of the 90% requirement follows:

Computation
of "substan-
tially all
voting com-
mon stock"
pooling
requirement

Total Sherman Company shares issued as of June 30, Year 2		100,000
Less: Shares in Sherman Company's treasury		500
Total Sherman Company shares outstanding as of June 30, Year 2		99,500
Less:		
Sherman Company shares owned by Patton Corporation Mar. 13, Year 2	7,500	
Sherman Company shares acquired by Patton Corporation for cash Mar. 26, Year 2	1,000	
Equivalent number of Sherman Company shares represented by Patton Corporation stock owned by Sherman Company at Mar. 13, Year 2 (6,000 ÷ 1½)	4,000	12,500
Effective number of Sherman Company shares acquired June 30, Year 2, in exchange for Patton Corporation stock		87,000
Application of 90% requirement (99,500 × 90%)		89,550

Thus, the 91,000 shares of Sherman Company capital stock actually exchanged on June 30, Year 2, are in effect restated to 87,000 shares. Since the restated amount is less than 90% of Sherman Company's 99,500 shares of capital stock outstanding, the business combination does not qualify for pooling accounting.

Restrictions on Treasury Stock To preclude the treasury stock abuses described on page 201, the Accounting Principles Board provided that any treasury stock issued by the combinor in a business combination qualifying for pooling accounting must have been acquired in accordance with a systematic plan of treasury stock acquisitions. The systematic plan of acquisitions must have been established for at least two years prior to the initiation of a business combination; and the treasury stock acquisitions must be required for stock option and compensation plans, or for other recurring stock distributions. Any "untainted" treasury stock issued to effect a pooling business combination should be accounted for as though retired and then issued as previously unissued stock.

No Pending Provisions For pooling accounting to be appropriate for a business combination, no additional capital stock must be contingently issuable to former shareholders of a combinee after a combination has been initiated. In addition, no capital stock must have been issued to an escrow agent pending the resolution of a contingency.

A business combination which meets the APB's specified conditions is accounted for as a pooling, regardless of the legal form of the combination (statutory merger, statutory consolidation, acquisition of stock, acquisition of assets). An acquisition of assets may be construed as an "exchange of voting common stock interests" if all the specified conditions for a pooling are met.

Presentation of business combinations in financial statements

Under both purchase accounting and pooling accounting, a balance sheet issued as of the date of a business combination accomplished through a statutory merger, statutory consolidation, or acquisition of assets includes all the assets and liabilities of the constituent companies. (The *consolidated* balance sheet issued following a business combination which results in a parent-subsidiary relationship is described in Chapters 6 and 7.) The income statement for the period in which a business combination is carried out will differ depending on whether purchase or pooling accounting is applied to record the business combination.

Purchase The income statement of the combinor for the period in which a purchase business combination occurred includes the operating results of the combinee *after the date of the business combination only.*

For example, under purchase accounting, Saxon Corporation's postmerger income statement for the year ended April 30, Year 6, would be identical to Saxon's premerger income statement shown in the pooling accounting illustration on page 207, except that net income would be $700,000 and selling, general, and administrative expenses would be $1,100,000. (The $200,000 out-of-pocket costs of the business combination are not charged to *expense* in purchase accounting; $66,250 is part of the cost to Saxon Corporation of Mason Company's net assets, and $133,750 is a reduction in Saxon's paid-in capital in excess of par.)

Pooling The income statement of the combined corporation for the period in which a pooling took place includes the results of operations of the constituent companies *as though the combination had been completed at the beginning of the period.* Comparative income statements or balance sheets for preceding periods must be restated in a comparable fashion. Intercompany transactions prior to the business combination must be eliminated from the combined income statements in a manner comparable to that described in Chapter 4 for branches.

This presentation stems from the concept that a business combination accounted for as a pooling is a *combining of stockholder interests* rather than an *acquisition of assets.* Because stockholder interests are combined, previous financial statements showing changes in those interests also are combined.

To illustrate, assume that the income statements of Saxon Corporation and Mason Company for the year ended April 30, Year 6 (prior to completion of their merger described earlier in this chapter), were as follows:

SAXON CORPORATION AND MASON COMPANY
Income Statements
For Year Ended April 30, Year 6

	Saxon Corporation	Mason Company
Revenue	$10,000,000	$5,000,000
Costs and expenses:		
Cost of goods sold	$ 7,000,000	$3,000,000
Selling, general, and administrative expenses	1,300,000*	962,000
Interest expense................................	150,000	100,500
Income taxes expense	1,050,000	562,500
Total costs and expenses	$ 9,500,000	$4,625,000
Net income	$ 500,000	$ 375,000

* Includes $200,000 expenses of business combination

Assume also that Mason Company's interest expense included $25,000 attributable to a loan from Saxon Corporation which had been repaid prior to April 30, Year 6.

The working paper for the post-merger income statement of Saxon Corporation under pooling accounting is illustrated below. The amounts in the Combined column would appear in Saxon Corporation's published post-merger income statement for the year ended April 30, Year 6.

Pooling of Interests

SAXON CORPORATION
Combining Income Statement Working Paper
For Year Ended April 30, Year 6

	Saxon Corporation	Mason Company	Combination eliminations	Combined
Revenue	$10,000,000	$5,000,000	(a) $(25,000)	$14,975,000
Costs and expenses:				
Cost of goods sold	$ 7,000,000	$3,000,000		$10,000,000
Selling, general, and administrative expenses ..	1,300,000	962,000		2,262,000
Interest expense	150,000	100,500	(a) $(25,000)	225,500
Income taxes expense ...	1,050,000	562,500		1,612,500
Total costs and expenses	$ 9,500,000	$4,625,000	$(25,000)	$14,100,000
Net income	$ 500,000	$ 375,000	$ -0-	$ 875,000

Explanation of combination eliminations:
(a) To eliminate intercompany interest received by Saxon Corporation from Mason Company.

Disclosure of business combinations in financial statements

Because of the complex nature of business combinations and their effects on the financial position and operating results of the combinor, extensive disclosure is required for the periods in which they occur. The following notes, from recent annual reports of Allegheny Ludlum Industries, Inc., and The Timken Company, respectively, illustrate the required disclosures for a purchase and a pooling of interests.

Purchase On February 28, 1975 the Corporation acquired all of the outstanding common stock of Standard-Thomson Corporation (Standard-Thomson) for cash and notes aggregating $15,483,000. Standard-Thomson is engaged in the manufacture and sale of thermo-mechanical and electro-mechanical controls and control components. The total purchase price was allocated to the net tangible assets acquired based on their estimated fair values, and included no goodwill. Since this acquisition was accounted for as a purchase, the results of operations of Standard-Thomson have been included in the consolidated statements of earnings from the date of acquisition.

The following table summarizes, on an unaudited pro forma basis, the consolidated results of the Corporation as though Standard-Thomson had been acquired on January 1, 1974:

	Year ended December 31,	
	1975	1974
	(In thousands, except earnings per share)	
Sales	$794,995	$1,006,952
Net earnings	29,874	46,616
Earnings per share of common stock:		
Primary..	4.98	8.47
Fully diluted	4.32	6.75

Pooling of Interests On April 25, 1975, the Company acquired Latrobe Steel Company for 611,100 shares of its Common Stock. The acquisition was accounted for as a pooling of interests and, accordingly, the accompanying financial statements include the accounts and operations of Latrobe for the years 1975 and 1974. Net sales and net income of the separate companies for the periods preceding the acquisition were:

	Three months ended Mar. 31, 1975 (Unaudited)	Year ended Dec. 31, 1974
Net sales:		
The Timken Company	$181,227,000	$665,492,127
The Latrobe Steel Company	18,139,000	73,454,464
Totals	$199,366,000	$738,946,591

	Three months ended Mar. 31, 1975 (Unaudited)	Year ended Dec. 31, 1974
Net income:		
The Timken Company	$ 14,774,000	$ 52,932,127
The Latrobe Steel Company	622,000	3,018,473
Totals	$ 15,396,000	$ 55,950,600

APPRAISAL OF ACCOUNTING STANDARDS FOR BUSINESS COMBINATIONS

The accounting standards for business combinations described and illustrated in preceding pages of this chapter have been criticized severely.

Criticism of purchase accounting

The principal criticisms of purchase accounting center on the recognition of *goodwill.* Many accountants take exception to the *residual* basis for valuing goodwill established by the Accounting Principles Board in *APB Opinion No. 16.* These critics contend that part of the amounts thus assigned to goodwill probably apply to other *identifiable* intangible assets. Accordingly, goodwill in a business combination should be valued *directly* by use of methods described in *Intermediate Accounting* of this series. Any remaining cost not directly allocated to *all* identifiable tangible and intangible assets and to goodwill would be apportioned to those assets based on the amounts assigned in the first valuation process.

The mandatory amortization of goodwill, prescribed by the Accounting Principles Board in *APB Opinion No. 17,* is considered by some accountants to be inappropriate for goodwill attributable to a business combination. These accountants recommend treating the amount assigned to goodwill in a business combination as a reduction of stockholders' equity of the combined enterprise.

The accounting described on page 192 for the excess of current fair values over total cost in a bargain-purchase business combination has also been challenged. Critics maintain there is no theoretical support for the arbitrary reduction of previously determined asset values by an apportioned amount of the bargain-purchase excess. They suggest the *negative goodwill* treatment described on page 192 for the *entire* bargain purchase excess.

Other accountants question whether current fair values of the *combinor's* net assets—especially goodwill—should be ignored in accounting for a business combination. They maintain it is inconsistent to reflect current fair values for net assets of the **combinee only,** in view of the significance of many business combinations involving large constituent companies.

Criticism of pooling accounting

The principal objections to pooling accounting are as follows:

1 Despite the elaborate framework for pooling accounting established by the APB, this accounting method is founded upon a delicate assumption. This assumption—that some business combinations involving exchanges of voting common stock result in a combining of stockholder interests rather than an acquisition of assets—is difficult to support in accounting theory. Two **Accounting Research Studies** recommended abolishing the pooling accounting method for business combinations between independent constituent companies.[8]

2 There is no explicit disclosure of the current fair value of the combinor's common stock exchanged in a business combination accounted for as a pooling. The disclosure required by **APB Opinion No. 16** is limited to stating the number and type of shares of stock issued in a pooling business combination. Thus, there is no way of ascertaining the current fair value of the consideration issued in the combination.

3 The assets of the combinee in a pooling business combination are not accounted for at their cost to the combinor. In the illustrated pooling accounting for the merger of Saxon Corporation and Mason Company (pages 195–196), the net assets of Mason Company were recorded in Saxon Corporation's accounts at the carrying amounts in Mason's accounts—$3,100,000. This amount is $716,250 less than the **cost** of Mason's net assets—$3,816,250 —reflected in the purchase accounting illustration.

4 A consequence of the misstatement of asset values is that earnings for periods subsequent to a pooling of interests are misstated.

FASB study of accounting for business combinations

In recognition of the unsatisfactory state of accounting for business combinations, the Financial Accounting Standards Board initiated a study of the subject shortly after the Board's inception. A lengthy **FASB Discussion Memorandum,** "An Analysis of Issues Related to Accounting for Business Combinations and Purchased Intangibles," was issued by the FASB in 1976. However, the related public hearing on business combinations accounting (the next step in the FASB procedures) was deferred until completion of the public hearing on the conceptual framework for accounting and reporting.

The **FASB Discussion Memorandum** described above includes the following:

[8] Arthur R. Wyatt, *Accounting Research Study No. 5,* "A Critical Study of Accounting for Business Combinations," AICPA (New York: 1963), p. 105; George R. Catlett and Norman O. Olson, *Accounting Research Study No. 10,* "Accounting for Goodwill," AICPA (New York: 1968), pp. 106, 109.

1 Six *basic issues* involving matters of concept or principle, and six related subissues.

2 Seventeen *implemental issues* involving choices about alternative procedures for giving effect to conceptual decisions

3 Fifteen *technical issues* dealing with aspects of applying accounting standards to specific business combinations

The following selections from the basic issues, implemental issues, and technical issues demonstrate the extensive scope of the FASB's study of accounting for business combinations.[9]

> BASIC ISSUE ONE: At the time of a combination, how should the identifiable assets and liabilities of the constituent companies be accounted for in the combined enterprise's financial statements?
>
> BASIC ISSUE TWO: How should positive goodwill be accounted for in a combination?
>
> BASIC ISSUE THREE: How should any positive goodwill recognized as an asset or as a deduction from stockholders' equity in the balance sheet subsequently be accounted for?
>
> BASIC ISSUE FOUR: How should any excess of the current value of a constituent company's net identifiable assets over the aggregate cost for that company be accounted for?
>
> IMPLEMENTAL ISSUE ONE: Should a combined enterprise's basic financial statements that give effect to . . . a combination (in which a new accounting basis would not be recognized) be presented as though the constituent companies have always been combined?
>
> IMPLEMENTAL ISSUE TWO: If equity securities are given to effect . . . a combination (in which a new accounting basis would not be recognized), how should the stockholders' equities of the constituent companies be accounted for?
>
> IMPLEMENTAL ISSUE THREE: How should any difference between the amount recognized for the consideration given and the sum of the amounts retained for the combinee's net assets be accounted for?
>
> IMPLEMENTAL ISSUE FOUR: How should a subsequent major disposition of assets related to . . . a combination (in which a new accounting basis would not be recognized) be accounted for?
>
> TECHNICAL ISSUE ONE: What special situations should be encompassed by any new accounting standards for business combinations?
>
> TECHNICAL ISSUE TWO: How should the income tax accounting problems stemming from combinations . . . be dealt with?
>
> TECHNICAL ISSUE THREE: How should costs incurred in connection with the evaluation, negotiation, and consummation of a combination be accounted for?

All accountants should welcome the successful completion of the business combinations study by the Financial Accounting Standards Board and the establishment of a sound conceptual basis for accounting for business combinations.

---

[9] *FASB Discussion Memorandum,* "An Analysis of Issues Related to Accounting for Business Combinations and Purchased Intangibles," FASB (Stamford: 1976), pp. 17, 19, 21, 24–25.

APPENDIX: SPECIFIED CONDITIONS FOR POOLING-OF-INTERESTS ACCOUNTING

1 Attributes of the combining companies.

   a Each of the combining companies is autonomous and has not been a subsidiary or division of another corporation within two years before the plan of combination is initiated.

   b Each of the combining companies is independent of the other companies.

2 Manner of combining interests.

   a The combination is effected in a single transaction or is completed in accordance with a specific plan within one year after the plan is initiated.

   b A corporation offers and issues only common stock with rights identical to those of the majority of its outstanding voting common stock in exchange for substantially all of the voting common stock interest of another company at the date the plan of combination is consummated.

   c None of the combining companies changes the equity interest of the voting common stock in contemplation of effecting the combination either within two years before the plan of combination is initiated or between the dates the combination is initiated and consummated; changes in contemplation of effecting the combination may include distributions to stockholders and additional issuances, exchanges, and retirements of securities.

   d Each of the combining companies reacquires shares of voting common stock only for purposes other than business combinations, and no company reacquires more than a normal number of shares between the dates the plan of combination is initiated and consummated.

   e The ratio of the interest of an individual common stockholder to those of other common stockholders in a combining company remains the same as a result of the exchange of stock to effect the combination.

   f The voting rights to which the common stock ownership interests in the resulting combined corporation are entitled are exercisable by the stockholders; the stockholders are neither deprived of nor restricted in exercising those rights for a period.

   g The combination is resolved at the date the plan is consummated and no provisions of the plan relating to the issue of securities or other consideration are pending.

3 Absence of planned transactions.

   a The combined corporation does not agree directly or indirectly to retire or reacquire all or part of the common stock issued to effect the combination.

   b The combined corporation does not enter into other financial arrangements for the benefit of the former stockholders of a combining company, such as a guaranty of loans secured by stock issued in the combination, which in effect negates the exchange of equity securities.

   c The combined corporation does not intend or plan to dispose of a significant part of the assets of the combining companies within two years after the combination other than disposals in the ordinary course of business of the former separate companies and to eliminate duplicate facilities or excess capacity.

SOURCE: *APB Opinion No. 16,* "Business Combinations," AICPA (New York: 1970), pp. 295–304.

REVIEW QUESTIONS

1 What is a **business combination?**

2 Differentiate between a **statutory merger** and a **statutory consolidation.**

3 What two methods may be used, individually or jointly, to determine an appropriate price to pay in a business combination?

4 State how each of the following out-of-pocket costs of a merger business combination treated as a purchase should be accounted for:
a Printing costs for proxy statement mailed to shareholders in advance of special meeting to ratify terms of the merger
b Legal fees for negotiating the merger
c CPA fees for auditing SEC registration statement covering shares of stock issued in the merger
d Printing costs for securities issued in the merger
e Legal fees for SEC registration statement covering shares of stock issued in the merger
f CPA fees for advice on income tax aspects of the merger

5 The term "goodwill" often appears in connection with business combinations.
a What is **goodwill?** Explain.
b What is **negative goodwill?** Explain.

6 a What is **contingent consideration** in a business combination?
b If a plan for a business combination includes a provision for contingent consideration, is pooling accounting appropriate for the combination? Explain.

7 How is the cost of a combinee allocated in a business combination treated as a purchase?

8 Distinguish between a **purchase** and a **pooling of interests** in terms of the entity relationships between the combining and the continuing units. (Do not discuss accounting differences.)

9 If a business combination meets the specified conditions requiring treatment as a pooling, what is the accounting effect as compared with a purchase interpretation?

10 Comment on the following quotation:

It is our judgment that the weight of logic and consistency supports the conclusion that business combinations between independent entities are exchange transactions involving a transfer of assets and that the accounting action to account for an exchange transaction is necessary to reflect properly the results of the business transaction.

11 Discuss some of the reasons for the popularity of pooling accounting for business combinations during the 1950s and 1960s.

12 Identify five abuses of pooling accounting during the 1960s.

13 How do the journal entries to the Paid-in Capital in Excess of Par account differ in purchase and pooling accounting?

14 What are **retrospective poolings?** How were they used in the Westec Corporation scandal?

15 Critics have charged that pooling accounting creates "instant earnings." How is this accomplished?

EXERCISES

Ex. 5-1 Select the best answer for each of the following multiple-choice questions.

1 Which of the following is not included in the cost of a combinee in a business combination accounted for as a purchase?

a Finder's fee for arranging the combination

b Contingent consideration determinable at the consummation date of the combination

c Costs of registering and issuing debt securities to the shareholders of the combinee

d None of the above

2 On February 28, Year 7, Solomon Company issued 10,000 shares of its no-par common stock (stated value $5 per share, current fair value $15 per share) for all 5,000 issued and outstanding shares of Manson Company's $1 par capital stock. The business combination met all the requirements for pooling accounting. On February 2, Year 7, prior to consummation of the business combination, the stockholders' equity accounts of Manson Company were as follows:

Capital stock, $1 par	$ 5,000
Paid-in capital in excess of par	30,000
Retained earnings	50,000
Total stockholders' equity	$85,000

The journal entry to record the business combination in the accounts of Solomon Company should include:

a A credit of $30,000 to the Paid-in Capital in Excess of Stated Value account

b A debit of $15,000 to the Paid-in Capital in Excess of Stated Value account (assuming a credit balance of at least $15,000 in that account)

c A credit of $5,000 to the Common Stock account

d None of the above

3 Which of the following was not an abuse of pooling accounting prior to the issuance of *APB Opinion No. 16,* "Business Combinations"?

a Creation of "instant earnings"

b Retrospective poolings

c Establishing an "Excess of Cost over Book Value" as an intangible asset

d None of the above

4 Negative goodwill in a statutory merger accounted for as a purchase business combination should be

a Offset against goodwill of the combinor

b Credited to the combinor's Paid-in Capital in Excess of Par account

c Credited to the combinor's Retained Earnings account

d Accounted for in some other way

Questions **5** and **6** are based on the following information: On December 1, Year 6, Morgan Company was merged into Stabler Company, with Morgan Company going out of existence. Both companies report on a calendar-year basis. The business combination should have been accounted for as a pooling, but it was accounted for mistakenly as a purchase.

5 As a result of this error, what was the effect upon Stabler Company's net income for the year ended December 31, Year 6?

a Overstated if Morgan had a net loss from December 1, Year 6, to December 31, Year 6

b Understated if Morgan had a net loss from January 1, Year 6, to November 30, Year 6

c Overstated if Morgan had net income from December 1, Year 6, to December 31, Year 6

d Understated if Morgan had net income from January 1, Year 6, to November 30, Year 6

6 What is the effect of this error upon Stabler Company's asset valuations at December 1, Year 6?

a Overstated under any circumstances

b Understated under any circumstances

c Overstated if the current fair value of Morgan's assets exceeded their carrying amounts

d Understated if the current fair value of Morgan's assets exceeded their carrying amounts

Ex. 5-2 The condensed balance sheet of Maltby Company at February 28, Year 7, with related current fair values of assets and liabilities, appears below:

MALTBY COMPANY
Balance Sheet
February 28, Year 7

	Carrying amount	Current fair value
Assets		
Current assets	$ 500,000	$ 580,000
Plant assets (net)	1,000,000	1,150,000
Other assets	300,000	350,000
Total assets	$1,800,000	
Liabilities & Stockholders' Equity		
Current liabilities	$ 300,000	300,000
Long-term debt	400,000	380,000
Capital stock, $1 par	500,000	
Paid-in capital in excess of par	200,000	
Retained earnings	400,000	
Total liabilities & stockholders' equity	$1,800,000	

On February 28, Year 7, Solaway Company issued 600,000 shares of its $1 par common stock (current fair value $25 per share) to Laura Maltby, sole stockholder of Maltby Company, for all 500,000 shares of Maltby Company capital stock owned by Laura Maltby, in a merger business combination qualifying for pooling accounting. Because the merger was negotiated privately and Laura Maltby signed a "letter agreement" not to dispose of the Solaway Company stock she received, the combination was not subject to SEC requirements. Thus, only $5,000 in legal fees was incurred to effect the merger; these fees were paid in cash by Solaway Company on February 28, Year 7.

Prepare, in good form, journal entries to record the business combination in the accounting records of (**a**) Solaway Company and (**b**) Maltby Company.

Ex. 5-3 Condensed balance sheets of Starling Corporation and Sampson Corporation at July 31, Year 9, appear on page 216.

	Starling Corporation	Sampson Corporation
Total assets	$700,000	$670,000
Total liabilities	$300,000	$300,000
Capital stock, $25 par	200,000	250,000
Paid-in capital in excess of par	80,000	130,000
Retained earnings (deficit)	120,000	(10,000)
Total liabilities & stockholders' equity	$700,000	$670,000

On July 31, Year 9, Starling Corporation and Sampson Corporation entered into a statutory consolidation. The new company, Starson Corporation, issued 75,000 shares of $10 par capital stock for all the outstanding capital stock of Starling and Sampson. Out-of-pocket costs of the business combination were immaterial.

a Prepare a journal entry to record the business combination in the accounts of Starson Corporation as a pooling.

b Prepare a journal entry to record the business combination in the accounts of Starson Corporation as a purchase. Assume that Sampson is the combinor; that current fair values of identifiable assets are $800,000 for Starling and $700,000 for Sampson; that each company's liabilities are fairly stated at $300,000; and that the current fair value of Starson capital stock is $12 per share.

Ex. 5-4 Select the best answer for each of the following multiple-choice questions.

1 A statutory consolidation is a business combination in which:

a An established company acquires all the voting common stock of one or more other established companies, which are then liquidated

b A new company acquires all the voting common stock of two or more established companies, which are then liquidated

c An established company acquires all the voting common stock of one or more other established companies, which are not liquidated

d Something else takes place

2 Generally, a debit to the Retained Earnings account of the combinor in a business combination is appropriate in:

a Purchase accounting only

b Pooling accounting only

c Either purchase accounting or pooling accounting

d Neither purchase accounting nor pooling accounting

Questions **3** and **4** are based on the following information: Acquisition Company purchased the net assets of Seller Company for $80,000. On the date of Acquisition's purchase, Seller had no long-term investments in marketable equity securities and $10,000 (carrying amount and current fair value) of liabilities. The current fair values of Seller Company's assets, when acquired, were:

Current assets	$ 40,000
Noncurrent assets	60,000
Total current fair values	$100,000

3 How should the $10,000 difference between the current fair value of the net assets acquired ($90,000) and the cost ($80,000) be accounted for by Acquisition Company?

a The $10,000 difference should be credited to the Retained Earnings account

b The noncurrent assets should be recorded at $50,000

c The current assets should be recorded at $36,000, and the noncurrent assets should be recorded at $54,000

d A deferred credit of $10,000 should be set up and amortized over a period not in excess of 40 years

4 Assume that Acquisition Company paid $110,000 for Seller Company's net assets and that all other information given above remains the same. What is the minimum annual difference between pre-tax accounting income and taxable income because of this purchase?

a Zero

b $500

c $2,000

d An amount which cannot be determined from the information given

5 Two calendar-year corporations combined on July 1, Year 5. The combination was accounted for properly as a pooling. How should the results of operations have been reported for the year ended December 31, Year 5?

a Combined from July 1 to December 31 and disclosed for the separate companies from January 1 to June 30

b Combined from July 1 to December 31 and disclosed for the separate companies for the entire year

c Combined for the entire year and disclosed for the separate companies from January 1 to June 30

d Combined for the entire year and disclosed for the separate companies for the entire year

Ex. 5-5 Armstrong Company issued voting preferred stock with a current fair value of $1,000,000 in exchange for all the outstanding common stock of Bailey Company. Bailey has tangible net assets with a carrying amount of $500,000 and a current fair value of $600,000. In addition, Armstrong issued voting preferred stock valued at $100,000 to an investment banker as a finder's fee for arranging the business combination.

Compute in good form the total increase in Armstrong Company's net assets resulting from the business combination with Bailey Company.

Ex. 5-6 Harris Company paid $50,000 cash for the net assets of Jackson Company, which consisted of the following:

	Carrying amount	Current fair value
Current assets	$10,000	$14,000
Plant assets (net)	40,000	55,000
Liabilities	(10,000)	(9,000)
Net assets	$40,000	$60,000

Compute in good form the amount at which Harris Company should record the plant assets acquired from Jackson Company.

Ex. 5-7 Nolan Company offered to exchange two shares of its common stock for each share of Osmond Company common stock. On the date of the offer Nolan held 3,000 shares of Osmond common and Osmond held 500 shares of Nolan common. In later cash transactions, Nolan purchased 2,000 shares of Osmond common and Osmond purchased 2,500 shares of Nolan common. At all times the number of common shares outstanding was 1,000,000 for Nolan and 100,000 for Osmond. After consummation of the business combination, Nolan held 100,000 Osmond common shares.

Compute in good form the number of shares considered exchanged in determining whether this combination should be accounted for by the pooling method.

Ex. 5-8 On November 1, Year 4, Rhodes Company issued 50,000 shares of its capital stock in exchange for all the capital stock of Thom Company. Out-of-pocket costs of the business combination were negligible. Rhodes tentatively recorded the additional shares of capital stock issued at par and debited Investment in Thom Company for $500,000. Thom Company was liquidated and became a division of Rhodes Company.

The net income of Rhodes Company and Thom Company during Year 4 were as follows:

	Jan. 1–Oct. 31	Nov. 1–Dec. 31
Rhodes Company	$420,000	$80,000*
Thom Company	350,000	
Thom Division of Rhodes Company		50,000

*Excludes any portion of Thom Division net income.

Condensed balance sheet and other data for Year 4 follow:

	Rhodes Company Oct. 31	Rhodes Company Dec. 31	Thom Company Oct. 31	Thom Division of Rhodes Company Dec. 31
Assets........................	$3,500,000	$4,080,000	$4,000,000	$4,150,000
Liabilities.....................	500,000	500,000	1,000,000	1,100,000
Capital stock, $10 par	2,000,000	2,500,000	2,000,000	-0-
Retained earnings	1,000,000	1,080,000	1,000,000	-0-
Market price per share of capital stock	100	130	20	-0-

Neither company paid dividends during Year 4. In recent months, Rhodes Company's capital stock has been selling at about 40 times earnings; prior to November 1, Year 4, Thom Company capital stock had been selling at 10 times earnings.

Answer the following questions, *ignoring expenses attributable to differences between current fair values and carrying amounts of Thom's net assets.* (Supporting computations should be in good form.)

a Assuming that the merger is accounted for as a pooling, what is Rhodes Company's net income for Year 4?

b What is the amount of the Year 4 earnings per share for Rhodes Company on a pooling basis?

c If the merger had been accounted for as a purchase, what would Rhodes Company's net income have been for Year 4?

d What is Rhodes Company's earnings per share for Year 4 on a purchase basis?

e What is the amount of retained earnings on a pooling basis at the end of Year 4?

f What is the amount of retained earnings on a purchase basis at the end of Year 4?

g Why did Rhodes Company issue capital stock having a total market value of

$5,000,000 in exchange for Thom Company capital stock which had a total market value of only $4,000,000 (200,000 shares at $20 per share = $4,000,000) at the date of the business combination?

SHORT CASES FOR ANALYSIS AND DECISION

Case 5-1 Talbert Company has engaged you to examine its financial statements in connection with a prospective merger or consolidation with Venice Company. Both methods of business combination are being considered under applicable corporate statutory law. Talbert is the larger of the two corporations and in substance is acquiring Venice Company.

Instructions Answer the following, setting forth reasons for any conclusions stated.
a Discuss the meaning of the terms **merger** and **consolidation** as used in corporate law, with particular emphasis on the legal difference between the two.
b What are the major legal requirements which must be met in order to accomplish either a merger or a consolidation?

Case 5-2 You have been engaged to examine the financial statements of Exeter Company for the year ended May 31, Year 6. You discover that on June 1, Year 5, Foster Company was merged into Exeter Company in a business combination qualifying for purchase accounting. You also find that both Exeter and Foster (prior to its liquidation) incurred legal fees, accounting fees, and printing costs for the business combination; both companies debited those costs to an intangible asset account entitled "Cost of Business Combination." In its journal entry to record the business combination with Foster Company, Exeter Company increased its Cost of Business Combination account by an amount equal to the balance in Foster's comparable account.

Instructions Evaluate Exeter Company's accounting for the out-of-pocket costs of the business combination with Foster Company.

Case 5-3 After extended negotiations East Corporation bought from West Company most of the latter's assets on June 30, Year 3. At the time of the sale West's accounts (adjusted to June 30, Year 3) reflected the following descriptions and amounts for the assets transferred:

	Cost	Contra accounts	Carrying amounts
Receivables	$ 83,600	$ 3,000	$ 80,600
Inventories	107,000	5,200	101,800
Land	20,000	-0-	20,000
Buildings	207,500	73,000	134,500
Fixtures and equipment	205,000	41,700	163,300
Goodwill	50,000	-0-	50,000
Totals	$673,100	$122,900	$550,200

You ascertain that the contra accounts were allowance for doubtful accounts, allowance to reduce inventories to market, and accumulated depreciation.

During the extended negotiations West held out for a consideration of approximately $600,000 (depending upon the level of the receivables and inventories). However, as of June 30, Year 3, West agreed to accept East's offer of $450,000 cash plus 1% of the net sales (as defined in the contract) of the next five years, with payments at the end of each year. West expects that East's total net sales during this period will exceed $15,000,000.

Instructions
a How should East Corporation record this transaction? Explain.
b Discuss the propriety of recording goodwill in the accounting records of East Corporation for this transaction.

Case 5-4 The boards of directors of Carter Corporation, Fulton Company, Russell, Inc., and Towne Corporation are meeting jointly to discuss plans for a merger. Each of the corporations has one class of common stock outstanding; Fulton also has one class of preferred stock outstanding. Although terms have not as yet been settled, Carter will be the surviving corporation. Because the directors want to conform to generally accepted accounting principles, they have asked you to attend the meeting as an advisor.

Instructions   Consider each of the following questions independently of the others and answer each in accordance with generally accepted accounting principles. Explain your answers.
a Assume that the merger will be consummated August 31, Year 5. Explain the philosophy underlying the accounting and how the balance sheet accounts of each of the four corporations will appear in Carter's balance sheet on September 1, Year 5, if the merger is accounted for as a:
(1) Pooling
(2) Purchase
b Assume that the merger will be consummated August 31, Year 5. Explain how the income statement accounts of each of the four corporations will be accounted for in Carter's income statement for the year ended December 31, Year 5, if the merger is accounted for as a:
(1) Pooling
(2) Purchase
c Some of the directors believe that the terms of the merger should be agreed upon immediately and that the method of accounting to be used may be chosen at some later date. Others believe that the terms of the merger and the accounting method to be used are very closely related. Which position is correct? Explain.
d Carter and Towne are comparable in size; Russell and Fulton are much smaller. How do these facts affect the choice of accounting method for the merger?
e Fulton was formerly a subsidiary of Garson Corporation, which has no other relationship to any of the four companies discussing the business combination. Garson voluntarily spun off Fulton 18 months ago. What effect, if any, do these facts have on the choice of accounting method for the merger?
f Carter holds 2,000 of Fulton's 10,000 outstanding shares of preferred stock and 15,000 of Russell's 100,000 outstanding shares of common stock. All of Carter's holdings were acquired during the first three months of Year 5. What effect, if any, do these facts have on the choice of accounting method?
g Since the directors feel that one of Towne's major divisions will not be compatible with the operations of the combined enterprise, they anticipate that it will be sold as soon as possible after the business combination is consummated. They expect to have no trouble in finding a buyer. What effect, if any, do these facts have on the choice of accounting method?

Case 5-5 Crawford Company and Krug Company, both of which have only voting common stock, are considering a merger whereby Crawford would be the surviving company. The terms of the business combination provide that the transaction would be carried out by Crawford exchanging one share of its unissued common stock for two shares of Krug's outstanding common stock. Prior to the date of the contemplated exchange, Crawford had purchased 5% of Krug's common stock, which it holds as an investment. Krug, at the same date, owns 2% of Crawford's common stock. All the remaining common stock of Krug will be acquired by Crawford in the contemplated exchange. Neither of the two companies has ever had any affiliation as a subsidiary or division of any other company.

Instructions

a How is a determination made as to whether a business combination is accounted for as a pooling or as a purchase? (Do not enumerate specific criteria.)

b Based only on the facts above, discuss the specific criteria which would qualify or disqualify the Crawford-Krug business combination for pooling accounting.

c What additional requirements (other than those discussed in **b** above) must be met in order for this business combination to be accounted for as a pooling?

Case 5-6 On February 15, Year 6, the negotiating officers of Shane Corporation agreed with George Miles, sole shareholder of Miles Company and Miles Industries, Inc., to acquire all of George Miles's stock ownership in the two companies in the following manner:

(1) 10,000 shares of Shane Corporation $1 par common stock (current fair value $25 per share) would be issued to George Miles on February 28, Year 6, for his 1,000 shares of $10 par capital stock of Miles Company. In addition, 10,000 shares of Shane common stock would be issued to George Miles on February 28, Year 11, if aggregate earnings of Miles Company for the five-year period then ended exceeded $150,000.

(2) $250,000 cash would be paid to George Miles on February 28, Year 6, for his 10,000 shares of $1 par capital stock of Miles Industries, Inc. In addition, $250,000 in cash would be paid to George Miles on February 28, Year 11, if aggregate earnings of Miles Industries, Inc., for the five-year period then ended exceeded $150,000.

Both Miles Company and Miles Industries, Inc., are to be merged into Shane Corporation on February 28, Year 6, and are to continue operations after that date as divisions of Shane Corporation. George Miles also agreed not to compete with Shane Corporation for the period March 1, Year 6, through February 28, Year 11. Because the merger was negotiated privately and George Miles signed a "letter agreement" not to dispose of the Shane Corporation stock received, the business combination was not subject to the jurisdiction of the SEC. Out-of-pocket costs of the business combination were negligible.

Key financial statement data of the three constituent companies as of February 28, Year 6 (prior to the merger), were as follows:

	Shane Corporation	Miles Company	Miles Industries, Inc.
Total assets	$25,000,000	$ 500,000	$ 600,000
Stockholders' equity	10,000,000	200,000	300,000
Net sales	50,000,000	1,500,000	2,500,000
Earnings per share	5	30	3

The controller of Shane Corporation prepared the following condensed journal entries to record the merger on February 28, Year 6:

Assets	500,000	
Liabilities		300,000
Common Stock		10,000
Common Stock to Be Issued		10,000
Paid-in Capital in Excess of Par		180,000

To record merger with Miles Company as a pooling.

Assets	650,000	
Goodwill	150,000	
Liabilities		300,000
Payable to George Miles		250,000
Cash		250,000

To record merger with Miles Industries, Inc., as a purchase, with
assets and liabilities of Miles Industries, Inc., recorded at current
fair values and goodwill to be amortized over a 40-year economic
life.

Instructions   Do you concur with the controller's journal entries? Discuss.

PROBLEMS

5-7. Ming Company merged into Soho Corporation in a business combination completed April 30, Year 5. Out-of-pocket costs paid by Soho Corporation April 30,
Year 5, in connection with the combination were as follows:

Finder's fee and legal fees relating to the business combination	$15,000
Cost associated with SEC registration statement for securities issued to complete the business combination	10,000
Total out-of-pocket costs of business combination	$25,000

The condensed individual balance sheets of the two companies immediately
prior to the merger were as follows:

SOHO CORPORATION AND MING COMPANY
Balance Sheets
April 30, Year 5

	Soho Corporation	Ming Company
Assets		
Current assets	$ 4,350,000	$ 3,000,000
Plant assets (net)	18,500,000	11,300,000
Patents	450,000	200,000
Deferred charges	150,000	-0-
Total assets	$23,450,000	$14,500,000

(continued)

Liabilities & Stockholders' Equity	Soho Corporation	Ming Company
Liabilities	$ 2,650,000	$ 2,100,000
Common stock, $10 par	12,000,000	-0-
Common stock, $5 par	-0-	3,750,000
Paid-in capital in excess of par	4,200,000	3,200,000
Retained earnings	5,850,000	5,450,000
Treasury stock, at cost, 100,000 shares	(1,250,000)	-0-
Total liabilities & stockholders' equity	$23,450,000	$14,500,000

You have obtained the following addition information:
(1) The current fair values of the identifiable assets and liabilities of Soho Corporation and Ming Company were as follows on April 30, Year 5:

SOHO CORPORATION AND MING COMPANY
Current Fair Values of Identifiable Net Assets
April 30, Year 5

	Soho Corporation	Ming Company
Current assets	$ 4,950,000	$ 3,400,000
Plant assets (net)	22,000,000	14,000,000
Patents...	570,000	360,000
Deferred charges	150,000	-0-
Liabilities..	(2,650,000)	(2,100,000)
Net assets	$25,020,000	$15,660,000

(2) There were no intercompany transactions prior to the business combination.
(3) Before the business combination, Soho Corporation had 3,000,000 shares of common stock authorized, 1,200,000 shares issued, and 1,100,000 shares outstanding. Ming Company had 750,000 shares of common stock authorized, issued, and outstanding. The treasury stock of Soho was "untainted."

Instructions Prepare journal entries in the accounting records of Soho Corporation to record the business combination with Ming Company under each of the following independent assumptions:

a Soho Corporation exchanged 400,000 shares of previously unissued common stock and 100,000 shares of treasury stock for all the outstanding common stock of Ming Company. All the conditions for pooling accounting enumerated in *APB Opinion No. 16,* "Business Combinations," were met.
b Soho Corporation paid $3,100,000 cash and issued 8% debentures at face amount of $16,900,000 for all the outstanding common stock of Ming Company. The current fair value of the debentures is equal to their face amount.

5-8 Gomez-Nako Company (a partnership) was organized on July 1, Year 1. Under the partnership contract $900,000 was invested by Gomez and $600,000 by Nako as initial capital; net income and net losses were to be shared in the same ratio as the initial capital investments. No additional capital investments have been made.

The June 30, Year 6, balance sheet of Gomez-Nako Company follows.

GOMEZ-NAKO COMPANY
Balance Sheet
June 30, Year 6

Assets

Cash	$ 500,500
Accounts receivable (net)	950,000
Inventories (lifo basis)	1,500,000
Short-term prepayments	18,000
Land	58,000
Building, machinery, and equipment (net)	1,473,500
Total assets	$4,500,000

Liabilities & Partners' Capitals

Current liabilities	$1,475,000
Gomez, capital	1,815,000
Nako, capital	1,210,000
Total liabilities & partners' capitals	$4,500,000

Gomez and Nako have engaged in lengthy discussions with the directors and executives of Quality Corporation during the past few months. With the permission of Gomez and Nako, the independent auditors of Quality Corporation conducted an examination of and expressed an unqualified opinion on the financial statements of Gomez-Nako Company as of June 30, Year 6.

Gomez agrees to accept 8,700 shares and Nako agrees to accept 5,800 shares of Quality Corporation common stock in exchange for all partnership interests. During the month of June, Year 6, the current fair value of Quality Corporation common stock was $265 per share. The stockholders' equity of Quality Corporation at June 30, Year 6, follows:

Common stock, $100 par	$2,000,000
Paid-in capital in excess of par	580,000
Retained earnings	2,496,400
Total stockholders' equity	$5,076,400

Instructions

a Prepare the necessary journal entry or entries in the accounting records of Quality Corporation to record the business combination as a pooling on July 1, Year 6.

b Prepare the necessary journal entry or entries in the accounts of Gomez-Nako Company to record the liquidation of the partnership.

5-9 A condensed balance sheet at March 31, Year 7, and related current fair value data for Miklos Company are presented on page 225.

MIKLOS COMPANY
Balance Sheet
March 31, Year 7

	Carrying amount	Current fair value
Assets		
Current assets	$ 500,000	$ 575,000
Plant assets (net)	1,000,000	1,200,000
Patent (net)	100,000	50,000
Total assets	$1,600,000	
Liabilities & Stockholders' Equity		
Current liabilities	$ 300,000	300,000
Long-term debt	400,000	450,000
Capital stock, $10 par	100,000	
Retained earnings	800,000	
Total liabilities & stockholders' equity	$1,600,000	

On April 1, Year 7, Sharpe Corporation issued 50,000 shares of its $5 par common stock (current fair value $14 per share) and $250,000 cash for the net assets of Miklos Company, in a business combination qualifying for purchase accounting. Of the $125,000 out-of-pocket costs paid by Sharpe on April 1, Year 7, $50,000 were legal fees and finders' fees related to the business combination.

Instructions Prepare the necessary journal entry or entries to record the business combination in the accounting records of Sharpe Corporation.

5-10 As of the close of business August 31, Year 2, Meno Company merged into Saffer Corporation in a business combination meeting the specified conditions for pooling accounting. Premerger income statements of the two companies for the year ended August 31, Year 2, were as follows:

SAFFER CORPORATION AND MENO COMPANY
Income Statements
For Year Ended August 31, Year 2

	Saffer Corporation	Meno Company
Revenue:		
Net sales	$800,000	$550,000
Interest	20,000	-0-
Rent	-0-	50,000
Total revenue	$820,000	$600,000
Costs and expenses:		
Cost of goods sold	$480,000	$300,000
Selling, general, and administrative expenses	75,000	50,000
Interest expense	15,000	10,000
Income taxes expense	150,000	144,000
Total costs and expenses	$720,000	$504,000
Net income	$100,000	$ 96,000

During the year prior to the merger, Meno Company had obtained from and repaid to Saffer Corporation a $100,000, 9%, 90-day loan; Saffer Corporation had rented for the entire year a sales office owned by Meno Company, with a monthly rental of $500 plus 1% of net sales; and Saffer Corporation had sold to Meno Company, at Saffer's regular markup, goods costing $120,000, all of which were resold during the year to outside customers at Meno's regular markup.

Instructions

a Prepare combination eliminations (in journal entry form) for Saffer Corporation's post-merger income statement for the year ended August 31, Year 2. Disregard income taxes.

b Prepare a working paper for the post-merger income statement of Saffer Corporation.

5-11 On June 30, Year 2, Millard Company and Manion Company entered into a statutory consolidation. A new company, Millman Corporation, issued 100,000 shares of its 500,000 authorized shares of no-par, $3 stated value common stock as follows:

(1) 60,000 shares for all 10,000 outstanding shares of Millard Company's $2 par capital stock

(2) 40,000 shares for all 15,000 outstanding shares of Manion Company's $1 par capital stock

Costs associated with the statutory consolidation (legal and audit fees, printing charges, SEC fees) aggregating $50,000 were paid in cash June 30, Year 2 (prior to the consolidation), by Millard Company on behalf of Millman Corporation. There were no other intercompany transactions.

Following are condensed financial statements of Millard Company and Manion Company for the year ended June 30, Year 2, prior to the consolidation:

MILLARD COMPANY AND MANION COMPANY

Financial Statements

For Year Ended June 30, Year 2

Balance Sheets	Millard Company	Manion Company
Assets		
Current assets	$ 200,000	$300,000
Receivable from Millman Corporation	50,000	-0-
Plant assets (net)	700,000	500,000
Other assets	60,000	10,000
Total assets	$1,010,000	$810,000
Liabilities & Stockholders' Equity		
Current liabilities	$ 160,000	$ 80,000
Long-term debt	200,000	90,000
Capital stock	20,000	15,000
Paid-in capital in excess of par	80,000	150,000
Retained earnings	550,000	475,000
Total liabilities & stockholders' equity	$1,010,000	$810,000

**Statements of Income
and Retained Earnings**

Net sales	$2,000,000	$3,000,000
Costs and expenses:		
Cost of goods sold.......................................	$1,200,000	$2,000,000
Selling, general, and administrative expenses	400,000	500,000
Interest expense	15,000	10,000
Income taxes expense	231,000	294,000
Total costs and expenses	$1,846,000	$2,804,000
Net income	$ 154,000	$ 196,000
Retained earnings, July 1, Year 1	396,000	279,000
Retained earnings, June 30, Year 2	$ 550,000	$ 475,000

Millard Company costs its inventories on the fifo basis; Manion Company uses lifo cost for inventories. As part of the consolidation agreement, Manion Company agreed to change its inventories valuation method from lifo to fifo. Relevant data for Manion Company are as follows:

	Lifo cost	Fifo cost
Inventories, June 30, Year 2	$100,000	$150,000
Inventories, June 30, Year 1	90,000	130,000

Instructions

a Prepare the adjusting journal entry at June 30, Year 2, to change Manion Company's inventories from lifo cost to fifo cost. Manion Company's combined federal and state income tax rate is 60%. (**Note:** In accordance with **APB Opinion No. 20,** "Accounting Changes," a change from lifo to another inventory costing method requires the retroactive adjustment of retained earnings.)

b Prepare the June 30, Year 2, journal entry or entries of Millman Corporation to record the statutory consolidation as a pooling.

c Prepare a working paper to compute pooled net income of Millman Corporation for the year ended June 30, Year 2.

5-12 Coolidge Corporation agreed to pay $750,000 cash and issue 50,000 shares of its $10 par ($20 current fair value per share) common stock on September 30, Year 4, for all the net assets of Hoover Company except cash. In addition, Coolidge Corporation agreed that if the current fair value of its common stock was not $20 per share or more on September 30, Year 5, a sufficient number of additional shares of common stock would be issued to the shareholders of Hoover Company on that date to make the aggregate current fair value of their Coolidge common shareholdings equal to $1,000,000.

The balance sheet of Hoover Company at September 30, Year 4, with related current fair values of assets and liabilities, appears on page 228.

HOOVER COMPANY
Balance Sheet
September 30, Year 4

	Carrying amount	Current fair value
Assets		
Cash	$ 100,000	$ 100,000
Accounts receivable (net)	300,000	300,000
Inventories	600,000	680,000
Short-term prepayments................................	20,000	20,000
10% investment in common stock of Truman Company ...	100,000	80,000
Land	500,000	650,000
Other plant assets (net)	1,000,000	1,250,000
Patent...	80,000	100,000
Total assets	$2,700,000	
Liabilities & Stockholders' Equity		
Current liabilities	$ 700,000	700,000
Long-term debt	500,000	480,000
Capital stock, $5 par	600,000	
Paid-in capital in excess of par	400,000	
Retained earnings	500,000	
Total liabilities & stockholders' equity	$2,700,000	

Out-of-pocket costs of the business combination paid by Coolidge Corporation on September 30, Year 4, were as follows:

Audit fees—SEC registration statement	$ 30,000
Finder's fee (2% of aggregate consideration)...............................	35,000
Legal fees—business combination	15,000
Legal fees—SEC registration statement....................................	20,000
Printing costs—securities and SEC registration statement	25,000
SEC registration fee	350
Total out-of-pocket costs of business combination	$125,350

Instructions

a Prepare as of September 30, Year 4, journal entries in the accounting records of Coolidge Corporation to reflect the above transactions.

b Assume that on September 30, Year 5, the current fair value of Coolidge Corporation's common stock was $18 per share. Prepare a journal entry to record the issuance of additional Coolidge Corporation common shares to shareholders of Hoover Company on that date and the payment of cash in lieu of fractional shares.

5-13 The board of directors of Calloway Corporation is considering a merger with Bruno Company. On page 229 are the most recent financial statements (condensed) and other financial data for the two companies, both of which use the same accounting principles and practices.

CALLOWAY CORPORATION AND BRUNO COMPANY
Balance Sheets
October 31, Year 8

	Calloway Corporation	Bruno Company
Assets		
Current assets	$ 500,000	$200,000
Plant assets (net)	1,000,000	500,000
Other assets	300,000	100,000
Total assets	$1,800,000	$800,000
Liabilities & Stockholders' Equity		
Current liabilities	$ 400,000	$100,000
Long-term debt	500,000	300,000
Capital stock, $10 par	600,000	100,000
Paid-in capital in excess of par	100,000	100,000
Retained earnings	200,000	200,000
Total liabilities & stockholders' equity	$1,800,000	$800,000

CALLOWAY CORPORATION AND BRUNO COMPANY
Statements of Income and Retained Earnings
For Year Ended October 31, Year 8

	Calloway Corporation	Bruno Company
Net sales	$5,000,000	$1,000,000
Costs and expenses:		
Costs of goods sold	$3,500,000	$ 600,000
Selling, general, and administrative expenses	1,000,000	200,000
Interest expense	200,000	50,000
Income taxes expense	180,000	90,000
Total costs and expenses	$4,880,000	$ 940,000
Net income	$ 120,000	$ 60,000
Retained earnings, Nov. 1, Year 7	80,000	140,000
Retained earnings, Oct. 31, Year 8	$ 200,000	$ 200,000
Earnings per share	$2.00	$6.00
Price-earnings ratio	10	5

Calloway Corporation's directors estimate that the out-of-pocket costs of the merger will be as follows:

Finder's fee and legal fees for the merger	$ 5,000
Costs associated with SEC registration statement	7,000
Total out-of-pocket costs of merger	$12,000

The discounted present values of Bruno Company's liabilities at October 31, Year 8, are equal to their carrying amounts. Current fair values of Bruno's assets at that date are as follows:

Current assets (difference from balance sheet amount attributable to inventories carried at fifo cost which were sold during year ended Oct. 31, Year 9) $230,000

Plant assets (difference from balance sheet amount attributable to land— $60,000 and to depreciable assets with a five-year remaining economic life—$40,000) 600,000

Other assets (difference from balance sheet amount attributable to lease- hold with a remaining term of four years) 120,000

Calloway Corporation's board of directors is considering two alternative plans for effecting the merger, as follows:

Plan 1 Issue 30,000 shares of capital stock for all the outstanding capital stock of Bruno Company in a business combination meeting the specified conditions for pooling accounting.

Plan 2 Issue 15,000 shares of capital stock with a current fair value of $20 per share, $100,000 cash, and an 8%, three-year note for $200,000 for all the outstanding capital stock of Bruno Company. The current fair value of the note is equal to its face amount.

Under either plan, Bruno Company would continue operations as a division of Calloway Corporation.

Instructions To assist Calloway Corporation's board of directors in their evalu- ation of the two plans, prepare a working paper to compute the following for each plan as though the merger had been effected as of October 31, Year 8:
a Net income and earnings per share of Calloway Corporation for the year ended October 31, Year 8.
b Net income and earnings per share of Calloway Corporation for the year end- ing October 31, Year 9, assuming the same basic sales and cost patterns for the year ended October 31, Year 8. Goodwill, if any, is to be amortized over 40 years.
Ignore income taxes in your computations.

5-14 Financial statements of Grant Corporation and Dale Corporation appear below:

GRANT CORPORATION AND DALE CORPORATION
Balance Sheets
June 30, Year 7

	Grant Corporation	Dale Corporation
Assets		
Cash	$ 25,500	$ 1,500
Notes and accounts receivable (net)	24,500	7,500
Inventories, at fifo cost	42,000	8,800
Receivable from Dale Corporation	7,600	-0-
Plant assets (net)	59,500	35,800
Other assets	4,500	200
Total assets	$163,600	$53,800

(continued)

	Grant Corporation	Dale Corporation
Liabilities & Stockholders' Equity		
Notes and accounts payable...........................	$ 20,700	$39,920
Payable to Grant Corporation	-0-	7,600
Income taxes payable	11,400	-0-
Other liabilities	1,500	2,200
Capital stock, $10 par	50,000	-0-
Capital stock, $100 par	-0-	25,000
Paid-in capital in excess of par	30,000	32,000
Retained earnings (deficit)	50,000	(52,920)
Total liabilities & stockholders' equity	$163,600	$53,800

GRANT CORPORATION AND DALE CORPORATION
Statements of Income and Retained Earnings (Deficit)
For Six Months Ended June 30, Year 7

	Grant Corporation	Dale Corporation
Revenue:		
Net sales	$150,000	$ 60,000
Other revenue	5,000	-0-
Total revenue	$155,000	$ 60,000
Costs and expenses:		
Cost of goods sold..................................	$105,000	$ 54,000
Selling, general, and administrative expenses	31,000	12,100
Income taxes expense	11,400	-0-
Total costs and expenses...........................	$147,400	$ 66,100
Net income (loss)	$ 7,600	$ (6,100)
Retained earnings (deficit), Jan. 1, Year 7	44,900	(46,820)
Subtotal..	$ 52,500	$(52,920)
Dividends	2,500	-0-
Retained earnings (deficit), June 30, Year 7..............	$ 50,000	$(52,920)

The pre-tax accounting income (loss) of the two corporations for the last six years is as follows (pre-tax accounting income and taxable income are the same):

	Grant Corporation	Dale Corporation
Year 1 (Year in which Dale Corporation was organized)	$18,000	$(4,000)
Year 2...	(7,500)	4,000
Year 3...	12,600	(15,000)
Year 4...	14,900	(6,000)
Year 5...	31,200	(7,000)
Year 6...	28,900	(11,100)

On July 1, Year 7, Dale Corporation transferred to Grant Corporation all its assets net of all liabilities, in exchange for unissued Grant Corporation capital stock. The terms of the merger provided that the current fair value of the stock in each corporation is to be its carrying amount, except that an allowance is to be made for the value of any net operating loss carryforward. Obtaining the benefit of the loss carryforward deduction was not the principal purpose of the merger. (Assume a combined federal and state income tax rate of 60% and that the state net operating loss carryover rules are the same as the federal rules, which require that an operating loss of the current year first be carried back three years and then forward seven years.)

Instructions

a Compute (1) the total number of shares of Grant Corporation capital stock to be distributed to shareholders of Dale Corporation and (2) the exchange ratio of Grant Corporation stock for Dale Corporation stock.

b Prepare a journal entry for Grant Corporation to record the merger with Dale Corporation as a pooling.

c Prepare a journal entry for Dale Corporation to record the merger with Grant Corporation. Assume that Dale Corporation does not record in its accounts the potential income tax benefit of its operating loss carryforward.

6

CONSOLIDATED FINANCIAL STATEMENTS: AT DATE OF PURCHASE BUSINESS COMBINATION

In Chapter 5 we used the terms *investor* and *investee* in our discussion of business combinations involving a combinor's acquisition of capital stock of a combinee corporation which is not liquidated. If the investor acquires more than 50% of the voting common stock of the investee, *a parent-subsidiary relationship* is established. The investee becomes a *subsidiary* of the acquiring *parent company* (investor) but remains a separate legal entity.

Strict adherence to the legal aspects of such a business combination would require the issuance of separate financial statements for the parent company and the subsidiary at the date of the business combination, and also for all subsequent periods of the affiliation. However, such strict adherence to legal form would ignore the *substance* of most parent-subsidiary relationships. A parent company and its subsidiary usually are a single *economic entity.* In recognition of this fact, *consolidated financial statements* are issued to report the financial position and operating results of a parent company and its subsidiaries as a single *accounting entity.*

Nature of consolidated financial statements

Consolidated financial statements are similar to the *combined* financial statements described in Chapter 4 for a home office and its branches.

Assets, liabilities, revenue, and expenses of the parent company and its subsidiaries are aggregated; intercompany transactions and balances are eliminated; and the final consolidated amounts are reported in the consolidated balance sheet, statements of income and retained earnings, and statement of changes in financial position.

However, the separate *legal entity* status of parent and subsidiary corporations necessitates working paper consolidation eliminations which generally are more complex than the eliminations described in Chapter 4 for a home office and its branches. Before illustrating consolidation eliminations, we shall examine some basic principles of consolidation.

Should all subsidiaries be consolidated?

A wide range of consolidation practices exists among major companies in the United States.[1] For example, the 31st edition of *Accounting Trends & Techniques* (published in 1977), the AICPA's annual survey of accounting practices in the published financial statements of 600 companies, reported the following:

1 A total of 379 companies consolidated all subsidiaries, while 215 companies excluded some subsidiaries from the consolidated financial statements. (The remaining 6 companies surveyed either did not issue consolidated financial statements or had no indication of subsidiaries.)

2 The principal types of subsidiaries *excluded* from consolidation were foreign subsidiaries, finance-related subsidiaries, and insignificant or inactive subsidiaries. "Finance-related subsidiaries" include finance companies, insurance companies, banks, and leasing companies.

In the authors' opinion, such wide variations in consolidation policy are undesirable and difficult to justify from a theoretical point of view. The purpose of consolidated financial statements is to present in a single accounting entity the combined resources, obligations, and operating results of a family of related corporations; consequently, there is no theoretical reason for excluding from consolidation any subsidiary which *is controlled.* The argument that finance-related subsidiaries should not be consolidated with parent manufacturing or retailing companies because of their unique features is difficult to justify when one considers the wide variety of production, marketing, and service companies that are consolidated in a *conglomerate* or highly diversified family of corporations.

---

[1] Adequate guidelines for consolidation policies have not been provided by the FASB or the AICPA; a limited step in this direction was contained in the following excerpt from *Accounting Research Bulletin No. 51;* "There is a presumption that consolidated statements are more meaningful than separate statements and that they are usually necessary for a fair presentation when one of the companies in the group directly or indirectly has a controlling financial interest in the other companies." *ARB No. 51,* "Consolidated Financial Statements," AICPA (New York: 1959), p. 41.

The meaning of "controlling financial interest"

Traditionally, an investor's direct or indirect ownership of more than 50% of an investee's voting common stock has been required to evidence the controlling financial interest underlying a parent-subsidiary relationship. However, even though such a stock ownership exists, other circumstances may negate the parent company's *actual* control of the subsidiary. For example, a subsidiary which is bankrupt or in court-supervised reorganization is not really controlled by its parent company. Also, a foreign subsidiary in a country having severe production, monetary, or income tax restrictions may in reality be subject to the authority of the foreign country rather than of its parent company.

It is important to recognize that a parent company's control of a subsidiary may be achieved *indirectly.* For example, if Plymouth Corporation owns 85% of the outstanding voting common stock of Selwyn Company and 45% of Talbot Company's common stock, while Selwyn Company also owns 45% of Talbot's common, both Selwyn and Talbot are controlled by Plymouth, because it effectively controls 90% of Talbot. This effective control consists of 45% held directly and 45% indirectly.

Criticism of traditional concept of control

Some accountants have challenged the conventional definition of *control* described in the preceding section. These accountants maintain that an investor owning less than 50% of an investee's voting common stock effectively may control the affiliate, especially if the remaining stock is scattered among a number of individual shareholders who do not attend shareholder meetings or give proxies. Effective control of an investee also is possible if the individuals comprising management of the investor corporation own a substantial number of shares of the investee or successfully solicit proxies from the investee's other shareholders. These arguments merit further study in the search for a less arbitrary definition of *control* than the one described in the preceding section.

Unconsolidated subsidiaries in consolidated financial statements

Current generally accepted accounting principles [2] require the use of the *equity method* of accounting for unconsolidated subsidiaries in consolidated financial statements. The equity method of accounting, which is discussed in depth in Chapters 8 and 9, reflects the parent company's share of the earnings of an unconsolidated subsidiary on a single line in the consolidated income statement. Use of the equity method of ac-

---

[2] *APB Opinion No. 18,* "The Equity Method of Accounting for Investments in Common Stock," AICPA (New York: 1971), pp. 353–354.

counting results in a figure for consolidated net income identical to that which would have resulted from consolidating the subsidiary.

CONSOLIDATION OF WHOLLY OWNED PURCHASED SUBSIDIARY AT DATE OF BUSINESS COMBINATION

To illustrate consolidated financial statements for a parent company and a wholly owned purchased subsidiary, assume that as of the close of business December 31, Year 10, Palm Corporation issued 10,000 shares of its common stock (current fair value $45 per share) for all the outstanding capital stock of Starr Company. Out-of-pocket costs of the business combination paid by Palm Corporation on December 31, Year 10, consisted of the following:

Finder's fee and legal fees relating to the business combination	*$50,000*
Costs associated with SEC registration statement	*35,000*
Total out-of-pocket costs of business combination	*$85,000*

Combinor's out-of-pocket costs of business combination

The business combination qualified for purchase accounting; Starr Company is to continue its corporate existence as a wholly owned subsidiary of Palm Corporation. Both companies use the same accounting principles and procedures, and no adjusting entries are required for either company prior to the business combination. The combined federal and state income tax rate for each company is 60%

Financial statements of Palm Corporation and Starr Company for the year ended December 31, Year 10, prior to consummation of the business combination, are presented below:

PALM CORPORATION AND STARR COMPANY
Separate Financial Statements
For Year Ended December 31, Year 10

	Palm Corporation	Starr Company
Income Statements		
Revenue		
Net sales	$ 990,000	$600,000
Interest revenue	10,000	-0-
Total revenue	$1,000,000	$600,000

(continued)

PALM CORPORATION AND STARR COMPANY
Separate Financial Statements
For Year Ended December 31, Year 10 (Continued)

	Palm Corporation	Starr Company
Income Statements		
Costs and expenses		
Cost of goods sold	$ 635,000	$410,000
Selling, general, and administrative expenses	80,000	30,000
Interest expense	50,000	30,000
Income taxes expense	141,000	78,000
Total costs and expenses	$ 906,000	$548,000
Net income	$ 94,000	$ 52,000
Statements of Retained Earnings		
Retained earnings, Jan. 1, Year 10	$ 65,000	$100,000
Net income	94,000	52,000
Subtotal	$159,000	$152,000
Dividends	25,000	20,000
Retained earnings, Dec. 31, Year 10	$134,000	$132,000
Balance Sheets		
Assets		
Cash	$100,000	$ 40,000
Inventories	150,000	110,000
Other current assets	110,000	70,000
Receivable from Starr Company	25,000	-0-
Plant assets (net)	450,000	300,000
Patent..	-0-	20,000
Total assets	$835,000	$540,000
Liabilities & Stockholders' Equity		
Payable to Palm Corporation	$ -0-	$ 25,000
Income taxes payable	66,000	10,000
Other liabilities	285,000	115,000
Common stock, $10 par	300,000	-0-
Capital stock, $5 par	-0-	200,000
Paid-in capital in excess of par	50,000	58,000
Retained earnings.............................	134,000	132,000
Total liabilities & stockholders' equity	$835,000	$540,000

The December 31, Year 10, current fair values of Starr Company's identifiable assets and liabilities were the same as their carrying amounts, except for the three assets listed on page 238.

Current fair values of selected assets of combinee		Current fair value, Dec. 31, Year 10
Inventories		$135,000
Plant assets (net)		365,000
Patent		25,000

Because Starr Company is continuing as a separate corporation and current generally accepted accounting principles do not sanction write-ups of assets of a going concern, Starr would make no journal entries associated with the business combination. Palm Corporation would record the combination as a purchase at December 31, Year 10, within the following journal entries:

Combinor's journal entries for purchase business combination			
Investment in Subsidiary (100,000 shares × $45)		450,000	
Common Stock (10,000 shares × $10)			100,000
Paid-in Capital in Excess of Par			350,000
To record issuance of 10,000 shares of common stock for all the outstanding capital stock of Starr Company in a business combination accounted for as a purchase.			
Investment in Subsidiary		50,000	
Paid-in Capital in Excess of Par		35,000	
Cash			85,000
To record payment of out-of-pocket costs of business combination with Starr Company. Finder's and legal fees relating to the combination are recorded as additional costs of the investment; costs associated with the SEC registration statement are recorded as an offset to the previously recorded proceeds from the issuance of common stock.			

The first journal entry above is similar to the entry illustrated in Chapter 5 (page 194) for a merger accounted for as a purchase. An Investment in Subsidiary account is debited with the current fair value of the common stock issued to effect the business combination, and the paid-in capital accounts are credited in the usual manner for any stock issuance. In the second entry, the *direct* out-of-pocket costs of the business combination are debited to the Investment in Subsidiary account, and the costs associated with the SEC registration statement, being costs of issuing stock, are applied to reduce the gross proceeds of the common stock issuance.

Unlike the journal entries for a merger accounted for as a purchase illustrated in Chapter 5, the above entries do not include any debits or credits to record individual assets and liabilities of Starr Company in the accounts of Palm Corporation. The reason is that Starr Company was not *liquidated* as in a merger; it remains a separate legal entity.

After the preceding journal entries have been posted, the affected ledger accounts of Palm Corporation (the combinor) appear as follows:

Ledger accounts of combinor affected by business combination

Cash

Date	Explanation	Debit	Credit	Balance
12/31/10	Balance forward			100,000 dr
12/31/10	Out-of-pocket costs of business combination		85,000	15,000 dr

Investment in Subsidiary

Date	Explanation	Debit	Credit	Balance
12/31/10	Issuance of stock in business combination	450,000		450,000 dr
12/31/10	Direct out-of-pocket costs of business combination	50,000		500,000 dr

Common Stock, $10 Par

Date	Explanation	Debit	Credit	Balance
12/31/10	Balance forward			300,000 cr
12/31/10	Issuance of stock in business combination		100,000	400,000 cr

Paid-in Capital in Excess of Par

Date	Explanation	Debit	Credit	Balance
12/31/10	Balance forward			50,000 cr
12/31/10	Issuance of stock in business combination		350,000	400,000 cr
12/31/10	Out-of-pocket costs of business combination	35,000		365,000 cr

Consolidating Balance Sheet Working Paper   Purchase accounting for the business combination of Palm Corporation and Starr Company requires a fresh start for the consolidated entity. This reflects the theory that a business combination which meets the requirements for purchase accounting is an *acquisition* of the combinee's assets (less liabilities) by the combinor. The operating results of Palm Corporation and Starr Company prior to the date of their business combination are those of two separate *economic*—as well as *legal*—entities. Accordingly, a consolidated balance sheet is the only financial statement issued at December 31, Year 10—the date of the business combination of Palm Corporation and Starr Company.

Preparation of a consolidated balance sheet usually requires the use of a *consolidating balance sheet working paper.* The form of the working paper, with the individual balance sheet amounts included for both Palm Corporation and Starr Company, is presented below:

Wholly owned purchased subsidiary at date of business combination

PALM CORPORATION AND SUBSIDIARY
Consolidating Balance Sheet Working Paper
December 31, Year 10

	Palm Corporation	Starr Company	Consolidation eliminations increase (decrease)	Consolidated
Assets				
Cash	$ 15,000	$ 40,000		
Inventories	150,000	110,000		
Other current assets . . .	110,000	70,000		
Intercompany receivable (payable)	25,000	(25,000)		
Investment in subsidiary	500,000	-0-		
Plant assets (net)	450,000	300,000		
Patent	-0-	20,000		
Goodwill	-0-	-0-		
Total assets	$1,250,000	$515,000		
Liabilities & Stockholders' Equity				
Income taxes payable . . .	$ 66,000	$ 10,000		
Other liabilities	285,000	115,000		
Common stock, $10 par	400,000	-0-		
Capital stock, $5 par . . .	-0-	200,000		
Paid-in capital in excess of par	365,000	58,000		
Retained earnings	134,000	132,000		
Total liabilities & stockholders' equity . .	$1,250,000	$515,000		

Developing the Consolidation Elimination Palm Corporation's Investment in Subsidiary account in the consolidating balance sheet working paper is similar to a home office's Investment in Branch account, as described in Chapter 4. However, Starr Company is a *separate corporation,* not a *branch;* therefore, Starr has the three conventional stockholders' equity accounts rather than the Home Office reciprocal account used by a branch. Accordingly, the consolidation elimination for the *intercompany* accounts of Palm Corporation and Starr Company must *decrease to zero* the Investment in Subsidiary account of Palm Corporation and the three stockholders' equity accounts of Starr Company. Decreases in assets are effected by *credits,* and decreases in stockholders' equity accounts are effected by *debits;* therefore, the consolidation elimination for Palm Corporation and subsidiary at December 31, Year 10 (the date of the purchase business combination) would be begun as follows (in journal entry form):

Elimination of intercompany accounts

Capital Stock—Starr	200,000	
Paid-in Capital in Excess of Par—Starr	58,000	
Retained Earnings—Starr	132,000	
	(390,000)	
Investment in Subsidiary—Palm		500,000

The footing of the debit items of the above partial consolidation elimination—$390,000, which represents the carrying amount of the net assets of Starr Company—is $110,000 less than the credit item—$500,000, which represents the cost of Palm Corporation's investment in Starr Company. As indicated on page 238, part of the $110,000 difference is attributable to the excess of current fair values over carrying amounts of certain *identifiable* assets of Starr Company. This excess is summarized as follows:

Differences between current fair values and carrying amounts of combinee's identifiable assets

	Current fair value	Carrying amount	Excess of current fair value over carrying amount
Inventories	$135,000	$110,000	$25,000
Plant assets (net)	365,000	300,000	65,000
Patent	25,000	20,000	5,000
Totals	$525,000	$430,000	$95,000

We already have indicated that current generally accepted accounting principles preclude the write-up of a going concern's assets. Thus, to conform to the requirements of purchase accounting for business combinations, the above differences must be incorporated in the consolidated balance sheet of Palm Corporation and subsidiary by means of the consolidation elimination. *Increases* in assets are recorded by *debits;* thus, the consolidation elimination for Palm Corporation and subsidiary begun on page 241 would be *continued* as follows:

<table>
<tr><td rowspan="7" style="text-align:right;">Use of consolidation elimination to reflect current fair values of combinee's identifiable assets</td><td>Capital Stock—Starr</td><td>200,000</td><td></td></tr>
<tr><td>Paid-in Capital in Excess of Par—Starr</td><td>58,000</td><td></td></tr>
<tr><td>Retained Earnings—Starr</td><td>132,000</td><td></td></tr>
<tr><td>Inventories–Starr ($135,000   – $110,000)</td><td>25,000</td><td></td></tr>
<tr><td>Plant assets (net)–Starr ($365,000   – $300,000)</td><td>65,000</td><td></td></tr>
<tr><td>Patent–Starr ($25,000   – $20,000)</td><td>5,000</td><td></td></tr>
<tr><td></td><td>485,000</td><td></td></tr>
<tr><td></td><td>   Investment in Subsidiary—Palm</td><td></td><td>500,000</td></tr>
</table>

The revised footing—$485,000—of the debit items of the above partial consolidation elimination is equal to the current fair value of the *identifiable* tangible and intangible net assets of Starr Company. Thus, the $15,000 difference ($500,000 − $485,000 = $15,000) between the cost of Palm Corporation's investment in Starr Company and the current fair value of Starr's identifiable net assets represents *goodwill* of Starr Company, in accordance with purchase accounting theory for business combinations, as described in Chapter 5 (pages 191 to 195). Consequently, the December 31, Year 10, consolidation elimination for Palm Corporation and subsidiary is completed with a $15,000 *debit* to Goodwill—Starr.

Completed Consolidating Working Papers   The completed consolidation elimination working paper for Palm Corporation and subsidiary and the related consolidating balance sheet working paper appear below:

Wholly owned purchased subsidiary at date of business combination

PALM CORPORATION AND SUBSIDIARY
Consolidation Elimination Working Paper
December 31, Year 10

<table>
<tr><td>(a) Capital Stock—Starr</td><td>200,000</td><td></td></tr>
<tr><td>Paid-in Capital in Excess of Par—Starr</td><td>58,000</td><td></td></tr>
<tr><td>Retained Earnings—Starr</td><td>132,000</td><td></td></tr>
</table>

(continued)

PALM CORPORATION AND SUBSIDIARY
Consolidation Elimination Working Paper
December 31, Year 10 (Continued)

Inventories—Starr ($135,000 − $110,000)	25,000	
Plant Assets (net)—Starr ($365,000 − $300,000)	65,000	
Patent—Starr ($25,000 − $20,000)	5,000	
Goodwill—Starr ($500,000 − $485,000)	15,000	
Investment in Subsidiary—Palm		500,000

To eliminate intercompany investment and equity accounts of subsidiary at date of business combination; and to allocate excess of cost over carrying amount of identifiable assets acquired, with remainder to goodwill.

Wholly owned purchased subsidiary at date of business combination

PALM CORPORATION AND SUBSIDIARY
Consolidating Balance Sheet Working Paper
December 31, Year 10

	Palm Corporation	Starr Company	Consolidation eliminations increase (decrease)	Consolidated
Assets				
Cash	$ 15,000	$ 40,000		$ 55,000
Inventories	150,000	110,000	(a) $ 25,000	285,000
Other current assets ..	110,000	70,000		180,000
Intercompany receivable (payable)	25,000	(25,000)		-0-
Investment in subsidiary	500,000	-0-	(a) (500,000)	-0-
Plant assets (net)	450,000	300,000	(a) 65,000	815,000
Patent	-0-	20,000	(a) 5,000	25,000
Goodwill	-0-	-0-	(a) 15,000	15,000
Total assets	$1,250,000	$515,000	$(390,000)	$1,375,000
Liabilities & Stockholders' Equity				
Income taxes payable	$ 66,000	$ 10,000		$ 76,000
Other liabilities	285,000	115,000		400,000
Common stock, $10 par	400,000	-0-		400,000
Capital stock, $5 par ..	-0-	200,000	(a) $(200,000)	-0-
Paid-in capital in excess of par	365,000	58,000	(a) (58,000)	365,000
Retained earnings	134,000	132,000	(a) (132,000)	134,000
Total liabilities & stockholders' equity	$1,250,000	$515,000	$(390,000)	$1,375,000

The following features of the consolidating balance sheet working paper at the date of the purchase business combination should be emphasized:

1 The consolidating balance sheet and consolidation elimination are working papers only. The consolidation elimination is not posted to either the parent company's or the subsidiary's accounting records.

2 The consolidation elimination is used to reflect differences between current fair values and carrying amounts of the subsidiary's net assets, because the subsidiary did not write up its assets to current fair values at the date of the business combination.

3 The Consolidation Eliminations column in the consolidating balance sheet working paper reflects *increases* and *decreases,* rather than *debits* and *credits.* Debits and credits are not appropriate in a working paper dealing with *financial statements* rather than *trial balances.*

4 Intercompany *receivables* and *payables* are placed on the same line of the consolidating balance sheet working paper and are combined to produce consolidated amounts of zero.

5 The respective corporations are identified in the components of the consolidation elimination. The reason for precise identification will be clarified in Chapter 10 dealing with elimination of intercompany profits.

6 The consolidated paid-in capital accounts are those of the parent company only. Subsidiaries' paid-in capital accounts *always* are eliminated in the process of consolidation.

7 Consolidated retained earnings at the date of the purchase business combination includes only the retained earnings of the parent company. This treatment is consistent with the theory that purchase accounting reflects a fresh start in an acquisition of assets (less liabilities), not a combining of existing stockholder interests.

8 The amounts in the Consolidated column of the consolidating balance sheet working paper reflect the financial position of a *single economic entity* comprising *two legal entities,* with all *intercompany* balances of the two entities eliminated.

Consolidated Balance Sheet   The amounts in the Consolidated column of the consolidating balance sheet working paper are presented in the customary fashion in the formal *consolidated balance sheet* of Palm Corporation and subsidiary.

CONSOLIDATION OF PARTIALLY OWNED PURCHASED SUBSIDIARY AT DATE OF BUSINESS COMBINATION

The consolidation of a parent company and its *partially owned* subsidiary differs from the consolidation of a wholly owned subsidiary in one major respect—the recognition of minority interest. *Minority interest* is a term applied to the claims of shareholders other than the parent company against the net income and net assets of the subsidiary. The minority interest in the subsidiary's net income is reported in the consolidated income statement, and the minority interest in the subsidiary's net assets is reported in the consolidated balance sheet.

To illustrate the consolidation techniques for a business combination involving a partially owned purchased subsidiary, assume the following facts. At the close of business April 30, Year 6, Post Corporation issued 57,000 shares of its common stock (current fair value $20 per share) in exchange for 38,000 of the 40,000 outstanding shares of Sage Company's capital stock in a business combination qualifying for purchase accounting. Thus, Post acquired a 95% interest in Sage, which became Post's subsidiary. Out-of-pocket costs of the business combination, paid in cash by Post on April 30, Year 6, were as follows:

Combinor's out-of-pocket costs of business combination	*Finder's fee and legal fees relating to the business combination* ...... $ 52,250
	Costs associated with SEC registration statement 72,750
	Total out-of-pocket costs of business combination $125,000

Financial statements of Post Corporation and Sage Company for the year ended April 30, Year 6, prior to consummation of the business combination, are presented on page 246. There were no intercompany transactions prior to the business combination.

The April 30, Year 6, current fair values of Sage Company's identifiable assets and liabilities were the same as their carrying amounts, except for the following assets:

	Current fair value, Apr. 30, Year 6
Current fair values of selected assets of combinee	
Inventories	$ 526,000
Plant assets (net)	1,290,000
Leasehold	30,000

Sage Company would make no journal entries related to the business combination, because Sage is continuing as a separate corporation and current generally accepted accounting principles do not permit the write-up of assets of a going concern. Post Corporation would record the business combination with Sage Company as a purchase by means of the two journal entries (below and at the top of page 247) on April 30, Year 6.

Combinor's journal entries for purchase business combination	*Investment in Subsidiary (57,000 shares × $20)* 1,140,000	
	Common Stock (57,000 shares × $1)	57,000
	Paid-in Capital in Excess of Par	1,083,000
	To record issuance of 57,000 shares of common stock for	
	38,000 of the 40,000 outstanding shares of Sage Company	
	in a business combination accounted for as a purchase.	

POST CORPORATION AND SAGE COMPANY
Separate Financial Statements
For Year Ended April 30, Year 6

	Post Corporation	Sage Company
Income Statements		
Net sales	$5,500,000	$1,000,000
Costs and expenses		
Cost of goods sold	$3,850,000	$ 650,000
Selling, general, and administrative expenses	600,000	100,000
Interest expense	75,000	40,000
Income taxes expense	585,000	126,000
Total costs and expenses	$5,110,000	$ 916,000
Net income	$ 390,000	$ 84,000
Statements of Retained Earnings		
Retained earnings, May 1, Year 5	$ 810,000	$ 250,000
Net income	390,000	84,000
Subtotal	$1,200,000	$ 334,000
Dividends	150,000	-0-
Retained earnings, Apr. 30, Year 6	$1,050,000	$ 334,000
Balance Sheets		
Assets		
Cash	$ 200,000	$ 100,000
Inventories	800,000	500,000
Other current assets	550,000	215,000
Plant assets (net)	3,500,000	1,100,000
Goodwill	100,000	-0-
Total assets	$5,150,000	$1,915,000
Liabilities & Stockholders' Equity		
Income taxes payable	$ 100,000	$ 76,000
Other liabilities	2,450,000	870,000
Common stock, $1 par	1,000,000	-0-
Capital stock, $10 par	-0-	400,000
Paid-in capital in excess of par	550,000	235,000
Retained earnings	1,050,000	334,000
Total liabilities & stockholders' equity	$5,150,000	$1,915,000

Combinor's journal entries for purchase business combination (continued)

Investment in Subsidiary	52,250	
Paid-in Capital in Excess of Par	72,750	
Cash		125,000

To record payment of out-of-pocket costs of business combination with Sage Company. Finder's fee and legal fees relating to the combination are recorded as additional costs of the investment; costs associated with the SEC registration statement are recorded as an offset to the previously recorded proceeds from the issuance of common stock.

After the preceding journal entries have been posted, the affected ledger accounts of Post Corporation appear as follows:

Ledger accounts of combinor affected by business combination

Cash

Date	Explanation	Debit	Credit	Balance
4/30/6	Balance forward			200,000 dr
4/30/6	Out-of-pocket costs of business combination		125,000	75,000 dr

Investment in Subsidiary

Date	Explanation	Debit	Credit	Balance
4/30/6	Issuance of stock in business combination	1,140,000		1,140,000 dr
4/30/6	Direct out-of-pocket costs of business combination	52,250		1,192,250 dr

Common Stock, $1 Par

Date	Explanation	Debit	Credit	Balance
4/30/6	Balance forward			1,000,000 cr
4/30/6	Issuance of stock in business combination		57,000	1,057,000 cr

Paid-in Capital in Excess of Par

Date	Explanation	Debit	Credit	Balance
4/30/6	Balance forward			550,000 cr
4/30/6	Issuance of stock in business combination		1,083,000	1,633,000 cr
4/30/6	Out-of-pocket costs of business combination	72,750		1,560,250 cr

Developing the Consolidation Elimination The preparation of the consolidation elimination for a parent company and a partially owned purchased subsidiary parallels that for a wholly owned purchased subsidiary described earlier in this chapter. First, the *intercompany* accounts are reduced to zero, as follows (in journal entry format):

Elimination of intercompany accounts of parent company and purchased subsidiary at date of business combination

Capital Stock—Sage	400,000	
Paid-in Capital in Excess of Par—Sage	235,000	
Retained Earnings—Sage	334,000	
	(969,000)	
Investment in Subsidiary—Post		1,192,250

The footing of the debit items of the above partial consolidation elimination—$969,000, which represents total stockholders' equity of Sage Company—is $223,250 less than the credit item—$1,192,250. Part of this $223,250 difference is the excess of the total of the cost of Post Corporation's investment in Sage Company and the *minority interest* in Sage Company over the carrying amounts of Sage's identifiable net assets. This excess may be identified as follows, from the data provided on pages 245 and 246:

Difference between current fair values and carrying amounts of combinee's identifiable assets

	Current fair value	Carrying amount	Excess of current fair value over carrying amount
Inventories	$ 526,000	$ 500,000	$ 26,000
Plant assets (net	1,290,000	1,100,000	190,000
Leasehold	30,000	-0-	30,000
Totals	$1,846,000	$1,600,000	$246,000

Under current generally accepted accounting principles, the above differences cannot be reflected in Sage Company's accounting records. Thus, to conform to the requirements of purchase accounting, the differences must be reflected in the consolidated balance sheet of Post Corporation and subsidiary by means of the consolidation elimination, which is continued as follows:

Use of con-solidation elimination to reflect current fair values of identifiable assets of purchased subsidiary at date of business combination	Capital Stock—Sage	400,000
	Paid-in Capital in Excess of Par—Sage	235,000
	Retained Earnings—Sage	334,000
	Inventories—Sage ($526,000 − $500,000)	26,000
	Plant Assets (net)—Sage ($1,290,000 − $1,100,000)	190,000
	Leasehold—Sage—($30,000 − $-0-)	30,000
		(1,215,000)
	Investment in Subsidiary—Post	1,192,250

The revised footing—$1,215,000—of the debit items of the above partial consolidation elimination represents the current fair value of Sage Company's *identifiable* net assets at April 30, Year 6.

Two items now must be recognized to complete the consolidation elimination for Post Corporation and subsidiary. First, the **minority interest** in the identifiable net assets of Sage company must be recognized with a **credit**. The minority interest is computed as follows:

Computation of minority interest in combinee's identifiable net assets	Current fair value of Sage Company's identifiable net assets	$1,215,000
	Minority interest percentage in Sage Company's identifiable net assets (100% minus Post Corporation's 95% interest)	5%
	Minority interest in Sage Company's identifiable net assets ($1,215,000 × 5%)	$ 60,750

Second, the goodwill purchased by Post Corporation in the business combination with Sage Company must be recorded with a **debit**. The goodwill is computed as follows:

Computation of goodwill purchased by combinor	Cost of Post Corporation's 95% interest in Sage Company	$1,192,250
	95% of $1,215,000 current fair value of Sage Company's identifiable net assets	1,154,250
	Goodwill purchased by Post Corporation	$ 38,000

The consolidation elimination for Post Corporation and subsidiary may now be completed as follows:

Partially owned purchased subsidiary at date of business combination

POST CORPORATION AND SUBSIDIARY
Consolidation Elimination Working Paper
April 30, Year 6

(a) Capital Stock—Sage	400,000	
Paid-in Capital in Excess of Par—Sage	235,000	
Retained Earnings—Sage	334,000	
Inventories—Sage ($526,000 − $500,000).............	26,000	
Plant Assets (net)—Sage ($1,290,000 − $1,100,000) ...	190,000	
Leasehold—Sage ($30,000 − $-0-)	30,000	
Goodwill—Post ($1,192,250 − $1,154,250)	38,000	
Investment in Subsidiary—Post		1,192,250
Minority Interest in Subsidiary.................		60,750

To eliminate intercompany investment and equity accounts of subsidiary at date of business combination; to allocate excess of cost over carrying amount of identifiable assets acquired, with remainder to goodwill; and to establish minority interest in subsidiary at date of business combination ($1,215,000 × 5% = $60,750).

Consolidating Balance Sheet Working Paper The consolidating balance sheet working paper at April 30, Year 6, for Post Corporation and subsidiary appears on page 251.

Alternative Methods for Valuing Minority Interest and Goodwill The computation of minority interest in subsidiary and goodwill in the preceding illustration was based on two premises. First, the *entire identifiable assets and liabilities* of a partially owned purchased subsidiary should be valued on a single basis—*current fair value.* Second, only the subsidiary goodwill *purchased* by the parent company should be recognized, in accordance with the historical cost principle for valuing assets.

Two alternative approaches to the procedure described above have been suggested. The first approach would assign current fair values to a partially owned purchased subsidiary's identifiable net assets *only to the extent of the parent company's ownership interest therein.* Under this

Partially owned purchased subsidiary at date of business combination

POST CORPORATION AND SUBSIDIARY
Consolidating Balance Sheet Working Paper
April 30, Year 6

	Post Corporation	Sage Company	Consolidation eliminations increase (decrease)		Consolidated
Assets					
Cash	$ 75,000	$ 100,000			$ 175,000
Inventories	800,000	500,000	(a) $	26,000	1,326,000
Other current assets ..	550,000	215,000			765,000
Investment in subsidiary	1,192,250	-0-	(a)	(1,192,250)	-0-
Plant assets (net)	3,500,000	1,100,000	(a)	190,000	4,790,000
Leasehold	-0-	-0-	(a)	30,000	30,000
Goodwill	100,000	-0-	(a)	38,000	138,000
Total assets	$6,217,250	$1,915,000	$	(908,250)	$7,224,000
Liabilities & Stockholders Equity					
Income taxes payable	$ 100,000	$ 76,000			$ 176,000
Other liabilities	2,450,000	870,000			3,320,000
Minority interest in subsidiary	-0-	-0-	(a) $	60,750	60,750
Common stock, $1 par	1,057,000	-0-			1,057,000
Capital Stock, $10 par .	-0-	400,000	(a)	(400,000)	-0-
Paid-in capital in excess of par	1,560,250	235,000	(a)	(235,000)	1,560,250
Retained earnings	1,050,000	334,000	(a)	(334,000)	1,050,000
Total liabilities & stockholders' equity	$6,217,250	$1,915,000	$	(908,250)	$7,224,000

approach, $233,700 ($246,000 × 95% = $233,700) of the total difference between current fair value and carrying amount of Sage Company's identifiable net assets summarized on page 248 would be reflected in the aggregate debits to inventories, plant assets, and leasehold in the consolidation elimination for Post Corporation and subsidiary at April 30, Year 6. The minority interest would be based upon the *carrying amounts* of Sage Company's identifiable net assets, rather than upon their *current fair values,* and would be computed as follows: $969,000 ×

5% = $48,450. Goodwill would be $38,000, as in the preceding illustration. Supporters of this approach argue that current fair values of a combinee's identifiable net assets should be reflected in consolidated financial statements only to the extent (percentage) that they have been **purchased** by the **combinor**. The balance of the combinee's net assets, and the related minority interest in the net assets, should be reflected in consolidated financial statements at the **historical cost–based** carrying amounts.

The other alternative approach to valuing minority interest and goodwill is to obtain a current fair value for **100%** of a partially owned purchased subsidiary's **total** net assets, either through independent measurement of the minority interest or by **inference** from the cost of the parent company's investment in the subsidiary. Independent measurement of the minority interest might be accomplished by reference to quoted market prices of publicly traded securities owned by minority shareholders of the subsidiary. The computation of minority interest and goodwill of Sage Company by inference from the cost of Post Corporation's investment in Sage is illustrated below.

Computation of minority interest and goodwill of partially owned purchased subsidiary based upon implied total current fair value of subsidiary	

Total cost of Post Corporation's investment in Sage Company	$1,192,250
Post Corporation's percentage ownership of Sage Company	95%
Implied current fair value of 100% of Sage Company's total net assets ($1,192,250 ÷ 0.95)	$1,255,000
Minority interest ($1,255,000 × 5%)	$ 62,750
Goodwill ($1,255,000 − $1,215,000, the current fair value of Sage Company's **identifiable** net assets)	$ 40,000

Supporters of the above approach contend that a **single valuation method** should be used for **all** net assets of a purchased subsidiary—including goodwill—regardless of the existence of a minority interest in the subsidiary. They further maintain that the goodwill should be attributed to the **subsidiary,** rather than to the **parent company,** as is done for a wholly owned purchased subsidiary, in accordance with the theory of purchase accounting for a business combination.

Summarizing the three approaches for valuing minority interest and goodwill of a partially owned purchased subsidiary, we have the following amounts derived from the April 30, Year 6, business combination of Post Corporation and Sage Company:

Comparison of three approaches for valuing minority interest and goodwill of partially owned purchased subsidiary

	Total identifiable net assets	Minority interest	Goodwill
1 Identifiable net assets recognized at current fair value; minority interest based on identifiable net assets	$1,215,000	$60,750	$38,000
2 Identifiable net assets recognized at current fair value only to extent of parent company's interest; balance of net assets and minority interest reflected at carrying amounts	1,202,700*	48,450	38,000
3 Current fair value, through independent measurement or inference, assigned to total net assets of subsidiary, including goodwill	1,255,000	62,750	40,000

* $969,000 + $233,700 = $1,202,700

In recognition of the significant conceptual differences between the three alternative methods which have been advanced for measuring minority interest and goodwill relative to a partially owned purchased subsidiary, the FASB has included the issue in its *FASB Discussion Memorandum* entitled "An Analysis of Issues Related to Business Combinations and Purchased Intangibles." The authors have chosen to reflect, in subsequent chapters of this book, the method illustrated in the combination elimination on page 250, not for its conceptual superiority, but because it has substantial usage in current accounting practice.[3]

Footnote disclosure of consolidation policy

The "Summary of Significant Accounting Policies" footnote required by *APB Opinion No. 22,* "Disclosure of Accounting Policies," should include a description of consolidation policy reflected in consolidated financial statements. The following excerpt from a recent annual report of American Biltrite, Inc., is typical:

> *Principles of Consolidation*—The consolidated financial statements include the accounts of the Company and its subsidiaries, all of which are wholly owned. All significant intercompany accounts are eliminated upon consolidation.
>
> The excess of net assets of acquired subsidiaries over cost is being amortized over ten-year periods from their respective dates of acquisition.

[3] *FASB Discussion Memorandum,* "An Analysis of Issues Related to Accounting for Business Combinations and Purchased Intangibles," (Stamford: 1976), p. 107, par. 371.

Advantages and shortcomings of consolidated financial statements

Consolidated financial statements are useful principally to stockholders and prospective investors of the parent company. These users of consolidated financial statements are provided with comprehensive financial information concerning the economic unit represented by the parent company and its subsidiaries, without regard for legal separateness of the affiliates.

Creditors of each consolidated enterprise and minority shareholders of subsidiaries find only limited use for consolidated financial statements, because such statements do not show the financial position or operating results of the individual companies comprising the consolidated group. In addition, creditors of the constituent companies cannot ascertain the asset coverages for their respective claims. But perhaps the most telling criticism of consolidated financial statements in recent years has come from financial analysts. These critics have pointed out that consolidated financial statements of highly diversified companies are impossible to categorize into a single industry or product classification. Thus, say the financial analysts, consolidated financial statements of a conglomerate cannot be used for comparative purposes. The problem of financial reporting by highly diversified companies is considered in Chapter 12.

REVIEW QUESTIONS

1 The use of consolidated financial statements for reporting to stockholders is common. Under some conditions, however, it is the practice to exclude certain subsidiaries from consolidation. List the conditions under which subsidiaries often are excluded from consolidated financial statements.

2 The principal limitation of consolidated financial statements is their lack of separate information about the assets, liabilities, revenue, and expenses of the individual companies included in the consolidation. List the problems which the reader of consolidated financial statements encounters as a result of this limitation.

3 What criteria could influence a parent company in its decision to include a subsidiary in consolidated financial statements, or to exclude the subsidiary? Explain.

4 Discuss the similarities and dissimilarities between consolidated financial statements for parent company and subsidiaries, and combined financial statements for segments (branches) of a single legal entity.

5 Are consolidation eliminations recorded in the accounting records of the parent company or of the subsidiary? Explain.

6 If a business combination resulting in a parent-subsidiary relationship is accounted for as a purchase, the identifiable net assets of the subsidiary must be reflected at their current fair values in the consolidated balance sheet at the date of the business combination. Does this require the subsidiary to record the current fair values in its accounting records? Explain.

7 The controller of Premier Corporation, which has just become the parent of Screed Company in a purchase-type business combination, inquires if a consolidated statement of changes in financial position is required for the year ended on the date of the combination. What is your reply? Explain.

8 Differentiate between a **consolidating balance sheet** and a **consolidated balance sheet.**

9 Describe three methods which have been proposed for valuing minority interest and related goodwill in the consolidated balance sheet of a parent company and its partially owned purchased subsidiary.

EXERCISES

Ex. 6-1 Select the best answer for each of the following multiple-choice questions.

1 Which of the following is the best theoretical justification for consolidated financial statements?
  a In form the companies are one entity; in substance they are separate
  b In form the companies are separate; in substance they are one entity
  c In form and substance the companies are one entity
  d In form and substance the companies are separate

2 For purposes of consolidated financial statements, **controlling financial interest** is defined as ownership of:
  a At least 20% of an investee company's voting common stock
  b 50% or more of an investee company's voting common stock
  c Any amount of an investee company's voting common stock
  d More than 50% of an investee company's voting common stock

3 Consolidation eliminations are entered on:
  a Both the parent company's and the subsidiary's accounting records
  b Neither the parent company's nor the subsidiary's accounting records
  c The parent company's accounting records only
  d The subsidiary's accounting records only

4 At the date of a purchase business combination resulting in a parent-subsidiary relationship, the difference between current fair values and carrying amounts of the subsidiary's net assets is:
  a Reflected in a consolidation elimination
  b Recorded in the applicable asset and liability accounts of the subsidiary
  c Recorded in the applicable asset and liability accounts of the parent company
  d Accounted for in some other manner

5 Consolidated financial statements are intended primarily for the use of:
  a Stockholders of the parent company
  b Taxing authorities
  c Management of the parent company
  d Creditors of the parent company

Ex. 6-2 On November 1, Year 4, Panama Corporation issued 10,000 shares of its $10 par ($30 per share current fair value) common stock for 99 of the 100 outstanding shares of Salvador Company's $100 par capital stock, in a business combination qualifying for purchase accounting. Out-of-pocket costs of the business combination were as follows:

Legal fees and finder's fee associated with the business combination	$16,800
Costs incurred for SEC registration statement for Panama's common stock .	20,000
Total out-of-pocket costs of business combination	$36,800

On November 1, Year 4, the current fair values of Salvador Company's identifiable net assets were equal to their carrying amounts. On that date, Salvador's stockholders' equity consisted of the following:

Capital stock, $100 par	$ 10,000
Paid-in capital in excess of par...	140,000
Retained earnings	70,000
Total stockholders' equity...	$220,000

Prepare in good form the journal entry or entries in Panama Corporation's accounting records to record the business combination with Salvador Company.

Ex. 6-3 Combinor Corporation and Combinee Company have been operating separately for five years. Each company has a minimal amount of liabilities and a simple capital structure consisting solely of voting common stock. Combinor, in exchange for 40% of its unissued voting common stock, acquired 80% of the common stock of Combinee. This was a "tax-free" stock-for-stock (Type B) exchange for federal income tax purposes. Combinee's identifiable net assets had a current fair value of $800,000 and a carrying amount of $580,000. The current fair value of the Combinor stock issued in the business combination was $700,000.

Compute the minority interest in subsidiary and the goodwill which would appear in the consolidated balance sheet of Combinor Corporation and subsidiary, using three alternative methods of computation.

Ex. 6-4 Solvang Company's balance sheet on December 31, Year 6, was as follows:

SOLVANG COMPANY
Balance Sheet
December 31, Year 6

Assets

Cash	$ 100,000
Accounts receivable (net)	200,000
Inventories..	500,000
Plant assets (net)	900,000
Total assets	$1,700,000

Liabilities & Stockholders' Equity

Current liabilities	$ 300,000
Long-term debt	500,000
Common stock, $1 par	100,000
Paid-in capital in excess of par...	200,000
Retained earnings	600,000
Total liabilities & stockholders' equity	$1,700,000

On December 31, Year 6, Pismo Company purchased all the outstanding common stock of Solvang for $1,500,000 cash. On that date, the current fair value of Solvang's inventories was $450,000 and the current fair value of Solvang's plant assets was $1,000,000. The current fair values of all other assets and liabilities of Solvang were equal to their carrying amounts.

a Compute in good form the amount of goodwill which should appear in the December 31, Year 6, consolidated balance sheet of Pismo Company and subsidiary as a result of the business combination.

b Compute in good form the amount of consolidated retained earnings which should appear in the December 31, Year 6, consolidated balance sheet of Pismo Corporation and subsidiary, assuming that Pismo's unconsolidated balance sheet on that date showed retained earnings of $2,000,000.

Ex. 6-5 Port Corporation acquired 70% of the outstanding capital stock of Sayle Company on July 31, Year 8. The unconsolidated balance sheet of Port immediately after the business combination and the consolidated balance sheet of Port Corporation and subsidiary are as follows:

PORT CORPORATION AND SUBSIDIARY
Unconsolidated and Consolidated Balance Sheets
July 31, Year 8

	Unconsolidated	Consolidated
Assets		
Current assets..................................	$106,000	$146,000
Investment in subsidiary	100,000	-0-
Plant assets (net)	270,000	370,000
Goodwill	-0-	8,100
Total assets	$476,000	$524,100
Liabilities & Stockholders' Equity		
Current liabilities	$ 15,000	$ 28,000
Minority interest in subsidiary	-0-	35,100
Capital stock	350,000	350,000
Retained earnings	111,000	111,000
Total liabilities & stockholders' equity	$476,000	$524,100

Of the excess payment for the investment in Sayle Company, $10,000 was ascribed to undervaluation of Sayle's plant assets; the balance of the excess payment was ascribed to goodwill. Current assets of Sayle include a $2,000 receivable from Port which arose before the business combination.

a Compute in good form the total current assets on Sayle Company's separate balance sheet as of July 31, Year 8.

b Compute in good form the total stockholders' equity on Sayle Company's separate balance sheet as of July 31, Year 8.

Ex. 6-6 On page 258 are the January 1, Year 3, balance sheets of two companies prior to their business combination:

PALACE CORPORATION AND SLAYTON COMPANY
Balance Sheets

January 1, Year 3	Palace Corporation	Slayton Company
Assets		
Cash	$ 3,000	$ 100
Inventories (at fifo cost, which approximates current fair value)	2,000	200
Plant assets (net).......................................	5,000	700*
Total assets	$10,000	$1,000
Liabilities & Stockholders' Equity		
Current liabilities......................................	$ 600	$ 100
Common stock, $1 par	1,000	100
Paid-in capital in excess of par	3,000	200
Retained earnings......................................	5,400	600
Total liabilities & stockholders' equity	$10,000	$1,000

*Current fair value at Jan. 1, Year 3, is $1,500.

a On January 1, Year 3, Palace Corporation acquired all the outstanding common stock of Slayton Company by paying $2,000 cash in a business combination qualifying for purchase accounting. Compute in good form the amount of goodwill which should appear in the consolidated balance sheet of Palace Corporation and subsidiary at January 1, Year 3.

b On January 1, Year 3, Palace Corporation acquired all the outstanding common stock of Slayton Company by paying $1,500 cash in a business combination qualifying for purchase accounting. Compute in good form the amount of plant assets which should appear in the consolidated balance sheet of Palace Corporation and subsidiary at January 1, Year 3.

Ex. 6-7 The consolidation elimination working paper at August 31, Year 5, for the consolidating balance sheet of Peachtree Corporation and Savannah Company is set forth below. As of the close of business that date, Peachtree Corporation acquired most of the outstanding capital stock of Savannah Company for cash.

PEACHTREE CORPORATION AND SUBSIDIARY
Consolidation Elimination Working Paper
August 31, Year 5

Capital Stock—Savannah	60,000	
Paid-in Capital in Excess of Par—Savannah	35,250	
Retained Earnings—Savannah	50,100	
Inventories—Savannah	3,900	
Plant Assets (net)—Savannah	28,500	
Patent—Savannah	4,500	
Goodwill—Peachtree	5,280	
Investment in Subsidiary—Peachtree		165,660
Minority Interest in Subsidiary		21,870

To eliminate intercompany investment and equity accounts of subsidiary at date of business combination; to allocate excess of cost over current fair values of identifiable net assets acquired to goodwill; and to establish minority interest in subsidiary at date of business combination accounted for as a purchase.

Answer the following questions (supporting computations should be in good form):

a What percentage of the outstanding capital stock of the subsidiary was acquired by the parent company?

b What was the aggregate current fair value of the subsidiary's identifiable net assets at August 31, Year 5?

c What value would be assigned to goodwill under the method which infers a total current fair value for the subsidiary's total net assets, based on the parent company's investment?

d What value would be assigned to minority interest in subsidiary under the method described in **c**?

Ex. 6-8 The condensed individual and consolidated balance sheets of Pawnee Corporation and its subsidiary, Sioux Company, at the date of their business combination appear below:

PAWNEE CORPORATION AND SUBSIDIARY
Individual and Consolidated Balance Sheets
June 30, Year 3

	Pawnee Corporation	Sioux Company	Consolidated
Assets			
Cash	$ 100,000	$ 40,000	$ 140,000
Inventories	500,000	90,000	610,000
Other current assets	250,000	60,000	310,000
Investment in subsidiary	420,000	-0-	-0-
Plant assets (net)	1,000,000	360,000	1,440,000
Goodwill	100,000	-0-	100,000
Total assets	$2,370,000	$550,000	$2,600,000
Liabilities & Stockholders' Equity			
Income taxes payable	$ 40,000	$ 35,000	$ 75,000
Other liabilities	580,600	195,000	775,600
Common stock	1,000,000	200,000	1,000,000
Paid-in capital in excess of par	429,400	210,000	429,400
Retained earnings (deficit)	320,000	(90,000)	320,000
Total liabilities & stockholders' equity .	$2,370,000	$550,000	$2,600,000

Reconstruct, in good form, the consolidation elimination working paper indicated by the above data.

SHORT CASES FOR ANALYSIS AND DECISION

Case 6-1 On May 31, Year 6, Plotke Company purchased at 100, $500,000 principal amount of Slotkin Company's 10-year, convertible debentures due May 31, Year 11. The debentures were convertible into 50,000 shares of Slotkin Company's voting common stock ($1 par), of which 40,000 shares were issued and outstanding May 31, Year 6. The controller of Plotke Company, who also is one of three Plotke officers who serve on the five-member board of directors of Slotkin Company, proposes to issue consolidated financial statements for Plotke Company and Slotkin Company as of May 31, Year 6.

Instructions Do you agree with the Plotke controller's proposal? Explain, including in your discussion appropriate financial statement disclosure of the "related party" status of Plotke Company and Slotkin Company.

Case 6-2 Because of irreconcilable differences of opinion, a dissenting group within the board of directors and management of West Company resigned and formed Yale Company to purchase a manufacturing division of West Company. After negotiation of the agreement but just before the closing and actual transfer of the property, Jacob Goode, a minority shareholder of West, notified Yale's directors that a prior stockholders' agreement with West empowered Goode to prevent the sale. The minority shareholder's claim was acknowledged by Yale's board of directors. Yale's board then organized Zulu Company to acquire the minority shareholder's interest in West for $75,000, and Yale advanced the cash to Zulu. Yale exercised control over Zulu as a subsidiary corporation with common directors and officers. Zulu paid the minority shareholder $75,000 (about twice the current fair value of his West stock) for his interest in West. Yale then purchased the manufacturing division from West.

Instructions
a Should the financial statements of Yale Company and Zulu Company be consolidated? Discuss.
b Assume that unconsolidated financial statements are prepared. Discuss the propriety of treating the $75,000 expenditure in the financial statements of Yale Company as:
   (1) An account receivable from Zulu Company
   (2) An investment in Zulu Company
   (3) Part of the cost of plant assets
   (4) A loss

Case 6-3 On January 2, Year 2, the board of directors of Pomerania Corporation assigned to a voting trust 15,000 shares of the 60,000 shares of Silesia Company capital stock owned by Pomerania. The trustee of the voting trust controls 40,000 of Silesia Company's 105,000 shares of issued capital stock, of which 5,000 shares are in Silesia's treasury. The term of the voting trust is three years.

Instructions Are consolidated financial statements appropriate for Pomerania Corporation and Silesia Company for the three years ending December 31, Year 4? Explain.

Case 6-4 In Year 6, Perry Corporation, a chain of discount stores, embarked upon a program of business combinations with its suppliers. On May 31, Year 6, the close of its fiscal year, Perry Corporation paid $8,500,000 cash and issued 100,000 shares of its common stock (current fair value $20 per share) for all 10,000 outstanding shares of capital stock of Sidney Company. Sidney Company was a furniture manufacturer whose products were featured in Perry Corporation's stores. Total stockholders' equity of Sidney Company on May 31, Year 6, was $9,000,000. Out-of-pocket costs attributable to the business combination itself (as opposed to the SEC registration statement for the 100,000 shares of Perry Corporation common stock) paid by Perry Corporation May 31, Year 6, totaled $100,000.

In the consolidated balance sheet of Perry Corporation and subsidiary at May 31, Year 6, the $1,600,000 difference between the parent company's cost and the carrying amounts of the subsidiary's net assets was allocated in accordance with purchase accounting as follows:

Inventories	$ 250,000
Plant assets	850,000
Patents..	300,000
Goodwill	200,000
Total excess of cost over carrying amounts of subsidiary's net assets	$1,600,000

Under terms of the indenture for a $1,000,000 debenture liability of Sidney Company, Perry Corporation is obligated to maintain Sidney Company as a separate corporation and to issue a separate balance sheet for Sidney each May 31. Perry Corporation's controller contends that Sidney Company's balance sheet for May 31, Year 6, should show net assets of $10,600,000—their cost to Perry Corporation. Sidney Company's controller disputes this valuation, claiming that generally accepted accounting principles require issuance of a **historical cost** balance sheet for Sidney Company at May 31, Year 6.

Instructions

a Present arguments in favor of the Perry controller's position.
b Present arguments in favor of the Sidney controller's position.
c Which position do you approve? Explain.

Case 6-5 On July 31, Year 5, Phillips Corporation transferred all right, title, and interest in several of its current research and development projects to Carl Stabler, sole shareholder of Stabler Company, in exchange for 55 of the 100 shares of Stabler Company capital stock owned by Carl Stabler. On the same date, Martha Morgan, who is not related to Phillips Corporation, Stabler Company, or Carl Stabler, purchased at $1,000 per share the remaining 45 shares of Stabler Company capital stock owned by Carl Stabler. Carl Stabler notified the directors of Phillips Corporation of his sale of the stock to Morgan.

Because Phillips Corporation had expensed the costs related to the research and development costs as the costs were incurred, Phillips' controller prepared the following journal entry to record the business combination with Stabler Company:

Investment in Subsidiary (55 shares × $1,000)	55,000	
Gain on Disposal of Intangible Assets		55,000

To record transfer of research and development projects to Carl Stabler in exchange for 55 shares of Stabler Company capital stock. Valuation of the investment is based upon an unrelated cash sale of Stabler Company stock on this date.

Instructions

a Do you concur with the above journal entry? Explain.
b Should the $55,000 gain appear in consolidated financial statements of Phillips Corporation and subsidiary as of July 31, Year 5? Explain.

PROBLEMS

6-6 As of the close of business September 30, Year 1, Poe Corporation issued 100,000 shares of its $5 par common stock (current fair value $12 per share) for 18,800 shares of the outstanding $20 par capital stock of Stowe Company. The $150,000 out-of-pocket costs of the business combination paid by Poe Corporation on September 30, Year 1, were allocable as follows: 60% to legal fees and finder's fee directly related to the business combination, and 40% to the SEC registration statement for Poe Corporation common stock issued in the business combination.

Immediately prior to the business combination, stockholders' equity accounts of the two companies were as follows:

	Poe Corporation	Stowe Company
Common stock or capital stock	$4,000,000	$ 400,000
Paid-in capital in excess of par	1,500,000	-0-
Retained earnings	3,000,000	700,000
Total stockholders' equity	$8,500,000	$1,100,000

Income tax effects, if any, may be ignored.

Instructions Prepare in good form Poe Corporation's journal entries to record the business combination with Stowe Company as a purchase.

6-7 On July 31, Year 10, Pon Corporation issued 20,000 shares of its $2 par common stock (current fair value $10 per share) for all 5,000 shares of outstanding $5 par capital stock of Spence Company, which is to remain a separate corporation. Out-of-pocket costs of the business combination, paid by Pon Corporation on July 31, Year 10, are shown below:

Finder's fee and legal fees related to the business combination	$20,000
Costs associated with SEC registration statement for Pon Corporation stock	10,000
Total out-of-pocket costs of business combination	$30,000

Spence Company's condensed balance sheet at July 31, Year 10, prior to the business combination, follows:

SPENCE COMPANY
Balance Sheet
July 31, Year 10

Assets

Current assets	$150,000
Plant assets (net)	300,000
Goodwill	20,000
Total assets	$470,000

(continued)

Liabilities & Stockholders' Equity

Current liabilities	*$120,000*
Long-term debt	*200,000*
Capital stock, $5 par	*25,000*
Paid-in capital in excess of par	*50,000*
Retained earnings	*75,000*
Total liabilities & stockholders' equity	*$470,000*

Spence Company's goodwill arose in Spence's July 31, Year 4, purchase of the net assets of Taylor Company.

Spence Company's assets and liabilities having July 31, Year 10, current fair values different from their carrying amounts were as follows:

	Current fair value	Carrying amount
Inventories	*$ 65,000*	*$ 60,000*
Plant assets (net)	*340,000*	*300,000*
Long-term debt	*190,000*	*200,000*

There were no intercompany transactions prior to the business combination.

Instructions

a Prepare Pon Corporation's journal entries at July 31, Year 10, in good form, to record the business combination with Spence Company as a purchase.

b Prepare the consolidation elimination working paper, in good form, for the consolidating balance sheet working paper of Pon Corporation and subsidiary at July 31, Year 10.

6-8 On October 31, Year 4, Pizula Corporation acquired 93% of the outstanding capital stock of Sills Company in exchange for 50,000 shares of Pizula Corporation $2 par ($10 current fair value per share) common stock. Out-of-pocket costs of the business combination paid by Pizula Corporation on October 31, Year 4, were as follows:

Legal fees and finder's fee related to the business combination	*$34,750*
Costs associated with SEC registration statement for Pizula Corporation stock	*55,250*
Total out-of-pocket costs of business combination	*$90,000*

There were no intercompany transactions between the two companies prior to the business combination. Sills Company is to be a subsidiary of Pizula Corporation.

Individual balance sheets of the two companies prior to the business combination are presented on page 264.

PIZULA CORPORATION AND SILLS COMPANY
Balance Sheets
October 31, Year 4

	Pizula Corporation	Sills Company
Assets		
Cash	$ 250,000	$ 150,000
Inventories	860,000	600,000
Other current assets	500,000	260,000
Plant assets (net)	3,400,000	1,500,000
Patents	-0-	80,000
Total assets	$5,010,000	$2,590,000
Liabilities & Stockholders' Equity		
Income taxes payable	$ 40,000	$ 60,000
Other current liabilities	390,000	854,000
Long-term debt	950,000	1,240,000
Common stock, $2	1,500,000	-0-
Capital stock, $10 par	-0-	100,000
Paid-in capital in excess of par	1,500,000	-0-
Retained earnings	630,000	336,000
Total liabilities & stockholders' equity	$5,010,000	$2,590,000

Other information
(1) Current fair values of Sills Company's identifiable net assets were the same as their carrying amounts at October 31, Year 4, except for the following:

Inventories	$ 620,000
Plant assets (net)	1,550,000
Patents	95,000
Long-term debt	1,225,000

(2) Income taxes, if any, may be ignored.

Instructions
a Prepare Pizula Corporation's journal entries at October 31, Year 4, in good form, to record the business combination with Sills Company as a purchase.
b Prepare the consolidation elimination working paper in good form, for October 31, Year 4, consolidating balance sheet working paper of Pizula Corporation and subsidiary.

6-9 On June 30, Year 7, Paragon Corporation issued a $300,000 note payable, due $60,000 per year with interest at 10% beginning June 30, Year 8, for 8,500 of the 10,000 outstanding shares of $10 par capital stock of Superb Company. Legal fees of $20,000 incurred by Paragon Corporation in connection with the business combination were paid June 30, Year 7.

Balance sheets of the two companies, immediately following the business combination, are presented on page 265.

PARAGON CORPORATION AND SUPERB COMPANY
Balance Sheets
June 30, Year 7

	Paragon Corporation	Superb Company
Assets		
Cash	$ 80,000	$ 60,000
Accounts receivable (net)	170,000	90,000
Inventories	370,000	120,000
Investment in subsidiary	320,000	-0-
Plant assets (net)	570,000	240,000
Goodwill	50,000	-0-
Total assets	$1,560,000	$510,000
Liabilities & Stockholders' Equity		
Accounts payable	$ 220,000	$120,000
Income taxes payable	100,000	40,000
10% note payable, due $60,000 annually	300,000	-0-
Capital stock, $10 par	250,000	100,000
Paid-in capital in excess of par	400,000	130,000
Retained earnings	290,000	120,000
Total liabilities & stockholders' equity	$1,560,000	$510,000

Other information
(1) An independent audit of Superb Company's financial statements for the year ended June 30, Year 7, disclosed that Superb's July 1, Year 6, inventories had been overstated $60,000 due to double counting; and that Superb had omitted from its June 30, Year 7, inventories merchandise shipped F.O.B. shipping point by a vendor June 30, Year 7, at an invoiced amount of $35,000. The effects of Superb's inventories errors are not reflected in Superb's balance sheet above.
(2) Both Paragon Corporation and Superb Company had combined federal and state income tax rates of 60%.
(3) Current fair values of Superb's net assets reflected in Superb's balance sheet above differed from carrying amounts as follows:

	Current fair value
Inventories	$150,000
Plant assets (net)	280,000

Instructions
a Prepare in good form the journal entry or entries to correct the inventories misstatements in Superb Company's financial statements for the year ended June 30, Year 7. Superb's accounting records have been closed for the year ended June 30, Year 7.
b Prepare a consolidation elimination working paper and a consolidating balance sheet working paper for Paragon Corporation and subsidiary at June 30, Year 7. The amounts for Superb Company should reflect the adjusting journal entry or entries prepared in **a,** above.

7

CONSOLIDATED FINANCIAL STATEMENTS: AT DATE OF POOLING BUSINESS COMBINATION

Consolidated financial statements prepared as of the date of a pooling business combination differ in several respects from consolidated financial statements as of the date of a purchase business combination. Among these differences are the following:

1 All four basic financial statements of the parent company and pooled subsidiary are consolidated as of the date of a pooling business combination, in accordance with the theory that a pooling is a combining of past and present shareholder interests. In contrast, only a consolidated balance sheet is appropriate at the date of a purchase business combination.

2 Current fair values of the subsidiary's net assets are not reflected in the consolidated balance sheet for a pooled subsidiary as they are for a purchased subsidiary.

3 Consolidated retained earnings at the date of a pooling business combination include the parent company's share of the subsidiary's retained earnings as of that date. In contrast, only the amount of the parent company's retained earnings is included in consolidated retained earnings at the date of a purchase business combination.

We shall now describe and illustrate (1) the consolidation of a wholly owned pooled subsidiary, and (2) the consolidation of a partially owned pooled subsidiary.

CONSOLIDATION OF WHOLLY OWNED POOLED SUBSIDIARY AT DATE OF BUSINESS COMBINATION

To illustrate the consolidated financial statements for a wholly owned pooled subsidiary at the date of the business combination, we shall return to the Palm Corporation–Starr Company business combination described in Chapter 6 (pages 236–237) and assume that the business combination qualified for pooling accounting rather than for purchase accounting. As indicated in Chapter 6, on December 31, Year 10, Palm Corporation issued 10,000 shares of its $10 par common stock for all the outstanding capital stock of Starr Company, and paid out-of-pocket costs of $85,000 in connection with the business combination. Separate financial statements of the two companies prior to the business combination appear on page 268.

The following journal entries would be made by Palm Corporation as of December 31, Year 10, to record the combination as a pooling:

Combinor's journal entries for pooling business combination

Investment in Subsidiary ($200,000 + $58,000 + $132,000) . . .	390,000	
Common Stock (10,000 shares × $10)		100,000
Paid-in Capital in Excess of Par ($258,000 − $100,000)		158,000
Retained Earnings of Subsidiary		132,000

To record issuance of 10,000 shares of common stock for all the outstanding capital stock of Starr Company in a business combination accounted for as a pooling.

Expenses of Business Combination	85,000	
Cash		85,000

To record payment of out-of-pocket costs of business combination with Starr Company.

The first of the preceding journal entries records Palm Corporation's investment in Starr Company's capital stock at the **carrying amount** of Starr's stockholders' equity on December 31, Year 10 ($200,000 + $58,000 + $132,000 = $390,000). In addition, a Retained Earnings of Subsidiary account is established to record the amount of Starr Company's retained earnings at December 31, Year 10. This separate account emphasizes that Starr Company's retained earnings are not a source of dividends to Palm Corporation shareholders, as is often true in a statutory merger. The first journal entry thus reflects the underlying theory of pooling accounting—the **combining of stockholder interests** concept—while recognizing the separate corporate identity (in a legal sense) of the pooled subsidiary.

In the second journal entry shown above, all out-of-pocket costs of the business combination are recorded as expenses. As explained in

PALM CORPORATION AND STARR COMPANY
Separate Financial Statements
For Year Ended December 31, Year 10

	Palm Corporation	Starr Company
Income Statements		
Revenue		
Net sales	$ 990,000	$600,000
Interest revenue	10,000	-0-
Total revenue	$1,000,000	$600,000
Costs and expenses		
Cost of goods sold	$ 635,000	$410,000
Selling, general, and administrative expenses	80,000	30,000
Interest expense	50,000	30,000
Income taxes expense	141,000	78,000
Total costs and expenses	$ 906,000	$548,000
Net income	$ 94,000	$ 52,000
Statements of Retained Earnings		
Retained earnings, Jan. 1, Year 10	$ 65,000	$100,000
Net income	94,000	52,000
Subtotal..	$ 159,000	$152,000
Dividends	25,000	20,000
Retained earnings, Dec. 31, Year 10	$ 134,000	$132,000
Balance Sheets		
Assets		
Cash	$ 100,000	$ 40,000
Inventories	150,000	110,000
Other current assets	110,000	70,000
Receivable from Starr Company	25,000	-0-
Plant assets (net)	450,000	300,000
Patent	-0-	20,000
Total assets..................................	$ 835,000	$540,000
Liabilities & Stockholders' Equity		
Payable to Palm Corporation	$ -0-	$ 25,000
Income taxes payable	66,000	10,000
Other liabilities	285,000	115,000
Common stock, $10 par	300,000	-0-
Capital stock, $5 par	-0-	200,000
Paid-in capital in excess of par	50,000	58,000
Retained earnings.............................	134,000	132,000
Total liabilities & stockholders' equity	$ 835,000	$540,000

Chapter 5, this procedure is required in a pooling business combination.

Although Palm Corporation's expenses are increased in the second journal entry on page 267, there is no adjustment of Palm's income taxes expense or liability accounts. Costs of a pooling business combination expensed for financial accounting are not deductible for income tax purposes. The U.S. Treasury Department considers such costs to be capital expenditures, rather than expenditures which may be either deducted when incurred or amortized over a period of years. The Treasury Department's position is contained in regulations for amortizable organizational expenditures.[1]

After the journal entries on page 267 have been posted, the affected financial statement items for Palm Corporation have the following balances:

Balances of financial statement items of combinor affected by business combination	

Selling, general, and administrative expenses ($80,000 + $85,000)*	$165,000
Net Income ($94,000 − $85,000)	9,000
Cash ($100,000 − $85,000)	15,000
Investment in subsidiary	390,000
Common stock, $10 par ($300,000 + $100,000)	400,000
Paid-in capital in excess of par ($50,000 + $158,000)	208,000
Retained earnings ($134,000 − $85,000)	49,000
Retained earnings of subsidiary	132,000

Controlling account for Expenses of Business Combination account.

In a pooling business combination involving a wholly owned subsidiary, the Investment in Subsidiary account is similar to the Investment in Branch account illustrated in Chapter 4 for a home office. However, the subsidiary's three stockholders' equity accounts (which total $390,000), rather than a single Home Office (or Parent Company) account, offset Palm Corporation's Investment in Subsidiary account.

Consolidating Financial Statements Working Paper When a business combination qualifies for pooling accounting, all four basic financial statements are consolidated for the period ended on the date of the combination. This is consistent with the assumption that a pooling is a combining of stockholder interests, rather than an acquisition of assets.

The consolidating financial statements working paper and the related consolidation eliminations working paper for Palm Corporation and subsidiary for the year ended December 31, Year 10, are presented on pages 271–272. All intercompany transactions and balances, including $10,000 interest received during Year 10 by Palm Corporation on its cash ad-

[1] U.S. Treasury Regulations, Section 1.248-1 (b).

vances to Starr Company, are eliminated in the process of consolidation.

In reviewing the consolidating financial statements working papers for a pooling business combination, the student should note the following points:

1 A separate consolidating statement of changes in financial position is not illustrated at this point in order to focus attention on more fundamental issues. Once the consolidated balance sheet, consolidated income statement, and consolidated statement of retained earnings are available, a consolidated statement of changes in financial position can be prepared from comparative consolidated statements and supplementary data relating to depreciation, amortization, and the like. A consolidated statement of changes in financial position is illustrated in Chapter 11.

2 Intercompany revenue and expenses are placed on the same line in adjacent columns of the consolidating income statement, so that they are eliminated without a formal consolidation elimination. There are no other intercompany items that require use of the Consolidation Eliminations column in the consolidating income statement.

3 Each pair of financial statements is consolidated in turn, in the sequence of the conventional accounting cycle. Thus, consolidated net income is carried forward to the consolidating statement of retained earnings, and the amount of consolidated retained earnings is carried forward to the consolidating balance sheet.

4 Dividends declared by Starr Company **are not eliminated** in the consolidating statement of retained earnings, because the dividends were paid to the former shareholders of Starr Company, not to Palm Corporation.

5 Consolidated retained earnings includes the retained earnings of both Palm Corporation and Starr Company, in accordance with pooling theory of accounting for a business combination. Thus, the separate Retained Earnings of Subsidiary account of Palm Corporation is eliminated, so that the individual Retained Earnings accounts of both parent company and subsidiary may be combined.

Consolidated Financial Statements The formal consolidated financial statements for Palm Corporation and subsidiary consist of the amounts in the Consolidated columns of the consolidating financial statements working paper. Because all intercompany transactions and balances have been eliminated in the computation of the consolidated amounts, these balances reflect only the transactions of Palm Corporation and Starr Company with **outside parties.**

There are no unusual features of a consolidated income statement or a consolidated balance sheet in a pooling business combination involving a wholly owned subsidiary. However, because a pooling represents an accounting change of the type classified as a **change in the reporting entity,**[2] the consolidated statement of retained earnings of Palm Corporation and subsidiary for the year ended December 31, Year 10, is illustrated at the top of page 273.

---

[2] *APB Opinion No. 20,* "Accounting Changes," AICPA (New York: 1971), p. 388.

Wholly owned pooled subsidiary at date of business combination

PALM CORPORATION AND SUBSIDIARY
Consolidating Financial Statements Working Paper
For Year Ended December 31, Year 10

	Palm Corporation	Starr Company	Consolidation eliminations increase (decrease)	Consolidated
Income Statement				
Revenue				
Net sales	$ 990,000	$600,000		$1,590,000
Intercompany revenue				
(expense)	10,000	(10,000)		-0-
Total revenue	$1,000,000	$590,000		$1,590,000
Cost and expenses				
Cost of goods sold	$ 635,000	$410,000		$1,045,000
Selling, general, and				
administrative expenses	165,000	30,000		195,000
Interest expense	50,000	20,000		70,000
Income taxes expense	141,000	78,000		219,000
Total costs and expenses . . .	$ 991,000	$538,000		$1,529,000
Net income	$ 9,000	$ 52,000		$ 61,000
Statement of Retained Earnings				
Retained earnings, Jan. 1,				
Year 10	$ 65,000	$100,000		$ 165,000
Net income	9,000	52,000		61,000
Subtotal	$ 74,000	$152,000		$ 226,000
Dividends	25,000	20,000		45,000
Retained earnings, Dec. 31,				
Year 10	$ 49,000	$132,000		$ 181,000
Balance Sheet				
Assets				
Cash	$ 15,000	$ 40,000		$ 55,000
Inventories	150,000	110,000		260,000
Other current assets	110,000	70,000		180,000
Intercompany receivable				
(payable)	25,000	(25,000)		-0-
Investment in subsidiary	390,000	-0-	(a) $(390,000)	-0-
Plant assets (net)	450,000	300,000		750,000
Patent	-0-	20,000		20,000
Total assets	$1,140,000	$515,000	$(390,000)	$1,265,000

(continued)

Wholly owned pooled subsidiary at date of business combination

PALM CORPORATION AND SUBSIDIARY
Consolidating Financial Statements Working Paper
For Year Ended December 31, Year 10 (continued)

	Palm Corporation	Starr Company	Consolidation eliminations increase (decrease)	Consolidated
Liabilities & Stockholders' Equity				
Income taxes payable	$ 66,000	$ 10,000		$ 76,000
Other liabilities	285,000	115,000		400,000
Common stock, $10 par	400,000	-0-		400,000
Capital stock, $5 par	-0-	200,000	(a) $(200,000)	-0-
Paid-in capital in excess of par	208,000	58,000	(a) (58,000)	208,000
Retained earnings	49,000	132,000		181,000
Retained earnings of subsidiary	132,000	-0-	(a) (132,000)	-0-
Total liabilities & stockholders' equity	$1,140,000	$515,000	$(390,000)	$1,265,000

Wholly owned pooled subsidiary at date of business combination

PALM CORPORATION AND SUBSIDIARY
Consolidation Eliminations Working Paper
December 31, Year 10

(a) Capital Stock—Starr 200,000
    Paid-in Capital in Excess of Par—Starr 58,000
    Retained Earnings of Subsidiary—Palm 132,000
        Investment in Subsidiary—Palm 390,000
    To eliminate intercompany investment and related accounts for stockholders' equity of subsidiary at date of business combination.

The "adjustment to reflect pooling of interests with Starr Company" in the statement on page 273 represents the retroactive application of the pooling accounting method to include Starr Company's beginning-of-year retained earnings of $100,000 with the retained earnings of Palm Corporation at the beginning of the year.

PALM CORPORATION AND SUBSIDIARY
Consolidated Statement of Retained Earnings
For Year Ended December 31, Year 10

Retained earnings, Jan. 1, Year 10:

As previously reported		$ 65,000
Adjustment to reflect pooling of interests with Starr Company		100,000
As restated		$165,000
Net income		61,000
Subtotal		$226,000
Dividends:		
Palm Corporation ($0.83⅓ per share)	$25,000	
Starr Company, prior to business combination	20,000	45,000
Retained earnings, Dec. 31, Year 10		$181,000

CONSOLIDATION OF PARTIALLY OWNED POOLED SUBSIDIARY AT DATE OF BUSINESS COMBINATION

Under the assumption that the Post Corporation–Sage Company business combination described in Chapter 6 (pages 245–246) qualified for pooling accounting rather than for purchase accounting, it will be used to illustrate consolidated financial statements for a partially owned pooled subsidiary at the date of the business combination. As indicated in Chapter 6, on April 30, Year 6, Post Corporation issued 57,000 shares of its common stock in exchange for 38,000 of the 40,000 outstanding shares of Sage Company's capital stock, and paid $125,000 out-of-pocket costs of the business combination. Separate financial statements of the two companies prior to the business combination appear below.

POST CORPORATION AND SAGE COMPANY
Separate Financial Statements
For Year Ended April 30, Year 6

	Post Corporation	Sage Company
Income Statements		
Net sales	$5,500,000	$1,000,000
Costs and expenses		
Costs of goods sold	$3,850,000	$ 650,000
Selling, general, and administrative expenses ...	600,000	100,000
Interest expense	75,000	40,000
Income taxes expense	585,000	126,000
Total costs and expenses	$5,110,000	$ 916,000
Net income	$ 390,000	$ 84,000

(continued)

POST CORPORATION AND SAGE COMPANY
Separate Financial Statements
For Year Ended April 30, Year 6 (continued)

Statements of Retained Earnings	Post Corporation	Sage Company
Retained earnings, May 1, Year 5	$ 810,000	$ 250,000
Net income	390,000	84,000
Subtotal	$1,200,000	$ 334,000
Dividends	150,000	-0-
Retained earnings, Apr. 30, Year 6	$1,050,000	$ 334,000

Balance Sheets

Assets		
Cash	$ 200,000	$ 100,000
Inventories...................................	800,000	500,000
Other current assets	550,000	215,000
Plant assets (net)	3,500,000	1,100,000
Goodwill......................................	100,000	-0-
Total assets	$5,150,000	$1,915,000

Liabilities & Stockholders' Equity		
Income taxes payable	$ 100,000	$ 76,000
Other liabilities................................	2,450,000	870,000
Common stock, $1 par	1,000,000	-0-
Capital stock, $10 par	-0-	400,000
Paid-in capital in excess of par................	550,000	235,000
Retained earnings	1,050,000	334,000
Total liabilities & stockholders' equity	$5,150,000	$1,915,000

Post Corporation's April 30, Year 6, journal entries to record the business combination with Sage Company as a pooling are presented below:

Combinor's journal entries for pooling business combination

Investment in Subsidiary [($400,000 + $235,000 + $334,000) × 95%]	920,550	
Common Stock (57,000 shares × $1)		57,000
Paid-in Capital in Excess of Par [($635,000 × 95%) − $57,000]		546,250
Retained Earnings of Subsidiary ($334,000 × 95%)		317,300

To record issuance of 57,000 shares of common stock for 38,000 of the 40,000 shares of outstanding capital stock of Sage Company in a business combination accounted for as a pooling.

Expenses of Business Combination	125,000	
Cash		125,000

To record payment of out-of-pocket costs of business combination with Sage Company.

Note that the first of the above journal entries records Post Corporation's **95% share** of the net assets (carrying amount $969,000) and retained earnings of Sage Company.

As pointed out on page 269, costs of a business combination expensed for financial accounting are not deductible or amortizable for income taxes. Thus, although the second of the above journal entries increases Post Corporation's expenses, Post's income taxes expense and liability accounts are not adjusted. The costs of the business combination represent a **permanent difference,** rather than a **timing difference,** between Post's pre-tax accounting income and taxable income. There is no income tax advantage to a pooling corporation for costs of the business combination, just as a purchasing corporation receives no income tax benefits from the amortization of purchased goodwill.

After the preceding journal entries have been posted, Post Corporation's relevant financial statement items have the following balances:

Balances of financial statement items of combinor affected by business combination

Selling, general, and administrative expenses ($600,000 + $125,000)* ..	$ 725,000
Net income ($390,000 − $125,000)	265,000
Cash ($200,000 − $125,000)	75,000
Investment in subsidiary	920,550
Common stock ($1,000,000 + $57,000)	1,057,000
Paid-in capital in excess of par ($550,000 + $546,250)	1,096,250
Retained earnings ($1,050,000 − $125,000)	925,000
Retained earnings of subsidiary	317,300

* Controlling account for Expenses of Business Combination account.

Consolidating Financial Statements Working Paper   The April 30, Year 6, consolidating financial statements working paper and related consolidation eliminations working paper for Post Corporation and subsidiary are set forth on pages 276–277.

Partially owned pooled subsidiary at date of business combination

POST CORPORATION AND SUBSIDIARY
Consolidating Financial Statements Working Paper
For Year Ended April 30, Year 6

	Post Corporation	Sage Company	Consolidation eliminations increase (decrease)	Consolidated
Income Statement				
Net sales	$5,500,000	$1,000,000		$6,500,000
Cost and expenses				
Cost of goods sold	$3,850,000	$ 650,000		$4,500,000
Selling, general, and ad-				
ministrative expenses	725,000	100,000		825,000
Interest expense	75,000	40,000		115,000
Income taxes expense	585,000	126,000		711,000
Minority interest in net				
income of subsidiary	-0-	-0-	(b) $ 4,200	4,200
Total costs and expenses ..	$5,235,000	$ 916,000	$ 4,200	$6,155,200
Net income	$ 265,000	$ 84,000	$(4,200)	$ 344,800
Statement of Retained Earnings				
Retained earnings, May 1,				
Year 5	$ 810,000	$ 250,000	(a) $(12,500)	$1,047,500
Net income	265,000	84,000	(4,200)	344,800
Subtotal	$1,075,000	$ 334,000	$(16,700)	$1,392,300
Dividends	150,000	-0-		150,000
Retained earnings, Apr. 30,				
Year 6	$ 925,000	$ 334,000	$(16,700)	$1,242,300
Balance Sheet				
Assets				
Cash	$ 75,000	$ 100,000		$ 175,000
Inventories	800,000	500,000		1,300,000
Other current assets	550,000	215,000		765,000
Investment in subsidiary	920,550	-0-	(a) $(920,550)	-0-
Plant assets (net)	3,500,000	1,100,000		4,600,000
Goodwill	100,000	-0-		100,000
Total assets	$5,945,550	$1,915,000	$(920,550)	$6,940,000

(continued)

POST CORPORATION AND SUBSIDIARY
Consolidating Financial Statements Working Paper
For Year Ended April 30, Year 6 (continued)

	Post Corporation	Sage Company	Consolidation eliminations increase (decrease)	Consolidated
Liabilities & Stockholders' Equity				
Income taxes payable	$ 100,000	$ 76,000		$ 176,000
Other liabilities	2,450,000	870,000		3,320,000
Minority interest in				
subsidiary	-0-	-0-	(a) $ 44,250	
			(b) 4,200	48,450
Common stock, $1 par	1,057,000	-0-	-0-	1,057,000
Capital stock, $10 par	-0-	400,000	(a) (400,000)	-0-
Paid-in capital in excess of				
par	1,096,250	235,000	(a) (235,000)	1,096,250
Retained earnings	925,000	334,000	(16,700)	1,242,300
Retained earnings of sub-				
sidiary	317,300	-0-	(a) (317,300)	-0-
Total liabilities &				
stockholders' equity	$5,945,550	$1,915,000	$(920,550)	$6,940,000

Partially owned pooled subsidiary at date of business combination

POST CORPORATION AND SUBSIDIARY
Consolidation Eliminations Working Paper
April 30, Year 6

(a) Capital Stock—Sage 400,000
    Paid-in Capital in Excess of Par—Sage 235,000
    Retained Earnings—Sage ($250,000 × 5%) 12,500
    Retained Earnings of Subsidiary—Post 317,300
        Investment in Subsidiary—Post 920,550
        Minority Interest in Subsidiary 44,250
    To eliminate intercompany investment and establish
    minority interest in subsidiary at beginning of year
    [($400,000 + $235,000 + $250,000) × 5% = $44,250].

(b) Minority Interest in Net Income of Subsidiary........... 4,200
        Minority Interest in Subsidiary 4,200
    To establish minority interest in net income of subsidiary
    for year ended April 30, Year 6 ($84,000 × 5% = $4,200).

The following should be stressed in a review of the consolidating financial statements working paper of Post Corporation and its partially owned subsidiary under the pooling theory:

1 The $4,200 debit to Minority Interest in Net Income of Subsidiary—consolidation elimination (b)—is posted to the consolidating income statement; the $12,500 debit to the Retained Earnings account of Sage Company—consolidation elimination (a)—is posted to the **beginning-of-year** line in the consolidating statement of retained earnings. All consolidation eliminations which affect consolidating statements other than the consolidating balance sheet are posted directly to the appropriate consolidating statements.

2 As in the previously illustrated consolidating financial statements working paper in this chapter, the net income totals of the consolidating income statement are brought forward intact to the consolidating statement of retained earnings, while the end-of-year retained earnings balances in the latter statement are forwarded to the consolidating balance sheet.

3 The combined effect of the $12,500 and $4,200 debit items of consolidation eliminations (a) and (b) is to include in consolidated retained earnings only Post Corporation's 95% interest in the end-of-year retained earnings of Sage Company. Thus, total consolidated retained earnings at April 30, Year 6, is composed of the following:

Composition of consolidated retained earnings	
Retained earnings of Post Corporation	*$ 925,000*
95% of Retained earnings of Sage Company ($334,000 × 95%)	*317,300*
Consolidated retained earnings	*$1,242,300*

4 The combined effect of the $44,250 and $4,200 credit items of consolidation eliminations (a) and (b) is to reflect the minority interest in subsidiary at April 30, Year 6, ($48,450) at its correct amount of 5% of Sage Company's total stockholders' equity ($400,000 + $235,000 + $334,000 = $969,000; $969,000 × 5% = $48,450) at that date.

Consolidated Financial Statements The consolidated financial statements for Post Corporation and subsidiary incorporate the amounts in the Consolidated columns of the consolidating financial statements working paper. The consolidated statement of retained earnings would be in the form illustrated on page 273 for Palm Corporation and Subsidiary.

Nature of minority interest

The appropriate classification and presentation of minority interest in the consolidated income statement and consolidated balance sheet has been a perplexing problem for accountants. Over the years, two theories for consolidated financial statements have been developed to account for minority interest—the **parent company theory** and the **entity theory.** One authority has described these two theories as follows:

> The "parent company" concept views consolidated statements as an extension of parent company statements, in which the investment account of the parent is replaced by the individual assets and liabilities underlying the parent's investment, and subsidiaries are viewed as almost the equivalent of branches. When subsidiary ownership is not complete, the consolidation

process segregates the minority interest in the partially owned subsidiary. *The minority interest is considered to be an outside group and a liability as far as the parent shareholder is concerned.*

. . . .

In contrast to the parent company concept, the "entity" concept views consolidated statements as those of an economic entity with *two classes of proprietary interest*—the major or dominant interest and the minority interest. It holds that in consolidation these interests should be treated consistently. The consolidated statements are not viewed as an extension of parent company statements; rather, they are viewed as an expression of the financial position and operating results of a distinct "consolidated entity" consisting of a number of related companies whose relationship arises from common control (based on powers conferred by share ownership). When related companies are viewed as parts of such an entity, the minority interest, instead of representing an accountability to an outside group by the parent, represents "*a part of capital.*"[3]

As indicated in the preceding quotation, the parent company theory of consolidated financial statements treats the minority interest in net assets of a subsidiary as a **liability.** This liability is increased each accounting period by an **expense** representing the minority's share of the subsidiary's net income (or decreased by the minority's share of the subsidiary's net loss). Dividends paid by the subsidiary to minority shareholders decrease the liability to them. Consolidated net income is **net** of the minority's share of the subsidiary's net income. The illustrated consolidating financial statements on pages 276–277 reflect the parent company theory of presenting minority interest.

In the entity theory, the minority interest in the subsidiary's net assets is included in the stockholders' equity section of the consolidated balance sheet. The consolidated income statement presents the minority interest in the subsidiary's net income as a subdivision of total consolidated net income. Thus, for Post Corporation and subsidiary, a condensed consolidated income statement for the year ended April 30, Year 6, would appear as follows under the entity theory:

Income statement: entity theory	**POST CORPORATION AND SUBSIDIARY**
	Consolidated Income Statement
	For Year Ended April 30, Year 6

Net sales	$6,500,000
Costs and expenses	6,151,000
Net income	$ 349,000
Distribution of net income:	
To majority interest	$ 344,800
To minority interest in subsidiary ($84,000 × 5%)	4,200
Total net income	$ 349,000

[3] *Consolidated Financial Statements,* Accountants International Study Group (Plaistow, England: 1973), p. 7.

In the authors' opinion, the entity theory of reporting minority interest overemphasizes the **legal aspects** of the separate corporate organizations comprising a parent–subsidiary relationship. In substance, minority shareholders are a special class of creditors of the consolidated entity, for in the usual case they exercise **no ownership control whatsoever** over the operations of either the parent company or the subsidiary. If consolidated financial statements are to present clearly the operating results and financial position of a single economic entity, the niceties of minority shareholders' ownership of a part of the subsidiary should be ignored. Consequently, the parent company theory of accounting for minority interest in subsidiary will be stressed throughout this book.

REVIEW QUESTIONS

1 Depending upon the accompanying circumstances, a business combination involving a parent company and a subsidiary may be accounted for as a purchase or as a pooling of interests. Discuss the differences between (1) a consolidated balance sheet prepared for a **purchase** and (2) a consolidated balance sheet prepared for a **pooling of interests.**

2 Explain the purpose of the account entitled Retained Earnings of Subsidiary.

3 For the year ended October 31, Year 2, Staley Company had net income of $60,000. As of the close of business that date, Pryor Corporation acquired most of the outstanding capital stock of Staley Company in exchange for Pryor's previously unissued common stock.

Consolidation eliminations for the year ended October 31, Year 2, included the following:

Minority Interest in Net Income of Subsidiary	1,200	
Minority Interest in Subsidiary		1,200

a Was the business combination of Pryor Corporation and Staley Company accounted for as a purchase or as a pooling of interests? Explain.
b What percentage of Staley Company's outstanding capital stock was exchanged for Pryor Corporation common stock? Explain.

4 Compare the **parent company theory** and the **entity theory** of consolidated financial statements as they relate to the classification of minority interest in the consolidated income statement and the consolidated balance sheet.

5 The retained earnings balances of Pelham Corporation and Skeene Company at September 30, Year 5, were $1,000,000 and $800,000, respectively. At the close of business that date Skeene Company became a subsidiary of Pelham Corporation when Pelham acquired 96% of Skeene's outstanding capital stock.

What is the amount of consolidated retained earnings in the consolidated balance sheet of Pelham Corporation and subsidiary at September 30, Year 5, if the business combination is accounted for as:
a A purchase? Explain.
b A pooling of interests? Explain.

EXERCISES

Ex. 7-1 Select the best answer for each of the following multiple-choice questions.

1 A Retained Earnings of Subsidary account is used at the date of a business combination accounted for as a:

a Purchase only

b Pooling only

c Purchase or as a pooling

d Merger

2 Consolidated financial statements prepared as of the date of a business combination involving a partially owned subsidiary must include the caption Minority Interest in Net Income of Subsidiary if the business combination was accounted for as a:

a Consolidation

b Purchase

c Pooling

d Purchase or as a pooling

3 What is the method of presenting minority interest in a consolidated balance sheet under the **entity theory** of consolidated financial statements?

a As a separate item within the liabilities section

b As a deduction from consolidated goodwill, if any

c By means of a note to the consolidated financial statements

d As a separate item within the stockholders' equity section

Questions **4** and **5** are based on the following information:

On June 30, Year 5, Porgy Company combined with Shad Company in a business combination qualifying for pooling accounting. Porgy exchanged six shares of its common stock for each share of Shad's outstanding capital stock. There were no intercompany transactions during the year ended June 30, Year 5. The balance sheets immediately before the business combination follow:

PORGY COMPANY AND SHAD COMPANY

Individual Balance Sheets

June 30, Year 5

	Porgy Company	Shad Company	
	Carrying amount	Carrying amount	Current fair value
Current assets	$ 40,000	$ 30,000	$ 45,000
Land	30,000	-0-	
Equipment (net)	150,000	120,000	140,000
Total assets	$220,000	$150,000	
Current liabilities	$ 35,000	$ 15,000	15,000
Notes payable	40,000	-0-	
Bonds payable..........................	-0-	100,000	100,000
Common stock, $1 par	75,000	-0-	
Capital stock, $5 par	-0-	50,000	
Retained earnings	70,000 *(10,000)*	(15,000)	
Total liabilities & stockholders' equity ..	$220,000	$150,000	

4 What was the retained earnings balance in the consolidated balance sheet at June 30, Year 5?

a $45,000   *b* $55,000   *c* $70,000   *d* $80,000

5 How should consolidated net income for the year ended June 30, Year 5, be computed?

    a Use only Porgy's net income, because the business combination occurred on the last day of the fiscal year.

    b Use only Shad's net income, because the business combination occurred on the last day of the fiscal year.

    c Add together both companies' net incomes, even though the business combination occurred on the last day of the fiscal year.

    d Add together both companies' net incomes and subtract the annual amortization of goodwill.

Ex. 7-2 On November 1, Year 4, Pender Company issued 10,000 shares of its $10 par ($30 current fair value) common stock for 99 of the 100 outstanding shares of Sontag Company's $100 par capital stock, in a business combination qualifying for pooling accounting. Out-of-pocket costs of the business combination were as follows:

Legal fees and finder's fee associated with the business combination	*$15,000*
Costs incurred for SEC registration statement for Pender's common stock ...	*20,000*
Total out-of-pocket costs of business combination	*$35,000*

On November 1, Year 4, Sontag Company's stockholders' equity was as follows:

Capital stock, $100 par	*$ 10,000*
Paid-in capital in excess of par	*140,000*
Retained earnings	*70,000*
Total stockholders' equity	*$220,000*

Prepare in good form the journal entry or entries in Pender Company's accounting records to record the business combination with Sontag Company.

Ex. 7-3 Phrygia Company issued voting common stock with a stated value of $90,000 in exchange for all the outstanding capital stock of Scythia Company, in a business combination accounted for properly as a pooling. The stockholders' equity accounts of Scythia Company at the date of the business combination were as follows:

Capital stock, $2 par	*$ 70,000*
Paid-in capital in excess of par	*7,000*
Retained earnings	*50,000*
Total stockholders' equity	*$127,000*

Compute the increase in Phrygia Company's stockholders' equity at the date of the business combination as a result of the combination.

Ex. 7-4 The January 1, Year 3, balance sheets of two companies prior to their business combination follow.

	Palacio Company	Sedgwick Company
	(in thousands of dollars)	
Assets		
Cash	$ 6,000	$ 200
Inventories	4,000	400
Plant assets (net)	10,000	1,400
Total assets	$20,000	$2,000
Liabilities & Stockholders' Equity		
Current liabilities	$ 1,200	$ 200
Common stock, $1 par	2,000	200
Paid-in capital in excess of par	6,000	400
Retained earnings	10,800	1,200
Total liabilities & stockholders' equity	$20,000	$2,000

On January 1, Year 3, Palacio Company acquired all the outstanding common stock of Sedgwick Company by issuing 200 shares of common stock (current fair value $20 per share) in a business combination qualifying for pooling accounting.

Compute the consolidated paid-in capital in excess of par in the January 1, Year 3, consolidated balance sheet of Palacio Company and subsidiary.

Ex. 7-5 On September 30, Year 7, Prosit Corporation combined with Skoal Company in a business combination qualifying for purchase accounting. Skoal Company's net income for the year ended September 30, Year 7, was $10,000, and Skoal neither declared nor paid dividends during the year. There were no intercompany transactions between the two companies prior to the business combination.

The consolidation elimination working paper for Prosit Corporation and subsidiary at September 30, Year 7, was as follows:

PROSIT CORPORATION AND SUBSIDIARY
Consolidation Elimination Working Paper (Purchase)
September 30, Year 7

Capital Stock—Skoal	50,000	
Paid-in Capital in Excess of Par—Skoal	60,000	
Retained Earnings—Skoal	70,000	
Inventories—Skoal	20,000	
Plant Assets (net)—Skoal	40,000	
Goodwill—Prosit	18,000	
Investment in Subsidiary—Prosit		234,000
Minority Interest in Subsidiary		24,000

To eliminate intercompany investment and equity accounts of subsidiary at date of business combination; to allocate excess of cost over carrying amounts of identifiable assets acquired, with remainder to goodwill; and to establish minority interest in subsidiary at date of business combination ($240,000 × 10% = $24,000).

Prepare a consolidation eliminations working paper for Prosit Corporation and subsidiary under the assumption the business combination of Prosit Corporation and Skoal Company had been accounted for as a pooling rather than as a purchase.

Ex. 7-6 On July 31, Year 7, Pinto Corporation issued its common stock for 9,700 shares of Savoy Company's 10,000 outstanding shares of $50 par capital stock. The business combination qualified for pooling accounting, and Savoy Company became a subsidiary of Pinto Corporation. Immediately following the business combination, Pinto's general ledger included the following account balances:

Investment in Subsidiary (Savoy Company) .... $1,789,650 dr.
Retained Earnings of Subsidiary (Savoy Company) .... 625,650 cr.

Savoy Company reported net income of $60,000 and paid no dividends for the year ended July 31, Year 7.

Prepare a consolidation eliminations working paper for Pinto Corporation and subsidiary as of July 31, Year 7.

Ex. 7-7 The consolidation eliminations working paper for Pritikin Corporation and its 99%-owned pooled subsidiary as of March 31, Year 2, the date of the business combination, follows:

PRITIKIN CORPORATION AND SUBSIDIARY
Consolidation Eliminations Working Paper
March 31, Year 2

Capital Stock—Scanlon 200,000
Paid-in Capital in Excess of Par—Scanlon 300,000
Retained Earnings of Subsidiary—Pritikin 396,000
Retained Earnings—Scanlon 3,200
    Investment in Subsidiary—Pritikin 891,000
    Minority Interest in Subsidiary 8,200
To eliminate intercompany investment and establish minority interest in subsidiary at beginning of year.

Minority Interest in Net Income of Subsidiary 800
    Minority Interest in Subsidiary 800
To establish minority interest in net income of subsidiary for year ended March 31, Year 2.

Prior to the business combination with Pritikin Corporation, Scanlon Company declared and paid dividends of $30,000 during the year ended March 31, Year 2.

Prepare a statement of retained earnings for Scanlon Company for the year ended March 31, Year 2, prior to the business combination with Pritikin Corporation.

SHORT CASES FOR ANALYSIS AND DECISION

Case 7-1 On January 2, Year 5, Preston Company paid $1,000,000 cash for all of Storey Company's outstanding capital stock. The carrying amount of Storey's net assets on January 2, Year 5, was $880,000. Both Preston and Storey have operated profitably for many years, both have December 31 fiscal years, and each has only one class of capital stock outstanding. The business combination should be accounted for by the purchase method, in which Preston should follow certain principles in allocating its investment cost to the assets acquired and liabilities assumed.

Instructions
a Describe the principles that Preston Company should follow in allocating its investment cost to the assets purchased and liabilities assumed, for a January 2, Year 5, consolidated balance sheet.
b Independent of your answer to *a,* assume that on January 2, Year 5, Preston Company acquired all of Storey Company's outstanding capital stock in exchange for Preston Company capital stock, and that all conditions for pooling accounting were met. Describe the principles that Preston Company should follow in applying the pooling accounting method to the business combination with Storey Company, in the preparation of a consolidated balance sheet on January 2, Year 5.

Case 7-2 The minority interest in a subsidiary might be presented several ways in a consolidated balance sheet. Discuss the propriety of reporting the minority interest in the consolidated balance sheet:
a As a liability
b As a part of stockholders' equity
c In a separate classification between liabilities and stockholders' equity

Case 7-3 On March 1, Year 6, Perlmuth Corporation entered into a business combination with Stabler Company which met the prerequisites for pooling accounting. A condition of the combination was that the Perlmuth Corporation common stock issued to Ralph Stabler, sole shareholder of Stabler Company, would be registered with the SEC. However, Perlmuth Corporation withdrew its registration statement for the common stock because of adverse stock market conditions. Accordingly, the business combination was never completed.

On April 30, Year 7, Progress Corporation issued its common stock, which was registered with the SEC, for all the outstanding capital stock of Stabler Company. All the requirements of pooling accounting appeared to be met in the Progress-Stabler business combination. However, upon learning of Perlmuth's aborted combination with Stabler Company, Walsh & Co., the new independent auditors for Progress Corporation, questioned whether the following provision for pooling accounting, set forth in *APB Opinion No. 16,* "Business Combinations," applied:

> Each of the combining companies is autonomous and has not been a subsidiary or division of another corporation within two years before the plan of combination is initiated.

Instructions   Does the Progress Corporation–Stabler Company business combination qualify for pooling accounting? Explain.

PROBLEMS

7-4 On page 286 is the consolidating statement of retained earnings working paper for Peary Corporation and subsidiary for the year ended the date Peary Corporation exchanged its common stock for 92% of the outstanding capital stock of Stratton Company in a pooling business combination:

PEARY CORPORATION AND SUBSIDIARY
Consolidating Statement of Retained Earnings
For Year Ended March 31, Year 7

	Peary Corporation	Stratton Company	Consolidation eliminations increase (decrease)	Consolidated
Retained earnings, Apr. 1, Year 6	$100,000	$50,000	(a) $(4,000)	$146,000
Net income	60,000	40,000	(3,200)	96,800
Subtotal	$160,000	$90,000	$(7,200)	$242,800
Dividends	20,000	-0-		20,000
Retained earnings, Mar. 31, Year 7	$140,000	$90,000	$(7,200)	$222,800

Prior to the business combination, Peary Corporation had 100,000 shares of common stock outstanding for many years.

Instructions Prepare in good form a consolidated statement of retained earnings for Peary Corporation and subsidiary for the year ended March 31, Year 7.

7-5 As of the close of business September 30, Year 1, Pickens Corporation issued 100,000 shares of its $5 par common stock (current fair value $12 per share) for 18,800 shares of the outstanding $20 par capital stock of Solis Company. The $150,000 out-of-pocket costs of the business combination paid by Pickens Corporation on September 30, Year 1, were allocable as follows: 60% to legal fees and finder's fee directly related to the business combination, and 40% to the SEC registration statement for Pickens Corporation common stock issued in the business combination.

   Immediately prior to the business combination, stockholders' equity accounts of the two companies were as follows:

	Pickens Corporation	Solis Company
Common stock or capital stock	$4,000,000	$ 400,000
Paid-in capital in excess of par	1,500,000	-0-
Retained earnings	3,000,000	700,000
Total stockholders' equity	$8,500,000	$1,100,000

Instructions Prepare in good form Pickens Corporation's journal entries to record the business combination with Solis Company as a pooling.

7-6 Individual statements of retained earnings for Perloff Corporation and Schwarz Company for the year ended May 31, Year 2 (prior to their business combination), follow.

PERLOFF CORPORATION AND SCHWARZ COMPANY
Statements of Retained Earnings
For Year Ended May 31, Year 2

	Perloff Corporation	Schwarz Company
Retained earnings, June 1, Year 1	$500,000	$290,000
Net income	100,000	80,000
Subtotal	$600,000	$370,000
Dividends	40,000	25,000
Retained earnings, May 31, Year 2	$560,000	$345,000

As of the close of business May 31, Year 2, Perloff Corporation issued 50,000 shares of its $1 par common stock for 54,600 of the 60,000 outstanding shares of $3 par capital stock of Schwarz Company. Total paid-in capital attributable to Schwarz's stock was $7 per share. The $80,000 out-of-pocket costs of the business combination, which qualified for pooling accounting, were paid by Perloff Corporation on May 31, Year 2. Each company had an effective combined federal and state income tax rate of 60%. There were no intercompany transactions prior to the date of the business combination.

Instructions Compute the following in good form:
a Minority interest in net income of Schwarz Company for the year ended May 31, Year 2.
b Consolidated net income for Perloff Corporation and subsidiary for the year ended May 31, Year 2.
c Minority interest in net assets of Schwarz Company at May 31, Year 2.
d Consolidated retained earnings for Perloff Corporation and subsidiary at May 31, Year 2.

7-7 The chief accountant of Purvis Corporation prepared the following journal entries as of March 31, Year 8:

Investment in Subsidiary	783,000	
Minority Interest in Subsidiary	16,000	
Common Stock		49,000
Paid-in Capital in Excess of Par of Subsidiary		300,000
Retained Earnings of Subsidiary		450,000

To record issuance of 4,900 shares of $10 par common stock for 9,800 of 10,000 outstanding shares of Semel Company $5 par capital stock in a business combination qualifying for pooling accounting; to bring forward Semel Company's Paid-in Capital in Excess of Par and Retained Earnings accounts at their carrying amounts in Semel's accounting records; and to provide for minority interest in Semel Company's net assets ($800,000) on March 31, Year 8.

Investment in Subsidiary	80,000	
Paid-in Capital in Excess of Par	70,000	
Cash		150,000

To record payment of out-of-pocket costs of business combination with Semel Company as follows:

(continued)

Finder's fee and legal fees relating to the business
  combination $80,000
Costs associated with SEC registration statement 70,000
    Total out-of-pocket costs of business combination $150,000

Instructions Prepare adjusting journal entries, in good form, to correct Purvis Corporation's accounting for its business combination with Semel Company on March 31, Year 8.

7-8 On July 31, Year 10, Perez Corporation issued 20,000 shares of its $2 par common stock (current fair value $10 per share) for all 5,000 shares of outstanding $5 par capital stock of Sakamoto Company, which is to remain a separate corporation. Out-of-pocket costs of the business combination, paid by Perez Corporation on July 31, Year 10, were as follows:

Finder's fee and legal fees relating to the business combination $20,000
Costs associated with SEC registration statement for Perez Corporation com-
  mon stock 10,000
    Total out-of-pocket costs of business combination $30,000

Sakamoto Company's condensed balance sheet at July 31, Year 10, prior to the business combination, follows:

SAKAMOTO COMPANY
Balance Sheet
July 31, Year 10

Assets
  Current assets $150,000
  Plant assets (net) 300,000
  Goodwill... 20,000
    Total assets $470,000

Liabilities & Stockholders' Equity
  Current liabilities $120,000
  Long-term debt 200,000
  Capital stock, $5 par 25,000
  Paid-in capital in excess of par..................................... 50,000
  Retained earnings 75,000
    Total liabilities & stockholders' equity $470,000

Sakamoto Company's goodwill arose in Sakamoto's July 31, Year 4, purchase of the net assets of Townsend Company.

Sakamoto Company's assets and liabilities having July 31, Year 10, current fair values different from their carrying amounts were as follows:

	Current fair value	Carrying amount
Inventories	$ 65,000	$ 60,000
Plant assets (net)	340,000	300,000
Long-term debt	190,000	200,000

There were no intercompany transactions prior to the business combination.

Instructions
a Prepare Perez Corporation's journal entries at July 31, Year 10, in good form, to record the business combination with Sakamoto Company as a pooling.
b Prepare the consolidation eliminations working paper, in good form, for consolidating financial statements working paper of Perez Corporation and subsidiary at July 31, Year 10.

7-9 On October 31, Year 4, Prouty Corporation acquired 93% of the outstanding capital stock of Stovall Company in exchange for 50,000 shares of Prouty's $2 par ($10 current fair value) common stock. Out-of-pocket costs of the business combination paid by Prouty Corporation on October 31, Year 4, were as follows:

Legal fees and finder's fee relating to the business combination	$34,750
Costs associated with SEC registration statement for Prouty Corporation common stock	55,250
Total out-of-pocket costs of business combination	$90,000

There were no intercompany transactions between the two companies prior to the business combination. Stovall Company is to be a subsidiary of Prouty Corporation.

Individual financial statements of the two companies prior to the business combination are presented below and at the top of page 290.

PROUTY CORPORATION AND STOVALL COMPANY
Financial Statements
For Year Ended October 31, Year 4

Income Statements	Prouty Corporation	Stovall Company
Net sales	$1,500,000	$ 800,000
Costs and expenses		
Cost of goods sold	$1,000,000	$ 480,000
Selling, general, and administrative expenses	150,000	80,000
Interest expense	50,000	25,000
Income taxes expense	180,000	129,000
Total costs and expenses	$1,380,000	$ 714,000
Net income	$ 120,000	$ 86,000

(continued)

PROUTY CORPORATION AND STOVALL COMPANY
Financial Statements
For Year Ended April 30, Year 6 (continued)

	Prouty Corporation	Stovall Company
Statements of Retained Earnings		
Retained earnings, Nov. 1, Year 3	$ 560,000	$ 250,000
Net income	120,000	86,000
Subtotal	$ 680,000	$ 336,000
Dividends	50,000	-0-
Retained earnings, Oct. 31, Year 4	$ 630,000	$ 336,000
Balance Sheets		
Assets		
Cash	$ 250,000	$ 150,000
Inventories	860,000	600,000
Other current assets	500,000	260,000
Plant assets (net)	3,400,000	1,500,000
Patents	-0-	80,000
Total assets	$5,010,000	$2,590,000
Liabilities & Stockholders Equity		
Income taxes payable	$ 40,000	$ 60,000
Other current liabilities	390,000	854,000
Long-term debt	950,000	1,240,000
Common stock, $2 par	1,500,000	-0-
Capital stock, $10 par	-0-	100,000
Paid-in capital in excess of par	1,500,000	-0-
Retained earnings	630,000	336,000
Total liabilities & stockholders' equity	$5,010,000	$2,590,000

Instructions
a Prepare Prouty Corporation's journal entries at October 31, Year 4, in good form, to record the business combination with Stovall Company as a pooling.
b Prepare the consolidating financial statements working paper and related consolidation eliminations working paper for October 31, Year 4, of Prouty Corporation and subsidiary.

8

CONSOLIDATED FINANCIAL STATEMENTS: SUBSEQUENT TO DATE OF PURCHASE BUSINESS COMBINATION

Subsequent to the date of a business combination, the parent company must account for the operating results of the subsidiary: the subsidiary's net income or net loss, and dividends declared and paid by the subsidiary. In addition, a number of intercompany transactions which frequently occur in a parent company–subsidiary relationship must be accounted for.

In this chapter, we shall describe and illustrate the accounting for operating results of purchased subsidiaries. Accounting for operating results of pooled subsidiaries and for intercompany transactions not involving a profit or a loss is illustrated in Chapter 9; Chapter 10 includes a discussion of accounting for intercompany transactions involving a profit or a loss.

ACCOUNTING FOR OPERATING RESULTS OF WHOLLY OWNED PURCHASED SUBSIDIARIES

In accounting for the operating results of purchased subsidiaries, a parent company may choose the *equity method* or the *cost method* of accounting.

Equity method

In the equity method of accounting, the parent company includes in its accounting records its share of the subsidiary's net income or net loss, adjusted for amortization of differences between current fair values and carrying amounts of a purchased subsidiary's net assets as of the date of the business combination, as well as its share of dividends declared by the subsidiary. Thus, the equity method of accounting for a subsidiary's operating results is similar to home office accounting for a branch's operations, as described in Chapter 4.

Proponents of the equity method of accounting maintain that the method is consistent with the accrual basis of accounting, because it recognizes increases or decreases in the value of the parent company's investment in the subsidiary when they are *realized* by the subsidiary as net income or net loss, not when they are *paid* by the subsidiary as dividends. Thus, proponents claim, the equity method stresses the *economic substance* of the parent company–subsidiary relationship: the two companies constitute a single economic entity for accounting purposes. Proponents of the equity method also claim that dividends declared by a subsidiary cannot constitute *revenue* to the parent company, as maintained by advocates of the cost method; instead, dividends are a liquidation of a portion of the parent company's investment in the subsidiary.

Cost method

In the cost method of accounting, the parent company accounts for the operation of a subsidiary only to the extent that dividends are declared by the subsidiary. Dividends declared by the subsidiary from net income subsequent to the business combination are *revenue* to the parent company; dividends declared by the subsidiary in excess of post-combination net income constitute a reduction of the parent company's investment in the subsidiary. Net income or net loss of the subsidiary is *not* recognized in the accounting records of a parent company when the cost method of accounting is used.

Supporters of the cost method contend that the method appropriately recognizes the *legal form* of the parent company–subsidiary relationship. Parent company and subsidiary are separate legal entities; accounting for a subsidiary's operations should recognize the separateness, according to proponents of the cost method. Thus, a parent company realizes revenue from an investment in a subsidiary when the subsidiary declares a dividend, not when the subsidiary reports net income.

Choosing between equity method and cost method

Consolidated financial statement balances will be the same, regardless of whether a parent company uses the equity method or the cost method to account for a subsidiary's operations. However, the consolidation eliminations used in the two methods are different, as illustrated in subsequent sections of this chapter.

The equity method of accounting is appropriate for **pooled** subsidiaries as well as **purchased** subsidiaries. The cost method, on the other hand, is compatible with **purchase accounting** only. In purchase accounting, the parent company's original investment in the subsidiary is recorded at **cost.** Hence, accounting for operating results of purchased subsidiaries by the cost method may be considered a logical extension of purchase accounting. However, in pooling accounting the parent company's investment at the date of the business combination is recorded at the carrying amount of the subsidiary's net assets. As a result, the parent company's Investment in Subsidiary account reflects the parent's equity in the subsidiary's net assets at the date of the business combination. The equity method of accounting for a pooled subsidiary's operations thus is consistent with pooling accounting illustrated in Chapter 9.

Illustration of equity method for wholly owned purchased subsidiary

Assume that Palm Corporation appropriately had used purchase accounting for the December 31, Year 10, business combination with its wholly owned subsidiary, Starr Company (see pages 236–238 for a description of the purchase business combination), and that Starr Company reported net income of $60,000 for the year ended December 31, Year 11. Assume further that on December 20, Year 11, Starr's board of directors declared a cash dividend of $0.60 per share on the 40,000 outstanding shares. The dividend was payable January 8, Year 12, to stockholders of record December 29, Year 11.

Starr Company's December 20, Year 11, journal entry to record the dividend declaration is as follows:

Wholly owned subsidiary's journal entry for declaration of dividend	*Dividends (40,000 shares × $0.60) 24,000*
	Intercompany Dividends Payable 24,000
	To record declaration of dividend payable Jan. 8, Year 12, to stockholders of record Dec. 29, Year 11.

Starr Company's credit to the Intercompany Dividends Payable account indicates that the liability for dividends payable to the parent company **must be eliminated** in the preparation of consolidated financial statements for the year ended December 31, Year 11.

Under the equity method of accounting, Palm Corporation would prepare the following journal entries to record the reported operating results of Starr Company for the year ended December 31, Year 11:

Year 11

Dec. 20 Intercompany Dividends Receivable   24,000
                  Investment in Subsidiary   24,000
         To record dividend declared by Starr Company,
         payable Jan. 8, Year 12, to stockholders of record
         Dec. 29, Year 11.

Dec. 31 Investment in Subsidiary   60,000
                  Intercompany Investment Income   60,000
         To record 100% of Starr Company's reported net
         income for the year ended Dec. 31, Year 11. (In-
         come tax effects are disregarded.)

The first journal entry above recognizes the dividends declared by the subsidiary in the Intercompany Dividends Receivable account, and is the counterpart of the subsidiary's journal entry to record the declaration of the dividend. The credit to the Investment in Subsidiary account in the first journal entry reflects an underlying premise of the equity method of accounting—dividends declared by a subsidiary represent a return of a portion of the parent company's investment in the subsidiary.

The second journal entry above recognizes the parent company's 100% share of the subsidiary's reported net income for Year 11. The subsidiary's reported net income *accrues* to the parent company under the equity method of accounting, similar to the accrual of interest on a note receivable.

The income tax effects of Palm Corporation's accrual of its share of Starr Company's reported net income are disregarded at this time. Income tax allocation problems associated with all aspects of parent company and subsidiary accounting are considered in Chapter 11.

Adjustment of Purchased Subsidiary's Reported Net Income   Because we have assumed in this chapter that Palm Corporation's business combination with Starr Company was accounted for as a *purchase,* Palm Corporation must prepare a third equity-method journal entry on December 31, Year 11, to adjust Starr Company's reported net income for depreciation and amortization attributable to the differences between the current fair values and carrying amounts of Starr's net assets as of the date of the Palm-Starr business combination. Because such differences are not recorded in the accounting records of the subsidiary, the subsidiary's *reported net income* is *overstated* from the point of view of the consolidated entity.

Let us assume that the December 31, Year 10, differences between the current fair values and carrying amounts of Starr Company's net assets were as follows:

<table>
<tr><td rowspan="9" style="font-style:italic">Differences between current fair values and carrying amounts of wholly owned purchased subsidiary's assets at date of business combination</td></tr>
</table>

Differences between current fair values and carrying amounts of wholly owned purchased subsidiary's assets at date of business combination	*Inventories*		$ 25,000
	Plant assets (net):		
	Land	$15,000	
	Building (economic life 15 years)	30,000	
	Machinery (economic life 10 years)	20,000	65,000
	Patent (economic life 5 years)		5,000
	Goodwill (economic life 30 years)		15,000
	Total		$110,000

Palm Corporation would prepare the following additional journal entry to reflect the effects of the difference between the current fair values and carrying amounts of Starr Company's net assets on Starr's reported net income for the year ended December 31, Year 11:

Parent company's equity-method journal entry to record operating results of wholly owned purchased subsidiary attributable to amortization of subsidiary's net assets	*Year 11*		
	Dec. 31 Intercompany Investment Income	30,500	
	Investment in Subsidiary		30,500
	To amortize differences between current fair values		
	and carrying amounts of Starr Company's net assets		
	at Dec. 31, Year 10, as follows:		
	Inventories—to cost of goods sold	$25,000	
	Building—depreciation ($30,000 ÷ 15) ...	2,000	
	Machinery—depreciation ($20,000 ÷ 10) .	2,000	
	Patent—amortization ($5,000 ÷ 5)	1,000	
	Goodwill—amortization ($15,000 ÷ 30) ..	500	
	Total difference applicable to Year 11 .	$30,500	
	(Income tax effects are disregarded.)		

After the three preceding journal entries are posted, Palm Corporation's Investment in Subsidiary and Intercompany Investment Income accounts appear as follows:

Ledger accounts of parent company using equity method of accounting for wholly owned purchased subsidiary	**Investment in Subsidiary**				
	Date	**Explanation**	**Debit**	**Credit**	**Balance**
	12/31/10	*Balance forward (page 239)*			*500,000 dr.*
	12/20/11	*Dividend declared by subsidiary*		*24,000*	*476,000 dr.*
	12/31/11	*Reported net income of subsidiary*	*60,000*		*536,000 dr.*
	12/31/11	*Amortization of differences between current fair values and carrying amounts of subsidiary's net assets*		*30,500*	*505,500 dr.*

Intercompany Investment Income

Date	Explanation	Debit	Credit	Balance
12/31/11	Reported net income of subsidiary		60,000	60,000 cr.
12/31/11	Amortization of differences between current fair values and carrying amounts of subsidiary's net assets	30,500		29,500 cr.

Consolidating Financial Statements Working Paper   The consolidating financial statements working paper and the related consolidation elimination working paper for Palm Corporation and subsidiary for the year ended December 31, Year 11, are below and on pages 297–298. The intercompany receivable and payable is the $24,000 dividend payable by Starr Company to Palm Corporation at December 31, Year 11. (The advances by Palm Corporation to Starr Company which were outstanding at December 31, Year 10, were repaid by Starr January 2, Year 11.)

Equity method: Wholly owned purchased subsidiary subsequent to business combination

PALM CORPORATION AND SUBSIDIARY
Consolidating Financial Statements Working Paper
For Year Ended December 31, Year 11

	Palm Corporation	Starr Company	Consolidation eliminations increase (decrease)	Consolidated
Income Statement				
Revenue				
Net sales	$1,100,000	$680,000		$1,780,000
Intercompany investment income	29,500	-0-	(a)$ (29,500)	-0-
Total revenue	$1,129,500	$680,000	$ (29,500)	$1,780,000
Costs and expenses				
Cost of goods sold	$ 700,000	$450,000	(a)$ 29,500	$1,179,500
Selling, general, and administrative expenses	151,000	80,000	(a) 1,000	232,000
Interest expense	49,000	-0-		49,000
Income taxes expense	120,000	90,000		210,000
Total costs and expenses	$1,020,000	$620,000	$ 30,500	$1,670,500
Net income	$ 109,500	$ 60,000	$ (60,000)	$ 109,500
Statement of Retained Earnings				
Retained earnings, Jan. 1, Year 11	$ 134,000	$132,000	(a)$(132,000)	$ 134,000
Net income	109,500	60,000	(60,000)	109,500
Subtotal	$ 243,500	$192,000	$(192,000)	$ 243,500

(continued)

*Equity method: Wholly owned purchased subsidiary subsequent to
business combination*

PALM CORPORATION AND SUBSIDIARY
Consolidating Financial Statements Working Paper
For Year Ended December 31, Year 11 (continued)

	Palm Corporation	Starr Company	Consolidation eliminations increase (decrease)	Consolidated
Dividends	30,000	24,000	(a) (24,000)	30,000
Retained earnings, Dec. 31, Year 1	$ 213,500	$168,000	$(168,000)	$213,500
Balance Sheet				
Assets				
Cash	$ 15,900	$ 72,100		$ 88,000
Intercompany receivable				
(payable)	24,000	(24,000)		-0-
Inventories	136,000	115,000		251,000
Other current assets	88,000	131,000		219,000
Investment in subsidiary	505,500	-0-	(a) $(505,500)	-0-
Plant assets (net)	440,000	340,000	(a) 61,000	841,000
Patent	-0-	16,000	(a) 4,000	20,000
Goodwill	-0-	-0-	(a) 14,500	14,500
Total assets	$1,209,400	$650,100	$(426,000)	$1,433,500
Liabilities & Stockholders' Equity				
Income taxes payable	$ 40,000	$ 20,000		$ 60,000
Other liabilities	347,900	204,100		552,000
Common stock, $10 par	400,000	-0-		400,000
Capital stock, $5 par	-0-	200,000	(a) $(200,000)	-0-
Paid-in capital in excess of par	208,000	58,000	(a) (58,000)	208,000
Retained earnings	213,500	168,000	(168,000)	213,500
Total liabilities & stockholders' equity	$1,209,400	$650,100	$(426,000)	$1,433,500

*Equity method: Wholly owned purchased subsidiary subsequent to
business combination*

PALM CORPORATION AND SUBSIDIARY
Consolidation Elimination Working Paper
December 31, Year 11

(a) Capital stock—Starr.............................	200,000
Paid-in Capital in Excess of Par—Starr	58,000
Retained Earnings—Starr	132,000

(continued)

Equity method: Wholly owned purchased subsidiary subsequent to business combination

PALM CORPORATION AND SUBSIDIARY
Consolidation Elimination Working Paper
December 31, Year 11 (continued)

Intercompany Investment Income—Palm	29,500	
Plant Assets (net)—Starr ($65,000 − $4,000)	61,000	
Patent—Starr ($5,000 − $1,000)	4,000	
Goodwill—Starr ($15,000 − $500)	14,500	
Cost of Goods Sold—Starr	29,500	
Selling, General, and Administrative Expenses— Starr	1,000	
Investment in Subsidiary—Palm		505,500
Dividends—Starr		24,000

To carry out the following:

(1) Eliminate intercompany investment and equity accounts of subsidiary at beginning of year, and subsidiary dividend.

(2) Provide for Year 11 depreciation and amortization on differences between business combination date current fair values and carrying amounts of Starr's net assets as follows:

	To cost of goods sold	To selling, general, and administrative expenses
Inventories sold ..	$25,000	$ -0-
Building depreciation	1,500	500
Machinery depreciation	2,000	
Patent amortization	1,000	-0-
Goodwill amortization	-0-	500
Totals	$29,500	$1,000

(3) Allocate remaining unamortized differences between combination date current fair values and carrying amounts of Starr's net assets to appropriate assets.

(Income tax effects are disregarded.)

The following aspects of the consolidating working paper for Palm Corporation and subsidiary should be emphasized:

1 The intercompany receivable and payable, placed in adjacent columns on the same line, are offset without a formal consolidation elimination.

2 The consolidation elimination cancels all intercompany transactions and balances not dealt with by the offset described in **1** above.

3 The consolidation elimination cancels the subsidiary's retained earnings balance **at the beginning of the year,** so that the three basic financial statements of the two companies each may be consolidated in turn. (All financial statements of a parent company and a purchased subsidiary are consolidated subsequent to the business combination.)

4 Three assumptions underlie the consolidation elimination: (a) the fifo method is used by Starr Company to account for inventories, thus, the $25,000 difference attributable to Starr's beginning inventories is allocable to cost of goods sold; (b) Starr Company's building depreciation is allocable 75% to cost of goods sold and 25% to selling, general, and administrative expenses; and (c) Starr's machinery depreciation and patent amortization are entirely allocable to cost of goods sold, and Starr's goodwill amortization is wholly allocable to selling, general, and administrative expenses.

5 Income tax effects of the consolidation elimination's increase in Starr Company's expenses are not included in the elimination. Income tax accounting in consolidated financial statements is considered in Chapter 11.

6 One of the effects of the consolidation elimination is to reduce the differences between the current fair values and the carrying amounts of the subsidiary's net assets at the business combination date. The effect of the reduction is as follows:

Aggregate difference at date of business combination (Dec. 31, Year 10)	$110,000
Reduction in consolidation elimination (a) ($29,500 + $1,000)	30,500
Unamortized difference at Dec. 31, Year 11	$ 79,500

The joint effect of Palm Corporation's use of the equity method of accounting and the annual consolidation elimination will be to extinguish the $79,500 difference above through Palm's Investment in Subsidiary account.

7 The parent company's use of the equity method of accounting results in the following equalities:

Parent company net income = consolidated net income
Parent company retained earnings = consolidated retained earnings

The above equalities exist when the equity method of accounting is used if there are no intercompany profits eliminated for the determination of consolidated net assets. Intercompany profits are discussed in Chapter 10.

8 Despite the equalities indicated above, **consolidated financial statements** are superior to **parent company financial statements** for the presentation of financial position and operating results of parent and subsidiary companies. The effect of the consolidating income statement for Palm Corporation and subsidiary is to reclassify Palm's $29,500 share of its subsidiary's adjusted net income into the revenue and expense components of that net income. Similarly, Palm's $505,500 investment in the subsidiary is reclassified by the consolidating balance sheet into the assets and liabilities comprising the subsidiary's net assets.

9 Purchase accounting theory requires the exclusion from consolidated retained earnings of a purchased subsidiary's retained earnings at date of a business combination. Palm Corporation's use of the equity method of accounting meets this requirement. Palm Corporation's retained earnings—which are equal to consolidated retained earnings—include Palm's $29,500 share of the subsidiary's adjusted net income for the year ended December 31, Year 11—the first year of the parent-subsidiary relationship.

Closing Entries   The equity method of accounting ignores legal form in favor of the economic substance of the relationship between a parent company and its subsidiary. However, state corporation laws necessitate a careful accounting for retained earnings available for dividends. Accordingly, Palm Corporation should prepare the following closing entry at December 31, Year 11, after the consolidating financial statements working paper has been completed:

Net Sales	*1,100,000*	
Intercompany Investment Income	*29,500*	
Costs and Expenses		*1,020,000*
Retained Earnings of Subsidiary		
($29,500 − $24,000)		*5,500*
Retained Earnings ($109,500 − $5,500)		*104,000*

Parent company's closing entry in equity method of accounting for purchased subsidiary

To close revenue and expense accounts; to transfer net income legally available for dividends to retained earnings; and to segregate 100% share of adjusted net income of subsidiary not distributed as dividends by the subsidiary.

The above closing entry excludes from Palm Corporation's retained earnings the amount of Palm's net income not available for dividends to Palm's shareholders—$5,500. This amount is computed as follows:

Adjusted net income of Starr Company recorded by Palm Corporation	*$29,500*
Less: Dividends paid by Starr Company to Palm Corporation	*24,000*
Amount of Starr Company's adjusted net income not distributed as a dividend to Palm Corporation	*$ 5,500*

Palm Corporation's Retained Earnings of Subsidiary account thus contains the amount of the purchased subsidiary's aggregate net income (less net losses) *since the date of the business combination* which has not been distributed by the subsidiary to the parent company as dividends.

Cost method of accounting for wholly owned purchased subsidiary

Because the cost method of accounting for a subsidiary's operating results is not stressed in this book, we shall not illustrate the cost method for a wholly owned purchased subsidiary. However, the cost method of accounting for a partially owned purchased subsidiary is illustrated on pages 309–314.

ACCOUNTING FOR OPERATING RESULTS OF PARTIALLY OWNED PURCHASED SUBSIDIARY

Illustration of equity method of accounting for partially owned purchased subsidiary

The Post Corporation–Sage Company consolidated entity described in Chapter 6 (pages 245–246) will be used to illustrate the equity method of accounting for the operating results of a partially owned purchased subsidiary.

Assume that Sage Company on March 24, Year 7, declared a $1 per share dividend payable April 16, Year 7, to shareholders of record April 1, Year 7, and that Sage Company reported net income of $90,000 for the year ended April 30, Year 7.

The following journal entries recognize the above-described dividend in Sage Company's accounts:

Partially owned subsidiary's journal entries for declaration and payment of dividend	*Year 7*

Mar. 24	Dividends (40,000 shares × $1)	40,000	
	Dividends Payable ($40,000 × 5%)		2,000
	Intercompany Dividends Payable		
	($40,000 × 95%)		38,000
	To record declaration of dividend payable Apr. 16, Year 7, to stockholders of record Apr. 1, Year 7.		
Apr. 16	Dividends Payable	2,000	
	Intercompany Dividends Payable	38,000	
	Cash		40,000
	To record payment of dividend declared Mar. 24, Year 7, to stockholders of record Apr. 1, Year 7.		

The following journal entries are required in the accounting records of Post Corporation:

Year 7

Mar. 24 Intercompany Dividends Receivable 38,000
            Investment in Subsidiary   38,000
            To record dividend declared by Sage Company, payable Apr. 16, Year 7, to stockholders of record Apr. 1, Year 7.

Apr. 16 Cash 38,000
            Intercompany Dividends Receivable   38,000
            To record receipt of dividend from Sage Company.

Apr. 30 Investment in Subsidiary ($90,000 × 95%) 85,500
            Intercompany Investment Income   85,500
            To record 95% of net income of Sage Company for the year ended Apr. 30, Year 7. (Income tax effects are disregarded.)

As pointed out on page 294, a **purchase** business combination involves a restatement of net asset values of the subsidiary. Sage Company's reported net income of $90,000 does not reflect cost expirations attributable to Sage's restated net asset values, **because the restatements were not reflected in Sage's accounts.** Consequently, the amortization of the difference between the current fair values of Sage Company's identifiable net assets at date of the business combination and the carrying amounts of those net assets must be accounted for by Post Corporation. Assume, as in Chapter 6 (page 248), that the difference was allocable to Sage's assets as follows:

Inventories .... $ 26,000
Plant assets (net):
  Land $60,000
  Building (economic life 20 years) 80,000
  Machinery (economic life 5 years) 50,000   190,000
Leasehold (economic life 6 years) 30,000
  Total $246,000

In addition, Post Corporation acquired in the business combination goodwill (to be amortized over 40 years) attributable to Sage Company in the amount of $38,000, computed as follows:

Computation of goodwill purchased by combinor		
Cost of Post Corporation's 95% interest in Sage Company		$1,192,250
Less: 95% of $1,215,000 aggregate current fair values of Sage Company's net assets		1,154,250
Goodwill purchased by Post Corporation (to be amortized over 40 years).		$ 38,000

Post Corporation prepares the following additional journal entry under the equity method of accounting to reflect the effects of the differences between current fair values and carrying amounts of the partially owned subsidiary's identifiable net assets:

Parent company's equity-method journal entry to record operating results of partially owned purchased subsidiary attributable to amortization of subsidiary's identifiable net assets

Intercompany Investment Income	42,750	
Investment in Subsidiary		42,750
To amortize differences between current fair values and carrying amounts of Sage Company's net assets at Apr. 30, Year 6:		
Inventories—to cost of good sold	$26,000	
Building—depreciation ($80,000 ÷ 20)	4,000	
Machinery—depreciation ($50,000 ÷ 5)	10,000	
Leasehold—amortization ($30,000 ÷ 6)	5,000	
Total difference applicable to Year 7	$45,000	
Amortization for Year 7: $45,000 × 95%...........	$42,750	
(Income tax effects are disregarded.)		

Next, Post Corporation prepares the following journal entry to record the amortization of goodwill purchased by Post in the business combination with Sage Company:

Parent company's equity-method journal entry to record amortization of goodwill

Amortization Expense ($38,000 ÷ 40 years)	950	
Investment in Subsidiary		950
To amortize goodwill acquired in business combination with partially owned purchased subsidiary over an economic life of 40 years.		

Note that the amortization of the goodwill is debited to Amortization Expense, not to Intercompany Investment Income. The reason for this treatment is explained on page 304.

After the preceding journal entries are posted, Post Corporation's Investment in Subsidiary and Intercompany Investment Income accounts appear as follows:

Investment in Subsidiary

Date	Explanation	Debit	Credit	Balance
4/30/6	Balance forward (page 247)			1,192,250 dr.
3/24/7	Dividend declared by subsidiary		38,000	1,154,250 dr.
4/30/7	Reported net income of subsidiary	85,500		1,239,750 dr.
4/30/7	Amortization of differences between current fair values and carrying amounts of subsidiary's identifiable net assets		42,750	1,197,000 dr.
4/30/7	Amortization of goodwill		950	1,196,050 dr.

Intercompany Investment Income

Date	Explanation	Debit	Credit	Balance
4/30/7	Reported net income of subsidiary		85,500	85,500 cr.
4/30/7	Amortization of differences between current fair values and carrying amounts of subsidiary's identifiable net assets	42,750		42,750 cr.

The $42,750 balance in Post Corporation's Intercompany Investment Income account represents 95% of the $45,000 adjusted net income ($90,000 − $45,000 = $45,000) of Sage Company for the year ended April 30, Year 7.

Amortization of Goodwill Attributable to Partially Owned Subsidiary As explained in Chapter 6 (page 249), goodwill in a business combination involving a partially owned subsidiary is attributed to the *parent company* rather than the *subsidiary* under the widely used accounting practice illustrated in this text. Consequently, amortization of the goodwill is debited to the Amortization Expense account of the parent company, with an offsetting credit to the Investment in Subsidiary account. Thus, this treatment differs from the amortization of goodwill attributable to a wholly owned subsidiary. As illustrated on page 295, amortization of a wholly owned subsidiary's goodwill is debited to the parent company's Intercompany Investment Income account.

The inconsistent treatment of goodwill in the two types of purchase business combinations is difficult to support. Proponents of a logical body of financial accounting theory will welcome the Financial Accounting Standards Board's resolution of this apparent inconsistency.

Consolidating Financial Statements Working Paper The consolidating financial statements working paper and the related consolidation eliminations working paper for Post Corporation and subsidiary for the year ended April 30, Year 7, are presented on pages 305–308.

Equity method: Partially owned purchased subsidiary subsequent to date of business combination

POST CORPORATION AND SUBSIDIARY
Consolidating Financial Statements Working Paper
For Year Ended April 30, Year 7

	Post Corporation	Sage Company	Consolidation eliminations increase (decrease)		Consolidated
Income Statement					
Revenue					
Net sales	$5,611,000	$1,089,000			$6,700,000
Intercompany investment					
income	42,750	-0-	(a) $	(42,750)	-0-
Total revenue	$5,653,750	$1,089,000	$	(42,750)	$6,700,000
Costs and expenses					
Cost of goods sold	$3,925,000	$ 700,000	(a) $	43,000	$4,668,000
Selling, general, and					
administrative expenses ..	556,950*	129,000	(a)	2,000	687,950
Interest and income taxes					
expense	710,000	170,000			880,000
Minority interest in net					
income of subsidiary	-0-	-0-	(b)	2,250	2,250
Total costs and expenses	$5,191,950	$ 999,000	$	47,250	$6,238,200
Net income	$ 461,800	$ 90,000	$	(90,000)	$ 461,800
Statement of Retained Earnings					
Retained earnings, May 1,					
Year 6	$1,050,000	$ 334,000	(a) $	(334,000)	$1,050,000
Net income	461,800	90,000		(90,000)	461,800
Subtotal	$1,511,800	$ 424,000	$	(424,000)	$1,511,800
Dividends	158,550	40,000	(a)	(40,000)	158,550
Retained earnings, Apr. 30,					
Year 7	$1,353,250	$ 384,000	$	(384,000)	$1,353,250
Balance Sheet					
Assets					
Inventories	$ 861,000	$ 439,000			$1,300,000
Other current assets	639,000	371,000			1,010,000
Investment in subsidiary ...	1,196,050	-0-	(a)	$(1,196,050)	-0-
Plant assets (net)	3,600,000	1,150,000	(a)	176,000	4,926,000
Leasehold	-0-	-0-	(a)	25,000	25,000
Goodwill	95,000	-0-	(a)	37,050	132,050
Total assets	$6,391,050	$1,960,000	$	(958,000)	$7,393,050

* Includes $950 amortization of goodwill.

(continued)

Equity method: Partially owned purchased subsidiary subsequent to date of business combination

POST CORPORATION AND SUBSIDIARY
Consolidating Financial Statements Working Paper
For Year Ended April 30, Year 7 (continued)

	Post Corporation	Sage Company	Consolidation eliminations increase (decrease)	Consolidated
Liabilities & Stockholders' Equity				
Liabilities	$2,420,550	$ 941,000		$3,361,550
Minority interest in subsidiary	-0-	-0-	(a) $ 58,750	
			(b) 2,250	61,000
Common stock, $1 par	1,057,000	-0-		1,057,000
Capital stock, $10 par	-0-	400,000	(a) (400,000)	-0-
Paid-in capital in excess of par	1,560,250	235,000	(a) (235,000)	1,560,250
Retained earnings	1,353,250	384,000	(384,000)	1,353,250
Total liabilities & stockholders' equity	$6,391,050	$1,960,000	$(958,000)	$7,393,050

Equity method: Partially owned purchased subsidiary subsequent to date of business combination

POST CORPORATION AND SUBSIDIARY
Consolidation Eliminations Working Paper
April 30, Year 7

(a) Capital Stock—Sage 400,000
    Paid-in Capital in Excess of Par—Sage 235,000
    Retained Earnings—Sage 334,000
    Intercompany Investment Income—Post 42,750
    Plant Assets (net)—Sage ($190,000 − $14,000) 176,000
    Leasehold—Sage ($30,000 − $5,000) 25,000
    Goodwill—Post ($38,000 − $950) 37,050
    Cost of Goods Sold—Sage 43,000

(continued)

Equity method: Partially owned purchased subsidiary subsequent to date of business combination

POST CORPORATION AND SUBSIDIARY
Consolidation Eliminations Working Paper
April 30, Year 7 (continued)

Selling, General, and Administrative Expenses—Sage . .	2,000	
Investment in Subsidiary—Post		1,196,050
Dividends—Sage		40,000
Minority Interest in Subsidiary		58,750

To carry out following:

(1) Eliminate intercompany investment and equity accounts of subsidiary at beginning of year, and subsidiary dividend.

(2) Provide for Year 7 depreciation and amortization on differences between business combination date current fair values and carrying amounts of Sage's net assets as follows:

	To cost of goods sold	To selling, general, and administrative expenses
Inventories sold . . .	$26,000	$ -0-
Building depreciation	2,000	2,000
Machinery depreciation	10,000	-0-
Leasehold amortization	5,000	-0-
Totals	$43,000	$2,000

(3) Allocate remaining unamortized differences between combination date current fair values and carrying amounts to appropriate assets.

(4) Establish minority interest in subsidiary at beginning of year ($60,750), less minority share of dividends declared by subsidiary during year ($40,000 × 5% = $2,000).

(Income tax effects are disregarded.)

(continued)

Equity method: Partially owned purchased subsidiary subsequent to date of business combination

POST CORPORATION AND SUBSIDIARY
Consolidation Eliminations Working Paper
April 30, Year 7 (continued)

(b) Minority Interest in Net Income of Subsidiary	2,250	
Minority Interest in Subsidiary		2,250

To establish minority interest in subsidiary's adjusted
net income for Year 7 as follows:

Net income reported by subsidiary	$90,000
Net reduction in elimination (a) above ...	(45,000)
Adjusted net income of subsidiary	$45,000
Minority share: $45,000 × 5%	$ 2,250

The following aspects of the equity-method consolidating financial statements working paper and consolidation eliminations working paper should be emphasized:

1 Three assumptions underlie consolidation elimination (a). First, the fifo method of inventory accounting is used by Sage Company. Thus, the $26,000 difference attributable to Sage's beginning inventories is allocable to cost of good sold. Second, Sage's building depreciation is allocable equally to cost of goods sold and to selling, general, and administrative expenses. Third, Sage's machinery depreciation and leasehold amortization are allocable solely to cost of goods sold.

2 Income tax effects of the increase in Sage Company's expenses are not included in elimination (a). Income tax accounting in consolidated financial statements is considered in Chapter 11.

3 Consolidation elimination (a) cancels Sage Company's retained earnings **at the beginning of the year.** This step is essential for the preparation of all three basic consolidating financial statements.

4 The parent company's use of the equity method of accounting results in the following equalities:

Parent company net income = consolidated net income
Parent company retained earnings = consolidated retained earnings

These equalities exist in the equity method of accounting if there are no intercompany profits eliminated for the determination of consolidated net assets. Intercompany profits are discussed in Chapter 10.

5 One of the effects of consolidation elimination (a) is to reduce the difference between the current fair values of the subsidiary's net assets at the business combination date and their carrying amounts at that date. The effect of the reduction is as follows:

Difference at date of business combination (Apr. 30, Year 6)	*$246,000*
Less: Reduction in consolidation elimination (a) ($43,000 + $2,000) ...	*45,000*
Difference at Apr. 30, Year 7	*$201,000*

The joint effect of Post Corporation's use of the equity method of accounting and the annual consolidation eliminations will be to extinguish the remaining $201,000 difference through Post's Investment in Subsidiary account. This will be illustrated in Chapter 10.

6 The minority interest in subsidiary at April 30, Year 7, may be verified as follows:

Sage Company's total stockholders' equity, Apr. 30, Year 7	*$1,019,000*
Add: Unamortized difference computed in **5,** *above*	*201,000*
Sage Company's adjusted stockholders' equity, Apr. 30, Year 7	*$1,220,000*
Minority interest therein: ($1,220,000 × 5%)	*$ 61,000*

7 The minority interest in net income of subsidiary is recognized in consolidation elimination (*b*) in the amount of $2,250 (5% of the adjusted net income of Sage Company) as an increase in minority interest in subsidiary and a decrease in consolidated net income.

Closing Entries As indicated in a previous section of this chapter, legal considerations necessitate the following closing entry for Post Corporation at April 30, Year 7:

Parent company's closing entry in equity method of accounting for purchased subsidiary

Net Sales	*5,611,000*	
Intercompany Investment Income	*42,750*	
Costs and Expenses		*5,191,950*
Retained Earnings of Subsidiary [($45,000 −		
$40,000) × 95%)]		*4,750*
Retained Earnings ($461,800 − $4,750)		*457,050*
To close revenue and expense accounts; to transfer net		
income legally available for dividends to retained earn-		
ings; and to segregate 95% share of adjusted net income		
of subsidiary not distributed as dividend by subsidiary.		

Illustration of cost method for partially owned purchased subsidiary

If Post Corporation used the cost method, rather than the equity method, of accounting for Sage Company's operating results for the year ended April 30, Year 7, Post would not prepare journal entries to reflect Sage's net income for the year. Post would record Sage's dividend declaration as follows on March 24, Year 7:

Intercompany Dividend Receivable 38,000
*   Intercompany Dividend Revenue 38,000*
To record dividend declared by Sage Company, payable Apr. 16,
Year 7, to stockholders of record Apr. 1, Year 7. (Income tax
effects are disregarded.)

Post Corporation's journal entry for receipt of the dividend from Sage would be the same under the cost method as under the equity method of accounting illustrated previously in this chapter.

Consolidated Financial Statements Working Paper   The consolidating financial statements working paper and the related consolidation eliminations working paper for Post Corporation and subsidiary for the year ended April 30, Year 7, appear below and on pages 311–313.

Cost method: Partially owned purchased subsidiary subsequent to date of business combination

POST CORPORATION AND SUBSIDIARY
Consolidating Financial Statements Working Paper
For Year Ended April 30, Year 7

	Post Corporation	Sage Company	Consolidation eliminations increase (decrease)	Consolidated
Income Statement				
Revenue				
Net sales	$5,611,000	$1,089,000		$6,700,000
Intercompany dividend revenue	38,000	-0-	(c) $ (38,000)	-0-
Total revenue	$5,649,000	$1,089,000	$ (38,000)	$6,700,000
Costs and expenses				
Cost of goods sold	$3,925,000	$ 700,000	(b) $ 43,000	$4,668,000
Selling, general, and administrative expenses	556,000	129,000	(b) 2,950	687,950
Interest and income taxes expense	710,000	170,000		880,000
Minority interest in net income of subsidiary	-0-	-0-	(d) 2,250	2,250
Total costs and expenses	$5,191,000	$ 999,000	$ 48,200	$6,238,200
Net income	$ 458,000	$ 90,000	$ (86,200)	$ 461,800

(continued)

Cost method: Partially owned purchased subsidiary subsequent to date of business combination

POST CORPORATION AND SUBSIDIARY
Consolidating Financial Statements Working Paper
For Year Ended April 30, Year 7 (continued)

	Post Corporation	Sage Company	Consolidation eliminations increase (decrease)	Con- solidated
Statement of Retained Earnings				
Retained earnings, May 1, Year 6	$1,050,000	$ 334,000	(a) $ (334,000)	$1,050,000
Net income	458,000	90,000	(86,200)	461,800
Subtotal	$1,508,000	$ 424,000	$ (420,200)	$1,511,800
Dividends	158,550	40,000	(c) (40,000)	158,550
Retained earnings, Apr. 30,				
Year 7	$1,349,450	$ 384,000	$ (380,200)	$1,353,250
Balance Sheet				
Assets				
Inventories	$ 861,000	$ 439,000	(a) $ 26,000	$1,300,000
			(b) (26,000)	
Other current assets	639,000	371,000		1,010,000
Investment in subsidiary	1,192,250	—	(a) (1,192,250)	-0-
Plant assets (net)	3,600,000	1,150,000	(a) 190,000	4,926,000
			(b) (14,000)	
Leasehold	-0-	-0-	(a) 30,000	25,000
			(b) (5,000)	
Goodwill	95,000	-0-	(a) 38,000	132,050
			(b) (950)	
Total assets	$6,387,250	$1,960,000	$ (954,200)	$7,393,050
Liabilities & Stockholders' Equity				
Liabilities	$2,420,550	$ 941,000		$3,361,550
Minority interest in subsidiary	-0-	-0-	(a) $ 60,750	61,000
			(c) (2,000)	
			(d) 2,250	
Common stock, $1 par	1,057,000	-0-		1,057,000
Capital stock, $10 par	-0-	400,000	(a) (400,000)	-0-
Paid-in capital in excess of par	1,560,250	235,000	(a) (235,000)	1,560,250
Retained earnings	1,349,450	384,000	(380,200)	1,353,250
Total liabilities &				
stockholders' equity	$6,387,250	$1,960,000	$ (954,200)	$7,393,050

Cost method: Partially owned purchased subsidiary subsequent to date of business combination

POST CORPORATION AND SUBSIDIARY
Consolidation Eliminations Working Paper
April 30, Year 7

(a) Capital Stock—Sage	400,000	
Paid-in Capital in Excess of Par—Sage	235,000	
Retained Earnings—Sage	334,000	
Inventories—Sage	26,000	
Plant Assets (net)—Sage	190,000	
Leasehold—Sage	30,000	
Goodwill—Post	38,000	
Investment in Subsidiary—Post		1,192,250
Minority Interest in Subsidiary		60,750

To eliminate intercompany investment and equity accounts of subsidiary at date of business combination; to allocate excess of cost over carrying amounts of identifiable assets acquired, with remainder to goodwill; and to establish minority interest in subsidiary at date of business combination ($1,215,000 × 5% = $60,750).

(b) Cost of Goods Sold—Sage	43,000	
Selling, General, and Administrative Expenses—Sage	2,000	
Selling, General, and Administrative Expenses—Post	950	
Inventories—Sage		26,000
Plant Assets (net)—Sage		14,000
Leasehold—Sage		5,000
Goodwill—Post		950

(1) To provide for Year 7 depreciation and amortization on differences between business combination date current fair values and carrying amounts of Sage's identifiable assets as follows:

	To cost of goods sold	To selling, general, and administrative expenses
Inventories sold	$26,000	$ -0-
Building depreciation	2,000	2,000
Machinery depreciation	10,000	-0-
Leasehold amortization	5,000	-0-
Totals	$43,000	$2,000

(continued)

Cost method: Partially owned purchased subsidiary subsequent to date of business combination

POST CORPORATION AND SUBSIDIARY
Consolidation Eliminations Working Paper
April 30, Year 7 (continued)

(2) To amortize goodwill acquired in business combination ($38,000 ÷ 40 = $950).

(Income tax effects are disregarded.)

(c) Intercompany Dividend Revenue—Post	38,000	
Minority Interest in Subsidiary	2,000	
Dividends—Sage		40,000

To eliminate intercompany dividends and minority
share thereof ($40,000 × 5% = $2,000).

(d) Minority Interest in Net Income of Subsidiary	2,250	
Minority Interest in Subsidiary		2,250

To establish minority interest in subsidiary's adjusted
net income for Year 7, as follows:

Net income reported by subsidiary	$90,000
Net reduction in elimination (b) above . . .	(45,000)
Adjusted net income of subsidiary	$45,000
Minority share: $45,000 × 5%	$ 2,250

The following points relative to the cost-method consolidation eliminations should be noted:

1 The consolidated amounts in the cost-method consolidating financial statements working paper are identical to the consolidated amounts in the equity-
method working paper (pages 305–306). This outcome results from the differing consolidation eliminations used in the two methods.

2 Three cost-method consolidation eliminations, (a), (b), and (c), are required
to accomplish what a single equity-method consolidation elimination, (a) on
pages 306–307, does. The reason is that the parent company's accounting
records are used in the equity method to reflect the parent company's share
of the subsidiary's adjusted net income or net loss.

3 Consolidation elimination (a) deals with the intercompany investment and
subsidiary equity accounts **at the date of the business combination.** This
consolidation elimination is identical to the one on page 250 of Chapter 6.
This accounting technique is necessary because the parent's Investment in
Subsidiary account is maintained at the **cost of the original investment** in the
cost method.

4 The parent company's cost-method net income and retained earnings are not
the same as the consolidated amounts. Thus, the consolidated amounts at
April 30, Year 7, may be proved as follows, to assure their accuracy:

Consolidated net income:

Net income of Post Corporation	$ 458,000
Less: Amortization of business combination goodwill	(950)
Add: Post Corporation's share of Sage Company's adjusted net income not distributed as dividends [($45,000 − $40,000) × 95%)]	4,750
Consolidated net income	$ 461,800

Consolidated retained earnings:

Retained earnings of Post Corporation	$1,349,450
Less: Amortization of business combination goodwill	(950)
Add: Post Corporation's share of adjusted net increase in Sage Company's retained earnings [($50,000 − $45,000) × 95%]	4,750
Consolidated retained earnings	$1,353,250

Concluding comments on equity and cost methods

In today's accounting environment, the equity method of accounting for a subsidiary's operations is preferable to the cost method for the following reasons:

1 The equity method emphasizes **economic substance** of the parent-company–subsidiary relationship, while the cost method emphasizes **legal form.** More and more, modern accounting stresses substance over form.

2 The equity method permits the use of **parent company journal entries** to reflect many items that must be included in **consolidation eliminations** in the cost method. Formal journal entries in the accounting records provide a better record than do working paper eliminations.

3 The equity method facilitates issuance of separate financial statements for the parent company, if required by Securities and Exchange Commission regulations or other considerations. Current generally accepted accounting principles require the equity method of accounting for unconsolidated subsidiaries in separate parent company financial statements.[1]

4 Except when intercompany profits (discussed in Chapter 10) exist in assets or liabilities to be consolidated, the parent company's net income and retained earnings are identical in the equity method to the related consolidated amounts. Thus, the equity method provides a useful self-checking technique.

5 As demonstrated in Chapter 9, the cost method is not considered appropriate for accounting for a pooled subsidiary's operations.

For these reasons, the equity method of accounting for a subsidiary's operations will be emphasized in the following chapters.

REVIEW QUESTIONS

1 "Consolidated financial statement balances will be the same, regardless of whether a parent company uses the equity method or the cost method to account for a subsidiary's operations." Why is this quotation true?

[1] APB Opinion No. 18, "The Equity Method of Accounting for Investments in Common Stock," AICPA (New York: 1971), pp. 353–354.

2 Both Parnell Corporation and Plankton Company have wholly owned subsidiaries. Parnell Corporation's general ledger has an Intercompany Dividend Revenue account, and an Intercompany Investment Income account appears in Plankton Company's ledger. Do both companies use the same method of accounting for their subsidiaries' operating results? Explain.

3 When there are no intercompany profits or losses in consolidated assets or liabilities, the equity method of accounting produces parent company net income which equals consolidated net income. The equity method also results in parent company retained earnings of the same amount as consolidated retained earnings. Why, then, are consolidated financial statements considered superior to the separate financial statements of the parent company when the parent company uses the equity method? Explain.

4 Describe the special features of closing entries for a parent company which accounts for its subsidiary's operating results by the equity method.

5 Plumstead Corporation's 92%-owned subsidiary declared a dividend of $3 per share on its 50,000 outstanding shares of common stock. How would Plumstead record this dividend under
a The equity method of accounting?
b The cost method of accounting?

6 Discuss some of the advantages which result from the use of the equity method, rather than the cost method, of accounting for a subsidiary's operating results.

7 Strake Company, a 90%-owned subsidiary of Peale Corporation, reported net income of $50,000 for the first fiscal year following the business combination. However, the consolidation elimination for the minority interest in the subsidiary's net income was in the amount of $3,500 rather than $5,000. Can this difference be justified? Explain.

8 Is a Retained Earnings of Subsidiary account required for a parent company using the cost method of accounting for the subsidiary's operations? Explain.

EXERCISES

Ex. 8-1 Select the best answer for each of the following multiple-choice questions:
1 Powell Corporation owns 80% of the outstanding capital stock of Sylvester Company, for which it uses the equity method of accounting. Compare the consolidated net income of Powell and Sylvester (X) with Powell's net income (Y) if it does not consolidate with Sylvester:
a $X > Y$ **c** $X < Y$
b $X = Y$ **d** The comparison cannot be determined.

2 A parent company which uses the equity method of accounting for its investment in a 70%-owned subsidiary, which reported a net income of $20,000 and paid $5,000 in dividends, made the following journal entries:

Investment in Subsidiary	14,000	
Intercompany Investment Income		14,000
Cash	3,500	
Intercompany Dividend Revenue		3,500

What effect will these journal entries have on the parent company's balance sheet?

    a Balance sheet will be fairly stated.
    b Investment in Subsidiary account will be overstated and Retained Earnings account will be understated.
    c Investment in Subsidiary account will be understated and Retained Earnings account will be understated.
    d Investment in Subsidiary account will be overstated and Retained Earnings account will be overstated.

3 A Retained Earnings of Subsidiary account appears in:
    a The consolidating financial statements working papers
    b The parent company's accounting records
    c The subsidiary's accounting records
    d Both *a* and *b*
    e Both *a* and *c*

4 A benefit (or benefits) of the equity method of accounting for a subsidiary's operating results is (or are) that, in the absence of intercompany profits or losses in assets and liabilities to be consolidated:
    a Parent company net income = consolidated net income
    b Parent company retained earnings = consolidated retained earnings
    c Both *a* and *b*
    d Neither *a* nor *b*

5 A parent company's debit to an Intercompany Dividends Receivable account indicates that, in accounting for the operating results of its subsidiary, the parent company uses:
    a The equity method of accounting
    b The cost method of accounting
    c The purchase method of accounting
    d Either *a* or *b*
    e Either *a* or *c*

Ex. 8-2 Paramount Corporation owns a 90% interest in a purchased subsidiary, Sorgen Company, which is accounted for by the cost method. During Year 5, Paramount had net income of $45,000 and Sorgen had net income of $20,000. Sorgen declared and paid a $4,000 dividend during Year 5. There were no differences between the current fair values and carrying amounts of Sorgen's net assets at the date of the business combination.
    Compute the consolidated net income of Paramount Corporation and subsidiary for Year 5.

Ex. 8-3 On March 31, Year 1, Parse Corporation acquired for cash 90% of the outstanding capital stock of Schick Company. The $100,000 excess of Parse's investment over 90% of the current fair value (and carrying amount) of Schick's identifiable net assets was allocable to goodwill having an estimated economic life of 25 years at March 31, Year 1. For the year ended March 31, Year 2, Schick Company reported a net loss of $30,000 and paid no dividends.
    What amount, disregarding income taxes, should Parse Corporation record in its Intercompany Investment Income account under the equity method of accounting for the year ended March 31, Year 2? Show computations.

Ex. 8-4 Following are all details of three ledger accounts of a parent company which uses the equity method of accounting for its subsidiary's operating results.

Intercompany Dividends Receivable

Aug. 16, Year 8	36,000	Aug. 27, Year 8	36,000

Investment in Subsidiary

Sept 1, Year 7	630,000	Aug. 16, Year 8	36,000
Aug. 31, Year 8	72,000	Aug. 31, Year 8	5,000

Intercompany Investment Income

Aug. 31, Year 8	5,000	Aug. 31, Year 8	72,000

What is the most logical explanation for each of the transactions recorded in the above ledger accounts?

Ex. 8-5 On January 1, Year 6, Pinter Corporation purchased 75% of the outstanding capital stock of Slattery Company for $345,000 cash. The investment is accounted for by the equity method. On that date, Slattery's net assets (carrying amount and current fair value) were $300,000. Pinter has determined that the excess of the cost of its investment in Slattery's identifiable net assets has an indeterminant economic life.

Slattery's net income for the year ended December 31, Year 6, was $50,000. During Year 6, Pinter received $15,000 cash dividends from Slattery. There were no other transactions between the two companies.

Compute the balance of Pinter Corporation's Investment in Subsidiary account (after adjustment) at December 31, Year 6, disregarding income taxes.

Ex. 8-6 Select the best answer for each of the following multiple-choice questions:

1 Which of the following describes the amount at which a parent company should carry its unconsolidated subsidiary in its separate financial statements for periods subsequent to the business combination?

a Original cost of the investment to the parent company

b Original cost of the investment adjusted for the parent company's share of the subsidiary's net income, net losses, and dividends

c Current fair value of the investment adjusted for dividends received

d Current fair value of the investment

2 In a parent company's unconsolidated financial statements, which accounts, other than Cash, are affected when a subsidiary's earnings and dividends are reflected?

a Dividend Revenue, Intercompany Investment Income, and Retained Earnings

b Dividend Revenue and Retained Earnings

c Investment in Subsidiary, Intercompany Investment Income, Dividend Revenue, and Retained Earnings

d Investment in Subsidiary, Intercompany Investment Income, and Retained Earnings

3 How is the portion of consolidated earnings to be assigned to minority interest in consolidated financial statements determined?

a The net income of the parent company is subtracted from the subsidiary's net income to determine the minority interest.

b The subsidiary's net income is allocated to the minority interest.

c The amount of the subsidiary's net income recognized for consolidation purposes is multiplied by the minority's percentage ownership.

d The amount of consolidated net income determined on the consolidating financial statements working paper is multiplied by the minority interest percentage at the balance sheet date.

4 When the equity method of accounting for an investment in a subsidiary is used, dividends from the subsidiary should be accounted for by the parent company as:

     a Revenue, unless paid from retained earnings of the subsidiary earned before the business combination

     b Revenue, if the dividends were declared from retained earnings

     c A reduction in the carrying amount of the Investment in Subsidiary account

     d A deferred credit

  5 What would be the effect on consolidated financial statements if an uncon-solidated subsidiary is accounted for by the equity method, but other sub-sidiaries are consolidated?

     a All the unconsolidated subsidiary's accounts will be included individually in the consolidated financial statements.

     b Consolidated retained earnings will not reflect the net income of the un-consolidated subsidiary.

     c Consolidated retained earnings will be the same as if the subsidiary had been included in the consolidation.

     d The parent company's dividend revenue from the unconsolidated sub-sidiary will be reflected in consolidated net income.

Ex. 8-7 Stellar Company, wholly owned subsidiary of Planetary Corporation, reported net income of $90,000 and paid dividends of $35,000 for the first year following the business combination. Goodwill computed in accordance with purchase accounting amounted to $64,000 at the date of the business combination, and had an estimated economic life of 20 years. Exclusive of Stellar's operations, Planetary Corporation had net income of $180,000 for the first year following the business combination.

    Disregarding income taxes, compute the net income of Planetary Corporation under (*a*) the equity method and (*b*) the cost method of accounting for the operating results of Stellar Company.

SHORT CASES FOR ANALYSIS AND DECISION

Case 8-1 Financial accounting usually emphasizes the economic substance of events even though the legal form may differ and suggest different treatment. For ex-ample, under the accrual basis of accounting, expenses are recognized when incurred (substance) rather than when cash is disbursed (form).

    Although the feature of substance over form exists in most generally ac-cepted accounting principles and practices, there are times when form prevails over substance.

    Instructions For each of the following topics, discuss the underlying theory in terms of both substance and form, that is, substance over form and possibly form over substance. Each topic should be discussed independently.

  a Consolidated financial statements

  b Equity method of accounting for investments in capital stock of subsidiaries and influenced investees

Case 8-2 You have recently been hired for the position of controller of Precision Corpora-tion, a manufacturer which has begun a program of expansion through busi-ness combinations. On February 1, Year 4, two weeks prior to your controller-ship appointment, Precision Corporation completed the acquisition of 85% of the outstanding common stock of Sloan Company for $255,000 cash. You are presently engaged in a discussion with Precision Corporation's chief accoun-tant concerning the appropriate accounting method for Precision's interest in Sloan Company's operating results. The chief accountant strongly supports the cost method of accounting, offering the following arguments:

  1 The cost method recognizes that Precision Corporation and Sloan Company are separate legal entities.

2 The existence of a minority interest in Sloan Company requires emphasis on the legal separateness of the two companies.

3 A parent company recognizes revenue under the cost method only when the subsidiary declares dividends. Such dividend revenue is consistent with the revenue realization principle of financial accounting. The Intercompany Investment Income account recorded in the equity method of accounting does not fit the definition of realized revenue.

4 Use of the equity method of accounting might result in Precision Corporation declaring dividends to its shareholders out of "paper" retained earnings which in reality belong to Sloan Company.

5 The cost method is consistent with other aspects of historical cost accounting, because working paper consolidation eliminations, rather than journal entries in ledger accounts, are used to recognize amortization of differences between current fair values and carrying amounts of Sloan Company's net assets.

Instructions Write a rebuttal to each of the chief accountant's arguments.

PROBLEMS

8-3 On January 1, Year 6, Paul Corporation made the following investments:
(1) Acquired for cash 80% of the outstanding capital stock of Samson Company at $70 per share. The stockholders' equity of Samson on January 1, Year 6, consisted of the following:

Capital stock, $50 par	$50,000
Retained earnings	20,000
Total stockholders' equity	$70,000

(2) Acquired for cash 70% of the outstanding capital stock of Spark Company at $40 per share. The stockholders' equity of Spark on January 1, Year 6, consisted of the following:

Capital stock, $20 par	$ 60,000
Paid-in capital in excess of par	20,000
Retained earnings	40,000
Total stockholders' equity	$120,000

Out-of-pocket costs of the two business combinations may be disregarded. An analysis of the retained earnings of each company for Year 6 follows:

	Paul Corporation	Samson Company	Spark Company
Balance, 1/1/6	$240,000	$20,000	$40,000
Net income (loss)	104,600*	36,000	(12,000)
Cash dividends paid	(40,000)	(16,000)	(9,000)
Balance, 12/31/6	$304,600*	$40,000	$19,000

*Before giving effect to journal entries in **a**(2), on page 320

Instructions
a Prepare journal entries for Paul Corporation to record the following for Year 6:

(1) Investments in subsidiaries
(2) Parent company's share of subsidiary's net income or net loss
(3) Subsidiary dividends received

b Compute the amount of minority interest in each subsidiary's stockholders' equity at December 31, Year 6.

c Compute the amount which should be reported as consolidated retained earnings of Paul Corporation and subsidiaries as of December 31, Year 6. Show all supporting computations. Disregard income taxes.

8-4 Pruitt Corporation purchased 82% of Spector Company's outstanding common stock for $328,000 cash on March 31, Year 8. Costs of the business combination may be ignored. Spector's stockholders' equity accounts on March 31, Year 8, were as follows:

Capital stock, $2 par	$ 50,000
Paid-in capital in excess of par	75,000
Retained earnings	135,000
Total stockholders' equity	$260,000

All of Spector Company's identifiable net assets were fairly valued at their March 31, Year 8, carrying amounts except for the following:

	Carrying amount	Current fair value
Land	$100,000	$120,000
Building (10-year economic life)	200,000	250,000
Patent (8-year economic life)	60,000	80,000

Any goodwill resulting from the business combination is amortized over the maximum period of 40 years. Spector Company uses the straight-line method for depreciation and amortization.

During the year ended March 31, Year 9, Spector Company reported net income of $1.20 per share and paid no dividends. There were no intercompany transactions between Pruitt Corporation and Spector Company.

Instructions
a Prepare Pruitt Corporation's journal entries to record Spector Company's operating results for the year ended March 31, Year 9.
b Prepare in good form the consolidation eliminations working paper for Pruitt Corporation and subsidiary at March 31, Year 9. Disregard income taxes.

8-5 The consolidation eliminations working paper for Prokop Corporation and its wholly owned subsidiary, Starbuck Company, at the date of the business combination was as follows:

PROKOP CORPORATION AND SUBSIDIARY
Consolidation Eliminations Working Paper
November 30, Year 1

Capital Stock—Starbuck	80,000
Paid-in Capital in Excess of Par—Starbuck	200,000
Retained Earnings—Starbuck	220,000

(continued)

PROKOP CORPORATION AND SUBSIDIARY
Consolidation Eliminations Working Paper
November 30, Year 1 (continued)

Inventories—Starbuck	20,000	
Goodwill—Starbuck	40,000	
Investment in Subsidiary—Prokop		560,000

To eliminate intercompany investment and equity accounts of subsidiary at date of business combination, and to allocate excess of cost over carrying amounts of identifiable assets acquired, with remainder to goodwill having an economic life of 40 years.

For the year ended November 30, Year 2, Starbuck Company reported net income of $90,000 and paid dividends of $30,000. Starbuck accounts for its inventories by the fifo costing method.

Instructions
a Prepare Prokop Corporation's journal entries to record the operating results of Starbuck Company for the year ended November 30, Year 2.
b Prepare the consolidation eliminations working paper for Prokop Corporation and subsidiary at November 30, Year 2. Disregard income taxes.

8-6 Perea Corporation, a wholesaler, purchased 80% of the issued and outstanding stock of Stengel Company, a retailer, on December 31, Year 2, for $120,000. At that date Stengel Company had one class of common stock outstanding at a par value of $100,000 and retained earnings of $30,000. Perea Corporation had a $50,000 deficit in retained earnings.

Perea Corporation purchased the Stengel Company stock from Stengel's major stockholder primarily to acquire control of signboard leases owned by Stengel Company. The leases will expire on December 31, Year 7, and Perea Corporation executives estimated that the leases, which cannot be renewed, were worth at least $20,000 more than their carrying amount when the Stengel Company stock was purchased.

The financial statements for both companies for the year ended December 31, Year 6, are as follows:

PEREA CORPORATION AND SUBSIDIARY
Financial Statements
For Year Ended December 31, Year 6

	Perea Corporation	Stengel Company
Income Statements		
Net sales	$420,000	$300,000
Costs and expenses:		
Cost of goods sold	$315,000	$240,000
Expenses	65,000	35,000
Total costs and expenses	$380,000	$275,000
Net income	$ 40,000	$ 25,000

(continued)

PEREA CORPORATION AND SUBSIDIARY
Financial Statements
For Year Ended December 31, Year 6 (continued)

	Perea Corporation	Stengel Company
Statements of Retained Earnings		
Retained earnings, Jan. 1, Year 6	$ 15,000	$ 59,000
Net income	40,000	25,000
Subtotal	$ 55,000	$ 84,000
Dividends	-0-	9,000
Retained earnings, Dec. 31, Year 6	$ 55,000	$ 75,000
Balance Sheets		
Assets		
Current assets	$172,000	$199,100
Investment in subsidiary	120,000	-0-
Land	25,000	10,500
Building and equipment	200,000	40,000
Accumulated depreciation	(102,000)	(7,000)
Signboard leases	-0-	42,000
Accumulated amortization	-0-	(33,600)
Total assets......................................	$415,000	$251,000
Liabilities & Stockholders' Equity		
Dividends payable	$ -0-	$ 9,000
Other current liabilities	60,000	67,000
Capital stock, $1 par	300,000	100,000
Retained earnings....................................	55,000	75,000
Total liabilities & stockholders' equity	$415,000	$251,000

Stengel Company declared a 9% cash dividend on December 20, Year 6, payable January 16, Year 7, to stockholders of record December 31, Year 6. Perea Corporation carries its investment at cost and had not recorded this dividend on December 31, Year 6. Neither company paid a dividend during Year 6.

Instructions
a Prepare adjusting entries for Perea Corporation at December 31, Year 6, to convert its accounting for Stengel Company's operating results to the equity method of accounting.
b Prepare the consolidating financial statements working paper at December 31, Year 6, and the related consolidation eliminations working paper. Balances for Perea Corporation should reflect the adjusting entries in **a**.
Disregard income taxes.

8-7 On June 30, Year 6, Petal Corporation acquired for cash of $19 per share all the outstanding voting common stock of Sepal Corporation. Both companies continued to operate as separate entities and both companies have calendar years.
(1) On June 30, Year 6, Sepal Corporation's condensed balance sheet was as follows:

SEPAL CORPORATION
Balance Sheet
June 30, Year 6

Assets

Cash	$ 700,000
Accounts receivable (net)	600,000
Inventories	1,400,000
Plant assets (net)	3,300,000
Other assets	500,000
Total assets	$6,500,000

Liabilities & Stockholders' Equity

Accounts payable and other current liabilities	$ 700,000
Long-term debt	2,600,000
Other liabilities	200,000
Common stock, $1 par	1,000,000
Paid-in capital in excess of par	400,000
Retained earnings	1,600,000
Total liabilities & stockholders' equity	$6,500,000

(2) On June 30, Sepal's assets and liabilities having current fair values that were different from the carrying amounts were as follows:

	Current fair value
Plant assets (net)	$16,400,000
Other assets	200,000
Long-term debt	2,200,000

The differences between current fair values and carrying amounts resulted in a debit or credit to depreciation or amortization for the consolidated statements for the six-month period ended December 31, Year 6, as follows:

Plant assets (net)	$500,000 debit
Other assets	10,000 credit
Long-term debt	5,000 debit
Total	$495,000 debit

(3) The amount paid by Petal in excess of the current fair value of the net assets of Sepal is attributable to expected future earnings of Sepal and will be amortized over the maximum allowable period.

(4) The Year 6 net income or net loss for both companies was as follows:

	Petal	Sepal
Jan. 1 to June 30	$ 250,000	$ (750,000)
July 1 to Dec. 31	1,070,000	1,250,000

The $1,070,000 net income of Petal includes the equity in the net income of Sepal.

(5) On December 31, Year 6, the condensed balance sheets for both companies were as follows:

PETAL CORPORATION AND SUBSIDIARY
Balance Sheets
December 31, Year 6

	Petal Corporation	Sepal Corporation
Assets		
Cash	$ 3,500,000	$ 625,000
Accounts receivable (net)	1,400,000	1,500,000
Inventories	1,000,000	2,500,000
Investment in subsidiary	19,720,000	-0-
Plant assets (net)	2,000,000	3,100,000
Other assets	100,000	475,000
Total assets	$27,720,000	$8,200,000
Liabilities & Stockholders' Equity		
Accounts payable and other current liabilities	$ 1,500,000	$1,100,000
Long-term debt	4,000,000	2,600,000
Other liabilities	750,000	250,000
Common stock, $1 par	10,000,000	1,000,000
Paid-in capital in excess of par	˙5,000,000	400,000
Retained earnings	6,470,000	2,850,000
Total liabilities & stockholders' equity	$27,720,000	$8,200,000

Instructions   Prepare a condensed consolidated balance sheet of Petal Corporation and its wholly owned subsidiary, Sepal Corporation, as of December 31, Year 6. Do not use a working paper, but show supporting computations in good form. Disregard income taxes.

9

CONSOLIDATED FINANCIAL STATEMENTS: SUBSEQUENT TO DATE OF POOLING BUSINESS COMBINATION

In this chapter, we shall consider the use of the equity method of accounting for the operating results of wholly owned and partially owned pooled subsidiaries. Then, we shall deal with accounting for intercompany transactions between a parent company and its subsidiaries (other than dividends) not involving a profit or loss.

Illustration of equity method of accounting for wholly owned pooled subsidiary

For purposes of illustrating the equity method of accounting for a wholly owned pooled subsidiary, let us turn once again to the December 31, Year 10, business combination of Palm Corporation and Sage Company, and assume that it has been accounted for as a pooling, as described in Chapter 7 (pages 267–273).

For the year ended December 31, Year 11, Starr Company reported net income of $60,000. Starr's board of directors on December 20, Year 11, declared a cash dividend of $0.60 per share on the 40,000 outstanding shares of Starr Company capital stock. The dividend was payable January 8, Year 12, to stockholders of record December 29, Year 11.

Under the equity method of accounting, Palm Corporation prepares the following journal entries to record the operating results of Starr Company for the year ended December 31, Year 11:

Year 11

Dec. 20 Intercompany Dividends Receivable (40,000 × $0.60).. 24,000

            Investment in Subsidiary 24,000

         To record dividend declared by Starr Company, payable Jan. 8, Year 12, to stockholders of record Dec. 29, Year 11.

31 Investment in Subsidiary 60,000

            Intercompany Investment Income 60,000

         To record 100% of Starr Company's reported net income for the year ended Dec. 31, Year 11. (Income tax effects are disregarded.)

After the preceding journal entries are posted, Palm Corporation's Investment in Subsidiary account appears as follows:

Investment in Subsidiary

Date	Explanation	Debit	Credit	Balance
12/31/10	Balance forward (page 269)			390,000 dr
12/20/11	Dividend declared by subsidiary		24,000	366,000 dr
12/31/11	Reported net income of subsidiary	60,000		426,000 dr

The $426,000 balance of Palm Corporation's Investment in Subsidiary account at December 31, Year 11, exactly offsets the stockholder's equity accounts of Starr Company at that date (see Starr Company's December 31, Year 11, balance sheet on page 328), as follows:

Starr Company's stockholder's equity accounts:

Capital stock, $5 par $200,000

Paid-in capital in excess of par................................... 58,000

Retained earnings 168,000

     Total stockholder's equity of Starr Company $426,000

The Investment in Subsidiary account thus reflects Palm Corporation's 100% interest in the net assets of Starr Company at Starr's carrying amount. In this way, the equity method of accounting is consistent with pooling accounting theory.

Consolidating Financial Statements Working Paper The consolidating financial statements working paper and the related consolidation elimination working paper for Palm Corporation and subsidiary for the year ended December 31, Year 11, are presented below and on page 328. The intercompany receivable and payable is the $24,000 dividend payable by Starr Company to Palm Corporation on December 31, Year 11. (The advances by Palm Corporation to Starr Company which were outstanding at December 31, Year 10, were repaid by Starr on January 2, Year 11.)

Equity method: Wholly owned pooled subsidiary subsequent to business combination

PALM CORPORATION AND SUBSIDIARY
Consolidation Elimination Working Paper
December 31, Year 11

(a) Capital Stock—Starr	200,000	
Paid-in Capital in Excess of Par—Starr	58,000	
Retained Earnings of Subsidiary—Palm	132,000	
Intercompany Investment Income—Palm	60,000	
Investment in Subsidiary—Palm		426,000
Dividends—Starr		24,000

To elimininate intercompany investment, related accounts for stockholder's equity of subsidiary, and investment income from subsidiary.

The following aspects of the consolidating working paper for Palm Corporation and subsidiary should be emphasized:

1 The intercompany receivable and payable, placed in adjacent columns on the same line, are offset without a formal consolidation elimination.

2 The consolidation elimination cancels all intercompany transactions and balances not dealt with by the offset described in **1** above.

3 **Consolidated net income** is the same as the **parent company's net income.** Also, **consolidated retained earnings** is equal to the total of the **parent company's** two retained earnings accounts, as demonstrated below:

Total of parent company's two retained earnings accounts equals consolidated retained earnings

Palm Corporation's retained earnings accounts:	
Retained earnings	$159,000
Retained earnings of subsidiary	132,000
Total (equal to consolidated retained earnings)	$291,000

Equity method: Wholly owned pooled subsidiary subsequent to business combination

PALM CORPORATION AND SUBSIDIARY
Consolidating Financial Statements Working Paper
For Year Ended December 31, Year 11

	Palm Corporation	Starr Company	Consolidation Eliminations Increase (Decrease)	Consolidated
Income Statement				
Revenue				
Net sales	$1,100,000	$680,000		$1,780,000
Intercompany investment income	60,000	-0-	(a) $ (60,000)	-0-
Total revenue	$1,160,000	$680,000	$ (60,000)	$1,780,000
Costs and expenses				
Costs of goods sold	$ 700,000	$450,000		$1,150,000
Selling, general, and administrative expenses	151,000	80,000		231,000
Interest expense	49,000	-0-		49,000
Income taxes expense	120,000	90,000		210,000
Total costs and expenses	$1,020,000	$620,000		$1,640,000
Net income	$ 140,000	$ 60,000	$ (60,000)	$ 140,000
Statement of Retained Earnings				
Retained earnings, Jan. 1, Year 11	$ 49,000	$132,000		$ 181,000
Net income	140,000	60,000	$ (60,000)	140,000
Subtotal	$ 189,000	$192,000	$ (60,000)	$ 321,000
Dividends	30,000	24,000	(a) (24,000)	30,000
Retained earnings, Dec. 31, Year 11	$ 159,000	$168,000	$ (36,000)	$ 291,000
Balance Sheet				
Assets				
Intercompany receivables (payables)	$ 24,000	$ (24,000)		$ -0-
Investment in subsidiary	426,000	-0-	(a) $(426,000)	-0-
Other assets	679,900	674,100		1,354,000
Total assets	$1,129,900	$650,100	$(426,000)	$1,354,000
Liabilities & Stockholders' Equity				
Liabilities	$ 230,900	$224,100		$ 455,000
Common stock, $10 par	400,000	-0-		400,000
Capital stock, $5 par	-0-	200,000	(a) $(200,000)	-0-
Paid-in capital in excess of par	208,000	58,000	(a) (58,000)	208,000
Retained earnings	159,000	168,000	(36,000)	291,000
Retained earnings of subsidiary	132,000	-0-	(a) (132,000)	-0-
Total liabilities & stockholders' equity	$1,129,900	$650,100	$(426,000)	$1,354,000

This equality is a direct result of Palm Corporation's use of the equity method of accounting for its investment in Starr Company.

4 The consolidation elimination cancels the parent company's Retained Earnings of Subsidiary account, because it carries a balance equal to the subsidiary's retained earnings *at the beginning of the year.* Only in this manner can each of the three sets of financial statements (income statement, statement of retained earnings, and balance sheet) be consolidated in turn.

Closing Entries   The equity method of accounting ignores legal form in favor of the economic substance of the relationship between a parent company and its subsidiary. However, state corporation laws necessitate a careful accounting for retained earnings available for dividends. Accordingly, Palm Corporation should prepare the following closing entry at December 31, Year 11, after the consolidating financial statements working paper has been completed:

<table>
<tr><td rowspan="10" style="text-align:right">*Parent company's closing entry under equity method of accounting for pooled subsidiary*</td></tr>
<tr><td>Net Sales..</td><td>1,100,000</td><td></td></tr>
<tr><td>Intercompany Investment Income....................</td><td>60,000</td><td></td></tr>
<tr><td>   Costs and Expenses ....</td><td></td><td>1,020,000</td></tr>
<tr><td>   Retained Earnings of Subsidiary ($60,000 −</td><td></td><td></td></tr>
<tr><td> $24,000)....................................</td><td></td><td>36,000</td></tr>
<tr><td>   Retained Earnings ($140,000 − $36,000) ....</td><td></td><td>104,000</td></tr>
<tr><td colspan="3">To close revenue and expense accounts; to transfer net income legally available for dividends to retained earnings; and to segregate 100% share of net income of subsidiary not distributed as dividends by subsidiary.</td></tr>
</table>

The above closing entry excludes from Palm Corporation's retained earnings the amount of Palm's recorded net income not available for dividends to Palm's shareholders—$36,000. This amount is computed as follows:

Net income of Starr Company recorded by Palm Corporation	$60,000
Less: Dividends paid by Starr Company to Palm Corporation	24,000
Amount of Starr Company's net income not distributed as a dividend to Palm Corporation	$36,000

In addition, the closing entry illustrated above increases Palm's Retained Earnings of Subsidiary account as follows:

<table>
<tr><td>Balance of
parent com-
pany's Re-
tained Earn-
ings of
Subsidiary
account after
closing entry</td><td>

Balance before closing entry $132,000
Amount of closing entry 36,000
Balance after closing entry (agrees with Starr Company's ending
  retained earnings) $168,000

</td></tr>
</table>

Illustration of equity method of accounting for partially owned pooled subsidiary

The Post Corporation–Sage Company pooling business combination described in Chapter 7 (pages 273–278) will be used to illustrate the equity method of accounting for the operating results of a partially owned pooled subsidiary.

Assume that Sage Company on March 24, Year 7, declared a $1 per share dividend payable April 16, Year 7, to shareholders of record April 1, Year 7, and that Sage Company reported net income of $90,000 for the year ended April 30, Year 7. The following journal entries recognize the above-described dividend in the accounting records of Sage Company:

<table>
<tr><td>Partially
owned sub-
sidiary's
journal entries
for declaration
and payment
of dividend</td><td>

Year 7
Mar. 24 Dividends (40,000 shares × $1) 40,000
              Dividends Payable ($40,000 × 5%) 2,000
              Intercompany Dividends Payable ($40,000 ×
                95%) 38,000
          To record declaration of dividend payable Apr. 16,
          Year 7, to stockholders of record Apr. 1, Year 7.

Apr. 16 Dividends Payable 2,000
        Intercompany Dividends Payable 38,000
              Cash 40,000
          To record payment of dividend declared Mar. 24, Year 7,
          to stockholders of record Apr. 1, Year 7.

</td></tr>
</table>

The following journal entries are required in the accounting records of Post Corporation:

<table>
<tr><td>Parent com-
pany's equity
method
journal entries
(cont.)</td><td>

Year 7
Mar. 24 Intercompany Dividends Receivable 38,000
              Investment in Subsidiary 38,000
          To record dividend declared by Sage Company, payable
          Apr. 16, Year 7, to stockholders of record Apr. 1, Year 7.

</td></tr>
</table>

to record
operating
results of
partially
owned pooled
subsidiary

Apr. 16 Cash	38,000	
Intercompany Dividends Receivable		38,000
To record receipt of dividend from Sage Company.		
Apr. 30 Investment in Subsidiary ($90,000 × 95%)	85,500	
Intercompany Investment Income		85,500
To record 95% of net income of Sage Company for the		
year ended Apr. 30, Year 7. (Income tax effects are		
disregarded.)		

After the preceding journal entries are posted, Post Corporation's Investment in Subsidiary account appears as follows:

Ledger
account of
parent com-
pany using
equity method
of accounting
for partially
owned pooled
subsidiary

Investment in Subsidiary

Date	Explanation	Debit	Credit	Balance
4/30/6	Balance forward (page 275)			920,550 dr
3/24/7	Dividend declared by subsidiary		38,000	882,550 dr
4/30/7	Reported net income of subsidiary	85,500		968,050 dr

The $968,050 balance of Post Corporation's Investment in Subsidiary account at April 30, Year 7, is equal to 95% of the total of Sage Company's stockholders' equity accounts at that date (see Sage Company's April 30, Year 7, balance sheet on page 332), as follows:

95% of total
stockholders'
equity ac-
counts of
partially
owned pooled
subsidiary
equal to
balance of
parent com-
pany's invest-
ment account

Sage Company's stockholders' equity accounts:	
Capital stock, $10 par	$ 400,000
Paid-in capital in excess of par	235,000
Retained earnings	384,000
Total stockholders' equity of Sage Company	$1,019,000
95% of Sage's stockholders' equity ($1,019,000 × 95%)	$ 968,050

Thus, the Investment in Subsidiary account reflects Post Corporation's 95% interest in the net assets of Sage Company at Sage's carrying amount. In this way, the equity method of accounting is consistent with pooling accounting theory.

Consolidating Financial Statements Working Paper The consolidating financial statements working paper and the related consolidation elimination working paper for Post Corporation and subsidiary for the year ended April 30, Year 7, are presented on pages 332–333.

Equity method: Partially owned pooled subsidiary subsequent to business combination

POST CORPORATION AND SUBSIDIARY
Consolidating Financial Statements Working Paper
For Year Ended April 30, Year 7

	Post Corporation	Sage Company	Consolidation Eliminations Increase (Decrease)	Consolidated
Income Statement				
Revenue				
Net sales	$5,611,000	$1,089,000		$6,700,000
Intercompany investment				
income	85,500	-0-	(a) $ (85,500)	-0-
Total revenue	$5,696,500	$1,089,000	$ (85,500)	$6,700,000
Costs and expenses				
Cost of goods sold	$3,925,000	$ 700,000		$4,625,000
Selling, general and				
administrative expenses . . .	556,000	129,000		685,000
Interest and income				
taxes expense	710,000	170,000		880,000
Minority interest in net				
income of subsidiary	-0-	-0-	(b) $ 4,500	4,500
Total costs and expenses .	$5,191,000	$ 999,000	$ 4,500	$6,194,500
Net income	$ 505,500	$ 90,000	$ (90,000)	$ 505,500
Statement of Retained Earnings				
Retained earnings, May 1,				
Year 6	$ 925,000	$ 334,000	(a) $ (16,700)	$1,242,300
Net income	505,500	90,000	(90,000)	505,500
Subtotal	$1,430,500	$ 424,000	$(106,700)	$1,747,800
Dividends	158,550	40,000	(a) (40,000)	158,550
Retained earnings, Apr. 30,				
Year 7	$1,271,950	$ 384,000	$ (66,700)	$1,589,250
Balance Sheet				
Assets				
Investment in subsidiary	$ 968,050	$ -0-	(a) $(968,050)	$ -0-
Other assets	5,195,000	1,960,000		7,155,000
Total assets	$6,163,050	$1,960,000	$(968,050)	$7,155,000
Liabilities & Stockholders'				
Equity				
Liabilities	$2,420,550	$ 941,000		$3,361,550
Minority interest in				
subsidiary	-0-	-0-	[(a) $ 46,450] [(b) 4,500]	50,950
Common stock, $1 par	1,057,000	-0-		1,057,000
Capital stock, $10 par	-0-	400,000	(a) (400,000)	-0-
Paid-in capital in excess of				
par	1,096,250	235,000	(a) (235,000)	1,096,250
Retained earnings	1,271,950	384,000	(a) (66,700)	1,589,250
Retained earnings of				
subsidiary	317,300	-0-	(a) (317,300)	-0-
Total liabilities &				
stockholders' equity	$6,163,050	$1,960,000	$(968,050)	$7,155,000

Equity method: Partially owned pooled subsidiary subsequent to business combination

POST CORPORATION AND SUBSIDIARY
Consolidation Eliminations Working Paper
April 30, Year 7

(a) Capital Stock—Sage	400,000	
Paid-in Capital in Excess of Par—Sage	235,000	
Retained Earnings—Sage ($334,000 × 5%)	16,700	
Retained Earnings of Subsidiary—Post	317,300	
Intercompany Investment Income—Post	85,500	
Investment in Subsidiary—Post		968,050
Dividends—Sage		40,000
Minority Interest in Subsidiary ($48,450−$2,000) ..		46,450

To eliminate intercompany investment and related accounts for stockholders' equity of subsidiary at beginning of year, and investment income from subsidiary; and to establish minority interest in subsidiary at beginning of year ($48,450) less minority dividends ($40,000 × 5% = $2,000).

(b) Minority Interest in Net Income of Subsidiary	4,500	
Minority Interest in Subsidiary		4,500

To establish minority interest in net income of subsidiary for year ended April 30, Year 7 ($90,000 × 5% = $4,500).

The following aspects of the consolidating working paper for Post Corporation and subsidiary are worthy of emphasis:

1 Consolidated net income is the same as the parent company's net income. Also, consolidated retained earnings is equal to the total of the **parent company's** two retained earnings accounts, as follows:

Total of parent company's two retained earnings accounts equals consolidated retained earnings

Post Corporation's retained earnings accounts:	
Retained earnings	$1,271,950
Retained earnings of subsidiary	317,300
Total (equal to consolidated retained earnings)	$1,589,250

2 The combined effect of the $46,450 and $4,500 credit entries of consolidation eliminations (a) and (b) is to present the minority interest in subsidiary at April 30, Year 7, at its correct amount of 5% of Sage Company's total stockholders' equity at that date ($400,000 + $235,000 + $384,000 = $1,019,000; $1,019,000 × 5% = $50,950).

Closing Entries　Palm Corporation prepares the following closing entry at April 30, Year 7, after the consolidating financial statements working paper has been completed:

<table>
<tr><td rowspan="8" style="text-align:right">Parent company's closing entry under equity method of accounting for pooled subsidiary</td><td>Net Sales ....</td><td style="text-align:right">5,611,000</td><td></td></tr>
<tr><td>Intercompany Investment Income ....</td><td style="text-align:right">85,500</td><td></td></tr>
<tr><td>　　Cost and Expenses ....</td><td></td><td style="text-align:right">5,191,000</td></tr>
<tr><td>　　Retained Earnings of Subsidiary　[($90,000 −</td><td></td><td></td></tr>
<tr><td>　　　$40,000) × 95%] ....</td><td></td><td style="text-align:right">47,500</td></tr>
<tr><td>　　Retained Earnings ($505,500 − $47,500) ....</td><td></td><td style="text-align:right">458,000</td></tr>
<tr><td colspan="3">To close revenue and expense accounts; to transfer net income legally available for dividends to retained earnings; and to segregate 95% share of net income of subsidiary not distributed as dividends by subsidiary.</td></tr>
</table>

The closing entry illustrated above increases Post Corporation's Retained Earnings of Subsidiary account as follows:

<table>
<tr><td rowspan="4" style="text-align:right">Balance of parent company's Retained Earnings of Subsidiary account after closing entry</td><td>Balance before closing entry ....</td><td style="text-align:right">$317,300</td></tr>
<tr><td>Amount of closing entry ....</td><td style="text-align:right">47,500</td></tr>
<tr><td>Balance after closing entry (equals 95% of $384,000, Sage Company's</td><td></td></tr>
<tr><td>　ending retained earnings balance) ....</td><td style="text-align:right">$364,800</td></tr>
</table>

ACCOUNTING FOR INTERCOMPANY TRANSACTIONS NOT INVOLVING PROFIT OR LOSS

Subsequent to the date of a business combination, a parent company and its subsidiaries may enter into a number of business transactions with each other. Both parent and subsidiary companies should account for these intercompany transactions in a manner which facilitates the consolidation process. To this end, separate ledger accounts should be established for all intercompany assets, liabilities, revenue, and expenses. These separate accounts clearly identify those intercompany items which must be eliminated in the preparation of consolidated financial statements. The accounting techniques described above are designed to assure that consolidated financial statements include only those balances and transactions resulting from the consolidated group's dealings with **outsiders.**

Among the numerous types of transactions (other than dividends) consummated between a parent company and its subsidiaries are the following:

Sales of merchandise (inventories)
Sales of land or depreciable assets
Sales of intangible assets
Loans on notes or open account
Leases of real or personal property
Rendering of services

The first three types of transactions listed above usually involve an element of profit or loss, which complicates the preparation of consolidated financial statements. Discussion of these intercompany transactions is deferred until Chapter 10.

Loans on notes or open account

Parent companies generally have more extensive financial resources or bank lines of credit than do their subsidiaries. Also, it may be more economical in terms of favorable interest rates for the parent company to carry out *all* the affiliated group's borrowings from financial institutions. Under these circumstances, the parent company will make loans to its subsidiaries for their working capital or other needs. Generally, the rate of interest on such loans exceeds the parent company's borrowing rate.

To illustrate, assume that during the year ended December 31, Year 12, Palm Corporation made the following cash loans to its wholly owned subsidiary, Starr Company, on promissory notes:

	Date of note	Term of note, months	Interest rate, %	Amount
Loans by parent company to wholly owned subsidiary	Feb. 1, Year 12	6	10	$10,000
	Apr. 1, Year 12	6	10	15,000
	Sept. 1, Year 12	6	10	21,000
	Nov. 1, Year 12	6	10	24,000

To differentiate properly between intercompany loans and loans with outsiders, Palm Corporation and Starr Company would use the accounts shown on page 336 to record the foregoing transactions (assuming all promissory notes were paid when due).

Ledger ac-
counts of
parent com-
pany and
subsidiary for
intercompany
loan trans-
actions

Palm Corporation Ledger

Intercompany Notes Receivable

Feb. 1	10,000	Aug. 1	10,000
Apr. 1	15,000	Oct. 1	15,000
Sept. 1	21,000		
Nov. 1	24,000		

Starr Company Ledger

Intercompany Notes Payable

Aug. 1	10,000	Feb. 1	10,000
Oct. 1	15,000	Apr. 1	15,000
		Sept. 1	21,000
		Nov. 1	24,000

Intercompany Interest Receivable

Dec. 31	1,100

Intercompany Interest Payable

Dec. 31	1,100

Intercompany Interest Revenue

Aug. 1	500
Oct. 1	750
Dec. 31	1,100

Intercompany Interest Expense

Aug. 1	500
Oct. 1	750
Dec. 31	1,100

In consolidating financial statements working paper for Palm Corporation and subsidiary for the year ended December 31, Year 12, the accounts illustrated above would appear as follows:

PALM CORPORATION AND SUBSIDIARY
Partial Consolidating Financial Statements Working Paper
For Year Ended December 31, Year 12

	Palm Corporation	Starr Company	Consolidation Eliminations	Consolidated
Income Statement				
Revenue				
Intercompany				
revenue				
(expenses)	$ 2,350	$ (2,350)		$ -0-
Balance Sheet				
Assets				
Intercompany				
receivables				
(payables)	$46,100	$(46,100)		$ -0-

It is apparent from the above illustration that careful identification of intercompany ledger account balances in the accounting records of the affiliated companies is essential for correct elimination of the intercompany items in the consolidating financial statements working paper.

Discounting of Intercompany Notes If an intercompany note receivable is discounted by the holder, the note in effect is payable to an *outsider*—the discounting bank. Consequently, discounted intercompany notes are *not eliminated* in the consolidating financial statements working paper.

Suppose, for example, that on December 1, Year 12, Palm Corporation had discounted the $24,000 note receivable from Starr Company at a 12% discount rate. Palm would prepare the following journal entry:

Parent company's journal entry for discounting of note receivable from subsidiary

Cash ($25,200 − $1,260)	23,940	
Interest Expense	260	
Intercompany Notes Receivable		24,000
Intercompany Interest Revenue ($24,000 × 10% × $\frac{1}{12}$) ..		200

To record discounting of 10%, six-month note receivable from Starr Company dated Nov. 1, Year 12 at a discount rate of 12%. Cash proceeds are computed as follows:

Maturity value of note [$24,000 + ($24,000 × 10% × $\frac{6}{12}$)]	$25,200
Discount ($25,200 × 12% × $\frac{5}{12}$)	1,260
Cash proceeds	$23,940

The preceding journal entry recognizes intercompany interest revenue for the one month the note was held by Palm Corporation. This approach is required because Starr Company will reflect in its accounts one month of intercompany interest expense on the note.

To assure proper accountability for the $24,000 note, Palm Corporation should notify Starr Company of the discounting. Starr Company would then prepare the following journal entry at December 1, Year 12:

Subsidiary journal entry for parent company's discounting of note payable by subsidiary to parent company

Intercompany Notes Payable	24,000	
Intercompany Interest Expense	200	
Notes Payable		24,000
Interest Payable		200

To transfer 10%, six-month note payable to Palm Corporation dated Nov. 1, Year 12, from intercompany notes to outsider notes. Action is necessary because Palm Corporation discounted the note on this date.

In the preceding journal entry, Starr Company credited Interest Payable rather than Intercompany Interest Payable for the $200 accrued interest on the note. This approach is required because the *discounting bank,* not Palm Corporation, is now the payee for the *total maturity value* of the note.

Under the note discounting assumption, the accounts related to intercompany notes would appear in the December 31, Year 12, consolidating financial statements working paper as follows:

PALM CORPORATION AND SUBSIDIARY
Partial Consolidating Financial Statements Working Paper
For Year Ended December 31, Year 12

	Palm Corporation	Starr Company	Consolidation Eliminations	Consolidated
Income Statement				
Revenue				
Intercompany				
revenue				
(expenses)	$ 2,150*	$ (2,150)*		$ -0-
Balance Sheet				
Assets				
Intercompany				
receivables				
(payables)	$21,700†	$(21,700)†		$ -0-

* $200 less than in illustration on page 336 because $24,000 discounted note earned interest for one month rather than two months.
† $21,000 note dated Sept. 1, Year 12, plus $700 accrued interest.

Leases of real or personal property

If a parent company leases real or personal property to a subsidiary, or vice versa, it is essential that both affiliates use the same accounting principles for the lease. If the lease is an *operating lease,*[1] the lessor affiliate should account for rental payments as revenue, and the lessee affiliate should record the payments as expense. For a *capital lease,*[1] the lessor affiliate should record a sale of the real or personal property, and the lessee affiliate should account for the lease as a "purchase" of the property. Accounting for a capital lease often involves intercompany profits or losses, which are discussed in Chapter 10.

To illustrate consolidation techniques for an intercompany *operating lease,* assume that Palm Corporation leases space for a sales office to Starr Company under a 10-year lease dated February 1, Year 12. The lease requires monthly rentals of $2,500 payable in advance the first day of each month beginning February 1, Year 12.

In the income statement section of the consolidating financial statements working paper for the year ended December 31, Year 12, Palm

[1] The accounting for operating leases and capital leases is included in the *Intermediate Accounting* book of this series.

Corporation's $27,500 rent revenue would be offset against Starr Company's rent expense in a manner similar to the offset of intercompany interest revenue and expense illustrated previously. There would be no intercompany assets or liabilities to be offset in an operating lease when rent is payable in advance at the beginning of each month.

Rendering of services

One affiliate may render various services to another, with resultant intercompany fee revenue and expenses. A common example is the **management fee** charged by a parent company to its subsidiaries. The object of this fee is to reimburse the parent company for managerial advice and supervision rendered to the subsidiaries.

Management fees often are billed monthly by the parent company, computed as a percentage of the subsidiary's net sales, number of employees, total assets, or some other measure. No new consolidation problems are introduced by intercompany fee revenue and expenses. However, care must be taken to make certain that both the parent company and the subsidiary record the fee billings in the same accounting period, because the billings typically are issued a few days after the end of the month.

Income taxes applicable to intercompany transactions

The intercompany revenue and expense transactions illustrated in this chapter do not include an element of intercompany profit or loss for the consolidated entity. This is true because the revenue of one affiliate exactly offsets the expense of the other affiliate in the income statement section of the consolidating financial statements working paper. Consequently, there are no income tax effects associated with the elimination of the intercompany revenue and expenses, whether the parent company and its subsidiaries file separate income tax returns or a consolidated income tax return.

Summary: Intercompany transactions and balances

The preceding sections have emphasized the necessity of clearly identifying intercompany ledger account balances in the accounting records of both the parent company and the subsidiary. This careful identification facilitates the elimination of intercompany items in the preparation of consolidated financial statements. Sometimes, the separate financial statements of a parent company and a subsidiary include differing balances for intercompany items which should offset. Before preparing the consolidating financial statements working paper, the accountant should prepare any necessary journal entries to correct intercompany balances or to bring such balances up to date.

REVIEW QUESTIONS

1 Describe the special features of the closing entry for a parent company which uses the equity method of accounting for the operating results of a pooled subsidiary.

2 How does the balance in a parent company's Retained Earnings of Subsidiary account for a pooled subsidiary differ from the balance of the same account for a purchased subsidiary?

3 Why is the equity method of accounting for a subsidiary's operating results consistent with the pooling theory of accounting for a business combination?

4 How should a parent company and subsidiary account for intercompany transactions and balances to assure their correct elimination in the preparation of consolidated financial statements? Explain.

5 What are five common intercompany transactions between a parent company and its subsidiary?

6 Princeton Corporation rents a sales office to its wholly owned subsidiary under an operating lease requiring rent of $500 per month. What are the income tax effects of the elimination of Princeton's $6,000 rent revenue and the subsidiary's $6,000 rent expense in the preparation of a consolidated income statement? Explain.

7 Is an intercompany note receivable which has been discounted at a bank eliminated in the preparation of a consolidated balance sheet? Explain.

EXERCISES

Ex. 9-1 On March 13, Year 7, Parker Corporation loaned $100,000 to its subsidiary, Sark Company, on a 90-day, 8% note. On April 12, Year 7, Parker Corporation discounted the Sark Company note at First National Bank at a 10% discount rate.

Compute the debit to the Cash account in Parker Corporation's journal entry to record the discounting of the Sark Company note.

Ex. 9-2 Southern Company, a 99%-owned pooled subsidiary of Packwood Corporation, reported net income of $100,000 and paid dividends of $40,000 for the year ended March 31, Year 4.

Compute the credit to the Retained Earnings of Subsidiary account in Packwood Corporation's closing entry at March 31, Year 4.

Ex. 9-3 Partridge Corporation uses the equity method of accounting for its 96%-owned pooled subsidiary, Swallow Company, with which it combined several years ago. For the year ended October 31, Year 6, Swallow Company reported net income of $60,000 and paid dividends of $40,000.

Compute the balance in Partridge Corporation's Intercompany Investment Income account at October 31, Year 6.

Ex. 9-4 On March 1, Year 2, Payton Corporation loaned $10,000 to its subsidiary, Slagle Company, on a 90-day, 7% promissory note. On March 31, Year 2, Payton Corporation discounted the Slagle Company note at the bank at a 10% discount rate.

Prepare Payton Corporation's journal entry to record the discounting of the note.

Ex. 9-5 Pender Corporation uses the equity method of accounting for the operating results of its 97%-owned pooled subsidiary, Sebo Company. For Year 6, Pender Corporation had net sales of $2,000,000 and total costs and expenses of $1,700,000. Sebo Company reported net income of $150,000 and declared dividends of $70,000.

Prepare Pender Corporation's journal entries to record its share of Sebo Company's dividends and net income for Year 6.

Ex. 9-6 Paley Corporation erroneously used the cost method of accounting for the operating results of its 94%-owned pooled subsidiary, Selma Company, with which Paley combined on May 31, Year 3. Details of Selma Company's Retained Earnings account for the three years since that date follow.

Retained Earnings

May 26, Year 4 Dividends	30,000	May 31, Year 3 Balance	470,000
May 31, Year 5 Net loss	20,000	May 31, Year 4 Net income	60,000
May 24, Year 6 Dividends	30,000	May 31, Year 6 Net income	80,000

Prepare an adjusting entry for Paley Corporation at May 31, Year 6, to convert its accounting for its subsidiary's operating results to the equity method. The entry should include the account or accounts necessary for Paley Corporation's income statement for the year ended May 31, Year 6.

Ex. 9-7 Saticoy Company, a wholly owned subsidiary of Porterville Corporation, reported net income of $70,000 and declared dividends of $20,000 for the year ended December 31, Year 6. Porterville Corporation had total revenue of $2,000,000, exclusive of intercompany investment income, and total costs and expenses of $1,200,000 for the year ended December 31, Year 6.

Prepare Porterville Corporation's closing entry at December 31, Year 6.

SHORT CASE FOR ANALYSIS AND DECISION

Case 9-1 As independent auditor of a new client, Aqua Water Company, you are reviewing the consolidating financial statements working paper prepared by Arthur Brady, Aqua Water Company's chief accountant. Aqua Water Company distributes water to homeowners in a suburb of a large city. Aqua Water Company purchases the water from Aqua Well Company, a subsidiary. Aqua Water organized Aqua Well five years ago and purchased all its capital stock for cash on that date. During the course of your audit, you have learned the following:

(1) Both Aqua Water Company and Aqua Well Company are public utilities subject to the jurisdiction of the state's Public Utilities Commission.

(2) Aqua Well charges Aqua Water for the transmission of water from wells to consumers. The transmission charge, at the customary utility rate, was approved by the state's Public Utilities Commission.

(3) Aqua Well charges Aqua Water separately for the volume of water delivered to Aqua Water's customers.

(4) Your audit working papers show the following audited amounts for the separate companies' financial statements:

	Aqua Water Company	Aqua Well Company
Total revenue	$3,500,000	$ 300,000
Net income	300,000	50,000
Total assets	5,700,000	1,000,000
Stockholders' equity	2,500,000	600,000

The consolidating financial statements working paper prepared by Aqua Water Company's chief accountant appears in order, except that Aqua Well's Transmission Revenue account of $60,000 is not offset against Aqua Water's Transmission Expense account of the same amount. The chief accountant explains that, because the transmission charge by Aqua Well is at the customary utility rate approved by the state's Public Utilities Commission, the charge should not be treated as intercompany revenue and expense. Furthermore, Brady points out, the consolidating financial statements working paper does offset Aqua Well Company's Water Sales account of $200,000 against Aqua Water Company's Water Purchases account of the same amount.

Instructions Do you concur with the chief accountant's position in this issue? Explain.

PROBLEMS

9-2 On January 1, Year 6, Peters, Inc., issued 200,000 additional shares of its voting common stock in exchange for 100,000 shares of Sorkin Company's outstanding voting common stock in a business combination appropriately accounted for as a pooling. The current fair value of Peters' voting common stock was $40 per share on the date of the business combination. The balance sheets of Peters and Sorkin immediately before the business combination contained the following information:

Peters, Inc.

Common stock, $5 par; authorized 1,000,000 shares; issued and outstanding 600,000 shares	$ 3,000,000
Paid-in capital in excess of par	6,000,000
Retained earnings	11,000,000
Total stockholders' equity	$20,000,000

Sorkin Company

Common stock, $10 par; authorized 250,000 shares; issued and outstanding 100,000 shares	$1,000,000
Paid-in capital in excess of par	2,000,000
Retained earnings	4,000,000
Total stockholders' equity	$7,000,000

Additional information is as follows:
(1) Net income for the year ended December 31, Year 6, was $1,150,000 for Peters and $350,000 for Sorkin. The net income for Peters does not include its share of Sorkin's net income.
(2) During Year 6, Peters paid $900,000 in dividends to its stockholders and Sorkin paid $210,000 in dividends to Peters.

Instructions Prepare the stockholders' equity section of the consolidated balance sheet of Peters, Inc., and its subsidiary, Sorkin Company at December 31, Year 6. Provide a supporting analysis for retained earnings. Disregard income tax considerations.

9-3 During the year ended October 31, Year 5, Strickland Company, 96%-owned pooled subsidiary of Prykop Corporation, reported net income of $50,000 and declared dividends of $20,000 on October 20, Year 5, payable November 10, Year 5, to stockholders of record October 31, Year 5.

Instructions
a Prepare journal entries for Prykop Corporation to record Strickland Company's operating results and dividend declaration for the year ended October 31, Year 5.
b Prepare the consolidation elimination for the minority interest in Strickland Company's net income for the year ended October 31, Year 5.

Disregard income taxes.

9-4 Photon Corporation owns 90% of the outstanding common stock of Spellman Company, acquired in a pooling business combination January 31, Year 1. For the year ended January 31, Year 2, Photon's Corporation's condensed unconsolidated income statement was as follows:

PHOTON CORPORATION
Income Statement
For Year Ended January 31, Year 2

Revenue

Net sales	$500,000
Intercompany investment income	27,000
Intercompany revenue	23,000
Total revenue	$550,000
Costs and expenses	510,000
Net income	$ 40,000

During the year ended January 31, Year 2, Spellman Company declared and paid dividends of $10,000.

Instructions Prepare in good form the closing entry for Photon Corporation at January 31, Year 2.

9-5 Pillsbury Corporation has begun making working capital loans to its wholly owned subsidiary, Sarpy Company, on 9% promissory notes. The following 120-day loans were made prior to June 30, Year 3, the close of the fiscal year:

May 1, Year 3	$15,000
May 31, Year 3	20,000

On June 6, Year 3, Pillsbury discounted the May 1 note at the bank, at a 12% discount rate.

Instructions Prepare journal entries to record the note transactions and related June 30, Year 3, adjustments:
a In the accounting records of Pillsbury Corporation.
b In the accounting records of Sarpy Company.

9-6 Pittsburgh Corporation completed a business combination with Syracuse Company on April 30, Year 7. Immediately thereafter, Pittsburgh began making cash advances on open account to Syracuse at a 10% annual interest rate. In addition, Syracuse agreed to pay a monthly management fee to Pittsburgh of 2% of monthly net sales. Payment was to be made no later than the tenth day of the month following Syracuse's accrual of the fee.

During your examination of the financial statements of Pittsburgh Corporation and Syracuse Company at July 31, Year 7, you discover that each company has set up only one account—entitled Intercompany Account—to record all intercompany transactions. Details of the two accounts at July 31, Year 7, are given below:

Pittsburgh Corporation Ledger
Intercompany Account—Syracuse Company

Date	Explanation	Ref.	Debit	Credit	Balance
May 2	Cash advance	CD	4,500		4,500 dr
May 27	Cash advance	CD	9,000		13,500 dr
June 11	Management fee	CR		2,000	11,500 dr
June 12	Repayment of May 2 advance	CR		4,550	6,950 dr
June 21	Cash advance	CD	10,000		16,950 dr
July 11	Management fee	CR		2,200	14,750 dr
July 27	Repayment of May 27 advance	CR		9,150	5,600 dr
July 31	Cash advance	CD	5,000		10,600 dr

Syracuse Company Ledger
Intercompany Account—Pittsburgh Corporation

Date	Explanation	Ref.	Debit	Credit	Balance
May 3	Cash advance	CR		4,500	4,500 cr
May 28	Cash advance	CR		9,000	13,500 cr
June 10	Management fee: $100,000 × 2%	CD	2,000		11,500 cr
June 11	Repayment of May 2 advance	CD	4,550		6,950 cr
June 22	Cash advance	CR		10,000	16,950 cr
July 10	Management fee: $110,000 × 2%	CD	2,200		14,750 cr
July 26	Repayment of May 27 advance	CD	9,150		5,600 cr

Your audit working papers show audited net sales of $330,000 for Syracuse Company for the three months ended July 31, Year 7. You agree to the companies' use of a 360-day year for computing interest.

Instructions Prepare in good form adjusting entries for Pittsburgh Corporation and Syracuse Company at July 31, Year 7. Establish appropriate separate intercompany accounts in the journal entries.

9-7 Ponce Corporation completed a pooling business combination with Skaggs Company on December 31, Year 6. 48,000 of Skaggs's 50,000 shares of outstanding common stock were exchanged in the combination.

Skaggs Company reported net income of $0.80 per share for Year 7 and declared dividends of $0.35 per share on December 13, Year 7, payable January 6, Year 8, to stockholders of record December 23, Year 7. There were no other intercompany transactions during Year 7.

Instructions Prepare journal entries to record:
a Skaggs Company's dividend declaration in its accounting records.
b Skaggs Company's operating results for Year 7 in Ponce's accounting records under the equity method of accounting.

9-8 On January 1, Year 3, Poll Corporation exchanged its capital stock for 100% of Strack Company's capital stock on a 1 for 4 basis. Poll's stock was selling on the market for $7 per share at the time, and the investment was recorded on this basis. The Poll stock exchanged was treasury stock that had been purchased for $4.50 per share three years prior to the business combination. The business combination qualified for pooling accounting. Out-of-pocket costs of the business combination may be ignored.

There was no market price available for Strack Company stock at the date of the business combination. The stockholders' equity per share of Strack stock was $1.60. Poll's board of directors justified the exchange ratio for the Strack stock on the grounds that the value of plant assets was understated.

The balance sheets of the two companies at December 31, Year 3, were as follows:

POLL CORPORATION AND STRACK COMPANY
Balance Sheets
December 31, Year 3

	Poll Corporation	Strack Company
Assets		
Cash	$ 50,000	$ (1,800)
Notes receivable	42,000	
Notes receivable discounted	(15,000)	
Accrued interest receivable	1,450	
Accounts receivable	68,000	68,800
Receivable from Strack Company	25,000	
Inventories	177,000	22,500
Investment in Strack Company	70,000	
Plant assets	290,000	240,000
Accumulated depreciation	(40,000)	(60,000)
Other assets	42,000	3,000
Total assets	$710,450	$272,500
Liabilities & Stockholders' Equity		
Notes payable	$ 45,000	$ 25,000
Accrued interest payable	300	1,750
Accounts payable	85,400	36,800
Payable to Poll Corporation		25,000
Other accrued liabilities	13,000	9,075
6% bonds payable, due Apr. 1, Year 13		100,000
Capital stock, $5 par	300,000	
Capital stock, $1 par		40,000
Paid-in capital in excess of par	150,000	
Retained earnings	116,750	34,875
Total liabilities & stockholders' equity	$710,450	$272,500

The following additional information is available:
(1) The income statement data for the two companies for the year ended December 31, Year 3, were as follows:

	Poll Corporation	Strack Company
Net sales	$600,000	$200,000
Costs and expenses	550,000	189,125
Net income	$ 50,000	$ 10,875

(2) Poll Corporation wired $13,000 to Strack Company's bank on January 2, Year 4, to cover the cash overdraft and to provide cash for working capital. The $13,000 was considered an additional advance to Strack.

(3) Strack's notes payable include a $10,000, 5% demand note payable to the president of Poll Corporation, who is not an officer of Strack Company. The note is dated July 1, Year 2, and interest is payable on July 1 and January 1. The remaining Strack Company notes payable are non-interest-bearing and are payable to Poll Corporation, which discounted them at the bank.

Instructions
a Prepare adjusting entries for Poll Corporation at December 31, Year 3.
b Prepare a consolidating balance sheet working paper at December 31, Year 3, and related consolidation eliminations working paper, in good form. Balances for Poll Corporation should reflect the adjusting entries in a.
Disregard income taxes.

10

CONSOLIDATED FINANCIAL STATEMENTS: INTERCOMPANY PROFITS AND LOSSES

Many transactions between a parent company and its subsidiary may involve an element of profit or loss. Among these transactions are intercompany sales of merchandise (inventories), intercompany sales of plant assets, and intercompany sales of intangible assets. Until intercompany profits or losses in such transactions are *realized* through the sale of the asset to an *outsider,* the profits or losses must be eliminated in the preparation of consolidated financial statements.

In addition, a parent or subsidiary company's purchase of its affiliate's bonds *in the open market* may result in a *realized* gain or loss *to the consolidated entity.* Because this realized gain or loss has not been reflected in the financial statements of either the parent company or the subsidiary at the date of the purchase of the bonds, it must be included in the consolidated financial statements.

In this chapter we shall discuss the consolidation eliminations for intercompany transactions of the types described above. We shall purposely illustrate intercompany transactions involving *profits,* because such transactions seldom involve losses.

Importance of eliminating or including intercompany profits and losses

At the outset, we must stress the importance of eliminating *unrealized* intercompany profits and losses and including *realized* gains or losses

in the preparation of consolidated income statements. Failure to eliminate **unrealized** amounts would result in consolidated income statements reflecting not only results of transactions with those **outside** the
consolidated entity, but also the result of **related-party** activities **within**
the affiliated group. Similarly, nonrecognition of **realized** gains and
losses would misstate consolidated net income. The parent company's
management would have free rein to manipulate net income if the accountant did not account for intercompany profits and losses properly
in the preparation of consolidated income statements.

INTERCOMPANY SALES OF MERCHANDISE (INVENTORIES)

Intercompany sales of merchandise are a natural outgrowth of a **vertical**
business combination, which involves a combinor and one or more of
its customers or suppliers as combinees. **Downstream** intercompany
sales of merchandise are those from a parent company to its subsidiaries. **Upstream** intercompany sales are those from subsidiaries to
the parent company. **Lateral** intercompany sales are between two subsidiaries of the same parent company.

The intercompany sales of merchandise between a parent company
and its subsidiary are similar to the intracompany shipments by a home
office to a branch, described in Chapter 4.

Intercompany sales of merchandise at cost

Intercompany sales of merchandise may be made at a price equal to the
selling company's cost. If so, the consolidation elimination is the same
whether all the goods were sold by the purchasing affiliate or whether
some of the goods remained in the purchaser's inventories at the date of
the consolidated financial statements. For example, assume that Palm
Corporation (the parent company) during the year ended December 31,
Year 12, sold merchandise costing $150,000 to Starr Company (the
subsidiary) **at a selling price equal to the cost** of the merchandise. Assume
further that Starr Company's December 31, Year 12, inventories included
$25,000 cost of merchandise obtained from Palm Corporation, and that
Starr still owed Palm $15,000 for merchandise purchases at December
31, Year 12. (Starr Company also purchased merchandise from other
suppliers during Year 12.)

The two companies would prepare the aggregate journal entries
illustrated on page 349 for the above transactions, assuming that both
companies used the perpetual inventory system.

The consolidating financial statements working paper for Palm Corporation and subsidiary for the year ended December 31, Year 12,
would include the data on page 350 with regard to intercompany sales
of merchandise only.

Journal entries related to parent company's sales of merchandise to subsidiary at cost

Explanations	Palm Corporation General Journal	Starr Company General Journal

(1) Palm sales of merchandise to Starr	Intercompany Accounts Receivable............. 150,000
	  Intercompany Sales 150,000
	
	Intercompany Cost of Goods Sold 150,000
	  Inventories 150,000
		Inventories 150,000
		  Intercompany Accounts Payable 150,000

(2) Starr payments to Palm for merchandise	Cash 135,000
	  Intercompany Accounts Receivable. 135,000
		Intercompany Accounts Payable 135,000
		  Cash 135,000

(3) Starr sales of merchandise purchased from Palm (Starr's sales prices are assumed)		Accounts Receivable 160,000
		  Sales 160,000
		
		Cost of Goods Sold 125,000
		  Inventories 125,000

PALM CORPORATION AND SUBSIDIARY
Partial Consolidating Financial Statements Working Paper
For Year Ended December 31, Year 12

	Palm Corporation	Starr Company	Consolidation Eliminations Increase (Decrease)	Consolidated
Income Statement				
Revenue				
Intercompany				
revenue				
(expenses)	$ -0-*	$ -0-	$-0-	$-0-
Balance Sheet				
Assets				
Intercompany				
receivable				
(payable)	$15,000	$(15,000)	$-0-	$-0-

* Palm Corporation's $150,000 intercompany sales and intercompany cost of goods sold are offset in Palm's separate income statement.

Note that Starr Company's cost of goods sold for Year 12 and inventories at December 31, Year 12, are not affected by consolidation eliminations. From a consolidated entity viewpoint, Starr's cost of goods sold and inventories are both stated at *cost;* no element of intercompany profit or loss is involved. In effect, Starr Company served as a *conduit* to outside customers for Palm Corporation's merchandise.

Intercompany profit in ending inventories

More typical than the intercompany sales of merchandise at cost described in the preceding section are intercompany sales involving a gross profit. The gross profit margin may be equal to, more than, or less than the margin on sales to outsiders. The intercompany gross profit is *realized* through the purchasing affilate's sales to outsiders. Consequently, any merchandise purchased from an affiliated company which remains unsold at the date of a consolidated balance sheet results in the *overstatement,* from a *consolidated* point of view, of the purchaser's ending inventories. The overstatement is equal to the amount of *unrealized* intercompany gross profit contained in the ending inventories. This overstatement is canceled through an appropriate consolidation elimination in the consolidating financial statements working paper.

Suppose, for example, that Sage Company (the partially owned subsidiary) during the year ended April 30, Year 8, began selling merchandise to Post Corporation (the parent company) at a gross profit margin of 20%. Sales by Sage to Post for the year totaled $120,000, of which $40,000 remained unsold by Post at April 30, Year 8. At that date, Post owed $30,000 to Sage for merchandise. Both companies used the perpetual inventory system.

The transactions described in the preceding paragraph would be recorded in summary form by the two companies as illustrated on page 352.

The intercompany gross profit in Sage Company's sales to Post Corporation during the year ended April 30, Year 8, is analyzed as follows:

Analysis of gross profit in partially owned subsidiary's sales of merchandise to parent company

	Selling price	Cost	Gross profit
Beginning inventories	$ -0-	$ -0-	$ -0-
Sales	120,000	96,000	24,000
Total	$120,000	$96,000	$24,000
Less: Ending inventories	40,000	32,000	8,000
Cost of goods sold	$ 80,000	$64,000	$16,000

This analysis demonstrates that the intercompany gross profit on sales by Sage Company to Post Corporation totaled $24,000, and that $16,000 of this intercompany profit was realized through Post Corporation's sales to outside customers. The remaining $8,000 of intercompany profit remains *unrealized* in Post Corporation's inventories at April 30, Year 8.

The following consolidation elimination would be required for Sage Company's intercompany sales of merchandise to Post Corporation for the year ended April 30, Year 8:

POST CORPORATION AND SUBSIDIARY
Partial Consolidation Eliminations Working Paper
April 30, Year 8

Intercompany Sales—Sage	120,000	
Intercompany Cost of Goods Sold—Sage		96,000
Cost of Goods Sold—Post		16,000
Inventories—Post		8,000

To eliminate intercompany sales, cost of goods sold, and unrealized profit in inventories. (Income tax effects are disregarded.)

Journal entries related to partially owned subsidiary's sales of merchandise to parent company at a gross profit

Explanations	Post Corporation General Journal		Sage Company General Journal	
(1) Sage sales of merchandise to Post	Inventories	120,000	Intercompany Accounts Receivable	120,000
	Intercompany Accounts Payable	120,000	Intercompany Sales	120,000
			Intercompany Cost of Goods Sold	96,000
			Inventories	96,000
(2) Post payments to Sage for merchandise	Intercompany Accounts Payable	90,000	Cash	90,000
	Cash	90,000	Intercompany Accounts Receivable	90,000
(3) Post sales of merchandise purchased from Sage (Post's sales prices are assumed)	Accounts Receivable	100,000		
	Sales	100,000		
	Cost of Goods Sold	80,000		
	Inventories	80,000		

The effects of the preceding consolidation elimination are threefold. First, it eliminates Sage Company's sales to Post Corporation and the related cost of goods sold. This avoids the overstatement of the **consolidated** amounts for sales and cost of goods sold, which should represent merchandise transactions with customers **outside** the consolidated entity. Second, the consolidation elimination removes the intercompany profit portion of Post Corporation's cost of goods sold, thus restating it to the cost of the **consolidated** entity. Finally, the elimination reduces the consolidated inventories to the actual cost for the consolidated entity.

Entering the preceding consolidation elimination in the consolidating financial statement working paper would result in the balances shown below (amounts for total sales to outsiders and cost of goods sold are assumed).

POST CORPORATION AND SUBSIDIARY				
Partial Consolidating Financial Statements Working Paper				
For Year Ended April 30, Year 8				
	Post Corporation	*Sage Company*	*Consolidation Eliminations Increase (Decrease)*	*Consolidated*
Income Statement				
Revenue				
Sales	$5,800,000	$1,200,000		$7,000,000
Intercompany				
sales	-0-	120,000	$(120,000)	-0-
Cost and expenses				
Cost of goods sold .	4,100,000	760,000	(16,000)	4,844,000
Intercompany cost				
of goods sold	-0-	96,000	(96,000)	-0-
Balance Sheet				
Assets				
Intercompany re-				
ceivable				
(payable)	$ (30,000)	$ 30,000		$ -0-
Inventories	900,000	475,000	$ (8,000)	1,367,000

Note that the $120,000 elimination of intercompany sales, less the $112,000 total ($16,000 + $96,000 = $112,000) of the cost of goods sold eliminations, equals $8,000—the amount of the intercompany profit eliminated from inventories. This $8,000 unrealized intercompany profit is attributable to Sage Company—the seller of the merchandise—and *must be taken into account in the determination of the minority interest in Sage Company's net income for the year ended April 30, Year 8.* The $8,000 also enters into the computation of Sage Company's retained earnings at April 30, Year 8. These matters are illustrated in the following section.

Intercompany profit in beginning and ending inventories

The consolidation elimination for intercompany sales of merchandise is complicated by intercompany profits in the **beginning** inventories of the purchaser. It is generally assumed that, on a first-in, first-out basis, the intercompany profit in the purchaser's **beginning** inventories is realized through sales to outsiders during the ensuing year. Only intercompany profit in **ending** inventories remains unrealized at the end of the year.

Continuing the illustration from the preceding section, assume that Sage Company's intercompany sales of merchandise to Post Corporation during the year ended April 30, Year 9, are analyzed as follows:

<table>
<tr><td rowspan="6">Analysis of gross profit in partially owned subsidiary's sales of merchandise to parent company</td><td></td><td>Selling price</td><td>Cost</td><td>Gross profit</td></tr>
<tr><td>Beginning inventories ....</td><td>$ 40,000</td><td>$ 32,000</td><td>$ 8,000</td></tr>
<tr><td>Sales ....</td><td>150,000</td><td>120,000</td><td>30,000</td></tr>
<tr><td>Total ....</td><td>$190,000</td><td>$152,000</td><td>$38,000</td></tr>
<tr><td>Less: Ending inventories ....</td><td>60,000</td><td>48,000</td><td>12,000</td></tr>
<tr><td>Cost of goods sold ....</td><td>$130,000</td><td>$104,000</td><td>$26,000</td></tr>
</table>

Sage Company's intercompany sales and intercompany cost of goods sold for the year ended April 30, Year 8, had been closed to Sage's Retained Earnings account. Consequently, Sage's April 30, Year 8, retained earnings was overstated by $7,600—95% of the amount of the unrealized intercompany profit in Post Corporation's April 30, Year 8, inventory. (The $400 remainder of the $8,000 unrealized profit at April 30, Year 8, is attributable to the minority interest in Sage Company, the **seller** of the merchandise.) The following consolidation elimination at April 30, Year 9, reflects these facts:

POST CORPORATION AND SUBSIDIARY
Partial Consolidation Eliminations Working Paper
April 30, Year 9

Retained Earnings—Sage ($8,000 × 95%)	7,600	
Minority Interest in Subsidiary ($8,000 × 5%)	400	
Intercompany Sales—Sage	150,000	
Intercompany Cost of Goods Sold—Sage		120,000
Cost of Goods Sold—Post		26,000
Inventories—Post		12,000

To eliminate intercompany sales, cost of goods sold, and
unrealized profit in inventories. (Income tax effects are disregarded.)

Intercompany profit in inventories and minority interest

Accountants have given considerable thought to the problem of intercompany profits in transactions of a partially owned subsidiary. There
is general agreement that all the intercompany profit in a partially owned
subsidiary's inventories should be eliminated for consolidated financial
statements. *This holds true whether the sales to the subsidiary are downstream from the parent company or are made by a wholly owned subsidiary of
the same parent.*

There has been no such agreement on the treatment of intercompany
profit in the parent company's or a subsidiary's inventories from upstream or lateral sales by a partially owned subsidiary. Two alternative
approaches have been suggested:

1 The first approach is elimination of intercompany profit only to the extent of
the parent company's ownership interest in the selling subsidiary's stock.
This approach builds upon the "parent company" concept of consolidated
financial statements (see Chapter 7, pages 278–279), in which the minority
interest is considered to be a *liability* of the consolidated entity. If the minority
shareholders are considered **outside creditors,** intercompany profit in the
parent company's inventories has been **realized** to the extent of the minority
shareholders' interest in the selling subsidiary's stock.

2 The second approach is elimination of all the intercompany profit. The "entity" concept of consolidated financial statements (see Chapter 7, page 279),
in which the minority interest is considered to be a *part of consolidated
stockholders' equity,* underlies this approach. If minority shareholders are
part owners of consolidated assets, their share of intercompany profits in
inventories has not been realized.

The AICPA sanctioned the second of the preceding approaches, in
the following passage from *Accounting Research Bulletin No. 51:*

> The amount of intercompany profit or loss to be eliminated . . . is not affected
> by the existence of a minority interest. The complete elimination of the inter-
> company profit or loss is consistent with the underlying assumption that the
> consolidated statements represent the financial position and operating re-

sults of a single business enterprise. The elimination of the intercompany profit or loss may be allocated proportionately between the majority and minority interests.[1]

Consequently, intercompany profits or losses in inventories resulting from *sales by a partially owned subsidiary* must be considered in the determination of minority interest in net income of the subsidiary, and in the computation of retained earnings of the subsidiary. The subsidiary's reported net income must be *increased* by the *realized* intercompany profit in the parent company's *beginning* inventories and *decreased* by the *unrealized* intercompany profit in the parent company's *ending* inventories. Failure to do so would attribute the *entire* intercompany profit effects to the *consolidated* net income.

Elimination of net profit versus elimination of gross profit

Some accounting theorists have discussed the propriety of eliminating intercompany *net* profit, rather than *gross* profit, in inventories of the consolidated entity. There is little theoretical support for such a proposal. First, elimination of intercompany *net* profit would in effect capitalize selling, general, and administrative expenses in consolidated inventories. Selling expenses are *always* period costs, and only in unusual circumstances are some general and administrative expenses capitalized in inventories as product costs. Second, determination of *net* profit for a particular merchandise item or product line requires many assumptions as to allocations of common costs. The resultant profit figure may be more a result of conjecture than an objectively determined amount.

INTERCOMPANY SALES OF PLANT ASSETS AND INTANGIBLE ASSETS

Intercompany sales of plant assets and intangible assets differ from intercompany sales of merchandise in two significant respects. First, intercompany sales of plant assets or intangibles between affiliated companies are rare transactions. In contrast, intercompany sales of merchandise recur frequently throughout each fiscal year, once a program of such sales has been established. Second, the relatively long economic lives of plant assets and intangible assets require the passage of many accounting periods before intercompany profits or losses on sales of these assets are realized in transactions with outsiders. Conversely, intercompany profits in consolidated inventories at the end of one accounting period usually are realized in sales to outsiders during the ensuing period.

These differences have their counterparts in the consolidation elimi-

---

[1] *ARB No. 51*, "Consolidated Financial Statements," AICPA (New York: 1959), p. 45.

nations for intercompany profits or losses on sales of plant assets or intangible assets described in the following sections.

Intercompany profit on sale of land

Suppose that, during the year ended April 30, Year 8, Post Corporation (the parent company) sold to Sage Company (the partially owned subsidiary) for $175,000 a parcel of undeveloped land which had cost Post $125,000. Sage Company acquired the land for a new building site. The two companies would record the transaction as follows (disregarding income tax effects to Post Corporation):

Journal entries for parent company's sale of land to partially owned subsidiary	Post Corporation General Journal		Sage Company General Journal	
	Cash 175,000		Land 175,000	
	Land	125,000	Cash	175,000
	Intercompany		To record purchase of	
	on Sale of	50,000	land from Post Corpo-	
	Land		ration.	
	To record sale of land			
	to Sage Company.			

In consolidated financial statements for the year ended April 30, Year 8, the land must be presented at its historical cost to the consolidated entity. Also, the $50,000 intercompany gain must be eliminated, because it has not been *realized* in a transaction with an outsider. Accordingly, the following consolidation elimination is required at April 30, Year 8:

POST CORPORATION AND SUBSIDIARY
Partial Consolidation Eliminations Working Paper
April 30, Year 8

Intercompany Gain on Sale of Land—Post 50,000
    Land—Sage 50,000
To eliminate unrealized intercompany profit on sale of land.
(Income tax effects are disregarded.)

The consolidation elimination above would appear as follows in the consolidating financial statements working paper for the year ended April 30, Year 8:

POST CORPORATION AND SUBSIDIARY
Partial Consolidating Financial Statements Working Paper
For Year Ended April 30, Year 8

	Post Corporation	Sage Company	Consolidation Eliminations Increase (Decrease)	Consolidated
Income Statement				
Revenue				
Intercompany				
gain on sale of				
land	$50,000	$ -0-	$(50,000)	$ -0-
Balance Sheet				
Assets				
Land	$ -0-	$175,000	$(50,000)	$125,000

Because land is not a depreciable asset, in subsequent years no journal entries affecting the land would be made by Sage Company unless the land were resold to an outsider (or back to Post Corporation).

Nevertheless, in ensuing years, as long as Sage Company owns the land, its $175,000 cost to Sage is overstated $50,000 for consolidated financial statement purposes. Because the $50,000 gain on the sale of the land was closed to Post Corporation's Retained Earnings account at April 30, Year 8, the following consolidation elimination is required for Year 9 and subsequent years:

POST CORPORATION AND SUBSIDIARY
Partial Consolidation Eliminations Working Paper
April 30, Year 9

Retained Earnings—Post	50,000	
Land—Sage		50,000

To eliminate unrealized intercompany profit in land. (Income tax effects are disregarded.)

The preceding consolidation elimination has no effect on the minority interest in the subsidiary, because *the gain was attributable to the parent company, the seller.*

Suppose that, instead of constructing a building on the land, Sage Company sold the land to an outsider for $200,000 during the year ended April 30, Year 10. Sage would prepare the following journal entry to record the sale:

Subsidiary's journal entry for sale of land to an outsider	Cash 200,000	
	Land	175,000
	Gain on Sale of Land	25,000
	To record sale of land to an outsider.	

The consolidated income statement for the year ended April 30, Year 10, must reflect the fact that, for **consolidated** purposes, a **$75,000 gain was realized** on Sage's sale of the land. This $75,000 gain consists of the $25,000 gain recorded by Sage, and the $50,000 intercompany gain on Post Corporation's sale of the land to Sage two years earlier. The following consolidation elimination at April 30, Year 10, is required:

POST CORPORATION AND SUBSIDIARY
Partial Consolidation Eliminations Working Paper
April 30, Year 10

Retained Earnings—Post	50,000	
Gain on Sale of Land—Sage		50,000
To attribute $50,000 unrealized profit on Post Corporation's sale of land to Sage Company to the gain on sale of land by Sage to an outsider. (Income tax effects are disregarded.)		

The $50,000 gain attributed to Sage Company in the preceding elimination would enter into the computation of the minority interest in Sage's net income for Year 10.

No further consolidation elimination would be required subsequent to Year 10.

Intercompany profit on sale of depreciable plant asset

Annual depreciation provisions cause a significant difference in the consolidation elimination for intercompany profit on the sale of a depreciable plant asset, compared to the eliminations described in the preceding section. Because the intercompany profit must be eliminated from the valuation of the depreciable asset for a consolidated balance sheet, the appropriate profit element must be eliminated from the related depreciation expense in the consolidated income statement. This is illustrated in the following pages.

Intercompany Profit at Date of Sale of Depreciable Plant Asset The consolidation elimination at date of sale for intercompany profit on the sale of a **depreciable plant asset** is identical to the comparable elimination for *land.* As of the date of sale, no depreciation has been recognized by the purchaser.

To illustrate, assume that on April 30, Year 8, Sage Company (the partially owned subsidiary) sold machinery to Post Corporation (the parent company). Details of the sale and of the machinery follow:

Selling price of machinery to Post Corporation	$60,000
Cost of machinery to Sage Company when acquired Apr. 30, Year 5	50,000
Estimated residual value:	
To Sage Company as of Apr. 30, Year 5	$ 4,000
To Post Corporation as of Apr. 30, Year 8	4,000
Estimated economic life:	
To Sage Company as of Apr. 30, Year 5	10 years
To Post Corporation as of Apr. 30, Year 8	5 years
Annual depreciation expense (straight-line method):	
To Sage Company—$46,000 × 10%	$ 4,600
To Post Corporation—$56,000 × 20%...............................	11,200

Details of machinery sold to parent company by partially owned subsidiary

The two companies would account for the sale at April 30, Year 8, as follows (disregarding income tax effects on Sage Company):

Journal entries for partially owned subsidiary's sale of machinery to parent company

Post Corporation General Journal	Sage Company General Journal
Machinery 60,000	Cash 60,000
Cash 60,000	Accumulated Depreciation 13,800
To record purchase of machinery from Sage Company	Machinery 50,000
	Intercompany Gain on Sale of Machinery 23,800
	To record sale of machinery to Post Corporation.

The following consolidation elimination would be required for consolidated financial statements at April 30, Year 8, the date of intercompany sale of the machinery:

POST CORPORATION AND SUBSIDIARY
Partial Consolidation Eliminations Working Paper
April 30, Year 8

Intercompany Gain on Sale of Machinery—Sage	23,800	
Machinery—Post		23,800
To eliminate unrealized intercompany profit on sale of machinery. (Income tax effects are disregarded.)		

The consolidation elimination above would result in the machinery being reflected in the consolidated balance sheet at its carrying amount to Sage Company—the seller—as follows:

Effect of elimination of unrealized intercompany profit on sale of machinery

Cost of machinery to Post Corporation (purchaser parent company) . . .	$60,000
Amount of consolidation elimination	23,800
Difference—equal to cost ($50,000), less accumulated depreciation ($13,800) of machinery to Sage Company (seller subsidiary)	$36,200

Elimination of the $23,800 intercompany gain on the sale of machinery *is taken into account in the determination of the minority interest in the net income of the partially owned subsidiary–the seller*—for Year 8. The $23,000 elimination also would enter into the computation of Sage Company's retained earnings, for consolidated purposes, at April 30, Year 8.

Intercompany Profit Subsequent to Date of Sale of Depreciable Plant Asset
An appropriate intercompany profit element must be eliminated from depreciation expense for a plant asset sold by one affiliate to another at a profit. The following consolidation elimination for Post Corporation and subsidiary at April 30, Year 9 (one year after the intercompany sale of machinery), illustrates this point:

POST CORPORATION AND SUBSIDIARY
Partial Consolidation Eliminations Working Paper
April 30, Year 9

Retained Earnings—Sage ($23,800 × 95%)	22,610	
Minority Interest in Subsidiary ($23,800 × 5%)	1,190	
Accumulated Depreciation—Post	4,760	
Machinery–Post		23,800
Depreciation Expense–Post		4,760

(continued)

> **POST CORPORATION AND SUBSIDIARY**
> **Partial Consolidation Eliminations Working Paper**
> **April 30, Year 9 (continued)**
>
> To eliminate unrealized intercompany profit in machinery and related depreciation. (Income tax effects are disregarded.) Profit element in depreciation computed as $23,800 × $\frac{1}{5}$ = $4,760, based on five-year estimated economic life of machinery.

Because Sage Company's gain on sale of the machinery was closed to Sage's Retained Earnings account, the preceding consolidation elimination corrects the resultant overstatement of Sage's beginning-of-year retained earnings from the viewpoint of the consolidated entity. In addition, the minority interest's share of the overstatement in the beginning retained earnings of Sage is recognized.

The intercompany profit eliminated from Post Corporation's depreciation expense may be verified as follows:

Verification of intercompany profit element in depreciation expense of parent company

Post's annual depreciation expense [($60,000 − $4,000) × $\frac{1}{5}$]	$11,200
Depreciation expense for a five-year economic life, based on Sage's carrying amount at date of sale [($36,200 − $4,000) × $\frac{1}{5}$]	6,440
Difference—equal to intercompany profit element in Post's annual depreciation expense	$ 4,760

Intercompany Profit in Depreciation and Minority Interest From the point of view of the consolidated entity, the intercompany profit element of annual depreciation expense represents a *realization* of a portion of the intercompany profit. Depreciation, in this view, is in effect an *indirect sale* of a portion of the machinery to the customers of Post Corporation—the purchaser of the machinery. The selling prices of Post's products produced by the machinery are established in amounts adequate to cover all costs of producing the products, including depreciation expense.

Thus, the $4,760 credit to Post Corporation's depreciation expense in the April 30, Year 9, consolidation elimination illustrated on page 361 in effect *increases* Sage Company's reported net income for consolidated purposes. *This increase must be considered in the computation of the minority interest in the subsidiary's net income for the year ended April 30, Year 9, and of the subsidiary's retained earnings at that date.*

Intercompany Profit in Later Years Consolidation eliminations for later years in the economic life of the machinery sold at an intercompany profit must reflect the fact that the intercompany profit element in annual depreciation expense in effect represents a *realization* of the intercompany profit. For example, the consolidation elimination for Post Corporation and subsidiary at April 30, Year 10 (two years following the intercompany sale of the machinery) is as follows:

POST CORPORATION AND SUBSIDIARY

Partial Consolidation Eliminations Working Paper

April 30, Year 10

Retained Earnings—Sage [($23,800 − $4,760) × 95%]	18,088	
Minority Interest in Subsidiary [(23,800 − $4,760) × 5%]	952	
Accumulated Depreciation—Post ($4,760 × 2)	9,520	
Machinery—Post		23,800
Depreciation Expense—Post		4,760

To eliminate unrealized intercompany profit in machinery and related depreciation. (Income tax effects are disregarded.)

The credit amounts of the preceding consolidation elimination for Year 10 are the same as those for Year 9. The credit amounts will remain unchanged for all consolidation eliminations during the remaining economic life of the machinery, because of the parent company's use of the straight-line method of depreciation. The $19,040 total of the debits to Sage Company's Retained Earnings account and to the minority interest in subsidiary represents the *unrealized* portion of the intercompany profit at the beginning of Year 10. Each succeeding year, the unrealized portion of the intercompany profit *decreases,* as indicated by the following summary of the consolidation elimination *debits* for those years:

POST CORPORATION AND SUBSIDIARY

Partial Consolidation Eliminations Working Paper—Debits Only

April 30, Year 11 through Year 13

	Year ended April 30		
	Year 11	Year 12	Year 13
Retained earnings—Sage	$13,566	$ 9,044	$ 4,522
Minority interest in subsidiary	714	476	238
Accumulated depreciation—Post	14,280	19,040	23,800

At the end of Year 13, the entire $23,800 of intercompany profit on the machinery has been realized through Post Corporation's annual depreciation charges. Thereafter, the following consolidation elimination is required for the machinery until it is sold or scrapped:

POST CORPORATION AND SUBSIDIARY
Partial Consolidation Eliminations Working Paper
April 30, Year 14

Accumulated Depreciation—Post	23,800	
Machinery—Post		23,800

To eliminate intercompany profit in machinery and related accumulated depreciation. (Income tax effects are disregarded.)

Intercompany profit on sale of intangible asset

The consolidation eliminations for intercompany profits on sales of intangible assets are similar to those for intercompany profits in depreciable plant assets. The unrealized intercompany profit of the selling affiliate is realized through annual amortization expense recorded by the purchasing affiliate.

PURCHASES OF AFFILIATE'S BONDS

The intercompany profits or losses on sales of merchandise, plant assets, and intangible assets are, at the date of sale, *unrealized* gains or losses resulting from transactions between two affiliated corporations. Intercompany gains and losses may be *realized by the consolidated entity* when one affiliate purchases in the open market bonds issued by another affiliate. The gain or loss on such a transaction is *imputed,* because the transaction is not consummated between the two affiliates. No realized or unrealized intercompany gain or loss would result from the *direct purchase* of one affilate's bonds by another affiliate, because the cost of the investment to the purchaser would be *exactly offset* by the issuance price of the debt.

Illustration of purchase of affiliate's bonds

Assume that on May 1, Year 7, Sage Company (the partially owned subsidiary) issued to the public $500,000 principal amount of 6% debentures (unsecured bonds) due May 1, Year 12. The debentures were issued at a price to yield an 8% return to investors. Interest was payable annually on May 1. Debenture issue costs are disregarded in this example.

The net proceeds of the debenture issue to Sage Company were $460,073, computed as follows:[2]

---

[2] *Intermediate Accounting* of this series contains comprehensive discussion of computations of debt issuance proceeds. The Appendix in the back of this text contains compound interest tables.

Computation of proceeds of bonds issued by partially owned subsidiary

Present value of $500,000 in five years @ 8%, with interest paid annually ($500,000 × 0.680583)	$340,292
Present value of $30,000 each year for five years @ 8% ($30,000 × 3.992710)	119,781
Proceeds of debenture issue	$460,073

During the year ended April 30, Year 8, Sage Company prepares the following journal entries for the debentures:

Partially owned subsidiary's journal entries for debentures

Year 7

May 1	Cash	460,073	
	Discount on Debentures Payable	39,927	
	Debentures Payable		500,000
	To record issuance of 6% debentures due May 1, Year 12, at a discount to yield 8%.		

Year 8

Apr. 30	Interest Expense ($460,073 × 8%)	36,806	
	Interest Payable		30,000
	Discount on Debentures Payable		6,806
	To record accrual of annual interest on 6% debentures.		

At April 30, Year 8, the balance of Sage Company's Discount on Debentures Payable account was $33,121 ($39,927 − $6,806 = $33,121).

Assume that on April 30, Year 8, Post Corporation (the parent company) had idle cash available for investment. With a market yield rate of 10% on that date, Sage Company's 6% debentures could be purchased at a substantial discount. Consequently, Post Corporation purchased in the open market on April 30, Year 8, $375,000 principal amount of the debentures for $327,452 plus $22,500 accrued interest for one year. The $327,452 purchase price is computed as follows:

Computation of parent company's purchase price for debentures of partially owned subsidiary

Present value of $375,000 in four years @ 10%, with interest paid annually ($375,000 × 0.683013)	$256,130
Present value of $22,500 each year for four years @ 10% ($22,500 × 3.169865)	71,322
Cost to Post Corporation of $375,000 principal amount of debentures .	$327,452

Post Corporation prepares the following journal entry at April 30, Year 8, to record the purchase of Sage Company's debentures:

<table>
<tr><td rowspan="6">Parent company's journal entry to record open-market purchase of debentures of partially owned subsidiary</td><td>Investment in Subsidiary's Debentures ....</td><td>327,452</td><td></td></tr>
<tr><td>Intercompany Interest Receivable ....</td><td>22,500</td><td></td></tr>
<tr><td>Cash ....</td><td></td><td>349,952</td></tr>
<tr><td>To record purchase of $375,000 principal amount of Sage</td><td></td><td></td></tr>
<tr><td>Company's 6% debentures due May 1, Year 12, and accrued</td><td></td><td></td></tr>
<tr><td>interest for one year.</td><td></td><td></td></tr>
</table>

Upon receiving notification of the parent company's purchase of the debentures, Sage Company prepares the following journal entry as of April 30, Year 8, to record the **intercompany** status of a portion of its debentures payable:

<table>
<tr><td rowspan="11">Partially owned subsidiary's journal entry to recognize parent company's open-market purchase of subsidiary's debentures</td><td>Debentures Payable ....</td><td>375,000</td><td></td></tr>
<tr><td>Discount on Intercompany Debentures Payable</td><td></td><td></td></tr>
<tr><td>($33,121 × $375,000/$500,000) ....</td><td>24,841</td><td></td></tr>
<tr><td>Interest Payable ($30,000 × $375,000/$500,000) ....</td><td>22,500</td><td></td></tr>
<tr><td>Intercompany Debentures Payable ....</td><td></td><td>375,000</td></tr>
<tr><td>Discount on Debentures Payable ....</td><td></td><td>24,841</td></tr>
<tr><td>Intercompany Interest Payable ....</td><td></td><td>22,500</td></tr>
<tr><td>To transfer to intercompany accounts all amounts attributable</td><td></td><td></td></tr>
<tr><td>to debentures payable purchased by parent company in open</td><td></td><td></td></tr>
<tr><td>market.</td><td></td><td></td></tr>
</table>

From the standpoint of the consolidated entity, Post Corporation's purchase of Sage Company's debentures is equivalent to the reacquisition of the debentures for the treasury at a **realized** gain of $22,707, computed as follows:

<table>
<tr><td rowspan="4">Computation of realized gain on parent company's open-market purchase of subsidiary's debentures</td><td>Carrying amount of Sage Company's debentures purchased by Post</td><td></td></tr>
<tr><td>Corporation at Apr. 30, Year 8 ($375,000 − $24,841) ....</td><td>$350,159</td></tr>
<tr><td>Cost of Post Corporation's investment ....</td><td>327,452</td></tr>
<tr><td>Gain on reacquisition of debentures ....</td><td>$ 22,707</td></tr>
</table>

The $22,707 realized gain *is not recorded* in the accounting records of either the parent company or the subsidiary. Instead, it is recognized *only* in the following consolidation elimination at April 30, Year 8:

POST CORPORATION AND SUBSIDIARY
Partial Consolidation Eliminations Working Paper
April 30, Year 8

Intercompany Debentures Payable—Sage	375,000	
Discount on Intercompany Debentures Payable—Sage		24,841
Investment in Subsidiary's Debentures—Post		327,452
Gain on Reacquisition of Debentures—Sage		22,707
To eliminate subsidiary's debentures purchased by parent,		
and to recognize gain on reacquistion of the debentures.		
(Income tax effects are disregarded.)		

Disposition of Gain on Reacquisition of Debentures The consolidation elimination illustrated above attributes the gain on Post Corporation's purchase of its subsidiary's debentures to Sage Company—the subsidiary. This treatment of the gain follows from the assumption that the parent company's open-market purchase of the subsidiary's debentures was, in effect, the acquisition of the debentures for the consolidated entity's treasury. The parent company acted as *agent* for the subsidiary in the open-market transaction; hence the gain is allocable to the subsidiary. Under this consolidated approach, the accounting for the gain on the reacquisition of the subsidiary's debentures is the same as if the *subsidiary itself* had reacquired the debentures.

The entire gain of $22,707 is reported in the consolidated income statement of Post Corporation and subsidiary for the year ended April 30, Year 8, in accordance with the provisions of *APB Opinion No. 26,* "Early Extinguishment of Debt." [3] If the gain is *material,* it is reported as an *extraordinary item,* as required by *FASB Statement No. 4,* "Reporting Gains and Losses from Extinguishment of Debt." [4]

Minority Interest in Gain on Reacquisition of Debentures As discussed in the preceding section, the gain on Post Corporation's reacquisition of its subsidiary's debentures is attributed to the subsidiary. It follows that *the gain should be considered in the computation of the minority interest in the subsidiary's net income for the year ended April 30, Year 8.* Also, the gain is included in the computation of the subsidiary's retained earnings at April 30, Year 8, for consolidated purposes.

[3] *APB Opinion No. 26,* "Early Extinguishment of Debt," AICPA (New York: 1973), pp. 501–502.
[4] *FASB Statement No. 4,* "Reporting Gains and Losses from Extinguishment of Debt," FASB (Stamford: 1975), p. 3, par. 8.

Accounting for gain in subsequent years

Affiliated
companies'
journal en-
tries for
debentures
for year
ended Apr. 30,
Year 9

In the four years following Post Corporation's purchase of Sage Company's debentures, the gain *realized but unrecorded* at the date of purchase is in effect *recorded* by the consolidated entity through the differences in the two affiliates' amortization of debenture discount. (It is essential that the affiliate which purchased the debentures undertake an amortization program consistent with that of the affiliate which issued the debentures.) To illustrate this concept, the accounting for the debenture interest by the two companies for the year ended April 30, Year 9, is presented below, and the relevant ledger accounts of both companies relative to the intercompany debentures are illustrated on pages 369–370 for the five years the debentures are outstanding.

	Post Corporation General Journal		*Sage Company General Journal*	
Year 8				
May 1	Cash 22,500		Intercompany Interest	
	Intercompany		Payable 22,500	
	Interest		Interest Payable 7,500	
	Receivable	22,500	Cash	30,000
	Receipt of accrued interest purchased on Sage Company's 6% debentures.		Payment of accrued interest on 6% debentures.	
Year 9				
Apr. 30	Intercompany Interest		Intercompany Interest	
	Receivable 22,500		Expense 28,013	
	Investment in		Interest Expense 9,338	
	Subsidiary's Debentures 10,245		Intercompany	
	Intercompany		Interest Payable .	22,500
	Interest Revenue .	32,745	Interest Payable ...	7,500
	Accrual of annual interest on Sage Company's 6% debentures. Interest computed as $327,452 × 10% = $32,745.		Discount on Intercompany Debentures Payable	5,513
			Discount on Debentures Payable .	1,838
			Accrual of annual interest on 6% debentures. Interest computed as follows:	
			Intercompany ($375,000 − $24,841) × 8% = $28,013	
			Other ($125,000 − $8,280) × 8% = $9,338	

Parent company's ledger accounts for intercompany debentures

Post Corporation Ledger
Investment in Subsidiary's Debentures

Date	Explanation	Debit	Credit	Balance
4/30/8	Purchase of $375,000 principal amount of debentures	327,452		327,452 dr
4/30/9	Amortization of discount ($32,745 − $22,500)	10,245		337,697 dr
4/30/10	Amortization of discount ($33,770 − $22,500)	11,270		348,967 dr
4/30/11	Amortization of discount ($34,897 − $22,500)	12,397		361,364 dr
4/30/12	Amortization of discount ($36,136 − $22,500)	13,636		375,000 dr

Intercompany Interest Revenue

Date	Explanation	Debit	Credit	Balance
4/30/9	($327,452 × 10%)		32,745	32,745 cr
4/30/9	Closing entry	32,745		-0-
4/30/10	($337,697 × 10%)		33,770	33,770 cr
4/30/10	Closing entry	33,770		-0-
4/30/11	($348,967 × 10%)		34,897	34,897 cr
4/30/11	Closing entry	34,897		-0-
4/30/12	($361,364 × 10%)		36,136	36,136 cr
4/30/12	Closing entry	36,136		-0-

Subsidiary's ledger accounts for intercompany debentures

Sage Company Ledger
Intercompany Debentures Payable

Date	Explanation	Debit	Credit	Balance
4/30/8	Debentures purchased by parent company		375,000	375,000 cr

Discount on Intercompany Debentures Payable

Date	Explanation	Debit	Credit	Balance
4/30/8	Debentures purchased by parent company	24,841		24,841 dr
4/30/9	Amortization ($28,013 − $22,500)		5,513	19,328 dr
4/30/10	Amortization ($28,454 − $22,500)		5,954	13,374 dr
4/30/11	Amortization ($28,930 − $22,500)		6,430	6,944 dr
4/30/12	Amortization ($29,444 − $22,500)		6,944	-0-

Intercompany Interest Expense

Date	Explanation	Debit	Credit	Balance
4/30/9	($375,000 − $24,841) × 8%	28,013		28,013 dr
4/30/9	Closing entry		28,013	-0-
4/30/10	($375,000 − $19,328) × 8%	28,454		28,454 dr
4/30/10	Closing entry		28,454	-0-
4/30/11	($375,000 − $13,374) × 8%	28,930		28,930 dr
4/30/11	Closing entry		28,930	-0-
4/30/12	($375,000 − $6,944) × 8%	29,444		29,444 dr
4/30/12	Closing entry		29,444	-0-

A comparison of the yearly entries to Post Corporation's Intercompany Interest Revenue account and Sage Company's Intercompany Interest Expense account demonstrates that the difference between the annual entries in the two accounts represents the *recording,* in the separate companies' accounting records, of the $22,707 gain *realized but unrecorded* when the parent company purchased the subsidiary's debentures in the open market. A summary of the differences between the two intercompany interest accounts appears below:

Differences between parent's Intercompany Interest Revenue account and subsidiary's Intercompany Interest Expense account total to realized gain on parent's purchase of subsidiary's debentures

Year ended April 30	Post Corporation's intercompany interest revenue	Sage Company's intercompany interest expense	Difference—representing recording of realized gain
Year 9	$ 32,745	$ 28,013	$ 4,732
Year 10	33,770	28,454	5,316
Year 11	34,897	28,930	5,967
Year 12	36,136	29,444	6,692
Totals	$137,548	$114,841	$22,707

Consolidation Elimination at April 30, Year 9 The consolidation elimination for the debentures and interest at April 30, Year 9, is as shown below.

POST CORPORATION AND SUBSIDIARY
Partial Consolidation Eliminations Working Paper
April 30, Year 9

Intercompany Interest Revenue—Post 32,745
Intercompany Debentures Payable—Sage 375,000
   Discount on Intercompany Debentures Payable—
    Sage 19,328

(continued)

POST CORPORATION AND SUBSIDIARY
Partial Consolidation Eliminations Working Paper
April 30, Year 9 (continued)

Investment in Subsidiary's Debentures—Post	337,697
Intercompany Interest Expense—Sage	28,013
Retained Earnings—Sage ($22,707 × 95%)	21,572
Minority Interest in Subsidiary ($22,707 × 5%)	1,135

To eliminate subsidiary's debentures owned by parent company, and related interest revenue and expense; and to increase subsidiary's beginning retained earnings by amount of unamortized realized gain on the reacquisition of the debentures. (Income tax effects are disregarded.)

The consolidation elimination above effectively reduces consolidated income before minority interest by $4,732 ($32,745 − $28,013 = $4,732). As indicated previously, the $4,732 is the difference between the eliminated intercompany interest revenue of the parent company and the subsidiary's intercompany interest expense. Failure to eliminate intercompany interest in this manner would result in a $4,732 overstatement of pre-minority interest consolidated income for Year 9, because the *entire* $22,707 realized gain on the reacquisition of the subsidiary's debentures was recognized in the consolidated income statement for Year 8—the year the debentures were reacquired.

The $4,732 reduction of consolidated income before minority interest is attributable to the subsidiary, because the original imputed gain to which the $4,732 relates was allocated to the subsidiary. Consequently, *the $4,732 must be considered in the computation of minority interest in net income of the subsidiary for the year ended April 30, Year 9.* The $4,732 also enters into the computation of the subsidiary's retained earnings at April 30, Year 9, for consolidated purposes.

The amounts associated with Sage Company's debentures are reflected in the consolidating financial statements working paper for the year ended April 30, Year 9, as illustrated on page 372.

POST CORPORATION AND SUBSIDIARY
Partial Consolidating Financial Statements Working Paper
For Year Ended April 30, Year 9

	Post Corporation	Sage Company	Consolidation Eliminations Increase (Decrease)	Consolidated
Income Statement				
Revenue				
Intercompany interest revenue	$ 32,745	$ -0-	$ (32,745)	$ -0-
Costs and expenses				
Intercompany interest expense	-0-	28,013	(28,013)	-0-
Statement of Retained Earnings				
Retained earnings, May 1, Year 8	$ x,xxx,xxx	$ xxx,xxx	$ 21,572	$ x,xxx,xxx
Balance Sheet				
Assets				
Investment in subsidiary's debentures	$ 337,697	$ -0-	$(337,697)	$ -0-
Liabilities & Stockholders' Equity				
Intercompany debentures payable	-0-	375,000	(375,000)	-0-
Discount on intercompany debentures payable	-0-	(19,328)	(19,328)	-0-
Minority interest in subsidiary ..	-0-	-0-	1,135	xxx,xxx

Consolidation Elimination at April 30, Year 10   The consolidation elimination at April 30, Year 10, is as follows:

POST CORPORATION AND SUBSIDIARY
Partial Consolidation Eliminations Working Paper
April 30, Year 10

Intercompany Interest Revenue—Post	33,770	
Intercompany Debentures Payable—Sage	375,000	
Discount on Intercompany Debentures Payable —Sage		13,374
Investment in Subsidiary's Debentures—Post		348,967
Intercompany Interest Expense—Sage		28,454
Retained Earnings—Sage ($22,707 − $4,732) × 95% .		17,076
Minority Interest in Subsidiary ($22,707 − $4,732) × 5%		899

To eliminate subsidiary's debentures owned by parent company, and related interest revenue and expense; and to increase subsidiary's beginning retained earnings by amount of unamortized realized gain on the reacquisition of the debentures. (Income tax effects are disregarded.)

Comparable consolidation eliminations would be appropriate for Years 11 and 12. After Sage Company paid the debentures in full at their May 1, Year 12, maturity date, no further consolidation eliminations for the debentures would be required.

Reissuance of intercompany debentures

The orderly amortization of a realized gain on the reacquisition of an affiliate's debentures is disrupted if the acquiring affiliate reissues the debentures before they mature. A *transaction* gain or loss on such a reissuance is not *realized* by the consolidated entity. Logic requires that a consolidation elimination must be prepared to treat the transaction gain or loss as premium or discount on the reissued debt, as appropriate. These complex issues are rarely encountered; hence they will not be illustrated here.

COMPREHENSIVE ILLUSTRATION OF CONSOLIDATING FINANCIAL STATEMENTS WORKING PAPERS

In Chapters 6 through 10 we have explained and illustrated a number of aspects of consolidating financial statements working papers. The comprehensive illustration which follows incorporates most of these aspects. The illustration is for Post Corporation and its partially owned subsidiary, Sage Company, for the year ended April 30, Year 9.

The ledger accounts for Post Corporation's Investment in Subsidiary, Retained Earnings, and Retained Earnings of Subsidiary, and for Sage

Company's Retained Earnings, are presented below and on page 375. Review of these accounts should aid in understanding the illustrative consolidating financial statements working paper and related consolidation eliminations working paper on pages 375–380.

Post Corporation Ledger
Investment in Subsidiary

Date	Explanation	Debit	Credit	Balance
4/30/6	Cost of business combination	1,192,250		1,192,250 dr
3/24/7	Dividends		38,000	1,154,250 dr
4/30/7	Reported net income	85,500		1,239,750 dr
4/30/7	Amortization of differences		42,750	1,197,000 dr
4/30/7	Amortization of goodwill		950	1,196,050 dr
3/22/8	Dividends		47,500	1,148,550 dr
4/30/8	Reported net income	99,750		1,248,300 dr
4/30/8	Amortization of differences		18,050	1,230,250 dr
4/30/8	Amortization of goodwill		950	1,229,300 dr
3/25/9	Dividends		57,000	1,172,300 dr
4/30/9	Reported net income	109,250		1,281,550 dr
4/30/9	Amortization of differences		18,050	1,263,500 dr
4/30/9	Amortization of goodwill		950	1,262,550 dr

Retained Earnings

Date	Explanation	Debit	Credit	Balance
4/30/6	Balance			1,050,000 cr
4/30/7	Dividends	158,550		891,450 cr
4/30/7	Net income ($461,800 − $4,750)		457,050	1,348,500 cr
4/30/8	Dividends	158,550		1,189,950 cr
4/30/8	Net income ($352,600 − $34,200)		318,400	1,508,350 cr
4/30/9	Dividends	158,550		1,349,800 cr
4/30/9	Net income ($460,200 − $34,200)		426,000	1,775,800 cr

Retained Earnings of Subsidiary

Date	Explanation	Debit	Credit	Balance
4/30/7	Undistributed income ($5,000 × 95%)		4,750	4,750 cr
4/30/8	Undistributed income ($36,000 × 95%)		34,200	38,950 cr
4/30/9	Undistributed income ($36,000 × 95%)		34,200	73,150 cr

Sage Company Ledger

Retained Earnings

Date	Explanation	Debit	Credit	Balance
4/30/6	Balance		334,000	334,000 cr
3/24/7	Dividends	40,000		294,000 cr
4/30/7	Net income		90,000	384,000 cr
3/22/8	Dividends	50,000		334,000 cr
4/30/8	Net income		105.000	439,000 cr
3/25/9	Dividends	60,000		379,000 cr
4/30/9	Net income		115,000	494,000 cr

Equity method: Partially owned purchased subsidiary subsequent to business combination

POST CORPORATION AND SUBSIDIARY

Consolidating Financial Statements Working Paper

For Year Ended April 30, Year 9

	Post Corporation	Sage Company	Consolidation Eliminations Increase (Decrease)		Consolidated
Income Statement					
Revenue					
Net sales	$5,900,000	$1,400,000			$7,300,000
Intercompany sales	-0-	150,000	(b)	$(150,000)	-0-
Intercompany interest					
revenue	32,745	-0-	(e)	(32,745)	-0-
Intercompany investment					
income................	91,200	-0-	(a)	(91,200)	-0-
Intercompany revenue					
(expenses)	14,000	(14,000)			-0-
Total revenue	$6,037,945	$1,536,000		$(273,945)	$7,300,000
Costs and expenses			(a)	$ 17,000	
			(b)	(26,000)	
Cost of goods sold	$4,300,000	$ 950,000	(d)	(4,760)	$5,236,240
Intercompany cost of					
goods sold	-0-	120,000	(b)	(120,000)	-0-
Selling, general, and					
administrative expenses .	671,302	141,149	(a)	2,000	814,451
Intercompany interest					
expense	-0-	28,013	(e)	(28,013)	-0-

(continued)

Equity method: Partially owned purchased subsidiary subsequent to business combination

POST CORPORATION AND SUBSIDIARY
Consolidating Financial Statements Working Paper
For Year Ended April 30, Year 9 (continued)

	Post Corporation	Sage Company	Consolidation Eliminations Increase (Decrease)		Consolidated
Interest expense	51,518	9,338			60,856
Income taxes expense	554,925	172,500			727,425
Minority interest in net income of subsidiary	-0-	-0-	(f)	4.601	4,601
Total costs and expenses	$5,577,745	$1,421,000		$(155,172)	$6,843,573
Net income	$ 460,200	$ 115,000		$(118,773)	$ 456,427
Statement of Retained Earnings					
Retained earnings, May 1, Year 8	$1,547,300	$ 439,000	(a) (b) (c) (d) (e)	$(439,000) (7,600) (50,000) (22,610) 21,572	$1,488,662
Net income	460,200	115,000		(118,773)	456,427
Subtotal	$2,007,500	$ 554,000		$(616,411)	$1,945,089
Dividends	158,550	60,000	(a)	(60,000)	158,550
Retained earnings, Apr. 30, Year 9	$1,848,950	$ 494,000		$(556,411)	$1,786,539

(continued)

POST CORPORATION AND SUBSIDIARY
Consolidating Financial Statements Working Paper
For Year Ended April 30, Year 9 (continued)

	Post Corporation	Sage Company	Consolidation Eliminations Increase (Decrease)		Consolidated
Balance Sheet					
Assets					
Intercompany receivables (payables)	$ (3,500)	$ 3,500			$ -0-
Inventories	950,000	500,000	(b) $	(12,000)	1,438,000
Other current assets	760,000	428,992			1,188,992
Investment in subsidiary ..	1,262,550	-0-	(a)	(1,262,550)	-0-
Investment in subsidiary's debentures	337,697	-0-	(e)	(337,697)	-0-
Plant assets (net)	3,700,000	1,300,000	(a) (d)	148,000 (19,040)	5,128,960
Land (for building site)	-0-	175,000	(c)	(50,000)	125,000
Leasehold	-0-	-0-	(a)	15,000	15,000
Goodwill	85,000	-0-	(a)	35,150	120,150
Total assets	$7,091,747	$2,407,492		$(1,483,137)	$8,016,102
Liabilities & Stockholders' Equity					
Debentures payable	$ -0-	$ 125,000			$ 125,000
Intercompany debentures payable	-0-	375,000	(e) $	(375,000)	-0-
Discount on debentures payable	-0-	(6,442)			(6,442)
Discount on intercompany debentures payable	-0-	(19,328)	(e)	(19,328)	-0-
Other liabilities	2,625,547	804,262			3,429,809
Minority interest in subsidiary	-0-	-0-	(a) (b) (d) (e) (f)	59,800 (400) (1,190) 1,135 4,601	63,946
Common stock, $1 par	1,057,000	-0-			1,057,000
Capital stock, $10 par	-0-	400,000	(a)	(400,000)	-0-
Paid-in capital in excess of par	1,560,250	235,000	(a)	(235,000)	1,560,250
Retained earnings	1,848,950	494,000		(556,411)	1,786,539
Total liabilities & stockholders' equity ...	$7,091,747	$2,407,492		$(1,483,137)	$8,016,102

Equity method: Partially owned purchased subsidiary subsequent to business combination

POST CORPORATION AND SUBSIDIARY
Consolidation Eliminations Working Paper
April 30, Year 9

(a) Capital Stock—Sage	400,000	
Paid-in Capital in Excess of Par—Sage	235,000	
Retained Earnings—Sage	439,000	
Intercompany Investment Income—Post	91,200	
Plant Assets (net)—Sage ($190,000 − $42,000)	148,000	
Leasehold—Sage ($30,000 − $15,000)	15,000	
Goodwill—Post ($38,000 − $2,850)	35,150	
Cost of Goods Sold—Sage	17,000	
Selling, General, and Administrative Expenses—Sage ..	2,000	
Investment in Subsidiary—Post		1,262,550
Dividends—Sage		60,000
Minority Interest in Subsidiary		59,800

To carry out the following:

(1) Eliminate intercompany investment and equity accounts of subsidiary at beginning of year, and subsidiary dividend.

(2) Provide for Year 9 depreciation and amortization on differences between combination date current fair values and carrying amount of Sage's identifiable assets, as follows:

	To cost of goods sold	To selling, general, and administrative expenses
Building depreciation	$ 2,000	$2,000
Machinery and equipment depreciation	10,000	-0-
Leasehold amortization ..	5,000	-0-
Totals	$17,000	$2,000

(3) Allocate remaining unamortized differences between combination date current fair values and carrying amounts to appropriate assets.

(4) Establish minority interest in subsidiary at beginning of year ($62,800), less minority share of dividends declared by subsidiary during year ($60,000 × 5% = $3,000).

(Income tax effects are disregarded.)

POST CORPORATION AND SUBSIDIARY
Consolidation Eliminations Working Paper
April 30, Year 9 (continued)

(b) Retained Earnings—Sage 7,600
    Minority Interest in Subsidiary 400
    Intercompany Sales—Sage 150,000
        Intercompany Cost of Goods Sold—Sage 120,000
        Cost of Goods Sold—Post 26,000
        Inventories—Post 12,000
    To eliminate intercompany sales and cost of goods sold,
    and unrealized profits in inventories. (Income tax effects
    are disregarded.)

(c) Retained Earnings—Post 50,000
        Land—Sage 50,000
    To eliminate unrealized intercompany profit in land. (Income tax effects are disregarded.)

(d) Retained Earnings—Sage 22,610
    Minority Interest in Subsidiary 1,190
    Accumulated Depreciation—Post 4,760
        Machinery—Post 23,800
        Depreciation Expense—Post 4,760
    To eliminate unrealized intercompany profit in machinery and in related depreciation. (Income tax effects are disregarded.)

(e) Intercompany Interest Revenue—Post 32,745
    Intercompany Debentures Payable—Sage 375,000
        Discount on Intercompany Debentures Payable—
        Sage 19,328
        Investment in Subsidiary's Debentures—Post ... 337,697
        Intercompany Interest Expense—Sage 28,013
        Retained Earnings—Sage 21,572
        Minority Interest in Subsidiary 1,135
    To eliminate subsidiary's debentures owned by parent company, and related interest revenue and expense; and to increase subsidiary's beginning retained earnings by amount of unamortized realized gain on the reacquisition of the debentures. (Income tax effects are disregarded.)

(continued)

POST CORPORATION AND SUBSIDIARY
Consolidation Eliminations Working Paper
April 30, Year 9 (continued)

(f) Minority Interest in Net Income of Subsidiary	4,601	
Minority Interest in Subsidiary		4,601

To establish minority interest in subsidiary's adjusted
net income for Year 9, as follows:

Net income reported by subsidiary	$115,000	
Adjustments due to consolidation elimi- nations:		
(a) ($17,000 + $2,000)	(19,000)	
(b) ($150,000 − $146,000)	(4,000)	
(d)	4,760	
(e) ($32,745 − $28,013)	(4,732)	
Adjusted net income of subsidiary	$ 92,028	
Minority share ($92,028 × 5%)	$ 4,601	

Following are important features of the consolidating financial statements working paper and related consolidation eliminations working paper for Post Corporation and subsidiary at April 30, Year 9:

1 Intercompany investment income of Post Corporation for Year 9 is computed as follows:

Computation of intercompany investment income

$115,000 (Sage Company's reported net income for Year 9) × 95%	$109,250
Less: $19,000 (Year 9 amortization of differences between current fair values and carrying amounts of Sage Company's net assets at date of business combination) × 95%	18,050
Intercompany investment income of Post Corporation for Year 9	$ 91,200

2 Post Corporation's intercompany revenue of $14,000 is a management fee from Sage Company, computed as 1% of Sage's $1,400,000 net sales for Year 9 ($1,400,000 × 1% = $14,000).

3 The income tax effects of Post Corporation's use of the equity method of accounting for its subsidiary's operating results are not reflected in Post's income taxes expense for Year 9. Income tax effects associated with the equity method of accounting are considered in Chapter 11.

4 Post Corporation's retained earnings balances in the consolidating statement of retained earnings are the totals of Post's two accounts for retained earnings, combined for convenience, as follows:

	Balance, May 1, Year 8	Balance, Apr. 30, Year 9
Post Corporation's retained earnings accounts:		
Retained earnings	$1,508,350	$1,775,800
Retained earnings of subsidiary	38,950	73,150
Totals	$1,547,300	$1,848,950

Combination of Post Corporation's retained earnings accounts

5 The net intercompany payable of Post Corporation at April 30, Year 9, consists of the following amounts:

Computation of net intercompany payables of parent company

Account payable to Sage Company for merchandise purchases		$40,000
Less: Interest receivable from Sage Company	$22,500	
Management fee receivable from Sage Company	14,000	36,500
Net intercompany payable		$ 3,500

6 Consolidation elimination (a) continues the amortization of differences between current fair values and carrying amounts of the subsidiary's net assets at date of the business combination of Post Corporation and Sage Company (see Chapter 8, page 309).

7 The $62,800 minority interest at beginning of year, as set forth in the explanation for consolidation elimination (a)(4), is computed as follows:

Computation of minority interest at beginning of year

Stockholders' equity of Sage Company at May 1, Year 8:		
Capital stock, $10 par		$ 400,000
Paid-in capital in excess of par		235,000
Retained earnings		439,000
Total stockholders' equity		$1,074,000
Add: Unamortized differences between current fair values and carrying amounts of Sage Company's net assets as of May 1, Year 8 (see page 302):		
Land	$60,000	
Building ($80,000 − $8,000)	72,000	
Machinery and equipment ($50,000 − $20,000)	30,000	
Leasehold ($30,000 − $10,000)	20,000	182,000
Total adjusted net assets of Sage Company, May 1, Year 8		$1,256,000
Minority interest therein ($1,256,000 × 5%)		$ 62,800

8 Consolidation eliminations *(b), (c), (d),* and *(e)* are identical to the eliminations illustrated in this chapter on pages 355, 358, 361, and 370–371, respectively. For posting to the consolidating financial statements working paper, consolidation elimination *(d)* was condensed. The credit to Depreciation Expense in elimination *(d)* is posted to Cost of Goods Sold in the consolidating income statement.

9 The $19,328 ***decrease*** in Discount on Intercompany Debentures Payable in the consolidating balance sheet is actually an ***increase*** for purposes of computing the $(1,483,137) total of the consolidation eliminations column for liabilities and stockholders' equity.

10 Because of the elimination of intercompany profits, consolidated net income does not equal the parent company's equity-method net income. Consolidated net income may be verified as follows:

Computation of consolidated net income

Post Corporation's net income		$460,200
Less: Post Corporation's share of adjustments to subsidiary's		
reported net income for intercompany profits:		
Consolidation elimination (b) ($150,000 − $146,000) ...	$(4,000)	
Consolidation elimination (d)	4,760	
Consolidation elimination (e) ($32,745 − $28,013)	(4,732)	
Total	$(3,972)	
Post Corporation's share [$(3,972) × 95%]		(3,773)
Consolidated net income		$456,427

11 Similarly consolidated retained earnings does not equal the total of the two parent company retained earnings accounts. Consolidated retained earnings may be verified as follows:

Computation of consolidated retained earnings

Total of Post Corporation's two retained earnings accounts *(4, p. 381)*		$1,848,950
Adjustments:		
Post Corporation's share of adjustments to subsidiary's reported		
net income (see *10,* above)		(3,773)
Intercompany profit in Post Corporation's retained earnings—		
consolidation elimination (c)		(50,000)
Post Corporation's share of adjustments to subsidiary's beginning		
retained earnings for intercompany profits:		
Consolidation elimination (b)	$ (7,600)	
Consolidation elimination (d)	(22,610)	
Consolidation elimination (e)	21,572	(8,638)
Consolidated retained earnings		$1,786,539

12 The consolidated balances in the consolidating financial statements working paper represent the financial position and operating results of Post Corporation and subsidiary resulting from the consolidated entity's transactions with **outsiders.** All intercompany transactions, profits, and balances have been eliminated in arriving at the consolidated amounts.

Concluding comments

The most common features of consolidating financial statements working papers have been discussed in this chapter and in Chapters 6 through 9. Chapter 11 includes the less frequent aspects of consolidations, as well as the more complex problems of consolidating financial statements working papers.

REVIEW QUESTIONS

1 How are consolidated financial statements affected if unrealized intercompany profits resulting from transactions between parent company and subsidiaries are not eliminated? Explain.

2 What consolidated financial statement categories are affected by intercompany sales of merchandise at a profit? Explain.

3 Some accountants advocate the elimination of intercompany profit in the parent company's ending inventories only to the extent of the parent's ownership interest in the selling subsidiary's stock. What argument can be advanced in opposition to this treatment of intercompany profit?

4 How do intercompany sales of plant assets and intangible assets differ from intercompany sales of merchandise?

5 Is intercompany profit on the sale of land ever **realized?** Explain.

6 Sayles Company, a 90% owned subsidiary of Partin Corporation, sold to Partin for $10,000 a machine with a carrying amount of $8,000, no residual value, and an estimated economic life of four years. Explain how the intercompany profit element of Partin Corporation's annual depreciation expense for the machine is accounted for in the consolidating financial statements working paper.

7 "No intercompany gain or loss should be recognized when a parent company purchases in the open market outstanding bonds of its subsidiary, because the transaction is not an **intercompany** transaction." Do you agree? Explain.

8 What accounting problems result from the reissuance by a subsidiary of parent company bonds acquired in the open market by the subsidiary? Explain.

9 Intercompany profits or losses in inventories, plant assets, or bonds result in consolidated net income which differs from the parent company's equity-method net income. Why is this true? Explain.

10 How is the intercompany profit in a subsidiary's **beginning** inventories resulting from the parent company's sales of merchandise to the subsidiary accounted for in a consolidation elimination? Explain.

EXERCISES

Ex. 10-1 Select the best answer for each of the following multiple-choice questions.

1 On January 2, Year 6, Purdue Corporation sold equipment costing $100,000
with accumulated depreciation of $25,000 to its wholly owned subsidiary,
Shubert Company. The selling price was $90,000. Purdue had been depreciat-
ing the equipment by the straight-line method over a 20-year economic life
with no residual value. Shubert continued this depreciation program. What
are the cost and accumulated depreciation, respectively, of this equipment
in the December 31, Year 6, consolidated balance sheet of Purdue Corporation and subsidiary?
a $75,000 and $3,750
b $90,000 and $4,500
c $90,000 and $29,500
d $100,000 and $30,000
e Some other amounts

2 On April 1, Year 6, a parent company purchased in the open market $750,000
principal amount of its subsidiary's 6% debentures due April 1, Year 11, with
interest payable annually on April 1, for $636,276—a 10% yield. The fiscal year
of both affiliates ends March 31. The parent company's April 1, Year 7,
journal entry for the receipt of interest on the debentures should include a
credit to the Intercompany Interest Revenue account in the amount of:
a $-0-   **b** $45,000   **c** $63,628   **d** $75,000   **e** None of the preceding

3 From a consolidated point of view, intercompany profit on a parent company's sale of land to its subsidiary is realized when:
a The parent company sells the land to the subsidiary
b The subsidiary uses the land to construct a factory for production of
finished goods
c The subsidiary sells the land to an outsider
d Some other event takes place

4 In the computation of minority interest in net income of a partially owned
subsidiary, the credit for Depreciation Expense—Parent in a consolidation
elimination for intercompany profit in a depreciable plant asset is attributed
to net income of:
a The parent company
b The subsidiary
c The consolidated entity
d None of the above

5 A consolidation elimination for a second year of intercompany sales, at a
markup over cost, by a partially owned subsidiary to its parent company
should include:
a A debit to Retained Earnings—Subsidiary
b A credit to Minority Interest in Subsidiary
c A credit to Cost of Goods Sold—Subsidiary
d None of the above

Ex. 10-2 Porterfield Corporation acquired a 70% interest in Samson Company in Year 2.
For the years ended December 31, Year 3 and Year 4, Samson reported net income of $80,000 and $90,000, respectively. During Year 3, Samson sold merchandise to Porterfield for $10,000 at a profit of $2,000. The merchandise was
resold during Year 4 by Porterfield to outsiders for $15,000.

Compute the minority interest in Samson's net income for Year 3 and Year 4. Disregard income taxes.

Ex. 10-3 On November 1, Year 5, Sofia Company, the 90%-owned subsidiary of Paris Corporation, issued to the public $100,000 principal amount of 5-year, 9% debentures, interest payable each November 1, for $103,993—an 8% yield. Bond issue costs may be disregarded.

On October 31, Year 6, Paris Corporation purchased in the open market $60,000 principal amount of Sofia Company's 9% debentures for $58,098—a 10% yield. The realized gain on the transaction reported in the October 31, Year 6, consolidated income statement of Paris Corporation and subsidiary was $3,889.

Compute the missing amounts in the consolidation elimination below. Round all amounts to the nearest dollar. Disregard income taxes.

PARIS CORPORATION AND SUBSIDIARY
Partial Consolidation Eliminations Working Paper
October 31, Year 7

Intercompany Interest Revenue—Paris		
Intercompany Debentures Payable—Sofia	60,000	
Premium on Intercompany Debentures Payable—Sofia		
Investment in Subsidiary's Debentures—Paris		
Intercompany Interest Expense—Sofia		
Retained Earnings—Sofia		
Minority Interest in Subsidiary		389

To eliminate subsidiary's debentures owned by parent company, and related interest revenue and expense; and to increase subsidiary's beginning retained earnings by amount of unamortized realized gain on the reacquisition of the debentures. (Income tax effects are disregarded.)

Ex. 10-4 Poland Corporation supplies all the merchandise sold by its wholly owned subsidiary, Serbia Company. Both Poland and Serbia use perpetual inventory systems. Poland bills merchandise to Serbia at a price 20% in excess of Poland's cost. For the fiscal year ended November 30, Year 8, Poland's sales to Serbia were $120,000 at billed prices. At billed prices, Serbia's December 1, Year 7, inventories were $18,000, and its November 30, Year 8, inventories were $24,000.

Prepare an analysis of intercompany sales, cost of goods sold, and profit in inventories for the year ended November 30, Year 8. Your analysis should show selling price, cost, and gross profit for each of the three intercompany items.

Ex. 10-5 On October 1, Year 4, Powell Corporation purchased new equipment for $14,500 from its 90%-owned subsidiary, Stowe Company. The equipment cost Stowe $9,000 and had an economic life of 10 years as of October 1, Year 4. Powell uses the sum-of-the-years'-digits depreciation method.

Prepare a consolidation elimination for Powell Corporation and subsidiary at September 30, Year 6. Disregard income taxes.

Ex. 10-6 Saucedo Company, the wholly owned subsidiary of Pacheco Corporation, issued 8%, five-year bonds May 1, Year 1, at their principal amount of $100,000. Interest is payable annually. On April 30, Year 2, Pacheco purchased in the open market 40% of Saucedo's outstanding bonds at a 10% yield, plus accrued interest.

Compute the amount of cash paid by Pacheco and the gain on the reacquisition of the bonds. Round all computations to the nearest dollar. Disregard income taxes.

Ex. 10-7 Pike Corporation acquired 90% of the outstanding common stock of Shad Company on August 1, Year 2. During the year ended July 31, Year 3, Pike made merchandise sales to Shad in the amount of $100,000; the merchandise was priced at 25% above Pike's cost. Shad had 20% of this merchandise in inventories at July 31, Year 3.

Prepare a consolidation elimination for Pike Corporation and subsidiary at July 31, Year 3. Disregard income taxes.

Ex. 10-8 On January 2, Year 1, Shanks Company, an 80%-owned subsidiary of Pasquale Corporation, sold to its parent company for $10,000 cash a machine with a carrying amount of $8,000, a five-year economic life, and no residual value. Both Pasquale and Shank use straight-line depreciation for all machinery.

Compute the missing amounts in the consolidation eliminations below. Use the identifying numbers for the missing amounts in your solution.

	December 31, Year 2	December 31, Year 4
Minority Interest in Subsidiary	(1)	(4)
Retained Earnings—Shanks	(2)	(5)
Accumulated Depreciation, Machinery—Pasquale .	(3)	(6)
Machinery—Pasquale	2,000	2,000
Depreciation Expense—Pasquale	400	400

To eliminate unrealized intercompany profit in machinery and in related depreciation. (Income tax effects are disregarded.)

SHORT CASES FOR ANALYSIS AND DECISION

Case 10-1 Sawhill Company, one of two wholly owned subsidiaries of Peasley Corporation, is in liquidation. On October 31, Year 8, Sawhill sold accounts receivable with a carrying amount of $50,000 to Shelton Company, the other wholly owned subsidiary of Peasley Corporation, for a gain of $10,000. Shelton Company debited the $10,000 to a deferred charge account, which is to be amortized in proportion to the amounts collected on the receivables Shelton acquired from Sawhill. The $10,000 gain appeared in the consolidated income statement of Peasley Corporation and Shelton Company for the year ended October 31, Year 8; Sawhill Company was not included in the consolidated financial statements on that date because it was in liquidation.

Instructions Evaluate the accounting described above.

Case 10-2 The existence of intercompany profits in consolidated inventories as a result of sales of merchandise by a partially owned subsidiary to its parent company has given rise to the following three viewpoints as to how such profits should be treated for consolidated financial statements:
a Only the parent company's share of intercompany profits in inventories should be eliminated.
b The entire amount of intercompany profits in inventories should be eliminated against the equities of the controlling and minority groups in proportion to their interests.

    c The entire amount of intercompany profits in inventories should be eliminated against consolidated retained earnings.

Instructions Present arguments to support each treatment.

Case 10-3 Prather Corporation has begun selling idle equipment from a discontinued product line to a wholly owned subsidiary, Sondheim Company, which requires the equipment in its operations. Prather had transferred the equipment from the Equipment account to an Idle Equipment account and had written down the equipment to net realizable value based on quotations from used machinery dealers. Depreciation expense on the idle equipment was terminated when the product line was discontinued.

    During Year 3, Prather Corporation's sales of idle equipment to Sondheim Company totaled $50,000; they were accounted for by Prather and Sondheim in the following aggregate journal entries:

Prather Corporation General Journal

Cash	50,000	
Sales of Idle Equipment		50,000
To record sales of idle equipment to Sondheim Company.		

Cost of Idle Equipment Sold	40,000	
Idle Equipment		40,000
To write off net realizable value of idle equipment sold to Sondhiem Company.		

Sondheim Company General Journal

Equipment	50,000	
Cash		50,000
To record purchases of used equipment from Prather Corporation.		

Depreciation: Equipment	5,000	
Accumulated Depreciation: Equipment		5,000
To provide, in accordance with regular policy, depreciation for one-half year in year of acquisition of equipment, based on economic life of five years and no residual value.		

    At December 31, Year 3, the controller of Prather Corporation prepared the following consolidation elimination:

Retained Earnings—Prather	10,000	
Equipment—Sondheim		10,000
To eliminate unrealized intercompany profit in equipment.		

Instructions Evaluate the journal entries and consolidation elimination presented above.

PROBLEMS

10-4 Pablo Corporation sells merchandise to its 90%-owned subsidiary, Smyth Company, at a markup of 25% on cost. Smyth Company sells merchandise to Pablo Corporation at a markup of 33⅓% on cost. Merchandise transactions between the two companies for the year ended June 30, Year 2, were as follows:

	Pablo sales to Smyth	Smyth sales to Pablo
July 1, Year 1, inventories of purchaser	$ 48,000	$ 30,000
Sales during year	600,000	800,000
Subtotal	$648,000	$830,000
Less: June 30, Year 2, inventories of purchaser	60,000	40,000
Cost of goods sold during year	$588,000	$790,000

Instructions Prepare in good form a consolidation eliminations working paper at June 30, Year 2, for Pablo Corporation and subsidiary. Disregard income taxes.

10-5 Pfister Corporation owns 90% of the outstanding capital stock of Steuber Company. On March 1, Year 4, Steuber sold to Pfister for $100,000 cash a warehouse recorded in Steuber's Leasehold Improvements account at that date at a carrying amount of $80,000. Pfister is amortizing the warehouse on the straight-line basis over the remaining life of the lease, which expires February 28, Year 14.

On March 1, Year 5, Pfister Corporation purchased in the open market for $48,264 cash (a 10% yield) one-half of Steuber Company's $100,000 principal amount 8% bonds due February 28, Year 7. The bonds had been issued at their principal amount March 1, Year 2, with interest payable annually on February 28.

Instructions Prepare in good form a consolidation eliminations working paper at February 28, Year 6, for Pfister Corporation and subsidiary. Disregard income taxes.

10-6 On July 1, Year 8, Pacific Corporation and its wholly owned subsidiary, Sommers Company, entered into the following transactions:
(1) Pacific sold to Sommers for $16,000 cash a machine with a carrying amount of $12,000 at date of sale. Sommers estimated an economic life of eight years and no residual value for the machine. Sommers uses straight-line depreciation for all plant assets.
(2) Pacific purchased in the open market for $361,571 (a 12% yield) four-fifths of Sommers' outstanding 8% debentures due June 30, Year 11. In Sommers' accounting records at July 1, Year 8, were the following balances:

8% debentures payable, due June 30, Year 11	$500,000
Discount on 8% debentures payable	24,870

The 8% debentures (interest payable each June 30) had been issued by Sommers July 1, Year 6, to yield 10%. Interest expense recorded by Sommers through Year 8 was as follows:

Year ended June 30, Year 7	$46,209
Year ended June 30, Year 8	46,830

Instructions Prepare in good form a consolidation eliminations working paper at June 30, Year 9, for Pacific Corporation and subsidiary. Disregard income taxes.

10-7 Powers Corporation acquired 80% of Snyder Company's 1,250 shares of $100 par common stock outstanding on July 1, Year 6, for $158,600, including out-of-pocket costs of the business combination. The excess of the current fair value of Snyder's net assets over their carrying amounts at July 1, Year 6, was attributable as follows:

To inventories $3,000

To equipment (five-year economic life at July 1, Year 6)................... 4,000

To goodwill (five-year economic life at July 1, Year 6)..................... Remainder
of excess

In addition, on July 1, Year 6, Powers Corporation purchased in the open market at their face amount $40,000 of Snyder Company's 6% bonds payable. Interest is payable by Snyder each July 1 and January 1.

Financial statements for Powers Corporation and Snyder Company for the period ended December 31, Year 6, appear below and on page 390. The following information also is available:

(1) Intercompany sales data for the six months ended December 31, Year 6, were as follows:

	Powers Corporation	Snyder Company
Intercompany payables at end of year....................	$13,000	$ 5,500
Intercompany purchases in inventories at end of year....	25,000	18,000

(2) On October 1, Year 6, Powers Corporation sold to Snyder Company for $12,000 equipment having a carrying amount of $14,000 at that date. Snyder Company established a five-year economic life, no residual value, and straight-line depreciation for the equipment.

POWERS CORPORATION AND SNYDER COMPANY
Financial Statements
For Period Ended December 31, Year 6

	Powers Corporation (year ended 12-31-6)	Snyder Company (six months ended 12-31-6)
Income Statements		
Revenue		
Net sales	$ 902,000	$400,000
Intercompany sales...............................	60,000	105,000
Intercompany interest revenue (expense)	1,200	(1,200)
Intercompany investment income	13,280	-0-
Intercompany loss on sale of equipment	(2,000)	-0-
Total revenue	$ 974,480	$503,800
Costs and expenses		
Cost of goods sold	$ 720,000	$300,000

(continued)

POWERS CORPORATION AND SNYDER COMPANY
Financial Statements
For Period Ended December 31, Year 6 (continued)

	Powers Corporation (year ended 12-31-6)	Snyder Company (six months ended 12-31-6)
Intercompany cost of goods sold	$ 50,000	$ 84,000
Operating expenses	124,480	99,800
Total costs and expenses	$ 894,480	$483,800
Net income	$ 80,000	$ 20,000

Statements of Retained Earnings

Retained earnings at beginning of period	$ 220,000	$ 50,000
Net income	80,000	20,000
Subtotal	$ 300,000	$ 70,000
Dividends	36,000	9,000
Retained earnings, Dec. 31, Year 6	$ 264,000	$ 61,000

Balance Sheets
Assets

Intercompany receivables (payables)	$ 100	$ (100)
Inventories, at fifo cost	300,000	75,000
Investment in subsidiary	164,340	-0-
Investment in subsidiary's bonds	40,000	-0-
Plant assets	794,000	280,600
Accumulated depreciation	(260,000)	(30,000)
Other assets	610,900	73,400
Total assets	$1,649,340	$398,900

Liabilities & Stockholders' Equity

Dividends payable	$ -0-	$ 1,600
Bonds payable	600,000	45,000
Intercompany bonds payable	-0-	40,000
Other liabilities	376,340	114,300
Capital stock, $100 par	360,000	125,000
Paid-in capital in excess of par	49,000	12,000
Retained earnings	264,000	61,000
Total liabilities & stockholders' equity	$1,649,340	$398,900

(3) Dividends were declared by Snyder Company as follows:

Sept. 30, Year 6	$1,000
Dec. 31, Year 6	8,000
Total dividends declared	$9,000

Instructions Prepare a consolidating financial statements working paper and related consolidation eliminations working paper for Powers Corporation and subsidiary for the year ended December 31, Year 6. Disregard income taxes.

10-8 On January 2, Year 1, Pritchard Corporation issued 5,000 shares of its $10 par capital stock in exchange for all 3,000 shares of Spangler Company's $20 par common stock outstanding on that date. Out-of-pocket costs of the business combination were negligible. The business combination qualified for pooling accounting, and Pritchard Corporation adopted the equity method of accounting for Spangler Company's operating results.

Condensed financial statements of the two companies for the year ended December 31, Year 1, are presented below and on page 392.

The following additional information is available:

(1) On December 31, Year 1, Spangler Company owed Pritchard Corporation $16,000 on open account and $8,000 on 6% demand notes dated July 1, Year 1 (interest payable at maturity). Pritchard Corporation discounted $3,000 of the notes received from Spangler Company with the First State Bank on July 1, Year 1, without notifying Spangler of this action.

(2) During Year 1, Pritchard Corporation sold to Spangler Company for $40,000 merchandise which cost $30,000. Spangler Company's December 31, Year 1, inventories included $10,000 of this merchandise priced at Spangler's cost.

PRITCHARD CORPORATION AND SPANGLER COMPANY
Financial Statements
For Year Ended December 31, Year 1

	Pritchard Corporation	Spangler Company
Income Statements		
Revenue		
Net sales	$500,000	$298,000
Intercompany sales	40,000	6,000
Intercompany interest revenue (expense)	150	(240)
Intercompany investment income	10,200	-0-
Intercompany gain on sale of equipment	-0-	2,000
Total revenue	$550,350	$305,760
Costs and expenses		
Cost of goods sold	$400,000	$225,000
Intercompany cost of goods sold	30,000	4,800
Operating expenses	88,450	65,760
Total costs and expenses	$518,450	$295,560
Net income	$ 31,900	$ 10,200
Statements of Retained Earnings		
Retained earnings, Jan. 1, Year 1	$ 67,000	$ 22,100
Net income	31,900	10,200
Subtotal	$ 98,900	$ 32,300
Dividends	-0-	4,500
Retained earnings, Dec. 31, Year 1	$ 98,900	$ 27,800
Balance Sheets		
Assets		
Intercompany receivables (payables)	$ 21,150	$(22,740)
Inventories	81,200	49,600

(continued)

PRITCHARD CORPORATION AND SPANGLER COMPANY
Financial Statements
For Year Ended December 31, Year 1 (continued)

	Pritchard Corporation	Spangler Company
Investment in subsidiary	112,300	-0-
Plant assets	83,200	43,500
Accumulated depreciation	(12,800)	(9,300)
Other assets	71,150	56,200
Total assets	$356,200	$117,260
Liabilities & Stockholders' Equity		
Liabilities	$ 56,700	$ 9,460
Capital stock, $10 par	120,000	-0-
Capital stock, $20 par	-0-	60,000
Paid-in capital in excess of par	58,500	20,000
Retained earnings	98,900	27,800
Retained earnings of subsidiary	22,100	-0-
Total liabilities & stockholders' equity	$356,200	$117,260

(3) On July 1, Year 1, Spangler Company sold equipment with a carrying amount of $15,000 to Pritchard Corporation for $17,000. Pritchard Corporation recorded depreciation on the equipment in the amount of $850 for Year 1. The economic life of the equipment at the date of sale was 10 years.

(4) Spangler Company shipped merchandise to Pritchard Corporation on December 31, Year 1, and recorded an account receivable of $6,000 for the sale. Spangler Company's cost for the merchandise was $4,800. Because the merchandise was in transit, Pritchard Corporation did not record the transaction. The terms of the sale were F.O.B. shipping point.

(5) Spangler Company declared a dividend of $1.50 per share on December 31, Year 1, payable on January 10, Year 2. Pritchard Corporation made no journal entry for the dividend declaration.

Instructions
a Prepare in good form any necessary adjusting entry or entries for Pritchard Corporation and Spangler Company at December 31, Year 1.
b Prepare a consolidating financial statements working paper and related consolidation eliminations working paper for Pritchard Corporation and subsidiary for the year ended December 31, Year 1. Disregard income taxes.

10-9 The condensed financial statements on pages 393 and 394 were prepared following completion of the December 31, Year 4, audit of Pye Corporation and its subsidiaries, Sidey Company and Shorer Company. The subsidiary investments are accounted for by the equity method of accounting.
The following additional information is available:

(1) Sidey Company was formed by Pye Corporation on January 2, Year 4. To secure additional capital, 25% of the capital stock was sold at par to outsiders. Pye purchased for cash the remaining capital stock at par.

(2) On July 1, Year 4, Pye acquired from stockholders 4,000 shares of Shorer Company's capital stock for $175,000. A condensed balance sheet for Shorer Company at July 1, Year 4, follows:

SHORER COMPANY
Balance Sheet
July 1, Year 4

Assets

Current assets	$165,000
Plant assets (net)	60,000
Total assets	$225,000

Liabilities & Stockholders' Equity

Current liabilities	$ 45,000
Capital stock, $20 par	100,000
Retained earnings	80,000
Total liabilities & stockholders' equity	$225,000

The current fair values of Shorer Company's identifiable net assets at July 1, Year 4, were the same as their carrying amounts at that date. Pye Corporation's board of directors determined that Shorer Company's goodwill had an economic life of five years.

PYE CORPORATION, SIDEY COMPANY, AND SHORER COMPANY
Financial Statements
For Periods Ended December 31, Year 4

	Pye Corporation (year ended 12-31-4)	Sidey Company	Shorer Company (six months ended 12-31-4)
Income Statements			
Revenue			
Net sales	$ 920,000	$245,000	$310,000
Intercompany sales	40,000	30,000	60,000
Dividend revenue	6,800	-0-	-0-
Gain on sale of plant assets	5,000	-0-	-0-
Intercompany gain on sale of plant			
assets	4,000	-0-	-0-
Intercompany revenue (expenses) ...	12,000	(6,000)	(6,000)
Intercompany investment (loss)—			
Sidey	(45,000)	-0-	-0-
Intercompany investment income—			
Shorer	108,800	-0-	-0-
Total revenue	$1,051,600	$269,000	$364,000
Costs and expenses			
Cost of goods sold	$ 788,000	$273,000	$168,000
Intercompany cost of goods sold ...	32,000	27,000	42,000
Operating expenses	73,200	29,000	18,000
Total costs and expenses	$ 893,200	$329,000	$228,000
Net income (loss)	$ 158,400	$ (60,000)	$136,000

(continued)

PYE CORPORATION, SIDEY COMPANY, AND SHORER COMPANY
Financial Statements
For Periods Ended December 31, Year 4 (continued)

	Pye Corporation	Sidey Company	Shorer Company (six months ended 12-31-4)
	(year ended 12-31-4)		
Statements of Retained Earnings			
Retained earnings at beginning of period	$ 611,000	$ -0-	$ 80,000
Net income (loss)	158,400	(60,000)	136,000
Subtotal	$ 769,400	$(60,000)	$216,000
Dividends	48,000	-0-	14,000
Retained earnings (deficit), Dec. 31, Year 4	$ 721,400	$(60,000)	$202,000
Balance Sheets			
Assets			
Intercompany receivables (payables)	$ 12,000	$ (6,000)	$ (6,000)
Inventories	242,900	70,000	78,000
Investment in Sidey Company	105,000	-0-	-0-
Investment in Shorer Company	269,500	-0-	-0-
Other investments.................	185,000	-0-	-0-
Plant assets (net)	279,000	51,000	78,000
Other assets	174,000	52,000	170,000
Total assets....................	$1,267,400	$167,000	$320,000
Liabilities & Stockholders' Equity			
Accounts payable	$ 46,000	$ 27,000	$ 18,000
Capital stock, $20 par	500,000	200,000	100,000
Retained earnings (deficit)	721,400	(60,000)	202,000
Total liabilities & stockholders' equity	$1,267,400	$167,000	$320,000

(3) The following intercompany sales of certain products were made during Year 4:

	Sales	Included in purchaser's Dec. 31, Year 4, inventories
Pye to Shorer.......................................	$ 40,000	$15,000
Sidey to Shorer	30,000	10,000
Shorer to Pye.......................................	60,000	21,900
Totals	$130,000	$46,900

(4) On January 2, Year 4, Pye Corporation sold a punch press to Sidey Company. The punch press was purchased on January 2, Year 2, and was being depreciated by the straight-line method over a ten-year economic life. Sidey Company computed depreciation by the same method based on the remaining economic life. Details of the sale were as follows:

Cost of punch press	$25,000
Less: Accumulated depreciation	5,000
Carrying amount	$20,000
Sales price	24,000
Gain on sale of punch press	$ 4,000

(5) Cash dividends were paid on the following dates in Year 4:

	Pye Corporation	Shorer Company
June 30	$22,000	$ 6,000
Dec. 31	26,000	14,000
Total cash dividends paid	$48,000	$20,000

(6) Pye Corporation billed each subsidiary $6,000 at year-end for management fees in Year 4. The invoices were paid in January, Year 5.

Instructions Prepare a consolidating financial statements working paper and related consolidation eliminations working paper for Pye Corporation and subsidiaries for the year ended December 31, Year 4. Disregard income taxes.

10-10 On June 30, Year 2, Pasini Corporation purchased all the outstanding common stock of Seymour Company for $3,605,000 cash and Pasini's common stock having a current fair value of $4,100,000. Out-of-pocket costs of the combination were negligible. At the date of the business combination, the carrying amounts and current fair values of Seymour's Company's assets and liabilities were as follows:

	Carrying amount	Current fair value
Cash	$ 160,000	$ 160,000
Accounts receivable (net)	910,000	910,000
Inventories	860,000	1,025,186
Building	9,000,000	7,250,000
Furniture, fixtures, and machinery	3,000,000	2,550,000
Accumulated depreciation	(5,450,000)	-0-
Intangible assets (net)	150,000	220,000
Total assets	$8,630,000	$12,115,186
Notes payable	$ 500,000	$ 500,000
Accounts payable	580,000	580,000
5% mortgage note payable	4,000,000	3,710,186
Total liabilities	$5,080,000	$ 4,790,186

Condensed financial statements of the two companies at December 31, Year 2, appear on pages 396 and 397.

By the year-end, December 31, Year 2, the net balance of Seymour Company's accounts receivable at June 30, Year 2, had been collected; the inventories on hand at June 30, Year 2, had been debited to cost of goods sold; the $500,000 note had been paid (on July 1, Year 2); and the accounts payable at June 30, Year 2, had been paid.

As of June 30, Year 2, Seymour Company's building and furniture, fixtures, and machinery had estimated economic lives of ten years and eight years, respectively. All intangible assets had an estimated economic life of 20 years. All depreciation and amortization is computed by the straight-line method.

As of June 30, Year 2, the 5% mortgage note payable had eight equal annual payments remaining, with the next payment due June 30, Year 3. The current fair value of the note was based on a 7% interest rate.

Prior to June 30, Year 2, there were no intercompany transactions between Pasini Corporation and Seymour Company; however, during the last six months of Year 2 the following intercompany transactions occurred:

(1) Pasini sold $400,000 of merchandise to Seymour. The cost of the merchandise to Pasini was $360,000. Of this merchandise, $75,000 remained on hand at December 31, Year 2.

(2) On December 31, Year 2, Seymour purchased in the open market $300,000 of Pasini's 7½% bonds payable for $303,849 including $22,500 interest receivable. Pasini had issued $1,000,000 of these five-year, 7½% bonds on January 1, Year 1, for $980,036 to yield 8%.

(3) Many of the management functions of the two companies have been combined since the business combination. Pasini charges Seymour a $30,000 per month management fee.

(4) At December 31, Year 2, Seymour owed Pasini two months' management fees and $18,000 for merchandise purchases.

PASINI CORPORATION AND SEYMOUR COMPANY
Financial Statements
For Periods Ended December 31, Year 2

	Pasini Corporation (year ended 12-31-2)	Seymour Company (six months ended 12-31-2)
Income Statements		
Revenue		
Net sales	$25,600,000	$6,000,000
Intercompany sales	400,000	-0-
Intercompany revenue (expenses)	180,000	(180,000)
Intercompany investment income	82,082	-0-
Total revenue	$26,262,082	$5,820,000
Cost and expenses		
Cost of goods sold	$17,640,000	$3,950,000
Intercompany cost of goods sold	360,000	-0-
Depreciation expense..........................	3,701,000	600,000
Amortization expense	-0-	3,750
Selling, general, and administrative expenses	3,130,000	956,000
Interest expense.............................	662,000	100,000
Total costs and expenses	$25,493,000	$5,609,750
Net income	$ 769,082	$ 210,250

(continued)

PASINI CORPORATION AND SEYMOUR COMPANY
Financial Statements
For Periods Ended December 31, Year 2 (continued)

	Pasini Corporation (year ended 12-31-2)	Seymour Company (six months ended 12-31-2)
Statements of Retained Earnings		
Retained earnings at beginning of period	$ 2,167,500	$ 650,000
Net income	769,082	210,250
Retained earnings, Dec. 31, Year 2	$ 2,936,582	$ 860,250
Balance Sheets		
Assets		
Intercompany receivables (payables)	$ 55,500	$ (55,500)
Inventories	2,031,000	1,009,500
Other current assets	2,326,457	1,026,526
Investment in subsidiary	7,787,082	-0-
Investment in Pasini Corporation 7½% bonds	-0-	281,349
Buildings	17,000,000	9,000,000
Furniture, fixtures, and machinery	4,200,000	3,000,000
Accumulated depreciation	(8,000,000)	(6,050,000)
Intangible assets (net)	-0-	146,250
Total assets	$25,400,039	$8,358,125
Liabilities & Stockholders' Equity		
Current liabilities	$ 2,017,343	$ 597,875
Mortgage notes payable	6,786,500	4,000,000
7½% bonds payable	700,000	-0-
Intercompany 7½% bonds payable	300,000	-0-
Discount on 7½% bonds payable	(9,020)	-0-
Discount on intercompany 7½% bonds payable ..	(3,866)	-0-
8¼% bonds payable	3,900,000	-0-
Common stock	8,772,500	2,900,000
Retained earnings	2,936,582	860,250
Total liabilities & stockholders' equity	$25,400,039	$8,358,125

Instructions Prepare a consolidating financial statements working paper and related consolidation eliminations working paper for Pasini Corporation and subsidiary for the year ended December 31, Year 2. Round all computations to the nearest dollar. Disregard income taxes.

11

CONSOLIDATED FINANCIAL STATEMENTS: SPECIAL PROBLEMS

In this chapter we shall consider the following special problems which may arise in the preparation of consolidated financial statements:

Installment acquisition of parent company's controlling interest in a subsidiary

Changes in parent company's ownership interest in a subsidiary

Subsidiary with preferred stock

Stock dividends distributed by a subsidiary

Treasury stock transactions of a subsidiary

Indirect shareholdings and parent company's stock owned by a subsidiary

Accounting for income taxes for a consolidated entity

Statement of changes in financial position for a consolidated entity

Installment acquisition of parent company's controlling interest in a subsidiary

A parent company may obtain control of a subsidiary company in a series of acquisitions of the subsidiary's capital stock, rather than in a single transaction constituting a business combination.

In accounting for installment acquisitions of stock in the eventual subsidiary, accountants are faced with a difficult question: At what point in the installment acquisition sequence should current fair values be determined for the subsidiary's identifiable net assets, in accordance with the purchase theory for business combinations?[1]

A practical answer to the preceding question is: Current fair values for the subsidiary's net assets should be ascertained at the date when the parent company attains control of the subsidiary. At that date, the business combination is completed, and purchase accounting should be applied.

However, this answer is not completely satisfactory, because current generally accepted accounting principles[2] require use of the equity method of accounting for investments in common stock sufficient to enable the investor to influence significantly the operating and financial policies of the investee company. A 20% common stock investment is presumed, in the absence of contrary evidence, to be the minimum ownership interest for exercising significant operating and financial influence over the investee company. Furthermore, *APB Opinion No. 18* requires retroactive application of the equity method of accounting when an investor's ownership interest reaches 20%. The following example illustrates these points.

Illustration of Installment Acquisition of Parent Company's Controlling Interest
Prinz Corporation acquired shares of Scarp Company's 10,000 shares of outstanding $5 par common stock as follows:

	Date	Number of shares of Scarp Company common stock acquired	Medium of payment by Prinz Corporation	Carrying amount of Scarp Company's identifiable net assets
Parent company's installment acquisition of controlling interest in subsidiary	Mar. 1, Year 2	1,000	$ 10,000 cash	$80,000
	Mar. 1, Year 3	2,000	22,000 cash	85,000
	Mar. 1, Year 4	6,500	28,000 cash 50,000 8%, 5- year note	90,000
	Totals	9,500	$110,000	

The above analysis indicates that Prinz made investments at a cost of $10, $11, and $12 per share in Scarp's common stock at dates when the net assets (or book value) per share of Scarp's common stock was $8, $8.50, and $9, respectively. The wisdom of ascertaining current fair values for Scarp's net assets at March 1, Year 4, the date Prinz attained control of Scarp, is apparent.

[1] As indicated in Chapter 5, pooling accounting is appropriate only for business combinations involving the exchange of 90% or more of the combinee company's voting common stock in a single transaction or in accordance with a specific plan.
[2] *APB Opinion No. 18*, "The Equity Method of Accounting for Investments in Common Stock," AICPA (New York: 1971), pp. 355–356.

Assume that, in addition to the Capital Stock account with a balance of $50,000 and a Paid-in Capital in Excess of Par account of $10,000, Scarp's Retained Earnings account showed the following changes:

Retained Earnings account of investee

	Retained Earnings			
Date	Explanation	Debit	Credit	Balance
Mar. 1, Year 2	Balance			20,000 cr
Feb. 10, Year 3	Dividends: $1 per share	10,000		10,000 cr
Feb. 28, Year 3	Net income		15,000	25,000 cr
Feb. 17, Year 4	Dividends: $1 per share	10,000		15,000 cr
Feb. 28, Year 4	Net income		15,000	30,000 cr

Parent Company's Journal Entries for Installment Acquisition Prinz would prepare the following journal entries (in addition to conventional end-of-period adjusting and closing entries) to record its investment in Scarp's common stock. (All dividends declared by Scarp are assumed to have been paid in cash on the declaration date.)

PRINZ CORPORATION
General Journal

Year 2
Mar. 1 Investment in Scarp Company 10,000
        Cash 10,000
        To record purchase of 1,000 shares of Scarp Company's outstanding common stock.

Year 3
Feb. 10 Cash 1,000
        Dividend Revenue............................ 1,000
        To record receipt of $1 per share cash dividend on 1,000 shares of Scarp Company common stock.

Mar. 1 Investment in Scarp Company 22,000
        Cash 22,000
        To record purchase of 2,000 shares of Scarp Company's common stock.

Mar. 1 Investment in Scarp Company 450
        Retained Earnings of Investee 450
        To convert accounting for investment in Scarp Company to equity method from cost method, and to record retroactively 10% share of operating results of

(continued)

PRINZ CORPORATION
General Journal (concluded)

Scarp Company for year ended Feb. 28, Year 3, as
follows:

Share of Scarp's reported net income, Year 3 ($15,000 × 10%)	$1,500
Less: Amortization of goodwill acquired in Mar. 1, Year 2, purchase: $10,000 cost, minus ($80,000 × 10%) = $2,000 goodwill; $2,000 ÷ 40 years = amortization for Year 3	50
Subtotal	$1,450
Less: Dividend revenue recorded in Year 3	1,000
Prior period adjustment to Retained Earnings of Investee account	$ 450

(Income tax effects are disregarded.)

Year 4

Feb. 17 Cash 3,000

           Investment in Scarp Company   3,000
To record receipt of $1 per share cash dividend on
3,000 shares of Scarp Company's common stock.

Feb. 28 Investment in Scarp Company 4,500

           Investment Income   4,500
To record share of Scarp Company's reported net
income for year ended Feb. 28, Year 4 ($15,000 ×
30% = $4,500). (Income tax effects are disregarded.)

Feb. 28 Investment Income   175

           Investment in Scarp Company   175
To record amortization of goodwill for Year 4 as
follows:

Purchase of Mar. 1, Year 2: $2,000 ÷ 40	$ 50	
Purchase of Mar. 1, Year 3: $22,000 cost, minus ($85,000 × 20%) = $5,000 goodwill; $5,000 ÷ 40 years = amortization for Year 4	125	
Total amortization	$175	

Mar. 1 Investment in Scarp Company 78,000

           Cash   28,000
           Notes Payable   50,000
To record purchase of 6,500 shares of Scarp Company's common stock for cash and an 8%, five-year
note.

Prinz's purchase of 6,500 shares of Scarp's outstanding common stock on March 1, Year 4, is in essence a business combination which should be accounted for as a purchase. Accordingly, Prinz should apply the principles of purchase accounting described in Chapters 5 and 6, including the valuation of Scarp's identifiable tangible and intangible net assets at their current fair values at March 1, Year 4. Any excess of the $78,000 cost of Prinz's investment over Prinz's 95% share of the current fair value of Scarp's identifiable net assets should be assigned to goodwill and amortized over a period of 40 years or less.

Criticism of Preceding Approach   The preceding illustration of accounting for the installment acquisition of an eventual subsidiary's common stock may be criticized for its handling of goodwill. On three separate dates spanning two calendar years, goodwill was recognized in Prinz's three purchases of outstanding common stock of Scarp. Furthermore, the three goodwill amounts are amortized over three different 40-year (or shorter) periods.

It might be argued that the current fair values of Scarp's identifiable net assets should be determined at each of the three dates Prinz purchased Scarp Company common stock. However, such a theoretically precise application of accounting principles for long-term investments in corporate securities appears unwarranted in terms of cost benefit analysis. Until Prinz attained control of Scarp, the amortization elements of Prinz's investment income presumably would not be material. Thus, the goodwill approach illustrated in the preceding section of this chapter appears to be practical and consistent with the following passage from *APB Opinion No. 18:*[3]

> The carrying amount of an investment in common stock of an investee that qualifies for the equity method of accounting . . . may differ from the underlying equity in net assets of the investee. . . . if the investor is unable to relate the difference to specific accounts of the investee, the difference should be considered to be goodwill and amortized over a period not to exceed forty years, . . .

Consolidating Financial Statements Working Paper for Prinz Corporation and Subsidiary   The consolidating financial statements working paper and related consolidation eliminations for Prinz Corporation and subsidiary at March 1, Year 4, and for subsequent periods would be prepared in accordance with the procedures for purchased subsidiaries outlined in Chapters 6, 8, and 10. Prinz's retroactive application of the equity method of accounting for its investment in Scarp's common stock results in the Investment in Scarp Company and Retained Earnings of Subsidiary (Investee) accounts as follows at March 1, Year 4:

---

[3] Ibid., p. 360.

Selected accounts of parent company

Investment in Scarp Company

Date	Explanation	Debit	Credit	Balance
3/1/2	Purchase of 1,000 shares	10,000		10,000 dr
3/1/3	Purchase of 2,000 shares	22,000		32,000 dr
3/1/3	Retroactive application of equity method of accounting	450		32,450 dr
2/17/4	Dividends		3,000	29,450 dr
2/28/4	Share of reported net income	4,500		33,950 dr
2/28/4	Amortization of goodwill		175	33,775 dr
3/1/4	Purchase of 6,500 shares	78,000		111,775 dr

Retained Earnings of Subsidiary (Investee)

Date	Explanation	Debit	Credit	Balance
3/1/3	Retroactive application of equity method of accounting		450	450 cr
2/28/4	Closing entry—share of Scarp Company adjusted net income not paid as a dividend [($4,500 − $175) − $3,000]		1,325	1,775 cr

If we assume that the current fair value of Scarp's identifiable net assets at March 1, Year 4, was $90,000, the same as the carrying amount of the net assets at that date, the consolidation elimination for Prinz and subsidiary at March 1, Year 4, would be as follows:

PRINZ CORPORATION AND SUBSIDIARY
Partial Consolidation Eliminations Working Paper
March 1, Year 4

Capital Stock, $5 par—Scarp	50,000	
Paid-in Capital in Excess of Par—Scarp	10,000	
Retained Earnings—Scarp ($30,000 − $1,775)	28,225	
Retained Earnings of Subsidiary (Investee)—Prinz	1,775	
Goodwill—Prinz {$1,900 + $4,875 + [$78,000 − ($90,000 × 65%)]}	26,275	
Investment in Subsidiary—Prinz		111,775
Minority Interest in Subsidiary		4,500

To eliminate intercompany investment and equity accounts of subsidiary at date of business combination; to allocate excess of cost over current fair value (equal to carrying amount) of identifiable net assets acquired to goodwill; and to establish minority interest in subsidiary at date of business combination ($90,000 × 5% = $4,500).

The $1,775 portion of Scarp's retained earnings attributable to Prinz's 30% ownership of Scarp common stock prior to the business combination is not eliminated. Thus, consolidated retained earnings at March 1, Year 4, the date of the purchase business combination, includes the $1,775 amount plus Prinz's own retained earnings.

For fiscal years subsequent to March 1, Year 4, Prinz would reflect in its accounting records 95% of the operating results of Scarp.

Changes in parent company's ownership interest in a subsidiary

Subsequent to the date of a business combination, a parent company may acquire stockholdings of the subsidiary's minority shareholders; or the parent company may sell some of its subsidiary stockholdings to outsiders. Also, the subsidiary itself may issue additional shares of capital stock to the public. We shall consider the accounting treatment for each of these situations in the following sections.

Parent Company Acquisition of Minority Interest Purchase accounting should be applied to the parent company's acquisition of all or part of the subsidiary's minority interest, even though the original business combination was accounted for as a pooling.[4] Any other approach would be inconsistent with pooling accounting theory.

To illustrate, assume that on March 1, Year 5, Prinz Corporation acquired for $7,000 the remaining 500 shares of Scarp Company's outstanding common stock owned by minority shareholders. If the minority interest in the consolidated balance sheet of Prinz and subsidiary amounted to $6,000 at February 28, Year 5, an implicit additional $1,000 of goodwill must be amortized by Prinz over a maximum period of 40 years, beginning March 1, Year 5. Under the equity method of accounting, Prinz would accrue 100% of Scarp's operating results for periods subsequent to March 1, Year 5.

If Prinz paid *less* than the carrying amount of the minority interest purchased, the appropriate accounting treatment of the difference is not clear. Presumably, the excess of minority interest carrying amount over Prinz's cost should be allocated pro rata to the carrying amounts of Scarp's noncurrent assets other than long-term investments in corporate securities. This approach would be consistent with the theory of purchase accounting set forth in Chapter 5 (pages 191–195). However, assuming that the difference between carrying amount and cost is immaterial, it may be treated as an offset to goodwill implicit in earlier purchases of Scarp's common stock and amortized over the remaining economic life of that goodwill.

---

[4] APB Opinion No. 16, "Business Combinations," AICPA (New York: 1970), p. 294.

Parent Company Sale of a Portion of Its Subsidiary Stockholdings   A parent company with a substantial ownership interest in a subsidiary may sell a portion of that interest for several reasons. Perhaps the parent company is short of cash, or the earnings of the subsidiary are unsatisfactory. The parent company may recognize that a subsidiary may be controlled effectively with just over 50% ownership of its voting common stock, and that an 80% or 90% ownership interest in a subsidiary may tie up resources unnecessarily. Some corporations which have engaged in business combinations during recent years have sold a portion of a newly acquired subsidiary's stock in order to generate cash for additional business combinations.

Sale of all of an ownership interest in a subsidiary involves accounting for and presentation of the disposal of a segment of a business. This topic is considered in Chapter 12.

Accounting for a parent company's sale of a part of its investment in a subsidiary is similar to the accounting for disposal of any noncurrent asset. The carrying amount of the subsidiary stock sold is removed from the parent company's Investment in Subsidiary account, and the difference between that carrying amount and the cash or current fair value of other consideration received is treated as a gain or loss on disposal of the stock. Under current generally accepted accounting principles, the gain or loss *is not considered to be an extraordinary item* for consolidated income statement presentation.[5]

Unless the original business combination with the subsidiary resulted from an installment acquisition of the subsidiary's stock, there is no significant change in the consolidation eliminations after the parent's sale of part of its ownership interest in the subsidiary. However, the minority interest in the subsidiary's net income and net assets increases. The parent company's equity-method journal entries for the subsidiary's operations are changed only for the decrease in the percentage of the parent's ownership interest in the subsidiary.

When control was acquired by installment purchases of the subsidiary's stock, *specific identification* should be used to account for the carrying amount of the subsidiary shares sold. There must be an accompanying adjustment in the parent company's application of the equity method of accounting for the subsidiary's operating results. For example, purchased goodwill may no longer be accounted for in the consolidating financial statements working paper if the block of subsidiary stock to which it applies was sold by the parent company.

Subsidiary's Issuance of Additional Shares to Outsiders   Instead of obtaining funds by selling a portion of its ownership interest in a subsidiary, the parent company may instruct the subsidiary to issue additional shares of stock to outsiders. The cash obtained would be available to the

[5] *APB Opinion No. 30,* "Reporting the Results of Operations," AICPA (New York: 1973), p. 566.

consolidated group. Unless the parent company acquires shares on a pro rata basis in the stock issuance, as in a stock rights offering, the parent's percentage ownership interest in the subsidiary will change. In addition, unless the subsidiary issues additional shares to outsiders at a price per share equal to the per-share carrying amount of the subsidiary's outstanding stock, there will be a realized gain or loss to the parent company. These two points are illustrated in the following section.

Illustration of Subsidiary's Issuance of Additional Stock to Outsiders   On January 2, Year 1, Paulson Corporation acquired 80% of the outstanding common stock of Spaulding Company for $240,000. Out-of-pocket costs of the business combination are disregarded in this illustration. Spaulding's stockholders' equity accounts at January 2, Year 1, were as follows:

Common stock, $5 par	$ 50,000
Paid-in capital in excess of par	75,000
Retained earnings	100,000
Total stockholders' equity	$225,000

Stockholders' equity of purchased subsidiary at date of business combination

The current fair values of Spaulding's identifiable net assets at January 2, Year 1, were equal to their carrying amounts. Thus, the $60,000 excess of the cost of Paulson's investment ($240,000) over 80% of the $225,000 current fair value of Spaulding's identifiable net assets ($225,000 × 80% = $180,000) was attributable to goodwill, which is amortized over 40 years.

For the year ended December 31, Year 1, Spaulding reported net income of $20,000 and paid cash dividends of $10,000 (or $1 per share). On December 31, Year 1, Spaulding issued 2,000 shares of common stock in a public offering at $33 per share, net of costs of issuing the stock. Thus, after the closing process, Spaulding's stockholders' equity at December 31, Year 1, amounted to $301,000 ($225,000 + $20,000 − $10,000 + $66,000 = $301,000), and consisted of the following account balances:

Common stock, $5 par ($50,000 + $10,000)	$ 60,000
Paid-in capital in excess of par ($75,000 + $56,000)	131,000
Retained earnings ($100,000 + $20,000 − $10,000)	110,000
Total stockholders' equity	$301,000

Stockholders' equity of purchased subsidiary after issuance of common stock to public

Paulson's Investment in Subsidiary account under the equity method of accounting appears below.

Parent company's Investment in Subsidiary account

Investment in Subsidiary

Date	Explanation	Debit	Credit	Balance
1/2/1	Purchase of 8,000 shares	240,000		240,000 dr
12/31/1	Dividend: $10,000 × 80%		8,000	232,000 dr
12/31/1	Share of reported net income: $20,000 × 80%	16,000		248,000 dr
12/31/1	Amortization of goodwill: $60,000 ÷ 40 years		1,500	246,500 dr
12/31/1	Gain on subsidiary's issuance of common stock to public	12,667		259,167 dr

The December 31, Year 1, increase of $12,667 in Paulson's Investment in Subsidiary account is offset by a credit to a nonoperating gain account. The $12,667 is Paulson's share of the increase in Spaulding's net assets resulting from Spaulding's issuance of stock to the public at $33 per share. The $33 per share issuance price exceeds the $30.81 carrying amount ($246,500 ÷ 8,000 shares = $30.81) per share of Paulson's investment in Spaulding prior to Spaulding's common stock issuance. The $12,667 debit to Paulson's Investment in Subsidiary account is computed as follows:

Computation of gain to parent company resulting from subsidiary's issuance of common stock to public

	Total		Paulson's share		Minority's share
Carrying amount of Spaulding Company's net assets after stock issuance to public	$301,000	(66⅔%)	$200,667	(33⅓%)	$100,333
Carrying amount of Spaulding Company's net assets before stock issuance to public	235,000	(80%)	188,000*	(20%)	47,000
Difference	$ 66,000		$ 12,667		$ 53,333

*Paulson's share of Spaulding's net assets...$188,000
Unamortized goodwill ($60,000 − $1,500) 58,500
Balance of Paulson's Investment in Subsidiary account $246,500

The analysis above reflects the effect of the decrease of Paulson's percentage interest to 66⅔% of Spaulding's outstanding common stock after the public stock issuance from 80% before the issuance. Nevertheless, the issuance price of $33 per share exceeded the $30.81 carrying amount per share of Paulson's original investment in Spaulding, thus resulting in the $12,667 nonoperating gain to Paulson.

The following consolidation eliminations would be appropriate for Paulson Corporation and subsidiary at December 31, Year 1, assuming that there were no other intercompany transactions or profits for Year 1:

PAULSON CORPORATION AND SUBSIDIARY
Partial Consolidation Eliminations Working Paper
December 31, Year 1

(a) *Common Stock—Spaulding* 60,000
    Paid-in Capital in Excess of Par—Spaulding 131,000
    Retained Earnings—Spaulding 100,000
    Goodwill—Paulson ($60,000 − $1,500) 58,500
    Intercompany Investment Income—Paulson
    ($20,000 × 80%) 16,000
        Investment in Subsidiary—Paulson 259,167
        Dividends—Spaulding 10,000
        Minority Interest in Subsidiary ($45,000 −
        $2,000 + $53,333) 96,333
    To eliminate intercompany investment and related equity
    accounts of subsidiary (retained earnings of subsidiary
    is at the beginning of year); to eliminate subsidiary's divi-
    dends declared; to record unamortized balance of the
    goodwill at Dec. 31, Year 1; and to provide for minority
    interest in subsidiary at beginning of year ($225,000 ×
    20% = $45,000), less dividends to minority shareholders
    ($10,000 × 20% = $2,000), plus minority interest's share of
    proceeds of public stock issuance ($66,000 − $12,667 =
    $53,333).

(b) *Minority Interest in Net Income of Subsidiary* 4,000
        Minority Interest in Subsidiary 4,000
    To provide for minority interest in subsidiary's Year 1 net
    income as follows: $20,000 × 20% = $4,000.

The **nonoperating gain** treatment accorded to the $12,667 increase in Paulson's interest in Spaulding is not accepted universally. As one authority has written:[6]

---

[6] *Consolidated Financial Statements,* Accountants International Study Group (Plaistow, England: 1973), p. 13.

... the SEC has adopted the position that the issue of shares by a subsidiary company to the public at an amount per share in excess of book value does not give rise to a gain to the parent interest in the consolidated income statement. In such circumstances, the SEC has generally required the gain to be credited direct to paid-in capital in consolidated financial statements. However, many accountants hold the view that consolidated paid-in capital should arise solely from transactions with stockholders of the parent company, and accordingly that subsidiary capital changes which affect the parent's share of stockholders' equity of the subsidiary should generally result in recognition of gain or loss or adjustment of goodwill on consolidation.

Subsidiary with preferred stock

Some combinees in a business combination have outstanding preferred stock. If a parent company acquires all of a subsidiary's preferred stock, together with all or a majority of its voting common stock, the consolidating financial statements working paper and related consolidation eliminations are similar to those illustrated in Chapters 6, 7, 8, and 9. If less than 100% of the subsidiary's preferred stock is acquired by the parent company, the preferences associated with the preferred stock must be considered in the determination of the minority interest in the net income and net assets of the subsidiary. The interest of minority preferred stockholders is not *residual,* as is the interest of minority common stockholders.

Illustration of Minority Interest in Subsidiary with Preferred Stock   Suppose, for example, that on July 1, Year 4, Praeger Corporation paid $200,000 (including direct out-of-pocket costs of the business combination) for 60% of Simmons Company's 10,000 shares of outstanding $1 par, 6% cumulative preferred stock and 80% of Simmons's 50,000 shares of outstanding $2 par common stock. The preferred stock has a liquidation preference of $1.10 per share and is callable at $1.20 per share plus cumulative preferred dividends in arrears. In addition to the two capital stock issues, Simmons had the following stockholders' equity accounts at July 1, Year 4:

Selected stockholders' equity accounts of purchased subsidiary	*Paid-in capital in excess of par* $30,000
	Retained earnings 50,000

There were no cumulative preferred dividends in arrears at July 1, Year 4. The current fair values of Simmons's identifiable net assets at July 1, Year 4, were equal to their carrying amounts at that date.

The presence of preferred stock raises two questions:

1 What part if any, does the preferred stock play in the determination of the goodwill purchased in the business combination?

2 Which per-share amount—$1 par, $1.10 liquidation preference, or $1.20 call price—should enter into the determination of the minority interest in Simmons's net assets at July 1, Year 4?

In the opinion of the authors, the following are logical answers to the two questions:

1 The preferred stock does not enter into the determination of the goodwill purchased in the business combination. Typically, preferred stockholders have no voting rights; thus, in a business combination, preferred stock may in substance be considered **debt** rather than **owners' equity.** Accordingly, the amount paid by the combinor for the subsidiary's **common stock** should be the measure of the goodwill.

2 The call price should be used in determining the minority interest of the preferred shareholders in Simmons's net assets at July 1, Year 4. The call price is usually the maximum claim on net assets imposed by the preferred stock contract. Furthermore, the call price is the amount which Simmons would pay, on a going-concern basis, to liquidate the preferred stock. Use of the preferred stock's liquidation value in the determination of the minority shareholders' interest in the subsidiary's net assets would stress a **quitting-concern** approach, rather than a going-concern assumption. Finally, the par of the preferred stock has no real significance as a measure of value for the preferred stock.

In accordance with the preceding discussion, Praeger would prepare the following journal entry to record the business combination with Simmons at July 1, Year 4. (Out-of-pocket costs of the combination are not accounted for separately in this illustration.)

Parent company's journal entry for purchase business combination involving subsidiary's preferred stock	Investment in Simmons Company Preferred Stock (6,000 shares × $1.20)	7,200	
	Investment in Simmons Company Common Stock ($200,000 − $7,200)	192,800	
	Cash		200,000
	To record business combination with Simmons Company under the purchase method of accounting.		

The consolidation elimination for Praeger and subsidiary at July 1, Year 4, follows:

PRAEGER CORPORATION AND SUBSIDIARY
Consolidation Eliminations Working Paper
July 1, Year 4

Preferred Stock—Simmons	10,000
Common Stock—Simmons	100,000
Paid-in Capital in Excess of Par—Simmons	30,000
Retained Earnings—Simmons	50,000

(continued)

PRAEGER CORPORATION AND SUBSIDIARY
Consolidation Eliminations Working Paper
July 1, Year 4 (concluded)

Goodwill—Praeger {$192,800 − [($190,000 − $12,000 call price of preferred stock) × 80%]}	50,400	
Investment in Simmons Company Preferred Stock—Praeger		7,200
Investment in Simmons Company Common Stock—Praeger		192,800
Minority Interest in Subsidiary—Preferred (4,000 shares × $1.20)		4,800
Minority Interest in Subsidiary—Common ($178,000 × 20%)		35,600

To eliminate intercompany investment and related equity accounts of subsidiary at date of business combination; to record excess of cost attributable to common stock over 80% share of current fair value of subsidiary's identifiable net assets as goodwill; and to provide for minority interest in subsidiary's preferred stock and in net assets applicable to common stock at date of business combination.

The following aspects of this elimination should be emphasized:

1 Simmons's goodwill is measured by the difference between the cost assigned to Praeger's investment in Simmons's common stock over Praeger's share of the current fair value of the subsidiary's net assets applicable to common stock. The subsidiary's preferred stock does not enter into the computation of the goodwill.

2 The minority interest in the subsidiary's preferred stock is measured by the 4,000 shares of preferred stock owned by minority shareholders multiplied by the $1.20 call price per share.

3 The minority interest in the subsidiary's common stock is computed as 20% of the $178,000 ($190,000 − $12,000 = $178,000) net asset value of Simmons's common stock.

Preferred Stock Considerations Subsequent to Date of Business Combination Regardless of whether Simmons's preferred dividend is paid or omitted in years subsequent to July 1, Year 4, the preferred dividend affects the computation of the minority interest of common shareholders in the net income of Simmons. For example, assume that Simmons reported net income of $50,000 for the year ended June 30, Year 5, and declared and paid the preferred dividend of $0.06 per share and a common dividend of $0.50 per share on June 30, Year 5. Praeger would record these elements of Simmons's operating results as follows at June 30, Year 5, under the equity method of accounting:

PRAEGER CORPORATION
General Journal
June 30, Year 5

Cash 20,360
     Investment in Simmons Company Common Stock   20,000
     Intercompany Dividend Revenue   360
To record receipt of dividends declared and paid by Simmons
Company as follows:
    Preferred stock: 6,000 × $0.06 .... $ 360
    Common stock: 40,000 shares × $0.50   20,000
      Total cash received $20,360

Investment in Simmons Company Common Stock 39,520
     Intercompany Investment Income   39,520
To record share of Simmons Company's reported net income
applicable to common stock as follows:
    Simmons Company's reported net income $50,000
    Less: Preferred dividend: (10,000 × $0.06)   600
    Net income attributable to common stock $49,400
    Parent company's share ($49,400 × 80%) $39,520

Amortization Expense 1,260
     Investment in Simmons Company Common Stock   1,260
To provide for parent company's Year 5 amortization of Simmons Company's goodwill purchased at date of business combination as follows:
    Simmons's goodwill purchased at date of business
      combination $50,400
    Amortization ($50,400 ÷ 40) .... $ 1,260

After the preceding journal entries were posted, Praeger's Investment in Simmons Company Common Stock account would appear as follows:

Investment account of parent company

Investment in Simmons Company Common Stock

Date	Explanation	Debit	Credit	Balance
7/1/4	Purchase of 40,000 shares	192,800		192,800 dr
6/30/5	Dividends		20,000	172,800 dr
6/30/5	Share of reported net income	39,520		212,320 dr
6/30/5	Amortization of goodwill		1,260	211,060 dr

If there were no other intercompany transactions or profits, the June 30, Year 5, consolidation eliminations working paper for Praeger Corporation and subsidiary would be as shown below:

PRAEGER CORPORATION AND SUBSIDIARY
Consolidation Eliminations Working Paper
June 30, Year 5

(a) Preferred Stock—Simmons 10,000
 Common Stock—Simmons 100,000
 Paid-in Capital in Excess of Par—Simmons 30,000
 Retained Earnings—Simmons 50,000
 Intercompany Dividend Revenue—Praeger 360
 Intercompany Investment Income—Praeger 39,520
 Goodwill—Praeger ($50,400 − $1,260) 49,140
  Investment in Simmons Company Preferred Stock
   —Praeger 7,200
  Investment in Simmons Company Common Stock
   —Praeger 211,060
  Minority Interest in Subsidiary—Preferred ($4,800
   − $240) 4,560
  Minority Interest in Subsidiary—Common
   [$35,600 − ($25,000 × 20%)] 30,600
  Dividends—Simmons ($600 + $25,000) 25,600
 To eliminate intercompany investment and related equity
 accounts of subsidiary at beginning of year; to eliminate
 subsidiary's dividends declared; to record unamortized
 balance of purchased goodwill at June 30, Year 5; and to
 provide for minority interest in subsidiary's preferred
 stock and common stock at beginning of year, less dividends to minority shareholders.

(b) Minority Interest in Net Income of Subsidiary 10,120
  Minority Interest in Subsidiary—Preferred 240
  Minority Interest in Subsidiary—Common
   [($50,000 − $600) × 20%] 9,880
 To provide for minority interest in net income of subsidiary
 for Year 5.

In the review of the June 30, Year 5, journal entries of Praeger and the consolidation eliminations working paper, the following should be noted:

1 Praeger Corporation's accounting for its investment in the subsidiary's preferred stock essentially is the cost method. This method is appropriate as long as the subsidiary declares and pays the cumulative preferred dividend annually. If the subsidiary had "passed" the preferred dividend of $600 for the year ended June 30, Year 5, Praeger would have recorded the "passed" preferred dividend under the equity method of accounting as follows:

Parent company's journal entry for "passed" preferred dividend of subsidiary	Investment in Simmons Company Preferred Stock 360	
	Intercompany Investment Income	360
	To accrue cumulative preferred dividend "passed" by subsidiary's board of directors ($600 × 60% = $360).	

The consolidation eliminations in the year of a "passed" cumulative preferred dividend would be the same as those illustrated above, except that the minority interest in the subsidiary's preferred stock would be $240 ($600 × 40% = $240) larger because of the effect of the "passed" dividend. (Of course, no common dividend could be declared if the cumulative preferred dividend were "passed.")

2 The net result of the preceding journal entries and consolidation eliminations is that the subsidiary's net income of $50,000 is allocated as follows:

	Total	Consolidated net income	Minority interest
Allocation of aubsidiary's net income to preferred and common shareholders			
To preferred shareholders: 10,000 shares × $0.06	$ 600	$ 360	$ 240
To common shareholders: in ratio of 80% and 20%	49,400	39,520	9,880
Net income of subsidiary	$50,000	$39,880	$10,120

Other Types of Preferred Stock   Treatment similar to that illustrated in the preceding section is appropriate for the minority interest in a subsidiary having other types of outstanding preferred stock. If the preferred stock were *noncumulative,* there would be no parent company accrual of "passed" dividends. If the preferred stock were *participating* (which seldom is the case), the subsidiary's retained earnings would be allocated to the minority interests in preferred stock and common stock according to the terms of the *participation clause.*

Stock dividends distributed by a subsidiary

If a parent company uses the equity method of accounting for the operating results of a subsidiary, the subsidiary's declaration and issuance of a stock dividend has no effect on the parent's Investment in Subsidiary account. As emphasized in **Intermediate Accounting** of this series, receipt of a stock dividend does not represent revenue to the investor.

After the declaration of a stock dividend not exceeding 20 to 25%, the subsidiary's retained earnings will have been reduced by an amount equal to the current fair value of the stock issued as a dividend. This reduction and the offsetting increase in the subsidiary's paid-in capital accounts must be incorporated in the consolidation eliminations subsequent to the issuance of the stock dividend. Thus, the amount of consolidated retained earnings is not affected by a subsidiary's stock dividend. As emphasized by the AICPA:[7]

> ... the retained earnings in the consolidated financial statements should reflect the accumulated earnings of the consolidated group not distributed to the shareholders of, or capitalized by, the parent company.

Treasury stock transactions of a subsidiary

Treasury stock held by a subsidiary at the date of a business combination logically should be treated as **retired** stock in the preparation of consolidated financial statements. A consolidation elimination should be prepared to account for the "retirement" of the treasury stock by the **par** or **stated value method.** For example, assume that Palance Corporation acquired all the outstanding capital stock of Sizemore Company on March 1, Year 6, for $147,000. Sizemore's stockholders' equity on that date was as follows:

Capital stock, $1 par	$ 50,000
Paid-in capital in excess of par	25,000
Retained earnings	50,000
Total paid-in capital and retained earnings	$125,000
Less: 1,000 shares of treasury stock, at cost	2,000
Total stockholders' equity	$123,000

Stockholders' equity of purchased subsidiary with treasury stock at date of business combination

The first consolidation elimination for Palance Corporation and subsidiary at March 1, Year 6, would be as follows:

[7] ARB No. 51, "Consolidated Financial Statements," AICPA (New York: 1959), p. 46.

PALANCE CORPORATION AND SUBSIDIARY
Consolidation Eliminations Working Paper
March 1, Year 6

Capital Stock—Sizemore 1,000
Paid-in Capital in Excess of Par—Sizemore 500
Retained Earnings—Sizemore 500
        Treasury Stock—Sizemore 2,000
To account for subsidiary's treasury stock as though it had been retired.

In the preceding elimination, paid-in capital in excess of par of the subsidiary is reduced by the pro rata portion ($25,000 ÷ 50,000 shares = $0.50 per share) applicable to the treasury stock. The remainder of the cost of the treasury stock is allocated to the subsidiary's retained earnings.

If, subsequent to the date of a business combination, a subsidiary acquires for the treasury some or all of the shares owned by minority shareholders, an elimination similar to the preceding one is appropriate. In addition, a gain or loss to the parent company must be recognized in a manner similar to that illustrated in a preceding section of this chapter for subsidiary issuances of common stock to the public.

Indirect shareholdings and parent company's stock owned by a subsidiary

In the early history of business combinations resulting in parent company–subsidiary relationships, complex indirect or reciprocal shareholdings were frequently encountered. **Indirect shareholdings** are those involving such relationships as one subsidiary and the parent company jointly owning a controlling interest in another subsidiary, or a subsidiary company being itself the parent company of its own subsidiary. **Reciprocal shareholdings** involve subsidiary ownership of shares of the parent company's voting common stock.

Business combinations in recent years generally have been far less complex than those described above. There usually has been a single parent company and one or more subsidiaries, and indirect shareholdings have been the exception rather than the rule. Accountants, faced with the problem of preparing a consolidating financial statements working paper for parent company–subsidiary relationships involving indirect shareholdings, must follow carefully the stock ownership percentages and apply the equity method of accounting for the various subsidiaries' operating results accordingly.

The traditional approach by accountants to problems of reciprocal shareholdings involved complex mathematical allocations of the individual affiliated companies' net income or loss to consolidated net income or loss and to minority interest. These allocations typically involved matrices or simultaneous equations.

Accountants have come to question the traditional approach to reciprocal shareholdings. The principal criticism is that strict application of mathematical allocations for reciprocal shareholdings violates the *going-concern* aspect of consolidated financial statements in favor of a *liquidation* approach. A related criticism is the emphasis of the traditional approach upon *legal form* of the reciprocal shareholdings, rather than upon *economic substance.* When a subsidiary acquires voting common stock of the parent company, it has been argued, the shares owned by the subsidiary are in essence *treasury stock* to the consolidated entity. The treasury stock treatment for reciprocal shareholdings was sanctioned by the American Accounting Association and by the AICPA as follows:

> Shares of the controlling company's capital stock owned by a subsidiary before the date of acquisition of control should be treated in consolidation as treasury stock. Any subsequent acquisition or sale by a subsidiary should likewise be treated in the consolidated statements as though it had been the act of the controlling company.[8]
>
> Shares of the parent held by a subsidiary should not be treated as outstanding stock in the consolidated balance sheet.[9]

The authors concur with the view that a subsidiary's shareholdings of parent company voting common stock in essence are treasury stock to the consolidated entity. This position is analogous to that set forth in Chapter 10 for intercompany bondholdings. There, the point was made that a subsidiary acquiring parent company bonds in the open market is acting on behalf of the parent in the reacquisition of the bonds for the consolidated entity's treasury.

Illustration of Parent Company Stock Owned by a Subsidiary On May 1, Year 7, Springer Company acquired in the open market for $50,000 cash 5,000 shares, or 5%, of the outstanding $1 par common stock of its parent company, Prospect Corporation. On April 30, Year 8 Prospect declared and paid a cash dividend of $1.20 per share.

Springer should make the following journal entries for its investment in Prospect:

---

[8] *Accounting and Reporting Standards for Corporate Financial Statements,* "Consolidated Financial Statements," AAA (Madison: 1957), p. 44.

[9] *ARB No. 51,* p. 45.

SPRINGER COMPANY
General Journal

Year 7			
May 1	Investment in Prospect Corporation	50,000	
	Cash		50,000
	To record purchase of 5,000 shares of parent company's outstanding common stock at $10 per share.		
Year 8			
Apr. 30	Cash	6,000	
	Intercompany Dividend Revenue		6,000
	To record dividend of $1.20 per share on 5,000 shares of parent company's common stock.		

The consolidation eliminations for Prospect Corporation and subsidiary at April 30, Year 8, would include the following:

PROSPECT CORPORATION AND SUBSIDIARY
Consolidation Eliminations Working Paper
April 30, Year 8

Treasury Stock—Prospect	50,000	
Investment in Prospect Corporation—Springer		50,000
To transfer subsidiary's investment in parent company's common stock to treasury stock category.		
Intercompany Dividend Revenue—Springer	6,000	
Dividends—Prospect		6,000
To eliminate parent company dividends received by subsidiary.		

The effect of the second elimination is to remove the parent company dividends applicable to the consolidated treasury stock. The result is that, in the consolidated statement of retained earnings, dividends are in the amount of $114,000 ($120,000 − $6,000 = $114,000), representing the $1.20 per share dividend on 95,000 shares of parent company common stock which are *outstanding* from the viewpoint of the consolidated entity. Thus, the principle that treasury stock does not receive dividends is not violated.

Accounting for income taxes for a consolidated entity

Accounting for income taxes for a consolidated entity has received considerable attention from accountants in recent years, primarily because of the growing emphasis in financial statements upon income tax allocation and disclosure. Accounting for income taxes in consolidated financial statements may be subdivided into three sections: (1) income taxes attributable to current fair values of a purchased subsidiary's identifiable net assets; (2) income taxes attributable to undistributed earnings of subsidiaries; and (3) income taxes attributable to intercompany profits.

Income Taxes Attributable to Current Fair Value of Purchased Subsidiary's Identifiable Net Assets   Income tax accounting requirements for business combinations often differ from financial accounting requirements. A business combination accounted for as a purchase, with accompanying revaluation of the combinee company's identifiable net assets, may meet the requirements for a "tax-free corporate reorganization" under the Internal Revenue Code, in which a new income tax basis of accounting may not be required for the combinee's net assets. Similarly, a business combination accounted for as a pooling, with no revaluation of the combinee's net assets, may not be a "tax-free corporate reorganization," and the income tax basis of the combinee's net assets may be changed. In such situations, a *permanent difference* may result between provisions for depreciation and amortization in the combinee company's financial statements and income tax returns.

In recognition of this problem, *APB Opinion No. 16,* "Business Combinations," included the following provision for income tax considerations in the valuation of a purchased combinee's net assets:[10]

> The market or appraisal values of specific assets and liabilities determined . . . (for a purchased combinee) may differ from the income tax bases of those items. Estimated future tax effects of differences between the tax bases and amounts otherwise appropriate to assign to an asset or a liability are one of the variables in estimating fair value. Amounts assigned to identifiable assets and liabilities should, for example, recognize that the fair value of an asset to an acquirer is less than its market or appraisal value if all or a portion of the market or appraisal value is not deductible for income taxes. The impact of tax effects on amounts assigned to individual assets and liabilities depends on numerous factors, including imminence or delay of realization of the asset value and the possible timing of tax consequences. Since differences between amounts assigned and tax bases are not timing differences . . . , the acquiring corporation should not record deferred tax accounts at the date of acquisition.

To illustrate the application of the above, assume that the business combination of Principia Corporation and its subsidiary, Sandusky Company, completed on June 1, Year 7, qualified for purchase accounting but met the requirements for a "tax-free corporate reorganization" for income tax purposes. Sandusky's building, which had a remaining economic life of ten years with no residual value on June 1, Year 7, had an appraised value of $100,000 and a carrying amount of $80,000 on that

---

[10] *APB Opinion No. 16,* pp. 320–321.

date. Assuming a combined federal and state income tax rate of 60%, Sandusky's building should be valued in the June 1, Year 7, consolidated balance sheet of Principia Corporation and subsidiary at $88,000, computed as follows:

Valuation of building for consolidation purposes

Appraised value of building, June 1, Year 7	$100,000
Less: Income taxes effect of nondeductible depreciation:	
($100,000 − $80,000) × 60%	12,000
Current fair value of building, June 1, Year 7	$ 88,000

Straight-line depreciation in the consolidated income statements of Principia Corporation and subsidiary for the ten years subsequent to the purchase business combination would include depreciation expense of $8,800 per year ($88,000 ÷ 10 years = $8,800) attributable to Sandusky's building. The $8,800 amount for annual depreciation is composed of the following:

Depreciation expense

Depreciation for income tax purposes ($80,000 ÷ 10 years)	$8,000
Depreciation, net of income taxes effect, on $20,000 difference between appraised value and carrying amount at date of business combination {[$20,000 × (1.00 − 0.60)] ÷ 10 years}	800
Total depreciation expense for consolidated income statement ($88,000 ÷ 10 years)	$8,800

Income Taxes Attributable to Undistributed Earnings of Subsidiaries Current accounting principles for income taxes associated with the undistributed earnings of subsidiaries are contained in *APB Opinion No. 23,* "Accounting for Income Taxes—Special Areas." The principal provisions of *APB Opinion No. 23* are as follows:[11]

The Board concludes that including undistributed earnings of a subsidiary in the pretax accounting income of a parent company, either through consolidation or accounting for the investment by the equity method, may result in a timing difference, in a difference that may not reverse until indefinite future periods, or in a combination of both types of differences, depending on the intent and actions of the parent company.

Timing difference. The Board believes it should be presumed that all undistributed earnings of a subsidiary will be transferred to the parent company. Accordingly, the undistributed earnings of a subsidiary included in consolidated income (or in income of the parent company) should be accounted for as a timing difference, except to the extent that some or all of the undistributed earnings meet the criteria in [the paragraph entitled "Indefinite reversal criteria"].

[11] *APB Opinion No. 23,* "Accounting for Income Taxes—Special Areas," AICPA (New York: 1972), pp. 446–447.

Indefinite reversal criteria. The presumption that all undistributed earnings will be transferred to the parent company may be overcome, and no income taxes should be accrued by the parent company, if sufficient evidence shows that the subsidiary has invested or will invest the undistributed earnings indefinitely or that the earnings will be remitted in a tax-free liquidation.

Thus, in the usual case, income tax allocation accounting is appropriate for undistributed earnings of a subsidiary. Measurement problems involved in computing the appropriate income taxes are no excuse for ignoring the required allocation, according to ***APB Opinion No. 23:***[12]

> Income taxes of the parent company applicable to a timing difference in undistributed earnings of a subsidiary are necessarily based on estimates and assumptions. For example, the tax effect may be determined by assuming that unremitted earnings were distributed in the current period and that the parent company received the benefit of all available tax-planning alternatives and available tax credits and deductions. The income tax expense of the parent company should also include taxes that would have been withheld if the undistributed earnings had been remitted as dividends.

Illustration of Income Tax Allocation for Undistributed Earnings of Subsidiaries Pinkley Corporation owns 75% of the outstanding capital stock of Seabright Company, which it acquired for cash on April 1, Year 2. Goodwill purchased by Pinkley in the business combination was $30,000; Seabright's identifiable net assets were fairly valued at their carrying amounts. For the year ended March 31, Year 3, Pinkley had pre-tax accounting income, exclusive of goodwill amortization and intercompany investment income under the equity method of accounting, of $100,000. Seabright's pre-tax accounting income was $50,000, and dividends paid by Seabright during Year 3 totaled $10,000. The combined federal and state income tax rate for both companies is 60%. Both federal and state income tax laws provide for a dividend received deduction rate of 85%. Neither Pinkley nor Seabright had any other timing differences; neither had any income subject to capital gains or preference income tax rates; and there were no intercompany profits resulting from transactions between Pinkley and Seabright.

Seabright's journal entry to accrue income taxes at March 31, Year 3, would be as follows:

Subsidiary's journal entry for accrual of income taxes		
Income Taxes Expense	*30,000*	
Income Taxes Payable		*30,000*
To provide for income taxes for Year 3 as follows: $50,000 ×		
60% = $30,000.		

At March 31, Year 3, Pinkley would prepare the following journal entries for income taxes payable, the subsidiary's operating results, and deferred income taxes:

[12] Ibid., p. 446.

PINKLEY CORPORATION
General Journal
March 31, Year 3

Amortization Expense	750	
Investment in Subsidiary		750

To record amortization of goodwill for Year 3: $30,000 ÷ 40 = $750.

Income Taxes Expense	60,000	
Income Taxes Payable...............................		60,000

To provide for income taxes for Year 3 on income exclusive of goodwill amortization (not deductible) and intercompany investment income as follows: $100,000 × 60% = $60,000.

Cash	7,500	
Investment in Subsidiary		7,500

To record dividend received from subsidiary: $10,000 × 75% = $7,500.

Investment in Subsidiary	15,000	
Intercompany Investment Income		15,000

To accrue share of subsidiary's reported net income for Year 3: $20,000* × 75% = $15,000.

Income Taxes Expense	1,350	
Income Taxes Payable...............................		675
Deferred Income Tax Liability		675

To provide for income taxes on intercompany investment income from subsidiary as follows:

Reported net income of subsidiary	$20,000
Less: Depreciation and amortization attributable to differences between current fair values and carrying amounts of subsidiary's net assets	-0-
Income of subsidiary subject to income taxes	$20,000
Parent company's share ($20,000 × 75%)	$15,000
Less: Dividend received deduction ($15,000 × 85%)	12,750
Amount subject to income taxes	$ 2,250
Income taxes expense ($2,250 × 60%)	$ 1,350
Taxes currently payable based on dividend received [($7,500 × 15%) × 60%)]	$ 675
Taxes deferred until earnings remitted by subsidiary	675
Income taxes expense	$ 1,350

* $50,000 − $30,000 = $20,000

Income Taxes Paid on Intercompany Profits   Current federal income tax laws and regulations permit an affiliated group of corporations to file a consolidated income tax return rather than separate returns. Intercompany profits and losses are eliminated in a consolidated income tax return just as they are in consolidated financial statements. An "affiliated group" for federal income tax purposes is defined as follows:[13]

> ... the term "affiliated group" means one or more chains of includible corporations connected through stock ownership with a common parent corporation which is an includible corporation if—
> (1) Stock possessing at least 80 percent of the voting power of all classes of stock and at least 80 percent of each class of the nonvoting stock of each of the includible corporations (except the common parent corporation) is owned directly by one or more of the other includible corporations; and
> (2) The common parent corporation owns directly stock possessing at least 80 percent of the voting power of all classes of stock and at least 80 percent of each class of the nonvoting stock of at least one of the other includible corporations
> As used in this subsection, the term "stock" does not include nonvoting stock which is limited and preferred as to dividends.

If a parent company and its subsidiaries do not qualify for the "affiliated group" status, or if they otherwise elect to file separate income tax returns, the following accounting principle governs the treatment of income taxes attributable to intercompany profits:[14]

> If income taxes have been paid on intercompany profits remaining within the group, such taxes should be deferred.

The deferral of income taxes provided or paid on intercompany profits can best be illustrated by returning to the intercompany profits examples in Chapter 10.

Income Taxes Attributable to Intercompany Profits in Inventories   For intercompany profits in inventories at the end of the first year of an affiliated group's operations, income tax allocation would accompany the consolidation elimination on page 351 for Post Corporation and Sage Company at April 30, Year 8, by means of the following additional elimination, assuming a combined federal and state income tax rate of 60%:

Elimination for income taxes attributable to intercompany profits in ending inventories	*Prepaid Income Taxes—Sage*	*4,800*
	Income Taxes Expense—Sage	*4,800*
	To defer income taxes provided on separate income tax returns of subsidiary applicable to unrealized intercompany profits in parent company's inventories at Apr. 30, Year 8: $8,000 × 60% = $4,800.	

---

[13] United States, *Internal Revenue Code of 1954,* sec. 1504(a).
[14] *ARB No. 51,* p. 46.

The $4,800 reduction in the income taxes expense of Sage Company (the partially owned subsidiary) would enter into the computation of the minority interest in the net income of the subsidiary.

With regard to intercompany profits in beginning and ending inventories (illustrated in the elimination on page 355) at April 30, Year 9, the following additional eliminations would be appropriate:

Eliminations for income taxes attributable to intercompany profits in ending and beginning inventories

Prepaid Income Taxes—Sage	*7,200*	
Income Taxes Expense—Sage		*7,200*

To defer income taxes provided on separate income tax returns of subsidiary applicable to unrealized intercompany profits in parent company's inventories at Apr. 30, Year 9: $12,000 × 60% = $7,200.

Retained Earnings—Sage ($4,800 × 95%)	*4,560*	
Minority Interest in subsidiary (4,800 × 5%)		*240*

To provide for income taxes attributable to realized intercompany profits in parent company's inventories at Apr. 30, Year 8: $8,000 × 60% = $4,800.

The second elimination above reflects the income tax effects of the *realization* by the consolidated group, on a first-in, first-out basis, of the intercompany profits in the parent company's *beginning* inventories.

Income Taxes Attributable to Intercompany Profits in Land   Under generally accepted accounting principles, gains and losses from sales of plant assets are not reported as extraordinary items.[15] Thus, intraperiod income tax allocation is not appropriate for such gains and losses. Accordingly, for the intercompany profit on sale of land illustrated in Chapter 10, the following elimination would accompany the one illustrated on page 357, assuming a combined federal and state "capital gains" income tax rate of 35%:

Elimination for income taxes attributable to intercompany profits in land—for period of sale

Prepaid Income Taxes—Post	*17,500*	
Income Taxes Expense—Post		*17,500*

To defer income taxes provided on separate income tax returns of parent company applicable to unrealized intercompany profit in subsidiary's land at Apr. 30, Year 8: $50,000 × 35% = $17,500.

In years subsequent to Year 8, as long as the subsidiary owned the land, the following elimination would be appropriate:

[15] *APB Opinion No. 30,* pp. 566 and 568.

Elimination for income taxes attribut- able to inter- company profits in land—for periods subsequent to sale	*Prepaid Income Taxes—Post* 17,500	
	Retained Earnings—Post	17,500
	To defer income taxes attributable to unrealized intercompany profit in subsidiary's land.	

In a year in which the subsidiary resold the land to an outsider, the appropriate elimination would be a debit to Income Taxes Expense—Post and a credit to Retained Earnings—Post, in the amount of $17,500.

Income Taxes Attributable to Intercompany Profit in a Depreciable Asset As pointed out in Chapter 10, the intercompany profit in the sale of a depreciable asset is realized through the periodic depreciation of the asset. Therefore, the related deferred income taxes "turn around" as depreciation expense is taken on the asset with intercompany profit in its carrying amount.

To illustrate, refer to the example in Chapter 10, pages 359–361. Assuming a combined federal and state income tax rate of 60%, the tax-deferral elimination at April 30, Year 8 (date of the intercompany sale of machinery), would be as follows:

Elimination for income taxes attrib- utable to intercompany profits in machinery— for period of sale	*Prepaid Income Taxes—Sage* 14,280	
	Income Taxes Expense—Sage	14,280
	To defer income taxes provided on separate income tax returns of subsidiary applicable to unrealized intercompany profit in parent company's machinery at Apr. 30, Year 8: $23,800 × 60% = $14,280.	

The $14,280 increase in the subsidiary's reported net income would be included in the computation of the minority interest in the subsidiary's net income for Year 8.

For the year ended April 30, Year 9, the elimination for income taxes attributable to the intercompany profit would be as follows:

Elimination for income taxes attrib- utable to intercompany profits in machinery— for first year subsequent to sale	*Income Taxes Expense—Sage* 2,856	
	Prepaid Income Taxes—Sage ($14,280 − $2,856) 11,424	
	Retained Earnings—Sage ($14,280 × 95%)	13,566
	Minority Interest in Subsidiary ($14,280 × 5%)	714
	To provide for income taxes expense on intercompany profit realized through parent company's depreciation: $4,760 × 60% = $2,856; and to defer income taxes attributable to remainder of unrealized profit.	

Comparable consolidation eliminations would be necessary at April 30, Years 10, 11, and 12.

Income Taxes Attributable to Intercompany Gain on Reacquisition of Debt
As pointed out in Chapter 10, a gain or loss is recognized in consolidated financial statements on one affiliate's open-market purchase of another affiliate's bonds or debentures. Thus, income taxes attributable to the gain or loss should be provided for in a consolidation elimination. The appropriate elimination to accompany the one illustrated on page 367 of Chapter 10 would be as follows, assuming that the combined income tax rate is 60% and that the gain is not material and thus is not reported as an extraordinary item in the income statement:

Elimination for income taxes attributable to intercompany gain on reacquisition of debentures —for period of reacquisition

Income Taxes Expense—Sage	13,624	
Deferred Income Tax Liability—Sage		13,624
To provide for income taxes attributable to subsidiary's realized gain on parent company's reacquisition of the subsidiary's debentures: $22,707 × 60% = $13,624.		

The additional expense of the subsidiary recorded in the preceding elimination would enter into the computation of the minority interest in net income of the subsidiary.

In years *subsequent* to the date of the reacquisition of the debentures, the *actual* income taxes expense of both the parent company and the subsidiary would reflect the effects of the intercompany interest revenue and expense. The income tax effects of the difference between intercompany interest revenue and expense would represent the "turnaround" of the $13,624 deferred income tax liability in the preceding elimination. For example, the elimination for income taxes which follows would be appropriate at April 30, Year 9, to accompany the related elimination on pages 370–371 of Chapter 10:

Elimination for income taxes attributable to intercompany gain on reacquisition of debentures —for first year subsequent to reacquisition

Retained Earnings—Sage ($13,624 × 95%)	12,943	
Minority Interest in Subsidiary ($13,624 × 5%)	681	
Income Taxes Expense—Sage ($4,732 × 60%)		2,839
Deferred Income Tax Liability—Sage ($13,624 − $2,839)		10,785
To reduce the subsidiary's recorded income taxes expense for amount attributable to **recorded** intercompany gain (for consolidation purposes) on subsidiary's debentures; and to provide for remaining deferred income taxes on unamortized portion of gain.		

Statement of changes in financial position for a consolidated entity

The consolidated financial statements issued by publicly owned companies include a statement of changes in financial position, generally prepared on a working capital basis. Such a statement may be prepared as described in the *Intermediate Accounting* text of this series; however, when the statement is prepared on a consolidated basis, a number of special problems arise. Some of these are described below:

1 Depreciation and amortization as reported in the consolidated income statement are added to combined net income, *including the minority share of net income,* in the consolidated statement of changes in financial position. The depreciation and amortization in a business combination accounted for as a purchase are based on the current fair values of the assets, including any goodwill, of subsidiaries at the dates of acquisition. Net income applicable to minority interest is included in the computation of working capital provided from operations, because 100% of working capital of subsidiaries is included in a consolidated balance sheet.

2 Only cash dividends paid by the parent company and the cash dividends paid by partially owned subsidiary companies *to minority shareholders* are reported as uses of working capital. Cash dividends paid by subsidiary companies to the parent company have no effect on consolidated working capital, because cash is transferred entirely *within the affiliated group* of companies. Dividends paid to minority stockholders which are material in amount should be listed separately or disclosed parenthetically in the consolidated statement of changes in financial position.

3 A purchase by the parent company of additional shares of stock directly from a subsidiary does not change the amount of consolidated working capital and thus would not be reported in a consolidated statement of changes in financial position. Any change in the amount of minority interest resulting from such purchases at amounts which differ from the carrying amounts of the subsidiary's net assets represents investment income (or loss) and is eliminated from combined net income in the computation of consolidated working capital provided from operations.

4 A purchase by the parent company of additional shares of stock from minority shareholders reduces consolidated working capital. Consequently, such a purchase is reported in the consolidated statement of changes in financial position as a financial resource (working capital or cash) applied.

5 A sale of part of the investment in a subsidiary company increases consolidated working capital (and the amount of minority interest) and thus is reported as a financial resource provided in the consolidated statement of changes in financial position. A gain or loss from such a sale represents an adjustment to combined net income in the measurement of working capital provided from operations.

Illustration of Consolidated Statement of Changes in Financial Position
Parent Corporation has owned 100% of the stock of Sub Company for several years. The business combination originally was treated as a pooling of interests. Sub Company has outstanding only one class of stock, and its total stockholders' equity at the end of Year 10 was $500,000. At the beginning of Year 11, Parent sold 30% of Sub's stock to outsiders for $205,000, which was $55,000 more than the carrying amount of the shares in Parent's accounting records. Sub reported a

net income of $100,000 and paid cash dividends of $60,000 near the end of Year 11. During Year 11, Parent issued additional common stock and cash of $200,000 in exchange for plant assets with a current fair value of $490,000.

The consolidated income statement for Year 11, the consolidated statement of retained earnings for Year 11, and the comparative consolidated balance sheet at December 31, Year 10 and Year 11, are presented below.

PARENT CORPORATION AND SUBSIDIARY
Consolidated Income Statement
For Year Ended December 31, Year 11

Sales and other revenue (including gain of $55,000 from sale of Sub Company stock)		$2,450,000
Costs and expenses:		
Cost of goods sold	$1,500,000	
Depreciation and amortization of intangibles	210,000	
Other operating expenses	190,000	1,900,000
Income before income taxes		$ 550,000
Income taxes expense		250,000
Combined net income		$ 300,000
Less: Minority interest in net income of subsidiary		30,000
Consolidated net income		$ 270,000

PARENT CORPORATION AND SUBSIDIARY
Consolidated Statement of Retained Earnings
For Year Ended December 31, Year 11

Balance, Jan. 1, Year 11	$670,000
Net income	270,000
Subtotal	$940,000
Dividends	160,000
Balance, Dec. 31, Year 11	$780,000

PARENT CORPORATION AND SUBSIDIARY
Consolidated Balance Sheet
December 31

	Year 11	Year 10
Assets		
Current assets	$1,200,000	$ 900,000
Plant assets	3,000,000	2,510,000
Less: Accumulated depreciation	(1,300,000)	(1,100,000)
Intangible assets (net)	240,000	250,000
Total assets	$3,140,000	$2,560,000

(continued)

PARENT CORPORATION AND SUBSIDIARY
Consolidated Balance Sheet
December 31 (concluded)

	Year 11	Year 10
Liabilities & Stockholders' Equity		
Current liabilities	$ 505,000	$ 490,000
Long-term debt	693,000	600,000
Minority interest	162,000	-0-
Common stock, $10 par	550,000	500,000
Paid-in capital in excess of par	450,000	300,000
Retained earnings	780,000	670,000
Total liabilities & stockholders' equity	$3,140,000	$2,560,000

A working paper for a consolidated statement of changes in financial position on a working capital basis for Year 11 is illustrated below and on page 430.

PARENT CORPORATION AND SUBSIDIARY
Working Paper for Consolidated Statement of Changes in
Financial Position (Working Capital Basis)
For Year Ended December 31, Year 11

	Account balances at Dec. 31, Year 10	Analysis of transactions for Year 11		Account balances at Dec. 31, Year 11
		Debit	Credit	
Working capital	$ 410,000	(x) $ 285,000		$ 695,000
Plant assets	2,510,000	(7) 290,000		3,000,000
		(8) 200,000		
Intangible assets (net)	250,000		(2) $ 10,000	240,000
Totals	$3,170,000			$3,935,000
Accumulated depreciation	$1,100,000		(2) 200,000	$1,300,000
Long-term debt	600,000		(5) 93,000	693,000
Minority interest	-0-	(9) 18,000	(3) 150,000	162,000
			(4) 30,000	
Common stock, $10 par	500,000		(6) 50,000	550,000
Paid-in capital in excess of par	300,000		(6) 150,000	450,000
Retained earnings	670,000	(9) 160,000	(1) 270,000	780,000
Totals	$3,170,000	$ 953,000	$ 953,000	$3,935,000

(continued)

PARENT CORPORATION AND SUBSIDIARY
Working Paper for Consolidated Statement of Changes in
Financial Position (Working Capital Basis)
For Year Ended December 31, Year 11 (concluded)

	Account balances at Dec. 31, Year 10	Analysis of transactions for Year 11		Account balances at Dec. 31, Year 11
		Debit	Credit	
Financial resources provided:				
Operations—net income		(1) $ 270,000		
Add: Depreciation and amortization		(2) 210,000		
Minority interest in net income of subsidiary		(4) 30,000		
Less: Gain on sale of Sub Company stock			(3) $ 55,000	
Sale of Sub Company stock .		(3) 205,000		
Increase in long-term debt ...		(5) 93,000		
Increase of common stock in exchange for plant assets ..		(6) 200,000		
Financial resources applied:				
Purchase of plant assets for cash			(7) 290,000	
Purchase of plant assets in exchange for common stock			(8) 200,000	
Payment of dividends, including $18,000 to minority shareholders of Sub Company			(9) 178,000	
Total financial resources provided and applied		$1,008,000	$ 723,000	
Increase in working capital			(x) 285,000	
		$1,008,000	$1,008,000	

A consolidated statement of changes in financial position for Parent
Company and Subsidiary for Year 11 is illustrated on page 431.

PARENT CORPORATION AND SUBSIDIARY
Consolidated Statement of Changes in Financial Position
(Working Capital Basis)
For Year Ended December 31, Year 11

Financial resources provided:

Working capital provided from operations:

Net income, including minority interest of $30,000	$300,000
Add: Depreciation and amortization of intangibles..............	210,000
Less: Gain on sale of Sub Company stock	(55,000)
Working capital provided from operations....................	$455,000
Sale of Sub Company stock	205,000
Long-term borrowing	93,000
Issuance of common stock in exchange for plant assets	200,000
Total financial resources provided	$953,000

Financial resources applied:

Purchase of plant assets for cash	$290,000	
Purchase of plant assets in exchange for common stock ..	200,000	
Payment of dividends, including $18,000 to minority share-holders of Sub Company	178,000	
Total financial resources applied		668,000
Increase in financial resources (working capital)		$285,000

Composition of working capital:

	End of Year 11	End of Year 10	Increase or (decrease) in working capital
Current assets	$1,200,000	$900,000	$300,000
Less: Current liabilities	505,000	490,000	(15,000)
Working capital	$ 695,000	$410,000	
Increase in working capital............................			$285,000

The following items in the consolidated statement of changes in financial position warrant special emphasis:

1 The working capital provided from operations includes the minority share of net income of Sub Company.

2 The working capital provided from operations excludes the gain from sale of Sub Company stock; thus the full proceeds of $205,000 are reported as a source of consolidated working capital.

3 Only the dividends paid to stockholders of Parent Corporation ($160,000) and to minority stockholders of Sub Company ($18,000) are reported as uses of consolidated working capital.

4 The issuance of common stock by Parent Corporation to acquire plant assets is an **exchange transaction** (as defined in **APB Opinion No. 19**) and is reported

as both a source and a use of consolidated working capital, even though no working capital accounts were affected directly by the exchange transaction.

Concluding comments

In this chapter we have discussed a number of special problems which might arise in the preparation of consolidated financial statements. We have purposely not discussed earnings per share computations for a consolidated entity, because in most circumstances the standards for earnings per share computations set forth in *Intermediate Accounting* of this series apply to the computation of consolidated earnings per share. The problems that arise in earnings per share computations when a subsidiary has securities which are common stock equivalents or are otherwise *dilutive* are highly technical and too specialized to warrant inclusion in our discussion of basic concepts.

REVIEW QUESTIONS

1 How is the equity method of accounting applied when a parent company attains control of a subsidiary in a series of stock acquisitions? Explain.

2 At what stage in the installment purchase of an eventual subsidiary's voting common stock should the parent company ascertain the current fair values of the subsidiary's identifiable net assets? Explain.

3 **APB Opinion No. 16,** "Business Combinations," requires use of the purchase method of accounting for parent company acquisitions of minority interest in a subsidiary, even though the original business combination was accounted for as a pooling. Discuss the reasoning supporting this requirement.

4 If a parent company purchases the minority interest in a subsidiary at less than its carrying amount, what accounting treatment is appropriate for the difference? Explain.

5 Why does a parent company realize a gain or a loss when a subsidiary issues voting common stock to the public at a price per share which differs from the carrying amount per share of the parent company's investment in the subsidiary's stock? Explain.

6 Explain how the minority interest in a subsidiary is affected by the parent company's ownership of 70% of the subsidiary's outstanding voting common stock and 60% of the subsidiary's outstanding 7%, cumulative, fully participating preferred stock.

7 Describe how the parent company's accounts are affected when a subsidiary purchases for its treasury all or part of its outstanding voting common stock owned by minority shareholders.

8 "The treasury stock treatment for shares of parent company voting common stock owned by a subsidiary overstates consolidated net income and understates the minority interest in net income of the subsidiary." Do you agree? Explain.

9 Shares of its own stock held by a corporation in its treasury are not entitled to dividends. However, a subsidiary receives dividends on shares of its parent company's outstanding voting common stock owned by the subsidiary. For consolidated financial statements, these parent company shares are considered equivalent to treasury stock of the consolidated entity. Is there an inconsistency in this treatment? Explain.

10 Discuss the following quotation:

(The "indefinite reversal criteria" provisions of **APB Opinion No. 23**) allow the decision to remit cash from a subsidiary to a parent to affect the income of the parent. This occurs because the full tax expense associated with the earnings of the subsidiary has not been recorded.

11 A parent company and its subsidiary file separate income tax returns. How do the consolidated deferred income taxes associated with the intercompany profit on the parent company's sale of a depreciable asset to its subsidiary "turn around"? Explain.

12 Are dividends paid to minority shareholders included in the consolidated statement of changes in financial position? Explain.

EXERCISES

Ex. 11-1 Select the best answer for each of the following multiple-choice questions:

1 At the end of Year 4, Piller Company owned 8,000 of the 9,000 shares of Salton Company capital stock outstanding. The stockholders' equity of Salton at the end of Year 4 was $360,000. Early in Year 5, Salton sold to the public an additional 1,000 shares of capital stock for $54,000. As a result of the sale of capital stock by Salton, Piller should:
  a Debit the Investment in Salton Company account for $48,000
  b Debit the Investment in Salton Company account for $11,200
  c Credit the Investment in Salton Company account for $11,200
  d Neither debit nor credit the Investment in Salton Company account

2 In an installment acquisition of a parent company's controlling interest in a subsidiary, the equity method of accounting for the investee's/subsidiary's operating results should be applied:
  a Prospectively when the parent company's capital stock ownership is sufficient to influence the investee
  b Prospectively when the parent company's capital stock ownership is sufficient to control the subsidiary
  c Retroactively when the parent company's capital stock ownership is sufficient to influence the investee
  d Retroactively when the parent company's capital stock ownership is sufficient to control the subsidiary

3 When a parent company acquires both preferred stock and common stock of the subsidiary in a business combination, goodwill arising from the combination should be computed based on:
  a Cost allocated to preferred stock only
  b Cost allocated to common stock only
  c Cost allocated to both preferred stock and common stock
  d Some other measure

4 In a consolidation elimination, the income tax effects of the realized gain on a parent company's open-market purchase of its subsidiary's bonds at a discount should include a:

  a Debit to Prepaid Income Taxes—Subsidiary
  b Credit to Deferred Income Tax Liability—Subsidiary
  c Debit to Prepaid Income Taxes—Parent Company
  d Credit to Deferred Income Tax Liability—Parent Company

5 Treasury stock held by a subsidiary at the date of a business combination should be treated in the preparation of a consolidated balance sheet:
  a As treasury stock of the consolidated entity
  b As authorized but unissued capital stock of the subsidiary
  c As treasury stock of the parent company
  d In some other manner

Ex. 11-2 In Year 5, Pryor Corporation formed a wholly owned foreign subsidiary. Year 5 pre-tax accounting income for the subsidiary was $500,000. The income tax rate of the country in which the foreign subsidiary was domiciled was 40%. None of the foreign subsidiary's earnings in Year 5 was paid as a dividend to Pryor; however, there is nothing to indicate that these earnings will not be remitted to Pryor in the future.

The country in which the foreign subsidiary is domiciled does not impose a tax on remittances to the United States. An income tax credit is allowed in the United States for income taxes payable in the country in which the foreign subsidiary is domiciled.

Assuming that the income tax rate in the United States is 48%, compute the total amount of income taxes expense relating to the foreign subsidiary that should be included in the consolidated income statement of Pryor Corporation and subsidiary for Year 5.

Ex. 11-3 On October 31, Year 5, Salvador Company, 80%-owned subsidiary of Panama Corporation, sold to its parent company for $20,000 a patent with a carrying amount of $15,000 to Salvador at that date. Remaining legal life of the patent on October 31, Year 5, was five years; the patent was expected to produce revenue for Panama during the entire five-year period. Panama and Salvador file separate income tax returns; their combined federal and state income tax rate is 60%.

Prepare the consolidation elimination or eliminations, including income tax allocation, for Panama Corporation and subsidiary with respect to the patent: (**a**) at October 31, Year 5; and (**b**) at October 31, Year 6.

Ex. 11-4 Prieto Corporation paid cash dividends of $250,000 and distributed a 5% stock dividend in Year 5. The market value of the shares distributed pursuant to the 5% stock dividend was $600,000. Prieto owns 100% of the common stock of S Company and 75% of the common stock of SS Company. In Year 5, S paid a cash dividend of $100,000 on the common stock and $25,000 on its $5 cumulative preferred stock. None of the preferred stock is owned by Prieto. In Year 5, SS paid cash dividends of $44,000 on its common stock, the only class of capital stock issued.

Compute the amount that should be reported as working capital applied to payment of dividends in the Year 5 consolidated statement of changes in financial position for Prieto Corporation and subsidiaries.

Ex. 11-5 The consolidated statement of changes in financial position for Paradise Corporation and its partially owned subsidiaries for Year 2 will be prepared on a working capital basis.

Using the letters below, indicate how each of the 13 items should be reported in the statement. A given item may be reported more than one way.

A–O = Add to combined net income in the determination of working capital provided from operations

D–O = Deduct from combined net income in the determination of consolidated working capital provided from operations

FP = A financial resource provided
FA = A financial resource applied
N = Not included or separately disclosed in the consolidated statement of changes in financial position

1 The minority interest in net income of subsidiaries is $37,500.
2 Paradise issued a bond payable to a subsidiary company in exchange for plant assets with a current fair value of $180,000.
3 Paradise distributed a 10% stock dividend; the additional shares issued had a current fair value of $675,000.
4 Paradise declared and paid a cash dividend of $200,000.
5 Long-term debt of Paradise in the amount of $2 million was converted into common stock.
6 A subsidiary sold plant assets to outsiders at a carrying amount of $80,000.
7 Paradise's share of the net income of an unconsolidated subsidiary totaled $28,000. The subsidiary did not pay cash dividends in Year 2.
8 Consolidated depreciation expense and amortization of intangibles totaled $285,000.
9 A subsidiary company amortized $3,000 of premium on bonds payable held by outsiders.
10 Paradise sold its entire holdings in an 80%-owned subsidiary for $3 million.
11 Paradise merged with Sun Company in a business combination accounted for as a pooling of interests: 150,000 shares of common stock with a current fair value of $4.5 million were issued by Paradise for 98% of Sun's capital stock.
12 Paradise received cash dividends of $117,000 from its consolidated subsidiaries.
13 The consolidated subsidiaries of Paradise paid cash dividends of $21,500 to minority stockholders.

Ex. 11-6 On August 1, Year 6, Packard Corporation purchased 1,000 of the 10,000 outstanding shares of Scopus Company's $1 par capital stock for $5,000. Scopus's identifiable net assets had a current fair value and carrying amount of $40,000 at that date. Scopus reported net income of $3,000 and declared and paid dividends of the same amount for the year ended July 31, Year 7. On August 1, Year 7, Packard purchased 4,500 more shares of Scopus's outstanding capital stock for $22,500. The current fair values and carrying amounts for Scopus's identifiable net assets were still $40,000 at that date. Scopus reported net income of $7,500 and paid no dividends for the year ended July 31, Year 8.

Prepare journal entries in Packard Corporation's accounting records for the above facts for the two years ended July 31, Year 8. Omit income tax effects. Journal entry explanations are not required.

Ex. 11-7 On August 1, Year 4, Princeton Corporation acquired 95% of the outstanding capital stock of Sycamore Company in a business combination accounted for as a pooling. Among the intercompany transactions between Princeton and Sycamore subsequent to August 1, Year 4, were the following:

(1) On May 31, Year 5, Sycamore declared a 10% stock dividend on its 10,000 outstanding shares of $10 par capital stock having a current fair value of $18 per share. The 1,000 shares of the stock dividend were issued June 18, Year 5.
(2) On July 28, Year 5, Sycamore purchased in the open market, for $15,000 cash, 1,000 of the 100,000 outstanding shares of Princeton's $1 par voting common stock. Princeton did not declare any dividends.

Prepare a consolidation eliminations working paper at July 31, Year 5, in good form, for Princeton Corporation and subsidiary. Disregard income taxes.

Ex. 11-8 Select the best answer for each of the following multiple-choice questions:
1 With respect to the difference between taxable income and pre-tax account-

ing income, the tax effect of the undistributed earnings of a subsidiary included in consolidated income normally should be:

a Accounted for as a timing difference
b Accounted for as a permanent difference
c Ignored because it must be based on estimates and assumptions
d Ignored because it cannot be presumed that all undistributed earnings of a subsidiary will be transferred to the parent company

2 Under the equity method of accounting for a subsidiary's operating results, the effect on the investor of dividends received from the investee usually is:

a A reduction of deferred income taxes and a reduction of investment
b A reduction of deferred income taxes and no effect on investment
c No effect on deferred income taxes and a reduction of investment
d No effect on deferred income taxes and no effect on investment

3 Sorter Company, a subsidiary of Polley Corporation, did not declare dividends from its Year 5 net income in Year 5. Polley should recognize income taxes on its share of Sorter's net income in its Year 5 financial statements only if:

a Sorter Company is a domestic corporation
b The net income will be remitted in a tax-free transaction within the foreseeable future
c The net income will be remitted in a taxable transaction on or before March 15, Year 6
d Remittance of the net income in a taxable transaction will not be postponed indefinitely

4 Accounting for the income tax effect of a difference between taxable income and pre-tax accounting income with respect to undistributed earnings of a subsidiary is similar to a situation involving:

a Profits on assets within the consolidated group which are eliminated in consolidated financial statements
b Profits on intercompany transactions which are taxed when reported in separate income tax returns
c Rents and royalties which are taxed when collected and deferred in financial statements until earned
d Profits on installment sales which are recognized in financial statements at the date of sale and reported in income tax returns when the installment receivables are collected

5 A Deferred Income Tax Liability account is credited in a consolidation elimination for the income tax effects of:

a Intercompany profits in inventories
b Intercompany profits in land
c Intercompany profits in a depreciable plant asset or an intangible asset
d All of the above
e None of the above

Ex. 11-9 The stockholders' equity section of Stegg Company's August 31, Year 2, balance sheet was as follows:

8% cumulative preferred stock, $1 par, dividends in arrears two years, authorized, issued, and outstanding 100,000 shares, callable at $1.10 per share plus dividends in arrears	$ 100,000
Common stock, $2 par, authorized, issued, and outstanding 100,000 shares	200,000
Paid-in capital in excess of par—common	150,000
Retained earnings	750,000
Total stockholders' equity	$1,200,000

On August 31, Year 2, Panay Corporation acquired for cash 50,000 shares of Stegg's outstanding preferred stock and 75,000 shares of Stegg's outstanding common stock for a total cost—including out-of-pocket costs—of $1,030,500. The current fair values of Stegg's identifiable net assets were equal to their carrying amounts at August 31, Year 2.

Answer the following questions (computations should be in good form):

a What amount of the $1,030,500 purchase price is assignable to Stegg's preferred stock?

b What is the minority interest of preferred shareholders in Stegg's net assets at August 31, Year 2?

c What is the amount of goodwill purchased by Panay August 31, Year 2?

d What is the minority interest of common shareholders in Stegg's net assets at August 31, Year 2?

SHORT CASES FOR ANALYSIS AND DECISION

Case 11-1 On January 2, Year 3, Phoenix Corporation acquired for cash all the outstanding capital stock of Scottsdale Company and 70% of the outstanding capital stock of Sonoma Company. Included among the assets of Scottsdale are investments in 80% of the outstanding capital stock of Spokane Company and 30% of the outstanding capital stock of Sonoma Company.

Instructions Discuss the accounting principles which Phoenix Corporation should use for its investment in Scottsdale Company and in its financial statements issued subsequent to the business combination with Scottsdale.

Case 11-2 On March 1, Year 1, Patotzka Corporation, a manufacturer, organized a wholly owned subsidiary finance company, Sterling Company, to purchase Patotzka's installment contracts for sales of its products. Patotzka purchased all 10,000 shares of Sterling's $5 par capital stock on March 1, Year 1.

By February 28, Year 4, Sterling had accumulated a retained earnings balance of $120,000, which also was reflected in Patotzka Corporation's Retained Earnings of Subsidiary account, under the equity method of accounting. As of the close of business February 28, Year 4, Sterling declared and issued a 100% stock dividend. In connection with the dividend, Sterling transferred $50,000 from its Retained Earnings account to its Capital Stock account.

The bank which provides Sterling's line of credit has requested separate financial statements for both Patotzka and Sterling, as well as consolidated financial statements, for the year ended February 28, Year 4. Patotzka's controller is concerned about the inconsistency resulting from the fact that Patotzka's Retained Earnings of Subsidiary account has a balance of $120,000 at February 28, Year 4, while Sterling's Retained Earnings account is $70,000 at that date. The controller asks your opinion of the propriety of transferring $50,000 from Patotzka's Retained Earnings of Subsidiary account to its Paid-in Capital in Excess of Par account.

Instructions What is your opinion of the controller's proposal? Explain.

Case 11-3 Scarborough Company, a wholly owned subsidiary of Poller Corporation, is in need of additional long-term financing. Under instructions from Poller, Scarborough offers 5,000 shares of its previously unissued $2 par capital stock to shareholders of Poller at a price of $10 per share. The offer is fully subscribed by Poller's shareholders, and the stock is issued for $50,000 cash on June 30, Year 6.

After the stock issuance, Poller owns 45,000 shares, or 90%, of the 50,000 shares of Scarborough capital stock outstanding; and shareholders of Poller own 5,000 shares, or 10%, of Scarborough's outstanding stock. By comparing

Poller's 90% interest in Scarborough's net assets after the capital stock issuance to the parent company's 100% interest in the subsidiary's net assets before the stock issuance, Poller's chief accountant computed a $4,000 nonoperating gain for entry into Poller's accounting records. The controller of Poller objected to the chief accountant's entry. The controller pointed out that the 5,000 shares of Scarborough capital stock were issued to Poller's shareholders, not to **outsiders,** and that it is a basic principle of accounting that a corporation cannot profit from capital stock issuances to its shareholders.

Instructions Evaluate the objections of Poller Corporation's controller.

PROBLEMS

11-4 Condensed balance sheets of Pellerin Corporation and its subsidiary, Sigmund Company, on the dates indicated, appear below:

PELLERIN CORPORATION AND SIGMUND COMPANY
Balance Sheets
Various Dates, Year 3

	Pellerin Corporation	Sigmund Company		
	Dec. 31, Year 3	Jan. 2, Year 3	Sept. 30, Year 3	Dec. 31, Year 3
Assets				
Cash	$ 400,000	$ 550,000	$ 650,000	$ 425,000
Fees and royalties receivable	-0-	250,000	450,000	500,000
Investment in Sigmund Company	2,358,000	-0-	-0-	-0-
Patents	-0-	1,000,000	850,000	800,000
Other assets	4,242,000	-0-	-0-	200,000
Total assets	$7,000,000	$1,800,000	$1,950,000	$1,925,000
Liabilities & Stockholders' Equity				
Liabilities	$ 400,000	$ 200,000	$ 150,000	$ 275,000
Capital stock, $10 par	5,000,000	1,000,000	1,000,000	1,000,000
Retained earnings	1,600,000	600,000	800,000	650,000
Total liabilities & stockholders' equity	$7,000,000	$1,800,000	$1,950,000	$1,925,000

Pellerin purchased 60,000 shares of Sigmund's outstanding capital stock January 2, Year 3, at a cost of $1,470,000; and 30,000 shares on September 30, Year 3, at a cost of $888,000. Pellerin obtained control over Sigmund for the valuable patents owned by Sigmund.

Sigmund amortizes the cost of patents on a straight-line basis. Any amount allocated to patents as a result of the business combination is to be amortized over the five-year remaining economic life of the patents as of January 2, Year 3.

Sigmund paid a cash dividend of $300,000 on December 31, Year 3. Pellerin has not recorded the declaration or the receipt of the dividend.

Instructions Prepare journal entries, in good form, for Pellerin Corporation at December 31, Year 3, to account for its investment in Sigmund Company by the equity method of accounting. Disregard income taxes.

11-5 Paine Corporation owns 99% of the outstanding capital stock of Spilberg Company, acquired July 1, Year 5, in a pooling, and 90% of the outstanding capital stock of Sykes Company, acquired July 1, Year 5, in a purchase which reflected goodwill of $52,200. All identifiable net assets of Sykes were fairly valued at their carrying amounts at July 1, Year 5. Goodwill is amortized over 40 years.

Condensed financial statements of Paine, Spilberg, and Sykes at June 30, Year 6, prior to income tax provisions and equity-method accruals in the accounts of Paine, appear below:

PAINE CORPORATION AND SUBSIDIARIES
Financial Statements
For Year Ended June 30, Year 6

	Paine Corporation	Spilberg Company	Sykes Company
Income Statements			
Revenue			
Net sales	$1,000,000	$ 550,000	$ 220,000
Intercompany sales	100,000	-0-	-0-
Total revenue	$1,100,000	$ 550,000	$ 220,000
Costs and expenses			
Cost of goods sold	$ 700,000	$ 357,500	$ 143,000
Intercompany cost of goods sold	70,000	-0-	-0-
Selling, general, and administrative			
expenses	130,000	92,500	27,000
Interest expense	50,000	-0-	-0-
Income taxes expense	-0-	60,000	30,000
Total costs and expenses	$ 950,000	$ 510,000	$ 200,000
Net income	$ 150,000	$ 40,000	$ 20,000
Statements of Retained Earnings			
Retained earnings, July 1, Year 5	$ 400,000	$ 300,000	$ 150,000
Net income	150,000	40,000	20,000
Subtotal	$ 550,000	$ 340,000	$ 170,000
Dividends	50,000	20,000	10,000
Retained earnings, June 30, Year 6	$ 500,000	$ 320,000	$ 160,000
Balance Sheets			
Assets			
Inventories	$1,000,000	$ 800,000	$ 700,000
Investment in Spilberg Company	990,000	-0-	-0-
Investment in Sykes Company	574,200	-0-	-0-
Other assets	1,501,300	1,260,000	790,000
Total assets	$4,065,500	$2,060,000	$1,490,000

(continued)

PAINE CORPORATION AND SUBSIDIARIES

Financial Statements

For Year Ended June 30, Year 6 (Concluded)

	Paine Corporation	Spilberg Company	Sykes Company
Liabilities & Stockholders' Equity			
Intercompany dividends payable	$ -0-	$ 19,800	$ 18,000
Other liabilities	1,965,500	1,020,200	882,000
Capital stock, $1 par	1,000,000	500,000	300,000
Paid-in capital in excess of par	600,000	200,000	130,000
Retained earnings	500,000	320,000	160,000
Total liabilities & stockholders' equity ...	$4,065,500	$2,060,000	$1,490,000

Intercompany profits in inventories resulting from Paine's sales to its subsidiaries during the year ended June 30, Year 6, are as follows:

In Spilberg Company's inventories—$6,000

In Sykes Company's inventories—$7,500

Instructions   Prepare in good form Paine Corporation's June 30, Year 6, journal entries for income taxes and equity-method accruals. Paine's combined federal and state income tax rate is 60%. All three companies declared dividends on June 30, Year 6.

11-6 Condensed individual and consolidated financial statements of Peterson Corporation and its wholly owned subsidiary, Swanson Company, for the year ended May 31, Year 4, appear below. The two companies use intercompany accounts only for receivables and payables.

PETERSON CORPORATION AND SUBSIDIARY

Individual and Consolidated Financial Statements

For Year Ended May 31, Year 4

	Peterson Corporation	Swanson Company	Consolidated
Income Statements			
Revenue			
Net sales	$10,000,000	$4,600,000	$12,900,000
Other revenue	270,000	20,000	38,250
Total revenue	$10,270,000	$4,620,000	$12,938,250
Costs and expenses			
Cost of goods sold	$ 6,700,000	$3,082,000	$ 8,085,300
Other operating expenses	2,920,000	1,288,000	4,209,250
Total costs and expenses	$ 9,620,000	$4,370,000	$12,294,550
Net income	$ 650,000	$ 250,000	$ 643,700

(continued)

PETERSON CORPORATION AND SUBSIDIARY
Individual and Consolidated Financial Statements
For Year Ended May 31, Year 4 (concluded)

	Peterson Corporation	Swanson Company	Consolidated
Statements of Retained Earnings			
Retained earnings, June 1, Year 3	$ 2,420,000	$ 825,000	$ 2,406,800
Net income	650,000	250,000	643,700
Subtotal	$ 3,070,000	$1,075,000	$ 3,050,500
Dividends	300,000	175,000	297,000
Retained earnings, May 31, Year 4	$ 2,770,000	$ 900,000	$ 2,753,500
Balance Sheets			
Assets			
Intercompany receivables (payables)..	$ 520,000	$ (520,000)	$ -0-
Marketable securities	400,000	150,000	530,000
Inventories	1,100,000	610,000	1,693,500
Investment in subsidiary	1,097,500	-0-	-0-
Other assets	2,800,000	1,370,000	4,170,000
Goodwill	-0-	-0-	47,500
Total assets	$ 5,917,500	$1,610,000	$ 6,441,000
Liabilities & Stockholders' Equity			
Liabilities	$ 2,075,000	$ 560,000	$ 2,635,000
Capital stock, $10 par	1,000,000	150,000	1,000,000
Retained earnings	2,770,000	900,000	2,753,500
Retained earnings of subsidiary	122,500	-0-	122,500
Treasury stock	(50,000)	-0-	(70,000)
Total liabilities & stockholders' equity	$ 5,917,500	$1,610,000	$ 6,441,000

Other information about the affiliated companies includes the following:
(1) All of Swanson's identifiable net assets were fairly valued at their carrying amounts at May 31, Year 2—the date of the Peterson-Swanson business combination. Thus, the $50,000 excess of Peterson's investment in Swanson over the carrying amounts of Swanson's identifiable net assets was attributable to goodwill with an estimated economic life of 40 years.
(2) Peterson sells merchandise to Swanson at Peterson's regular markup.
(3) Swanson owns 1,000 shares of Peterson's outstanding capital stock.

Instructions Reconstruct the consolidation eliminations for Peterson Corporation and subsidiary at May 31, Year 4. Omit explanations and disregard income taxes.

11-7 Condensed financial statements of Pomerania Corporation and its two subsidiaries for the year ended December 31, Year 8, appear on pages 442–443.

POMERANIA CORPORATION AND SUBSIDIARIES
Financial Statements
For Year Ended December 31, Year 8

	Pomerania Corporation	Slovakia Company	Sylvania Company
Income Statements			
Revenue			
Net sales	$1,120,000	$900,000	$700,000
Intercompany sales	140,000	-0-	-0-
Intercompany investment income	44,000	-0-	-0-
Total revenue	$1,304,000	$900,000	$700,000
Costs and expenses			
Cost of goods sold	$ 800,000	$650,000	$550,000
Intercompany cost of goods sold	100,000	-0-	-0-
Operating expenses......................	300,000	150,000	130,000
Total costs and expenses	$1,200,000	$800,000	$680,000
Net income................................	$ 104,000	$100,000	$ 20,000
Statements of Retained Earnings			
Retained earnings, Jan. 1, Year 8	$ 126,200	$107,000	$100,000
Net income.................................	104,000	100,000	20,000
Subtotal..................................	$ 230,200	$207,000	$120,000
Dividends	22,000	75,000	-0-
Retained earnings, Dec. 31, Year 8............	$ 208,200	$132,000	$120,000
Balance Sheets			
Assets			
Intercompany receivables (payables)	$ 63,400	$ (41,000)	$ (22,400)
Inventories	290,000	90,000	115,000
Investment in Slovakia Company stock	305,600	-0-	-0-
Investment in Slovakia Company bonds	20,800	-0-	-0-
Investment in Sylvania Company preferred stock	7,000	-0-	-0-
Investment in Sylvania Company common stock	196,000	-0-	-0-
Other assets..............................	836,400	555,000	510,000
Total assets	$1,719,200	$604,000	$602,600
Liabilities & Stockholders' Equity			
Dividends payable	$ 22,000	$ 6,000	$ -0-
Bonds payable	285,000	125,000	125,000
Intercompany bonds payable	-0-	25,000	-0-
Discount on bonds payable	(8,000)	(10,000)	-0-
Discount on intercompany bonds payable ...	-0-	(2,000)	-0-

(continued)

POMERANIA CORPORATION AND SUBSIDIARIES
Financial Statements
For Year Ended December 31, Year 8 (concluded)

	Pomerania Corporation	Slovakia Company	Sylvania Company
Other liabilities	$ 212,000	$ 78,000	$107,600
Preferred stock, $20 par...................	400,000	-0-	50,000
Common stock, $10 par	600,000	250,000	200,000
Retained earnings	208,200	132,000	120,000
Total liabilities & stockholders' equity	$1,719,200	$604,000	$602,600

Additional information available includes the following:
(1) Pomerania Corporation's Investment in Slovakia Company Stock account appears as follows:

Investment in Slovakia Company Stock

Date	Explanation	Debit	Credit	Balance
Year 8				
Jan. 2	Cost of 5,000 shares	71,400		71,400 dr
June 30	20% of dividend declared		9,000	62,400 dr
June 30	20% of net income for Jan. 2–June 30	12,000		74,400 dr
July 1	Cost of 15,000 shares	223,200		297,600 dr
Dec. 31	80% of dividend declared		24,000	273,600 dr
Dec. 31	80% of net income for July 1–Dec. 31	32,000		305,600 dr

(2) The accountant for Pomerania made no equity-method journal entries for Pomerania's investments in Sylvania's preferred and common stock. Pomerania acquired 250 shares of Sylvania's fully participating noncumulative preferred stock for $7,000 and 14,000 shares of Sylvania's common stock for $196,000 on January 2, Year 8. Out-of-pocket costs of the business combination were negligible.
(3) Sylvania's December 31, Year 8, inventories included $22,400 of merchandise acquired from Pomerania for which no payment had been made.
(4) Pomerania acquired in the open market twenty-five $1,000 principal amount 6% bonds of Slovakia for $20,800 on December 31, Year 8. The bonds have a December 31 interest payment date, and a maturity date of December 31, Year 10.
(5) Slovakia owed Pomerania $17,000 at December 31, Year 8, for a noninterest-bearing cash advance.

Instructions
a Prepare adjusting journal entry or entries for Pomerania Corporation at December 31, Year 8, in good form, to account for investments in Sylvania Company preferred and common stock by the equity method. Disregard income taxes.
b Prepare a consolidating financial statements working paper and related consolidation eliminations working paper, in good form, for Pomerania Corporation and subsidiaries at December 31, Year 8. Disregard income taxes.

11-8 Plover Corporation purchased for $151,000 cash, including direct out-of-pocket costs of the business combination, 100% of the common stock and 20% of the preferred stock of Starling Company on June 30, Year 1. On that date, Starling's retained earnings balance was $41,000. The current fair values of Starling's identifiable assets and liabilities and preferred stock did not differ materially from their carrying amounts at June 30, Year 1.

The individual financial statements of Plover and Starling for Year 2 appear below:

PLOVER CORPORATION AND SUBSIDIARY
Financial Statements
For Year Ended December 31, Year 2

	Plover Corporation	Starling Company
Income Statements		
Revenue		
Net sales	$1,562,000	$ -0-
Intercompany sales	238,000	-0-
Earned revenue on contracts	-0-	1,210,000
Intercompany earned revenue on contracts	-0-	79,000
Interest revenue	19,149	-0-
Intercompany investment income	42,500	-0-
Intercompany dividend revenue	500	-0-
Intercompany gain on sale of land	4,000	-0-
Intercompany interest revenue (expense)	851	(851)
Total revenue	$1,867,000	$1,288,149
Costs and expenses		
Cost of goods sold	$ 942,500	$ -0-
Intercompany cost of goods sold	212,500	-0-
Cost of earned revenue on contracts	-0-	789,500
Intercompany cost of earned revenue on contracts	-0-	62,500
Selling, general, and administrative expenses	497,000	360,000
Interest expense	49,000	31,149
Total costs and expenses	$1,701,000	$1,243,149
Net income	$ 166,000	$ 45,000
Statements of Retained Earnings		
Retained earnings, Jan. 1, Year 2	$ 139,311	$ 49,500
Net income	166,000	45,000
Subtotal	$ 305,311	$ 94,500
Dividends	-0-	2,500
Retained earnings, Dec. 31, Year 2	$ 305,311	$ 92,000
Balance Sheets		
Assets		
Intercompany receivables (payables)	$ 35,811	$ 21,189
Costs and estimated earnings in excess of billings on uncompleted contracts	-0-	30,100

(continued)

PLOVER CORPORATION AND SUBSIDIARY
Financial Statements
For Year Ended December 31, Year 2 (concluded)

	Plover Corporation	Starling Company
Inventories	217,000	117,500
Investment in subsidiary	202,000	-0-
Land	34,000	42,000
Other plant assets (net)	717,000	408,000
Other assets	153,000	84,211
Total assets	$1,358,811	$ 703,000
Liabilities & Stockholders' Equity		
Dividends payable	$ -0-	$ 2,000
Mortgage notes payable	592,000	389,000
Other liabilities	203,000	70,000
5% noncumulative, nonparticipating preferred stock,		
$1 par	-0-	50,000
Common stock, $10 par	250,000	100,000
Retained earnings	305,311	92,000
Retained earnings of subsidiary	8,500	-0-
Total liabilities & stockholders' equity	$1,358,811	$ 703,000

Transactions between Plover and Starling during the year ended December 31, Year 2, follow:

(1) On January 2, Year 2, Plover sold land with an $11,000 carrying amount to Starling for $15,000. Starling made a $3,000 down payment and signed an 8% mortgage note payable in 12 equal quarterly payments of $1,135, including interest, beginning March 31, Year 2.

(2) Starling produced equipment for Plover under two separate contracts. The first contract, which was for office equipment, was begun and completed during Year 2 at a cost to Starling of $17,500. Plover paid $22,000 cash for the equipment on April 17, Year 2. The second contract was begun on February 15, Year 2, but will not be completed until May of Year 3. Starling has incurred $45,000 costs under the second contract as of December 31, Year 2, and anticipates additional costs of $30,000 to complete the $95,000 contract. Starling accounts for all contracts under the percentage-of-completion method of accounting. Plover has made no journal entry in its accounting records for the uncompleted contract as of December 31, Year 2. Plover depreciates all its equipment over a 10-year estimated economic life with no residual value. Plover takes a half year's depreciation in the year of purchase.

(3) On December 1, Year 2, Starling declared a 5% cash dividend on its preferred stock, payable January 15, Year 3, to stockholders of record December 14, Year 2.

(4) Plover sells merchandise to Starling at an average markup of 12% of cost. During the year, Plover billed Starling $238,000 for merchandise shipped, for which Starling paid $211,000 by December 31, Year 2. Starling has $11,200 of this merchandise on hand at December 31, Year 2.

Instructions

a Reconstruct the Intercompany Receivables (Payables) accounts of the affiliates as of December 31, Year 2.

b Prepare in good form any necessary adjusting journal entry or entries as of December 31, Year 2, based on your analysis in **a** above.

c Prepare a consolidating financial statements working paper and related consolidation eliminations working paper for Plover Corporation and subsidiary for Year 2. Round all computations to the nearest dollar. Disregard income tax considerations.

11-9 Pickens Corporation acquired 10% of the 100,000 outstanding shares of $2.50 par common stock of Skiffens Company on December 31, Year 6, for $38,000. An additional 70,000 shares were acquired for $331,800 on June 30, Year 8 (at which time there was no material difference between the current fair values and carrying amounts of Skiffens Company's identifiable net assets). Out-of-pocket costs of the business combination were negligible.

The financial statements of Pickens Corporation and subsidiary for the year ended December 31, Year 8, appear below:

PICKENS CORPORATION AND SUBSIDIARY

Financial Statements

For Year Ended December 31, Year 8

	Pickens Corporation	Skiffens Company
Income Statements		
Revenue		
Net sales	$ 840,000	$360,000
Intercompany sales	80,600	65,000
Intercompany gain on sale of equipment	9,500	-0-
Intercompany interest revenue	2,702	-0-
Intercompany investment income	44,800	-0-
Total revenue	$ 977,602	$425,000
Costs and expenses		
Cost of goods sold	$ 546,000	$252,000
Intercompany cost of goods sold	56,420	48,750
Interest expense	32,000	9,106
Intercompany interest expense	-0-	2,276
Other operating expenses	271,382	56,868
Total costs and expenses	$ 905,802	$369,000
Net income	$ 71,800	$ 56,000
Statements of Retained Earnings		
Retained earnings, Jan. 1, Year 8	$ 595,000	$136,000
Net income	71,800	56,000
Subtotal	$ 666,800	$192,000
Dividends	20,000	11,000
Retained earnings, Dec. 31, Year 8	$ 646,800	$181,000

(continued)

PICKENS CORPORATION AND SUBSIDIARY
Financial Statements
For Year Ended December 31, Year 8 (concluded)

	Pickens Corporation	Skiffens Company
Balance Sheets		
Assets		
Intercompany receivables (payables)	$ 35,800	$(35,800)
Inventories	180,000	96,000
Investment in Skiffens Company stock	405,800	-0-
Investment in Skiffens Company bonds	27,918	-0-
Plant assets (net)	781,500	510,000
Accumulated depreciation	(87,000)	(85,000)
Other assets	333,782	146,500
Total assets	$1,677,800	$631,700
Liabilities & Stockholders' Equity		
Dividends payable	$ 20,000	$ 2,200
Bonds payable	400,000	120,000
Intercompany bonds payable	-0-	30,000
Discount on bonds payable	-0-	(4,281)
Discount on intercompany bonds payable	-0-	(1,070)
Other liabilities	97,000	24,851
Capital stock, $2.50 par	500,000	250,000
Paid-in capital in excess of par	14,000	29,000
Retained earnings	646,800	181,000
Total liabilities & stockholders' equity	$1,677,800	$631,700

The following information is available:

(1) An analysis of Pickens Corporation's Investment in Skiffens Company Stock account:

Date	Description	Amount
Dec. 31, Year 6	Investment	$ 38,000
June 30, Year 8	Investment	331,800
Dec. 15, Year 8	Dividend: $11,000 × 80%	(8,800)
Dec. 31, Year 8	Net income for Year 8: $56,000 × 80%	44,800
Dec. 31, Year 8	Balance	$405,800

(2) An analysis of the companies' Retained Earnings accounts appears at the top of page 448.

	Pickens Corporation	Skiffens Company
Balance, Dec. 31, Year 6	$540,000	$101,000
Net income for Year 7	55,000	40,000
Cash dividends in Year 7	-0-	(5,000)
Balance, Dec. 31, Year 7	$595,000	$136,000
Net income, first half of Year 8	31,000	23,000
Net income, second half of Year 8	40,800	33,000
Cash dividends declared, Dec. 15, Year 8	(20,000)	(11,000)
Balance, Dec. 31, Year 8	$646,800	$181,000

(3) Data on intercompany sales for Year 8:

	Pickens Corporation	Skiffens Company
Year-end inventory of intercompany merchandise purchases, on first-in, first-out basis	$26,000	$22,000
Intercompany payables at year-end	12,000	7,000

(4) Pickens acquired $30,000 principal amount of Skiffen's 6% bonds in the open market January 2, Year 8, for $27,016—a 10% yield. Skiffens had issued the bonds on January 2, Year 6, to yield 8% and has been paying the interest each December 31.

(5) On September 1, Year 8, Pickens Corporation sold equipment with a cost of $40,000 and accumulated depreciation of $9,300 to Skiffens Company for $40,200. Skiffens Company recorded the equipment at a cost of $49,500, with accumulated depreciation of $9,300. At September 1, Year 8, the equipment had an estimated economic life of 10 years and no residual value.

(6) Skiffens Company owed Pickens Corporation $32,000 at December 31, Year 8, for noninterest-bearing cash advances.

Instructions

a Prepare in good form any necessary adjusting journal entries indicated by the above information. Disregard income taxes. Any amortization required by **APB Opinion No. 17,** "Intangible Assets," should be over a 40-year economic life.

b Prepare a consolidating financial statements working paper and related consolidation eliminations working paper for Pickens Corporation and subsidiary at December 31, Year 8. Disregard income taxes.

11-10 On January 2, Year 6, Plummer Corporation purchased a controlling interest of 75% in the outstanding capital stock of Sinclair Company for $96,000, including direct out-of-pocket costs of the business combination. Financial statements for the two companies for the year ended December 31, Year 6, appear on pages 449–450.

PLUMMER CORPORATION AND SINCLAIR COMPANY
Financial Statements
For Year Ended December 31, Year 6

	Plummer Corporation	Sinclair Company
Income Statements		
Revenue		
Net sales	$772,000	$426,000
Intercompany sales	78,000	104,000
Intercompany dividend revenue	-0-	750
Intercompany gain on sale of machinery	-0-	800
Intercompany investment income	30,600	-0-
Other revenue	9,000	2,900
Total revenue	$889,600	$534,450
Costs and expenses		
Cost of goods sold	$445,000	$301,200
Intercompany cost of goods sold	65,000	72,800
Depreciation expense	65,600	11,200
Selling, general, and administrative expenses	149,900	52,375
Income taxes expense	80,100	58,125
Total costs and expenses	$805,600	$495,700
Net income	$ 84,000	$ 38,750
Statements of Retained Earnings		
Retained earnings, Jan. 1, Year 6	$378,000	$112,000
Net income	84,000	38,750
Subtotal	$462,000	$150,750
Dividends	7,500	10,000
Retained earnings, Dec. 31, Year 6	$454,500	$140,750
Balance Sheets		
Assets		
Marketable securities	$ -0-	$ 18,000
Intercompany receivables (payables)	15,250	(15,250)
Inventories	275,000	135,000
Other current assets	309,100	106,000
Investment in subsidiary	123,600	-0-
Plant assets	518,000	279,000
Accumulated depreciation	(298,200)	(196,700)
Total assets	$942,750	$326,050

(continued)

PLUMMER CORPORATION AND SINCLAIR COMPANY
Financial Statements
For Year Ended December 31, Year 6 (concluded)

	Plummer Corporation	Sinclair Company
Liabilities & Stockholders' Equity		
Dividends payable	$ 6,750	$ -0-
Income taxes payable	80,100	58,125
Other current liabilities	215,400	91,175
Capital stock, $10 par	150,000	-0-
Capital stock, $5 par	-0-	22,000
Paid-in capital in excess of par	36,000	14,000
Retained earnings	454,500	140,750
Total liabilities & stockholders' equity	$942,750	$326,050

The following information is available:
(1) Sinclair's stockholders' equity accounts at January 2, Year 6, were as follows:

Capital stock, $5 par	$ 20,000
Paid-in capital in excess of par	10,000
Retained earnings	112,000
Total stockholders' equity	$142,000

(2) Sinclair's marketable securities consist of 1,500 shares of Plummer capital stock purchased on June 15, Year 6, in the open market for $18,000.
(3) On December 10, Year 6, Plummer declared a cash dividend of $0.50 per share payable January 10, Year 7, to stockholders of record December 20, Year 6. Sinclair paid a cash dividend of $1 per share on June 30, Year 6, and distributed a 10% stock dividend on September 30, Year 6. The stock's ex-dividend current fair value was $15 per share on September 30, Year 6.
(4) Sinclair sold machinery with a carrying amount of $4,000, no residual value, and a remaining economic life of five years to Plummer for $4,800 on December 31, Year 6.
(5) Sinclair's depreciable plant assets had a composite estimated remaining economic life of five years at January 2, Year 6.
(6) Data on intercompany sales of merchandise follow:

	In purchaser's inventory, Dec. 31, Year 6	Amount payable by purchaser, Dec. 31, Year 6
Plummer Corporation to Sinclair Company ...	$24,300	$24,000
Sinclair Company to Plummer Corporation ...	18,000	8,000

(7) Both companies are subject to a combined federal and state income tax rate of 60%. Plummer is entitled to a dividend received deduction of 85%. Each company will file separate income tax returns for Year 6. Except for Plummer's Intercompany Investment Income account, there are no timing differences for either company.

Instructions

a Prepare December 31, Year 6, adjusting journal entry or entries, in good form, to provide for income tax allocation in the accounts of Plummer Corporation due to Plummer's use of the equity method of accounting for the subsidiary's operating results.

b Prepare a consolidating financial statements working paper and related consolidation eliminations, including those for income tax allocation, for Plummer Corporation and subsidiary at December 31, Year 6.

11-11 On February 1, Year 5, Pullard Corporation purchased all the outstanding common stock of Staley Company for $5,850,000, including direct out-of-pocket costs of the business combination, and 20% of Staley's preferred stock for $150,000. On the date of the business combination, the carrying amounts and current fair values of Staley's identifiable assets and liabilities were as follows:

	Carrying amount	Current fair value
Cash	$ 200,000	$ 200,000
Notes receivable	85,000	85,000
Accounts receivable (net)	980,000	980,000
Inventories	828,000	700,000
Land	1,560,000	2,100,000
Other plant assets	7,850,000	10,600,000
Accumulated depreciation	(3,250,000)	(4,000,000)
Other assets	140,000	50,000
Total assets	$8,393,000	$10,715,000
Notes payable	$ 115,000	$ 115,000
Accounts payable	400,000	400,000
7% subordinated debentures	5,000,000	5,000,000
Total liabilities	$5,515,000	$5,515,000
Preferred stock, noncumulative, nonparticipating; $5 par and call price per share; authorized, issued, and outstanding 150,000 shares	$ 750,000	
Common stock; $10 par; authorized, issued, and outstanding 100,000 shares	1,000,000	
Paid-in capital in excess of par (common stock)	122,000	
Retained earnings	1,006,000	
Total stockholders' equity	$2,878,000	
Total liabilities & stockholders' equity	$8,393,000	

Financial statements of Pullard and Staley for the period ended October 31, Year 5, appear on pages 452–453.

PULLARD CORPORATION AND STALEY COMPANY
Financial Statements
For Period Ended October 31, Year 5

	Pullard Corporation (year ended 10/31/5)	Staley Company (9 mos. ended 10/31/5)
Income Statements		
Revenue		
Net sales	$18,042,000	$5,530,000
Intercompany sales	158,000	230,000
Intercompany investment income	505,150	-0-
Interest revenue	26,250	1,700
Intercompany interest revenue...............	78,750	-0-
Total revenue	$18,810,150	$5,761,700
Costs and expenses		
Cost of goods sold...........................	$10,442,000	$3,010,500
Intercompany cost of goods sold	158,000	149,500
Depreciation expense	1,103,000	588,750
Selling, general, and administrative expenses .	3,448,500	1,063,900
Interest expense	806,000	190,650
Intercompany interest expense	-0-	78,750
Total costs and expenses...................	$15,957,500	$5,082,050
Net income....................................	$ 2,852,650	$ 679,650
Statements of Retained Earnings		
Retained earnings, beginning of period	$12,683,500	$1,006,000
Net income....................................	2,852,650	679,650
Retained earnings, Oct. 31, Year 5	$15,536,150	$1,685,650
Balance Sheets		
Assets		
Cash	$ 822,000	$ 530,000
Notes receivable	-0-	85,000
Accounts receivable (net)	2,723,700	1,346,400
Intercompany receivables	12,300	-0-
Inventories	3,204,000	1,182,000
Investment in Staley Company common stock .	6,355,150	-0-
Investment in Staley Company preferred stock	150,000	-0-
Investment in Staley Company debentures	1,500,000	-0-
Land	4,000,000	1,560,000
Other plant assets	17,161,000	7,850,000
Accumulated depreciation	(6,673,000)	(3,838,750)
Other assets	263,000	140,000
Total assets	$29,518,150	$8,854,650

(continued)

PULLARD CORPORATION AND STALEY COMPANY
Financial Statements
For Period Ended October 31, Year 5 (concluded)

	Pullard Corporation (year ended 10/31/5)	Staley Company (9 mos. ended 10/31/5)
Liabilities & Stockholders' Equity		
Notes payable	$ -0-	$ 115,000
Accounts payable	1,342,000	169,700
Intercompany accounts payable	-0-	12,300
7% subordinated debentures	-0-	3,500,000
Intercompany 7% subordinated debentures ...	-0-	1,500,000
Long-term debt	10,000,000	-0-
Preferred stock, $5 par	-0-	750,000
Common stock, $10 par	2,400,000	1,000,000
Paid-in capital in excess of par	240,000	122,000
Retained earnings	15,536,150	1,685,650
Total liabilities & stockholders' equity	$29,518,150	$8,854,650

By the fiscal year-end, October 31, Year 5, the following transactions had taken place:

(1) The balance of Staley's net accounts receivable at February 1, Year 5, had been collected.

(2) Staley's inventories at February 1, Year 5, had been debited to cost of goods sold. Staley uses a perpetual inventory system.

(3) Prior to February 1, Year 5, Pullard had purchased at face amount $1,500,000 of Staley's 7% subordinated debentures. The debentures mature on August 31, Year 11, with interest payable annually each August 31.

(4) As of February 1, Year 5, Staley's other plant assets had a composite remaining economic life of six years. Staley used the straight-line method of depreciation, with no residual value. Staley's depreciation expense for the nine months ended October 31, Year 5, was based on the former depreciation rates in effect prior to the business combination.

(5) The other assets consist entirely of long-term investments made by Staley and do not include any investment in Pullard.

(6) During the nine months ended October 31, Year 5, the following intercompany sales occurred:

	Pullard to Staley	Staley to Pullard
Net sales	$158,000	$230,000
Included in purchaser's inventories, Oct. 31, Year 5	36,000	12,000
Balance unpaid, Oct. 31, Year 5..........................	16,800	22,000

Pullard sells to Staley at cost. Staley sells to Pullard at regular selling price, including a normal gross profit margin of 35%. There were no intercompany sales prior to February 1, Year 5.

(7) Neither company declared dividends during the period covered by their separate financial statements.

(8) Staley's goodwill recognized in the business combination was $1,400,000. The companies' policy is to amortize intangible assets over a 20-year economic life, and to include the amortization among general expenses.

(9) The $505,150 balance in Pullard's Intercompany Investment Income account is computed as follows:

Net income reported by Staley for nine months ended Oct. 31, Year 5 .... $679,650
Less: Amortization of differences between current fair values and carrying
    amounts of Staley's identifiable net assets at Feb. 1, Year 5:
    Inventories—to cost of goods sold .... $(128,000)
    Other plant assets—depreciation ($6,600,000 − $4,600,000) ×
    $1/6 \times 3/4$ year 250,000
    Goodwill—amortization $1,400,000 × $1/20$ × $3/4$ year 52,500   174,500
Balance, Oct. 31, Year 5 .... $505,150

Instructions Prepare a consolidating financial statements working paper and related consolidation eliminations working paper for Pullard Corporation and subsidiary at October 31, Year 5. Round all computations to the nearest dollar. Disregard income taxes

11-12 Presented below are the separate financial statements of Pennington Corporation and its subsidiary, Singleton Company, for the year ended December 31, Year 5:

PENNINGTON CORPORATION AND SINGLETON COMPANY
Financial Statements
For Year Ended December 31, Year 5

	Pennington Corporation	Singleton Company
Income Statements		
Revenue		
Net sales	$3,904,000	$1,700,000
Intercompany sales	96,000	-0-
Intercompany investment income	232,000	-0-
Intercompany dividend revenue	75,000	-0-
Total revenue	$4,307,000	$1,700,000
Costs and expenses		
Cost of goods sold	$2,902,000	$1,015,000
Intercompany cost of goods sold	80,000	-0-
Interest expense	-0-	7,800
Other operating expenses	400,000	377,200
Total costs and expenses	$3,382,000	$1,400,000
Net income	$ 925,000	$ 300,000

(continued)

PENNINGTON CORPORATION AND SINGLETON COMPANY
Financial Statements
For Year Ended December 31, Year 5 (concluded)

	Pennington Corporation	Singleton Company
Statements of Retained Earnings		
Retained earnings, Jan. 1, Year 5	$2,100,000	$ 640,000
Net income	925,000	300,000
Subtotal	$3,025,000	$ 940,000
Dividends	170,000	100,000
Retained earnings, Dec. 31, Year 5	$2,855,000*	$ 840,000
Balance Sheets		
Assets		
Cash	$ 486,000	$ 249,600
Accounts receivable (net)	190,000	185,000
Intercompany receivables	45,000	-0-
Inventories	475,000	355,000
Investment in subsidiary's stock	954,000	-0-
Investment in subsidiary's bonds	58,000	-0-
Plant assets (net)	2,231,000	530,000
Total assets	$4,439,000	$1,319,600
Liabilities & Stockholders' Equity		
Accounts payable	$ 384,000	$ 62,000
Bonds payable	-0-	60,000
Intercompany bonds payable	-0-	60,000
Discount on bonds payable	-0-	(1,200)
Discount on intercompany bonds payable	-0-	(1,200)
Common stock, $10 par	1,200,000	250,000
Paid-in capital in excess of par	-0-	50,000
Retained earnings	2,855,000*	840,000
Total liabilities & stockholders' equity	$4,439,000	$1,319,600

* Includes $352,000 balance of Retained Earnings of Subsidiary account

Additional information

(1) On January 2, Year 3, Pennington acquired from John Singleton, the sole shareholder of Singleton Company, for $440,000 cash, both a patent with a current fair value of $40,000 and 80% of the outstanding common stock of Singleton Company. Out-of-pocket costs of the business combination were negligible. The total stockholder's equity of Singleton Company on January 2, Year 3, was $500,000, and the current fair values of Singleton's identifiable assets and liabilities were equal to their carrying amounts on that date. Pennington debited the entire $440,000 to the Investment in Subsidiary's Stock account. The patent, for which no amortization has been provided by Pennington, had a remaining economic life of four years as of January 2, Year 3.

(2) On July 1, Year 5, Pennington reduced its investment in Singleton Company to 75% by selling Singleton common stock for $70,000 to an unaffiliated company. Pennington recorded the $70,000 as a credit to the Investment in Subsidiary's Stock account.

(3) For the six months ended June 30, Year 5, Singleton had net income of $140,000. Pennington recorded 80% of this amount in its accounting records prior to the sale of Singleton stock.

(4) During Year 4, Singleton sold merchandise to Pennington for $130,000, at a markup of 30% on Singleton's cost. On January 1, Year 5, $52,000 of this merchandise remained in Pennington's inventories. The merchandise was sold in February, Year 5, at a gross profit of $8,000.

(5) In November, Year 5, Pennington sold merchandise to Singleton for the first time. Pennington's cost for this merchandise was $80,000, and the sale was made at 120% of cost. Singleton's inventories at December 31, Year 5, included merchandise purchased from Pennington in the amount of $24,000.

(6) On December 31, Year 5, a $45,000 payment was in transit from Singleton to Pennington.

(7) In December, Year 5, Singleton declared and paid cash dividends of $100,000 to its stockholders.

(8) On December 31, Year 5, Pennington purchased for $58,000, 50% of Singleton's outstanding bonds. The management of Pennington intends to keep the Singleton bonds until their maturity, December 31, Year 9.

Instructions
a Prepare journal entries to correct the accounts of Pennington Corporation at December 31, Year 5. Disregard income taxes.
b Prepare a consolidating financial statements working paper and related consolidation eliminations working paper for Pennington Corporation and subsidiary for the year ended December 31, Year 5. Amounts for Pennington Corporation should reflect the journal entries in **a**. Disregard income taxes.

11-13 Pastore Corporation acquired an 80% interest in Seville Company on December 31, Year 5, for a total consideration of $1 million. The purchase price consisted of $850,000 cash and $150,000 current fair value of securities of Redeker, Inc., which had been held by Pastore as a long-term investment. The investment is accounted for by Pastore under the equity method of accounting. The consolidated balance sheet for the two companies December 31, Year 5, follows:

PASTORE CORPORATION AND SUBSIDIARY
Consolidated Balance Sheet
December 31, Year 5

Assets		Liabilities & Stockholders' Equity	
Cash	$ 750,000	Accounts payable	$1,000,000
Accounts receivable (net)	1,300,000	Notes payable (current)	1,500,000
Inventories	2,250,000	Minority interest	250,000
Plant assets	3,850,000	Capital stock	1,000,000
Less: Accumulated		Paid-in capital in excess of par	800,000
depreciation	(1,400,000)	Retained earnings	2,200,000
		Total liabilities &	
Total assets	$6,750,000	stockholders' equity	$6,750,000

The excess of the carrying amount of Seville capital stock over the cost of Pastore's investment was $250,000, which included the amount imputed to the minority interest. The excess was deducted from Seville's plant assets and pre-business combination net income in the accounting records of Seville.

On July 2, Year 6, Pastore sold a 10% interest in Seville for $150,000. The net income, cash dividends, and depreciation expense for each company for Year 6 are summarized below (net income of Pastore includes intercompany investment income from Seville and the gain or loss on the sale of Seville's capital stock):

	Pastore Corporation	Seville Company
Net income for first half of Year 6	$260,000	$72,500
Net income for second half of Year 6	273,500	82,500
Cash dividends paid in December, Year 6	100,000	30,000
Depreciation expense for Year 6	225,000	55,000

The separate unclassified balance sheets for Pastore Corporation and Seville Company at December 31, Year 6, are given below:

PASTORE CORPORATION AND SEVILLE COMPANY
Balance Sheets
December 31, Year 6

Assets	Pastore Corporation	Seville Company	Liabilities & Stockholders' Equity	Pastore Corporation	Seville Company
Cash	$ 695,000	$ 260,000	Accounts payable	$ 569,000	$ 450,000
Accounts receivable (net) .	900,000	500,000	Notes payable ...	1,100,000	310,000
Inventories	1,600,000	750,000	Bonds payable .	500,000	-0-
Investment in Seville Company (equity method)	962,500	-0-	Capital stock	1,000,000	500,000
			Paid-in capital in excess of par	800,000	-0-
Plant assets ...	3,500,000	1,250,000	Retained earnings	2,633,500	875,000
Less: Accumulated depreciation	(1,055,000)	(625,000)	Total liabilities & stockholders'		
Total assets .	$6,602,500	$2,135,000	equity	$6,602,500	$2,135,000

Instructions (Disregard income taxes)
a Compute the consolidated net income for Year 6.
b Prepare a consolidated balance sheet at December 31, Year 6, without using a working paper.
c Prepare a consolidated statement of changes in financial position on a working capital basis for Year 6. A working paper is not required.
d Reconcile the amount of minority interest at December 31, Year 5, with the amount of minority interest at December 31, Year 6.

12

SEGMENT REPORTING; INTERIM STATEMENTS; FINANCIAL FORECASTS

In this chapter we shall deal with three issues which have received much attention from accounting authorities in recent years. Segment reporting, interim financial statements, and financial forecasts have been the subject of pronouncements by the FASB, the AICPA, and the SEC. In addition, the Cost Accounting Standards Board and other professional organizations have issued standards or position papers on one or more of these topics.

SEGMENT REPORTING

The FASB has defined an *industry segment* as follows:[1]

> *Industry segment.* A component of an enterprise engaged in providing a product or service or a group of related products and services primarily to unaffiliated customers (i.e., customers outside the enterprise) for a profit.

Another term usually considered synonymous with industry segment is *line of business.*

The wave of *conglomerate* business combinations in recent years, involving constituent companies in different industries or markets, led to consideration of appropriate methods for reporting financial data for industry segments.

[1] *FASB Statement No. 14,* "Financial Reporting for Segments of a Business Enterprise," FASB (Stamford: 1976), p. 5, par. 10.

Background of segment reporting

The FASB has traced a chronological history of segment reporting from the start of hearings in 1964 before the U.S. Senate Judiciary Committee's Subcommittee on Antitrust and Monopoly. The Subcommittee was considering economic concentration in American industry, especially in the so-called *conglomerate,* or *diversified,* business enterprises.

Out of these hearings came a great deal of discussion among academicians, Congressmen, SEC officials, financial analysts, business executives, and AICPA representatives regarding the propriety of financial reporting for segments of an entity. The concept of segment reporting was controversial, because it was opposed to the philosophy that *consolidated financial statements,* rather than separate financial statements, fairly present the financial position and operating results of a single economic entity, regardless of the legal, industry-segment, or product-line structure of the entity.

In 1976, the FASB issued *FASB Statement No. 14,* "Financial Reporting for Segments of a Business Enterprise." The principal provisions of this statement were as follows:[2]

> When an enterprise issues a complete set of financial statements that present financial position at the end of the enterprise's fiscal year and results of operations and changes in financial position for that fiscal year in conformity with generally accepted accounting principles, those financial statements shall include certain information relating to:
>
> a) The enterprise's operations in different industries . . .
>
> b) Its foreign operations and export sales . . .
>
> c) Its major customers . . .
>
> If such statements are presented for more than one fiscal year, the information required by this Statement shall be presented for each such year, . . .

FASB Statement No. 14 also required the disclosure of segment information in interim financial statements. However, in *FASB Statement No. 18,* "Financial Reporting for Segments of a Business Enterprise—Interim Financial Statements," issued in 1977, the FASB rescinded that requirement. Interim financial statements are discussed in another section of this chapter.

In 1978, *FASB Statement No. 21* suspended the applicability of *FASB Statement No. 14* to nonpublic companies, pending completion of a project to determine whether nonpublic companies should have financial statement presentation and disclosure requirements which are more limited than those for public companies.

Major issues in segment reporting

In an *FASB Discussion Memorandum,* "An Analysis of Issues Related to Financial Reporting for Segments of a Business Enterprise," published

---

[2] Ibid., pp. 1–2, par. 3.

prior to *FASB Statement No. 14,* the FASB identified 11 issues, involving 23 separate questions, to be considered in segment reporting. We shall consider only the following two issues:

1 What approach should be taken in specifying segments to be reported externally?
2 What segment information related to the results of operations (income statement) should be reported?

Following our consideration of these issues, we shall present the stand taken on each issue in *FASB Statement No. 14.*

Specification of segments

The *FASB Discussion Memorandum* suggests the following alternative bases for segmentation of a business enterprise:[3]

    A. Organizational lines, such as divisions, branches or subsidiaries, or other legal or nonlegal entities.
    B. Area of economic activity. For example:
        Industries in which the enterprise operates
        Product lines and types of services rendered
        Markets
        Geographical areas
    C. More than one basis of segmentation

Basing segments on the organizational lines of an enterprise has the advantage of ease of identification of segments because the segments are identical to the organizational structure. Such a basis appears to ignore economic substance of segments in favor of legal or other form. Rarely does each organizational subdivision of an enterprise carry on its operations in a single economic activity.

An industry in which a segment operates usually is more precisely definable than is the product line related to a segment. However, many authorities on segment reporting have commented upon the overlapping and indistinct boundaries between industries and product lines.

Other proponents have gone on record in favor of segmentation according to the *market* for a segment's goods or services—such as commercial, defense contracts, and the like. Another proposed segmentation basis is geographical areas, such as foreign and domestic segments.

The FASB essentially took a compromise position with respect to the alternatives described above by its requirement that financial statements of an enterprise must include information about the enterprise's operations in different industries, operations in foreign areas, export sales, and major customers.

---

[3] *FASB Discussion Memorandum,* "An Analysis of Issues Related to Financial Reporting for Segments of a Business Enterprise" (Stamford, Conn.: 1974), p. 14, par. 54.

Operations in Different Industries   The FASB established the following guidelines for reporting operations in different industries:[4]

> The reportable segments of an enterprise shall be determined by (a) identifying the individual products and services from which the enterprise derives its revenue, (b) grouping those products and services by industry lines into industry segments . . . , and (c) selecting those industry segments that are significant with respect to the enterprise as a whole . . . .

The FASB decided that none of the systems which had been developed for classifying business activities was satisfactory for determining the industry segments of all enterprises. Accordingly, the FASB left to enterprise management the determination of an enterprise's industry segments. The Board recommended use of the enterprise's *profit centers,* the smallest units of activity for which revenue and expense information is accumulated for internal management purposes, as a starting point in the identification of the enterprise's industry segments.

After an enterprise has identified its industry segments, its *reportable segments* must be determined. The FASB decided that an industry segment is *significant,* and thus a reportable segment, if it meets one or more of the following tests:[5]

> a) Its revenue (including both sales to unaffiliated customers and intersegment sales or transfers) is 10% or more of the combined revenue (sales to unaffiliated customers and intersegment sales or transfers) of all of the enterprise's industry segments.
> b) The absolute amount of its operating profit or operating loss is 10% or more of the greater, in absolute amount, of:
>   (i) The combined operating profit of all industry segments that did not incur an operating loss, or
>   (ii) The combined operating loss of all industry segments that did incur an operating loss. . . .
> c) Its identifiable assets are 10% or more of the combined identifiable assets of all industry segments.

The FASB also provided for the following limitations on reportable segments:[6]

> *1* The combined revenue from sales to unaffiliated customers of *all reportable segments* must constitute at least 75% of the combined revenue from sales to unaffiliated customers of *all industry segments.*
> *2* The number of reportable segments generally *should not exceed ten.* Closely related industry segments might be combined into a single reportable segment to achieve the limit of ten.
> *3* Disclosures required for reportable segments do not apply to a *dominant segment,* defined as a segment whose revenue, operating profit or loss, and identifiable assets each constitute more than 90% of related combined totals for all industry segments, with no other industry segment meeting the 10% test. However, the financial statements of an enterprise having a dominant industry segment, or operating in a single industry, must identify the industry.

[4] *FASB Statement No. 14,* p. 8, par. 11.
[5] Ibid., p. 10, par. 15.
[6] Ibid., pp. 11, 12, pars. 17, 19, 20.

Operations in Foreign Areas and Export Sales   In *FASB Statement No. 14,* the FASB required enterprises which operate in *foreign geographic areas* (individual foreign countries or groups of countries) to report information for each *significant foreign geographic area,* and in the aggregate for all other foreign geographic areas which are not significant. A foreign geographic area is considered significant if its revenue from sales to unaffiliated customers or its identifiable assets are at least 10% of related total amounts in the enterprise's financial statements. Comparable information is required for the enterprise's domestic operations, unless the domestic operations do not meet the same 10% test for significance.[7] Further, the FASB required information regarding export sales in the financial statements of enterprises whose export sales exceed 10% of total sales to unaffiliated customers.[8]

Major Customers   The FASB also required disclosure of the revenue from sales to any single customer, or from aggregate sales to domestic or foreign governments, which represent 10% or more of total sales of the enterprise. Also, the industry segment making the sales must be identified.

Segment operating results to be reported

The *FASB Discussion Memorandum* offered the following alternatives for presenting a segment's operating results for a fiscal period:[9]

  A. Segment sales should be reported.

  B. Some measure of segment income should be reported (e.g., net income or some intermediate level of income).

  C. A complete or condensed segment income statement should be presented.

Segment Sales   Prior to the issuance of *FASB Statement No. 14,* there appeared to be no serious opposition to the position that sales of an industry segment represent a minimum reporting level. An unresolved issue was whether a segment's *intersegment sales or transfers* to another segment should be included in the reported sales for a segment. Although the *FASB Discussion Memorandum* indicated there is some support for inclusion of intersegment transfers in a segment's reported sales, there were opposition arguments:[10]

> Those who argue for exclusion of intersegment transfers from segment sales contend that (1) financial accounting should recognize only those revenues which have been realized through a bargained market transaction; (2) the transfer price is not objectively verifiable because there has been no

[7] Ibid., p. 17, par. 32.
[8] Ibid., p. 18, par. 36.
[9] *FASB Discussion Memorandum,* p. 25, par. 105.
[10] Ibid., p. 27, par. 113.

arm's-length transaction; (3) the level of segment activity, including inter-segment transfers, may be affected by internal production decisions; and (4) the total reported segment sales, including intersegment transfers, will differ from consolidated figures unless appropriate eliminations are presented.

Despite the validity of the above arguments, the FASB sanctioned inclusion of intersegment sales or transfers in the revenue of a reportable segment, as follows:[11]

> *Revenue.* Sales to unaffiliated customers and sales or transfers to other industry segments of the enterprise shall be separately disclosed in presenting revenue of a reportable segment. . . . for purposes of this Statement sales or transfers to other industry segments shall be accounted for on the basis used by the enterprise to price the intersegment sales or transfers. The basis of accounting for intersegment sales or transfers shall be disclosed. If the basis is changed, disclosure shall be made of the nature of the change and its effect on the reportable segments' operating profit or loss in the period of change.

Measure of Segment Income   Perhaps the most controversial aspect of segment reporting was whether some measure of segment income should be developed. The nature of the controversy over reporting income for segments is discernible in the following questions developed by the FASB:[12]

> Should common costs which are not traceable to individual segments be allocated to the various segments and, if so, on what basis?
> Should interest expense be attributed to segments?
> Should unusual or infrequently occurring items be attributed to segments?
> Should income from investee companies accounted for by the equity method be attributed to segments?
> Should income taxes be allocated to segments and, if so, on what basis?

The two extreme positions on reporting income for segments were (*a*) *a net income* should be reported for each segment, and (*b*) *no income amount* whatsoever should be reported for a segment. Proponents of a net income presentation for segments, while recognizing that a number of assumptions may underlie the computation of net income, maintained that difficulties of estimation and computation should not preclude the reporting of a segment net income figure useful to investors and creditors.

The opposition argument was that the arbitrary nature of many allocations of common costs, interest, and income taxes to segments makes the resultant net income figures misleading rather than informative. Opponents of reporting segment income cited as one allocation problem the difficulty of allocating income taxes to segments. Income tax allocation is difficult because of the existence of various tax avoidance alternatives to a diversified entity, the differences between income tax liabilities when a consolidated income tax return is filed as opposed to

[11] *FASB Statement No. 14,* p. 13, par. 23.
[12] *FASB Discussion Memorandum,* p. 26, par. 106.

separate returns, and the existence of net operating loss carrybacks and carryforwards.

Some accountants advocated a compromise position between the two extremes. These accountants supported a segment contribution approach for reporting a segment's income. **Segment contribution** is defined as segment sales less **traceable expenses,** those expenses directly identified with a particular segment.[13]

The FASB took the following position on disclosure of segment income:[14]

> *Profitability.* Operating profit or loss . . . , defined . . . (as a segment's revenue minus all operating expenses, including expenses not directly traceable to the segment,) . . . shall be presented for each reportable segment. As part of its segment information, an enterprise shall explain the nature and amount of any unusual or infrequently occurring items . . . reported in its consolidated income statement that have been added or deducted in computing the operating profit or loss of a reportable segment. . . . Methods used to allocate operating expenses among industry segments in computing operating profit or loss should be consistently applied from period to period (but, if changed, disclosure shall be made of the nature of the change and its effect on the reportable segments' operating profit or loss in the period of change).

The FASB required that expenses not directly traceable to a segment should be allocated to each benefited segment on a reasonable basis. However, the following should never be included in the computation of the operating profit or loss of a reportable segment:[15]

Revenue earned at the corporate level and not derived from the operations of any industry segment

General corporate expenses (incurred at an enterprise's central administrative office)

Interest expense

Domestic and foreign income taxes

Equity in income or loss from unconsolidated subsidiaries and other unconsolidated investees

Gain or loss on discontinued operations

Extraordinary items

Minority interest

Cumulative effect of a change in accounting principles

A "reasonable basis" for the allocation of expenses not directly traceable to a segment might be found in a pronouncement of the Cost Accounting Standards Board (CASB). In **Cost Accounting Standard 403,** "Allocation of Home Office Expenses to Segments," the CASB provided a three-factor formula for the allocation of residual home office expenses to segments. The percentage of residual home office expenses to be allocated to a segment was the arithmetic average of the following three percentages for the same fiscal period:[16]

[13] Ibid., pp. 29–30, par. 133
[14] *FASB Statement No. 14,* pp. 6, 13, pars. 10, 24.
[15] Ibid., pp. 6–7, par. 10.
[16] *Cost Accounting Standard 403,* sec. 403.50(c)(1).

1 Segment payroll dollars divided by total payroll dollars of all segments
2 Segment operating revenue (including intersegment transfers out, and reduced by intersegment transfers in) divided by total operating revenue of all segments
3 Segment average plant assets and inventories, at carrying amounts, divided by total carrying amount of average plant assets and inventories of all segments

Illustration of Allocation of Nontraceable Expenses   To illustrate the allocation of nontraceable expenses to industry segments under the provisions of *Cost Accounting Standard 403,* assume the following data for the home office and two industry segments of Multiproduct Corporation for the year ended April 30, Year 7. There were no intersegment transfers for the year.

Data for home office and two industry segments

	Home office	Pharma-ceutical products	Food products	Total
Net sales	$ -0-	$550,000	$ 450,000	$1,000,000
Traceable expenses	$ -0-	$300,000	$ 350,000	$ 650,000
Nontraceable expenses	200,000	-0-	-0-	200,000
Total expenses	$200,000	$300,000	$ 350,000	$ 850,000
Income before income taxes				$ 150,000
Income taxes expense				90,000
Net income.....................				$ 60,000
Payroll dollars	$ 60,000	$160,000	$ 240,000	$ 460,000
Average plant assets and inventories	$ 80,000	$620,000	$1,380,000	$2,080,000

The three-factor formula under *Cost Accounting Standard 403* would be computed as follows for Multiproduct Corporation:

Computation of three-factor formula

	Pharmaceutical products		Food products	
Ratio of segment payroll dollars	$ 160,000 / $ 400,000	= 40%	$ 240,000 / $ 400,000	= 60%
Ratio of segment operating revenue	$ 550,000 / $1,000,000	= 55%	$ 450,000 / $1,000,000	= 45%
Ratio of average plant assets and inventories	$ 620,000 / $2,000,000	= 31%	$1,380,000 / $2,000,000	= 69%
Total		126%		174%
Arithmetic average (divide by 3)		42%		58%

The $200,000 nontraceable expenses of the home office of Multiproduct Corporation would be allocated to the two segments as follows:

To Pharmaceutical Products segment: $200,000 × 42%	$ 84,000
To Food Products segment: $200,000 × 58%	116,000
Total nontraceable expenses	$200,000

Pre-tax accounting income (loss) for the two industry segments of Multiproduct Corporation would thus be computed as follows:

	Pharmaceutical products	Food products	Total
Net sales	$550,000	$450,000	$1,000,000
Traceable expenses	$300,000	$350,000	$ 650,000
Nontraceable expenses	84,000	116,000	200,000
Total expenses	$384,000	$466,000	$ 850,000
Operating profit (loss)	$166,000	$(16,000)	$ 150,000

The authors question the wisdom of applying such an arbitrary formula to the allocation of nontraceable expenses to segments for financial reporting purposes. The CASB allocation formula appears to be one of expediency rather than theoretical soundness. This is borne out in the preceding illustration by the operating loss attributed to the Food Products segment of Multiproduct Corporation.

Disclosure of Identifiable Assets and Other Information for Reportable Segments In addition to revenue and operating profit or loss, the following additional disclosures were required by the FASB for reportable segments:[17]

1 Identifiable assets, including tangible and intangible assets used exclusively by an industry segment and an allocated portion of assets used jointly by two or more industry segments, but excluding assets maintained for general corporate purposes and intersegment loans, advances, or investments
2 Depreciation, depletion, and amortization
3 Additions to plant assets
4 Equity in net income and net assets of unconsolidated subsidiaries and influenced investees whose operations are integrated vertically with those of the segment

[17] FASB Statement No. 14, pp. 7, 14, pars. 10, 26, 27.

5 Effect of a change in accounting principle on segment operating profit or loss

Presentation of segment information

The FASB approved the following alternative methods for disclosure of information about the reportable segments of a business enterprise:[18]

a) Within the body of the financial statements, with appropriate explanatory disclosures in the footnotes to the financial statements.

b) Entirely in the footnotes to the financial statements.

c) In a separate schedule that is included as an integral part of the financial statements. If, in a report to securityholders, that schedule is located on a page that is not clearly a part of the financial statements, the schedule shall be referenced in the financial statements as an integral part thereof.

In the appendix, pages 481-483, the segment information disclosures of Union Pacific Corporation and Subsidiary Companies and Tenneco Inc, from the 1977 annual reports, are presented.

SEC requirements for segment information

In 1977 the SEC issued *Accounting Series Release No. 236,* "Industry Segment Reporting." In *ASR No. 236* the SEC adopted *Regulation S-K,* a new integrated disclosure regulation, to apply to industry segments of companies supervised by the SEC. The SEC's requirements essentially parallel those of *FASB Statement No. 14.*

Reporting the effects of disposal of a segment of a business

To this point, we have discussed accounting standards developed by the Financial Accounting Standards Board for financial reporting for segments of a business enterprise. We shall conclude our consideration of segment reporting with the reporting for effects of the disposal of a segment of a business.

In 1973, the Accounting Principles Board issued *APB Opinion No. 30,* "Reporting the Results of Operations." The APB's conclusions included the following with respect to disposal of a segment of a business:[19]

> For purposes of this Opinion, the term *discontinued operations* refers to the operations of a segment of a business . . . that has been sold, abandoned, spun off, or otherwise disposed of or, although still operating, is the subject of a formal plan for disposal. . . . The Board concludes that the results of continuing operations should be reported separately from discontinued operations and that any gain or loss from disposal of a segment of a business . . . should be reported in conjunction with the related results of discontinued operations and not as an extraordinary item. Accordingly, operations of a segment that has been or will be discontinued should be reported separately as a component of income before extraordinary items and the

[18] Ibid., p. 15, par. 28.
[19] *APB Opinion No. 30,* pp. 558–559.

cumulative effect of accounting changes (if applicable) in the following manner:

Income from continuing operations before income taxes	$XXXX	
Provision for income taxes	XXXX	
Income from continuing operations		$XXXX
Discontinued operations (Note _____):		
Income (loss) from operations of discontinued Division X (less applicable income taxes of $_____)	$XXXX	
Loss on disposal of Division X, including provision of $ _____ for operating losses during phase-out period (less applicable income taxes of $_____)	XXXX	XXXX
Net income		$XXXX

Amounts of income taxes applicable to the results of discontinued operations and the gain or loss from disposal of the segment should be disclosed on the face of the income statement or in related notes. Revenues applicable to the discontinued operations should be separately disclosed in the related notes.

In clarifying the methods for computing the gain or loss on discontinued operations, the APB differentiated between the measurement date and the disposal date. The *measurement date* was defined as the date on which management having authority to approve the action commits itself to a formal plan to dispose of a segment of the business. The *disposal date* was defined as the date of closing the sale of the segment, or ceasing operations of an abandoned segment.[20] The period between the measurement date and the disposal date is known as the *phase-out period.* If management expects a *loss* on the disposal of a segment, the estimated loss should be recorded at the measurement date. An expected *gain* on disposal of a segment should be recognized when realized—typically on the disposal date.[21]

INTERIM FINANCIAL STATEMENTS

Generally, financial statements are published for the fiscal year of the accounting entity. However, many companies issue complete financial statements for interim accounting periods during the course of a fiscal year. For example, a closely held company with outstanding bank loans may be required to provide monthly or quarterly financial statements to the lending bank. However, interim financial statements usually are associated with the *quarterly reports* issued by publicly owned companies to their shareholders, the SEC, and the stock exchanges which list their stock. The New York Stock Exchange's listing agreement requires listed companies to publish quarterly financial reports. Companies subject to

[20] Ibid., pp. 561–562.
[21] Ibid., p. 562.

the periodic reporting requirements of the SEC must file Form 10-Q with the Commission 45 days after the end of each of the first three quarters of their fiscal years. In addition, the SEC requires disclosure of operating results for each quarter of the fiscal year in an unaudited note to annual financial statements.

Problems in interim financial statements

Except for 10-Q quarterly reports filed with the SEC, the form, content, and accounting practices for interim financial statements and reports were left to the discretion of the issuing companies until 1973. In that year, the Accounting Principles Board issued *Opinion No. 28,* "Interim Financial Reporting." Prior to the issuance of *Opinion No. 28,* there were unresolved problems regarding interim financial statements and reports. These problems included the following:

1 Enterprises employed a wider variety of accounting practices and estimating techniques for interim financial statements than they used in the annual financial statements examined by independent auditors. The companies' implicit view was that any misstatements in interim financial statements would be taken care of by auditors' adjustments for the annual financial statements.

2 Seasonal fluctuations in revenue and irregular incurrence of costs and expenses during the course of a business entity's fiscal year limited the comparability of operating results for interim periods of the fiscal year. Furthermore, time constraints in the issuance of interim statements limited the available time for accumulating accurate end-of-period data on inventories, payables, and related expenses.

3 Accountants held divergent views on the theoretical issues underlying interim financial statements. These differing views were described as follows:[22]

> Some view each interim period as a basic accounting period and conclude that the results of operations for each interim period should be determined in essentially the same manner as if the interim period were an annual accounting period. Under this view deferrals, accruals, and estimations at the end of each interim period are determined by following essentially the same principles and judgments that apply to annual periods.
>
> Others view each interim period primarily as being an integral part of the annual period. Under this view deferrals, accruals, and estimations at the end of each interim period are affected by judgments made at the interim date as to results of operations for the balance of the annual period. Thus, an expense item that might be considered as falling wholly within an annual accounting period (no fiscal year-end accrual or deferral) could be allocated among interim periods based on estimated time, sales volume, productive activity, or some other basis.

Misleading interim financial statements

The problems discussed in the preceding section led to a number of notorious examples of published interim income statements with substantial quarterly earnings, and fiscal year financial statements showing a substantial net loss. One such example was Mattel, Inc., a manu-

---

[22] *APB Opinion No. 28,* "Interim Financial Reporting," AICPA (New York: 1973), p. 521.

facturer of toys and leisure-time products whose stock was traded on the New York Stock Exchange. The SEC filed in court a complaint that Mattel, Inc., had issued false and misleading interim earnings reports for the first three quarters of a fiscal year. The reports showed first quarter net income of $3.9 million; second quarter net income of $6.1 million; and third quarter net income of $6.4 million—for a three-quarters net income of $16.4 million. According to the SEC, Mattel ultimately reported a net loss of $32 million for the entire fiscal year. The SEC charged Mattel with failing to make adequate interim adjustments for doubtful accounts receivable, sales returns, excess and obsolete inventories, and amortization of tool costs. Further, Mattel was accused of failing to disclose that it had deferred significant amounts of expenses from the first three quarters of the fiscal year to the fourth quarter of that year.

APB Opinion No. 28

In 1973, the Accounting Principles Board issued **APB Opinion No. 28,** "Interim Financial Reporting." The stated objectives for the **Opinion** were to provide guidance on accounting and disclosure issues peculiar to interim reporting and to set forth minimum disclosure requirements for interim financial reports of publicly traded companies.[23] Part I of the **Opinion** dealt with standards for determining interim financial information and Part II covered disclosure of summarized interim financial data by publicly traded companies. In **APB Opinion No. 28,** the APB adopted the viewpoint that interim periods should be accounted for as integral parts of the relevant annual period.

In Part I of **APB Opinion No. 28,** the APB established guidelines for the following components of interim financial reports: revenue, costs associated with revenue, all other costs and expenses, and income tax provisions. These guidelines are discussed in the following sections.

Revenue According to **APB Opinion No. 28,** revenue from products sold or services rendered should be recognized as earned during an interim period on the same basis as followed for the full year. Further, businesses having significant seasonal variations in revenue should disclose the seasonal nature of their activities.[24]

Costs Associated with Revenue Costs and expenses associated directly with or allocated to products sold or services rendered include raw materials costs, direct labor costs, and factory overhead. **APB Opinion No. 28** required the same accounting for these costs and expenses in interim financial reports as in fiscal year financial statements.[25] However,

[23] Ibid., p. 522.
[24] Ibid., pp. 523, 527.
[25] Ibid., p. 524.

the *Opinion* provided the following exceptions with respect to determination of cost of goods sold for interim financial reports:[26]

1 Companies which use the gross profit method at interim dates to estimate cost of goods sold should disclose this fact in interim financial reports. In addition, any material adjustments reconciling estimated interim inventories with annual physical inventories should be disclosed.

2 Companies which use the lifo inventory method and which **temporarily** deplete base lifo inventories during an interim reporting period should include in cost of goods sold for the interim period the estimated cost of replacing the depleted lifo base.

3 Lower-of-cost-or-market write-downs of inventories should be provided for interim periods as for complete fiscal years, unless the interim date market declines in inventory are considered **temporary,** and not applicable at the end of the fiscal year. If an inventory market write-down in one interim period is offset by an inventory market price **increase** in a subsequent interim period, a gain is recognized in the subsequent period to the extent of the loss provided in preceding interim periods of the fiscal year.

For example, assume that Reynolds Company, which uses lower-of-cost-or-market fifo accounting for its single merchandise item, had 10,000 units of merchandise with fifo cost of $50,000, or $5 per unit, in inventory at the beginning of Year 3. Assume further for simplicity that Reynolds Company made no merchandise purchases during Year 3. Quarterly sales, and end-of-quarter replacement costs for inventory, were as follows during Year 3:

Quarterly sales and end-of-quarter replacement costs for inventory

Quarter	Quarterly sales (units)	End-of-quarter inventory replacement cost (per unit)
1	2,000	$6
2	1,500	4
3	2,000	7
4	1,200	3

If the market decline in the second quarter was not considered to be **temporary,** Reynolds Company's cost of goods sold for the four quarters of Year 3 would be computed as follows:

Computation of quarterly cost of goods sold

Quarter	Computation for quarter	Cost of goods sold For quarter	Cumulative
1	2,000 × $5	$10,000	$10,000
2	(1,500 × $5) + (6,500 × $1)	14,000	24,000
3	(2,000 × $4) − $4,500*	3,500	27,500
4	(1,200 × $5) + (3,300 × $2)	12,600	40,100

* 4,500 units remaining in inventory multiplied by $1 write-up to original cost.

[26] Ibid., pp. 524–525.

The $40,100 cumulative cost of goods sold for Reynolds Company for Year 3 may be verified as follows:

6,700 units sold during Year 3, at $5 fifo cost per unit...................	$33,500
Write-down of Year 3 ending inventory to replacement cost (3,300 units × $2)..	6,600
Cost of goods sold for Year 3..	$40,100

4 Companies using standard costs for inventories and cost of goods sold generally should report standard cost variances for interim periods as they do for fiscal years. Planned materials price variances and volume or capacity variances should be deferred at the end of interim periods if the variances are expected to be absorbed by the end of the fiscal year.

All Other Costs and Expenses   The following guidelines for all costs and expenses other than those associated with revenue are set forth in *APB Opinion No. 28:*[27]

Costs and expenses other than product costs should be charged to income in interim periods as incurred, or be allocated among interim periods based on an estimate of time expired, benefit received or activity associated with the periods. Procedures adopted for assigning specific cost and expense items to an interim period should be consistent with the bases followed by the company in reporting results of operations at annual reporting dates. However, when a specific cost or expense item charged to expense for annual reporting purposes benefits more than one interim period, the cost or expense item may be allocated to those interim periods.

Some costs and expenses incurred in an interim period, however, cannot be readily identified with the activities or benefits of other interim periods and should be charged to the interim period in which incurred. Disclosure should be made as to the nature and amount of such costs unless items of a comparable nature are included in both the current interim period and in the corresponding interim period of the preceding year.

Arbitrary assignment of the amount of such costs to an interim period should not be made.

Gains and losses that arise in any interim period similar to those that would not be deferred at year-end should not be deferred to later interim periods within the same fiscal year. . . .

The amounts of certain costs and expenses are frequently subjected to year-end adjustments even though they can be reasonably approximated at interim dates. To the extent possible such adjustments should be estimated and the estimated costs and expenses assigned to interim periods so that the interim periods bear a reasonable portion of the anticipated annual amount. Examples of such items include inventory shrinkage, allowance for uncollectible accounts, allowance for quantity discounts, and discretionary year-end bonuses.

APB Opinion No. 28 includes a number of specific applications of the preceding guidelines.

[27] Ibid., pp. 525–526, 527.

Income Tax Provisions   The techniques for computing income tax provisions in interim financial reports were described as follows in *APB Opinion No. 28:*[28]

> At the end of each interim period the company should make its best estimate of the effective tax rate expected to be applicable for the full fiscal year. The rate so determined should be used in providing for income taxes on a current year-to-date basis. The effective tax rate should reflect anticipated investment tax credits, foreign tax rates, percentage depletion, capital gains rates, and other available tax planning alternatives. However, in arriving at this effective tax rate no effect should be included for the tax related to significant unusual or extraordinary items that will be separately reported or reported net of their related tax effect in reports for the interim period or for the fiscal year.

To illustrate, assume that at the end of the first quarter of Year 7, Carter Company's actual first quarter and forecasted fiscal year operating results were as follows:

Actual first quarter and forecasted fiscal year pre-tax accounting income	First quarter (actual)	Fiscal year (estimated)
Revenue	$400,000	$1,800,000
Costs and expenses other than income taxes	300,000	1,500,000
Income before income taxes	$100,000	$ 300,000

Assume further that there were no *timing differences* between Carter Company's pre-tax accounting income and taxable income, but that the company had the following estimated *permanent differences* between pre-tax accounting income and federal and state taxable income for the fiscal year:

Estimated permanent differences	
Dividend exclusion	$17,000
Goodwill amortization	5,000

If Carter Company's *nominal* federal and state income tax rates total 60%, the company would estimate its *effective* combined income tax rate for Year 7 as follows:

[28] Ibid., pp. 527–528.

Computation of estimated effective income tax rate		
Estimated income before income taxes		$300,000
Add: Nondeductible goodwill amortization		5,000
Less: Dividend exclusion		(17,000)
Estimated taxable income		$288,000
Estimated combined federal and state income taxes ($288,000 × 60% = $172,800)..		$172,800
Estimated effective combined federal and state income tax rate for Year 7 ($172,800 ÷ $300,000 = 57.6%)		57.6%

Carter Company's journal entry for income taxes for the first quarter of Year 7 would be as follows:

Journal entry for income taxes for first quarter of fiscal year		
Income Taxes Expense	57,600	
Income Taxes Payable		57,600
To provide for estimated federal and state income taxes for the first quarter of Year 7 as follows: $100,000 × 57.6% = $57,600.		

For the second quarter of Year 7, Carter Company again would estimate an effective combined federal and state income tax rate based on more current projections for permanent differences between pre-tax accounting income and taxable income for the entire year. However, the new effective rate **would not be retroactively applied** to restate the first quarter's tax expense. For example, assume that Carter's second quarter estimate of the effective combined federal and state income tax rate was 58.2% and that Carter's pre-tax income for the second quarter was $120,000 (or $220,000 for first two quarters). Carter would prepare the following journal entry for income taxes expense for the second quarter of Year 7:

Journal entry for income taxes for second quarter of fiscal year		
Income Taxes Expense	70,440	
Income Taxes Payable		70,440
To provide for estimated federal and state income taxes for the second quarter of Year 7 as follows:		
$220,000 × 58.2%	$128,040	
Less: Income taxes provided for first quarter	57,600	
Income taxes expense for second quarter	$ 70,440	

The preceding example of the computation of income taxes expense for an interim period is highly simplified. Many complex aspects of income taxes, such as net operating loss carrybacks and carryforwards, complicate the computations of income taxes for interim periods. *FASB Interpretation No. 18,* "Accounting for Income Taxes in Interim Periods," provides guidance for complex interim period income tax computations.

Reporting accounting changes in interim periods

In 1974, the FASB issued *FASB Statement No. 3,* "Reporting Accounting Changes in Interim Financial Statements," as an amendment to *APB Opinion No. 28.* Following are the two principal provisions of *FASB Statement No. 3:*[29]

> If a cumulative effect type accounting change is made during the *first* interim period of an enterprise's fiscal year, the cumulative effect of the change on retained earnings at the *beginning of that fiscal year* shall be included in net income of the first interim period (and in last-twelve-months-to-date financial reports that include that first interim period).
>
> If a cumulative effect type accounting change is made in *other than the first* interim period of an enterprise's fiscal year, *no* cumulative effect of the change shall be included in net income of the period of the change. Instead, financial information for the pre-change interim periods of the fiscal year in which the change is made shall be restated by applying the newly adopted accounting principle to those pre-change interim periods. The cumulative effect of the change on retained earnings at the *beginning of that fiscal year* shall be included in restated net income of the first interim period of the fiscal year in which the change is made (and in any year-to-date or last-twelve-months-to-date financial reports that include the first interim period). Whenever financial information that includes those pre-change interim periods is presented, it shall be presented on the restated basis.

Disclosure of Interim Financial Data   As a minimum, *APB Opinion No. 28* provided that the following data should be included in publicly traded companies' interim financial reports to shareholders. The data are to be reported for the just-completed quarter and the year to date, or twelve months to date of the quarter's end.[30]

a. Sales or gross revenues, provision for income taxes, extraordinary items (including related income tax effects), cumulative effect of a change in accounting principles or practices, and net income.
b. Primary and fully diluted earnings per share data for each period presented, . . .
c. Seasonal revenue, costs or expenses.
d. Significant changes in estimates or provisions for income taxes.
e. Disposal of a segment of a business and extraordinary, unusual or infrequently occurring items.
f. Contingent items.
g. Changes in accounting principles or estimates.
h. Significant changes in financial position.

[29] *FASB Statement No. 3,* "Reporting Accounting Changes in Interim Financial Statements," FASB (Stamford: 1974), p. 4, par. 9, 10.
[30] *APB Opinion No. 28,* p. 532.

An example of the presentation of interim financial data, from the 1977 annual report of Walt Disney Productions, appears below.

NOTE 6

OPERATIONS BY QUARTER (UNAUDITED):

A summary of certain information pertaining to operating results for each quarter of fiscal years 1977 and 1976 is shown below (in thousands of dollars, except for per share data).

	December 31	March 31	June 30	September 30
1977				
Revenues	*$119,529*	*$139,996*	*$165,103*	*$205,197*
Operating income before corporate expenses	*27,453*	*39,716*	*44,772*	*67,710*
Income before taxes on income	*22,528*	*33,886*	*38,855*	*62,078*
Net income	*11,828*	*17,786*	*20,355*	*31,978*
Earnings per common and common equivalent share	*.37*	*.56*	*.64*	*1.00*
1976				
Revenues	*115,736*	*139,502*	*148,671*	*179,987*
Operating income before corporate expenses	*26,123*	*40,250*	*41,061*	*52,851*
Income before taxes on income	*21,169*	*34,029*	*35,865*	*49,136*
Net income	*11,169*	*18,029*	*18,865*	*26,536*
Earnings per common and common equivalent share	*.35*	*.56*	*.59*	*.84*

Conclusions on interim financial statements

APB Opinion No. 28, FASB Statement No. 3, and *FASB Interpretation No. 18* represent a substantial effort to upgrade the quality of interim financial statements. However, controversy continues on the subject of interim financial reporting—especially concerning the APB's premise that an interim period should be accounted for as a portion of the applicable annual period. In recognition of this controversy and other problems of interim financial reporting, the FASB has undertaken a comprehensive study of the topic, and has issued a *Discussion Memorandum* entitled "Interim Financial Accounting and Reporting."

FINANCIAL FORECASTS

The AICPA has defined a *financial forecast* for an enterprise as an estimate of the most probable financial position, results of operations, and changes in financial position for one or more future periods.[31] Accountants, financial executives, and financial analysts have debated extensively the propriety of including financial forecasts in annual and interim financial reports to shareholders. Among the arguments on the propriety of published financial forecasts are the following:

Arguments in support of published financial forecasts

Proponents of the publishing of enterprise financial forecasts advance the following arguments in support of their position:

1 Publication of financial forecasts would make them available to all interested parties, rather than to a few financial analysts and institutional investors.
2 The availability of an enterprise's published financial forecasts would make the enterprise more competitive in the search for scarce debt and equity capital.
3 Disclosure of assumptions underlying published financial forecasts would alert users to the uncertainties and risks inherent in forecasting.
4 Forecasts already are used for managerial purposes by most progressive companies. Thus, publication of financial forecasts would not add unduly to the costs of financial communications of those companies.
5 Mathematical models and computers have enhanced substantially the reliability of forecasting techniques.

Arguments in opposition to published financial forecasts

Following are the principal objections to published financial forecasts expressed by opponents:

1 Unsophisticated users of published financial forecasts might consider them to be commitments rather than estimates. These users would not comprehend the uncertainties and risks in the forecasting process.
2 Enterprises which did not attain forecasted results might lose the confidence of current and prospective shareholders and creditors.
3 The forecasts used for managerial purposes are designed more for motivation and control than for achievability.
4 Potential legal liability in published financial forecasts might lead to ultra-conservative forecasting or manipulation of actual operating results by managements.
5 Economic disruptions such as inflation, energy and commodity shortages, increasing labor costs, and high interest rates make financial forecasts for periods longer than one or two months extremely unreliable.

Despite the persuasiveness of the arguments in support of financial

[31] *Statement of Position 75-4,* "Presentation and Disclosure of Financial Forecasts," AICPA (New York: 1975), p. 2.

forecasts, the opponents' counterarguments have considerable merit, especially the last one.

The SEC's position on financial forecasts

A few years ago, the SEC held public hearings on the propriety of the inclusion of financial forecasts in filings with the Commission. As a result of the hearings and other comments received, the SEC took the position (**Release No. 33-5699**) that filing of financial forecasts with the Commission should be **voluntary,** not **mandatory.** To encourage voluntary filings, the SEC authorized the development of a "safe harbor rule" to protect the management of forecast-issuing enterprises from shareholder suits resulting from the enterprise's failure to achieve forecasted results.

AICPA pronouncement on financial forecasts

Because of the SEC's interest in financial forecasts, the AICPA issued **Statement of Position 75-4,** "Presentation and Disclosure of Financial Forecasts," to provide guidance for enterprises which published financial forecasts. Among the AICPA's recommendations were the following:[32]

1 Preferably, financial forecasts should be presented in the format of the historical financial statements expected to be issued, except that the customary notes to financial statements are not required for forecasts.

2 As a minimum, financial forecasts should include, as applicable: sales or gross revenue; gross profit; provision for income taxes; net income; disposal of a segment of a business; extraordinary, unusual or infrequently occurring items; primary and fully diluted earnings per-share date for each period presented; and significant anticipated changes in financial position.

3 Financial forecasts should be prepared on a basis consistent with the accounting principles expected to be used in the historical financial statements for the forecast periods; and a summary of significant accounting policies should accompany the forecast or be incorporated by reference.

4 Financial forecasts should reflect monetary amounts representing the single most probable forecasted result. Such point estimates may be supplemented by ranges or probabilistic statements for key measures such as sales and net income.

5 Assumptions considered by management to be most significant, or key factors on which enterprise financial results depend, should be disclosed in financial forecasts, in a "Summary of Significant Forecast Assumptions." In addition there should be disclosed the basis or rationale for the assumptions, and relative impact of variations in the assumptions which would affect significantly the forecasted data.

6 The period to be covered by a financial forecast should be determined by management after consideration of their ability to forecast and the needs of users of the forecast.

7 Financial forecasts should be labeled clearly and presented separately from historical financial statements.

[32] Ibid., pp. 3–8.

8 Unless financial forecasts are not intended to be updated, or a release of historical financial statements covering the forecast period is imminent, outdated forecasts should be superseded by revised forecasts to reflect significant changes in assumptions, actual results, or unanticipated events and circumstances. The reasons for updating should be disclosed in the revised forecast.

Importance of assumptions in forecasting

A frequently heard statement is that "a financial forecast is only as good as the assumptions which underlie it." The AICPA recognized the importance of assumptions in a lengthy discussion in *Statement of Position 75-4.* Among the points made by the AICPA were the following:[33]

1 Communication of all assumptions underlying a financial forecast is not feasible.

2 Unforeseen changes in conditions may make significant certain assumptions which previously had been considered unimportant.

3 Significant assumptions which are disclosed need not be presented in such a manner or in such detail as would affect adversely the competitive position of the enterprise.

4 Significant assumptions to be disclosed include the following:

a Assumptions for which a reasonably anticipated variation may affect significantly the forecasted results

b Assumptions about anticipated conditions that are expected to differ significantly from current conditions

c Other assumptions considered important to the forecast or to its interpretation

Illustration of financial forecast

An illustrative financial forecast which includes many of the recommendations of the AICPA's *Statement of Position 75-4* follows.

ORACLE CORPORATION
Financial Forecast Data (Note)
For Year Ending July 31, Year 8

Net sales	$2,500,000
Gross profit on sales	1,000,000
Income from continuing operations before income taxes	700,000
Provision for income taxes	420,000
Loss on disposal of Sinclair Division, less applicable income taxes	50,000
Net income	230,000
Earnings from continuing operations per common share	$2.80
Earnings per common share	$2.30

---

[33] Ibid., pp. 5–6.

The Summary of Significant Forecast Assumptions is an integral part of this financial forecast.

Note: *The financial forecast for the year ending July 31, Year 8, has been prepared on a basis consistent with the significant accounting policies described [in] this annual report.*

Summary of Significant Forecast Assumptions
This financial forecast is based on management's assumptions concerning future events and circumstances. The assumptions disclosed herein are those which management believes are significant to the forecast or are key factors upon which the financial results of the enterprise depend. Some assumptions inevitably will not materialize, and unanticipated events and circumstances may occur subsequent to July 15, Year 7, the date of this forecast. Therefore, the actual results achieved during the forecast period will vary from the forecast and the variations may be material.

(1) The company expects its raw material costs to rise, on an overall basis, commensurate with the rate of monetary inflation. The forecast assumes any raw material cost increases can be recovered in the form of higher sales prices for the company's products. Labor costs have been forecasted using rates provided in the company's union contract, which does not expire until June 30, Year 9.

(2) At certain times in the year, the company is dependent on short-term bank borrowing. The company's forecast of interest expense is based on the seasonal borrowing patterns of prior years for financing inventories and receivables. The company does not expect to incur any long-term borrowing and anticipates no major changes in the prime rate from its present level of 8½%.

(3) Manufacture of the company's major products depends on the availability of relatively small quantities of petroleum by-products. The company has no guaranteed source for these raw materials. The forecast assumes continued availability of these raw materials.

(4) Earnings per share data have been computed under the same procedures used for historical financial statements purposes.

Conclusion

Considerable effort continues to be expended by accountants and others in research and in setting standards for the three topics discussed in this chapter—segment reporting, interim financial statements, and financial forecasts. We can anticipate releases on one or more of these topics in the future from the FASB, the AICPA, and the SEC. The standards, principles, and guidelines described in this chapter thus may be changed in the coming years.

APPENDIX: Examples of Segment Reporting

Financial Review (continued)
Business Segments (Note 1)

Union Pacific Corporation and
Subsidiary Companies

(Thousands of Dollars)

	1977	1976	1975	1974	1973
Revenues:					
Transportation	$1,313,567	$1,174,544	$1,004,342	$1,000,266	$ 882,245
Oil and Gas	1,141,044	826,746	731,528	591,128	327,109
Mining	47,190	24,809	19,145	5,594	4,065
Land	26,615	21,256	19,674	15,942	20,931
Equity and other income	25,879	17,609	75,413[a]	10,474	9,074
Total Revenues	$2,554,295	$2,064,964	$1,850,102	$1,623,404	$1,243,424
Operating Profit (Loss):					
Transportation	$ 214,991	$ 179,604	$ 148,294	$ 186,036	$ 170,669
Oil and Gas	162,589	113,628	14,778[b]	30,276[b]	57,331
Mining	17,783	10,210	7,883	1,701	911
Land	3,509	5,865	3,239	3,640	(97)
Total Operating Profit	398,872	309,307	174,194	221,653	228,814
Equity and other income	25,879	17,609	75,413[a]	10,474	9,074
Interest expense	(66,817)	(60,672)	(48,352)	(39,992)	(30,655)
Corporate expenses	(19,945)	(19,063)	(13,678)	(11,551)	(10,121)
Income Before Federal Income Taxes	$ 337,989	$ 247,181	$ 187,577	$ 180,584	$ 197,112
Assets at December 31:					
Transportation	$2,796,562	$2,587,498	$2,459,493	$2,267,539	$2,151,990
Oil and Gas	1,055,093	827,806	710,555	491,575	400,303
Mining	98,982	80,230	59,472	41,822	30,787
Land	102,661	115,476	120,147	126,712	125,604
Corporate	63,127	82,736	68,581	100,805	119,692
Total Assets	$4,116,425	$3,693,746	$3,418,248	$3,028,453	$2,828,376
Depreciation, Depletion, Amortization and Retirements:					
Transportation	$ 86,397	$ 80,288	$ 75,310	$ 71,744	$ 68,634
Oil and Gas	58,925	47,894	121,941[b]	90,397[b]	32,245
Mining	1,122	312	795	557	129
Land	682	719	852	1,014	944
Corporate	503	503	357	140	—
Total Depreciation, Depletion, Amortization and Retirements	$ 147,629	$ 129,716	$ 199,255	$ 163,852	$ 101,952
Capital Expenditures[c]:					
Transportation	$ 204,189	$ 177,943	$ 205,780	$ 195,760	$ 139,420
Oil and Gas	147,243	187,135	205,917	189,566	45,309
Mining	12,339	12,958	20,335	8,596	68
Land	450	273	2,620	6,311	2,744
Corporate	—	—	5,098	3,780	—
Total Capital Expenditures	$ 364,221	$ 378,309	$ 439,750	$ 404,013	$ 187,541

(a) Includes a $59,878,000 before tax gain from sale of interests in British North Sea.
(b) 1975 includes a $60,774,000 provision for losses associated with Champlin's interest in nine tracts off the Gulf Coast of Florida based upon unsuccessful drilling results. The 1975 provision together with a $60,000,000 provision recorded in 1974 completely reserved Champlin's $120,774,000 investment in such leases.
(c) Excludes advances to and capital expenditures of unconsolidated affiliated companies.

The accompanying accounting policy disclosures and notes to financial statements are an integral part of this information.

1. Business Segments

In accordance with FASB Statement No. 14 effective in 1977, certain financial and operating data is presented on a business segment basis on page 32 of the Financial Review. Information appearing therein for the years ended December 31, 1977 and 1976 is an integral part of these financial statements. Rail freight operations involve the movement of a wide array of minerals, farm products and manufactured goods. Oil and gas operations include the exploration, development and production of crude oil and natural gas and the refining, processing, transporting and marketing of petroleum products. Mining operations are responsible for developing Union Pacific's reserves of coal, trona (natural soda ash) and uranium. Land operations involve the sale, lease and development of prime properties to industrial and commercial customers. The Corporation operates principally in the United States.

Revenues by segment relate substantially to unaffiliated customers. Revenues less operating expenses constitute operating profit (loss). Identifiable assets by industry are those assets that are used in the Corporation's operations in each industry. Corporate assets are principally cash and marketable securities.

Tenneco Inc

SEGMENT AND GEOGRAPHIC AREA INFORMATION AT DECEMBER 31,1977 AND FOR THE YEAR THEN ENDED:

	Segment							Geographic Area		
	Integrated Oil	Natural Gas Pipelines	Construction and Farm Equipment	Shipbuilding	Other	Reclass. and Elim.	Consolidated	Reclass. and Elim.	United States	Foreign
					(Millions)					
Sales and operating revenues from unaffiliated companies	$1,504.6	$1,820.6	$1,505.6	$784.9	$1,824.6	$ —	$7,440.3	$ —	$6,445.8	$ 994.5
Transfers between segments or geographic areas	199.4	15.3	—	—	9.7	(224.4)	—	(240.3)	217.3	23.0
Total sales and operating revenues	$1,704.0	$1,835.9	$1,505.6	$784.9	$1,834.3	$(224.4)	$7,440.3	$ (240.3)	$6,663.1	$1,017.5
Operating profit	$ 408.3	$ 296.1	$ 114.7	$ 56.3	$ 177.9	$ —	$1,053.3	$ —	$ 948.4	$ 104.9
Equity in net income of affiliated companies	.2	1.3	4.5	—	29.6	—	35.6	—	13.1	22.5
General corporate expenses	(10.0)	(8.2)	(8.3)	(6.3)	(10.0)	—	(42.8)	—	(42.8)	—
Income before interest, federal income taxes and minority interests	$ 398.5	$ 289.2	$ 110.9	$ 50.0	$ 197.5	$ —	$1,046.1	$ —	$ 918.7	$ 127.4
Identifiable assets	$2,601.6	$1,815.5	$1,240.1	$629.7	$1,905.6	$(237.4)	$7,955.1	$ (27.3)	$6,776.2	$1,206.2
Investment in affiliated companies	1.2	21.7	139.8	—	160.5	—	323.2	—	151.4	171.8
Total assets	$2,602.8	$1,837.2	$1,379.9	$629.7	$2,066.1	$(237.4)	$8,278.3	$ (27.3)	$6,927.6	$1,378.0
Other disclosures: Depreciation, depletion and amortization expense	$ 158.1	$ 131.1	$ 27.3	$ 17.1	$ 56.2	$ —	$ 389.8			
Capital expenditures	$ 386.3	$ 92.3	$ 78.6	$ 33.7	$ 123.5	$ —	$ 714.4			

NOTE: Products are transferred between segments and geographic areas on a basis intended to reflect as nearly as possible the "market value" of the products.

REVIEW QUESTIONS

1 What is an *industry segment* of an enterprise?

2 Is the concept of segment reporting consistent with the theory of consolidated financial statements? Explain.

3 Outline the segment reporting requirements of *FASB Statement No. 14,* "Financial Reporting for Segments of a Business Enterprise."

4 Identify three suggested alternative bases for segmentation of a business enterprise.

5 What arguments were advanced in opposition to inclusion of *intersegment sales or transfers* in a segment's reported sales?

6 Why was the question of whether some measure of segment income should be reported so controversial? Explain.

7 What advantages were claimed for a *segment contribution approach* for reporting a segment's income?

8 Describe the formula for the allocation of residual home office expenses set forth in *Cost Accounting Standard 403,* "Allocation of Home Office Expenses to Segments."

9 Differentiate between the *measurement date* and the *disposal date* for the discontinuance of a segment of an enterprise.

10 Discuss the provisions of *APB Opinion No. 28,* "Interim Financial Reporting," dealing with the accounting for costs associated with revenue in interim financial statements.

11 Explain the technique included in *APB Opinion No. 28,* "Interim Financial Reporting," for the computation of income tax provisions in interim financial statements.

12 Does the SEC require disclosure of a company's forecasted data in that company's filings with the Commission? Explain.

13 List three arguments advanced by proponents of published financial forecasts for business enterprises.

14 Discuss the role of assumptions in the preparation of financial forecasts.

EXERCISES

Ex. 12-1 Select the best answer for each of the following multiple-choice questions.

1 Which of the following is a required disclosure in the income statement for the disposal of a segment of an enterprise?
a The gain or loss on disposal should be reported as an extraordinary item
b Results of operations of a discontinued segment should be disclosed immediately below extraordinary items

     c Earnings per share from both continuing operations and net income should be disclosed in the income statement

     d Revenue and expenses applicable to the discontinued segment should be disclosed in the income statement

2 Minimum disclosure requirements for enterprises issuing interim financial information include

     a An interim statement of changes in financial position and an interim balance sheet

     b Primary and fully diluted earnings per share data for each period presented

     c Sales and cost of goods sold for the current interim period and the year-to-date

     d The contribution margin by product line for the current interim period and the year-to-date

3 Which of the following reporting practices is permissible for interim financial reporting?

     a Use of the gross profit method for pricing interim inventories

     b Use of the direct costing method for determining manufactured inventories

     c Deferral of unplanned variances under a standard cost system until year-end

     d Deferral of declines in the market value of inventories until year-end

4 In its consideration of interim financial reporting, how did the Accounting Principles Board conclude that such reporting should be viewed?

     a As a special type of reporting that need not comply with generally accepted accounting principles

     b As useful only if enterprise activity is spread evenly throughout the year so that estimates are unnecessary

     c As reporting for a basic accounting period

     d As reporting for an integral part of an annual period

5 Which of the following is not a consideration in reporting for industry segments of an enterprise?

     a Allocation of nontraceable expenses

     b Pricing of intersegment transfers

     c Identification of the segments

     d Consolidation policy

Ex. 12-2 Penner Corporation, a holding company, has two operating subsidiaries; one manufactures wheelbarrows and the other manufactures toothbrushes. The wheelbarrow subsidiary has been unprofitable, and in December, Year 5, Penner contracted to sell that subsidiary to an unrelated company for $60,000. The sale will be effective April 1, Year 6. Penner will continue to operate the wheelbarrow subsidiary during the first three months of Year 6, even though those operations are expected to result in a pre-tax loss of $10,000 for the three months.

    At December 31, Year 5, Penner's investment in the wheelbarrow subsidiary had a carrying amount of $100,000. Both the $40,000 loss on the sale of the investment and the $10,000 operating loss will be deductible in Penner's Year 6 income tax return, resulting in an anticipated tax saving of $27,500 at a combined federal and state income tax rate of 55%.

    Compute the loss on the disposal of the wheelbarrow subsidiary that should appear in the consolidated income statement of Penner Corporation and subsidiaries for Year 5.

Ex. 12-3 The nontraceable expenses of Maryland Company's home office for Year 8 totaled $150,000. Other financial data for Maryland's home office and two industry segments follow:

	Home office	Industry Segment A	Industry Segment B
Payroll dollars	$50,000	$200,000	$150,000
Net sales (operating revenue)	-0-	600,000	400,000
Average plant assets and inventories	80,000	400,000	320,000

Allocate the nontraceable expenses of Maryland Company to its two industry segments in accordance with the provisions of **Cost Accounting Standard 403.** Round all percentage computations to the nearest tenth.

Ex. 12-4 On January 2, Year 6, Ashland Corporation paid property taxes on its plant assets for Year 6 in the amount of $40,000. In March, Year 6, Ashland made customary annual major repairs to plant assets in the amount of $120,000. The repairs will benefit the entire Year 6. In April, Year 6, Ashland incurred a $420,000 loss from a market decline of inventories which was considered to be permanent.

Show how the above items should be reported in Ashland's quarterly income statements for Year 6. Supporting computations should be in good form.

Ex. 12-5 Ehrlich Corporation's accounting records for the year ended May 31, Year 2, included the following data for its three industry segments:

	Industry Segment 1	Industry Segment 2	Industry Segment 3
Net sales to outsiders	$500,000	$400,000	$300,000
Intersegment transfers out	40,000	50,000	60,000
Traceable expenses:			
Intersegment transfers in	70,000	60,000	20,000
Other	300,000	200,000	200,000

Nontraceable expenses of Ehrlich totaled $120,000 for the year ended May 31, Year 2. Ehrlich allocates these expenses on the basis of segment sales to outsiders.

Compute the operating profit or loss of each of Ehrlich's three industry segments for the year ended May 31, Year 2, in accordance with the provisions of **FASB Statement No. 14,** "Financial Reporting for Segments of a Business Enterprise."

Ex. 12-6 Indiana Company's accounting records for the year ended August 31, Year 4, include the following data with respect to its Wabash Division. Sale of that division to Expansive Enterprises, Inc., for $300,000 was authorized by Indiana's board of directors on August 31, Year 4. Closing date of the sale was expected to be February 28, Year 5.

INDIANA COMPANY
Wabash Division
Selected Accounting Data

Net sales, year ended Aug. 31, Year 4	$200,000
Costs and expenses, year ended Aug. 31, Year 4	150,000
Estimated operating losses, six months ending Feb. 28, Year 5	30,000
Estimated carrying amount of net assets at Feb. 28, Year 5	330,000

Indiana Company's combined federal and state income tax rate is 60%.

Prepare a partial income statement for Indiana Company for the year ended August 31, Year 4, to present the above data.

Ex. 12-7 Natoka Company sells a single product, which it purchases from three different vendors. On May 1, Year 8, Natoka's inventory of the product consisted of 1,000 units priced at fifo cost of $7,500. Natoka's merchandise transactions for the year ended April 30, Year 9, were as follows:

Quarter	Units purchased	Cost per unit purchased	Units sold	End-of-quarter replacement cost per unit
1	5,000	$8.00	4,500	$8.50
2	6,000	8.50	7,000	9.00
3	8,000	9.00	6,500	8.50*
4	6,000	8.50	5,500	9.50

*Decline not considered to be temporary

Compute Natoka's cost of goods sold for each of the four quarters of the year ended April 30, Year 9. Show computations.

Ex. 12-8 Fitzhugh Oil Company's actual pre-tax operating results for the first two quarters of its fiscal year ending April 30, Year 4, and its related estimates for the entire fiscal year, were as follows:

	Year ending April 30, Year 4		
	First quarter (actual)	Second quarter (actual)	Full year (estimated)
Revenue	$600,000	$700,000	$2,700,000
Costs and expenses other than income taxes	400,000	450,000	2,000,000
Income before income taxes	$200,000	$250,000	$ 700,000

Fitzhugh's financial executives anticipated no timing differences between pre-tax accounting income and taxable income for the year ending April 30, Year 4. However, the executives estimated the following permanent differences between pre-tax accounting income and taxable income for the first and second quarters:

	Estimate of permanent differences for year ending April 30, Year 4	
	Made for first quarter	Made for second quarter
Dividend exclusion	$ 15,000	$ 20,000
Excess of statutory depletion over cost depletion	150,000	140,000
Goodwill amortization	50,000	50,000

Fitzhugh's combined federal and state income tax rate is expected to be 60% for the year ending April 30, Year 4.

Prepare journal entries for Fitzhugh's estimated income taxes expense for the first quarter and second quarter of the year ending April 30, Year 4. Round all effective income tax rate percentages to the nearest tenth.

Ex. 12-9 Selected assumptions underlying Rayburn Company's financial forecast for the year ending November 30, Year 9, follow:

1 Markups on merchandise will be 25% of gross purchase cost.

2 Merchandise purchases will be made on account with terms of 1/10, net 60. Purchase discounts always will be taken and will be recorded in the Purchase Discounts account.

3 Payments of each month's purchases will be made as follows:
   60% in month of purchase
   40% during first 10 days of first month following month of purchase

4 Merchandise inventories at end of each month will be maintained at 30% of the following month's cost of goods sold.

5 Merchandise sales on account will continue to bear terms of 2/10, net 30. Cash sales will not be subject to discount.

6 Collections of each month's sales on account will be made as follows:
   50% in month of sale
   45% in month following month of sale

7 5% of each month's sales on account will be doubtful of collection.

8 70% of collections on account in the month of sale will be subject to discount; 10% of the collections in the succeeding month will be subject to discount.

9 Forecasted sales for the first four months of the year ending November 30, Year 9, are as follows:

	Gross sales on account	Cash sales
Year 8:		
December	$1,900,000	$400,000
Year 9:		
January	1,500,000	250,000
February	1,700,000	350,000
March	1,600,000	300,000

Compute in good form the following items for Rayburn's financial forecast for the year ending November 30, Year 9:

a Forecasted gross purchases for January, Year 9

b Forecasted inventories at December 31, Year 8

c Forecasted payments to suppliers during February, Year 9

d Forecasted sales discounts to be taken by customers making remittances during February, Year 9

e Forecasted total collections from customers during February, Year 9

SHORT CASES FOR ANALYSIS AND DECISION

Case 12-1 The Financial Accounting Standards Board requires the reporting of financial data for segments of a business enterprise.

Instructions

a What does financial reporting for segments of a business enterprise involve?

b Identify the reasons why financial data should be reported for segments of a business enterprise.

c Identify the possible disadvantages of reporting financial data for segments of a business enterprise.

d Identify the accounting difficulties inherent in segment reporting.

Case 12-2 Chester Corporation, a publicly owned company listed on a major stock exchange, forecasted operations for Year 5 as follows:

CHESTER CORPORATION
Forecasted Income Statement
For Year Ending December 31, Year 5

Net sales (1,000,000 units)	$6,000,000
Cost of goods sold	3,600,000
Gross profit on sales	$2,400,000
Selling, general, and administrative expenses	1,400,000
Operating income	$1,000,000
Nonoperating revenue and expenses	-0-
Income before income taxes	$1,000,000
Income taxes (current and deferred)	550,000
Net income	$ 450,000
Earnings per share of common stock	$4.50

Chester has operated profitably for many years and has experienced a seasonal pattern of sales volume and production similar to the following ones forecasted for Year 5:

Sales volume is expected to follow a quarterly pattern of 10%, 20%, 35%, 35%, respectively, because of the seasonality of the industry. Also, due to production and storage capacity limitations it is expected that production will follow a pattern of 20%, 25%, 30%, 25%, per quarter, respectively.

At the conclusion of the first quarter of Year 5, the controller of Chester prepared and issued the following interim income statement for public release:

CHESTER CORPORATION
Income Statement
For Quarter Ended March 31, Year 5

Net sales (100,000 units)	$ 600,000
Cost of goods sold	360,000
Gross profit on sales	$ 240,000
Selling, general, and administrative expenses	275,000
Operating loss	$ (35,000)
Loss from warehouse fire	(175,000)
Loss before income taxes	$(210,000)
Income taxes	-0-
Net loss	$(210,000)
Loss per share of common stock	$(2.10)

The following additional information is available for the first quarter just completed, but was not included in the public information released:

(1) The company uses a standard cost system in which standards are set at currently attainable levels on an annual basis. At the end of the first quarter, underapplied fixed factory overhead (volume variance) of $50,000 was treated as an asset. Production during the first quarter was 200,000 units, of which 100,000 were sold.

(2) The selling, general, and administrative expenses were forecasted on a basis of $900,000 fixed expenses for the year plus $0.50 variable expenses per unit of sales.

(3) The warehouse fire loss met the conditions of an extraordinary loss. The warehouse had an undepreciated cost of $320,000; $145,000 was recovered from insurance on the warehouse. No other gains or losses are anticipated this year from similar events or transactions, nor has Chester had any similar losses in preceding years; thus, the full loss will be deductible as an ordinary loss for income tax purposes.

(4) The effective income tax rate, for federal and state taxes combined, is expected to average 55% of income before income taxes for Year 5. There are no permanent differences between pre-tax accounting income and taxable income.

(5) Earnings per share were computed on the basis of 100,000 shares of capital stock outstanding. Chester has only one class of stock issued, no long-term debt outstanding, and no stock option plan.

Instructions

a Without reference to the specific situation described above, what are the standards of disclosure for interim financial data (published interim financial reports) for publicly traded companies? Explain.

b Identify the weaknesses in form and content of Chester's interim income statement, without reference to the additional information.

c For each of the five items of additional information, indicate the preferable treatment for each item for interim-reporting purposes and explain why that treatment is preferable.

Case 12-3 Pastime Corporation, a holding company, owns 100% of the outstanding capital stock of three subsidiary companies. Each of the subsidiaries has forecasted pre-tax income for Year 7, but Pastime has forecasted a pre-tax loss for that year. Accordingly, Pastime plans to file consolidated federal and state income tax returns for Year 7, to take advantage of offsetting its forecasted pre-tax loss against the taxable income of the three subsidiaries.

A major creditor of Pastime has requested separate financial statements for Pastime and each of the three subsidiaries for Year 7. The controller of Pastime is uncertain how to present income taxes expense or credit in the separate income statements of each company.

Instructions What advice would you give the controller of Pastime? Explain.

PROBLEMS

12-4 Bridger Corporation, a diversified manufacturing company, had four separate operating divisions engaged in the manufacture of products in each of the following industries: food products, health aids, textiles, and office equipment.

Financial data for the two years ended December 31, Year 8 and Year 7, are presented on page 491.

	Net sales		Cost of goods sold		Operating expenses	
	Year 8	Year 7	Year 8	Year 7	Year 8	Year 7
Food products...	$3,500,000	$3,000,000	$2,400,000	$1,800,000	$ 550,000	$ 275,000
Health aids	2,000,000	1,270,000	1,100,000	700,000	300,000	125,000
Textiles	1,580,000	1,400,000	500,000	900,000	200,000	150,000
Office equipment	920,000	1,330,000	800,000	1,000,000	650,000	750,000
Totals	$8,000,000	$7,000,000	$4,800,000	$4,400,000	$1,700,000	$1,300,000

On January 1, Year 8, Bridger adopted a plan to sell the assets and product line of the office equipment division at an anticipated gain. On September 1, Year 8, the division's assets and product line were sold for $2,100,000 cash, at a gain of $640,000 (exclusive of operations during the phase-out period).

The company's textiles division had six manufacturing plants which produced a variety of textile products. In April, Year 8, the company sold one of these plants and realized a gain of $130,000. After the sale, the operations at the plant that was sold were transferred to the remaining five textile plants which the company continued to operate.

In August, Year 8, the main warehouse of the food products division, located on the banks of the Colton River, was flooded when the river overflowed. The resulting damage of $420,000 is not included in the financial data given above. Historical records indicate that the Colton River normally overflows every four to five years, causing flood damage to adjacent property.

For the two years ended December 31, Year 8 and Year 7, the company earned interest revenue on investments of $70,000 and $40,000, respectively.

For the two years ended December 31, Year 8 and Year 7, the company's net income was $960,000 and $670,000, respectively.

Income taxes expense for each of the two years should be computed at a rate of 50%.

Instructions   Prepare in good form a comparative income statement for Bridger Corporation for the two years ended December 31, Year 8 and Year 7. Footnotes and earnings per share disclosures are not required.

12-5 Cedarwood Company has an excellent financial forecasting system. For the year ending July 31, Year 6, Cedarwood forecasted pre-tax accounting income of $800,000. The company did not anticipate any timing differences between pre-tax accounting income and taxable income. However, the following permanent differences between accounting and taxable income for Year 6 were forecasted:

Dividend exclusion	$150,000
Goodwill amortization	20,000
Officers' life insurance premium expense	15,000

In addition, Cedarwood anticipated investment tax credits of $50,000 for Year 6. The company's combined federal and state income tax rate is 60%, and federal and state laws coincided with respect to determination of taxable income.

Cedarwood's quarterly pre-tax accounting income for the year ended July 31, Year 6, is summarized at the top of page 492.

Quarter ended:

Oct. 31, Year 5	*$180,000*
Jan. 31, Year 6	*230,000*
Apr. 30, Year 6	*195,000*
July 31, Year 6	*215,000*

During Year 6, Cedarwood did not alter its forecast of pre-tax accounting income for the year. However, effective January 31, Year 6, the company revised its permanent difference estimate for the Year 6 dividend exclusion to $180,000 from $150,000, and its investment tax credit estimate for the year to $80,000 from $50,000. The actual amounts for the permanent differences and investment credit computed by the company as of July 31, Year 6, were as follows:

Dividend exclusion	*$175,000*
Goodwill amortization	*20,000*
Officers' life insurance premium expense	*16,000*
Investment tax credit	*90,000*

Instructions

a Compute the effective combined federal and state income tax rates which Cedarwood should use for its quarterly interim financial statements for the year ended July 31, Year 6. Round all percentage computations to the nearest tenth.

b Prepare Cedarwood's journal entries for income taxes at October 31, Year 5, and January 31, April 30, and July 31, Year 6.

12-6 The general ledger of Vincent Company included the following amounts for the year ended December 31, Year 6:

Cost of goods sold—continuing operations	$ 8,000,000
Estimated loss on disposal of Southern Division, to be completed in first	
quarter of Year 7	*50,000*
Income taxes expense ($540,000 × 60%)	*324,000*
Interest expense	*100,000*
Judgment paid in lawsuit of **Justin Company v. Vincent Company,** *initiated*	
in Year 4	*80,000*
Loss from bankruptcy of major customer	*150,000*
Loss from operations of Southern Division, discontinued effective Dec. 31,	
Year 6	*120,000*
Net sales—continuing operations	*10,000,000*
Selling, general, and administrative expenses—continuing operations	*800,000*
Uninsured loss from earthquake at Northern Division	*160,000*

Vincent's combined federal and state income tax rate is 60%. The company had no timing or permanent differences between pre-tax accounting income and taxable income, and no investment tax credits for Year 6. Prior to Year 6, there had not been an earthquake in Vincent's locality for more than 50 years.

Instructions Prepare an income statement for Vincent for the year ended December 31, Year 6, in accordance with the provisions of **APB Opinion No. 30,** "Reporting the Results of Operations." Disregard earnings per share disclosures.

12-7 Gregory Company, a manufacturer of molded plastic containers, determined in October, Year 8, that it needed cash to continue operations. The company began negotiating for a one-month bank loan of $100,000 which would be discounted at 6% per annum on November 1. In considering the loan, the bank requested a forecasted income statement and a cash forecast for the month of November, Year 8.

The following information is available:

(1) Sales were forecasted at 120,000 units per month in October, Year 8, December, Year 8, and January, Year 9, and at 90,000 units in November, Year 8. The selling price is $2 per unit. Sales are billed on the fifteenth and last day of each month, with terms of 2/10, net 30. Past experience indicates that sales are even throughout the month and 50% of the customers pay the billed amount within the discount period. The remainder pay at the end of 30 days, except for doubtful accounts, which average ½% of gross sales. On its income statement the company deducts from sales the estimated amounts for cash discounts on sales and doubtful accounts expense.

(2) The inventory of finished goods on October 1 was 24,000 units. The finished goods inventory at the end of each month is to be maintained at 20% of sales anticipated for the following month. There is no goods in process inventory.

(3) The inventory of raw materials on October 1 was 22,800 pounds. At the end of each month the raw materials inventory is to be maintained at not less than 40% of production requirements for the following month. Materials are purchased as needed in minimum quantities of 25,000 pounds per shipment. Raw material purchases of each month are paid in the next succeeding month, with terms of net 30 days.

(4) All salaries and wages are paid on the fifteenth and last day of each month for the period ending on the date of payment.

(5) All factory overhead and selling and administrative expenses are paid on the tenth of the month following the month in which incurred. Selling expenses are forecasted at 10% of gross sales. Administrative expenses, which include depreciation expense of $500 per month on office furniture and fixtures, total $33,000 per month.

(6) The standard cost of a molded plastic container, based on normal production of 100,000 units per month, is as follows:

Materials—½ pound	$0.50
Labor	.40
Variable factory overhead	.20
Fixed factory overhead	.10
Total standard cost	$1.20

Fixed factory overhead includes depreciation on factory equipment of $4,000 per month. Overabsorbed or underabsorbed factory overhead is included in cost of goods sold.

(7) The cash balance on November 1 is expected to be $10,000.

Instructions Prepare the following for Gregory Company, assuming that the bank loan is granted. (Do not consider income taxes.)

a Working papers computing inventory forecasts by months for:
  (1) Finished goods production in units for October, November, and December, Year 8.
  (2) Raw materials purchases in pounds for October and November, Year 8.

b A forecasted income statement for the month of November, Year 8.

c A cash forecast for the month of November, Year 8, showing the beginning balance, receipts (itemized by dates of collection), disbursements, and ending balance.

12-8 Holden Corporation has three stores, each of which is an industry segment, in a state which recently enacted legislation permitting municipalities within the state to levy an income tax on corporations operating within their respective municipalities. The legislation established a uniform income tax rate which the municipalities may levy, and regulations which provided that the tax is to be computed on income derived within the taxing municipality after a reasonable and consistent allocation of nontraceable expenses. Nontraceable expenses, which have not been allocated to individual stores previously, include warehouse, delivery, and corporate office expenses.

Each of the municipalities in which Holden operates a store has levied the corporate income tax as provided by state legislation, and management is considering two plans for allocating nontraceable expenses to the stores. The Year 9 operating results for each store, before nontraceable expenses and income taxes, were as follows:

| | Store | | | |
	Hastings	Irving	Jamestown	Total
Net sales	$416,000	$353,600	$270,400	$1,040,000
Cost of goods sold	215,700	183,300	140,200	539,200
Gross profit on sales	$200,300	$170,300	$130,200	$ 500,800
Less local operating expenses:				
Fixed	$ 60,800	$ 48,750	$ 50,200	$ 159,750
Variable	54,700	64,220	27,448	146,368
Total	$115,500	$112,970	$ 77,648	$ 306,118
Income before nontraceable expenses and income taxes	$ 84,800	$ 57,330	$ 52,552	$ 194,682

Nontraceable expenses in Year 9 were as follows:

Warehouse and delivery expenses:

Warehouse depreciation $20,000

Warehouse operations 30,000

Delivery expenses .... 40,000 $ 90,000

Corporate office expenses:

Advertising $18,000

Corporate office salaries 37,000

Other corporate office expenses 28,000   83,000

Total nontraceable expenses $173,000

Additional information includes the following:
(1) One-fifth of the warehouse space is used to house the corporate office, and depreciation on this space is included in other corporate office expenses. Warehouse operating expenses vary with the quantity of merchandise sold.

(2) Delivery expense varies with distance and the number of deliveries. The distances from the warehouse to each store and the number of deliveries made in Year 9 were as follows:

Store	Miles	Number of deliveries
Hastings	120	140
Irving	200	64
Jamestown	100	104

(3) All advertising is arranged by the corporate office and is distributed in the areas in which stores are located.

Instructions

a For each of the following plans for allocating nontraceable expenses, compute the income of each store that would be subject to the municipal income tax levy on corporation income:

Plan 1 Allocate all nontraceable expenses on the basis of sales volume.

Plan 2 First, allocate corporate office salaries and other corporate office expenses evenly to warehouse operations and each store; second, allocate the resulting warehouse operations expenses, warehouse depreciation, and advertising to each store on the basis of sales volume; and third, allocate delivery expense to each store on the basis of delivery miles times number of deliveries.

b Which plan would you advise management to adopt? Explain.

12-9 Principia Corporation was incorporated January 2, Year 4, with a public issuance of 3 million shares of $1 par capital stock on that date for net proceeds of $5,750,000, net of out-of-pocket costs of the stock issuance. Immediately thereafter, Principia organized three wholly owned subsidiaries—Seattle Company and Boston Company in the United States, and London Company in the United Kingdom. Principia paid $1,500,000 cash for each subsidiary's 1,500,000 authorized shares of $1 par capital stock.

The consolidating financial statements working paper for Principia and subsidiaries is presented on pages 496–497. Other information is as follows:

(1) Each of the affiliated companies constitutes a different industry segment.

(2) Principia, Seattle, and Boston operate in the North America geographic area, and London operates in the Western Europe geographic area.

(3) None of the companies declared or paid dividends in Year 4.

(4) Each of the companies files separate income tax returns at an effective income tax rate of 60%.

(5) Intercompany receivables and payables represent loans or advances. (Receivables and payables arising from intercompany sales of merchandise were paid in full at December 31, Year 4.)

(6) $50,000 of Principia's selling, general, and administrative expenses represents nontraceable expenses allocable to each industry segment in the ratio of the *average* of each segment's Year 4 sales to outsiders and December 31, Year 4, plant asset balances. The remainder of Principia's selling, general, and administrative expenses represents general corporate expenses.

(7) Cash not required for each segment's current operations is forwarded to Principia for the purchase of short-term investments.

PRINCIPIA CORPORATION AND SUBSIDIARIES
Consolidating Financial Statements Working Paper
For Year Ended December 31, Year 4
(000 omitted)

	Principia Corporation	Seattle Company	Boston Company	London Company*	Consolidation eliminations increase (decrease)		Consolidated
Income Statement							
Revenue							
Net sales	$ 500	$ 400	$ 300	$ 200			$1,400
Intercompany sales	40	30	20	10	(b)	$ (100)	-0-
Intercompany investment income	32	-0-	-0-	-0-	(a)	(32)	-0-
Interest revenue	20	-0-	-0-	-0-			20
Total revenue	$ 592	$ 430	$ 320	$ 210		$ (132)	$1,420
Costs and expenses							
Cost of goods sold	$ 375	$ 320	$ 210	$ 130	(b)	$ (10)	$1,025
Intercompany cost of goods sold	32	24	16	8	(b)	(80)	-0-
Selling, general, and administrative expenses	133	60	40	50			283
Interest expense	-0-	6	9	7			22
Income taxes expense	15	12	27	9	(b)	(6)	57
Total costs and expenses	$ 555	$ 422	$ 302	$ 204		$ (96)	$1,387
Net income and retained earnings	$ 37	$ 8	$ 18	$ 6		$ (36)	$ 33

Balance Sheet

					Eliminations		
Assets							
Short-term investments	$ 80	$ -0-	$ -0-	$ -0-			$ 80
Inventories	500	600	700	800	(b)	$ (10)	2,590
Other current assets	700	800	600	500		6	2,600
Prepaid income taxes	-0-	-0-	-0-	-0-	(b)		6
Intercompany receivables (payables)	80	(60)	50	(70)			-0-
Investments in subsidiaries	4,532	-0-	-0-	-0-	(a)	(4,532)	-0-
Plant assets (net)	800	900	700	600			3,000
Intangible assets (net)	40	60	50	70			220
Total assets	$6,732	$2,300	$2,100	$1,900		$(4,536)	$8,496
Liabilities & Stockholders' equity							
Current liabilities	$ 945	$ 692	$ 432	$ 227			$2,296
6% bonds payable	-0-	100	150	167			417
Capital stock, $1 par	3,000	1,500	1,500	1,500	(a)	$(4,500)	3,000
Paid-in capital in excess of par	2,750	-0-	-0-	-0-			2,750
Retained earnings	37	8	18	6		(36)	33
Total liabilities & stockholders' equity	$6,732	$2,300	$2,100	$1,900		$(4,536)	$8,496

Explanation of consolidation eliminations
(a) To eliminate intercompany investment and related equity accounts of subsidiaries.
(b) To eliminate intercompany sales, cost of goods sold, and unrealized profits in inventories, and to defer income taxes applicable to unrealized profits.
* Amounts translated to dollars from British pounds

Instructions Prepare the following for Principia Corporation and subsidiaries for Year 4 in accordance with the provisions of *FASB Statement No. 14,* "Financial Reporting for Segments of a Business Enterprise":

a Working paper to determine whether each industry segment constitutes a significant segment.

b Disclosures of information about the operations of Principia Corporation and subsidiaries in different industries. Use the following format:

PRINCIPIA CORPORATION AND SUBSIDIARIES
Information about the Companies' Operations in Different Industries
For Year Ended December 31, Year 4
(000 omitted)

	Principia industry	Seattle industry	Boston industry	London industry	Elimi- nations	Con- solidated
Sales to unaffiliated customers	500	400	300	200		1400
Intersegment sales	40	30	20	10	(100)	
Total revenue ..	540	430	320	210		
Operating profit (loss)	407 135 118	344 75 11	226 51 43	138 59 13	(10)	175
Interest revenue ..						20
General corporate expenses						83
Interest expense .						22
Income before income taxes ...						90
Identifiable assets at Dec 31, Year 4	2040	2360	2050	1970	(4)	8416
Corporate assets						80
Total assets at Dec. 31, Year 4						8496

c Disclosures of information about the operations of Principia Corporation and subsidiaries in different geographic areas. Use the following format:

PRINCIPIA CORPORATION AND SUBSIDIARIES
Information about the Companies' Operations in Different Geographic Areas
For Year Ended December 31, Year 4
(000 omitted)

	North America	Western Europe	Elimi-nations	Con-solidated
Sales to unaffiliated customers	1200	200		1400
Transfers between geographic areas ...	90	10	⟨100⟩	
Total revenue	1290	210		
Operating profit	172	13	⟨10⟩	175
Interest revenue				20
General corporate expenses				83
Interest expense				22
Income before income taxes				90
Identifiable assets at Dec. 31, Year 4 ...	6470	1970	⟨4⟩	8416
Corporate assets				80
Total assets at Dec. 31, Year 4				8496

Supporting computations should be in good form. Footnotes are not required. Disregard requirements for disclosure of export sales, major customers, depreciation and amortization, and additions to plant assets.

13

FINANCIAL REPORTING BY MULTINATIONAL COMPANIES

A *multinational company* (sometimes called a *transnational corporation*) is a business enterprise which carries on operations in more than one nation, through a network of branches, divisions, and subsidiaries. These companies obtain raw materials and debt or equity capital in countries where such resources are plentiful. Multinational companies manufacture their products in nations where wages and other operating costs are lowest, and they sell their products in countries which provide the most profitable markets. Many of the largest multinational companies are headquartered in the United States. One source has estimated the total number of multinational companies in the United States at 200. Among the largest of these companies are General Motors Corporation, Exxon Corporation, Ford Motor Company, General Electric Company, and International Business Machines Corporation.

In this chapter, we shall discuss the three principal accounting and reporting issues of multinational companies—variations in international accounting standards, accounting for transactions involving foreign currencies, and consolidated or combined financial statements for a United States company and its foreign subsidiaries or branches.

VARIATIONS IN INTERNATIONAL ACCOUNTING STANDARDS

The wide variety of accounting standards and practices among the nations of the world presents a substantial problem to the multinational company. The international public accounting firm of Arthur Andersen & Co. commented upon this problem as follows:[1]

> No internationally recognized standards of accounting exist today. In the case of certain basic concepts, there is some consensus in practice among several of the more industrialized countries of the world, and this consensus is likely to be more pronounced in the case of larger multinational companies, especially those that are audited by accounting firms associated with an international practice. Yet even among the world's principal industrial countries, significant variations in accounting standards can be found. Since accounting problems have been approached from various perspectives, differing, and often conflicting, solutions have been developed.
>
> The principal problems that impede the development of internationally recognized accounting standards and that must be overcome before such standards can be established include:
>> Failure of accountants and users to consider or agree on the objectives of financial statements.
>> Differences in the extent to which the accounting profession has developed in various countries.
>> Influence of income tax laws on financial reporting.
>> Provisions of company laws.
>> Requirements of governmental and other regulatory bodies.
>> Failure to consider differences among countries in basic economic factors affecting financial reporting.
>> Inconsistencies in practices recommended by the accounting professions in different countries.

Actions to narrow differences in international accounting and auditing standards

Three organizations involved in the quest for greater uniformity in international accounting and auditing standards are the Accountants International Study Group, the International Accounting Standards Committee, and the International Federation of Accountants.

The Accountants International Study Group, formed jointly by the AICPA and the Institutes of Chartered Accountants of Canada, England and Wales, Scotland, and Ireland, prior to its recent disbanding issued a number of reports which surveyed accounting thought and practices of the Study Group's member countries. These reports covered areas such as materiality, consolidated financial statements, going-concern problems, interim financial reporting, independence of auditors, and revenue recognition.

The International Accounting Standards Committee originally comprised representatives from the professional accounting societies of Australia, Canada, France, Germany, Japan, Mexico, Netherlands, United Kingdom and Ireland, and the United States. Subsequently, associate membership status was given to accounting profession representatives of several other countries. The Committee's stated goal was to formulate and solicit general acceptance of basic international stand-

[1] *Accounting Standards for Business Enterprises throughout the World,* Arthur Andersen & Co. (Chicago: 1974), pp. 2–3.

ards in accounting, financial reporting, and auditing. Several of the pronouncements which the Committee has issued recommended accounting standards comparable in most respects to those used in the United States. The work of the International Accounting Standards Committee, which is headquartered in London, may in time exercise a great deal of influence on accounting standards for multinational companies.

The International Federation of Accountants, headquartered in New York, began with a membership of 63 professional accounting organizations of 49 countries. Its orientation is the professional practice of accounting and auditing; thus, it seeks international uniformity in education and training of accountants, professional ethics, and auditing standards.

ACCOUNTING FOR TRANSACTIONS INVOLVING FOREIGN CURRENCIES

In most countries, a foreign country's currency is treated as though it were a **commodity,** or a **money-market instrument.** In the United States, for example, foreign currencies are bought and sold by the international banking departments of commercial banks. These foreign currency transactions are entered into on behalf of the bank's multinational company customers, and for the bank's own account.

The buying and selling of foreign currencies as though they were commodities result in variations in the **exchange rate** between the currencies of two countries. For example, a daily newspaper at the end of 1977 quoted the exchange rates for foreign banknotes shown below:

Prices for foreign currencies

Prices for Foreign Banknotes, as Quoted on the Last Business Day (in dollars)			
	Buying	Selling	Buying year ago
Argentina (Peso)	.0015	.002	.003
Australia (Dollar)	1.06	1.13	1.02
Austria (Schilling)	.063	.066	.057
Belgium (Franc)	.027	.03	.026
Brazil (Cruzeiro)	.04	.05	.06
Britain (Pound)	1.83	1.93	1.67
Canada (Dollar)	.90	.92	.97
China-Taiwan (Dollar)	.023	.026	.02
Colombia (Peso)	.02	.03	.02
Denmark (Krone)	.16	.18	.16
Egypt (Pound)	1.28	1.35	1.28
Finland (Markka)	.23	.25	.25

(cont.)

Price for Foreign Banknotes, as Quoted on the Last Business Day (in dollars)

	Buying	Selling	Buying year ago
France (Franc)	.20	.22	.19
Greece (Drachma)	.023	.029	.02
Hong Kong (Dollar)	.20	.22	.18
India (Rupee)	.07	.11	.07
Indonesia (Rupiah)	.0016	.002	z
Italy (Lira)	.00100	.00125	.001
Japan (Yen)	.0039	.0043	.0032
Malaysia (Ringgit)	.34	.40	.34
Mexico (Peso)	.04	.05	.04
Netherlands (Guilder)	.43	.45	.39
New Zealand (Dollar)	.78	.95	.68
Norway (Krone)	.18	.20	.18
Pakistan (Rupee)	.04	.08	.05
Philippines (Peso)	.11	.14	.10
Portugal (Escudo)	.02	.026	.026
Singapore (Dollar)	.34	.41	.34
South Korea (Won)	.0013	.0020	.0013
Spain (Peseta)	.011	.013	.013
Sweden (Krona)	.20	.22	.23
Switzerland (Franc)	.4850	.5100	.40
Thailand (Baht)	.04	.05	z
Turkey (Lira)	.03	.05	.05
Uruguay (Peso)	.15	.18	.20
Venezuela (Bolivar)	.22	.24	.22
West Germany (Mark)	.45	.47	.41

Supplied by one major New York bank.
z—Not available.

The quoted rates are *spot rates* applicable to current exchanges of money. *Forward market rates* apply to foreign currency transactions which are to be consummated at a future date. The *agio* (or *spread*) between the buying rates and the selling rates represents the gross profit to a trader in foreign currency. If, for example, a United States multinational company required £10,000 (10,000 British pounds), it would have had to pay the foreign currency trader $19,300 (£10,000 × $1.93 selling spot rate) in the market for foreign banknotes illustrated above.

Factors influencing fluctuations in exchange rates include the individual nation's balance of payments surpluses or deficits, differing global rates of inflation, money-market variations (such as interest rates) in individual countries, capital investment levels, and monetary activities of central banks.

FASB Statement No. 8

In 1975, the FASB issued **FASB Statement No. 8,** "Accounting for the Translation of Foreign Currency Transactions and Foreign Currency Financial Statements." In that pronouncement, the FASB established uniform accounting standards for matters involving foreign currencies, thereby eliminating a number of questionable accounting practices which had been used by United States multinational companies. In the following sections, we shall discuss the accounting standards established by the FASB for foreign currency transactions.

Transactions involving foreign currencies

A multinational company headquartered in the United States engages in sales, purchases, and loans with independent entities in foreign countries, as well as with its branches, divisions, or subsidiaries in other countries. If the transactions with independent foreign entities are consummated in terms of the United States dollar, no accounting problems arise for the United States multinational company. The sale, purchase, or loan transaction is recorded in dollars in the accounting records of the United States company; the independent foreign entity must obtain the dollars necessary to complete the transaction through the foreign exchange department of its bank.

Often, however, the transactions outlined above are negotiated and settled in terms of the foreign entity's **local currency.** In such circumstances, the United States company must account for the transaction denominated in foreign currency in terms of United States dollars. This accounting, described as **foreign currency translation,** is accomplished by applying the exchange rate between the foreign currency and the United States dollar.

To illustrate, assume that on April 18, Year 6, Worldwide Corporation purchased merchandise from a West German supplier at a cost of 100,000 deutsche marks (symbol DM). The April 18, Year 6, selling spot rate was DM1 = $0.45. Because Worldwide was a customer of good credit standing, the West German supplier made the sale on 30-day open account.

Assuming that Worldwide uses a perpetual inventory system, the company would record the April 18, Year 6, purchase as follows:

Journal entry for purchase of merchandise from West German supplier	Inventories.. 45,000	
	Accounts Payable	45,000
	To record purchase on 30-day open account from West German supplier for DM 100,000, translated at selling spot rate of DM1 = $0.45 (DM 100,000 × $0.45 = $45,000).	

The *selling* spot rate was used in the above journal entry, because it was the rate at which the liability to the West German supplier could have been settled on April 18, Year 6.

Exchange gains and losses

During the period that the account payable to the West German supplier remains unpaid, the spot rate for deutsche marks may change. If the spot rate *decreases,* Worldwide will realize an *exchange gain;* if the spot rate *increases,* Worldwide will incur an *exchange loss.* Exchange gains and losses are included in the determination of net income for the period in which the spot rate changes.[2]

To illustrate, assume that on April 30, Year 6, the selling spot rate for deutsche marks was DM1 = $0.446, and Worldwide prepares financial statements monthly. The company would prepare the following journal entry with respect to the account payable to the West German supplier:

<table>
<tr><td rowspan="8">Journal entry to record exchange gain on date financial statements prepared</td><td colspan="3"></td></tr>
<tr><td>Accounts Payable ....</td><td>400</td><td></td></tr>
<tr><td>   Exchange Gains and Losses ....</td><td></td><td>400</td></tr>
<tr><td colspan="3">To record exchange gain applicable to April 18, Year 6, purchase from West German supplier, as follows:</td></tr>
<tr><td>   Liability recorded at April 18, Year 6 .... $45,000</td><td></td><td></td></tr>
<tr><td>   Liability translated at spot rate DM1 = $0.446</td><td></td><td></td></tr>
<tr><td>   (DM 100,000 × $0.446 = $44,600) .... 44,600</td><td></td><td></td></tr>
<tr><td>   Exchange gain .... $ 400</td><td></td><td></td></tr>
</table>

Assume further that the selling spot rate on May 18, Year 6, was DM1 = $0.44. The May 18, Year 6, journal entry for Worldwide's payment of the liability to the West German supplier would be as follows:

<table>
<tr><td rowspan="6">Journal entry for payment of liability to West German supplier</td><td colspan="3"></td></tr>
<tr><td>Accounts Payable ....</td><td>44,600</td><td></td></tr>
<tr><td>   Exchange Gains and Losses ....</td><td></td><td>600</td></tr>
<tr><td>   Cash ....</td><td></td><td>44,000</td></tr>
<tr><td colspan="3">To record payment for DM 100,000 draft to settle liability to West German supplier, and recognition of exchange gain (DM 100,000 × $0.44 = $44,000).</td></tr>
</table>

[2] *FASB Statement No. 8,* "Accounting for the Translation of Foreign Currency Transactions and Foreign Currency Financial Statements," FASB (Stamford: 1975), pp. 7–8, par. 17.

Two-Transaction Perspective and One-Transaction Perspective   The journal entries on pages 504-505 reflect the *two-transaction perspective* for viewing a foreign trade transaction. Under this concept, which was sanctioned by the FASB in *FASB Statement No. 8,* Worldwide's dealings with the West German supplier essentially were *two separate transactions.* One transaction was the purchase of the merchandise; the second was the purchase of the foreign currency required to pay the liability for the merchandise purchased. Supporters of the two-transaction perspective argue that an importer's or exporter's assumption of a risk in the exchange rate for a foreign currency is a financial decision, not a merchandising decision.

Advocates of an opposing viewpoint, the *one-transaction perspective,* maintain that Worldwide's total exchange gains of $1,000 ($400 + $600 = $1,000) on its transaction with the West German supplier should be applied to reduce the cost of the merchandise acquired from the West German supplier. Under this approach, Worldwide would not prepare a journal entry on April 30, Year 6, but would prepare the following journal entry on May 18, Year 6 (assuming that one-fourth of the merchandise purchased on April 18 remained unsold on May 18):

Journal entry under one-transaction perspective	Accounts Payable 45,000	
	Cost of Goods Sold ($1,000 × ¾)	750
	Inventories ($1,000 × ¼)	250
	Cash	44,000
	Payment for DM 100,000 draft (DM 100,000 × $0.44 = $44,000) to settle liability to West German supplier, and allocation of resultant exchange gain to cost of goods sold and to inventories.	

In effect, supporters of the one-transaction perspective for foreign trade activities consider the original amount recorded for a foreign merchandise purchase as an *estimate,* subject to adjustment when the exact cash outlay required for the purchase is known. Thus, the one-transaction proponents emphasize the *cash-payment* aspects of the transaction, rather than the *bargained-price* aspects as of the date of the foreign trade transaction.

The authors concur with the FASB's support for the two-transaction perspective for foreign trade activities and for loans receivable and payable denominated in a foreign currency. In the authors' view, the separability of the merchandising and financing aspects of a foreign trade transaction is an undeniable fact. In delaying payment of a foreign trade purchase transaction, an importer has made a decision to assume the risk of fluctuations in the exchange rate for the foreign currency required to pay for the purchase. This risk assumption is measured by the exchange gain or loss recorded at the time of payment for the purchase. To offset the exchange gain or loss against the cost of the merchandise would be a violation of the widely accepted accounting prohibition against setoffs.

Forward exchange contracts

The preceding example of accounting for exchange gains and losses assumed that Worldwide Corporation bore the risk of fluctuations in the exchange rate for deutsche marks. Worldwide could have **hedged** the risk on April 18, Year 6, by purchasing a 30-day forward exchange contract for DM 100,000 at the forward market rate. A **forward exchange contract** is an agreement to exchange currencies of different countries on a specified date at the forward market rate in effect when the contract was made. The forward market rate usually is higher than the spot rate for the currency, in recognition of the currency dealer's assumption of the risk of fluctuations in exchange rates. The forward market rate increases as the term to maturity of the forward exchange contract.

Accounting for Forward Exchange Contracts In *FASB Statement No. 8* and *FASB Statement No. 20,* "Accounting for Forward Exchange Contracts," the FASB established separate accounting standards for the following types of forward exchange contracts:

1 Contracts to hedge foreign currency commitments in general
2 Contracts to hedge an identifiable foreign currency commitment which meets specified conditions
3 Contracts for speculation in a foreign currency
4 Contracts to hedge a foreign currency exposed net asset or net liability position

We shall discuss the first three types of forward exchange contracts in this section. The fourth type of forward exchange contract is dealt with in the section on consolidated or combined financial statements of multinational companies.

Forward Exchange Contract to Hedge Foreign Currency Commitments in General Returning to the illustration of Worldwide Corporation, assume that on April 5, Year 6, in anticipation of initiating import transactions with various West German suppliers, Worldwide purchased a 60-day forward exchange contract for DM 500,000. Because Worldwide had no specific commitment to pay deutsche marks on April 5, Year 6, the forward exchange contract was not a hedge of an *identifiable* foreign currency commitment. Applicable exchange rates for deutsche marks on April 5, Year 6, were as follows:

Spot rates:	DM 1 =
Buying	$0.443
Selling	0.452
Forward market rates:	
30-day contracts	0.464
60-day contracts	0.478
90-day contracts	0.489

Thus, the cost of the DM 500,000, 60-day forward exchange contract purchased by Worldwide on April 5, Year 6, was $239,000 (DM 500,000 × $0.478 = $239,000).

The *discount* on the forward exchange contract, measured by the foreign currency amount of the contract multiplied by the difference between the forward market rate and the spot rate at the date of the contract, is a financing cost which is apportioned to expense over the life of the contract.

Worldwide's April 5, Year 6, journal entry to record the purchase of the forward exchange contract would be as follows:

Investment in Forward Exchange Contract (DM 500,000 ×		
$0.452 selling spot rate)	226,000	
Deferred Interest [DM 500,000 × ($0.478 − $0.452)]	13,000	
Forward Exchange Contract Payable (DM 500,000 ×		
$0.478 forward market rate)		239,000
To record purchase of DM 500,000 forward exchange contract		
for 60 days at forward market rate of DM 1 = $0.478.		

During the 60-day term of the DM 500,000 forward exchange contract, Worldwide would realize an exchange gain or loss whenever the *spot rate* for deutsche marks changed. For example, assuming that the selling spot rate for deutsche marks on April 30, Year 6, was DM 1 = $0.446 and that Worldwide prepares monthly financial statements, the following journal entry would be required on April 30, Year 6:

Exchange Gains and Losses [DM 500,000 × ($0.452 − $0.446)]...	3,000	
Interest Expense ($13,000 × 25/60)	5,417	
Investment in Forward Exchange Contract		3,000
Deferred Interest		5,417
To recognize exchange loss on forward exchange contract result-		
ing from decrease of spot exchange rate for deutsche marks to		
$0.446 from $0.452, and to amortize expired discount to April 30,		
Year 6, on contract.		

If the selling spot rate for deutsche marks was DM 1 = $0.449 on May 31, Year 6, the following journal entry would be appropriate on that date:

Journal entry to record exchange gain on forward exchange contract	Investment in Forward Exchange Contract [DM 500,000 × ($0.449 − $0.446)] 1,500
	Interest Expense ($13,000 × 31/60) 6,717
	Exchange Gains and Losses............................ 1,500
	Deferred Interest 6,717
	To recognize exchange gain on forward exchange contract resulting from increase of spot exchange rate for deutsche marks to $0.449 from $0.446, and to amortize expired discount to May 31, Year 6, on contract.

Assuming a selling spot rate of DM = $0.451 on June 4, Year 6, the maturity date of Worldwide's 60-day forward exchange contract, the two journal entries would be:

Journal entry to record exchange gain on forward exchange contract	Investment in Forward Exchange Contract [DM 500,000 × ($0.451 − $0.449)] 1,000
	Interest Expense ($13,000 × 4/60) 866
	Exchange Gains and Losses............................ 1,000
	Deferred Interest 866
	To recognize exchange gain on forward exchange contract resulting from increase of spot exchange rate for deutsche marks to $0.451 from $0.449, and to amortize expired discount to June 4, Year 6, on contract.
Journal entry to record payment of forward exchange contract	Investment in Deutsche Marks (DM 500,000 × $0.451) 225,500
	Forward Exchange Contract Payable (DM 500,000 × $0.478) ... 239,000
	Investment in Forward Exchange Contract 225,500
	Cash 239,000
	To record payment of DM 500,000 forward exchange contract, and receipt of deutsche marks.

After the preceding journal entries were posted, Worldwide's Investment in Forward Exchange Contract and Deferred Interest ledger accounts would appear as follows:

Selected
ledger
accounts
related to
forward
exchange
contract

Investment in Forward Exchange Contract

Date	Explanation of transactions	Debit	Credit	Balance
4/5/6	Purchase of 60-day, DM 500,000 contract	226,000		226,000 dr
4/30/6	Exchange loss		3,000	223,000 dr
5/31/6	Exchange gain	1,500		224,500 dr
6/4/6	Exchange gain	1,000		225,500 dr
6/4/6	Receipt of deutsche marks		225,500	-0-

Deferred Interest

Date	Explanation of transactions	Debit	Credit	Balance
4/5/6	Discount on forward exchange contract	13,000		13,000 dr
4/30/6	Amortization		5,417	7,583 dr
5/31/6	Amortization		6,717	866 dr
6/4/6	Amortization		866	-0-

Summarizing, Worldwide incurred interest expense of $13,000, and a net exchange loss of $500 ($3,000 − $1,500 − $1,000 = $500), during the 60-day period of its DM 500,000 forward exchange contract. In return Worldwide benefited from knowing what its total outlay for deutsche marks would be on June 4, Year 6, the maturity date of the forward exchange contract. Upon receipt of the deutsche marks, Worldwide could pay for imports from West German suppliers at a known dollar amount as the suppliers' invoices became due.

Forward Exchange Contract to Hedge Identifiable Foreign Currency Commitment In *FASB Statement No.8* and *FASB Statement No. 20,* the FASB established the following conditions for a forward exchange contract intended to hedge an identifiable foreign currency commitment:[3]

1 The life of the forward contract extends from the foreign currency commitment date to the anticipated transaction date or a later date.

2 The forward contract is denominated in the same currency as the foreign currency commitment.

3 The foreign currency commitment is firm and uncancelable.

For a forward exchange contract meeting the above conditions, and in an amount not exceeding the related foreign currency commitment, the following are deferred and included in the dollar amount of the related foreign currency transaction:

1 The discount or premium on the forward exchange contract applicable to the period of the commitment

[3] Ibid., p. 11, par. 27; *FASB Statement No. 20,* "Accounting for Forward Exchange Contracts," FASB (Stamford: 1977), p. 5, par. 13.

2 Exchange gains during the term of the contract

3 Exchange losses during the term of the contract, unless deferral would cause the recognition of a loss, such as a write-down of inventories to net realizable value, in a subsequent period

The amount of a forward exchange contract meeting the conditions for a hedge of an identifiable foreign currency commitment may exceed the amount of the related commitment. If so, any exchange gain or loss applicable to the amount of the forward exchange contract in excess of the commitment is deferred only to the extent that the forward contract provides a hedge on an *after–income taxes* basis. Such a deferred gain or loss is offset against the related income taxes on the exchange gains or losses in the period the income taxes are reflected in the accounting records. Exchange gains and losses which are not deferred are reflected in the income statement when the exchange rate changes.

To illustrate the accounting for a forward exchange contract which is a hedge of an identifiable foreign currency commitment, assume that Worldwide Corporation on May 1, Year 6, issued a purchase order to a West German supplier at a total price of DM 175,000. Delivery and payment were scheduled for June 30, Year 6.

To hedge against fluctuations in the exchange rate for deutsche marks, Worldwide purchased on May 1, Year 6, a firm, uncancelable forward exchange contract for the receipt of DM 175,000 on June 30, Year 6. Selected exchange rates for deutsche marks during Year 6 were as follows:

		DM 1 =		
Exchange rates for deutsche marks		**May 1**	**May 31**	**June 30**
Spot rates:				
Buying		$0.454	$0.449	$0.455
Selling		0.462	0.458	0.466
Forward market rates:				
30-day contracts		0.477	0.472	0.487
60-day contracts		0.493	0.488	0.495
90-day contracts		0.519	0.502	0.520

Worldwide's journal entries for purchase of the forward exchange contract, receipt of the merchandise from the West German supplier, payment of the forward exchange contract, and payment of the supplier's invoice, are presented on pages 512–513.

The result of the preceding journal entries is that the merchandise purchased by Worldwide from the West German supplier is valued at the total cost, including financing costs, of the transaction with the German supplier. These costs are summarized as follows:

CHAPTER 13

<table>
<tr><td rowspan="5">Total cost of merchandise purchased from West German supplier</td><td>Invoice cost of merchandise (DM 175,000 × $0.466 selling spot rate on date received) ....</td><td>$81,550</td></tr>
<tr><td>Discount on forward exchange contract for deutsche marks ....</td><td>5,425</td></tr>
<tr><td>Net deferred exchange gain on forward exchange contract ....</td><td>(700)</td></tr>
<tr><td>Total cost of merchandise ....</td><td>$86,275</td></tr>
</table>

The illustrated accounting is appropriate because the forward exchange contract was acquired to hedge an identifiable foreign currency commitment rather than general, unspecified commitments. Purchase of such a contract enabled Worldwide to predetermine its total cost of the merchandise purchased from the West German supplier at $86,275, the total cash outlay for the forward exchange contract.

WORLDWIDE CORPORATION
General Journal

Year 6

May 1 Investment in Forward Exchange Contract
(DM 175,000 × $0.462 selling spot rate) 80,850
Deferred Interest 5,425
Forward Exchange Contract Payable
(DM 175,000 × $0.493 forward market rate) .. 86,275
To record purchase of DM 175,000 forward exchange
contract for 60 days, at forward market rate of
DM 1 = $0.493.

31 Deferred Exchange Gains and Losses
[DM 175,000 × ($0.462 − $0.458)] 700
Investment in Forward Exchange Contract ... 700
To defer exchange loss resulting from decrease of
spot exchange rate for deutsche marks to DM 1 =
$0.458 from DM 1 = $0.462.

June 30 Investment in Forward Exchange Contract
[DM 175,000 × ($0.466 − $0.458)] 1,400
Deferred Exchange Gains and Losses 1,400
To defer exchange gain resulting from increase of
spot exchange rate for deutsche marks to DM 1 =
$0.466 from DM 1 = $0.458.

(continued)

WORLDWIDE CORPORATION
General Journal (concluded)

Year 6

June 30	*Inventories ($81,550 − $700 + $5,425)*	86,275	
	Deferred Exchange Gains and Losses		
	($1,400 − $700)	700	
	Deferred Interest		5,425
	Accounts Payable (DM 175,000 × $0.466)		81,550
	To record purchase of merchandise from West German supplier for DM 175,000, translated at selling exchange rate of DM 1 = $0.466, and to increase cost of merchandise for discount on forward exchange contract, less deferred net exchange gain on contract.		
30	*Forward Exchange Contract Payable*	86,275	
	Investment in Deutsche Marks	81,550	
	Investment in Forward Exchange Contract ($80,850 − $700 + $1,400)		81,550
	Cash		86,275
	To record payment of forward exchange contract, and receipt of deutsche marks.		
30	*Accounts Payable*	81,550	
	Investment in Deutsche Marks		81,550
	To record settlement of liability to West German supplier.		

Forward Exchange Contract for Speculation   There is no separate accounting treatment for the discount or premium on a forward exchange contract acquired for speculation in the foreign currency involved. The speculation forward exchange contract is similar to a short-term investment in a marketable bond which will not be held to maturity; thus, the accounting for discount or premium is similar for these two investments.

The exchange gain or loss on a speculation forward exchange contract is computed by multiplying the foreign currency amount of the contract by the difference between (1) the forward market rate available for the remainder of the contract and (2) the contracted forward market rate or the forward market rate last used to compute an exchange gain or loss. Exchange gains and losses on speculation forward exchange contracts are included in the computation of net income for the period in which the forward market rate changes.

To illustrate, assume the following exchange rates for deutsche marks during Year 6:

Exchange rates for deutsche marks	DM 1 =		
	May 1	May 31	June 30
Spot rates:			
Buying	$0.454	$0.449	$0.455
Selling	0.462	0.458	0.466
Forward market rates:			
30-day contracts	0.477	0.472	0.487
60-day contracts	0.493	0.488	0.495
90-day contracts	0.519	0.502	0.520

On May 1, Year 6, Speculators, Inc., purchased a 60-day forward exchange contract for DM 200,000, in anticipation of an increase in the spot rates for deutsche marks during the 60-day period.

The journal entries of Speculators, Inc., for the forward exchange contract, assuming that the company prepares monthly financial statements, are presented below.

SPECULATORS, INC.
General Journal

Year 6

May 1 Investment in Forward Exchange Contract
    (DM 200,000 × $0.493) 98,600
        Forward Exchange Contract Payable 98,600
    To record purchase of DM 200,000 forward exchange contract for 60 days, at forward market rate of DM 1 = $0.493.

31 Exchange Gains and Losses
    [DM 200,000 × ($0.493 − $0.472)] 4,200
        Investment in Forward Exchange Contract ... 4,200
    To recognize exchange loss on forward exchange contract resulting from difference between contracted forward market rate (DM 1 = $0.493) and forward market rate for remaining 30-day term of contract (DM 1 = $0.472).

June 30 Investment in Deutsche Marks 94,400
    Forward Exchange Contract Payable 98,600
        Investment in Forward Exchange Contract
        ($98,600 − $4,200) 94,400
        Cash 98,600
    To record payment of DM 200,000 forward exchange contract, and receipt of deutsche marks.

(cont.)

> **SPECULATORS, INC.**
> **General Journal (concluded)**
>
> Year 6
> June 30   Cash (DM 200,000 × $0.455) 91,000
>   Exchange Gains and Losses [DM 200,000 ×
>   ($0.472 − $0.455)] 3,400
>   Investment in Deutsche Marks 94,400
>   To record sale of DM 200,000 at buying spot rate of
>   DM 1 = $0.455, and resultant exchange loss.

The increase in the spot rates for deutsche marks which Speculators, Inc., had anticipated did not occur; thus, the company incurred an exchange loss of $7,600 ($4,200 + $3,400 = $7,600) on the forward exchange contract for speculation.

Summary of Accounting for Forward Exchange Contracts   The preceding discussion of accounting for forward exchange contracts is summarized in the table on page 516.

CONSOLIDATED OR COMBINED FINANCIAL STATEMENTS FOR FOREIGN SUBSIDIARIES OR BRANCHES

When a United States multinational company prepares consolidated or combined financial statements which include the assets, liabilities, and operations of foreign subsidiaries or branches, the United States company must *translate* the amounts in the financial statements of the foreign entities from *local currency* to United States dollars. Similar treatment must be given to the assets and income statement amounts associated with foreign subsidiaries which are not consolidated, and with other foreign investees for which the United States company uses the equity method of accounting.

If the exchange rate for the foreign currency of the country in which a foreign subsidiary or branch operated remained constant instead of fluctuating, translation of the investee's financial statements to United States dollars would be simple. All financial statement amounts would be translated to United States dollars at the constant exchange rates.

We have already noted, however, that exchange rates fluctuate frequently. Thus, the accountant charged with translating amounts in a foreign investee's financial statements to United States dollars faces a problem similar to that involving inventory valuation during a period of price fluctuations. Which exchange rate or rates should be used to translate the foreign investee's financial statements? A number of answers were proposed for this question prior to the issuance of *FASB*

Accounting for Forward Exchange Contracts

Purpose of contract	Discount or premium on contract		Exchange gains or losses on contract	
	Measurement	Accounting	Measurement	Accounting
Hedge of foreign currency commitments in general	Difference between forward market rate and spot rate at date of contract	Apportioned to expense over term of contract	Difference between spot rate at date of measurement and date of contract (or date of most recent measurement)	Included in income statement for period in which exchange rate changes
Hedge of identifiable foreign currency commitment	Difference between forward market rate and spot rate at date of contract	Amount related to period of commitment deferred and included in dollar basis of related foreign currency transaction	Difference between spot rate at date of measurement and date of contract (or date of most recent measurement)	Gains deferred and included in dollar basis of related foreign currency transaction to extent amount of contract does not exceed amount of commitment. Gain on amount in excess of commitment deferred to extent amount provides a hedge on an after–income tax basis. Gain attributable to remainder of any excess included in income statement for period in which exchange rate changes Losses comparably deferred unless deferral would lead to recognition of loss in subsequent period
Speculation	Difference between forward market rate and spot rate at date of contract	Not accounted for separately	Difference between forward market rate for remaining term of contract and contract rate or rate last used to compute exchange gain or loss	Included in income statement for period in which exchange rate changes

Statement No. 8. The several methods for foreign currency translation may be grouped into three basic classes: *current/noncurrent, monetary/ nonmonetary,* and *current rate.* (A fourth method, the *temporal method,* essentially is the same as the monetary/nonmonetary method.) The three classes differ principally in translation techniques for balance sheet accounts.

Current/noncurrent method

In the *current/noncurrent method* of translation, current assets and current liabilities are translated at the exchange rate in effect at the balance sheet date of the foreign investee (the *current rate*). All other assets and liabilities, and the elements of owners' equity, are translated at the *historical rates* in effect at the time the assets, liabilities, and equities first were recorded in the accounting records. In the income statement, depreciation and amortization are translated at historical rates applicable to the related assets, while all other expenses and revenue items are translated at an *average* exchange rate for the accounting period.

The current/noncurrent method of translating foreign investees' financial statements was sanctioned by the AICPA for many years following World War II. This method supposedly best reflected the *liquidity* aspects of the foreign investee's financial position. However, the current/noncurrent method has few adherents among today's accountants. The principal theoretical objection to the current/noncurrent method is that, with respect to inventories, it represents a departure from historical cost. Inventories are translated at the *current rate,* rather than at *historical rates,* when the current/noncurrent method of translating foreign currency accounts is followed.

Monetary/nonmonetary method

The *monetary/nonmonetary method* of translating foreign currencies focuses upon the characteristics of assets and liabilities of the foreign investee, rather than upon their balance sheet classifications. This method is founded upon the same monetary/nonmonetary aspects of assets and liabilities that are employed in general price-level accounting. *Monetary assets and liabilities*—those representing claims or obligations expressed in a fixed monetary amount—are translated at the current exchange rate. All other assets, liabilities, and owners' equity accounts are translated at appropriate historical rates. In the income statement, average exchange rates are applied to all revenue and expenses except depreciation, amortization, and cost of goods sold, which are translated at appropriate historical rates.

Supporters of the monetary/nonmonetary method emphasized its retention of the historical cost concept in the foreign investee's financial statements. Because the foreign investee's financial statements are consolidated or combined with those of the United States multinational company, consistent accounting principles are applied in the consolidated or combined financial statements.

Current rate method

Critics of the monetary/nonmonetary method point out that this method emphasizes the *parent company* aspects of a foreign investee's financial position and operating results. By reflecting the foreign investee's changes in assets and liabilities, and operating results, as though they were made in the parent company's *reporting currency,* the monetary/nonmonetary method misstates the actual financial position and operating relationships of the foreign investee.

The critics of the monetary/nonmonetary method of foreign currency translation have proposed the *current rate method.* Under the current rate method, all balance sheet accounts other than owners' equity accounts are translated at the current exchange rate. Owners' equity accounts are translated at historical rates.

To emphasize the *local currency* aspects of the foreign investee's operations, all revenue and expense may be translated at the current rate. Otherwise, an average exchange rate is used for all revenue and expenses.

Standards for translation established by the FASB

In *FASB Statement No. 8,* the FASB did not accept entirely any of the three translation methods described above. Instead, adapting most of the features of the monetary/nonmonetary method, the FASB established the following standards for translation of foreign currency financial statements:[4]

> ... balances representing cash and amounts receivable or payable that are denominated in the local currency shall be translated into dollars at the current rate.
>
> For assets and liabilities other than those described ... (above) ... the particular measurement basis used shall determine the translation rate. Several measurement bases are used in financial accounting under present generally accepted accounting principles. A measurement may be based on a price in a past exchange (for example, historical cost), a price in a current purchase exchange (for example, replacement cost), or a price in a current sale exchange (for example, market price). Foreign statements may employ various measurement bases. Accordingly, accounts in foreign statements that are carried at exchange prices shall be translated in a manner that retains their measurement bases as follows:
>
> a) Accounts carried at prices in past exchanges (past prices) shall be translated at historical rates.
>
> b) Accounts carried at prices in current purchase or sale exchanges (current prices) or future exchanges (future prices) shall be translated at the current rate.
>
> Revenue and expense transactions shall be translated in a manner that produces approximately the same dollar amounts that would have resulted had the underlying transactions been translated into dollars on the dates they occurred. Since separate translation of each transaction is usually impractical, the specified result can be achieved by using an average rate for the period. However, revenue and expenses that relate to assets and liabilities translated at historical rates shall be translated at the historical rates used to translate the related assets or liabilities.

The table on page 519 summarizes the FASB's provisions for translation of assets and liabilities denominated in a foreign currency.

[4] *FASB Statement No. 8, p. 6,* pars. 12 and 13.

Rates Used to Translate Assets and Liabilities

	Translation rates	
	Current	Historical
Assets		
Cash on hand and demand and time deposits	X	
Marketable equity securities:		
Carried at cost		X
Carried at current fair value	X	
Accounts and notes receivable and related unearned discount	X	
Allowance for doubtful accounts and notes receivable	X	
Inventories:		
Carried at cost		X
Carried at current replacement price or current selling price	X	
Carried at net realizable value	X	
Carried at contract price (produced under fixed-price		
contracts)	X	
Short-term prepayments		X
Refundable deposits	X	
Advances to unconsolidated subsidiaries	X	
Plant assets		X
Accumulated depreciation		X
Cash surrender value of life insurance	X	
Patents, trademarks, licenses, and formulas		X
Goodwill		X
Other intangible assets		X
Liabilities		
Accounts and notes payable and bank overdrafts	X	
Accrued expenses payable	X	
Accrued losses on firm purchase commitments	X	
Refundable deposits	X	
Deferred revenue		X
Bonds payable or other long-term debt	X	
Unamortized premium or discount on bonds or notes payable	X	
Accrued pension obligations	X	
Obligations under warranties	X	

SOURCE: Adapted from *FASB Statement No. 8,* "Accounting for the Translation of Foreign Currency Transactions and Foreign Currency Financial Statements," FASB (Stamford: 1975, p. 20.

The appropriate historical or current exchange rate generally would be the rate applicable to conversion of the foreign currency for dividend remittances.[5] Accordingly, a United States multinational company having foreign branches, investees, or subsidiaries typically would use the

[5] Ibid., p. 13, par. 30.

buying spot rate at the balance sheet date or applicable historical date to translate the foreign currency financial statements.

In recognition of the complexity of a strict application of historical rates to assets such as inventories and to related cost of goods sold, the FASB permitted the use of averages or other methods of approximation, provided the results obtained did not differ materially from amounts developed from application of required translation standards.[6] The FASB specifically required the use of weighted averages of applicable exchange rates for translation of income statement items not translated at historical rates.[7]

Also in *FASB Statement No. 8,* the FASB required interperiod income tax allocation for timing differences in the recognition of exchange gains and losses for financial accounting and for income tax accounting.

Illustration of translation of foreign currency financial statements

In this section, we shall illustrate the translation of a foreign branch's financial statements. To simplify the illustration, we shall model it upon the Rex Pen Company home office–branch illustration in Chapter 4, with inventories billed to the branch in excess of cost. We shall assume further that both the home office and the branch use the perpetual inventory system, and that the branch is located in France.

The Year 1 transactions illustrated in Chapter 4 are repeated below. Following each transaction is the exchange rate for French francs (F) at the date of the transaction.

Transactions for Year 1
(1) Cash of $1,000 was sent to the branch (F1 = $0.20).
(2) Merchandise with a cost of $60,000 was shipped to the branch at a billed price of $90,000 (F1 = $0.20).
(3) Equipment was purchased by the branch for F 2,500, to be carried in the home office accounting records (F1 = $0.20).
(4) Sales by the branch on credit amounted to F 500,000 (F1 = $0.16). Cost of goods sold was F 337,500.
(5) Collections of accounts receivable by the branch amounted to F 248,000 (F1 = $0.25).
(6) Payments for operating expenses by the branch totaled F 80,000 (F1 = $0.25).
(7) Cash of F 156,250 was remitted by the branch to home office (F1 = $0.24).
(8) Operating expenses incurred by the home office charged to the branch totaled $3,000 (F1 = $0.24).
The exchange rate at the end of Year 1 was F1 = $0.23.

The preceding transactions would be recorded by the home office and by the branch with the journal entries on page 521.

[6] Ibid., pp. 11–12, par. 29.
[7] Ibid., p. 22, par. 45.

REX PEN COMPANY
Home Office and Branch General Journals
For Year 1

Home Office Accounting Records ($)			Branch Accounting Records (F)		
(1) Investment in			Cash	5,000	
Branch X	1,000		Home Office		5,000
Cash		1,000			
(2) Investment in					
Branch X	90,000		Inventories	450,000	
Allowance			Home Office		450,000
for Over-					
valuation					
of Inven-					
tories:					
Branch X		30,000			
Inventories		60,000			
(3) Equipment:			Home Office	2,500	
Branch X	500		Cash		2,500
Investment					
in Branch					
X		500			
(4) None			Accounts		
			Receivable	500,000	
			Cost of Goods		
			Sold	337,500	
			Sales		500,000
			Inventories .		337,500
(5) None			Cash	248,000	
			Accounts		
			Receivable		248,000
(6) None			Operating		
			Expenses	80,000	
			Cash		80,000
(7) Cash	37,500		Home Office	156,250	
Investment			Cash		156,250
in Branch					
X		37,500			
(8) Investment in			Operating		
Branch X	3,000		Expenses	12,500	
Operating			Home Office		12,500
Expenses		3,000			

In the home office accounting records, the Investment in Branch X ledger account would appear (in dollars before the accounts are closed), as follows:

Home office reciprocal account with branch (in dollars)

Investment in Branch X

Explanation of transactions	Debit	Credit	Balance
Cash sent to branch	$ 1,000		$ 1,000 dr
Merchandise shipped to branch	90,000		91,000 dr
Equipment purchased by branch, recorded in home office accounting records		$ 500	90,500 dr
Cash received from branch		37,500	53,000 dr
Operating expenses billed to branch	3,000		56,000 dr

In the branch accounting records, the Home Office ledger account would appear (in francs before the accounts are closed), as follows:

Branch reciprocal account with home office (in francs)

Home Office

Explanation of transactions	Debit	Credit	Balance
Cash received from home office		F 5,000	F 5,000 cr
Merchandise received from home office		450,000	455,000 cr
Equipment purchased by branch	F 2,500		452,500 cr
Cash sent to home office	156,250		296,250 cr
Operating expenses billed by home office		12,500	308,750 cr

The branch trial balance (in francs) would be as follows at the end of Year 1:

REX PEN COMPANY
Branch X Trial Balance
December 31, Year 1

	Debit	Credit
Cash	F 14,250	
Accounts receivable	252,000	
Inventories	112,500	
Home office		F308,750
Sales		500,000
Cost of goods sold	337,500	
Operating expenses	92,500	
Totals	F808,750	F808,750

Translation of Branch Trial Balance Translation of the branch trial balance is illustrated below:

REX PEN COMPANY
Translation of Branch X Trial Balance
December 31, Year 1

	Balance, francs dr (cr)	× Exchange rate	= Balance, dollars dr (cr)
Cash	F 14,250	$0.23 (1)	$ 3,278
Accounts receivable	252,000	0.23 (1)	57,960
Inventories	112,500	0.20 (2)	22,500
Home office	(308,750)	(3)	(56,000)
Sales	(500,000)	0.215 (4)	(107,500)
Cost of goods sold	337,500	0.20 (2)	67,500
Operating expenses	92,500	0.215 (4)	19,887
Subtotals	F -0-		$ 7,625
Exchange gain	-0-		(7,625)
Totals	F -0-		$ -0-

(1) Current rate (at end of Year 1)
(2) Historical rate (when goods were shipped to branch by home office)
(3) Balance of Investment in Branch X account in home office accounting records
(4) Average of beginning (F1 = $0.20) and ending (F1 = $0.23) exchange rates for Year 1

In the review of the translation of the branch trial balance the following should be noted:

1 Monetary assets are translated at the current rate; the single nonmonetary asset—inventories—is translated at the appropriate historical rate.

2 To achieve quickly the same result as a translation of the Home Office account transactions at appropriate historical rates, the balance of the home office's Investment in Branch X account (in dollars) is substituted for the branch's Home Office account (in francs). All equity accounts—regardless of legal form of the investee—are translated at historical rates.

3 A simple average of beginning-of-year and end-of-year exchange rates is used to translate revenue and expense accounts other than cost of goods sold, which is translated at the appropriate historical rates. In practice, a quarterly, monthly, or even daily weighted average might be computed.

4 A balancing figure labeled as an "exchange gain" is used to reconcile the total debits and total credits of the branch's translated trial balance. This exchange gain is included in the determination of the branch's net income for Year 1.

After the branch trial balance has been translated from francs to dollars, combined financial statements for home office and branch may be prepared as illustrated previously in Chapter 4.

Translation of financial statements of foreign subsidiaries

In the translation of a foreign subsidiary's financial statements from the local currency to United States dollars prior to consolidation with the United States parent company, techniques comparable to those used for translation of branches are appropriate. Monetary assets and liabilities of the foreign subsidiary other than intercompany items are translated at the current exchange rate; nonmonetary assets and liabilities and stockholders' equity accounts are translated at appropriate historical rates. The foreign subsidiary's arm's-length revenue and expenses other than depreciation, amortization, and cost of goods sold are translated at average exchange rates. The latter three expenses are translated at appropriate historical rates.

All intercompany receivables, payables, revenue, and expenses in the foreign subsidiary's accounting records are translated at the United States dollar amounts in the comparable United States parent company accounts. This technique represents a "shortcut" translation of the subsidiary's accounts at appropriate exchange rates.

If the foreign subsidiary is not consolidated with the United States parent company, the same translation techniques described above are necessary before the parent company accounts for the foreign subsidiary's operations under the equity method of accounting described in Chapter 8.

Forward exchange contracts for foreign currency exposed positions

A multinational company's investment in a foreign branch, subsidiary, or influenced investee creates an exposed net asset position or an exposed net liability position. A foreign investee with an excess of assets translated at the current rate over liabilities translated at the current rate has an *exposed net asset position.* For example, Branch X of Rex Pen Company (illustrated in the preceding section) has an exposed net asset position of F266,250 (cash, F14,250 + accounts receivable, F252,000 = F266,250). An *exposed net liability position* results from the reverse situation.

An investor multinational company may sell or purchase forward exchange contracts to hedge its foreign investee's exposed net asset or net liability position. The discount or premium on such a forward exchange contract is amortized to expense over the term of the contract, and the exchange gains or losses are reflected in the income statement for the period in which the exchange rate changes.[8]

Financial statement disclosures of foreign currency matters

In *FASB Statement No. 8,* the FASB required the following disclosures in a multinational company's financial statements or in the notes accompaning the financial statements:[9]

[8] Ibid., p. 9, par. 23.
[9] Ibid., pp. 13–14, pars. 32, 33, 34.

The aggregate exchange gain or loss included in determining net income for the period shall be disclosed in the financial statements or in a note thereto. For the purpose of that disclosure, gains and losses on forward contracts ... (other than contracts to hedge identifiable foreign currency commitments) ... shall be considered exchange gains or losses.

Effects of rate changes on reported results of operations, other than the effects included in the disclosure required by (the above) paragraph ... shall, if practicable, be described and quantified. If quantified, the methods and the underlying assumptions used to determine the estimated effects shall be explained. ...

An enterprise's financial statements shall not be adjusted for a rate change that occurs after the date of the financial statements or after the date of the foreign statements of a foreign operation that are consolidated or combined with or accounted for by the equity method in the financial statements of the enterprise. However, disclosure of the rate change and its effects, if significant, may be necessary.

The note below, from the 1977 Annual Report of International Telephone and Telegraph Corporation, illustrates several of the disclosure requirements included in *FASB Statement No. 8:*

Foreign Currency Translation: Generally, net assets are translated from foreign currencies into United States dollars at the rates of exchange in effect at year end, except for inventories and certain other investments, deferred business development costs, property and certain deferred taxes which are translated at historic rates of exchange.

Income accounts are translated at the average rates of exchange prevailing during the year, except for those accounts related to assets and liabilities translated at historic rates of exchange, which are similarly translated at historic rates. Gain or loss on forward exchange contracts is recognized when translation rates are changed to reflect new currency values.

Including insurance and finance subsidiaries, net foreign exchange gains (losses) arising from the conversion of foreign currencies and the translation of balance sheet items are included in income as shown below (in thousands of dollars):

	1977	1976
Before minority interest and income taxes	*$(70,393)*	*$ (7,227)*
After minority interest and income taxes	*(66,970)*	*(13,203)*
Per share	*(.50)*	*(.10)*

In addition, translation of the 1977 income statement at average rates of exchange that differed from those used in the prior year affected earnings favorably by $72,124,000 or $.54 per share.

Criticism of *FASB Statement No. 8*

In issuing *FASB Statement No. 8,* the FASB brought to the financial statements of United States multinational companies the uniformity which had been lacking in the past. Prior to the issuance of *FASB Statement No.*

8, some multinational companies used the current/noncurrent method for translating foreign currency financial statements, but many other companies used the monetary/nonmonetary method or a hybrid method. Many multinational companies deferred net exchange gains from translation of foreign currency financial statements, and offset subsequent exchange losses against the deferred gains. The result was a "smoothing" of the effects of exchange gains and losses.

FASB Statement No. 8, with its requirement for the inclusion in the income statement of exchange gains and losses, except those deferred as described on pages 510–513, brought severe criticism from many multinational companies. These companies complained that the wide fluctuations in exchange rates for many foreign currencies caused significant "paper" fluctuations in net income. Such fluctuations, claimed the critics, were beyond the control of management and were confusing to users of financial statements. Supporters of *FASB Statement No. 8* countered that fluctuations in exchange rates are historical facts and that deferring exchange gains and losses, rather than recognizing them as they occur, is misleading to users of financial statements.

In response to the criticism described above, the FASB commissioned a research project to determine any impact of *FASB Statement No 8* on the market prices of multinational companies' common stock.

REVIEW QUESTIONS

1 What is a *multinational company?*

2 Identify four of the principal problems that impede the development of internationally recognized accounting standards.

3 Differentiate between the Accountants International Study Group and the International Accounting Standards Committee.

4 Define the following terms associated with foreign currencies:
   a Exchange rate
   b Forward market rate
   c Selling rate
   d Spot rate

5 Today's newspaper listed quoted prices for the Japanese yen (¥) as follows:
   Buying rate: ¥1 = $0.0039
   Selling rate: ¥1 = $0.0043
How many United States dollars would a United States importer have had to exchange for ¥50,000 at the above prices to settle an account payable in that amount to a Japanese supplier? Explain.

6 On March 27, Year 3, a United States multinational company purchased merchandise on 30-day credit terms from a Philippines exporter at an invoice cost of ₱80,000. (₱ is the symbol for the Philippines peso.) What United States dollar amount would the United States company credit to Accounts

Payable if the March 27, Year 3, exchange rates for Philippine pesos were as follows:

Buying rate: ₱1 = $0.11
Selling rate: ₱1 = $0.14

7 How does a United States multinational company **hedge** against the risk of fluctuations in exchange rates for foreign currencies? Explain.

8 Explain the **one-transaction perspective** regarding the nature of an exchange gain or loss.

9 What arguments are advanced in support of the **two-transaction perspective** for exchange gains and losses? Explain.

10 Should exchange gains or losses be recorded in the accounting records prior to collection of a receivable or payment of a liability in foreign currency? Explain.

11 Why has **FASB Statement No. 8** been criticized by multinational companies?

12 Differentiate between the **current/noncurrent method** and the **current rate method** of translating foreign currencies.

13 What is a **forward exchange contract?**

14 What exchange rate is used to translate the Intercompany Accounts Payable account of a foreign subsidiary of a United States parent company? Explain.

15 What disclosures relating to foreign currency matters are required in the financial statements or footnotes of United States multinational companies?

EXERCISES

Ex. 13-1 Select the best answer for each of the following multiple-choice questions.
1 Exchange gains and losses resulting from the translation of foreign currency financial statements into dollars should be included:
 a As an ordinary item in net income for the period in which the exchange rate changes
 b As an extraordinary item in net income for the period in which the exchange rate changes
 c In the balance sheet as a deferred item
 d As an ordinary item in net income if gains, but deferred if losses

2 Arnold Company has a receivable from a foreign customer which is payable in the local currency of the foreign customer. The account receivable for 900,000 local currency units (LCU) has been translated to $315,000 in Arnold's December 31, Year 5, balance sheet. On January 15, Year 6, the account receivable was collected in full when the exchange rate was LCU 1 = $0.33⅓. What journal entry should Arnold prepare to record the collection of this account receivable?

 a Cash 300,000
  Accounts Receivable 300,000

```
 b  Cash .................................................  300,000
     Exchange Gains and Losses .............................   15,000
        Accounts Receivable ................................                 315,000


 c  Cash .................................................  300,000
     Deferred Exchange Losses .............................   15,000
        Accounts Receivable ................................                 315,000


 d  Cash .................................................  315,000
     Accounts Receivable ...................................                 315,000
```

3 A material loss arising from the devaluation of the currency of a foreign country in which a multinational company was conducting operations through a branch would be reported in the company's year-end financial statements as

a An asset to be offset against subsequent gains from foreign currency revaluations

b A factor in the determination of income before extraordinary items for the year in which the loss occurred

c An extraordinary item for the year in which the loss occurred

d A prior period adjustment, unless the foreign branch had begun operations during the year in which the loss occurred

4 Sequoia Company owns a foreign subsidiary which reported net income for Year 3 of 4,800,000 local currency units (LCU), appropriately translated to $800,000. On October 15, Year 3, when the exchange rate was LCU 1 = $0.175, the foreign subsidiary paid to Sequoia a dividend of LCU 2,400,000. The dividend represented the net income of the foreign subsidiary for the six months ended June 30, Year 3, during which period the weighted-average exchange rate was LCU 1 = $0.172. The exchange rate at December 31, Year 3, was LCU 1 = $0.169. What exchange rate should be used to translate the dividend for the December 31, Year 3, consolidated financial statements of Sequoia Company and subsidiary?

a LCU 1 = $0.175   **c** LCU 1 = $0.169
b LCU 1 = $0.172   **d** LCU 1 = $0.167

5 A multinational company is translating a foreign subsidiary's financial statements from the foreign currency to dollars for the December 31, Year 7, consolidated financial statements. The average exchange rate for Year 7 should be used to translate

a Cash at December 31, Year 7
b Land purchased in Year 5
c Retained earnings at January 1, Year 7
d Sales for Year 7

6 In the preparation of consolidated or combined financial statements for a United States multinational company and its foreign branches or subsidiaries, the balances in the foreign currency financial statements must be translated to dollars. The objective of the translation process is to obtain currency valuations that

a Are conservative
b Reflect current monetary equivalents
c Are expressed in United States dollars and are in conformity with generally accepted accounting principles in the United States
d Reflect the translated items at unexpired historical cost

Ex. 13-2 Armand Company is translating the financial statements of its foreign subsidiary to United States dollars on December 31, Year 2. On that date, the foreign subsidiary had long-term accounts receivable of 1,500,000 local currency units (LCU) and LCU 2,400,000 long-term debt. The exchange rate in effect when the specific transactions involving those foreign currency amounts occurred was LCU 1 = $0.50. The exchange rate on December 31, Year 2, was LCU 1 = $0.66⅔.

Compute the United States dollar amount of the foreign subsidiary's long-term accounts receivable and long-term debt at December 31, Year 2.

Ex. 13-3 On November 16, Year 6, Progress Company, a United States multinational company, purchased raw materials from a foreign supplier for 100,000 units of the supplier's local currency (LCU). On November 30, Year 6, Progress prepared interim financial statements. On December 16, Year 6, Progress purchased a draft for LCU 100,000 and remitted it to the foreign supplier. Selected exchange rates for one unit (LCU 1) of the foreign supplier's local currency were as follows:

	Spot rates		30-day
	Buying	*Selling*	*forward market rate*
Nov. 16, Year 6	$0.50	$0.52	$0.53
Nov. 30, Year 6	0.51	0.53	0.54
Dec. 16, Year 6	0.49	0.51	0.52

Prepare journal entries required for Progress Corporation's purchase from the foreign supplier.

Ex. 13-4 The foreign subsidiary of Christopher Company, a United States multinational company, has plant assets at December 31, Year 5, with a cost of 3,600,000 local currency units (LCU). Of this amount, plant assets with a cost of LCU 2,400,000 were acquired in Year 3, when the exchange rate was LCU 1 = $0.625; and plant assets with a cost of LCU 1,200,000 were acquired in Year 4, when the exchange rate was LCU 1 = $0.556. The exchange rate at December 31, Year 5, was LCU 1 = $0.500, and the weighted-average exchange rate for Year 5 was LCU 1 = $0.521. The foreign subsidiary depreciates plant assets by the straight-line method over a 10-year economic life with no residual value.

Compute for Year 5 the depreciation expense for Christopher Company's foreign subsidiary, in United States dollars.

Ex. 13-5 On August 6, Year 7, Cavalier Corporation, a United States multinational company which uses the perpetual inventory system, purchased from a Belgium supplier on 30-day open account goods costing 80,000 Belgian francs. On that date, various exchange rates for Belgian francs (BF) were as follows:

Spot rates:
Buying: BF1 = $0.025
Selling: BF1 = $0.029

30-day forward market rate: BF1 = $0.031

Also on August 6, Year 7, Cavalier Corporation purchased a 30-day firm, uncancelable forward exchange contract for BF 80,000.

Prepare journal entries to record the August 6, Year 7, transactions described above, as well as the related transactions on September 5, Year 7, on which date the selling spot rate was BF 1 = $0.029. Cavalier does not close its accounting records or prepare interim financial statements monthly.

Ex. 13-6 On January 2, Year 6, Exeter Company established a branch in a foreign country. In connection with your preparation of combined financial statements for the home office and branch of Exeter at December 31, Year 6, you note the following accounts in the trial balance of the branch. In addition, you learn that all transfers of funds from the home office of Exeter to the foreign branch are executed at the selling spot rate.

3 1 Sales
4 2 Home Office
1 3 Accounts Receivable, Trade
4 4 Office Equipment (purchased in the United States and paid for in United States dollars)
1 5 Factory Building
1 6 Inventories, Dec. 31, Year 6
2 7 Mortgage Note Payable on Factory Building (due Dec. 31, Year 16)
4 8 Inventories, Jan. 2, Year 6 (received from home office)
2 9 Notes Payable to Bank (due Jan. 31, Year 7)
1 10 Accumulated Depreciation: Factory Building

Indicate at which of the following exchange rates each of the above accounts would be translated into United States dollars:

(1) The selling spot rate at the date of payment, acquisition, or entry in the accounting records
(2) The selling spot rate at December 31, Year 6
(3) An average of selling spot rates for Year 6
(4) None of the above (If you select this answer, indicate what rate you would use.)

Ex. 13-7 Transatlantic Corporation, a United States multinational company with subsidiaries in foreign countries, prepares consolidated financial statements which include all subsidiaries. The accounting records and financial statements of the foreign subsidiaries are maintained in the respective local currencies of the countries in which they operate.

a Explain the translation of the subsidiaries' financial statements to United States dollars with respect to each of the following items:

(1) Accounts receivable, trade
(2) Sales
(3) Building
(4) Accrued payroll
(5) Depreciation, building
(6) Intercompany accounts payable to Transatlantic Corporation

b Explain the nature of any difference between the total debits and total credits of a foreign subsidiary's trial balance after it has been translated to United States dollars.

Ex. 13-8 On June 30, Year 6, Peninsular Corporation, a United States multinational company, sold merchandise costing $75,000 to a Portuguese customer, receiving in exchange a 60-day, 12% note for 2,500,000 escudos (Esc). The buying rate for escudos on June 30, Year 6, was Esc 1 = $0.04. On August 29, Year 6, Peninsular received from the Portuguese customer a draft for Esc 2,550,000, which Peninsular converted on that date to United States dollars at the buying rate for escudos of Esc 1 = $0.05.

Prepare journal entries for Peninsular to record the June 30, Year 6, sale, under the perpetual inventory system, and the August 29, Year 6, conversion of the Portuguese customer's Esc 2,550,000 draft to United States dollars.

SHORT CASES FOR ANALYSIS AND DECISION

Case 13-1 During January, Year 12, Winstead Corporation, a United States multinational company, established a subsidiary, Archer Company, in a foreign country. Winstead owns 90% of Archer's outstanding capital stock; the remaining 10% is owned by citizens of the foreign country.

Instructions

a What criteria should Winstead use to determine whether to prepare consolidated financial statements with Archer for the year ended December 31, Year 15? Explain.

b Independent of your answer to **a**, assume that consolidated financial statements are appropriate for Winstead Corporation and Archer Company. Before consolidated financial statements can be prepared, individual items in Archer's financial statements for the year ended December 31, Year 15, must be translated from the foreign currency to dollars. For each of the ten items listed below, taken from Archer's financial statements for the year ended December 31, Year 15, specify what exchange rate is appropriate for translation of the item, and explain why that rate is appropriate. Number your answers to correspond with each item listed below:

  (1) Cash
  (2) Trade accounts receivable (all from Year 15 revenue)
  (3) Supplies inventory (all purchased during last quarter of Year 15)
  (4) Land (purchased in Year 12)
  (5) Short-term note payable to Foreign National Bank.
  (6) Capital stock, no par or stated value (all issued in January, Year 12)
  (7) Retained earnings, January 1, Year 15
  (8) Sales
  (9) Depreciation expense on plant assets
  (10) Salaries expense

Case 13-2 Hitchcock Corporation, a United States multinational company, has a subsidiary in Austria. On April 1, Year 3, Hitchcock purchased for $50,000 a draft for 500,000 Austrian schillings (S) and remitted it to the Austrian subsidiary as a long-term, noninterest-bearing advance. The advance was to be repaid ultimately in United States dollars.

You were engaged as independent auditor for the examination of the March 31, Year 4, consolidated financial statements of Hitchcock and subsidiaries (including the Austrian subsidiary). On March 31, Year 4, the selling spot rate for schillings was S1 = $0.05. Hitchcock's controller translated the Payable to Parent Company account in the Austrian subsidiary's balance sheet from S500,000 to $25,000 (S500,000 × $0.05 = $25,000). Because the $25,000 translated balance of the subsidiary's Payable to Hitchcock Corporation account did not offset the $50,000 balance of Hitchcock's Receivable from Austrian Subsidiary account as of March 31, Year 4, Hitchcock's controller prepared the following consolidation elimination at March 31, Year 4:

Exchange Loss—Austrian Subsidiary *25,000*
    Receivable from Austrian Subsidiary—Hitchcock *25,000*
To record exchange loss resulting from decline in exchange rate for
schillings to S1 = $0.05 on March 31, Year 4, from S1 = $0.10 on April
1, Year 3.

Instructions   Evaluate the accounting treatment described above.

Case 13-3 West Coast Corporation, a United States multinational company, has a branch in Hong Kong. The Hong Kong branch purchases locally all its merchandise acquired for resale. The branch sells to Hong Kong customers exclusively, and measures its cost of goods sold by the fifo method.

For many years, the exchange rate between the United States dollar and the Hong Kong dollar (HK$) has remained stable. However, there were substantial fluctuations in the exchange rate during Year 6, as evidenced by the following selling spot rates for Hong Kong dollars on the dates of the Hong Kong branch's purchases of merchandise:

Year 6	Exchange rate
Jan. 2	HK$1 = $0.20
Apr. 1	HK$1 = $0.16
July 1	HK$1 = $0.24
Oct. 1	HK$1 = $0.22
Dec. 31	HK$1 = $0.26

Instructions Discuss the propriety of translating the Year 6 cost of goods sold of West Coast's Hong Kong branch to United States dollars at the following alternative exchange rates:
a Historical fifo rates
b Average rate
c Current rate (as of December 31, Year 6)

PROBLEMS

13-4 Exchange rates for the British pound (£) on various dates in Year 3 were as follows:

	£1 =		
	Aug. 1	Aug. 31	Sept. 30
Spot rates:			
Buying	$1.80	$1.82	$1.83
Selling	1.90	1.91	1.92
Forward market rates:			
30-day contracts	1.92	1.94	1.94
60-day contracts	1.94	1.96	1.97
90-day contracts	1.97	1.99	1.98

On August 1, Year 3, Grandamerica Corporation, a United States multinational company which prepares interim financial statements monthly, purchased a 60-day forward exchange contract for £50,000.

Instructions Prepare all necessary journal entries for Grandamerica's forward exchange contract during its 60-day term under the following assumptions:
a The contract was purchased for speculation.
b The contract was purchased as a hedge of the exposed net liability position of Grandamerica's London branch.
c The contract was firm and uncancelable, and was purchased as a hedge of a £50,000 purchase order issued by Grandamerica on August 1, Year 3, to a British supplier to be delivered and paid for on September 30, Year 3.
Omit journal entry explanations.

13-5 The trial balance in local currency units (LCU) of the Foreign Branch of Diverse Company at April 30, Year 7, the end of the branch's first month of operations, is presented at the top of page 533.

DIVERSE COMPANY: FOREIGN BRANCH
Trial Balance
April 30, Year 7

	Balance, LCU Dr (Cr)
Cash	10,000
Accounts receivable	50,000
Inventories (1,600 units at fifo cost)	124,375
Home office	(104,557)
Sales (2,100 units at LCU 133)	(279,300)
Cost of goods sold..	152,281
Operating expenses	47,201
Total	-0-

Additional information is as follows:
(1) Foreign Branch sells a single product, which it acquires from the home office of Diverse Company.
(2) The Investment in Foreign Branch ledger account in the accounting records of the home office of Diverse Company (prior to end-of-period adjusting and closing entries) follows:

Investment in Foreign Branch ($)

Date	Explanation of transactions	Debit	Credit	Balance
4/1/7	Cash sent to branch	10,000		10,000 dr
4/1/7	1,000 units of merchandise shipped to branch @ $80 per unit	80,000		90,000 dr
4/3/7	Equipment purchased by branch (recorded in Home Office accounts)		5,500	84,500 dr
4/10/7	1,200 units of merchandise shipped to branch @ $81 per unit	97,200		181,700 dr
4/20/7	1,500 units of merchandise shipped to branch @ $82 per unit	123,000		304,700 dr
4/29/7	Cash received from branch		210,00(	94,700 dr
4/30/7	Operating expenses billed to branch	25,000		119,700 dr

(3) The Home Office ledger account in the accounting records of the Foreign Branch of Diverse Company (prior to end-of-period closing entries) follows:

Home Office (LCU)

Date	Explanation of transactions	Debit	Credit	Balance
4/2/7	Cash received from home office		9,091	9,091 cr
4/2/7	1,000 units of merchandise received from home office @ LCU 72.73		72,730	81,821 cr
4/2/7	Equipment purchased by branch	5,000		76,821 cr
4/11/7	1,200 units of merchandise received from home office @ LCU 72.32		86,784	163,605 cr
4/21/7	1,500 units of merchandise received from home office @ LCU 78.10		117,150	280,755 cr
4/28/7	Cash sent to home office	200,000		80,755 cr
4/30/7	Operating expenses billed by home office		23,810	104,565 cr

(4) Exchange rates for the local currency units (LCU) of the country in which Foreign Branch operates were as follows during April, Year 7:

Apr. 1–Apr. 6... LCU 1 = $1.10
Apr. 7–Apr. 18.. LCU 1 = 1.12
Apr. 19–Apr. 30... LCU 1 = 1.05

Instructions Translate the April 30, Year 7, trial balance of the Foreign Branch of Diverse Company to dollars from local currency units. Compute all exchange rates to the nearest cent.

13-6 On December 1, Year 5, Chicago Corporation formed a foreign subsidiary which issued all of its currently outstanding common stock on that date. Selected captions from the subsidiary's balance sheets, all of which are shown in local currency units (LCU), are as follows:

	November 30	
	Year 7	Year 6
Accounts receivable (net of allowance for doubtful accounts of 2,200 LCU at Nov. 30, Year 7, and 2,000 LCU at Nov. 30, Year 6)	40,000 LCU	35,000 LCU
Inventories, at cost	80,000	75,000
Plant assets (net of accumulated depreciation of 31,000 LCU at Nov. 30, Year 7, and 14,000 LCU at Nov. 30, Year 6)	163,000	150,000
Long-term debt	100,000	120,000
Common stock, authorized 10,000 shares, par 10 LCU per share, issued and outstanding 5,000 shares at Nov. 30, Year 7, and Nov. 30, Year 6	50,000	50,000

Additional information is as follows:

(1) Exchange rates are as follows:

Dec. 1, Year 5–June 30, Year 6 .... 2 LCU to $1
July 1, Year 6–Sept. 30, Year 6.................................... 1.8 LCU to $1
Oct. 1, Year 6–May 31, Year 7..................................... 1.7 LCU to $1
June 1, Year 7–Nov. 30, Year 7 .... 1.5 LCU to $1
Average monthly rate for fiscal year ended Nov. 30, Year 6 .... 1.9 LCU to $1
Average monthly rate for fiscal year ended Nov. 30, Year 7 .... 1.6 LCU to $1

(2) An analysis of the accounts receivable (net) balance follows:

	Year ended November 30	
	Year 7	Year 6
Accounts receivable:		
Balance at beginning of year	37,000 LCU	-0- LCU
Sales (36,000 LCU per month in Year 7 and 31,000 LCU per month in Year 6)	432,000	372,000
Collections	(423,600)	(334,000)
Write-offs (April, Year 7, and November, Year 6)	(3,200)	(1,000)
Balance at end of year	42,200 LCU	37,000 LCU

	Year ended November 30	
	Year 7	Year 6
Allowance for doubtful accounts:		
Balance at beginning of year	2,000 LCU	-0- LCU
Provision for doubtful accounts	3,400	3,000
Write-offs (April, Year 7, and November, Year 6)	(3,200)	(1,000)
Balance at end of year	2,200 LCU	2,000 LCU

(3) An analysis of inventories for which the first-in, first out (fifo) inventory method is used, follows:

	November 30	
	Year 7	Year 6
Inventories at beginning of year	75,000 LCU	-0- LCU
Purchases (May, Year 7, and May, Year 6).............	335,000	375,000
Goods available for sale	410,000	375,000
Inventories at end of year	80,000	75,000
Cost of goods sold	330,000 LCU	300,000 LCU

(4) On December 1, Year 5, Chicago's foreign subsidiary purchased land for 24,000 LCU and depreciable plant assets for 140,000 LCU. On June 4, Year 7, additional depreciable plant assets were purchased for 30,000 LCU. Plant assets are being depreciated on a straight-line basis over a 10-year economic life with no residual value. A full year's depreciation is taken in the year of purchase.

(5) On December 15, Year 5, 7% serial bonds with a principal amount of 120,000 LCU were issued. These bonds mature serially each year through December 15, Year 11, and interest is paid semiannually on June 15 and December 15. The first principal payment was made on December 15, Year 6.

Instructions Prepare a working paper to translate the selected captions above into United States dollars at November 30, Year 7, and November 30, Year 6, respectively. Show supporting computations in good form. Round all exchange rates to the nearest cent.

13-7 New Orleans Corporation, a United States multinational company with an April 30 fiscal year, had the following transactions, among others, during March and April, Year 8:

		Exchange rate		
		Spot		Forward
Date	Explanation of transactions	Buying	Selling	market
Year 8				
Mar. 6	Purchased goods from Brazilian supplier on 30-day open account, cost 100,000 cruzeiros (Cr$). Purchased firm, uncancelable 30-day forward exchange contract for Cr$100,000.	$0.12	$0.13	$0.135

(cont.)

		Exchange rate		
		Spot		Forward
Date	Explanation of transactions	Buying	Selling	market
Year 8 Mar. 18	Purchased goods from Danish supplier on 30-day open account, cost 75,000 kronen (DKr).	0.16	0.18	0.184
25	Sold goods to Swiss customer on 30-day open account for 50,000 francs (Sfr). Cost of goods sold $15,000.	0.36	0.38	0.382
Apr. 4	Purchased goods from Spanish supplier on 30-day open account for 150,000 pesetas (Ptas).	0.015	0.02	0.025
5	Liquidated Cr$100,000 forward exchange contract, and paid Brazilian supplier for Mar. 6 purchase.	0.12	0.13	0.136
17	Purchased draft for DKr75,000 for payment to Danish supplier for Mar. 18 purchase.	0.17	0.19	0.195
24	Received draft for Sfr50,000 from Swiss customer for sale of Mar. 25. Exchange draft for U.S. dollar credit to bank checking account.	0.37	0.39	0.393
30	Obtained exchange rate quotation for Spanish pesetas.	0.02	0.025	0.03

Instructions

a Prepare journal entries for New Orleans Corporation to record the above transactions in United States dollars, under the perpetual inventory system.

b Prepare the necessary adjusting journal entry or entries for New Orleans Corporation at April 30, Year 8. The company does not prepare monthly interim financial reports.

13-8 On August 1, Year 8, Westpac Corporation, a United States multinational company, established a sales branch in Singapore. The transactions of Westpac's home office with the Singapore branch, and the branch's own transactions, during August, Year 8, are set forth below. Following each transaction is the appropriate spot exchange rate for Singapore dollars (S$).

(1) Cash of $50,000 sent to branch (S$1 = $0.45)

(2) Merchandise with a cost of $75,000 shipped to branch at a billed price of $100,000 (S$1 = $0.45)

(3) Rent of leased premises for August paid by branch, S$1,000 (S$1 = $0.45)

(4) Store and office equipment purchased by branch for S$5,000, to be carried in home office accounting records (S$1 = $0.45)

(5) Sales by branch on credit, S$25,000 (S$1 = $0.46). Cost of goods sold, S$15,000

(6) Collections of accounts receivable by branch, S$20,000 (S$1 = $0.455)

(7) Payment of operating expenses by branch, S$5,000 (S$1 = $0.47)

(8) Cash remitted to home office by branch, S$10,000 (S$1 = $0.44)

(9) Operating expenses incurred by home office charged to branch, $2,000 (S$1 = $0.445)

(10) Uncollectible account receivable written off by branch, S$1,000 (S$1 = $0.44)

Instructions Prepare journal entries for the home office of Westpac Corporation in United States dollars, and for the Singapore branch in Singapore dollars, to record the above transactions. Both segments use the perpetual inventory system and the direct write-off method of accounting for uncollectible accounts. Round all amounts to the nearest dollar. Omit journal entry explanations.

13-9 Houston Corporation, a United States multinational company, acquired Centralamerica Company on January 2, Year 3, by the purchase at carrying amount of all outstanding capital stock. Centralamerica is located in Nicaduras, whose monetary unit is the peso ($N). Centralamerica's accounting records were continued without change. A trial balance, in pesos, on January 2, Year 3, follows:

CENTRALAMERICA COMPANY
Trial Balance (pesos)
January 2, Year 3

	Debit	Credit
Cash	$N 3,000	
Accounts receivable	5,000	
Inventories	32,000	
Plant assets	204,000	
Accumulated depreciation		$N 42,000
Accounts payable		81,400
Capital stock		50,000
Retained earnings		70,600
Totals	$N244,000	$N244,000

Centralamerica's trial balance, in pesos, at December 31, Year 4, follows:

CENTRALAMERICA COMPANY
Trial Balance (pesos)
December 31, Year 4

	Debit	Credit
Cash	$N 25,000	
Accounts receivable	20,000	
Allowance for doubtful accounts		$N 500
Receivable from Houston Corporation	33,000	
Inventories	110,000	
Plant assets	210,000	
Accumulated depreciation		79,900
Notes payable		60,000
Accounts payable		22,000
Income taxes payable		40,000
Capital stock		50,000
Retained earnings		100,600
Sales—local		170,000
Sales—foreign		200,000

(cont.)

CENTRALAMERICA COMPANY
Trial Balance (pesos)
December 31, Year 4 (concluded)

	Debit	Credit
Cost of goods sold	$N207,600	
Depreciation expense	22,400	
Selling and administrative expenses	60,000	
Income taxes expense	40,000	
Gain on sale of plant assets		$N 5,000
Totals	$N728,000	$N728,000

The following additional information is available:
(1) All of Centralamerica's foreign sales are made to Houston Corporation and are accumulated in the account Sales—Foreign. The balance in the Receivable from Houston Corporation account is the total of unpaid invoices. All foreign sales are billed in United States dollars. The reciprocal accounts in Houston's accounting records show total Year 4 purchases as $471,000 and the total of unpaid invoices as $70,500.
(2) Depreciation is computed by the straight-line method over a 10-year economic life for all depreciable assets, with no residual value. Machinery costing $N20,000 was purchased on December 31, Year 3, and no depreciation was recorded for this machinery in Year 3. There have been no other depreciable assets acquired since January 2, Year 3, and no assets are fully depreciated.
(3) Certain assets that were in the Plant Assets account at January 2, Year 3, were sold on December 31, Year 4. For Year 4 a full year's depreciation was recorded before the assets were removed from the accounting records. Information regarding the sale follows:

Cost of assets	$N14,000
Accumulated depreciation	4,900
Carrying amount	$N 9,100
Proceeds of sale	14,100
Gain on sale of plant assets	$N 5,000

(4) No journal entries have been made in the Retained Earnings account of the subsidiary since its acquisition other than the net income for Year 3. The Retained Earnings account at December 31, Year 3, was translated to $212,000.
(5) The prevailing exchange rates follow:

	Dollars per peso
Jan. 2, Year 3	$2.00
Year 3 average	2.10
Dec. 31, Year 3	2.20
Year 4 average	2.30
Dec. 31, Year 4	2.40

(6) The December 31, Year 4, inventories translate to $258,500. Cost of goods sold for Year 4 translates to $481,632.

Instructions Prepare a working paper to translate the December 31, Year 4, trial balance of Centralamerica Company from pesos to dollars. The working paper should show the trial balance in pesos, the exchange rate, and the trial balance in dollars. Supporting computations should be in good form.

13-10 Miami Corporation, a United States multinational company, established a branch in Brazentina in Year 2 to purchase local products for resale by the home office and to sell company products locally.

You were engaged to examine the company's combined financial statements for the year ended December 31, Year 9. You engaged a licensed professional accounting firm in Brazentina to examine the branch accounts. The firm reported that the branch accounts were fairly stated in pesos (B), except that a Brazentina franchise fee and any possible adjustments required by home office accounting procedures were not recorded. Trial balances for the branch and the home office as of December 31, Year 9, appear below and on page 540.

Your examination disclosed the following information:

(1) The Brazentina peso was devalued July 1, Year 9, from B1 = $0.25 to B1 = $0.20. The former exchange rate had been in effect since Year 1.

(2) Included in the balance of the home office's Investment in Branch account was a $4,000 billing for merchandise shipped during Year 9. The branch did not receive the shipment during Year 9. Home office sales to the branch are marked up 33⅓% on cost and shipped F.O.B. home office. Branch sales to home office are made at branch cost. There were no seasonal fluctuations in branch sales to outsiders during the year.

(3) The branch had beginning and ending inventories valued at fifo cost of B80,000 [exclusive of the amount in (2), above], of which one-half at each date had been acquired from the home office. The home office had December 31, Year 9, inventories valued at fifo cost of $520,000.

(4) The Branch account balance is the unamortized portion of a $15,000 fee paid in January, Year 8, to a United States firm for marketing research for the branch. Currency restrictions prevented the branch from paying the fee, which was paid by the home office. The home office agreed to accept merchandise from the branch over a five-year period, during which the fee is to be amortized.

(5) There were no changes in the branch's plant assets during Year 9.

(6) The government of Brazentina imposes a franchise fee of 10 pesos per 100 pesos of net income before franchise fee of the branch, in exchange for certain exclusive trading rights granted to the branch. The fee is payable each May 1 for the preceding calendar year's trading rights; it had not been recorded by the branch at December 31, Year 9.

MIAMI CORPORATION
Home Office and Branch
Trial Balances
December 31, Year 9

	Branch (pesos) dr (cr)	Home office (dollars) dr (cr)
Cash	B 110,000	$ 90,000
Accounts receivable, trade	150,000	160,000
Inventories, Jan. 1, Year 9	80,000	510,000
Short-term prepayments	-0-	18,000
Investment in branch	-0-	10,000
Branch	-0-	12,000
Plant assets	1,000,000	750,000

(cont.)

MIAMI CORPORATION
Home Office and Branch
Trial Balances
December 31, Year 9 (concluded)

	Branch (pesos) dr (cr)	Home office (dollars) dr (cr)
Accumulated depreciation	(650,000)	(350,000)
Current liabilities.......................................	(220,000)	(240,000)
Long-term debt	(230,000)	(200,000)
Home office	(30,000)	-0-
Capital stock	-0-	(300,000)
Retained earnings, Jan. 1, Year 9	-0-	(145,000)
Sales...	(1,680,000)	(4,035,000)
Intracompany sales	-0-	(160,000)
Purchases	1,180,000	3,010,000
Intracompany purchases	-0-	140,000
Depreciation expense	100,000	50,000
Other operating expenses	190,000	680,000
Totals	B -0-	$ -0-

Instructions Prepare a working paper to combine the income statement and balance sheet of Miami Corporation's home office and Brazentina branch, with all amounts stated in United States dollars. Formal combined financial statements are not required. Do not prepare formal adjusting entires or combination eliminations; instead, explain the adjustments and eliminations, including supporting computations, at the bottom of the working paper. Disregard income taxes.

The following columnar headings are suggested for your working paper:
Branch trial balance (in pesos):
  Unadjusted—dr (cr)
  Adjustments—dr (cr)
  Adjusted—dr (cr)
Exchange rate
Branch trial balance (in dollars)—dr (cr)
Home office trial balance (in dollars):
  Unadjusted—dr (cr)
  Adjustments—dr (cr)
  Adjusted—dr (cr)
Combination eliminations—increase (decrease)
Combined income statement—dr (cr)
Combined balance sheet—dr (cr)

13-11 Individual financial statements of San Diego Corporation, a United States multinational company, and its two subsidiaries for the year ended December 31, Year 6, appear on page 541. ($ is the symbol for the Mexican peso as well as for the United States dollar.)

Additional data regarding the companies follow:
(1) On December 31, Year 5, San Diego acquired 900 of the 1,000 issued and outstanding shares of capital stock of United States Subsidiary for $9,000, and all 1,000 shares of the issued and outstanding capital stock of Mexico Subsidiary for $12,000. The tangible and identifiable intangible net assets of

SAN DIEGO CORPORATION AND SUBSIDIARIES
Financial Statements
For Year Ended December 31, Year 6

	San Diego Corporation (dollars)	United States Subsidiary (dollars)	Mexico Subsidiary (pesos)
Income Statements			
Revenue			
Sales	$400,000	$21,000	$381,000
Intercompany sales to United States			
Subsidiary	10,000	-0-	-0-
Total revenue	$410,000	$21,000	$381,000
Costs and expenses			
Cost of goods sold	$300,000	$15,000	$300,000
Intercompany cost of goods sold	7,500	-0-	-0-
Depreciation expense	3,000	550	17,500
Selling expenses	34,500	2,400	16,500
General and administrative expenses ..	35,000	1,650	18,000
Income taxes expense	15,000	400	15,000
Total costs and expenses	$395,000	$20,000	$367,000
Net income	$ 15,000	$ 1,000	$ 14,000
Statements of Retained Earnings			
Retained earnings, Jan. 1, Year 6	$ 25,000	$ 2,000	$ 7,000
Net income	15,000	1,000	14,000
Subtotal	$ 40,000	$ 3,000	$ 21,000
Dividends	-0-	1,000	-0-
Retained earnings, Dec. 31, Year 6	$ 40,000	$ 2,000	$ 21,000
Balance Sheets			
Assets			
Cash	$ 10,000	$ 1,500	$ 10,000
Accounts receivable (net)	30,000	8,000	35,000
Intercompany receivables (payables) ..	4,000	(900)	-0-
Inventories	20,000	-0-	83,000
Investment in United States Subsidiary	9,000	-0-	-0-
Investment in Mexico Subsidiary	12,000	-0-	-0-
Plant assets	45,000	5,500	175,000
Accumulated depreciation	(15,000)	(2,000)	(75,000)
Total assets	$115,000	$12,100	$228,000
Liabilities & Stockholders' Equity			
Accounts payable	$ 25,000	$ -0-	$ 7,000
Dividends payable	-0-	100	-0-
Long-term debt	-0-	-0-	100,000
Capital stock, 1,000 shares	50,000	10,000	100,000
Retained earnings	40,000	2,000	21,000
Total liabilities & stockholders' equity	$115,000	$12,100	$228,000

both investee companies were fairly valued at their carrying amounts on December 31, Year 5. San Diego planned to use the equity method of accounting for its investments in both subsidiaries.

(2) Both of San Diego's subsidiaries depreciate plant assets on the straight-line basis over 10-year economic lives, with no residual values. None of the subsidiaries' plant assets was fully depreciated at December 31, Year 5, or at December 31, Year 6. There were no additions to or retirements of Mexico Subsidiary's plant assets during Year 6.

(3) On December 31, Year 6, San Diego shipped merchandise billed at $4,000 to United States Subsidiary.

(4) On December 18, Year 6, United States Subsidiary declared a dividend of $1 per share, payable January 16, Year 7, to stockholders of record January 10, Year 7.

(5) Exchange rates for the Mexican peso were as follows:

Dec. 31, Year 5, through Mar. 31, Year 6 .... $U.S. 0.12

Apr. 1, Year 6, through Dec. 31, Year 6 .... $U.S. 0.08

Instructions

a Prepare a working paper to translate Mexico Subsidiary's financial statements from Mexican pesos to United States dollars. Use **weighted** average of exchange rates where appropriate. Translate Mexico Subsidiary's inventories at $U.S. 7,885, and its cost of goods sold at $U.S. 31,500.

b Prepare necessary adjusting entries for San Diego and for United States Subsidiary at December 31, Year 6.

c Prepare a consolidating financial statements working paper, and related consolidation eliminations working paper, for San Diego and subsidiaries at December 31, Year 6. Your working papers should reflect the translated balances in *a* and the adjustments in *b.* Disregard income taxes.

14

BANKRUPTCY AND CORPORATE REORGANIZATION

Business failures are a common occurrence in the United States economy. According to the national credit rating company Dun & Bradstreet, Inc., there were more than 11,000 business failures in 1975—a number representing 0.43% of the approximately 2.7 million concerns in business that year.[1] As might be expected, mismanagement and poor accounting records are the most commonly cited causes of business failures.

The situation which precedes the typical business failure is inability to pay liabilities as they become due. Unsecured creditors often resort to lawsuits to satisfy their unpaid claims against a company. Secured creditors may force foreclosure proceedings for real property or may repossess personal property which collateralizes a *security agreement.* The Internal Revenue Service may seize the properties of a business enterprise which has failed to pay FICA and income taxes withheld from employees.

A business may be unable to pay its liabilities as they become due even though the current fair values of its assets exceed its liabilities. For example, a company may experience a severe cash shortage in times of "double-digit" price inflation because of the lag between the purchase

[1] U.S. Department of Commerce, *Pocket Data Book: U.S.A. 1976* (Washington: 1976), p. 262.

or production of goods at inflated costs and the recovery of the inflated costs through increased selling prices.

More typical of the failing business than the conditions described in the preceding paragraph is the state of *insolvency,* which is defined in the United States Bankruptcy Act as follows:[2]

> A person shall be deemed insolvent within the provisions of this Act whenever the aggregate of his property, exclusive of any property which he may have conveyed, transferred, concealed, removed, or permitted to be concealed or removed, with intent to defraud, hinder, or delay his creditors, shall not at a fair valuation be sufficient in amount to pay his debts.

The terms *insolvent* and *bankrupt* often are used as interchangeable adjectives. Such usage is technically incorrect; *insolvent* refers to a person's or company's financial condition, and *bankrupt* refers to a legal state. In this chapter we shall discuss various legal and accounting issues associated with bankruptcy, as well as with arrangements with creditors and corporate reorganizations.

BANKRUPTCY

Article 1, Section 8 of the Constitution of the United States authorized Congress to establish uniform laws on the subject of bankruptcies throughout the United States. For the first eighty-nine years under the Constitution, the United States had a national bankruptcy law for only a total of sixteen years. During the periods in which national bankruptcy laws were not in effect, state laws on insolvency prevailed. In 1898 the present Bankruptcy Act was enacted; it has been amended frequently and extensively since that time. Enactment of the Bankruptcy Act in effect caused state laws on insolvency to be relatively dormant.

The Bankruptcy Act

The Bankruptcy Act contains fourteen effective chapters. The first seven chapters of the Act cover ordinary bankruptcy. Chapter 8 of the Act, entitled "Provisions for the Relief of Debtors," has only one effective section: Section 77, titled "Reorganization of Railroads Engaged in Interstate Commerce." Chapter 9 of the Act deals with the composition of indebtedness of certain taxing agencies or instrumentalities. Chapters 10 and 11 of the Act, which will be covered in the final sections of this chapter, deal with corporate reorganizations and arrangements, respectively. The three remaining chapters of the Bankruptcy Act are as follows: Chapter 12, "Real Property Arrangements by Persons Other than Corporations"; Chapter 13, "Wage Earners' Plans"; and Chapter 14, "Maritime Commission Liens." Chapters 8, 9, 12, 13, and 14 of the Act are very specialized and will not be covered in this discussion.

[2] *United States Bankruptcy Act,* sec. 1(19).

Section 2075 of Title 28, Chapter 131 of the U.S. Code provides that the United States Supreme Court may prescribe by general rules the various legal practices and procedures under the Bankruptcy Act. Thus, the Bankruptcy Rules established by the Supreme Court constitute important interpretations of provisions of the Bankruptcy Act.

Ordinary bankruptcy

The legal process known as *ordinary bankruptcy* involves the liquidation of the assets of a bankrupt individual or business enterprise and the distribution of the cash proceeds to the bankrupt's creditors. Creditors having *security interests* collateralized by specific assets of the debtor are entitled to obtain satisfaction of their claims from the assets pledged as collateral. The Bankruptcy Act provides for priority treatment for certain other unsecured creditors; their claims are satisfied in full, if possible, from proceeds of realization of the debtor's noncollateralized assets. Unsecured creditors without priority receive *dividends,* in proportion to the amounts of their claims, from the remaining proceeds of liquidation of the debtor's assets.

Voluntary Petition   The Bankruptcy Act provide that any "person," except a municipal, railroad, insurance, or banking corporation, or a savings and loan association, may file a petition in a federal district court to be adjudicated a *voluntary bankrupt.* The official form for a voluntary bankruptcy petition must be accompanied by supporting schedules of the petitioner's debts and property. The debts are classified as follows: (1) creditors having priority; (2) creditors holding security; and (3) creditors having unsecured claims without priority. The debtor's property is reported as follows: real property; personal property; property not otherwise scheduled; and property claimed as exempt. Valuations of property are at *market* or *current fair values.* Also accompanying the voluntary bankruptcy petition is a *statement of affairs* (not to be confused with the *accounting* statement of affairs illustrated in a subsequent section of this chapter), which contains a series of questions concerning all aspects of the debtor's financial condition and operations.

Creditors Having Priority   The Bankruptcy Act provides that the following debts are to have priority over other unsecured debts, and are to be paid in full out of a bankrupt's estate before any dividends are paid to other unsecured creditors:

1 Costs and expenses of administering the bankrupt's estate
2 Unpaid wages and commissions not in excess of $600 per claimant, earned by employees within three months before the date of filing of the voluntary petition
3 Costs incurred by creditors in successfully opposing the discharge of a bankrupt, or in providing evidence, leading to conviction, of a crime committed by the bankrupt during the bankruptcy proceeding

4 Taxes owed to the United States or to any state or subdivision thereof, unless the taxes are released by a discharge in bankruptcy

5 Debts, other than for taxes, having priority under United States law (for example, amounts owed to agencies of the United States), and rent owed to a lessor entitled to priority under applicable state law

Property Claimed as Exempt   Certain property of a bankruptcy petitioner is not includable in the bankrupt's estate. The Bankruptcy Act excludes from coverage of the Act the various allowances provided in the laws of the United States or of the state of the bankrupt's residence. Typical of these allowances are residential property exemptions provided by homestead laws and exemptions for life insurance policies payable on death to the spouse or a relative of the bankrupt.

Involuntary Petition   If a debtor other than the types excluded in the Bankruptcy Act owes unpaid amounts to twelve or more unsecured creditors who are not employees, relatives, stockholders, or other "insiders," three or more of the creditors having unsecured claims totaling $500 or more may file in a federal district court a creditor's petition for bankruptcy, also known as an *involuntary petition.* If less than twelve creditors are involved, one or more creditors having unsecured claims of $500 or more may file the petition. Excluded from the involuntary bankruptcy petition process are wage earners earning $1,500 or less per year, farmers, savings and loan associations, and municipal, railroad, insurance, or banking corporations. The petitioning creditors must claim that the debtor owes debts aggregating $1,000 or more, and that the debtor committed an act of bankruptcy within four months preceding the filing of the petition.

Acts of Bankruptcy   The Bankruptcy Act identify six acts of bankruptcy by a debtor, as follows:

1 Concealing, removing, or permitting to be concealed or removed, any part of the debtor's assets, in order to hinder, delay, or defraud creditors; or fraudulently making or allowing a transfer of property.

2 Transferring assets to a creditor while the debtor is insolvent, with the objective of enabling the creditor to obtain a greater percentage of the unpaid claim than some other creditor of the same classification. (Such a transfer of assets is called a *preference.)*

3 Permitting a creditor to obtain a lien upon any part of the debtor's property while the debtor is insolvent, and not having discharged the lien on a timely basis.

4 Making a general assignment of assets to a trustee for conversion into cash for the benefit of creditors.

5 Permitting or initiating, while the debtor is insolvent or unable to pay debts as they mature, the appointment of a receiver or trustee to take charge of the debtor's property.

6 Admitting in writing an inability to pay debts and a willingness to be adjudicated a bankrupt.

Role of court in ordinary bankruptcy

The federal district court in which a voluntary or involuntary petition for bankruptcy is filed oversees all aspects of the bankruptcy proceedings.

The officer of the court in charge of the bankruptcy proceedings is the *referee.* Referees are appointed for a six-year term by the judges of bankruptcy courts. Jurisdiction and duties of referees are set forth in the Bankruptcy Act.

Adjudication   One of the first acts of the referee is to either dismiss or adjudicate the voluntary or involuntary bankruptcy petition. *Adjudication* is defined as the determination, whether by decree or by operation of law, *that a person or a business enterprise is a bankrupt.*[3] The filing of a voluntary petition in bankruptcy is in effect adjudication; in an involuntary petition, adjudication is made by the referee after a hearing at which the debtor may attempt to refute the creditor's charges that the debtor committed an act of bankruptcy. Any suits which are pending against a debtor for whom a voluntary or involuntary bankruptcy petition is filed are *stayed* until adjudication or dismissal of the petition; after adjudication, such suits are further stayed until the question of the bankrupt's discharge is determined by the court.

Receiver   Before or after adjudication, a *receiver* may be appointed by the bankruptcy court to preserve the assets of a bankrupt's estate and protect the interest of creditors. The receiver, like the referee, is an officer of the bankruptcy court. A receiver, as instructed by the court, may take possession of, but not title to, the property of a bankrupt, conduct the business of the bankrupt, or represent the bankrupt's estate in any legal proceedings.

Accounting duties of the receiver include taking a physical inventory of the bankrupt's property (unless an inventory was filed with the bankruptcy petition), maintaining records of cash and properties received and disposed of, and reporting on the financial condition and administration of the bankrupt's estate at periodic intervals and at the end of the receivership.

Appraisal of Bankrupt's Estate   The bankruptcy court is required by the Bankruptcy Act to obtain an appraisal of all the real and personal property included in a bankrupt's estate. The purpose of the appraisal is to facilitate sale of the bankrupt's property and use of the sales proceeds for dividends to unsecured, nonpriority creditors. Estate property cannot be sold for less than 75% of appraised value without court approval.

Role of Bankrupt's Creditors   Within a period of 10 to 30 days after an adjudication, the bankruptcy court must call a meeting of the bankrupt's

[3] Ibid., sec. 1(2).

creditors. At this first meeting of creditors, the presiding referee may allow or disallow creditors' claims which have been submitted. Also at the first meeting, the "outsider" creditors appoint a trustee or three trustees to manage the bankrupt's estate. A majority vote in number and amount of claims of all unsecured and nonpriority creditors present is required for actions by creditors. Creditors must submit their claims within six months after the date of the first meeting of creditors in order for the claims to be allowed against the bankrupt's estate. Creditors must receive from the court at least 30 day's notice of the last day set for filing objections to a bankrupt's discharge.

Role of Trustee The trustee elected by the creditors or appointed by the court assumes custody of and title to the bankrupt's nonexempt property, either directly or from a receiver if one had been previously appointed by the bankruptcy court. The principal duties of the trustee are to continue operating the bankrupt's business if directed by the court, liquidate the property of the bankrupt's estate, and pay dividends to unsecured nonpriority creditors within 10 days after they are declared by the referee. The trustee is responsible for keeping accounting records similar to those described for receivers on page 547.

The Bankruptcy Act empowers the trustee to invalidate a preference (page 546) received within four months of the filing of a bankruptcy petition by a creditor who had reasonable cause to believe that the debtor was insolvent at the time of the preference. The trustee may recover from the creditor the money or property constituting the preference and include it in the bankrupt's estate.

Dividends to Creditors Dividends are declared by the referee and paid by the trustee to unsecured, nonpriority creditors. The Bankruptcy Act describes procedures for and timing of dividend declarations.

Discharge of Bankrupt Once the bankrupt's property has been liquidated, all secured and priority creditor claims have been paid, and all possible dividends have been paid to unsecured, nonpriority creditors, the bankrupt may receive a *discharge,* defined as the release of the bankrupt from all unliquidated debts, except the following:[4]

1 Taxes which became payable by the bankrupt to the United States or to any state or subdivision within three years preceding the bankruptcy, including taxes attributable to improper preparation of tax returns by the bankrupt
2 Liabilities resulting from the bankrupt's obtaining money or property under false pretenses or representations, or willful conversion of the property of others
3 Debts not scheduled by the bankrupt in support of the bankruptcy petition, such creditors not being informed of the bankruptcy proceedings
4 Debts arising from embezzlement or other fraudulent acts by the bankrupt acting in a fiduciary capacity

[4] Ibid., sec. 1(15), sec. 17a.

5 Wages and commissions entitled to priority (see pages 545–546) but remaining unpaid
6 Liabilities for amounts furnished to the bankrupt by an employee of the bankrupt, to secure performance of terms of the employment contract
7 Amounts due for alimony or child support
8 Liabilities for willful and malicious injuries to the person or property of others (other than the conversion described in **2** above)

A bankrupt will not be discharged if any crimes, misstatements, or other malicious acts were committed by the bankrupt in connection with the court proceedings. In addition, a bankrupt will not be discharged if the current bankruptcy petition was filed within six years of a previous bankruptcy discharge to the same bankrupt.

Role of accountant in ordinary bankruptcy

The accountant's role in ordinary bankruptcy proceedings is concerned with proper reporting of the financial condition of the debtor or debtor company, and adequate accounting and reporting for the receiver or trustee for the bankrupt's estate.

Financial condition of debtor company: Statement of affairs

A company which enters ordinary bankruptcy proceedings is a *quitting concern,* not a *going concern.* Consequently, the balance sheet, which reports the financial position of a going concern, is inappropriate for a company in bankruptcy.

The financial statement designed for a company entering bankruptcy is the *statement of affairs* (not to be confused with the legal bankruptcy form with the same title described on page 545). The purpose of the statement of affairs is to present the assets and liabilities of the debtor company from a *liquidation* viewpoint, because liquidation is the outcome of ordinary bankruptcy. Thus, assets in the statement of affairs are valued at *current fair values;* carrying amounts of the assets are presented on a memorandum basis. In addition, assets and liabilities in the statement of affairs are classified according to the rankings and priorities set forth in the Bankruptcy Act; the current/noncurrent classification used in a balance sheet for a going concern is not appropriate for the statement of affairs.

Illustration of Statement of Affairs   The balance sheet of Sanders Company at June 30, Year 4, the date the company filed a voluntary bankruptcy petition, is presented on page 550.

SANDERS COMPANY
Balance Sheet
June 30, Year 4

Assets

Current assets:

Cash	$ 2,700
Notes receivable and accrued interest, less allowance for doubtful notes, $6,000	13,300
Accounts receivable, less allowance for doubtful accounts, $23,240	16,110

Inventories, at fifo cost:

Finished goods	12,000
Goods in process	35,100
Raw materials	19,600
Factory supplies	6,450
Short-term prepayments	950
Total current assets	$106,210

Plant assets, at cost:

Land	$20,000	
Buildings, less accumulated depreciation, $33,750	41,250	
Machinery, less accumulated depreciation, $32,100	48,800	
Tooling, less accumulated amortization, $2,300	14,700	
Total plant assets		124,750
Total assets		$230,960

Liabilities & Stockholders' Equity

Current liabilities:

Notes payable:

Pacific National Bank, including accrued interest		$ 15,300
Suppliers, including accrued interest		51,250
Accounts payable		52,000
Accrued salaries and wages		8,850
Property taxes payable		2,900
Accrued interest on bonds		1,800
FICA and income taxes withheld and accrued		1,750
Total current liabilities		$133,850
First mortgage bonds payable		90,000
Total liabilities		$223,850

Stockholders' equity:

Capital stock, $100 par, 750 shares authorized and issued	$75,000	
Deficit	(67,890)	7,110
Total liabilities & stockholders' equity		$230,960

Other information available from notes to financial statements and from estimates of current fair values of assets follows:

1 Notes receivable with a principal amount plus accrued interest totaling $15,800, and an estimated realizable value of $13,300, collateralize the notes payable to Pacific National Bank.

2 Finished goods are estimated to be salable at a markup of 33⅓% over cost, with disposal costs estimated at 20% of selling prices. Estimated cost to complete goods in process is $15,400, of which $3,700 would be cost of raw materials and factory supplies used. Estimated selling prices of goods in process when completed total $40,000, with disposal costs estimated at 20% of selling prices. Estimated realizable values for raw materials and factory supplies not required to complete goods in process are $8,000 and $1,000, respectively. All short-term prepayments are expected to be used up in the course of liquidation.

3 Land and buildings, which have an appraised value of $95,000, collateralize the first mortgage bonds payable. Machinery with a carrying amount of $18,200 and estimated realizable value of $10,000 collateralizes notes payable to suppliers in the amount of $12,000, including accrued interest. Estimated realizable value of the remaining machinery is $9,000, net of disposal costs of $1,000. Estimated realizable value of tooling, after its use in completing the goods in process inventory, is $3,255.

4 Accrued salaries and wages are debts having priority under the Bankruptcy Act.

The statement of affairs for Sanders Company at June 30, Year 4, is presented on pages 552–553. The following points should be stressed in the review of the June 30, Year 4, statement of affairs for Sanders.

1 The "Carrying amount" columns in the statement of affairs serve as a tie-in to the balance sheet of Sanders at June 30, Year 4, as well as a basis for determination of expected losses or gains on liquidation of Sanders's assets.

2 Assets are assigned to one of three categories: pledged with fully secured creditors, pledged with partially secured creditors, and free. This categorization of assets facilitates the computation of estimated amounts available for unsecured creditors—those with priority and those without priority.

3 Liabilities are ranked into the categories reported by a debtor in the schedules supporting a voluntary bankruptcy petition (see page 545): priority, fully secured, partially secured, and unsecured.

4 A *contra,* or *offset,* technique is used where the legal right of setoff exists. For example, amounts due to fully secured creditors are deducted from the estimated current fair value of the assets serving as collateral; and liabilities with priority are deducted from estimated amounts available to unsecured creditors from the proceeds of asset liquidation.

5 An "estimated settlement per dollar of unsecured liabilities" can be computed by dividing the estimated amount available for unsecured creditors by the total unsecured liabilities, thus:

$$\frac{\$62,865}{\$95,250} = 66 \text{ cents on the dollar}$$

The above computation enables the bankruptcy referee to estimate the aggregate dividends which will be available to unsecured, nonpriority creditors in a bankruptcy proceeding.

SANDERS COMPANY
Statement of Affairs
June 30, Year 4

Carrying amount	Assets	Current fair value	Estimated amount available	Loss or (gain) on realization
	Assets pledged with fully secured creditors:			
$ 20,000	Land ....}	$95,000		$(33,750)
41,250	Building ....}			
	Less: Fully secured claims (contra)	91,800	$ 3,200	
	Assets pledged with partially secured creditors:			
13,300	Notes and interest receivable (deducted contra)	$13,300		
18,200	Machinery (deducted contra)	$10,000		8,200
	Free assets:			
2,700	Cash	$ 2,700	2,700	
-0-	Notes and interest receivable	-0-	-0-	
16,110	Accounts receivable	16,110	16,110	
	Inventories:			
12,000	Finished goods .	12,800	12,800	(800)
35,100	Goods in process	20,300*	20,300*	14,800
19,600	Raw materials ...	8,000	8,000	11,600
6,450	Factory supplies	1,000	1,000	5,450
950	Short-term prepayments	-0-	-0-	950
30,600	Machinery	9,000	9,000	21,600
14,700	Tooling	3,255	3,255	11,445
	Total estimated amount available .	$76,365		$ 39,495

*Estimated selling price $40,000
Less: Estimated "out-of-pocket" completion costs
    ($15,4000 − $3,700) .... (11,700)
       Estimated disposal costs ($40,000 × 20%) .. (8,000)
Net realizable value $20,300

(cont.)

SANDERS COMPANY
Statement of Affairs
June 30, Year 4 (concluded)

Carrying amount	Assets	Current fair value	Estimated amount available	Loss or (gain) on realization
	Less: Liabilities with priority (contra)	$13,500		
	Estimated amount available for unsecured creditors		$62,865	
	Estimated deficiency to unsecured creditors		32,385	
$230,960			$95,250	

Carrying amount	Liabilities & stockholders' equity			Amount unsecured
	Liabilities with priority:			
$ 8,850	Accrued salaries and wages	$ 8,850		
2,900	Property taxes payable	2,900		
1,750	FICA and income taxes withheld and accrued	1,750		
	Total (deducted contra)	$13,500		
	Fully secured creditors:			
90,000	First mortgage bonds payable	$90,000		
1,800	Accrued interest on bonds payable	1,800		
	Total (deducted contra)	$91,800		
	Partially secured creditors:			
15,300	Notes and accrued interest payable to Pacific National Bank	$15,300		
	Less: Net realizable value of notes pledged as collateral (contra)	13,300		$ 2,000
12,000	Notes and accrued interest payable to suppliers	$12,000		
	Less: Estimated realizable value of machinery pledged as collateral (contra)	10,000		2,000
	Unsecured creditors:			
39,250	Notes payable to suppliers			39,250
52,000	Accounts payable			52,000
7,110	Stockholders' equity			
$230,960				$95,250

Some accountants recommend the preparation of a *statement of estimated deficiency to unsecured creditors* as an adjunct to the statement of affairs. This supplementary statement appears unnecessary, because the information it contains is included entirely in the "Estimated amount available" column of the statement of affairs. If the balance sheet prepared on the same date as a statement of affairs includes adequate allowances for doubtful accounts and for estimated liabilities, the statement of affairs will be adequate for a comprehensive analysis of the financial condition of a "quitting concern."

Accounting and reporting for receiver or trustee

As pointed out previously in this chapter, a receiver or trustee must keep records of cash and other assets received and disposed of for the bankrupt's estate, and report on the financial condition and administration of the bankrupt's estate at periodic intervals *(interim reports)* and at the end of the receivership or trusteeship. Traditionally, the accounting records and reports used for receivers and trustees have been extremely detailed and elaborate. However, the provisions of the applicable Bankruptcy Rule are very general; therefore, simple accounting records and reports should be adequate. The authors therefore recommend the following with respect to the accounting records for a bankrupt debtor:

1 Maintenance of the accounting records of the debtor should be continued during the period that a receiver or trustee carries on the operations of the debtor's business.

2 An *accountability* technique should be used once the trustee begins liquidation of the bankrupt's assets. In the accountability method of accounting the assets and liabilities for which the trustee is responsible are recorded in the accounting records of the trustee at their statement of affairs valuations, with an offset to a memorandum-type balancing account with a title such as Estate Deficit. Appropriate cash receipts and cash payments journal entries would be made for the trustee's liquidation of assets and payment of liabilities. No "gain" or "loss" account is necessary because the business in liquidation does not require a statement of operations. Differences between cash amounts realized and carrying amounts of the related assets or liabilities are debited or credited directly to the Estate Deficit account.

3 The interim and final reports of the trustee to the bankruptcy court will be a statement of cash receipts and disbursements, a statement of realization and liquidation, and, for interim reports, supporting schedules of assets not yet realized and liabilities not yet liquidated.

Illustration of Accountability Technique   Assume that Arline Wells, the trustee in the voluntary bankruptcy proceedings for Sanders Company (see pages 549–553), took custody of and title to the assets of Sanders at June 30, Year 4. The accountant for the trustee would prepare the following journal entry on June 30, Year 4:

SANDERS COMPANY, IN BANKRUPTCY
Arline Wells, Trustee
General Journal
June 30, Year 4

Cash	2,700	
Notes and Interest Receivable	13,300	
Accounts Receivable	16,110	
Finished Goods Inventory	12,800	
Goods in Process Inventory	20,300	
Raw Materials Inventory	8,000	
Factory Supplies	1,000	
Land and Building	95,000	
Machinery	19,000	
Tooling	3,255	
Estate Deficit	32,385	
Notes and Interest Payable		66,550
Accounts Payable		52,000
Accrued Salaries and Wages		8,850
Property Taxes Payable		2,900
FICA and Income Taxes Withheld and Accrued		1,750
Accrued Interest on Bonds		1,800
First Mortgage Bonds Payable		90,000

To record current fair values of assets and liabilities of Sanders Company, in voluntary bankruptcy proceedings.

When the trustee liquidates the assets of Sanders, the journal entry would be a debit to Cash, a credit to the appropriate asset account, and a debit or credit to the Estate Deficit account for a loss or gain on liquidation, respectively. Cost of administering the estate also would be debited to the Estate Deficit account.

Statement of Realization and Liquidation   The traditional statement of realization and liquidation was a complex and not very readable accounting presentation. A form of realization and liquidation statement which should be more useful to the bankruptcy court than the traditional statement is illustrated on page 556. This financial statement is based on the assumed activities of the trustee for the bankrupt estate of Sanders Company during the month of July, Year 4, including operating the business long enough to complete the goods in process inventory.

An accompanying statement of cash receipts and payments for the month ended July 31, Year 4, would show the sources of the $39,654 total realization proceeds, and the dates, check numbers, payees, and amounts of the $13,500 paid for liabilities with priority and the $1,867

SANDERS COMPANY, IN BANKRUPTCY
Arline Wells, Trustee
Statement of Realization and Liquidation
For Month Ended July 31, Year 4

Estate deficit, June 30, Year 4 .... $32,385
Assets realized:

	Current fair value, June 30, Year 4	Realization proceeds	Loss or (gain)	
Accounts receivable ...	$14,620	$12,807	$ 1,813	
Finished goods inventory	12,800	11,772	1,028	
Goods in process inventory	14,820	15,075	(255)	
Totals	$42,240	$39,654		2,586

Liabilities with priority liquidated at carrying amounts:

Accrued salaries and wages	$ 8,850	
Property taxes payable	2,900	
FICA and income taxes withheld and accrued	1,750	
Total	$13,500	

Estate administration expenses paid 1,867
Estate deficit, July 31, Year 4 .... $36,838

paid for estate administration expenses. Supporting schedules would summarize assets not yet realized and liabilities not yet liquidated.

Concluding comment on ordinary bankruptcy

Ordinary bankruptcy, covered by Chapters 1 through 7 of the Bankruptcy Act, involves liquidation of the bankrupt's estate. In many cases, an insolvent business may be restored to a sound financial footing if it can defer payment of its debts. Chapter 11 of the Bankruptcy Act, dealing with arrangements, enables a business to continue operations under court protection from creditor lawsuits, while it formulates a plan to pay its debts.

ARRANGEMENTS

An *arrangement* is defined in Chapter 11 of the Bankruptcy Act as any plan of a debtor for the settlement, satisfaction, or extension of the time of payment of *unsecured debts,* upon any terms.[5] An arrangement in-

[5] Ibid., sec. 306(1).

cludes provisions modifying or altering the rights of some or all unsecured creditors.

Petition for arrangement

Although any debtor eligible for ordinary bankruptcy (see page 545) also is eligible to file a petition for an arrangement under Chapter 11 of the Bankruptcy Act, generally only debtors with no large liabilities payable to the public file petitions for arrangements. The petition for an arrangement must state that the debtor is insolvent or unable to pay debts as they mature. The petition must also set forth provisions of the debtor's proposed arrangement, or must state that the debtor intends to propose an arrangement.

A petition for a corporation debtor includes an exhibit of key components of the corporation's financial position, as well as the supporting schedules and statement of affairs required for an ordinary bankruptcy petition. The court in which the petition is filed has exclusive jurisdiction over the debtor and the debtor's property, wherever located, until provisions of the arrangement have been performed. The filing of the petition operates as a stay of the commencement or continuation of any court or other proceedings against the debtor or the property of the debtor.

Appointment of receiver or control by debtor

The Bankruptcy Act provides that the court, upon the application of any interested party such as a stockholder or creditor of the debtor company, may appoint a receiver of the property of the debtor. The receiver has the power, subject to court control, to operate the business and manage the property of the debtor for as long as the court authorizes. The receiver must file periodic reports with the court as directed. If a receiver is not appointed, the debtor continues in possession and ownership of its property, and continues to operate the business.

Role of creditors

The court must hold a first meeting of creditors not less than 25 nor more than 40 days after the debtor files the petition for an arrangement. The notice of the first meeting generally is accompanied by a copy of the debtor's proposed arrangement and a summary of the debtor's assets, including any appraisals, and liabilities. At the first meeting, the judge or referee of the court receives proof of creditors' claims and may allow or disallow them. The creditors' written acceptances of the proposed arrangement also are received by the court at the first meeting of creditors.

Confirmation of arrangement

If, at the first meeting of creditors, all or a majority of creditors affected by the arrangement have accepted the arrangement in writing, the court confirms the arrangement once the debtor has deposited funds with a fiduciary. The funds deposited should be adequate to pay liabilities with priority, any amounts to be distributed to creditors as part of the arrangement, and amounts adequate to cover the costs of the bankruptcy proceedings. Once the arrangement is confirmed, it is binding upon the debtor, upon all creditors (whether or not they have accepted it in writing), and upon any person issuing securities or acquiring property under the arrangement. The effect of the confirmation of the arrangement is to discharge the debtor from all unsecured liabilities, except as provided for in the arrangement, and except for debts not dischargeable in bankruptcy (see pages 548–549).

Although Chapter 11 of the Bankruptcy Act does not require stockholders to accept an arrangement in order for the court to confirm it, some state laws or corporate bylaws of the debtor may require such approval. The board of directors of the debtor corporation should submit the plan of arrangement to stockholders for their approval if the plan requires a change in the capital structure of the corporation.

Accounting for an arrangement

The accountant for a debtor involved in a Chapter 11 arrangement proceeding must account for all provisions of the arrangement as confirmed by the court.

To illustrate the accounting for an arrangement, assume that Sanders Company (see pages 549–554) filed a petition for an *arrangement,* rather than for *ordinary bankruptcy,* on June 30, Year 4. The proposed arrangement, which was approved by stockholders and all unsecured creditors and confirmed by the court, included the following:

1 Deposit $25,000 with escrow agent, as soon as cash becomes available, to cover liabilities with priority and costs of bankruptcy proceedings.
2 Amend articles of incorporation to provide for 10,000 shares of authorized capital stock of $1 par. The new capital stock is to be exchanged on a share-for-share basis for the 750 shares of old $100 par capital stock already issued to shareholders.
3 Extend due date of unsecured notes payable to suppliers totaling $15,250 for four years, until May 31, Year 9. Increase the interest rate on the notes from 10% to 12%, the current fair rate of interest.
4 Exchange 1,600 shares of new $1 par capital stock (at current fair value of $15 a share) for unsecured notes payable to suppliers totaling $24,000.
5 Pay vendors 70 cents per dollar of accounts payable owed.

Illustrative Journal Entries for Arrangement   The following journal entries, numbered to correspond with the provisions of the arrangement outlined above, were recorded by Sanders Company in connection with the confirmed arrangement, when cash became available from operations:

SANDERS COMPANY
General Journal

(1) Cash with Escrow Agent 25,000
      Cash   25,000
    To record deposit of cash with escrow agent under terms of
    Chapter 11 bankruptcy arrangement.

    Accrued Salaries and Wages 8,850
    Property Taxes Payable 2,900
    FICA and Income Taxes Withheld and Accrued 1,750
        Cash with Escrow Agent   13,500
    To record escrow agent's payment of liabilities with priority
    at June 30, Year 4.

    Costs of Bankruptcy Proceedings 11,000
        Cash with Escrow Agent   11,000
    To record escrow agent's payment of costs of bankruptcy
    proceedings.

(2) Capital Stock, $100 par 75,000
        Capital Stock, $1 par   750
        Paid-in Capital in Excess of Par   74,250
    To record issuance of 750 shares of $1 par capital stock in
    exchange for 750 shares of $100 par capital stock.

(3) 10% Notes Payable to Suppliers, due May 31, Year 5 15,250
        12% Notes Payable to Suppliers, due May 31, Year 9   15,250
    To record extension of due dates of notes payable to sup-
    pliers and increase of interest rate from 10% to 12%.

(4) Notes Payable to Suppliers 24,000
        Capital Stock, $1 par   1,600
        Paid-in Capital in Excess of Par   22,400
    To record exchange of 1,600 shares of $1 par capital stock
    for $24,000 principal amount of notes payable, at current fair
    value of $15 a share.

(5) Accounts Payable 52,000
        Cash   36,400
        Gain from Discharge of Indebtedness in Bankruptcy   15,600
    To record payment of $0.70 per dollar of accounts payable
    to vendors.

After the arrangement had been carried out, the following journal entry would be appropriate for eliminating the $67,890 accumulated deficit of Sanders Company at June 30, Year 4 (assuming approval of stockholders):

Paid-in Capital in Excess of Par 63,290		
Gain from Discharge of Indebtedness in Bankruptcy 15,600		
Costs of Bankruptcy Proceedings		11,000
Retained Earnings.....................................		67,890
To eliminate deficit at June 30, Year 4, and close bankruptcy gain and costs to Paid-in Capital in Excess of Par account.		

The effect of the preceding journal entries is to show a "clean slate" for Sanders Company as a result of the Chapter 11 bankruptcy arrangement and the write-off of the accumulated deficit existing at the date of the petition for arrangement. The extension of due dates of some debts, conversion of other debts into equity securities, and liquidation of accounts payable at less than their face amount, should enable Sanders to resume operations as a going concern. For a reasonable number of years subsequent to the arrangement, Sanders should "date" the retained earnings in its balance sheets to disclose that the earnings were accumulated after the arrangement with unsecured creditors.

Disclosure of arrangements

Because of the unusual and pervasive effects of arrangements under Chapter 11 of the Bankruptcy Act, full disclosure in financial statements or footnotes is essential for the period in which an arrangement is carried out. The following, from a recent prospectus of The Miller-Wohl Company, Inc., is an example of such disclosure:

1973 Arrangement with Creditors

Prior to February 1973, the Company, in addition to its present business, also operated 26 discount department stores, engaged in the business of wholesale distribution to department and discount stores of housewares, small appliances, toys and similar hard goods and operated retail fabric stores and leased fabric departments in discount department stores.

As a result of substantial losses experienced by the discount department stores, the Company experienced a deterioration in its financial position. It became increasingly difficult to obtain merchandise for the Company's operations. When a number of creditors commenced legal proceedings against and sought to attach assets of the Company in September 1972, it filed a petition for an Arrangement with creditors under Chapter XI of the Bankruptcy Act. Operating under the court protection afforded in Chapter XI proceedings, the Company was able to effect the orderly sale or termination of the operations of its discount department stores, disposed of its wholesaling and fabric operations and closed approximately 50 unprofitable or marginally profitable women's apparel stores. In connection with the store closings, the Company generally obtained court orders approving the disaffirmance of the related lease obligations, many of which had a substantial portion of the lease term remaining, which had the effect of limiting the landlords' claims to a maximum of three years' rent.

The Company negotiated an Arrangement with its creditors which was confirmed by the Court in November 1973, terminating the Chapter XI proceedings. A total of approximately $35,300,000 in general creditor claims was approved by the Court. Under the Arrangement, general creditors have received to date cash payments totaling approximately $15,600,000, including amounts paid in settlement of future payments to which creditors were entitled under the terms of the Arrangement. Creditors receiving the payments provided for under the Arrangement have received to date cash payments totaling approximately 48% of their claims. The Arrangement provided for the issuance of one share of the Company's Common Stock, as constituted on the date the Arrangement was confirmed, for each $100 of claims. The Company has issued a total of approximately 529,000 shares (adjusted for the September 1975 stock distribution) in respect of such claims. Such creditors are entitled to receive additional future cash payments of 2½% of their claims on each of February 15, 1976, 1977 and 1978, and up to an additional 1% of their claims on May 15 of each of such years if and to the extent that net income of the Company for the immediately preceding fiscal year exceeds approximately $900,000. Assuming that the net income of the Company exceeds this amount in each of these years, the Company will be obligated to pay an aggregate of an additional approximately $3,000,000 to such creditors. The balance of the creditors' claims has been discharged.

CORPORATE REORGANIZATION

Chapter 10 of the Bankruptcy Act provides for the court-supervised reorganization of a corporation which is insolvent or unable to pay its debts as they mature. For all but very small corporations, the reorganization is carried out by a court-appointed trustee. Chapter 10 reorganizations are used primarily by large corporations with extensive debt owed to the public. In recent years, a number of widely publicized corporate reorganizations have involved corporations which were victims of "management fraud."

Petition for reorganization

The Bankruptcy Act provides that any one of the following may file a petition for a corporate reorganization:

1 A corporation which is insolvent or unable to pay its debts when they mature
2 Three or more creditors of a corporation, as described in *1*, with claims aggregating $5,000 or more
3 A trustee under an indenture for securities of a corporation as described in *1*

The petition must show the reasons why reorganization is required, and why an arrangement under Chapter 11 of the Bankruptcy Act is inadequate for relief. In addition, a petition filed by creditors or by an indenture trustee must state one of the following:

1 That the corporation was adjudicated a bankrupt in a pending proceedings in bankruptcy; or

2 That a receiver or trustee has been appointed for or has taken charge of all or the greater portion of the property of the corporation in a pending equity proceeding; or

3 That an indenture trustee or a mortgagee under a mortgage is, because of a default, in possession of all or the greater portion of the property of the corporation; or

4 That a proceeding to foreclose a mortgage or to enforce a lien against all or the greater portion of the property of the corporation is pending; or

5 That the corporation has committed an act of bankruptcy within four months prior to the filing of the petition.

The bankruptcy court judge approves a petition unless dissatisfied as to the petition's compliance with provisions of Chapter 10 of the Bankruptcy Act. If a petition is filed by creditors or by an indenture trustee, the debtor corporation is subpoenaed by the court. The corporation can contest the allegations of a creditor's or indenture trustee's petition. The judge's approval of a petition operates as a stay of any pending ordinary bankruptcy, mortgage foreclosure, equity receivership, or lien enforcement proceeding against the debtor corporation.

Appointment of trustee

After approval of a petition involving a corporation with debts aggregating $250,000 or more, the bankruptcy court judge appoints one or more trustees for the corporation. Among the powers and duties of the trustee are the following:

1 Prepare and file in court a list of creditors of each class and their claims and a list of stockholders of each class

2 Investigate the acts, conduct, property, liabilities, and business operations of the corporation, consider the desirability of continuing operations, and formulate a plan for such continuance for submission to the judge

3 Report to the judge any facts acertained as to fraud against or mismanagement of the corporation

Plan of reorganization

The plan of reorganization submitted by the trustee to the bankruptcy court judge is given to the debtor corporation, its creditors, stockholders, and trustees, the Secretary of the Treasury, and the Securities and Exchange Commission. The plan must include provisions altering or modifying the interests and rights of the creditors and stockholders of the corporation, as well as a number of additional provisions. The judge must submit plans for corporations with more than $3 million of indebtedness to the SEC for review and advisory comment; submission of other plans to the SEC for comment is optional with the judge. Before a plan of reorganization is confirmed by the bankruptcy court, the plan must be deemed *feasible* as well as *fair* and *equitable* to the various creditor and stockholder groups. To be feasible, the plan should afford reasonable prospect of financial integrity and success for the reorganized corporation.

Once a plan of reorganization is approved by the judge of the bankruptcy court, the trustee submits the plan, the judge's opinion thereon, and the report of the SEC to all creditors and stockholders affected by the plan. In order for the plan to be confirmed by the judge, two-thirds of all affected creditors, and a majority of the shareholders of a solvent corporation, must approve the plan. Confirmation of the plan of reorganization by the judge makes the plan binding upon the corporation, upon all creditors and stockholders of the corporation, and upon any other corporation issuing securities or acquiring property under the plan.

Accounting for a corporate reorganization

The accounting problems associated with a corporate reorganization are similar to those involved in arrangements, as illustrated on pages 558–560. Journal entries are made to reflect write-downs of assets; reductions of par or stated value of capital stock (with recognition of resultant paid-in capital in excess of par or stated value); extensions of due dates of notes payable; exchanges of debt securities for equity securities; and the elimination of a deficit. The journal entries for a Chapter 10 corporate reorganization thus resemble the entries to record a *quasi-reorganization,* as illustrated in *Intermediate Accounting* of this series. In essence, the only difference for accounting purposes between a Chapter 10 corporate reorganization and a quasi-reorganization is the authority for the journal entries. Chapter 10 corporate reorganization journal entries result from a directive of the bankruptcy court, while journal entries for a quasi-reorganization are authorized by action of stockholders.

It is important for the accountant to be thoroughly familiar with the plan of a corporate reorganization, in order to account properly for its implementation. The accountant must be careful to avoid charging post-reorganization operations with losses which arose before the organization.

Footnote disclosure of corporate reorganizations

The elaborate and often complex issues involved in a corporate reorganization must be disclosed in a note to the financial statements for the period in which the plan of reorganization was carried out. The following abridged footnote appeared in an annual report of Anta Corporation, successor to two corporations which were victims of major management fraud.

Anta Corporation was formed (effective July 1, 1972) by the reorganization under Chapter X of the Federal Bankruptcy Act of Four Seasons Nursing Centers of America, Inc., and Four Seasons Equity Corporation and their subsidiaries (the reorganized companies). A Court-appointed Board of Directors assumed responsibility for the operations of the Company on September 15, 1972.

The Plan of Reorganization provided for the issuance of common stock of the Company at the rate of one share of $1 par value stock for each $7 of unsecured indebtedness (over $200) of the reorganized companies, and for distribution to persons who suffered losses as a result of acquiring for value any stock, warrant or other security of the reorganized companies before July 22, 1970 and who filed a claim for such losses with the Trustee, on a pro rata basis (based on the dollar amount of loss) of one-half the number of shares of common stock issued to unsecured creditors. All previously issued common stock, warrants and options have been canceled under the Terms of the Plan. Creditors who had approved claims against the reorganized companies for work performed or material delivered (Class B-2) were paid in cash in full under the terms of the Plan of Reorganization. . . .

Reorganization compared to an arrangement

Some of the significant differences between a corporate reorganization under Chapter 10 of the Bankruptcy Act and an arrangement under Chapter 11 of the Act are as follows:

1 Only a corporation can reorganize; an arrangement can be carried out by the various classes of debtors eligible for ordinary bankruptcy.

2 Reorganization involves all classes of a corporation's creditors and shareholders; an arrangement involves only unsecured creditors.

3 A trustee is appointed for all but the smallest corporations undergoing reorganization; in many cases the debtor continues to operate a business involved in arrangement proceedings.

4 Two-thirds of a corporation's creditors must approve a reorganization; a majority of unsecured creditors can approve an arrangement.

5 The Securities and Exchange Commission reviews and advises the bankruptcy court on plans for reorganization. The SEC has no such role in arrangements, although the SEC is authorized to apply to the court to dismiss a Chapter 11 arrangement proceeding and require the petitioning corporation to reorganize under the more stringent provisions of Chapter 10 of the Bankruptcy Act.

Proposed change in bankruptcy law

In February 1978, the United States House of Representatives passed and sent to the Senate H.R. 8200, a bill which would repeal the Bankruptcy Act and replace it with Title 11, "Bankruptcy," of the United States Code. If enacted, the bill would become fully effective October 1, 1983. Among the significant provisions of the bill are the following:

1 A system of federal bankruptcy courts and judges would be established to replace federal district courts in the administration of bankruptcies.

2 United States trustees would be appointed and supervised by the Attorney General for each judicial district. The United States trustees would serve as trustees in certain bankruptcy reorganizations and would appoint and supervise panels of private trustees to handle ordinary bankruptcies.

3 The office of referee would be abolished. Trustees would perform duties formerly assigned to referees under the Bankruptcy Act.

4 A single Chapter 11, "Reorganization," would replace present Bankruptcy Act Chapters 10 and 11.

The enactment of the above legislation, despite its significant changes in the administration of bankruptcies, would have no major effects on the accounting for bankruptcies described in this chapter.

Concluding comments

In this chapter we have highlighted the principal aspects of bankruptcy and corporate reorganization, without becoming involved in extensive details of these highly complex areas of accounting. Most accountants may be exposed to bankruptcy proceedings at some time during their professional career; thus a knowledge of the basic legal issues in bankruptcy and corporate reorganization is essential to an understanding of the accounting issues involved. Accountants who serve receivers or trustees in bankruptcy proceedings should consult the Bankruptcy Act and legal counsel for guidance in the various accounting matters involved.

REVIEW QUESTIONS

1 Define *insolvency* as that term is used in the United States Bankruptcy Act.

2 What are *Bankruptcy Rules?*

3 Identify the various classes of creditors whose claims are dealt with in ordinary bankruptcy.

4 What are *dividends* in a bankruptcy proceeding?

5 Differentiate between a *voluntary* and an *involuntary* bankruptcy petition.

6 Can any corporation file a voluntary bankruptcy petition? Explain.

7 What is a *statement of affairs* under the Bankruptcy Act?

8 List the unsecured debts having priority over other unsecured debts under the provisions of the Bankruptcy Act.

9 Who can file an *involuntary petition* in ordinary bankruptcy?

10 Identify four *acts of bankruptcy.*

11 Differentiate between the following officers of a bankruptcy court: *referee, receiver,* and *trustee.*

12 What are the effects of a *discharge* in a bankruptcy proceedings? Explain.

13 What use is made of the accounting financial statement known as a *statement of affairs?* Explain.

14 Describe the **accountability** method of accounting used by a trustee in bankruptcy.

15 What is an **arrangement** under the Bankruptcy Act?

16 Describe the role of stockholders of a bankrupt company involved in Chapter 11 arrangement proceedings.

17 What is a **corporate reorganization** under the Bankruptcy Act?

18 Describe three differences between arrangements and corporate reorganizations under the Bankruptcy Act.

EXERCISES

Ex. 14-1 Select the best answer for each of the following multiple-choice questions:

1 Under which chapter or chapters of the Bankruptcy Act is the reorganization of a corporation which is insolvent or unable to pay its debts processed?
   a Chapters 1 to 7 **b** Chapter 9 **c** Chapter 11 **d** Other

2 In ordinary bankruptcy, creditors having priority are:
   a Fully secured
   b Unsecured
   c Partially secured
   d Either fully secured or partially secured
   e Any of the above

3 An Estate Deficit account appears in:
   a A statement of affairs for a bankrupt
   b The accounting records of a bankrupt maintained by a receiver
   c The accounting records of a bankrupt maintained by a trustee
   d Any of the above
   e None of the above

4 A statement of affairs is:
   a A legal document accompanying a voluntary bankruptcy petition
   b An accounting financial statement for a "quitting concern"
   c Both **a** and **b**
   d Neither **a** nor **b**

5 Which of the following provable debts is not discharged by bankruptcy?
   a Hospital bills
   b Wages earned more than three months prior to commencement of bankruptcy proceedings
   c Liability for breach of a fiduciary duty resulting from a fraud committed by the debtor-fiduciary
   d Rent payments due which have accrued within three months of the filing of the bankruptcy petition

6 Your client is entitled to a rent priority in bankruptcy; accordingly, the client:
   a Will have the claim satisfied prior to those of general creditors, even though general creditors receive nothing
   b Ranks equally with all other creditors entitled to priority
   c Has a claim superior to the claims of secured creditors
   d Is precluded from asserting the priority if it was obtained within three months of the filing of the bankruptcy petition

Ex. 14-2 Among the provisions of Savich Company's arrangement confirmed by the bankruptcy court on November 30, Year 6, under provisions of Chapter 11 of the Bankruptcy Act, were the following:

1 Amend articles of incorporation to provide for 100,000 shares of $2 par authorized capital stock, 1,000 shares to be exchanged on a share-for-share basis for 1,000 shares of $50 par capital stock currently outstanding.

2 Issue 1,000 shares of $2 par capital stock with a current fair value of $10 a share and $10,000 cash to unsecured trade creditors, in full settlement of their claims totaling $25,000.

Prepare journal entries for the above provisions of Savich Company's arrangement at November 30, Year 6.

Ex. 14-3 The statement of affairs for Wilbur Corporation shows that approximately $0.77 on the dollar probably will be paid to unsecured creditors. The corporation owes Jurgens Company $23,000 on a note, including accrued interest of $940. Inventories with a current fair value of $19,200 collateralize the note payable.

Compute the amount that Jurgens should receive from Wilbur Corporation, assuming that actual payments to unsecured creditors consist of 77% of total acknowledged claims.

Ex. 14-4 Compute the amount that will probably be paid to each class of creditors, using the following data taken from the statement of affairs for Irving Corporation:

Assets pledged with fully secured creditors (current fair value, $75,000)	$ 90,000
Assets pledged with partially secured creditors (current fair value, $52,000) ..	74,000
Free assets (current fair value, $40,000)	70,000
Liabilities with priority	7,000
Fully secured creditors	30,000
Partially secured creditors	60,000
Unsecured creditors	112,000

Ex. 14-5 The following information for Hartford Book Company was obtained by an accountant retained by the company's major creditors:

a Furniture and fixtures: Carrying amount, $70,000; current fair value, $60,500; pledged on a note payable of $42,000 on which unpaid interest of $800 has accrued.

b Book manuscripts owned: Carrying amount, $15,000; current fair value, $7,200; pledged on a note payable of $9,000; interest is paid to date on the note.

c Books in process of production: Accumulated cost (direct materials, direct labor, and factory overhead), $37,500; net realizable value upon completion, $60,000; additional out-of-pocket costs of $14,200 will be required to complete the books in process.

Prepare the headings for the asset side of a statement of affairs and illustrate how each of the three items described above should be shown in the statement.

Ex. 14-6 From the traditional statement of realization and liquidation shown below, prepare a more concise statement of realization and liquidation similar to the one illustrated on page 556:

HOGAN COMPANY, IN BANKRUPTCY

Walter Frank, Trustee

Statement of Realization and Liquidation

For Month of January, Year 2

Assets to be realized:		Liabilities to be liquidated:	
Accounts receivable	$ 7,500	Accounts payable	$30,000
Inventories	12,500	Notes payable	5,000
Equipment	10,000	Interest payable	150
Subtotal	$30,000	Subtotal	$35,150

(cont.)

HOGAN COMPANY, IN BANKRUPTCY

Walter Frank, Trustee

Statement of Realization and Liquidation

For Month of January, Year 2 (concluded)

Supplementary charges:		Liabilities assumed:	
Administration expenses	2,950	Interest payable	50
Interest expense	50	Assets realized:	
Liabilities liquidated:		Accounts receivable	6,500
Accounts payable	6,000	Inventories	14,500
Liabilities not liquidated:		Assets not realized:	
Accounts payable	24,000	Equipment	10,000
Notes payable	5,000	Net loss	2,000
Interest payable	200		
Total	$68,200	Total	$68,200

Ex. 14-7 In auditing the financial statements of Osborne Company as of December 31, Year 10, you find the following items had been debited or credited to the Retained Earnings account during the six months immediately following a Chapter 10 corporate reorganization, which was finalized and made effective July 1, Year 10:

a Debit of $25,000 arising from an additional income tax assessment applicable to Year 9.

b Credit of $48,000 resulting from gain on sale of equipment which was no longer used in the business. This equipment had been written down by a $50,000 increase in the Accumulated Depreciation account at July 1, Year 10.

c Debit of $15,000 resulting from the loss on plant assets destroyed in a fire on November 2, Year 10.

d Debit of $32,000 representing cash dividends declared on preferred stock.

e Credit of $60,400, the net income for the six-month period ended December 31, Year 10.

For each of these items, state whether you believe it to be correctly debited or credited to the Retained Earnings account. Give a brief reason for your conclusion.

SHORT CASES FOR ANALYSIS AND DECISION

Case 14-1 Folsom Corporation has filed a voluntary petition for bankruptcy on February 1, Year 7. Among its creditors are the following:

(1) Ward Company

Ward sold Folsom two tractor trailers in August, Year 6, and filed and recorded its financing statement on December 15, Year 6, after it learned that Folsom was in severe financial difficulty. The outstanding balance due Ward is $9,000, which is the current fair value of the two tractor trailers. Ward is attempting to recover its outstanding balance.

(2) Second National Bank

Second National holds a first mortgage on the real estate where Folsom has its principal plant, office, and warehouse. The mortgage is for $280,750, representing the unpaid balance due on the original $350,000 mortgage note. The property was sold for $290,000, its current fair value as established by bids received by the trustee. The mortgage was executed two years ago and filed and recorded at that time.

(3) *James Company*

James, a major supplier of parts, delivered $10,000 of parts to Folsom on January 17, Year 7. Upon delivery, James received $5,000 cash and insisted on receiving the balance by the end of the month. When the balance was not received, James obtained from Folsom a financing statement which James filed on February 2.

(4) *Sixty-five wage earners*

This class of employee is mainly composed of the machine operators and others employed in Folsom's plant and warehouse. They were not paid for the final month. All were paid at the minimum wage level and each has a claim for $400, for a total of $26,000.

(5) *Federal, state, and local taxing authorities*

Folsom owes $6,800 in delinquent income, property, and payroll taxes.

(6) *Administration costs*

These total $12,000.

(7) *Various general creditors*

Excluding items (1) through (6) above, general creditors have provable claims of $1,614,900. The bankrupt's total estate consists of $850,000 of assets in addition to the real estate described in (2).

Instructions

a Discuss the legal implications and the resulting rights of each of the persons or entities described above in (1) through (7) as a result of the facts given and the application of bankruptcy law to them. Give reasons for any conclusions stated.

b What is the bankruptcy dividend (percentage on the dollar) that each general creditor will receive? Show calculations in good form.

Case 14-2 Ford Corporation is insolvent. It has 20 unsecured creditors and 3 creditors who have liens on its assets. Ford, while insolvent, paid $20,000 to Jones Company, one of its unsecured creditors, in partial payment of goods sold and delivered by Jones to Ford six months earlier. Adams Company, one of the secured creditors, loaned Ford cash ten months ago and, two months ago, when it knew Ford was insolvent, obtained from Ford a security interest in the company's accounts receivable which Adams perfected under applicable state law. Collins Company, another of the secured creditors, sold Ford machinery six months ago and obtained a security interest therein which was not perfected. Barton Company, the remaining secured creditor, holds a mortgage on Ford's plant which it obtained two years ago and which was filed and recorded under applicable state law.

Instructions

a Has Ford committed an act of bankruptcy? Explain.

b Assuming that Ford has committed an act of bankruptcy, how many of its creditors must join in an involuntary petition in bankruptcy? How much in provable claims must such petitioning creditors have? Explain.

c Assume that an involuntary petition has been filed against Ford and Ford has been adjudicated bankrupt, all other facts recited above remaining the same. Discuss the rights of Adams, Collins, and Barton in relation to Ford's trustee in bankruptcy.

d Assuming that Jones received a preference, might the trustee be able to recover the $20,000 from Jones? Explain.

Case 14-3 During your examination of the financial statements of Zuber Corporation, you note that as of September 30, Year 5:

(1) Current liabilities exceed current assets at current fair value.

(2) Total assets at current fair value substantially exceed total liabilities.

(3) Cash position is poor and current payables are past due.

(4) Trade creditors and secured creditors are pressing for payment, and several lawsuits have been commenced against Zuber.

Further investigation reveals the following:

On August 31, Year 5, Zuber made a $1,000 payment to Davis Company on a $20,000 mortgage indebtedness over one year past due. The current fair value of the mortgaged property on August 31, Year 5, was $35,000.

On September 20, Year 5, a trade creditor, Mann Company, obtained a judgment against Zuber, which under applicable law constitutes a lien on Zuber's real property.

On September 22, Year 5, Zuber paid a substantial amount to Case Company, a supplier, on an account over one year old.

On September 27, Year 5, Zuber executed and delivered a financing statement to Forbes Company, a vendor, from which Zuber had purchased machinery six months earlier. Forbes filed and perfected the financing statement.

Instructions

a As of September 30, Year 5, did any of the above transactions constitute acts of bankruptcy? Explain.

b As of September 30, Year 5, could the creditors of Zuber file an involuntary petition in bankruptcy against Zuber if a sufficient number of them having a sufficient amount of claims decide to do so? Explain.

c Independent of your answers to parts a and b, assume the same facts set out above except that Zuber's total liabilities exceed total assets at current fair value, and that on October 2, Year 5, Zuber filed a voluntary petition in bankruptcy, and a trustee has been appointed.

(1) What are the rights, if any, of the trustee against each of the creditors involved in the four transactions stated in the problem? Explain.

(2) What are the general requirements for creditors to be entitled to vote on and participate in a bankruptcy proceeding? Explain for each of the four creditors involved whether it meets these requirements, and why.

PROBLEMS

14-4 The following information is available at October 10, Year 5, for Archer Company, which is having considerable difficulty paying its liabilities as they become due:

	Carrying amount
Cash	$ 4,000
Accounts receivable (net): Current fair value equal to carrying amount	46,000
Inventories: Net realizable value, $18,000; pledged on	
$21,000 of notes payable	39,000
Plant assets: Current fair value, $67,400; pledged on mortgage note payable	134,000
Accumulated depreciation	27,000
Supplies: Current fair value, $1,500	2,000
Wages payable, all earned during latest month	5,800
Property taxes payable	1,200
Accounts payable	60,000
Notes payable, $21,000 secured	40,000
Mortgage note payable, including interest of $400	50,400
Capital stock, $5 par	100,000
Deficit	59,400

Instructions
a Prepare a statement of affairs using the form illustrated on pages 552–553.
b Prepare a working paper showing the estimated percentage of claims each group of creditors should reasonably expect to receive if Archer Company petitions for bankruptcy.

14-5 Ransom Corporation was in financial difficulty because of declining sales and poor cost controls. Its stockholders and principal creditors had asked for an estimate of the financial results of the sale of the assets, the payment of liabilities, and the liquidation of the corporation. The independent accountants for Ransom Corporation subsequently prepared the statement of affairs which appears on pages 572–573.

On January 2, Year 4, Ransom Corporation filed a voluntary petition for bankruptcy under the Bankruptcy Act. Richard Takaki was appointed as trustee by the bankruptcy court to take custody of the assets, make payments to creditors, and implement an orderly liquidation of the company. In January, Year 4, the trustee completed the following transactions:

Jan. 2 Recorded the assets and liabilities of Ransom Corporation in a separate set of accounting records. The assets were recorded at current fair value and all liabilities were recorded at the estimated amounts payable to the various groups of creditors.

Jan. 7 Sold the land and buildings at an auction for $52,000 cash and paid $42,550 to the mortgagee. The payment included interest of $50 which accrued in January.

Jan. 10 Made cash payments as follows:

Wages payable	$1,500
FICA and income taxes withheld and accrued	800
Completion of inventories	400
Liquidation costs	600

Jan. 31 Cash receipts for the period from January 8 to January 31 were

Collection on accounts receivable at carrying amount, including $10,000 assigned accounts	17,500
Sale of inventories	18,000
Sale of Public Service Company bonds	920

Jan. 31 Additional cash payments were:

Liquidation costs	1,250
Note payable to bank (from proceeds of collection of assigned accounts receivable)	10,000
Dividend of $0.50 on the dollar to unsecured creditors	30,500

Instructions
a Prepare the journal entries for the transactions listed above in the accounting records of the trustee.
b Prepare a statement of realization and liquidation for the month of January, Year 4. Use the form illustrated on page 556.
c Prepare a trial balance for the trustee at January 31, Year 4.

14-6 Caine Corporation advises you that it is facing bankruptcy proceedings. As the company's independent CPA, you are aware of its financial condition.

The unaudited balance sheet of Caine Corporation at July 10, Year 10, and additional information are presented on page 574:

RANSOM CORPORATION
Statement of Affairs
December 31, Year 3

Carrying amount	Assets	Current fair value	Estimated amount available	Loss or (gain) on realization
	Assets pledged with fully secured creditors:			
$ 4,000	Land	$20,000		$(16,000)
25,000	Buildings	30,000		(5,000)
	Total	$50,000		
	Less: Fully secured claims (contra)	42,500	$ 7,500	
	Assets pledged with partially secured creditors:			
10,000	Accounts receivable (deducted contra)	$10,000		
	Free assets:			
700	Cash	$ 700	700	
10,450	Accounts receivable	10,450	10,450	
40,000	Inventories $19,350			
	Less: Cost to complete 400	18,950	18,950	21,050
9,100	Factory supplies	-0-	-0-	9,100
5,750	Public Service Company bonds	900	900	4,850
38,000	Machinery and equipment	18,000	18,000	20,000
	Total estimated amount available		$56,500	$34,000
	Less: Liabilities with priority (contra)		5,500	
	Estimated amount available for unsecured creditors		$51,000	
	Estimated deficiency to unsecured creditors		10,000	
$143,000			$61,000	

Carrying amount	Liabilities & stockholders' equity		Amount unsecured
	Liabilities with priority:		
$ 1,500	Wages payable	$ 1,500	
800	FICA and income taxes withheld and accrued	800	
	Estimated liquidation costs payable	3,200	
	Total (deducted contra)	$ 5,500	
	Fully secured creditors:		
42,000	Mortgage note payable	$42,000	
500	Accrued interest payable	500	
	Total (deducted contra)	$42,500	
	Partially secured creditors:		
25,000	Notes payable to bank	$25,000	
	Less: Assigned accounts receivable	10,000	$15,000
	Unsecured creditors:		
20,000	Notes payable to suppliers		20,000
26,000	Accounts payable		26,000
27,200	Stockholders' equity		
$143,000			$61,000

CAINE CORPORATION
Balance Sheet
July 10, Year 10

Assets

Cash	$ 12,000
Short-term investments, at cost	20,000
Accounts receivable, less allowance for doubtful accounts	90,000
Finished goods inventory	60,000
Raw materials inventory	40,000
Short-term prepayments	5,000
Land	13,000
Buildings (net)	90,000
Machinery (net)	120,000
Goodwill	20,000
Total assets	$470,000

Liabilities & Stockholders' Equity

Notes payable to bank	$135,000
Accounts payable	94,200
Accrued wages	15,000
Mortgage notes payable	130,000
Capital stock	100,000
Retained earnings (deficit)	(4,200)
Total liabilities & stockholders' equity	$470,000

Additional information

(1) Cash includes a $500 travel advance which has been spent.

(2) Accounts receivable of $40,000 have been pledged as collateral for notes payable to banks in the amount of $30,000. Credit balances of $5,000 are netted in the accounts receivable total. All accounts are expected to be collected except those for which an allowance has been established.

(3) Short-term investments consist of government bonds costing $10,000 and 500 shares of Owens Company stock. The current fair value of the bonds is $10,000; the current fair value of the stock is $18 per share. The bonds have accrued interest receivable of $200. The short-term investments are pledged as collateral for a $20,000 note payable to bank.

(4) Estimated realizable value of finished goods is $50,000 and of raw materials is $30,000. For additional out-of-pocket costs of $10,000 the raw materials would realize $59,900 as finished goods.

(5) Short-term prepayments will be exhausted during the liquidation period.

(6) The appraised value of plant assets is as follows: Land, $25,000; buildings, $110,000; machinery, $65,000.

(7) Accounts payable include $15,000 withheld FICA and income taxes and $6,000 due to creditors who had been reassured by the president of Caine that they would be paid. There are unrecorded employer's FICA taxes in the amount of $500.

(8) Wages payable are not subject to any limitations under the Bankruptcy Act.

(9) Mortgage notes payable consist of $100,000 on land and buildings, and a $30,000 installment contract on machinery. Total unrecorded accrued interest for these liabilities amounts to $2,400.

(10) Probable judgment on a pending damage suit is estimated at $50,000.

(11) Costs to be incurred in connection with the liquidation are estimated at $10,000.

(12) You have not submitted an invoice for $5,000 for the April 30, Year 10, annual audit of Caine, and you estimate a $1,000 fee for liquidation work.

Instructions

a Prepare a statement of affairs for Caine Corporation at July 10, Year 10.

b Prepare a working paper which explains the amount of the estimated deficiency to unsecured creditors of Caine Corporation.

14-7 On June 30, Year 6, Anne Asch was appointed receiver of Rogers Company. The company's general ledger trial balance on that date is presented below:

ROGERS COMPANY

Trial Balance

June 30, Year 6

Cash	$ 14,135	
Notes receivable	29,000	
Accrued interest on notes receivable	615	
Accounts receivable	19,500	
Stock subscriptions receivable	5,000	
Allowance for doubtful notes and accounts		$ 800
Inventories	48,000	
Land	10,000	
Building	50,000	
Accumulated depreciation: Building		15,000
Machinery and equipment	33,000	
Accumulated depreciation: Machinery and equipment		19,000
Furniture and fixtures	21,000	
Accumulated depreciation: Furniture and fixtures		9,500
Goodwill	8,000	
Organization costs	1,600	
Note payable to City Bank		18,000
Notes payable to Municipal Trust Co.		6,000
Notes payable to vendors		24,000
Accrued interest on notes payable		1,280
Accounts payable		80,520
Wages payable		1,400
FICA and income taxes withheld and accrued		430
Mortgage bonds payable		32,000
Accrued interest payable on mortgage bonds		1,820
Capital stock		65,000
Capital stock subscribed		5,000
Retained earnings—deficit	39,900	
Totals	$279,750	$279,750

Additional information

(1) Notes receivable of $25,000 were pledged to collateralize the $18,000 note payable to City Bank. Interest of $500 was accrued on the pledged notes and $600 was accrued on the $18,000 note payable to the bank. All the pledged notes were collectible. Of the remaining notes receivable, a $1,000 non-interest-bearing note was uncollectible.

(2) Accounts receivable include $7,000 from Boren Company, which currently is being liquidated. Creditors expect to realize $0.40 on the dollar. The allowance for doubtful accounts is adequate to cover any other uncollectible accounts. A total of $3,200 of the remaining collectible accounts receivable was pledged as collateral for the notes payable to Municipal Trust Co. of $6,000 with accrued interest of $180 at June 30, Year 6.

(3) The subscriptions receivable from stockholders for no-par capital stock are due July 31, Year 6, and are considered fully collectible.

(4) Inventories are valued at cost and are expected to realize 25% of cost on a forced liquidation sale after the write-off of $10,000 of obsolete stock.

(5) Land and buildings, which are appraised at 110% of their carrying amount, are mortgaged as collateral for the bonds. Interest of $1,820 was accrued on the bonds to June 30, Year 6. The company expects to realize 20% of the cost of its machinery and equipment, and 50% of the cost of its furniture and fixtures after incurring refinishing costs of $800.

(6) Estimated costs of liquidation are $4,500. Depreciation, prepayments, and accruals have been adjusted to June 30, Year 6.

(7) The company has net operating loss carryovers for income tax purposes of $22,000 for Year 4, and $28,000 for Year 5. Assume the income tax rate in effect for those years was 50%.

Instructions

a Prepare a statement of affairs classifying assets according to their availability for secured and unsecured creditors and classifying liabilities according to their legal priority and secured status. The column headings below are suggested for the statement:

For assets:	Carrying amount	Assets	Current fair value	Estimated amount available	Loss or (gain) on realization

For liabilities and stockholders' equity:	Carrying amount	Liabilities & stockholders' equity		Amount unsecured

b Compute the estimated settlement per dollar of unsecured liabilities.

14-8 Martin Corporation had $105,000 of dividends in arrears on its preferred stock at March 31, Year 20. While retained earnings were adequate to permit the payment of accumulated dividends, the company's management did not wish to weaken its working capital position. They also realized that a portion of the plant assets was no longer used by the company. Therefore, management proposed the following reorganization, which was approved by stockholders, to be effective as of April 1, Year 20:

(1) The preferred stock was to be exchanged for $300,000 of 5% debentures. Dividends in arrears were to be settled by the issuance of $120,000 of $10 par, 5%, noncumulative preferred stock.

(2) Common stock was to be assigned a par of $50 per share.

(3) Goodwill was to be written off; plant assets were to be written down, based on appraisal and estimates of economic value, by a total of $103,200 consisting of $85,400 increase in the Accumulated Depreciation account and $17,800 decrease in plant assets; other current assets were to be written down by $10,460 to reduce receivables and inventories to net realizable values.

The condensed balance sheet at March 31, Year 20, is presented below:

MARTIN CORPORATION
Balance Sheet
March 31, Year 20

Assets

Cash		$ 30,000
Other current assets		252,890
Plant assets	$1,458,250	
Less: Accumulated depreciation	512,000	946,250
Goodwill		50,000
Total assets		$1,279,140

Liabilities & Stockholders' Equity

Current liabilities	$ 132,170
7% cumulative preferred stock, $100 par ($105,000 dividends in arrears)	300,000
Common stock, no-par, 9,000 shares outstanding	648,430
Paid-in capital in excess of par: preferred stock	22,470
Retained earnings	176,070
Total liabilities & stockholders' equity	$1,279,140

Instructions

a Prepare journal entries to give effect to the reorganization as of April 1, Year 20. Give complete explanations with each entry and comment on any possible options in recording the reorganization.

b Prepare a balance sheet at April 30, Year 20, assuming that net income for April was $15,000. The operations resulted in $11,970 increase in cash, $18,700 increase in other current assets, $7,050 increase in current liabilities, and $8,620 increase in the Accumulated Depreciation account.

14-9 Osman Corporation is considering dissolution because one of the three stockholders, Adam Wright, cannot get along with the other two, Ben Yates and Carla Zorb. At the end of Year 7, Yates and Zorb agree to reorganize the corporation into a partnership.

The information relative to the reorganization plan follows:

(1) The balance sheet of Osman Corporation at December 31, Year 7, is shown below:

OSMAN CORPORATION
Balance Sheet
December 31, Year 7

Assets

Current assets:	
Cash	$105,000
Accounts receivable (net of $22,000 allowance)	135,000
Inventories	225,000
Short-term prepayments	4,500
Total current assets	$469,500

(cont.)

OSMAN CORPORATION
Balance Sheet
December 31, Year 7 (concluded)

Assets

Building, stated at appraisal value determined at Dec. 31, Year 7	$125,000	
Less: Accumulated depreciation	27,500	$97,500
Investment in land		20,000
Other assets		10,000
Total assets		$597,000

Liabilities & Stockholders' Equity

Current liabilities:

Note payable to Adam Wright, a stockholder		$ 30,000
Accounts payable		110,000
Accrued liabilities		32,000
Total current liabilities		$172,000

Stockholders' equity:

Preferred stock, $100 par (liquidation value $110); authorized, 1,000 shares; in treasury, 400 shares; outstanding, 600 shares	$100,000	
Common stock, no-par; stated value $1; authorized, 200,000 shares; issued and outstanding, 100,000 shares	100,000	
Paid-in capital in excess of stated value	150,000	
Total paid-in capital	$350,000	
Capital from appraisal of building in Year 7	50,000	
Retained earnings	72,250	
Subtotal	$472,250	
Less: Treasury stock, 400 shares of preferred stock (at cost)	47,250	425,000
Total liabilities & stockholders' equity		$597,000

(2) The capital stock records of Osman Corporation at December 31, Year 7, indicate that the three stockholders have retained their respective interests since the corporation was organized five years ago as follows:

Stockholder	Total invested	Preferred		Common	
		Shares	Amount	Shares	Amount
Ben Yates	$115,000	300	$30,000	35,000	$ 85,000
Carla Zorb	105,000	100	10,000	40,000	95,000
Adam Wright	90,000	200	20,000	25,000	70,000
Totals	$310,000	600	$60,000	100,000	$250,000

(3) In accordance with the reorganization plan, the corporation will acquire Wright's stock, and thereafter the corporation will be liquidated by an appropriate disposition of its net assets.
(4) In order to finance the acquisition of Wright's stock, the building was appraised as a basis for an $80,000 mortgage loan arranged by the corporation with an insurance company. The appraisal was made at December 31, Year 7, and was recorded in the accounting records as follows:

	Market value per appraisal	Cost	Appraisal capital
Building..	$125,000	$70,000	$55,000
Less: Accumulated depreciation	27,500	22,500	5,000
Totals	$ 97,500	$47,500	$50,000

(5) Wright's stock is to be acquired for cash of $110 per share for the preferred stock and $3 per share for the common stock. The stock acquired from Wright is to be retired.
(6) After the acquisition of Wright's stock, disposition of the net assets of the corporation in complete liquidation of the corporation is to be made as follows:
 (a) The note payable to Wright is to be paid in cash.
 (b) The treasury stock is to be canceled, and the preferred stock owned by Yates and Zorb is to be retired at $110 a share.
 (c) The investment in land is to be transferred to Zorb at its current fair value of $36,000.
 (d) The remaining assets are to be acquired and the liabilities (including the $80,000 mortgage loan) are to be assumed by a partnership organized by Yates and Zorb. Yates is to withdraw cash from the partnership as necessary to equalize his capital account with that of Zorb.

Instructions Prepare a working paper giving effect to the reorganization of Osman Corporation into a partnership as of December 31, Year 7, in accordance with the agreement among the three stockholders. Use the following columnar headings in the working paper:

Accounts	Osman Corporation balance sheet Dec. 31, Year 7		Transactions to implement reorganization		Yates & Zorb Partnership balance sheet Dec. 31, Year 7	

15

ACCOUNTING FOR ESTATES AND TRUSTS

Estates and *trusts* are accounting entities, as well as taxable entities under the provisions of federal income tax laws and regulations. The individuals or corporations which manage the assets of estates and trusts are *fiduciaries;* they exercise stewardship for those assets in accordance with the provisions of a *will,* a *trust document,* or state laws.

In this chapter we shall deal first with certain aspects of estates, including wills, and then discuss and illustrate the accounting for estates; the last section covers the legal and accounting aspects of trusts.

LEGAL AND ACCOUNTING ASPECTS OF ESTATES

State laws (generally termed *probate codes*) regulate the administration and distribution of estates of decedents, missing persons, and other individuals subject to protection of the court. The many variations among the probate codes of the fifty states led to the drafting of a *Uniform Probate Code* developed by the National Conference of Commissioners on Uniform State Laws and approved by the American Bar Association. Although the Uniform Probate Code has not yet been adopted by all states, we shall use the Code to illustrate certain legal issues underlying accounting for estates.

Provisions of Uniform Probate Code governing estates

The Uniform Probate Code identifies an **estate** as all the property of a decedent, trust, or other person whose affairs are subject to the Code.[1] **Person** is defined as an individual, a corporation, an organization, or other legal entity. Thus, the Code establishes the accounting entity status of an estate.

The Uniform Probate Code also provides that the real and personal property of a decedent is to be awarded to the persons specified in the will. In the absence of a will—a condition known as **intestacy**—the decedent's property goes to heirs, as enumerated in the Code. Thus, as the Code points out, the intentions of a **testator** (a person creating a will) control the disposition of a decedent's property.[2]

Wills   The Uniform Probate Code provides that a will shall be in writing, signed by the testator, or in the testator's name by some other person in the testator's presence and by the testator's direction, and also signed by at least two witnesses. The chief exception to these requirements is a **holographic will**—a will having its material provisions and signature in the handwriting of the testator.

Probate of Wills   Probate of a will is action by the probate court (also known as **surrogate** or **orphan's** court) to validate the will. The Uniform Probate Code provides for two types of probate—**informal** and **formal.** Informal probate is initiated by the application of an interested party filed with a court official known as a **registrar.** After thorough review of the completeness and propriety of an application for informal probate, the registrar issues a written statement of informal probate, thus making the will effective.

Formal probate is litigation to determine whether a decedent left a valid will, and it is initiated by a petition filed by an interested party requesting the probate court to order probate of the will. The petition also may request a finding that the decedent died intestate. During the court hearings, any party to the formal probate proceedings may oppose the will; however, the burden of proof that the will is invalid is on the contestant of the will. After completion of the hearings, the court enters an order for formal probate of a will found to be valid, or an order that the decedent died **intestate** (without a valid will). Generally, no formal or informal probate proceedings may be undertaken more than three years after the decedent's death.

Appointment of Personal Representative   In both informal and formal probate proceedings, the probate court appoints a **personal representative** of the decedent to administer the decedent's estate. A personal repre-

[1] Uniform Probate Code, Sec. 1-201(11).

[2] Ibid., Sec. 2-603.

sentative named in the decedent's will is called an **executor.** If the decedent died intestate, the court-appointed personal representative is known as an **administrator.** The Uniform Probate Code requires the probate court to issue **letters testamentary** to the personal representative before administration of the estate can begin. Because personal representatives are fiduciaries, they must observe standards of care in administering estates that prudent persons would observe in dealing with the property of others. The personal representative is entitled to reasonable compensation for services.

Powers and Duties of Personal Representative   The personal representative of a decedent is empowered to take possession and control of the decedent's property, and to have title to the property in trust for the benefit of creditors and beneficiaries of the estate. The personal representative has many additional powers, such as: (1) the right to continue any single proprietorship business of the decedent for not more than four months following the date of the personal administrator's appointment; and (2) the authority to allocate items of revenue and expenses of the estate to either **estate principal** (corpus) or **estate income,** as provided by the will or by law. The allocations to estate principal and estate income comprise the chief accounting problem for an estate and are discussed in a subsequent section of this chapter.

Not later than 30 days after appointment, the personal representative must inform the decedent's **devisees** or heirs of the appointment. (A **devisee** is any person or trust named in a will to receive real or personal property of the decedent in a transfer known as a **devise.**) Within three months after appointment, the personal representative must prepare an inventory of property owned by the decedent at date of death, together with a listing of any liens against the property. The property in the inventory must be valued at current fair value at date of death; to this end, the personal representative may retain the services of an appraiser. The inventory is filed with the probate court, and copies are provided to interested parties who request them. If, after the filing of the original inventory, other assets of the decedent are discovered, the personal representative must file a supplementary inventory with the probate court.

Exempt Property and Allowances   Like the Bankruptcy Act discussed in Chapter 14, the Uniform Probate Code provides for certain exemptions from claims against the estate assets, even by devisees. These exemptions are as follows:

1 *Homestead allowance.*   The decedent's surviving spouse, or surviving minor and dependent children, are entitled to an aggregate **homestead allowance** of $5,000. This allowance is in addition to any share of the estate passing to the spouse or children by the will.
2 *Exempt property.*   The decedent's surviving spouse or children are entitled to an aggregate $3,500 value of automobiles, household furniture and furnishings, appliances, and personal effects.

3 *Family allowance.* The surviving spouse and children who were being supported by the decedent are entitled to a reasonable cash allowance, payable in a lump sum not exceeding $6,000 or in installments not exceeding $500 per month for one year, during the administration of the estate. The family allowance has priority over all claims against the estate, but does not have priority over the homestead allowance.

Claims of Creditors against the Estate Upon formal appointment, a personal representative is required to publish a notice once a week for three successive weeks, in a newspaper of general circulation, requesting creditors of the estate to present their claims within four months after the date of the first publication, or be forever barred. If the estate assets not exempt under the Uniform Probate Code are insufficient to pay all claims in full, the personal representative shall pay claims in the following order:

1 Expenses of administering the estate
2 Decedent's funeral expenses and medical and hospital expenses of the decedent's last illness
3 Debts and taxes with preference under federal or state laws
4 All other claims

Four months after publication of the first notice to estate creditors, the personal representative initiates payment of claims in the order outlined above, after first providing for homestead, family, and support allowances.

Distributions to Devisees The personal representative also has the duty of distributing estate assets to the devisees named in the will. The assets are to be distributed in kind to the extent possible, rather than first being converted to cash and then distributed in cash.

If estate assets which are not exempt are insufficient to cover creditors' claims as well as all devises, the devises *abate*—or are reduced—in the sequence provided for in the decedent's will. If the will is silent as to order of abatement, the Uniform Probate Code provides the following abatement sequence:

1 Property not specifically mentioned in the will
2 *Residuary devises,* which are devises of all estate property remaining after general and specific devises are satisfied
3 *General devises,* which are gifts of a sum of money or a number of countable monetary assets, such as 500 shares of Mercury Company common stock
4 *Specific devises,* which are gifts of identified objects, such as named paintings, automobiles, stock certificates, or real property

Devises may be granted to the devisees *in trust,* which requires the establishment of a *testamentary trust,* or one provided for by a will. Trusts are discussed in a subsequent section of this chapter.

Estate and Inheritance Taxes The federal estate tax assessed against the net assets of an estate, and inheritance taxes assessed by various states against devisees and heirs of a decedent, often called **death taxes,** must be apportioned to the various devisees in the manner outlined in the will. If the will is silent on apportionment, the Uniform Probate Code applies. The Code provides that the estate and inheritance taxes are to be apportioned to the various devisees in the ratio of each devisee's interest to the aggregate interests of all devisees.

Closing the Estate   No earlier than six months after the date of appointment, a personal representative may close an estate by filing a statement with the probate court. The written content of this statement is described in the Uniform Probate Code; this legal statement usually is accompanied by a financial statement known as a **charge and discharge statement.**

Provisions of Revised Uniform Principal and Income Act governing estates

We have previously noted that the chief accounting problem for an estate is the allocation of revenue and expenses of the estate to **estate principal** or **estate income.** This allocation is important because many wills provide that income from the assets of a testamentary trust may be paid to an **income beneficiary,** while the principal of a trust is paid to a **principal beneficiary** or **remainderman.** A proper accounting for principal and income by the personal representative of a decedent is essential before the estate is closed.

The Revised Uniform Principal and Income Act provides guidelines for allocation in the absence of instructions in the will or trust agreement. Through 1978, many states had adopted all or part of this Act, often with modifications. The provisions of the Revised Uniform Principal and Income Act include the following:

1 **Income** is defined as the return in money or property derived from the use of principal, including rent, interest, cash dividends, or any other revenue received during administration of a decedent's estate.
2 **Principal** is defined as property set aside by its owner to be held in trust for eventual delivery to a remainderman. Principal includes proceeds of insurance on principal assets, stock and liquidating dividends, and allowances for depreciation. Any accrued rent or other revenue at the date of death of the testator is principal.
3 Premium or discount on investments in bonds included in principal is not amortized. All proceeds from sale or redemption of bonds are principal.
4 Income is charged with a reasonable provision for depreciation, computed in accordance with generally accepted accounting principles, on all depreciable assets except property used by a beneficiary such as a residence or a personal automobile. Income also is charged with expenses of administering and preserving income-producing estate property, such as property taxes, ordinary repairs, and insurance premiums.
5 Principal is charged with expenditures incurred in preparing principal property for sale or rent, cost of investing and reinvesting principal assets, major

repairs to principal assets, and income taxes on receipts or gains allocable to principal.

6 Court costs, attorneys' fees, and accountants' fees for periodic reporting to the probate court, as well as trustees' fees, are apportioned between principal and income.

Illustration of accounting for an estate

Now that we have reviewed certain legal issues involved in estates, we shall illustrate the accounting for estates, including the charge and discharge statement rendered by the personal representative at the closing of the estate. Estate accounting is carried out in accordance with the *accountability* method previously illustrated in Chapter 14. The accounting records of the personal representative reflect only those items for which the representative is accountable, under the equation Assets = Accountability.

Our illustration is based on the following data:

1 Jessica Davis, a single woman who lived alone, died March 18, Year 3, after a brief illness which required her to be hospitalized. Her will, approved for informal probate on March 25, Year 3, contained the following devises:

  a $10,000 in cash to each of three household employees: Alice Martin, cook; Angela Wilson, housekeeper; Nolan Ames, gardener and maintenance man. Devisees must waive claims for unpaid wages at date of death.

  b 200 shares of Preston Company common stock to Nancy Grimes, a niece.

  c Paintings, other art objects, clothing, jewelry, and personal effects to Frances Grimes, a married woman, the only living sister of Jessica Davis.

  d Residence, furniture, and furnishings to Wallace Davis, a single man, the only living brother of Jessica Davis.

  e $5,000 cash to Universal Charities, a nonprofit organization.

  f Residue of estate in trust to Nancy Grimes; income to be paid at the end of each calendar quarter to Grimes until her twenty-first birthday October 1, Year 8, at which time the principal also is paid to Grimes.

2 Paul Hastings, attorney for Jessica Davis and executor of her estate, published the required newspaper notice to creditors on March 26, April 2, and April 9, Year 3. The following claims were received from creditors within the four-month statutory period:

List of claims against estate of Jessica Davis	*Description of claims*	*Amount*
	Funeral expenses (Watts Mortuary)	$ 810
	Hospital bills (Suburban Hospital)......................................	1,928
	Doctor's fees (Charles Carson, M.D.)..................................	426
	Morningside Department Store	214
	Various residence bills	87
	Total claims against estate	$3,465

3 Hastings prepared final individual federal and state income tax returns for Jessica Davis for the period January 1 to March 18, Year 3. The federal return showed income tax due in the amount of $457; the state return showed no tax due.

4 Hastings prepared the following inventory of property owned by Jessica Davis at March 18, Year 3:

<table>
<tr><td rowspan="2" style="text-align:right">List of
property
included in
estate of
Jessica Davis</td><td>**Description of property**</td><td>**Current fair value
Mar. 18, Year 3**</td></tr>
<tr><td>Bank checking account ....</td><td>$ 2,157</td></tr>
<tr><td></td><td>Bank savings account (including accrued interest) ....</td><td>30,477</td></tr>
<tr><td></td><td>Savings and loan association 2-year certificate of deposit
   maturing June 30, Year 3 (including accrued interest) ....</td><td>26,475</td></tr>
<tr><td></td><td>Accrued salary earned for period Mar. 1 to Mar. 8, Year 3 ....</td><td>214</td></tr>
<tr><td></td><td>Claim against medical insurance carrier ....</td><td>1,526</td></tr>
<tr><td></td><td>Social security benefits receivable ....</td><td>14,820</td></tr>
<tr><td></td><td>Proceeds of life insurance policy (payable to estate) ....</td><td>25,000</td></tr>
<tr><td></td><td>Marketable securities:</td><td></td></tr>
<tr><td></td><td>   Common stock of Preston Company, 200 shares ....</td><td>8,000</td></tr>
<tr><td></td><td>   Common stock of Arthur Corporation, 100 shares ....</td><td>6,500</td></tr>
<tr><td></td><td>Residence ....</td><td>40,800*</td></tr>
<tr><td></td><td>Furniture and furnishings ....</td><td>2,517</td></tr>
<tr><td></td><td>Paintings and other art objects ....</td><td>16,522</td></tr>
<tr><td></td><td>Clothing, jewelry, personal effects ....</td><td>625</td></tr>
<tr><td></td><td>Automobile ....</td><td>2,187</td></tr>
<tr><td></td><td>   Total current fair value of estate property ....</td><td>$177,820</td></tr>
</table>

* Subject to unpaid trust deed note of $15,500 due $500 monthly on the last day of the month, plus interest at 10% per year on the unpaid balance.

5 Subsequent to preparing the above inventory, Hastings discovered a certificate for 600 shares of Campbell Company common stock with a current fair value of $18,000.

6 Hastings prepared the federal estate tax return for the Estate of Jessica Davis, Deceased. The return showed a tax due of $18,556. Hastings also prepared state inheritance tax returns for the devisees showing aggregate taxes due of $5,020.

7 Hastings administered the estate, charging a fee of $2,500, and closed the estate by filing the required legal statement and a charge and discharge statement prepared by a CPA who was a member of Hastings's law firm.

The journal entries on pages 587–590 would be entered in the accounting records for the Estate of Jessica Davis, Deceased. (Dates for journal entries are assumed.) Comments relating to specific journal entries which require particular emphasis start on page 591.

PAUL HASTINGS, EXECUTOR
Of the Will of Jessica Davis, Deceased
General Journal

Year 3

Mar. 18 Principal Cash 2,157
Savings Account 30,477
Certificate of Deposit 26,475
Accrued Salary Receivable 214
Medical Insurance Claim Receivable 1,526
Social Security Benefits Receivable 14,820
Life Insurance Claim Receivable 25,000
Marketable Securities 14,500
Residence 40,800
Furniture and Furnishings 2,517
Paintings and Other Art Objects 16,522
Clothing, Jewelry, Personal Effects 625
Automobile 2,187
    Note Payable Secured by Deed of Trust 15,500
    Accrued Interest Payable
    ($15,500 × 10% × 18/360) 78
    Estate Principal Balance
    ($177,820 − $15,578) 162,242
To record inventory of property owned by decedent
Jessica Davis at date of death, net of lien against
residence.

25 Marketable Securities 18,000
    Assets Discovered 18,000
To record supplemental inventory for property discovered subsequent to filing of original inventory.

31 Principal Cash 70,511
Income Cash 55
    Savings Account 30,477
    Accrued Salary Receivable 214
    Social Security Benefits Receivable 14,820
    Life Insurance Claim Receivable 25,000
    Interest Revenue 55
To record liquidation of various assets in cash,
including $55 interest received on savings account
for period Mar. 18–31, Year 3.

(cont.)

PAUL HASTINGS, EXECUTOR
Of the Will of Jessica Davis, Deceased
General Journal (continued)

Mar. 31	Distributions to Income Beneficiaries	55	
	Income Cash		55

To distribute income cash payable to residuary devisee Nancy Grimes, as required by the will.

Apr. 2	Principal Cash	2,050	
	Loss on Disposal of Principal Assets	137	
	Automobile		2,187

To record sale of automobile at a loss.

4	Devises Distributed	5,000	
	Principal Cash		5,000

To record distribution of general devise to Universal Charities.

16	Liabilities Paid	3,922	
	Principal Cash		3,922

To record following liabilities paid:

Funeral expenses (Watts Mortuary)	$ 810
Hospital bills (Suburban Hospital)	1,928
Doctor's fees (Charles Carson, M.D.) . . .	426
Final federal income tax	457
Morningside Department Store	214
Various residence bills	87
Total	$3,922

19	Principal Cash	1,526	
	Medical Insurance Claim Receivable		1,526

To record collection of medical insurance claim.

24	Income Cash	1,500	
	Principal Cash	1,000	
	Payable to Devisees		1,000
	Dividend Revenue		1,500

To record receipt of quarterly cash dividends on common stock, as follows:

(cont.)

PAUL HASTINGS, EXECUTOR
Of the Will of Jessica Davis, Deceased
General Journal (continued)

Preston Company:
200 shares × $5 a share $1,000
Arthur Corporation:
100 shares × $3 a share 300
Campbell Company:
600 shares × $2 a share 1,200
Total $2,500

Apr. 25 Receivable from Devisees......................... 23,576
    Principal Cash 23,576
To record payment of federal estate tax and state
inheritance taxes on behalf of devisees, as follows:
Federal estate tax $18,556
State inheritance taxes 5,020
Total $23,576

26 Principal Cash 6,295
    Receivable from Devisees................... 6,295
To record receipt of cash from specific devisees
for their shares of federal estate tax and state inherit-
ance taxes, as follows:
Frances Grimes: $23,576 × 10.2% $2,405
Wallace Davis: $23,576 × 16.5% 3,890
Total $6,295

27 Devises Distributed 30,000
    Receivable from Devisees................... 4,173
    Principal Cash 25,827
To record payment of cash to general devisees, less
amounts receivable for their shares of federal estate
tax and state inheritance taxes, as follows:
$10,000 devises payable to Alice Martin, Angela
Wilson, Nolan Ames: $10,000 × 3 ..... $30,000
Shares of death taxes:
($23,576 × 5.9%) × 3 4,173
Net cash paid $25,827

(cont.)

PAUL HASTINGS, EXECUTOR
Of the Will of Jessica Davis, Deceased
General Journal (concluded)

Apr. 30	Note Payable Secured by Deed of Trust	15,500	
	Accrued Interest Payable	78	
	Devises Distributed	52,886	
	Payable to Devisees	1,000	
	Marketable Securities		8,000
	Residence		40,800
	Furniture and Furnishings		2,517
	Paintings and Other Art Objects		16,522
	Clothing, Jewelry, Personal Effects		625
	Principal Cash		1,000

To transfer to devisee Nancy Grimes cash for dividend received on Preston Company common stock, and to record distribution of devises as follows:

General devise to Nancy Grimes:		
200 shares of Preston Company common stock	$ 8,000	
Specific devise to Frances Grimes:		
Paintings, other art objects, clothing, jewelry, personal effects	17,147	
Specific devise to Wallace Davis:		
Residence, net of deed of trust, with furniture and furnishings	27,739	
Total	$52,886	

May 1	Administrative Expenses	2,500	
	Principal Cash		2,500
	To record payment for executor's fee.		
3	Devises Distributed	85,797	
	Distributions to Income Beneficiaries	1,500	
	Principal Cash		21,714
	Income Cash		1,500
	Certificate of Deposit		26,475
	Marketable Securities		24,500
	Receivable from Devisees		13,108

To record distribution of residuary devise (principal and income) to Third National Bank, trustee for Nancy Grimes, devisee.

Mar. 18 Journal Entry This entry records the executor's inventory of estate assets, including accrued interest and accrued salary at the date of death. Since the decedent was a single woman, there was no homestead allowance, family allowance, or exempt property. The deed of trust note applicable to the residence is recorded as a liability for accountability purposes. Claims of creditors *are not* recorded as liabilities because the accounting records for an estate are not designed to record all aspects of the estate's financial position. Only the executor's accountability for assets is reflected in the accounting records for an estate.

Mar. 31 Journal Entries A separate cash account, entitled Income Cash, is used to record cash receipts attributable to income. In accordance with provisions of the will, the income attributable to the residuary devise to Nancy Grimes is distributed to the devisee at the end of the calendar quarter.

Apr. 2 Journal Entry No depreciation was recorded on the automobile prior to its sale, because it was not a revenue-producing asset for the estate.

Apr. 16 Journal Entry The Liabilities Paid account represents a reduction of the executor's accountability for estate assets; it is neither an asset account nor an expense account.

Apr. 24 Journal Entry Dividends received on marketable securities required segregation in the accounting records because the securities are allocable to separate devises, as follows:

> Preston Company common stock, $1,000: Allocable to general devise to Nancy Grimes
>
> Arthur Corporation and Campbell Company common stock, $1,500: Allocable to residuary devise to Nancy Grimes

Although Nancy Grimes is the recipient of both devises, the residuary devise ultimately will be placed in trust for the devisee.

Apr. 25 Journal Entry The will of Jessica Davis was silent regarding allocation of estate and inheritance taxes. Consequently, in accordance with the provisions of the Uniform Probate Code, the federal estate tax and state inheritance taxes are allocated in the ratio of interests of devisees, other than the nontaxable nonprofit organization, in the estate. The following working paper shows these ratios:

Ratios of devisee interests in estate of Jessica Davis	Devisee	Current fair value of estate interest	Ratio to total of all estate interests
	Alice Martin............................	$ 10,000	5.9%
	Angela Wilson	10,000	5.9
	Nolan Ames	10,000	5.9
	Nancy Grimes (general devise)	8,000	4.7
	Frances Grimes.....................	17,147 (1)	10.2
	Wallace Davis	27,739 (2)	16.5
	Nancy Grimes (residuary devise)	85,797	50.9
	Totals	$168,683	100.0%

(1) $16,522 + $625 = $17,147
(2) ($40,800 + $2,517) − ($15,500 + $78) = $27,739

Apr. 26 and Apr. 27 Journal Entries   The executor requested the specific devisees to pay in cash their shares of the federal estate tax and state inheritance taxes. The executor withheld the general devisees' death taxes from the cash payable to them.

May 1 Journal Entry   The entire fee of the executor was charged to estate principal because the time spent by Paul Hastings on income assets was nominal. The allocation of fees is more appropriate for a trust than for an estate of relatively short duration.

May 3 Journal Entry   No adjusting entries are required for interest on the certificate of deposit or any declared but unpaid dividends on the marketable securities. An accrual-basis cutoff for an estate is appropriate only at the time the executor prepares the inventory of estate property in order to facilitate the distinction between estate principal and estate income. If the will provides that accrual-basis accounting must be used, the executor must comply.

In the preceding illustration, federal and state income taxes on the estate were disregarded. In addition, it was assumed that devisee Wallace Davis immediately occupied the decedent's residence, so that depreciation on the residence was not required as it would be if rent revenue were realized from a lease. A further assumption was that devisee Wallace Davis paid the March 31 and April 30, Year 3, installments on the trust deed note secured by the residence.

Trial Balance of Estate Accounts   Following is a trial balance of the accounts of the Estate of Jessica Davis at May 3, Year 3:

PAUL HASTINGS, EXECUTOR
Of the Will of Jessica Davis, Deceased
Trial Balance
May 3, Year 3

Principal

Estate principal balance		$162,242
Assets discovered		18,000
Loss on disposal of principal assets	$ 137	
Liabilities paid	3,922	
Devises distributed	173,683	
Administrative expenses	2,500	
Totals	$180,242	$180,242

Income

Interest revenue		$ 55
Dividend revenue		1,500
Distributions to income beneficiaries	$ 1,555	
Totals	$ 1,555	$ 1,555

Charge and Discharge Statement   The executor's charge and discharge statement for the Estate of Jessica Davis is presented below and on pages 594–596. The items in the statement were taken from the trial balance of the Estate of Jessica Davis which appears above. Although the executor's activities essentially ended May 3, the Uniform Probate Code precludes closing an estate earlier than six months after the issuance of letters testamentary.

PAUL HASTINGS, EXECUTOR
Of the Will of Jessica Davis, Deceased
Charge and Discharge Statement
For Period March 18 through September 18, Year 3

First, as to Principal

I charge myself as follows:

Inventory, Mar. 18, Year 3 (Schedule 1)	$162,242	
Assets discovered (Schedule 2)	18,000	$180,242

I credit myself as follows:

Loss on disposal of principal assets (Schedule 3)	$ 137	
Liabilities paid (Schedule 4)	3,922	
Devises distributed (Schedule 5)	173,683	
Administrative expenses (Schedule 6)	2,500	180,242
Balance, Sept. 18, Year 3		$ -0-

(cont.)

PAUL HASTINGS, EXECUTOR
Of the Will of Jessica Davis, Deceased
Charge and Discharge Statement
For Period March 18 through September 18, Year 3 (concluded)

Second, as to Income

I charge myself as follows:

Interest revenue (Schedule 7).......................	$ 55	
Dividend revenue (Schedule 8)	1,500	$ 1,555

I credit myself as follows:

Distributions of income (Schedule 9)...............	1,555

Balance, Sept. 18, Year 3	$ -0-

PAUL HASTINGS, EXECUTOR
Of the Will of Jessica Davis, Deceased
Schedules Supporting Charge and Discharge Statement
For Period March 18 through September 18, Year 3

Schedule 1—Inventory, Mar. 18, Year 3

Bank checking account...		$ 2,157
Bank savings account (including accrued interest)		30,477
Savings and loan association 2-year certificate of deposit maturing June 30, Year 3 (including accrued interest)		26,475
Accrued salary earned for period Mar. 1–8, Year 3		214
Claim against medical insurance carrier		1,526
Social security benefits receivable................................		14,820
Proceeds of life insurance policy (payable to estate)...............		25,000
Marketable securities:		
Common stock of Preston Company, 200 shares		8,000
Common stock of Arthur Corporation, 100 shares		6,500
Residence	$40,800	
Less: Balance of trust deed note payable; including accrued interest of $78	15,578	25,222
Furniture and furnishings		2,517
Paintings and other art objects....................................		16,522
Clothing, jewelry, personal effects		625
Automobile		2,187
Total		$162,242

(cont.)

PAUL HASTINGS, EXECUTOR
Of the Will of Jessica Davis, Deceased
Schedules Supporting Charge and Discharge Statement
For Period March 18 through September 18, Year 3 (continued)

Schedule 2—Assets discovered

On Mar. 25, Year 3, a certificate for 600 shares of Campbell Company common stock was discovered among the decedent's personal effects. All other securities were located in the decedent's safe-deposit box at Third National Bank .... $ 18,000

Schedule 3—Loss on disposal of principal assets

Sale of automobile, Apr. 3, Year 3:

Carrying amount	$ 2,187
Less: Cash proceeds	2,050
Loss	$ 137

Schedule 4—Liabilities paid

Watts Mortuary	$ 810
Suburban Hospital	1,928
Charles Carson, M.D.	426
Final federal income tax	457
Morningside Department Store	214
Various residence bills	87
Total	$ 3,922

Schedule 5—Devises distributed

General devise to Universal Charities: Cash	$ 5,000
General devise to Alice Martin: Cash	10,000
General devise to Angela Wilson: Cash	10,000
General devise to Nolan Ames: Cash	10,000
General devise to Nancy Grimes: 200 shares of Preston Company common stock	8,000
Specific devise to Frances Grimes: Paintings, other art objects, clothing, jewelry, personal effects	17,147
Specific devise to Wallace Davis: Residence, net of deed of trust note payable, with furniture and furnishings	27,739
Residuary devise to Nancy Grimes: Cash, certificate of deposit, 100 shares of Arthur Corporation common stock, 600 shares of Campbell Company common stock	85,797
Total	$173,683

Schedule 6—Administrative expenses

Fee of executor (charged entirely to principal because income administration activities were nominal) .... $ 2,500

(cont.)

PAUL HASTINGS, EXECUTOR
Of the Will of Jessica Davis, Deceased
Schedules Supporting Charge and Discharge Statement
For Period March 18 through September 18, Year 3 (concluded)

Schedule 7—Interest revenue

Bank savings account, Mar. 18–31, Year 3	$ 55

Schedule 8—Dividend revenue

Arthur Corporation common stock	$ 300
Campbell Company common stock	1,200
Total	$ 1,500

Schedule 9—Distributions of income

Mar. 31, Year 3: To residuary devisee Nancy Grimes	$ 55
May 3, Year 3: To Third National Bank, trustee for Nancy Grimes ..	1,500
Total	$ 1,555

The charge and discharge statement shows the executor's *accountability,* not the financial position or cash transactions of the estate. The statement discloses the charges to the executor for estate principal and estate income assets for which the executor is accountable, and the credits to the executor for the dispositions made of estate assets.

Closing Entry for Estate Once the executor's closing statement and charge and discharge statement have been accepted by the probate court, the accountant for the estate may prepare an appropriate closing entry. The September 18, Year 3, closing entry for the Estate of Jessica Davis would be as follows:

Journal entry	Estate Principal Balance	162,242	
to close estate	Assets Discovered	18,000	
of Jessica	Interest Revenue	55	
Davis	Dividend Revenue	1,500	
	Loss on Disposal of Principal Assets		137
	Liabilities Paid		3,922
	Devises Distributed		173,683
	Administrative Expenses		2,500
	Distributions to Income Beneficiaries		1,555
	To close estate of Jessica Davis in accordance with probate court authorization.		

Concluding comments on accounting for estates

The example of estate accounting in this chapter was simplified in terms of details and time required for the liquidation of the estate. In practice, many estates—especially those involved in formal probate proceedings—take many months and sometimes years to settle. For many estates, preparation of the federal estate tax return is a complex task. Furthermore, the estate of an *intestate* decedent involves complicated legal issues. The accountant involved in accounting for an estate must be familiar with provisions of the decedent's will and with appropriate state probate laws and principal and income laws, and should work closely with the attorney for the estate.

LEGAL AND ACCOUNTING ASPECTS OF TRUSTS

A trust created by a will, as illustrated in the preceding sections of this chapter, is termed a *testamentary trust.* A trust created by the act of a living person is known as an *inter vivos,* or *living,* trust. The parties to a trust are (1) the *settlor* (also known as the *donor* or *trustor*)—the individual creating the trust, (2) the *trustee*—the fiduciary individual or corporation holding legal title to the trust property and carrying out the provisions of the *trust document* for a fee, and (3) the *beneficiary*—the party for whose benefit the trust was established. As we have noted previously in this chapter, the income from trust property may be distributed to an *income beneficiary,* but the principal of a trust ultimately goes to a *principal beneficiary* or *remainderman.*

Provisions of Uniform Probate Code affecting trusts

Article VII of the Uniform Probate Code contains four parts: trust registration, jurisdiction of courts concerning trusts, duties and liabilities of trustees, and powers of trustees. The Code requires that a trustee of a trust must register the trust with the appropriate state probate court. Registration subjects the trust to the jurisdiction of the court. The court's jurisdiction may include appointing or removing a trustee, reviewing the trustee's fees, and reviewing or settling interim or final accountings of the trustee. The trustee is required by the Code to administer the trust expeditiously for the benefit of the beneficiaries, and to use standards of care appropriate for a prudent person in dealing with the property of others. The trustee must keep the trust beneficiaries reasonably informed as to the administration of the trust, and furnish the beneficiaries a statement of the trust accounts annually (or more frequently if necessary) and at the termination of the trust.

Provisions of Revised Uniform Principal and Income Act governing trusts

The provisions for allocations between principal and income included in the Revised Uniform Principal and Income Act (see pages 584–585) are applicable to trusts as well as to estates.

Illustration of accounting for a trust

The journal entries in the accounting records of a trust usually differ from those of an estate because of the longer life of a trust. Whereas the personal representative for an estate attempts to complete the administration of the estate as expeditiously as possible, the trustee for a trust must comply with the provisions of the trust document during the stated term of the trust. Accordingly, the trustee's activities include investment of trust property in revenue-producing assets and maintenance of accounting records for both trust principal and trust income.

To illustrate the accounting issues for a trust, we shall return to the testamentary trust created by the will of Jessica Davis (see page 585). The trust was created by the residuary devise to Nancy Grimes, which required the trustee to pay income from the trust to Grimes at the end of each calendar quarter until her twenty-first birthday, October 1, Year 8, at which time the trust principal would be paid to Grimes. Thus Grimes is both the income beneficiary and the remainderman.

The journal entries below illustrate the activities of Third National Bank, trustee for Nancy Grimes, during the calendar quarter ended June 30, Year 3. The journal entries for the Nancy Grimes Trust are *cash-basis* entries; there is no need to accrue interest or dividends on the trust assets because financial position or operations statements normally are not prepared for the trust.

NANCY GRIMES TRUST
Third National Bank, Trustee
General Journal

Year 3

May 3	Principal Cash	21,714	
	Income Cash	1,500	
	Certificate of Deposit	26,475	
	Marketable Securities	24,500	
	Trust Principal Balance		72,689
	Trust Income Balance		1,500

To record receipt of principal and income assets in trust from Paul Hastings, executor of estate of Jessica Davis.

(cont.)

NANCY GRIMES TRUST
Third National Bank, Trustee
General Journal (concluded)

May 6	Marketable Securities	19,900	
	Accrued Interest Purchased	180	
	Principal Cash		20,080

To record purchase of following securities:

$15,000 principal amount of 12%, 20-year bonds of Warren Company, due Mar. 31, Year 23, purchased at 100	$15,000	
Accrued interest purchased	180	
$5,000 face amount of 60-day commercial paper of Modern Finance Company, due July 5, Year 3, purchased at 12% discount	4,900	
Total cash outlay	$20,080	

June 30	Principal Cash	26,475	
	Income Cash	612	
	Certificate of Deposit.......................		26,475
	Interest Revenue		612

To record proceeds of matured certificate of deposit and interest since Mar. 18, Year 3.

30	Administrative Expenses...........................	250	
	Expenses Chargeable to Income	250	
	Principal Cash		250
	Income Cash		250

To record payment of trustee fee for period May 3–June 30, Year 3, chargeable equally to principal and to income.

30	Marketable Securities	25,000	
	Principal Cash		25,000

To record purchase of 5-year, 8% U.S. Treasury notes due June 30, Year 8, at face amount.

30	Distributions to Income Beneficiary	1,862	
	Income Cash		1,862

To record regular quarterly distribution to income beneficiary Nancy Grimes.

The May 3, Year 3, opening journal entry for the trust is the counterpart of the journal entry for the Estate of Jessica Davis on the same date (see page 590), except that the amount receivable from the trust beneficiary for federal estate tax and state inheritance tax was offset against the gross amount of the devise, and the $72,689 difference ($85,797 − $13,108 = $72,689) was recorded as the trust principal balance.

Trial Balance of Trust Accounts   The June 30, Year 3, trial balance of the Nancy Grimes Trust is as follows:

NANCY GRIMES TRUST
Third National Bank, Trustee
Trial Balance
June 30, Year 3

Principal

Principal cash	$ 2,859	
Marketable securities	69,400	
Accrued interest purchased	180	
Trust principal balance		$72,689
Administrative expenses	250	
Totals	$72,689	$72,689

Income

Trust income balance		$ 1,500
Interest revenue		612
Expenses chargeable to income	$ 250	
Distributions to income beneficiary	1,862	
Totals	$ 2,112	$ 2,112

Charge and Discharge Statement for Trust   A charge and discharge statement for the trustee of the Nancy Grimes Trust would resemble the comparable statement for an estate illustrated on pages 593–596. The major difference would be a schedule for the details of the $72,439 trust principal balance at June 30, Year 3 ($72,689 − $250 = $72,439).

Periodic Closing Entry for Trust   A closing entry should be made for a trust at the end of each period for which a charge and discharge statement is prepared in order to clear the nominal accounts for the next reporting period. The June 30, Year 3, closing entry for the Nancy Grimes Trust would be as follows:

Periodic	*Trust Principal Balance*	250	
closing	*Trust Income Balance*	1,500	
entry for	*Interest Revenue*	612	
a trust	*Administrative Expenses*		250
	Expenses Chargeable to Income		250
	Distributions to Income Beneficiary		1,862
	To close nominal accounts of trust.		

At the time specified in the trust document for transfer of the trust principal to the remainderman, a journal entry would be made to charge the Distributions to Principal Beneficiary account and credit the various trust principal asset accounts. A closing entry for the termination of the trust would then be required, in the form of the comparable estate journal entry illustrated on page 596.

REVIEW QUESTIONS

1 Is the Uniform Probate Code in effect throughout the United States?

2 Define the following terms:
  a Estate
  b Intestacy
  c Testator
  d Executor
  e Administrator
  f Letters testamentary
  g Devise
  h Remainderman
  i Inter vivos trust
  j Settlor

3 Compare *informal probate* with *formal probate* of a will.

4 Compare the standards of care required of a *personal representative* with the standards of care required of a *trustee.*

5 Why must there be a sharp distinction between *principal* and *income* in the administration of an estate?

6 Describe the *exempt property and allowances* provisions of the Uniform Probate Code.

7 What type of *devise* is each of the following? Explain.
  a The beach house at 1411 Ocean Avenue
  b $25,000 cash
  c $60,000 face amount of U.S. Treasury bonds
  d 1,000 shares of Rogers Corporation common stock represented by certificate no. G-1472
  e All my remaining property

8 Is **accrual-basis accounting** ever used for an estate or a trust? Explain.

9 Explain the requirements for **depreciation accounting** contained in the Revised Uniform Principal and Income Act.

10 Describe the use of the Assets Discovered account in the accounting for an estate.

11 Compare a personal representative's **charge and discharge statement** with the financial statements issued by a business enterprise.

12 Discuss the similarities and differences in the journal entries for estates and for trusts.

EXERCISES

Ex. 15-1 Marjorie Singer is trustee of a testamentary trust established in the will of Carla Cohen. The principal of the trust consists of stocks, bonds, and a building subject to a mortgage. The will provides that trust income is to be paid to the surviving husband, Luka Cohen, during his lifetime, that the trust will terminate upon his death, and that the principal is then to be distributed to the Soledad School for Girls. Indicate whether each of the following statements is true or false:

a A cash dividend received on one of the trust securities may not be used without compensating the husband.

b A 5% stock dividend on Z Co. stock should be distributed to Luka Cohen.

c The cost of insurance on the office building should be deducted from the income paid to Luka Cohen.

d Monthly principal payments to amortize the mortgage note are deducted from income.

e Proceeds from fire insurance on the office building would be a part of the trust principal.

f The cost of exercising stock warrants is chargeable to trust income.

g The Soledad School for Girls is the residuary beneficiary of the trust established under Carla Cohen's will.

h If Luka Cohen and the Soledad School for Girls agree to terminate the trust and divide the trust principal, the trustee would have to comply with their wishes.

Ex. 15-2 Indicate whether each of the following items would be charged to principal or to income of a testamentary trust, assuming that the Revised Uniform Principal and Income Act is to be followed.

a Depreciation on building

b Legal fees for managing trust assets

c Special assessment tax levied on real estate for street improvements

d Interest on mortgage note payable

e Loss on disposal of trust investments

f Major repairs to property prior to disposal of the property

Ex. 15-3 Indicate how each of the following cash disbursements should be classified in the charge and discharge statement for an estate:

a Executor's fees

b Estate and inheritance taxes

c Fire insurance premiums

d Special assessments which add permanent value to real estate

e Monthly allowance to beneficiaries

f Expenses of probating the will of decedent

g Legal fees for defending claims against the estate

h Funeral and terminal-illness expenses

Ex. 15-4 Selected transactions completed by the executor of the estate of Charles Fellner, who died on October 15, Year 10, are listed below:

Oct. 20 Inventory of estate assets (at current fair value) was filed with the court as follows:

Cash	$ 56,700
Real estate	148,000
Capital stock of Jenson Company	60,000
9% bonds of Guam Corporation ($40,000 face amount)..........	40,000
Accrued interest on bonds of Guam Corporation	600
Personal and household effects	23,500

Oct. 29 A certificate for 50 shares of IBM Corporation capital stock valued at $9,000 was found in the coat pocket of an old suit belonging to the decedent.

Nov. 10 A dividend of $520 was received on the capital stock of Jenson Company. The stock was willed as a specific devise to Rollo Fellner.

Nov. 15 Liabilities of Charles Fellner in the amount of $30,000 were paid.

Nov. 22 Administrative expenses of $3,240 were paid. All expenses are chargeable to principal.

Nov. 29 The bonds of Guam Corporation were sold at 98, plus accrued interest of $1,050.

Nov. 30 The capital stock of Jenson Company and the cash dividend of $520 were transferred to Rollo Fellner.

Prepare journal entries to record the transaction listed above in the accounting records of the executor for the estate of Charles Fellner.

Ex. 15-5 Scott Robinson, executor for the estate of Leland Clason, who died on August 10, Year 2, prepared the following trial balance at February 10, Year 3:

Principal cash	$ 26,000	
Income cash	490	
Estate principal balance		$117,000
Assets discovered		1,800
Gains on disposal of principal assets		1,200
Administrative expenses	3,000	
Liabilities paid	24,500	
Devises distributed ...⁻..................................	66,500	
Interest revenue		3,590
Distributions to income beneficiaries	2,000	
Expenses chargeable to income	1,100	
Totals	$123,590	$123,590

Prepare a charge and discharge statement for the period August 10, Year 2, through February 10, Year 3. Do not prepare supporting schedules.

Ex. 15-6 Pursuant to the will of Gabriela Bonita, the balance of her estate after probate is to be transferred to a testamentary trust. The following trial balance was prepared from the accounts of the estate at June 30, Year 5:

Principal cash	$115,000	
Income cash	6,750	
Marketable securities	105,000	
Estate principal balance		$265,000
Assets discovered		13,000
Gains and losses on disposal of principal assets		12,000
Administrative expenses	5,400	
Liabilities paid	16,000	
Devises distributed	48,600	
Interest revenue		4,000
Dividend revenue		4,500
Expenses chargeable to income	1,750	
Totals	$298,500	$298,500

a Prepare the journal entry to close the accounts of the estate.
b Prepare the journal entry to open the accounting records for the trust.

SHORT CASES FOR ANALYSIS AND DECISION

Case 15-1 The estate of Michael Ferron included the following items at the date of death, April 16, Year 2:

(1) Sunrise Company 10% bonds due June 16, Year 12; principal amount $100,000, current fair value at April 16, Year 2 (excluding accrued interest), $103,500; interest payable June 16 and December 16 of each year.
(2) Polanco Corporation common stock, 5,000 shares, dividend of $1 declared April 1, payable May 1 to stockholders of record April 14.
(3) Polanco Corporation 8% cumulative preferred stock, 1,000 shares. (Dividends are paid semiannually on January 1 and July 1, and there are no dividends in arrears.)

Instructions
a The executor of the estate asks you for advice as to which items constitute income and which constitute principal of the estate.
b Suppose that dividends were in arrears on the Polanco Corporation 8% cumulative preferred stock; would your answer to **a** be any different? If so, in what way? Explain.

Case 15-2 Carl Lau transferred a manufacturing business and 10,000 shares of MP Company common stock to Fidelity Trust Company to be held in trust for the benefit of his son, Robert, for life, with the remainder to go to Robert's son, Edward. Fidelity Trust Company insured the business with Boston Insurance Company by buying two policies. One policy was a standard fire insurance policy covering the buildings and equipment. The other policy covered any loss of income during periods when the business was inoperable as a result of fire or other catastrophe. The buildings and equipment subsequently were destroyed by fire, and Boston Insurance Company paid claims under both policies to Fidelity Trust Company.

Shortly after the 10,000 common shares of MP Company had been transferred to Fidelity Trust Company, MP Company declared a dividend of 10 common shares of Monte Oil Corporation for each 100 shares of MP Company common stock held. The Monte Oil Corporation common stock had been purchased as an investment by MP Company.

During the same year MP Company directors declared that the common stock would be split on a basis of two new shares for each old share. After the distribution of the new shares, Fidelity Trust Company decided to sell 10,000 shares of MP Company common stock.

Instructions How should Fidelity Trust Company handle the events which have been described above as to distribution between the income beneficiary and the remainderman? State reasons for making the distribution in the manner which you recommend.

Case 15-3 In analyzing the accounts of James Fairmont, executor of the estate of Luis Como, who died January 16, Year 7, you review the will and other documents, which reveal that (1) Como's son had been specifically bequeathed the decedent's only rental property and 6% bonds of Padre Corporation, $50,000 maturity value, due March 1, Year 21; (2) Como's daughter was the beneficiary of a life insurance policy (face amount $100,000) on which the decedent had paid the premiums; and (3) Como's widow had been left the remainder of the estate in trust, with full powers of appointment.

Your examination also reveals the following transactions occurring from the time of Como's death to March 1, Year 7:

(1) Jan. 20 $3,105 was received in connection with the redemption of $3,000 face amount of Camm Corporation 7% bonds due January 15, Year 7.

(2) Jan. 20 $500 was received from Pittson Corporation as a cash dividend of $1 per share on common stock declared December 1, Year 6, payable January 15, Year 7, to stockholders of record January 2, Year 7.

(3) Jan. 20 $5,040 was paid to Backe and Co., brokers, for the purchase of five Seaboard Co. 8% bonds due June 30, Year 18.

(4) Jan. 21 30 shares of common stock were received from Ragusa Company, constituting an ordinary 2% stock dividend declared December 14, Year 6, distributable January 20, Year 7, to stockholders of record January 15, Year 7.

(5) Feb. 1 $200 quarterly interest was paid by the executor on a promissory note due January 31, Year 8.

(6) Feb. 1 Como's physician was paid $2,500 for services rendered during Como's last illness.

(7) Feb. 2 $600 was collected from Zappa Corporation, as a cash dividend of $0.25 per share on common stock declared January 18, Year 7, payable January 30, Year 7, to stockholders of record January 27, Year 7.

(8) Feb. 3 $575 rental revenue for February was received and deposited in the bank.

(9) Feb. 10 $890 was paid for real estate taxes covering the period from February 1 to July 31, Year 7.

(10) Mar. 1 $1,802 was paid to the Internal Revenue Service as the remaining income tax owed by the decedent for Year 6 taxable income.

Instructions Indicate whether each transaction should be
Allocated between principal and income
Allocated between principal and beneficiaries (devisees)
Attributed solely to income

(cont.)

Attributed solely to principal
Attributed solely to beneficiaries (devisees)
Give reasons supporting your conclusions as to how each transaction should be handled.

Case 15-4 Thomas Wall, a resident of Buffalo, New York, died September 1, Year 1. Wall's will established a trust providing that the income, after costs of administration, be paid to his widow Maria during her lifetime.
During the first year of the trust, the trustee received the following:
(1) Dividend revenue:

Cash dividends declared Aug. 5, Year 1, payable to stockholders of record
Aug. 30 .... $ 9,200
Cash dividends declared at various times from Sept. 2, Year 1, to July 31,
Year 2 27,500
Stock dividend declared on Dec. 1, Year 1, and received Dec. 28, Year 2, a
total of 75 shares of Scynthian Art Company common stock. The current
fair value of the stock at date of declaration was $40 per share.

(2) Interest revenue:

Semiannual interest on municipal bonds paid on Dec. 1, Year 1 .... $ 4,000
Semiannual interest on municipal bonds paid on June 1, Year 2 (bonds
were purchased by trustee) 5,500
Semiannual interest on corporate bonds paid on Feb. 28 and Aug. 31,
Year 2 (for the two periods) 21,200

(3) Marketable securities with an inventory valuation of $45,000 were sold for $49,280.
The trustee's expenses and fees paid in accordance with the provisions of the trust agreement totaled $4,444.

Instructions
a Prepare an income statement for the year ended August 31, Year 2, to show the amount to which Maria Wall is entitled in accordance with the terms of the trust agreement.
b For those items not considered income, explain why they are excluded.

PROBLEMS

15-5 Harry Hall died on June 5, Year 1. Donald Bates was named executor of the estate in the will prepared by Hall's attorney three years ago. On December 31, Year 1, the accountant for the executor prepared the following trial balance:

DONALD BATES, EXECUTOR
Of the Will of Harry Hall, Deceased
Trial Balance
December 31, Year 1

Principal cash	$ 32,000	
Income cash	3,000	
Investments in bonds	168,300	
Investments in common stocks	70,000	
Household effects	9,500	
Gains on disposal of principal assets		$ 2,200
Assets discovered		16,800
Liabilities paid	26,200	
Administrative expenses	9,000	
Devises distributed	10,000	
Estate principal balance		306,000
Dividend revenue		4,200
Interest revenue		8,500
Expenses chargeable to income	720	
Distributions to income beneficiaries	8,980	
Totals	$337,700	$337,700

Instructions   The amount in the Estate Principal Balance account represents the inventory of assets at June 5, Year 1. Prepare a charge and discharge statement for the estate of Harry Hall. Supporting schedules are not required for any items except the listing of assets comprising the estate principal balance at December 31, Year 1.

15-6 Margaret Earl died on March 1, Year 8, leaving a valid will in which she named Perry Moore as executor and trustee of her assets pending final distribution to Alex Parr, a nephew. The will instructed the executor to transfer Earl's personal effects and automobile to the nephew, to pay estate taxes, outstanding liabilities, and administrative expenses of the estate, and to transfer the remaining assets to a trust for the benefit of the nephew. Income from the estate and the trust is to be paid to the nephew, who will receive the principal (corpus) upon graduation from medical school.

An inventory of the estate at March 1, Year 8, consisted of the following assets:

Cash	$ 19,440
Certificate of deposit at Chicago Federal Savings and Loan Association; includes accrued interest of $1,100	101,100
Personal effects	13,200
Automobile	2,800
Investment in common stocks	72,000

The following transactions were completed by the executor before the trust assets were transferred to the Margaret Earl Trust on December 10, Year 8:

(1) Discovered a savings account of $6,290 in the name of Margaret Earl. (Debit Principal Cash.)

(2) Paid administrative expenses for the estate, $5,200. All expenses are chargeable to principal.

(3) Sold common stock with a carrying amount of $20,000 for $21,020, net of commissions.

(4) Transferred personal effects and automobile to Alex Parr.

(5) Received income as follows (there were no expenses chargeable to income): Interest, $5,200 (includes accrued interest on certificate of deposit at March 1. Year 8); dividends, $1,400.

(6) Distributed the income of the estate to Alex Parr.

(7) Paid liabilities of decedent, $8,050.

(8) Paid estate taxes, $32,000. (Debit the account Estate Taxes Paid.)

Instructions

a Prepare journal entries to record the transactions and to close the accounting records for the estate. Disregard homestead allowance, exempt property, and family allowance.

b Prepare a charge and discharge statement immediately prior to the transfer of estate assets to the Margaret Earl Trust. Do not prepare any supporting schedules.

c Prepare a journal entry to establish the accounting records for the testamentary trust.

15-7 Samson Rue died in Year 1, and under the terms of the will the devisees were listed as follows:

(1) Gladys Rue, widow of Samson Rue, was left a general devise of $100,000 payable immediately, and in addition a life interest in 50% of the residuary estate, with the right of appointment.

(2) Ellen Rue, daughter, was left 25% of the residuary estate. One-half of this was left outright, and the other half was to remain in trust, with the right of appointment.

(3) Pauline Rue, daughter, was left a life interest in 15% of the residuary estate, with the right of appointment.

(4) George Rue, son, was left a 10% interest in the residuary estate, to be paid outright.

Samson Rue's will specified that the executor had the power to defer the sale of any estate assets and to hold such assets in trust until, in the opinion of the executor, conditions were favorable, and to make intermediate distributions of principal from the funds so realized to the beneficiaries. The income from the estate (or trust) was to be distributed annually in the proportion of the beneficiaries' interests.

On December 31, Year 3, the following advances on principal were made:

Ellen Rue *$300,000*

George Rue *200,000*

The general devise to Gladys Rue had not been paid as of December 31, Year 3.

The trustee rendered the first accounting to the probate court at December 31, Year 3, on which date all income, after payment of all expenses applicable to income, was paid to the beneficiaries.

The probate court's decree on the accounting of December 31, Year 3, specified that (1) in considering the distribution of future income, all intermediate payments of principal should be treated as advances to the beneficiaries; (2) in order to make a fair and equitable division of income, interest at 8% per year is to be charged or credited to the beneficiaries subsequent to Year 3.

The income for Year 4 amounted to $840,000 after all expenses applicable to income had been paid. No other distribution of principal had taken place.

Instructions Prepare a journal entry to record the payments to income beneficiaries at December 31, Year 4. Support the journal entry with a statement showing how the amounts payable to the beneficiaries were determined. Disregard homestead allowance, exempt property, and family allowance.

15-8 Robert Green died December 31, Year 1, and left all property in trust to his daughter, Sally. Income was to be paid to her as she needed it, and at her death the trust principal was to go to Robert Green's nephew, Nicholas Green. Any income (including accrued interest) not paid to Sally at her death would be paid to her estate. Robert Green appointed Paul Pool trustee at a fee of $3,100 per year. All expenses of settling the estate were paid and accounted for by the executor before the trustee assumed responsibility for the trust.

   Sally Green died on October 1, Year 5, and left all her property in trust to her cousin, Nora Loomis. Paul Pool, who also was appointed executor and trustee of Sally Green's estate, agreed not to charge additional fees for these services. All income subsequent to October 1, Year 5, was to be paid to Nora Loomis as soon as the income was received by the trustee. The estate of Sally Green consisted solely of Sally's unexpended income from the Robert Green Trust. Principal cash of the Robert Green Trust was invested immediately at 8% interest, payable quarterly.

   From October 1, Year 5, to December 31, Year 6, Nicholas Green received "advances" from the income of his uncle's trust. On December 31, Year 6, the remainder of the trust was turned over to Nicholas Green.

   The property received by Paul Pool under the will of Robert Green on January 1, Year 2, consisted of the following:

(1) 20,000 shares of Armco Corporation common stock with a current fair value of $25 per share.
(2) $150,000 bonds of Armco Corporation, paying interest on June 30 and December 31 at 9% per year. The bonds had a current fair value equal to their face amount.

   In the five years ended December 31, Year 6, the trustee received the following dividends on the Armco Corporation common stock: February 1, Year 2, Year 3, and Year 4, $25,000 per year; February 1, Year 5, and Year 6, $30,000 per year. The trustee made the following payments:

Trustee's fees and expenses: $3,100 per year

To beneficiaries:

Sally Green, income beneficiary of the Robert Green Trust, from December 31, Year 1, to October 1, Year 5:

Year 2	*$18,625*
Year 3	*17,500*
Year 4	*19,375*
Year 5	*28,500*

Nicholas Green, principal beneficiary of the Robert Green Trust, from October 1, Year 5, to December 31, Year 6:

Year 5	*$ 8,500*
Year 6	*23,000*

Nora Loomis, beneficiary of the Sally Green Trust, from October 1, Year 5, to December 31, Year 6:

Year 5 and Year 6, all trust income as determined on cash basis of accounting.

The trustee of the Robert Green Trust kept the remaining cash in a checking account, where it earned no interest for the beneficiaries.

Instructions

a Prepare a statement for the Robert Green Trust from December 31, Year 1, to October 1, Year 5, showing the undistributed income comprising the Sally Green Trust. Assume that interest on the Armco Corporation bonds was accrued by the trustee from July 1 to October 1, Year 5. Disregard homestead allowance, exempt property, and family allowance.

b Compute the amount to be distributed to Nicholas Green at December 31, Year 6.

c Compute the income received by Nora Loomis from the Sally Green Trust in Year 5 and in Year 6.

15-9 Chester Evans died in an accident on May 31, Year 1. The will provided that all liabilities and expenses were to be paid and that the property was to be distributed as follows:

(1) Personal residence to Tuesday Evans, widow of Chester Evans.

(2) U.S. Treasury 6% bonds and Permian Company common stock—to be placed in trust. All income to go to Tuesday Evans during her lifetime, with the right of appointment upon her death.

(3) Sonar Corporation 9% bonds—bequeathed to Lulu Evans Crane, daughter of Chester Evans.

(4) Cash—a bequest of $15,000 to Mario Evans, son of Chester Evans.

(5) Residue of estate—to be divided equally between the two children of Chester Evans—Lulu Evans Crane and Mario Evans.

The will further provided that during the administration period Tuesday Evans was to be paid $500 a month out of estate income. Estate and inheritance taxes are to be borne by the residue of the estate. Mario Evans was named as executor and trustee.

An inventory of the decedent's property was prepared. The inventory of estate assets follows:

Personal residence	$ 95,000
Jewelry—diamond ring	14,600
Portland National Bank—checking account; balance May 31, Year 1	143,000
$100,000 U.S. Treasury 6% bonds, due Year 20, interest payable Mar. 1 and Sept. 1 (includes accrued interest of $1,500)	101,500
$10,000 Sonar Corporation 9% bonds, due Year 10, interest payable May 31 and Nov. 30	9,900
Permian Company common stock, 800 shares	64,000
Dividends receivable on Permian Company common stock	800
XY Company common stock, 700 shares	70,000

The executor opened an estate checking account and transferred the decedent's checking account balance to it. Other deposits through July 1, Year 2, were as follows:

Interest collected on $100,000 U.S. Treasury 6% bonds:

Sept. 1, Year 1	$ 3,000
Mar. 1, Year 2	3,000

Dividends received on Permian Company common stock:

June 15, Year 1, declared May 7, Year 1, payable to holders of record May 27, Year 1..	800
Sept. 15, Year 1	800
Dec. 15, Year 1	1,200
Mar. 15, Year 2	1,500
June 15, Year 2	1,500

Net proceeds of June 19, Year 1, sale of XY Company 700 shares of common stock 68,810

Payments were made from the estate's checking account through July 1, Year 2, for the following:

Liabilities of decedent paid (including funeral expenses)	$12,000
Additional prior years' federal and state income taxes, plus interest, to May 31, Year 1..	1,810
Year 1 income taxes of Chester Evans for the period Jan. 1, Year 1, through May 31, Year 1, in excess of amounts paid by the decedent on declarations of estimated tax	9,100
Federal and state fiduciary income taxes, fiscal years ending June 30, Year 1, and June 30, Year 2	2,400
Estate and inheritance taxes	73,000
Monthly payments to Tuesday Evans, 13 payments of $500	6,500
Attorney's and accountant's fees (allocated entirely to principal)..............	25,000

The executor, Mario Evans, waived his fee. However, he desired to receive his father's diamond ring in lieu of the $15,000 cash devise. All parties agreed to this in writing, and the court's approval was secured. All other specific devises were delivered by July 15, Year 1.

Instructions

a Prepare a charge and discharge statement as to principal and income, with supporting schedules, to accompany the attorney's formal court accounting on behalf of the executor of the Estate of Chester Evans for the period from May 31, Year 1, through July 1, Year 2. In accordance with the will, the executor accrued the interest and dividends on the estate investments to July 1, Year 2. Disregard homestead allowance, exempt property, and family allowance.

b Prepare a summary showing the allocation of principal and income assets at July 1, Year 2, between the trust for the benefit of Tuesday Evans and the residual estate to be divided between Lulu Evans Crane and Mario Evans.

15-10 The will of Lowell Adams directed that the executor, Samuel Reed, liquidate the entire estate within two years of the date of death and pay the net proceeds and income to the Boys Republic. Lowell Adams, a bachelor, died on February 1, Year 10, after a brief illness.

An inventory of the decedent's property was prepared, and the current fair value of all items was determined. The preliminary inventory, before the computation of any appropriate income accruals on inventory items, follows:

	Current fair value
United California Bank checking account	$ 8,500
$60,000 Sun City bonds, interest rate 6%, payable Jan. 1 and July, maturity date July 1, Year 14	59,000
2,000 shares Rex Corporation common stock.............................	220,000
Term life insurance: beneficiary, Estate of Lowell Adams	20,000
Residence ($86,500) and furniture ($8,000)	94,500

During Year 10 the following transactions occurred:
(1) The interest on the Sun City bonds was collected. The bonds were sold on July 1, for $59,000, and the proceeds and interest accrued at February 1, Year 10 ($300) were paid to the Boys Republic.
(2) Rex Corporation paid cash dividends of $1 per share on March 1 and December 1, and distributed a 10% stock dividend on July 1. All dividends were declared 45 days before each payment date and were payable to holders of record as of 40 days before each payment date. In September, 1,000 shares were sold at $105 per share, and the proceeds were paid to the Boys Republic.
(3) Because of a depressed real estate market, the personal residence was rented furnished at $300 per month commencing April 1, Year 10. The rent was paid monthly, in advance. Real estate taxes of $1,200 for the calendar Year 10 were paid. The house and furnishings have estimated economic lives of 40 years and 8 years, respectively. The part-time gardener was paid four months' wages totaling $500 on April 30 for services performed, and then was released.
(4) The United California Bank checking account was closed, and the balance of $8,500 was transferred to a bank account for the estate.
(5) The proceeds of the term life insurance were received on March 1 and deposited in a bank account for the estate.
(6) The following disbursements were made:
   (a) Funeral expenses and expenses of last illness, $3,500.
   (b) Balance due on Year 9 income taxes of deceased, $700.
   (c) Attorney's and accountant's fees, $15,000, of which $1,000 was allocated to income.
(7) On December 31, the balance of the undistributed income, except for $250, was paid to the beneficiary. The balance of the cash on hand derived from the principal of the estate also was paid to the beneficiary on December 31. At December 31, the executor resigned and waived all fees.

Instructions Prepare a charge and discharge statement, together with supporting schedules, for the executor of the Estate of Lowell Adams for the period February 1–December 31, Year 10. Disregard depreciation.

16

GOVERNMENT ENTITIES: FUNDS AND PROGRAMS

The student beginning the study of accounting for government entities temporarily must set aside many of the familiar accounting principles for business enterprises. Such fundamental concepts of accounting theory for business enterprises as the nature of the accounting entity, the primacy of the income statement, and the pervasiveness of accrual accounting have limited relevance in accounting for government entities. Consequently, we shall begin our discussion with those features of government entities which give rise to unique accounting concepts. In the second section of the chapter we shall deal with the various theoretical issues of accounting for government entities. The chapter will be concluded with specific examples of accounting for governmental units.

NATURE OF GOVERNMENT ENTITIES

When thinking of government entities of the United States, one tends to focus on the federal government, or on the governments of the 50 states. However, in addition to those major government entities and the governments of the several U.S. territories, there are the following governmental units in the United States:[1]

---

[1] *Audits of State and Local Governmental Units,* AICPA (New York: 1974), p. 4.

More than 3,000 counties

Nearly 17,000 townships

More than 18,000 municipalities

Almost 16,000 school districts

Nearly 24,000 special districts (port authorities, airports, public buildings, libraries, and others)

Despite the wide range in size and scope of governance, the government entities listed above have a number of characteristics in common. Among these characteristics are the following:

1 *Organization to serve the citizenry.* A basic tenet of governmental philosophy in the United States is that government entities exist to serve the citizens subject to their jurisdiction. Thus, the citizens as a whole establish government entities through the constitutional and charter process. Business enterprises, in contrast, are created by only a limited number of individuals.

2 *General absence of the profit motive.* With few exceptions, government entities render services to the citizenry without the objective of profiting from those services. Business enterprises are motivated to a great extent to earn profits.

3 *Taxation as the principal source of revenue.* The citizenry subject to a government's jurisdiction provides resources to the governmental unit principally through taxation. Many of these taxes are paid on a self-assessment basis. There is no comparable revenue source for business enterprises.

4 *Impact of the legislative process.* Operations of governmental units are for the most part initiated by various legislative enactments, such as operating budgets, borrowing authorizations, and tax levies. Business enterprises are also affected by federal, state, and local laws and regulations, but not to such a direct extent.

5 *Stewardship for resources.* A primary responsibility of governmental entities in financial reporting is to demonstrate adequate stewardship for resources provided by their citizenry. Business enterprises have a comparable responsibility to their owners, but not to the same extent as government entities.

The five preceding characteristics of government entities are major determinants of accounting theory for such entities.

THEORY OF ACCOUNTING FOR GOVERNMENT ENTITIES

In accounting for business enterprises, **economic substance** of financial transactions is emphasized over their **legal form.** Thus, capital leases which are in substance installment purchases of personal property are accounted for as such in the financial statements of business enterprises. Similarly, minority interest in a consolidated subsidiary, although in form a part of consolidated stockholders' equity, is substantively treated as a liability under the "parent company theory" of consolidated financial statements.

In contrast, accounting for governmental units emphasizes **legal form** over **economic substance.** This emphasis is necessitated by the characteristics of government entities discussed in the preceding section of this chapter—especially the impact of the legislative process and the stewardship for resources. Emphasis on legal form for governmental units is manifested in several aspects of governmental accounting. Among these are the following:

The governmental accounting entity

The modified accrual basis of accounting

Recording of expenditures rather than expenses

Recording of purchase orders for merchandise and services

Recording the budget

The governmental accounting entity

Accounting for business enterprises emphasizes the economic entity as an accounting unit. Thus, a partnership is considered to be an accounting entity separate from partners; and consolidated financial statements are issued for a group of affiliated—but legally separate—corporations which comprise a single economic entity under common control.

There is generally no single accounting entity for a specific governmental unit, such as a city or a county. Instead, the accounting entity for governmental units is the fund. A *fund* is described by the National Council on Governmental Accounting as follows:[2]

> A fund is defined as an independent fiscal and accounting entity with a self-balancing set of accounts recording cash and other financial resources, together with all related liabilities and residual equities or balances, and changes therein, which are segregated for the purpose of carrying on specific activities or attaining certain objectives in accordance with special regulations, restrictions, or limitations.

Thus, accounting for a single governmental unit generally involves several different funds. The National Council on Governmental Accounting has recommended eight types of funds, as follows:[3]

Governmental Funds

(1) *The General Fund*—to account for all unrestricted resources except those required to be accounted for in another fund.

(2) *Special Revenue Funds*—to account for the proceeds of specific revenue sources (other than special assessments, expendable trusts, or for major capital projects) that are restricted by law or administrative action to expenditure for specified purposes.

(3) *Capital Projects Funds*—to account for financial resources segregated for the acquisition of major capital facilities (other than those financed by Special Assessment and Enterprise Funds).

(4) *Debt Service Funds*—to account for the accumulation of resources for, and the payment of, interest and principal on general long-term debt.

(5) *Special Assessment Funds*—to account for the financing of public improvements or services deemed to benefit the properties against which special assessments are levied.

[2] *Exposure Draft: GAAFR Restatement Principles,* National Council on Governmental Accounting (Chicago: 1978), p. 10.

[3] Ibid., pp. 14–15.

Proprietary Funds
(6) *Enterprise Funds*—to account for operations that are financed and operated in a manner similar to private business enterprises—where the stated intent is that the costs (expenses, including depreciation) of providing goods or services to the general public on a continuing basis be financed or recovered primarily through user charges—or where periodic determination of revenues earned, expenses incurred, and/or net income is deemed appropriate for capital maintenance, public policy, management control, accountability, or other purposes.
(7) *Internal (or Intragovernmental) Service Funds*—to account for the financing of goods or services provided by one department or agency to other departments or agencies of the governmental unit, or to other governmental units, on a cost-reimbursement basis.

Fiduciary Funds
(8) *Trust and Agency Funds*—to account for assets held by a governmental unit as trustee or agent for individuals, private organizations, and/or other governmental units. These include (a) Expendable Trust Funds, (b) Nonexpendable Trust Funds, (c) Pension Trust Funds, and (d) Agency Funds.

In addition, the National Council on Governmental Accounting recommended that governmental units maintain two **self-balancing groups of accounts**—the general fixed assets and general long-term debt groups.

Every governmental unit has a general fund. Additional funds should be established as required by legislative action and the maintenance of adequate custodianship for resources of the governmental unit. Accounting for each of the eight types of funds and two groups of accounts will be discussed in subsequent sections of this chapter. At this point, we must emphasize that a governmental unit does not have a single accounting entity to account for all its financial resources, obligations, revenues, and expenditures.

The modified accrual basis of accounting

Except for enterprise funds and internal (or intragovernmental) service funds, which reflect sales of merchandise and services, governmental accounting does not emphasize the results of the governmental unit's operations for a fiscal year. Financial reporting for governments instead focuses upon the stewardship provided for the governmental unit's assets. One consequence is that a **modified accrual basis** of accounting is appropriate for the five governmental funds and for expendable trust funds. The conventional accrual basis of accounting is used for the two proprietary funds, nonexpendable trust funds, and pension trust funds.

What is the **modified accrual basis** of accounting? The AICPA has described the modified accrual basis as follows:[4]

Revenues are recorded as received in cash except for (a) revenues susceptible to accrual and (b) revenues of a material amount that have not been received at the normal time of receipt.

. . . .

[4] *Audits of State and Local Governmental Units,* pp. 14, 16.

Expenditures are recorded on the accrual basis, except in the instances discussed below.

Disbursements for inventory items may be considered as expenditures at the time of purchase or at the time the items are used.

Normally expenditures are not divided between years by the recording of prepaid expenses, for example prepaid insurance.

Interest on long-term debt, commonly accounted for in debt service funds, normally should be recorded as an expenditure on its due date. . . .

Few revenues of the five governmental funds and expendable trust funds are susceptible to accrual. For example, there is no basis for the accrual of self-assessed taxes such as income taxes, sales taxes, and taxes on gross business receipts. Similarly, fees for business licenses, marriage licenses, and comparable permits generally are recorded when received in cash, because these fees are not billable in advance of the service or granting of a permit.

Perhaps the most commonly accrued revenue of a governmental unit is property taxes. These taxes customarily are billed by the governmental unit to the property owner and generally are payable in the fiscal year for which billed.

In summary, cash basis accounting is appropriate for many revenues of the five governmental funds and expendable trust funds.

Recording of expenditures rather than expenses

Because of the lack of emphasis upon operating results, funds other than the two proprietary funds account for authorized *expenditures* of the government's resources, rather than accounting for *expenses* of operations. There is no attempt to match *cost expirations* against *realized revenues* in funds other than enterprise funds and internal (or intragovernmental) service funds. As a result, depreciation is recorded only in enterprise funds and internal (or intragovernmental) service funds, and, if required by the trust indenture, in nonexpendable trust funds. In addition, depreciation may be recorded in the general fixed assets group of accounts, which are nothing more than memorandum records.[5] Similarly, there is no uncollectible taxes expense in the general fund or in special revenue funds, because tax revenues susceptible to accrual are recorded in an amount *net* of the estimated uncollectible portion of the related receivables, as illustrated on page 623.

Recording of purchase orders for merchandise and services

Because of the need for the expenditures of governmental units to be in accordance with authorizations of appropriate legislative bodies, an *encumbrance* accounting technique is used for the general fund, special revenue funds, capital projects funds, and special assessment funds. When a purchase order for merchandise or services is issued to a sup-

[5] Ibid., p. 18.

plier by one of the preceding funds, a journal entry similar to the following is made in the accounting records of the fund:

Journal entry
for encum-
brances

Encumbrances	18,413	
Reserve for Encumbrances		18,413
To record encumbrance for purchase order no. 1685 issued to Wilson Company.		

When the supplier's invoice for the ordered merchandise or services is received by the governmental unit, it is recorded and the related encumbrance is reversed as follows:

Journal
entries for
receipt of
invoice and
reversal of
encum-
brances

Expenditures	18,507	
Vouchers Payable		18,507
To record invoice received from Wilson Company under purchase order no. 1685.		
Reserve for Encumbrances	18,413	
Encumbrances		18,413
To reverse encumbrance for purchase order no. 1685 issued to Wilson Company.		

As indicated by the preceding example, the invoice amount may differ from the amount of the governmental unit's purchase order because of such items as shipping charges and sales taxes.

The encumbrance technique is a memorandum method for making certain that total expenditures for a fiscal year do not exceed authorized amounts. Encumbrance journal entries are not necessary for normal recurring expenditures such as salaries and wages, utilities, and rent. The encumbrance technique used in accounting for government entities has no counterpart in accounting for business enterprises.

Recording the budget

Budgets are key elements of legislative control over governmental units. The executive branch of a governmental unit proposes the budgets, the legislative branch reviews, modifies, and enacts the budgets, and finally the executive branch approves the budgets and carries out their provisions.

The two basic classifications of budgets for governmental units are the same as those for business enterprises—operating budgets and capital budgets. *Operating budgets* include the *estimated revenues* and amounts appropriated for *expenditures* for a specific fiscal year of the government unit. Operating budgets are appropriate for the general fund and special revenue funds; they are also sometimes used for debt service funds. An expendable trust fund also may have an operating budget, depending upon the terms of the *trust indenture. Capital budgets,* which are used to control the expenditures for construction projects or other plant asset acquisitions, are appropriate for capital projects funds and special assessment funds. The operating or capital budgets are *recorded in the accounting records* of all these funds, to aid in accounting for compliance with legislative authorizations.

As mentioned previously, the operations of the two proprietary funds are similar to those of business enterprises. Consequently, operating budgets are used by these funds as a managerial planning and control device rather than as a legislative control tool. Thus, operating budgets of enterprise funds and internal (or intragovernmental) service funds usually are not recorded in the accounting records of these funds.

Types of Operating Budgets   One or more of four types of operating budgets may be used by a governmental unit. A *traditional budget* emphasizes the *object* of each authorized expenditure, by department. For example, under the legislative activity of the general government function, the traditional budget may include authorized expenditures for personal services, supplies, and capital outlays.

A *program budget* stresses measurement of total cost of a specific governmental unit *program,* regardless of how many departments of the governmental unit are involved in the program. Object of expenditure information is of secondary importance in a program budget.

In a *performance budget,* there is an attempt to relate the input of governmental resources to the output of governmental services. For example, the total estimated expenditures of the enforcement section of the taxation department might be compared to the aggregate collections of additional tax assessments budgeted for the fiscal year.

The fourth type of operating budget for a governmental unit is the *planning, programming, budgeting system* (PPBS). This budgeting technique has been described as follows:[6]

> PPBS attempts to apply concepts of program and performance budgeting to the tasks of identifying the fundamental objectives of a government; selections are made from among alternative ways of attaining these objectives, on the basis of the full analysis of respective cost implications and expected benefit results of the alternatives.

Regardless of which types of operating budgets are used by a governmental unit, the final budget adopted by the governmental unit's legislative body will include *estimated revenues* for the fiscal year and the *appropriations* for expenditures authorized for that year. If the estimated reve-

[6] Ibid., pp. 27–28.

nues of the budget exceed appropriations (as required by law for many governmental units), there will be a **budgetary surplus;** if appropriations exceed estimated revenues in the budget, there will be a **budgetary deficit.**

Journal Entry for a General Fund Budget   To illustrate the recording of an operating budget in the accounting records of a general fund, assume that the Town of Verdant Glen in June of Year 5 adopted the following condensed operating budget for its General Fund for the fiscal year ending June 30, Year 6:

Budget of general fund	*Estimated revenues:*	
	General property taxes	*$700,000*
	Other	*100,000*
	Total estimated revenues	*$800,000*
	Appropriations:	
	General government *$420,000*	
	Other *340,000*	
	Total appropriations	*760,000*
	Excess of estimated revenues over appropriations (budgetary surplus).	*$ 40,000*

The journal entry to record the above budget on July 1, Year 5, would be as follows:

Journal entry for budget of general fund	*Estimated Revenues* *800,000*		
	Appropriations		*760,000*
	Fund Balance		*40,000*
	To record operating budget adopted for fiscal year ending June 30, Year 6.		

An analysis of each of the accounts in the preceding journal entry follows:

1 The Estimated Revenues account may be considered a **pseudo asset** account, because it reflects revenues expected to be received by the General Fund during the fiscal year. It is not a genuine asset, because it does not fit the accounting definition of an asset as an economic resource of an enterprise that is recognized and measured in conformity with generally accepted accounting principles.[7] Thus, the Estimated Revenues account is in substance a memorandum account, useful for control purposes only, which will be closed prior to the issuance of financial statements for the General Fund at the end of the fiscal year on June 30, Year 6.

---

[7] *APB Statement No. 4,* "Basic Concepts and Accounting Principles Underlying Financial Statements of Business Enterprises," AICPA (New York: 1970), p. 49.

2 The Appropriations account may be considered a **pseudo liability** account, because it reflects the legislative body's commitments to expend General Fund resources as authorized in the operating budget. The Appropriations account is not a genuine liability, because it does not fit the definition of a liability as an economic obligation that is recognized and measured in conformity with generally accepted accounting principles.[8] The Appropriations account, like the Estimated Revenues account, is a memorandum account useful for control purposes only, which will be closed prior to issuance of year-end financial statements for the General Fund.

3 The Fund Balance account, as its title implies, is an account which balances the asset and liability accounts of a general fund. Although similar to the owners' equity accounts of a business enterprise in this balancing feature, the Fund Balance account does not purport to show any ownership interest in a general fund's assets.

The journal entry to record the Town of Verdant Glen General Fund's operating budget for Fiscal Year 6 would be accompanied by detailed entries to subsidiary ledgers for both estimated revenues and appropriations. The budget of the Town of Verdant Glen General Fund purposely was condensed; in practice, the general fund's estimated revenues and appropriations would be detailed by source and function, respectively, into one or more of the following widely used subsidiary ledger categories:

Estimated revenues:	Appropriations:
Taxes	General government
Licenses and permits	Public safety
Intergovernmental revenues	Public works
Charges for services	Health and welfare
Fines and forfeits	Culture—recreation
Miscellaneous[9]	Debt service
	Intergovernmental expenditures
	Miscellaneous[10]

In summary, budgets of a governmental unit are recorded in the accounting records of the five governmental funds. An expendable trust fund also may record a budget if required to do so by the trust indenture. The recording of the budget initiates the accounting cycle for each of the funds listed above. Recording the budget also facilitates the preparation of financial statements which compare budgeted and actual amounts of revenues and expenditures.

ILLUSTRATIONS OF ACCOUNTING FOR GOVERNMENT ENTITIES

Having considered several of the theoretical issues in accounting for government entities, we shall now discuss and illustrate the journal

[8] Ibid., p. 50.
[9] *Governmental Accounting, Auditing, and Financial Reporting,* National Council on Governmental Accounting (Ann Arbor: 1968), pp. 188–190.
[10] Ibid., pp. 192–201.

entries for most of the eight types of funds identified previously, as well as for the general fixed assets and general long-term debt groups of accounts.

Accounting for the general fund

As indicated in the first part of this chapter, a general fund is used to account for all transactions of a governmental unit not properly accounted for in one of the other seven types of funds. Thus, the general fund as an accounting entity serves the same *residual* purpose as the general journal provides as an accounting record. Although the general fund is residual, it usually accounts for the largest aggregate dollar amounts of the governmental unit's revenues and expenditures.

In illustrating the accounting for a general fund, we shall expand the example of the Town of Verdant Glen used in the preceding section of this chapter.

Illustration of Accounting for a General Fund   Assume that the balance sheet of the Town of Verdant Glen General Fund at June 30, Year 5 *(prior* to the journal entry for the Fiscal Year 6 budget illustrated on page 620), was as follows:

TOWN OF VERDANT GLEN GENERAL FUND
Balance Sheet
June 30, Year 5

Assets	
Cash	$160,000
Inventory of supplies	40,000
Total assets	$200,000
Liabilities, Reserve, & Fund Balance	
Vouchers payable	$ 80,000
Reserve for inventory of supplies	40,000
Fund balance	80,000
Total liabilities, reserve, & fund balance	$200,000

The Reserve for Inventory of Supplies account is analogous to an appropriation of retained earnings in a business enterprise. It represents a reservation of the General Fund's Fund Balance account, so that the $40,000 nonexpendable portion of the General Fund's total assets will not be appropriated for expenditures in the legislative body's adoption of the next operating budget for the General Fund.

Assume that, in addition to the budget illustrated on page 620, the Town of Verdant Glen General Fund had the following summarized transactions for the fiscal year ended June 30, Year 6:

1 Property taxes were billed in the amount of $720,000, of which $14,000 was of doubtful collectibility.

2 Property taxes collected in cash totaled $650,000; other revenues collected in cash totaled $102,000.

3 Property taxes in the amount of $13,000 were found to be uncollectible.

4 Purchase orders were issued to vendors and suppliers in the total amount of $360,000.

5 Expenditures for the year totaled $760,000, of which $90,000 applied to additions to inventory of supplies, and $350,000 applied to $355,000 of the purchase orders issued during the year.

6 Cash payments on vouchers payable totaled $770,000.

7 Supplies with a cost of $80,000 were used during the year.

8 All uncollected property taxes at June 30, Year 6, were determined to be delinquent.

The following journal entries, numbered to correspond to the transactions outlined above, would be recorded in the accounting records of the Town of Verdant Glen General Fund during the year ended June 30, Year 6:

TOWN OF VERDANT GLEN GENERAL FUND
General Journal

1 *Taxes Receivable—Current*	720,000	
Estimated Uncollectible Current Taxes		*14,000*
Revenues		*706,000*
To accrue property taxes billed and to provide for estimated		
uncollectible portion.		

As indicated earlier, the modified accrual basis of accounting for a general fund permits the accrual of property taxes, because they are **billed** to the property owners by the Town of Verdant Glen. Because expense accounting is not appropriate for a general fund, the estimated uncollectible property taxes are **offset** against the total taxes billed; the net amount is the **actual** revenue from property taxes for the year.

2 *Cash*	752,000	
Taxes Receivable—Current		650,000
Revenues		102,000
To record cash collections of property taxes and other		
revenues for the year.		

Under the modified accrual basis of accounting, revenues not susceptible to accrual are recorded on the cash basis. However, any taxes or other revenues collected in advance of the fiscal year to which they apply would be credited to a liability account in the Town of Verdant Glen General Fund.

3 *Estimated Uncollectible Current Taxes*	*13,000*	
Taxes Receivable—Current		*13,000*
To write off receivable for property taxes which are uncollectible.		

The foregoing journal entry represents a shortcut approach. In an actual situation, uncollectible property taxes would first be transferred, together with estimated uncollectible amounts, to the Taxes Receivable —Delinquent account from the Taxes Receivable—Current account. Any amounts collected on these delinquent taxes would include revenues for interest and penalties required by law. Any uncollected delinquent taxes would be transferred, together with estimated uncollectible amounts, to the Tax Liens Receivable account. After the passage of an appropriate statutory period, the governmental unit might satisfy its tax lien by selling the property on which the taxes were levied.

4 *Encumbrances*	*360,000*	
Reserve for Encumbrances		*360,000*
To record purchase orders issued during the year.		

Encumbrance journal entries are designed to prevent the overexpending of an appropriated amount in the budget. The journal entry to the Encumbrances account would be posted in detail to reduce the unexpended balances of each applicable appropriation in the subsidiary ledger for appropriations. The unexpended balance of each appropriation thus is reduced for the amount committed by the issuance of the applicable purchase orders.

5a *Expenditures*	*670,000*	
Inventory of Supplies	*90,000*	
Vouchers Payable		*760,000*
To record expenditures for the year.		

The Expenditures account is debited with all expenditures, regardless of purpose, except for additions to the inventory of supplies. Principal and interest payments on debt, additions to the governmental unit's plant assets, payments for services to be received in the future—all are debited to Expenditures rather than to asset or liability accounts. (Expenditures for debt principal and interest and plant asset additions also are recorded *on a memorandum basis* in the general long-term debt and general fixed assets groups of accounts, respectively.)

The accounting for general fund expenditures described above emphasizes once again the importance of the operating budget in the accounting for a general fund. Expenditures are chargeable to amounts appropriated by the legislative body of the governmental unit. The detail items making up the $670,000 total debit to the Expenditures account in the preceding journal entry are posted to the appropriations subsidiary ledger as reductions of unexpended balances of each appropriation.

5b	Reserve for Encumbrances	355,000	
	Encumbrances		355,000
	To reverse encumbrances applicable to vouchered expenditures totaling $350,000.		

Recording actual expenditures of $350,000 relevant to purchase orders totaling $355,000 makes this amount of the previously recorded encumbrances no longer necessary. Accordingly, $355,000 of encumbrances is reversed; the reversal is posted to the detailed appropriations subsidiary ledger as well as to the general ledger.

6	Vouchers Payable	770,000	
	Cash		770,000
	To record payment of vouchered liabilities during the year.		
7	Expenditures	80,000	
	Inventory of Supplies............................		80,000
	To record cost of supplies used during the year.		
	Fund Balance	10,000	
	Reserve for Inventory of Supplies		10,000
	To increase inventory of supplies reserve to agree with balance in Inventory of Supplies account at end of year.		

The immediately preceding journal entry represents a reservation of a portion of the Fund Balance account to prevent its being appropriated improperly to finance a deficit operating budget for the General Fund for Year 7. Only cash and other monetary assets of a general fund are available for appropriation to finance authorized expenditures of the succeeding fiscal year.

8 Taxes Receivable—Delinquent	57,000	
Estimated Uncollectible Current Taxes	1,000	
Taxes Receivable—Current		57,000
Estimated Uncollectible Delinquent Taxes		1,000
To transfer delinquent taxes and related estimated uncollectible amounts from the current classification.		

The preceding journal entry clears the Taxes Receivable—Current account and the related contra account for uncollectible amounts so that they will be available for accrual of property taxes for the next fiscal year ending June 30, Year 7.

After all the preceding journal entries (including the budget entry on page 620) have been posted, the trial balance for the Town of Verdant Glen General Fund at June 30, Year 6, would be as follows:

TOWN OF VERDANT GLEN GENERAL FUND
Trial Balance
June 30, Year 6

Cash	$ 142,000	
Taxes receivable—delinquent	57,000	
Estimated uncollectible delinquent taxes		$ 1,000
Inventory of supplies	50,000	
Vouchers payable		70,000
Reserve for encumbrances		5,000
Reserve for inventory of supplies		50,000
Fund balance		110,000
Estimated revenues	800,000	
Appropriations		760,000
Revenues		808,000
Expenditures	750,000	
Encumbrances	5,000	
Totals	$1,804,000	$1,804,000

Closing Entries for a General Fund Before financial statements are prepared for the Town of Verdant Glen General Fund for the year ended June 30, Year 6, the budgetary and actual revenue, expenditure, and encumbrance accounts must be closed. The June 30, Year 6, closing entries for the Town of Verdant Glen General Fund would be as follows:

Closing entries for general fund

Revenues	808,000	
Estimated Revenues		800,000
Fund Balance		8,000
To close estimated and actual revenues accounts.		
Appropriations	760,000	
Expenditures		750,000
Encumbrances		5,000
Fund Balance		5,000
To close Appropriations, Expenditures, and Encumbrances accounts.		

The foregoing journal entries do not close the Reserve for Encumbrances account. Thus, the reserve represents a restriction on the fund balance at June 30, Year 6, because the Town of Verdant Glen General Fund is committed in Fiscal Year 7 to make estimated expenditures of $5,000 attributable to budgetary appropriations carried over from Fiscal Year 6. If the Reserve for Encumbrances account had been closed in the preceding journal entry, the Fund Balance account would have been overstated by $5,000. The Fund Balance account must represent the balance of the General Fund's assets which are available for appropriation for a **deficit budget** in Fiscal Year 7.

On July 1, Year 6—the beginning of Fiscal Year 7—the following journal entry would be appropriate for the $5,000 balance in the Reserve for Encumbrances account at June 30, Year 6:

Journal entry for outstanding encumbrances at beginning of fiscal year

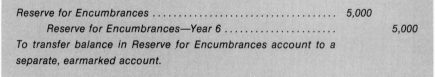

Reserve for Encumbrances	5,000	
Reserve for Encumbrances—Year 6		5,000
To transfer balance in Reserve for Encumbrances account to a separate, earmarked account.		

The journal entry above clears the Reserve for Encumbrances account for entries applicable to the general fund's operating budget for Fiscal Year 7. When the invoices applicable to the $5,000 reserve for encumbrances for Year 6 are received during Fiscal Year 7, a separate Expenditures—Year 6 account would be debited for the actual amount of the invoices. One of the closing entries at June 30, Year 7, would close the Expenditures—Year 6 account and the Reserve for Encumbrances—Year 6 account to the Fund Balance account.

Financial Statements for a General Fund We have stated previously that the results of operations (that is, net income or net loss) are not significant for a general fund. Therefore, the following three financial statements (the statement of revenues, expenditures, and encumbrances; the statement of changes in fund balance; and the balance sheet) should be prepared for the Town of Verdant Glen General Fund for the year ended June 30, Year 6.

TOWN OF VERDANT GLEN GENERAL FUND
Statement of Revenues, Expenditures, and Encumbrances
For Year Ended June 30, Year 6

	Budget	Actual	Over (under) budget
Revenues			
Taxes	$700,000	$706,000	$ 6,000
Other	100,000	102,000	2,000
Total revenues	$800,000	$808,000	$ 8,000
Expenditures and Encumbrances*			
General government	$420,000	$409,000	$(11,000)
Other	340,000	346,000	6,000
Total expenditures	$760,000	$755,000	$ (5,000)
Excess of revenues over expenditures and encumbrances	$ 40,000	$ 53,000	$ 13,000

* Breakdown of actual amounts between General Government and Other categories is assumed.

TOWN OF VERDANT GLEN GENERAL FUND
Statement of Changes in Fund Balance
For Year Ended June 30, Year 6

Fund balance, July 1, Year 5	$ 80,000
Add: Excess of revenues over expenditures and encumbrances	53,000
Subtotal	$133,000
Less: Increase in reserve for inventory of supplies	10,000
Fund balance, June 30, Year 6	$123,000

TOWN OF VERDANT GLEN GENERAL FUND
Balance Sheet
June 30, Year 6

Assets

Cash	$142,000
Property taxes receivable, less allowance of $1,000 for uncollectible amounts	56,000
Inventory of supplies	50,000
Total assets	$248,000

Liabilities, Reserves, & Fund Balance

Vouchers payable	$ 70,000
Encumbrances outstanding	5,000
Reserve for inventory of supplies	50,000
Fund balance	123,000
Total liabilities, reserves, & fund balance	$248,000

The following aspects of the Town of Verdant Glen General Fund financial statements should be emphasized:

1 The statement of revenues, expenditures, and encumbrances compares budgeted to actual amounts. This comparison aids in the appraisal of the stewardship for the General Fund's resources and the compliance with legislative appropriations. (Expenditures in excess of appropriated amounts generally are not permitted unless a supplementary appropriation is made by the legislative body of the governmental unit.)

2 The $8,000 excess of actual revenues over estimated revenues in the statement of revenues, expenditures, and encumbrances coincides with the amount credited to the Fund Balance account in the General Fund's June 30, Year 6, closing entry for estimated and actual revenues. The $5,000 excess of budgeted appropriations over actual expenditures and encumbrances also agrees with the amount credited to the Fund Balance account in the related General Fund closing entry at June 30, Year 6.

3 The excess of *actual* revenues over *actual* expenditures and encumbrances appears in the General Fund's statement of changes in fund balance. The *budgeted* excess of estimated revenues over appropriations does not appear in the statement of changes in fund balance, although it does appear in the statement of revenues, expenditures, and encumbrances.

4 The assets of the Town of Verdant Glen General Fund include only monetary assets and inventory. Expenditures for prepayments (other than supplies) and for plant assets are not recorded as assets in the General Fund.

5 The $123,000 fund balance at June 30, Year 6, is available, if required, for appropriation for a deficit budget for Fiscal Year 7. As pointed out earlier in this chapter, many government entities are not authorized to enact deficit budgets.

Concluding Comments on Accounting for a General Fund The preceding illustration of accounting for and financial statements of a general fund obviously has been simplified. For example, *interfund accounts* and transactions between the General Fund and other funds of the Town of Verdant Glen were not included in the illustration. "Receivable from" and "Payable to" accounts with other funds of the governmental unit are appropriate for interfund transactions. Accounting for interfund transactions is similar to accounting for intercompany transactions between affiliated corporations.

Accounting for special revenue funds

Special revenue funds are very similar to the general fund. They are established to account for the collections and expenditures associated with specialized revenue sources which are earmarked by law or regulation to finance specified governmental operations. Rubbish collection, freeway construction, and rapid transit systems are examples of governmental activities accounted for in special revenue funds.

Account titles, budgetary processes, and financial statements for special revenue funds are similar to those for general funds; therefore, they are not illustrated in this section.

On occasion, there may be a question as to whether a particular governmental program should be accounted for in a special revenue fund or in an enterprise fund. The National Council on Governmental Accounting summarized this issue as follows:[11]

> As a general rule, the distinguishing characteristic of a Special Revenue Fund is that most of the revenue involved in the operation comes from tax and non-tax sources not directly related to services rendered rather than from direct charges to users of the services. If a facility or program is financed entirely or predominantly by charges to users, the financial transactions involved should be accounted for in an Enterprise Fund. . . .

Accounting for capital projects funds

Capital projects funds of a governmental unit record the receipt and disbursement of cash for the governmental unit's plant assets, other than those financed by special assessments and government enterprises. The resources for a capital projects fund usually are derived from proceeds of general obligation bonds, but the resources may also come from current tax revenues or from grants or shared revenues of other governmental units.

As stated previously, a capital budget, rather than an operating budget, is the control device appropriate for a capital projects fund. The capital budget should deal with both the authorized expenditures for the project and the bonds or other sources of revenues for the project.

Journal Entries for a Capital Projects Fund Neither an Estimated Revenues account nor an Appropriations account is needed to record the capital budget for a capital projects fund. The capital projects fund is not an

[11] Ibid., p. 28.

authorized taxing agency; it merely receives proceeds of general obligation bond issuances or general fund and special revenue fund tax levies.
Furthermore, no annual legislative authorizations are required for the
expenditures of a capital projects fund, because the capital budget
covers all authorized expenditures of the fund during the life of the project. The Fund Balance account of a capital projects fund may be viewed
as serving the same purpose as an Appropriations account of the general fund, special revenue fund, or debt service fund. The opening
journal entry for a capital projects fund financed entirely with the proceeds of a general obligation bond issue is as follows:

*Opening
journal
entry for
capital
projects
fund
financed
by proceeds
of general
obligation
bond issue*

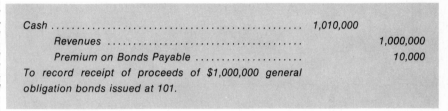

Cash	1,010,000	
Revenues		1,000,000
Premium on Bonds Payable		10,000

*To record receipt of proceeds of $1,000,000 general
obligation bonds issued at 101.*

The proceeds of the bond issue represent **revenues** to the capital projects fund; that fund does not assume the liability for the bonded indebtedness. The liability for the bonds is reflected in the general long-term
debt group of accounts until the bonds mature. At maturity date, the
bond liability is recorded in the debt service fund and removed from the
general long-term debt group of accounts.

Typically, the principal amount of the general obligation bonds represents the total capital budget for the capital projects fund. Accordingly,
the $10,000 bond premium in the preceding journal entry would be
transferred to the debt service fund, which must pay periodic interest
and the bond principal at maturity.

If the bonds had been issued at a discount, the customary accounting
treatment would be to offset the discount against the Revenues account
of the capital projects fund. Any deficiency in the capital projects fund's
cash at the date of completion of the project usually would be financed
from the general fund.

For a capital projects fund financed by a transfer of cash from the
general fund, the opening journal entry would not reflect revenues. For
example, if we assume that the project was to be financed from tax
revenues of the general fund, the capital projects fund's opening journal
entry would be as follows:

Opening
journal entry
for capital
projects fund
financed
by tax
revenues of
general fund

Receivable from General Fund   500,000

    Fund Balance   500,000

To record amount receivable from General Fund for author-

ized capital project.

In the general fund, a companion journal entry would debit Expenditures and credit Payable to Capital Projects Fund in the amount of $500,000.

Following the opening journal entry, subsequent journal entries for the capital projects fund would include encumbrance journal entries for construction contracts and purchase orders issued, and expenditures journal entries for payments to contractors, architects, and suppliers. These journal entries would be similar to those illustrated for a general fund. In addition, temporarily idle cash of the capital projects fund might be invested in short-term, interest-bearing securities. Any interest earned on the investments would be transferred from the capital projects fund to the debt service fund or to the general fund, depending on the source of the original financing of the capital projects fund.

Expenditures for construction recorded in the capital projects fund are accompanied in the general fixed assets group of accounts by a closing entry at the end of the fiscal year with a debit to Construction Work in Progress and a credit to Investment in Fixed Assets from Capital Projects Fund. The accounting for the general fixed assets group of accounts is illustrated in a subsequent section of this chapter.

At the end of each fiscal year prior to completion of a capital project, the Revenues, Expenditures, and Encumbrances accounts of the capital projects fund are closed to the Fund Balance account. Upon completion of the project, the entire capital projects fund is closed by a transfer of any unused cash to the debt service fund or the general fund, as appropriate. Any cash deficiency in the capital projects fund probably would be made up by the general fund; this financing would be credited to the Revenues account of the capital projects fund, because it was not contemplated in the original budget for the project.

Financial Statements for a Capital Projects Fund   Three financial statements are issued for a capital projects fund at the close of each fiscal year prior to completion of the project. The statement of revenues—estimated and actual—is similar in content to the revenues portion of the general fund statement illustrated on page 628. The statement of changes in fund balance shows the fund balance at the beginning of the fiscal year, increased by the year's actual revenues and decreased by the total expenditures and encumbrances for the fiscal year. The statement concludes with the fund balance at the end of the fiscal year.

The balance sheet for a capital projects fund shows the fund's assets —cash, short-term investments, and receivables. Liabilities, reserve for encumbrances, and fund balance round out the capital projects fund's balance sheet. To reiterate, the assets constructed with resources of the capital projects fund do not appear in that fund's balance sheet. Constructed plant assets appear in the governmental unit's general fixed assets group of accounts. Furthermore, any general obligation bonds issued to finance the capital projects fund are not a liability of this fund. Prior to the maturity date or dates of the bonds, the liability is carried in the general long-term debt group of accounts. At the date the bonds mature, the related liability is transferred to the debt service fund from the general long-term debt group of accounts.

Accounting for debt service funds

Payments of principal and interest on all long-term debt of a government entity other than special assessment bonds, revenue bonds, and general obligation bonds serviced by an enterprise fund are accounted for in debt service funds. *Special assessment bonds* are repaid from the proceeds of special assessment levies against specific properties receiving benefits from the special assessment improvements; accordingly, these bonds are accounted for in special assessment funds. *Revenue bonds* are payable from the earnings of a governmental enterprise and are accounted for in the appropriate enterprise fund. In some cases, *general obligation bonds,* which are supported by the full faith and credit of the issuing governmental unit, will be repaid from the resources of a governmental enterprise. These general obligation bonds should be reported as liabilities of the appropriate enterprise fund.

We must stress that the liability for bonds payable from resources of a debt service fund is not recorded in that fund until the debt matures. Prior to maturity date, the bond liability is recorded in the general long-term debt group of accounts.

The three customary types of general obligation long-term debt whose servicing is recorded in debt service funds are the following:

Serial bonds, with principal payable in annual installments over the life of the issue

Term bonds, with principal payable in total at a fixed maturity date from proceeds of an accumulated sinking fund

Notes, maturing more than one year from date of issuance

Journal Entries for a Debt Service Fund   A governmental unit's debt service fund operates in a manner similar to a business enterprise's pension fund. An actuarially determined amount, based on required debt servicing expenditures for the governmental unit's fiscal year, is recorded in the accounting records of the debt service fund at the beginning of the fiscal year. In effect, this amount is the operating budget for the debt service fund for the fiscal year.

The budget for a term bond, which requires the accumulation of a sinking fund, is recorded in the accounting records of the debt service fund as follows:

Opening
journal entry
for debt
service fund
for term
bonds

Required Additions	50,500	
Required Earnings	1,500	
Appropriations		12,200
Fund Balance		39,800

*To record budget for required additions and earnings for term
bond sinking fund, and for required expenditures for interest
and fiscal agent's fee.*

For a serial bond, which requires annual payments of principal as well as interest, the debt service fund's budget entry would use the same Estimated Revenues and Appropriations accounts as the budget entry for a general fund illustrated on page 620.

We previously have pointed out that the modified accrual basis of accounting is appropriate for a debt service fund. Thus, any property taxes specifically earmarked for servicing of a governmental unit's term or serial general obligation bonds may be accrued as revenues in the debt service fund. The accounting for such a tax accrual is the same as that for the general fund.

On the due date for any principal and interest payments by the debt service fund, the Expenditures account is debited and related Bonds Payable and Interest Payable accounts are credited. (The general long-term debt group of accounts simultaneously would be relieved of the corresponding amounts, as explained on page 640.) A debt service fund does not accrue interest which is not payable at the end of the fiscal year, because that interest has not been provided for in the debt service fund's budget for the fiscal year. A debt service fund does not issue purchase orders or contracts; thus the encumbrance accounting technique is not required.

For a term bond, which requires the accumulation of a sinking fund, the journal entries for a debt service fund include the investment of cash in interest-bearing securities and the collection of interest. Under the modified accrual basis of accounting, interest revenue accrued on investments at the end of the governmental unit's fiscal year is recorded in the accounting records of the debt service fund.

Financial Statements for a Debt Service Fund   The statement of changes in fund balance for a debt service fund usually is appended to the statement of revenues and expenditures, because the only change in the fund balance is the excess of revenues over expenditures. Further, a comparison of budgeted to actual revenues and expenditures is unnecessary for a debt service fund, because of the limited sources of revenues and types of expenditures. Footnote disclosure is appropriate for the actuarially determined required additions to a debt service fund for a term bond. A balance sheet for a debt service fund might appear as follows:

TOWN OF VERDANT GLEN DEBT SERVICE FUND
Balance Sheet
June 30, Year 6

Assets

Cash	$ 10,000
Cash with fiscal agent	54,000
Investments, at amortized cost plus accrued interest	80,000
Property taxes receivable, less allowance of $2,000 for uncollectible	
amounts	10,000
Total assets	$154,000

Liabilities & Fund Balance

Bonds payable	$ 50,000
Interest payable	4,000
Fund balance	100,000
Total liabilities & fund balance	$154,000

The balance sheet above discloses that cash has been deposited with the Town of Verdant Glen's fiscal agent (ordinarily a bank trust department) to pay bonds and interest which have matured at June 30, Year 6. The fiscal agent, however, has not yet completed redemption of the matured bonds and interest coupons.

Accounting for special assessment funds

A special assessment fund accounts for the assets, liabilities, revenues, and expenditures attributable to special tax assessments, payable in installments, which are levied on property owners in the governmental unit's jurisdiction. These tax assessments finance construction projects primarily for the benefit to property owners.

Accounting for a special assessment fund is in many respects a composite of the accounting for a debt service fund and a capital projects fund. The accounting records of a special assessment fund include both the proceeds and the servicing of the *special assessment bonds* which are issued to finance the construction project prior to the collection of special assessments receivable.

Journal Entries for a Special Assessment Fund   Like a capital projects fund, a special assessment fund might have a capital budget. The following journal entry would record the capital budget:

<table>
<tr><td rowspan="7">Opening journal entry for capital budget of special assessment fund</td></tr>
</table>

Opening journal entry for capital budget of special assessment fund	*Special Assessments Receivable—Current* 100,000	
	Special Assessments Receivable—Deferred 900,000	
	Fund Balance	1,000,000
	To record levy of special assessments, payable in ten equal annual installments, with interest at 8% on unpaid balance.	

The special assessment fund then would record the issuance of special assessment serial bonds, usually equal in amount to the deferred special assessments receivable, with a debit to Cash and a credit to Bonds Payable. Any premium or discount on the bonds would be recorded in the special assessment fund and amortized through interest expense in the customary manner, because the special assessment fund services its own bonds. The accrual basis of accounting is used for the special assessment fund, except that interest revenues on assessments receivable and interest expense on special assessment bonds payable are accrued only if fully matured and not yet received or paid. Delinquent assessments receivable, encumbrances, and expenditures are recorded in the same way as illustrated previously for the general fund. At the end of each fiscal year prior to completion of the construction project financed by the special assessments, the Interest Revenues, Interest Expense, Expenditures, and Encumbrances accounts are closed to the Fund Balance account. Complementary closing entries would be made to the Construction Work in Progress account in the general fixed assets group of accounts.

At the beginning of each fiscal year following the establishment of the special assessment fund, the current installments of the special assessments receivable are transferred from the Special Assessments Receivable—Deferred account to the Special Assessments Receivable—Current account. Payments of matured serial special assessment bonds are recorded in the accounting records of the fund in the usual manner for the liquidation of interest-bearing debt.

Financial Statements for a Special Assessment Fund   The financial statements for a special assessment fund are the statement of cash receipts and disbursements, statement of changes in fund balance, and balance sheet. Unlike a capital projects fund, a special assessment fund does not issue a statement of revenues—estimated and actual, because a special assessment fund's revenue consists only of interest on deferred special assessments receivable.

Accounting for enterprise funds

Enterprise funds account for the operations of commercial-type activities of the governmental unit, such as utilities, airports, seaports, and recreational facilities. These commercial-type enterprises sell services to the public (and in some cases to other activities of the governmental unit) at a profit. Consequently, the accounting for enterprise funds is more like business enterprise accounting than the accounting for any other governmental fund.

For example, accrual accounting is used for an enterprise fund, with short-term prepayments, depreciation expense, and doubtful accounts expense recorded in the fund's accounting records. The enterprise fund's accounting records also include the plant assets owned by the enterprise, as well as the liabilities for revenue bonds and any general obligation bonds payable by the enterprise fund. Encumbrance accounting is not used for enterprise funds, and the operating budget is not recorded in the accounting records of an enterprise fund. Retained earnings of an enterprise fund may be debited with cash remittances to the general fund, like dividends paid by a business enterprise.

Financial Statements for an Enterprise Fund   The financial statements for an enterprise fund are analogous to those for a business enterprise— a statement of revenue and expenses (income statement), statement of retained earnings, balance sheet, and statement of changes in financial position. However, there are a number of differences between the accounting records of an enterprise fund and those of a business enterprise. Among these differences are the following:

1 Enterprise funds are not subject to federal and state income taxes. However, an enterprise fund may be required to make payments in lieu of property or franchise taxes to the general fund.

2 There is no capital stock in an enterprise fund's balance sheet. Instead, Contributions accounts set forth the assets contributed to the enterprise fund by the general fund, by customers of the enterprise fund, or by other public agencies.

3 An enterprise fund has many restricted assets. Cash deposits made by customers of a utility enterprise fund, which are to assure the customers' payment for utility services, are restricted for cash or interest-bearing investments to offset the enterprise fund's liability for the customers' deposits. Cash received from proceeds of revenue bonds issued by the enterprise fund is restricted to payments for construction of plant assets financed by issuance of the bonds. Part of the cash generated by the enterprise fund's operations must be set aside and invested for payment of interest and principal of the revenue bond liabilities of the enterprise fund.

4 A number of retained earnings reserves appear in the accounting records of an enterprise fund. These reserves are equal to the cash and investments restricted to payment of revenue bond interest and principal.

The statement of revenue and expenses (income statement) of an enterprise fund may be on a budget-to-actual comparison basis, even though the operating budget is not recorded in the accounting records of the fund. In the enterprise fund's balance sheet, the restricted assets of the fund, the liabilities payable from restricted assets, and the retained earnings reserves are segregated and clearly labeled.

There is a difference among accounting authorities as to the appropriate balance sheet presentation of the governmental unit's general obligation bonds which are to be paid by an enterprise fund. The National Council on Governmental Accounting has recommended that the liability for such general obligation bonds be recorded in the general long-term debt group of accounts and that a liability account entitled Advance from Municipality—General Obligation Bonds be set up in the enterprise fund to offset the cash received from the issuance of the general obligation bonds.[12] The position of the AICPA is that the actual liability for the general obligation bonds should appear in the balance sheet of the enterprise fund (as stated earlier in this chapter) and that a footnote to the statement of general long-term debt of the governmental unit should describe the obligation for payment of the bonds if the enterprise fund fails to do so.[13] The AICPA's position seems the sounder of the two alternatives, from a theoretical point of view, and is supported by the authors.

Accounting for internal (or intragovernmental) service funds

An internal (or intragovernmental) service fund is established to sell merchandise and services to other departments of the governmental unit, but not to the public at large. This type of fund is created to assure uniformity and economies in the procurement of merchandise and services for the governmental unit as a whole, such as stationery supplies and the maintenance and repairs of motor vehicles.

An internal service fund operates like a business enterprise, except that it is not profit-motivated. Its Billings to Departments revenues account should be sufficient to cover all its operating costs and expenses, with perhaps a modest profit margin. In this way, the resources of an internal service fund are "revolving"; the original contribution from the general fund to establish the internal service fund is expended for supplies, operating equipment, and employees' salaries or wages, and the amounts expended are then recouped through billings to other departments of the governmental unit.

Although an internal service fund should use an operating budget for managerial planning and control purposes, the budget need not be recorded in the accounting records of the fund. The accrual basis of accounting, including the perpetual inventory system and depreciation of plant assets, is required for an internal service fund. Encumbrance accounting is not mandatory but may be useful in controlling the purchase orders of the internal service fund.

The financial statements for an internal service fund consist of a combined statement of operations and retained earnings and a balance sheet. Because an internal service fund is not profit-motivated, the term

[12] Ibid., p. 57.
[13] *Audits of State and Local Governmental Units*, p. 79.

net income should not be used in the statement of operations. "Excess of revenues over expenses" or a similar caption is more appropriate. Like an enterprise fund, an internal service fund has no owners' equity in its balance sheet. A Contribution from General Fund account represents the general fund's "investment" in the internal service fund.

Accounting for trust and agency funds

Trust and agency funds are used to account for assets held by a governmental unit as a *custodian.* Agency funds are of short duration; they typically account for such items as sales taxes, payroll taxes, and other deductions withheld from salaries of governmental unit employees for transmittal to a federal or state tax collection unit.

Trust funds of a governmental unit are longer-lived than agency funds. An *expendable* trust fund is one whose principal and income both may be expended to achieve the objectives of the trust. A Government Employees' Retirement Trust Fund is an example of an expendable trust fund, for both principal and income of a Retirement Trust Fund are expended for retired government employees' pensions. A *nonexpendable* trust fund is one whose income is expended to carry out the objectives of the trust; the principal remains intact. For example, an *endowment* established by the grantor of a trust may specify that the income from the endowment is to be expended by the governmental unit for student scholarships, but the endowment principal is not to be expended. A nonexpendable trust fund requires two separate trust fund accounting entities—one for principal and one for revenues. Accounting for the two separate trust funds requires a careful distinction between transactions affecting the principal—such as changes in the investment portfolio—and transactions affecting income—such as cash dividends and interest on the investment portfolio. The trust indenture, which is the legal document establishing the trust, should delineate distinctions between principal and income. If the trust indenture is silent with respect to such distinctions, the trust law of the governmental unit governs separation of principal trust fund and revenue trust fund transactions.

Because the governmental unit serves as a custodian for a trust fund, accounting for a trust fund should comply with the trust indenture under which the fund was established. Among the provisions which might affect the accounting for a trust fund are requirements that the operating budget for the trust fund be recorded in its accounting records and that depreciation be recorded for an endowment principal trust fund which includes depreciable assets.

The accrual basis of accounting is appropriate for nonexpendable and pension trust funds and agency funds; the modified accrual basis of accounting is used for expendable trust funds. Financial statements required for trust and agency funds are a statement of cash receipts and disbursements, a statement of changes in fund balance, and a balance sheet.

General fixed assets and general long-term debt groups of accounts

A governmental unit's general fixed assets and general long-term debt groups of accounts are not funds; they are memorandum accounts. Their purpose is to provide in one record the governmental unit's plant assets and long-term liabilities which are not recorded in one of the governmental unit's other funds. We have pointed out earlier that plant assets are recorded, as appropriate, in enterprise, trust, and internal service funds; and that bond liabilities are recorded, as appropriate, in debt service, enterprise, and special assessment funds.

The AICPA has suggested that the "improvements other than buildings" category of governmental unit-owned assets need not be recorded in the general fixed assets group of accounts, because they are immovable and of value only to the governmental unit.[14] These assets generally are termed "land improvements" in accounting for a business enterprise.

Assets in the general fixed assets group of accounts are recorded at their cost to the government or at their current fair value if donated to the governmental unit. The offsetting memorandum account is entitled Investment in General Fixed Assets from Capital Projects Fund, or other sources.

As pointed out earlier, depreciation may be recorded in the general fixed assets group of accounts, with a debit to the appropriate Investment in General Fixed Assets account and a credit to an Accumulated Depreciation account. When a plant asset is sold or retired by the governmental unit, the memorandum accounts in the general fixed assets group are relieved of the carrying amount of the asset; the sales proceeds are recorded as miscellaneous revenues in the general fund.

General obligation bonds of a governmental unit, both serial and term, which are not recorded in an enterprise fund are recorded as memorandum credits in the general long-term debt group of accounts. The offsetting memorandum debit entry is to an account entitled Amount to Be Provided for Payment of (Serial or Term) Bonds. When cash and other assets for the ultimate payment of a bond issue have been accumulated in a debt service fund, an Amount Available in Debt Service Fund account is debited and the Amount to Be Provided for Payment of Bonds account is credited. When the bonds are paid by the debt service fund, the memorandum accounts are reversed in the general long-term debt group of accounts in a closing entry at the end of the fiscal year.

[14] Ibid., p. 17.

Combined financial statements for governmental units

The annual report for a governmental unit's fiscal year is a complex mass of financial data if separate financial statements are presented in the report for each fund and group of accounts. Consequently, accountants have considered various methods for condensing the financial data within manageable bounds.

It is generally agreed that *consolidated-type* financial statements issued for affiliated business enterprises are inappropriate for the funds and account groups of a governmental unit. Despite the presence of "Receivable from" and "Payable to" interfund receivable and payable accounts, the various types of funds and account groups are too heterogeneous and subject to too many legal restrictions to be consolidated into a single reporting entity.

The AICPA has sanctioned the presentation of individual balance sheets of a governmental unit's funds and account groups in adjacent columns of a *combined* balance sheet, with a "memorandum only" total column which aggregates the columnar amounts.[15] The total column *does not* purport to show the financial position of the entire governmental unit.

Checklist of accounting for government entities

The discussion in this chapter of accounting for government entities is summarized in a checklist on page 642.

Criticism of accounting for government entities

The accounting standards for government entities have been criticized extensively in recent years. Since the severe financial crises of New York and other major United States cities, critics of accounting for government entities have claimed that ponderous financial reports of government entities, necessitated by the many funds and budgets, prevent a clear analysis of the financial condition of the entities. For example, a recent study found that the 1974 annual report of General Motors Corporation, which reported gross revenue of $31 billion and 734,000 employees, presented its operating results and financial position in 24 pages, of which 10 pages were devoted to written explanations of the company's operations. In contrast, the 1974 annual report of a city with gross revenues of $1 billion and 50,000 employees included more than 200 pages of detailed schedules, many of which were relevant only to internal management.[16]

The National Council on Governmental Accounting, a group of 21

---

[15] Ibid., pp. 20–21.
[16] "Financial Disclosure Practices of the American Cities: A Public Report," *Journal of Accountancy* (December, 1976), p. 80.

Checklist of Accounting for Government Entities

	Governmental Funds					Proprietary Funds		Trust or agency funds	General fixed assets group of accounts	General long-term debt group of accounts
	General fund	Special revenue fund	Capital projects fund	Debt service fund	Special assessment fund	Enterprise fund	Internal (or intra-governmental) service fund			
Records operating or capital budget	X	X	X	X	X			X		
Uses accrual basis of accounting						X	X	X(3)		
Uses modified accrual basis of accounting	X	X	X	X	X			X(3)		
Records taxes or assessments receivable	X	X		X	X					
Uses encumbrance technique	X	X	X		X					
Records plant assets						X	X	X	X	
Records depreciation						X	X	X	X	
Records proceeds of bond issuances			X		X	X				
Records liability for bonds issued	X	X		X(1)	X	X				X
Records payment of bonds				X	X	X				
Financial statements issued:									(4)	(4)
Balance sheet	X	X	X	X(2)	X	X	X	X		
Statement of revenues and expenditures	X	X	X	X	X					
Statement of operations						X	X			
Statement of cash receipts and disbursements					X					
Statement of changes in fund balance	X	X	X	X(2)	X			X		
Statement of changes in retained earnings						X	X			
Statement of changes in financial position						X				

(1) At maturity date of bonds only.
(2) Statement of revenues and expenditures is combined with statement of changes in fund balance.
(3) Expendable trust funds use modified accrual basis of accounting; other trust and agency funds use accrual basis of accounting.
(4) The two groups of accounts issue **trial balances** rather than **financial statements.**

local, state, and federal governmental accountants and managers, has long been responsible for establishing accounting principles for state and local governmental units. In 1978, it issued for comment an exposure draft of proposed changes in governmental accounting principles as stated in *Governmental Accounting, Auditing, and Financial Reporting* (GAAFR) issued in 1968. In addition to some minor proposed changes in basic accounting practices, the following format was recommended for the annual report of a governmental unit:[17]

  1 *Introductory Section*
  (Table of contents, letter(s) of transmittal, and other material deemed appropriate by management)
  2 *Financial Section*
    a *Auditor's Report*
    b *Combined Statements—Overview*
      (1) Combined Balance Sheet—All Fund Types and Account Groups
      (2) Combined Statement of Revenues, Expenditures, and Changes in Fund Balances—All Governmental Fund Types
      (3) Combined Statement of Revenues, Expenses, and Changes in Retained Earnings (or Equity)—All Proprietary Fund Types
      (4) Combined Statement of Changes in Financial Position—All Proprietary Fund Types
      (Fiduciary funds may be reported in (2) and (3) above, as appropriate, or separately.)
    c *Fund and Account Group Statements and Schedules*
      (1) Combining Statements—By Fund Type (where governmental unit has more than one fund of a fund type)
      (2) Individual fund and account group statements and/or schedules (as necessary for fair presentation in conformity with generally accepted accounting principles and to demonstrate compliance with legal provisions)
      (3) Supplemental schedules as desired by the government (e.g., Combined Schedule of Cash Receipts, Disbursements, and Balances—All Funds)
    d *Notes to the Financial Statements*
    (The Summary of Significant Accounting Policies and other notes to the financial statements necessary for adequate disclosure)
  3 *Statistical Tables*

In addition to the current efforts of the National Council on Governmental Accounting, the FASB has placed financial reporting concepts for governmental entities on its agenda. Because of the current activities of the National Council on Governmental Accounting, the precise role of the FASB in the setting of accounting standards for governmental entities is not clear at this time.

Prototype consolidated financial statements of United States Government

An interesting recent innovation in accounting for government entities has been the issuance by the United States Government of prototype

[17] *Exposure Draft: GAAFR Restatement Principles,* pp. 50–51.

consolidated financial statements. According to the Secretary of the Treasury, these financial statements represent a step in the evolution of comprehensive and understandable government financial reporting. The appendix which follows includes prototype consolidated financial statements of the United States Government for the period ended September 30, 1976.

Appendix: Prototype Consolidated Financial Statements of United States Government

United States Government
Consolidated Statement of Financial Position
as of September 30, 1976, and June 30, 1976 and 1975

(amounts in billions)

Assets

(What the Government owns—resources that are available to pay obligations or to provide public services in the future)

	1976		1975
	Sept. 30	June 30	June 30
Cash and monetary reserves			
Operating cash in the Treasury	$17.4	$14.8	$7.6
International monetary reserves *(Note 1)*	17.9	17.1	16.2
Other cash	6.3	7.1	5.2
	41.6	39.0	29.0
Receivables (net of allowances)			
Accounts receivable	5.4	3.9	5.5
Accrued taxes receivable *(Note 2)*	14.1	10.1	11.8
Loans receivable *(Note 3)*	100.2	106.4	82.7
Advances and prepayments	6.7	3.6	1.3
	126.4	124.0	101.3
Inventories (at cost) *(Note 4)*			
Goods for sale	13.5	13.2	11.2
Work in process	.8	.8	.7
Raw materials	1.4	1.6	2.8
Materials and supplies for Government use	35.4	35.5	31.2
Stockpiled materials and commodities	12.5	12.3	11.6
	63.6	63.4	57.5
Property and equipment (at cost)			
Land *(Note 5)*	7.6	7.5	7.0
Buildings, structures, and facilities *(Note 6)*	92.7	92.5	92.1
Military hardware *(Note 7)*	133.5	133.5	126.6
Equipment *(Note 7)*	42.9	42.6	41.1
Construction in progress	16.2	16.6	18.0
Other	1.7	1.8	2.1
	294.6	294.5	286.9
Accumulated depreciation *(Note 8)*	(147.2)	(145.1)	(136.5)
	147.4	149.4	150.4
Deferred charges and other assets	20.2	18.6	16.7
Total assets	$399.2	$394.4	$354.9

The accompanying notes are an integral part of this statement.

United States Government
Consolidated Statement of Financial Position
as of September 30, 1976, and June 30, 1976 and 1975

(amounts in billions)

Liabilities

(What the Government owes—obligations incurred in the
past that will require cash or other resources in the future)

	1976 Sept. 30	1976 June 30	1975 June 30
Accounts payable	$53.7	$45.7	$46.9
Unearned revenue	9.8	9.5	8.3
Borrowings from the public *(Note 9)*	494.6	476.6	394.4
Accrued pensions under retirement and disability plans *(Note 10)*			
Military personnel	119.3	117.3	96.6
Civilian employees	133.9	130.9	118.0
Social security	630.8	603.1	499.5
Veterans	113.4	113.6	117.3
	997.4	964.9	831.4
Loss reserves for guarantee and insurance programs *(Note 11)*	27.9	25.3	15.1
Other liabilities	42.5	41.8	39.4
Total liabilities	1,625.9	1,563.8	1,335.5

Fiscal Deficit

(The accumulated amount by which the costs of Government
activities have exceeded Government revenues)

Fiscal deficit beginning of period	(1,169.4)	(980.6)	(833.2)
Current period fiscal deficit	(29.6)	(85.2)	(63.9)
Current noncash provision for social security *(Note 12)*	(27.7)	(103.6)	(83.5)
Fiscal deficit end of period	(1,226.7)	(1,169.4)	(980.6)
Total liabilities and fiscal deficit	$399.2	$394.4	$354.9

The accompanying notes are an integral part of this statement.

United States Government Consolidated Statement of Operations for the Transitional Quarter (TQ) ended September 30, 1976, and the Years ended June 30, 1976 and 1975

(amounts in billions)

	1976	1976	1975
Revenues	TQ	June 30	June 30
Levied under the Government's sovereign power			
Individual income taxes	$38.8	$131.6	$122.4
Corporate income taxes	12.5	39.7	37.4
Social insurance taxes and contributions ...	25.8	92.7	86.4
Excise taxes	4.5	16.9	16.6
Estate and gift taxes	1.5	5.2	4.6
Customs duties	1.2	4.1	3.7
Miscellaneous	4.4	9.8	9.7
	88.7	300.0	280.8
Earned through Government business-type operations			
Sale of goods and services	5.7	14.8	11.8
Interest	2.4	16.3	11.9
Other	4.0	17.6	16.8
	12.1	48.7	40.5
Total revenues	100.8	348.7	321.3
Expenses by function (see also summary of expenses by object and agency)			
Agriculture	1.9	10.7	14.5
Commerce and transportation	6.3	17.6	15.4
Community and regional development	3.8	13.4	6.2
Education, training, employment, and social services	6.6	17.9	14.4
General government	3.2	12.2	7.9
General science, space and technology	1.4	4.3	3.7
Health	11.6	34.1	27.1
Income security			
Military personnel	4.8	28.1	23.1
Civilian employees	5.5	21.2	17.0
Social insurance	26.3	81.7	72.6
Veterans	1.6	4.7	14.2
Other	9.8	37.5	28.4
Interest	8.1	37.1	32.7
International affairs	4.3	12.0	8.1
Law enforcement and justice	1.2	3.4	2.8
National defense	22.6	65.6	73.3
Natural resources, environment, and energy	4.9	13.6	7.8
Revenue sharing and general purpose fiscal assistance	2.3	6.7	6.6
Veterans benefits and services	4.2	12.1	9.4
Total expenses	130.4	433.9	385.2
Current period fiscal deficit	$(29.6)	$(85.2)	$(63.9)

The accompanying notes are an integral part of this statement.

Summary of Expenses by Object and Agency

	1976		1975
	TQ	June 30	June 30
Expenses by object			
Salaries and employee benefits	$8.3	$67.8	$63.9
Vendor services and supplies	24.1	68.5	67.3
Depreciation	2.1	8.6	7.7
Pensions, health and life insurance	10.1	57.3	48.8
Casualty insurance and indemnities	35.5	103.0	87.1
Grants, subsidies, and contributions	42.2	91.6	77.7
Interest	8.1	37.1	32.7
Total expenses	$130.4	$433.9	$385.2
Expenses by agency			
Legislative Branch	$.2	$.8	$.7
The Judiciary	.1	.3	.3
Executive Branch			
Office of the President	4.3	11.5	22.1
Departments			
Agriculture	5.8	22.1	8.0
Commerce	.8	2.3	1.7
Defense	27.8	97.2	96.8
Health, Education and Welfare	43.2	132.1	107.9
Housing and Urban Development	4.4	15.6	9.7
Interior	1.5	4.2	3.3
Justice	.8	2.5	2.2
Labor	7.7	26.4	17.0
State	.4	1.2	.9
Transportation	3.8	12.7	9.0
Treasury: Interest	8.1	37.1	32.7
Other	3.2	9.8	9.8
Independent Agencies	18.3	58.1	63.1
Total expenses	$130.4	$433.9	$385.2

The accompanying notes are an integral part of this statement.

Introductory Statement to Notes

As is true of accounting in other types of economic entities governmental accounting exists for the purpose of providing complete and accurate financial information, in proper form and on a timely basis, to those responsible for and concerned with the operations of governmental units and agencies. While the Federal Government presently prepares many types of statements for specialized users, these prototype Federal Consolidated Financial Statements have been prepared to serve the common needs of a variety of users, with emphasis on the general public, to help promote understanding of the overall financial condition of the Federal Government and to promote a more informed understanding of government's place in our economy. It is important to note that this report is a prototype: Many aspects of the financial statements require further analysis. Only as the various problems are resolved can fully satisfactory statements be prepared. A change in the fiscal year required that amounts be reflected in the Consolidated Statement of Financial Position as of September 30, 1976, June 30, 1976, and June 30, 1975. The revenues and expenses for the three month Transition Quarter (July 1, 1976, to September 30, 1976) are shown separately in the Consolidated Statement of Operations.

The sources used in developing the statements were predominantly Treasury publications, supplemented by reports from both the civilian and military sectors of the Federal Government. For the most part, these publications and reports are a product of the agencies' accounting systems, which by law must conform in all material respects to the accounting principles, standards, and related requirements prescribed by the Comptroller General of the United States. The maintenance of accounts on the accrual basis is a basic requirement for all Federal agencies. As of December 31, 1976, there were 338 accounting systems subject to approval by the Comptroller General. (The Comptroller General has approved the principles and standards of 98 percent of these accounting systems and the designs of 52 percent of the systems.) The great majority of information in this report is derived from these systems.

The accompanying financial statements include the accounts of all significant agencies and funds included in the Unified Budget of the United States Government. Agencies such as the U.S. Postal Service, the Export-Import Bank of the United States, and the Federal Financing Bank, which are classified as "off-budget" (not included in the budget), have also been included in the financial statements because they are wholly owned and are clearly within the scope of Government operations. Government-sponsored enterprises such as Federal Land Banks have been excluded because they are privately owned. The Federal Reserve System is excluded. Although the Government's power to tax and to create money may be considered its most important assets, these are not included in these statements because the concepts have not been developed to the point where valuation is possible.

Although the Advisory Committee on Federal Consolidated Financial Statements has generally agreed that assets should be shown on a current value basis, the current value method best suited for each type of asset has not yet been determined. The Valuation Methods Schedule (page 26) lists various current value methods applicable to each type of asset. This is one of the many conceptual as well as practical problems that the Treasury has begun to address and must resolve to improve the usefulness of these statements.

Notes to Financial Statements

1. International monetary reserves

This category as of the latest period shown, September 30, 1976, comprises the following items: $11.6 billion in gold, which has been recorded at $42.22 per ounce, the statutory price at which gold is monetized by the issuance of Gold Certificates to the Federal Reserve System; $2.4 billion of Special Drawing Rights, which are an international reserve asset; and $3.9 billion representing the United States reserve position with the International Monetary Fund.

2. Accrued taxes receivable

The September 30, 1976, total for taxes receivable represents $6.0 billion (net) for delinquent taxes and $8.1 billion of accrued corporate taxes. The amounts as of June 30, 1975, were $6.4 billion and $5.4 billion, respectively. No accrual has been made for individual income taxes. (A method for accruing these taxes is scheduled for study.) Likewise, assessed tax deficiencies pending settlement have not been included.

3. Loans receivable

Outstanding loans and allowances for losses have been recorded as reported by the various lending agencies. No attempt has been made to evaluate the adequacy of the allowance for losses, but it is presumed to be understated and is under study. Interest rates and loan repayment terms vary considerably for outstanding loans, with rates ranging from 2 percent to 12 percent and terms from as short as 90 days to well over 40 years.

4. Inventories

Inventories include nondepreciable personal property and are generally stated at cost. The September 30, 1976, total for inventories comprises $47.8 billion for the Department of Defense and $15.8 billion for other agencies. The amounts as of June 30, 1975, were $42.8 billion and $14.7 billion, respectively. The inventory accounts do not include the weapons stockpile of the Energy Research and Development Administration, since the extent of this inventory is classified information.

5. Land

Land is valued at the cost paid by the Government. The cost of land acquired through donation, exchange, bequest, forfeiture, or judicial process is estimated by the General Services Administration at amounts the Government would have paid if purchased at the date of acquisition. Pending study of valuation methods, the outer continental shelf, other offshore lands, and the 704 million acres of public domain lands have not been included. In 1972 a committee of the House of Representatives estimated the value of public domain lands (93 percent of the total on-shore acreage owned by the Federal Government) to be $29.9 billion. Acreage owned by the Federal Government as of September 30, 1976, exclusive of off-shore lands, is summarized below by predominant usage.

Usage	Acres (millions)
Forest and wildlife	504.6
Grazing	163.5
Parks and historic sites	26.0
Alaska oil and gas reserves	23.0
Military (except airfields)	18.4
Flood control and navigation	8.1
Reclamation and irrigation	6.0
Industrial	2.9
Alaska native reserves	2.8
Airfields	1.9
Research and development	1.6
Power development and distribution	1.5
Other usages	1.8
Total	762.1

6. Buildings, structures, and facilities

This category consists of all real property owned by the Federal Government except land. The total reflects the acquisition cost of buildings and the costs of acquiring or erecting dams, utility systems, monuments, roads and bridges. The September 30, 1976, total for this category represents $61.7 billion for the Department of Defense and $31.0 billion for other agencies. The amounts as of June 30, 1975, were $57.2 billion and $34.9 billion, respectively.

7. Depreciable personal property

Equipment and military hardware are recorded at acquisition cost and include only depreciable personal property which is currently in use or in usable condition. The major components of each category are summarized below.

	Sept. 30, 1976	June 30, 1975
(amounts in billions)		
Military hardware		
Aircraft and related equipment	$57.3	$51.6
Ships and service craft	39.7	38.0
Combat and tactical vehicles	19.9	17.8
Missiles and related equipment	11.3	10.6
Other	5.3	8.6
Total	$133.5	$126.6
Equipment		
Department of Defense		
Industrial plant equipment	$14.3	$13.9
Communication and electronics	4.2	4.9
Other	4.5	3.5
	23.0	22.3
Other agencies	19.9	18.8
Total	$42.9	$41.1

8. Accumulated depreciation

Most Government agencies do not calculate depreciation on property and equipment. For such agencies, accumulated depreciation was estimated on a straight line basis, based on available information. The useful lives applied to each classification of asset are as follows: buildings, structures, and facilities—50 years; ships and service craft—30 years; industrial plant equipment—20 years; all other depreciable assets—10 years.

Reported amounts were used for those agencies, for example, Tennessee Valley Authority and U.S. Postal Service, that do depreciate property and equipment. These agencies account for approximately 6 percent of the total accumulated depreciation reflected in the Consolidated Statement of Financial Position.

9. Borrowings from the public

The gross amount of Federal debt outstanding has been reduced by intragovernmental holdings net of unamortized premiums and discounts. The largest such reduction reflects the holdings of Government trust funds. Significant intragovernmental holdings of Federal debt securities are summarized below. For additional information on borrowings from the public, see the Federal Debt Maturity Schedule in the supplementary section (page 24).

	Sept. 30, 1976	June 30, 1975
(amounts in billions)		
Social Security Administration		
Federal Old Age and Survivors	$37.1	$39.9
Federal Disability Insurance	6.4	8.1
Federal Hospital Insurance	11.0	9.8
Federal Supplementary Medical Insurance	1.2	1.4
	55.7	59.2
Civil Service Commission		
Civil Service Retirement and Disability	42.7	38.6
Other	2.5	2.0
	45.2	40.6
Department of Labor—Unemployment	4.9	7.2
Department of Transportation		
Highway	9.0	9.6
Other	2.7	1.9
	11.7	11.5
Veterans Administration	8.3	8.1
Federal Deposit Insurance Corporation	6.6	6.2
Other	3.6	4.5
Total	$136.0	$137.3

As of September 30, 1976, foreign and international investors held approximately $75.0 billion of the debt outstanding with the public. The amount as of June 30, 1975, was $66.0 billion.

10. Accrued pensions under retirement and disability plans

The accounting for accrued pensions is subject to several different assumptions, definitions, and methods of calculation for the various retirement and disability plans. Specific methods applied to each of the major pension accruals are summarized below. Liabilities for approximately 30 other Government pension plans are not included because of insufficient data. Further study and analysis is required for adequate valuation and disclosure of pension liabilities.

Military personnel and civilian employees: Liabilities have been recorded based on the estimated present value of accrued benefits, as actuarially computed by the administering agencies.

Social security: Estimates for social security are based on the present value of the projected excess of benefits over contributions for present participants for the next 75 years.

Veterans: The liability for Veterans Administration benefits represents the computed present value of annual benefit payments estimated by the Veterans Administration to the year 2000.

11. Loss reserves for guarantee and insurance programs

For additional information on loss reserves for guarantee and insurance programs, see the Commitments and Contingencies Schedule in the supplementary section (pages 22-23).

12. Current noncash provision for social security

The noncash provision for social security represents changes in the social security accrued liabilities between periods based on a 30-year amortization of the actuarial deficit. Accounting methods for this provision require additional study.

The noncash amounts are not included in the Statement of Operations because a substantial but indeterminate portion is not applicable to the current period. The Statement of Operations does include cash benefit payments.

13. Contingencies

Several Government agencies insure businesses and individuals against various types of risks. The amount of insurance coverage in force, representing the maximum risk exposure of the Government, is $1,566.9 billion as of September 30, 1976.

The Government also guarantees loans by non-Government enterprises to businesses and individuals. These guarantees become liabilities of the Government only when the Government is required to honor its guarantees. Loan guarantees in force at September 30, 1976, are $194.4 billion. For further information on contingencies, see the Commitments and Contingencies Schedule in the supplemental section (pages 22-23).

14. Open-ended programs and fixed costs

The Government also commits itself to provide services by passing laws that make spending mandatory. Since a significant amount of future spending is fixed by law, it is very probable that the Government will pay for these programs in future years. Listed below are the programs for the Transition Quarter and Fiscal Year 1976 that can be terminated only if a law is changed.

	TQ	1976
	(amounts in billions)	
Payments for individuals		
Social security and railroad retirement	$20.7	$76.2
Federal employees' retirement and insurance	4.3	15.6
Unemployment assistance	4.2	19.8
Veterans benefits	2.9	13.9
Medicare and Medicaid	7.0	26.3
Housing payments	.6	2.5
Public assistance related programs	4.9	20.2
	44.6	174.5
Net interest	7.0	26.8
General revenue sharing	1.6	6.2
Other open-ended programs and fixed costs	3.3	9.4
Total	$56.5	$216.9

REVIEW QUESTIONS

1 What characteristics of government entities have a significant influence on the accounting for governmental units? Explain.

2 What is a *fund* in accounting for government entities?

3 What is the support for each of the following aspects of accounting theory for government entities?
 a The modified accrual basis of accounting
 b The encumbrance accounting technique
 c Recording the budget in the accounting records

4 Differentiate between a *program budget* and a *performance budget.*

5 The Estimated Revenues account of a governmental unit's general fund sometimes is alluded to as a *pseudo asset.* Why is this true?

6 What does the reference to a general fund as *residual* mean? Explain.

7 a What are the basic financial statements for a governmental unit's general fund?
 b What are the major differences between the financial statements of a governmental unit's general fund and the financial statements of a business enterprise?

8 What revenues of a general fund usually are accrued? Explain.

9 Distinguish between the Expenditures account of a governmental unit's general fund and the expense accounts of a business enterprise.

10 The accounting records for the City of Worthington General Fund include an account titled Reserve for Inventory of Supplies. Explain the purpose of this account.

11 Under what circumstances are general obligation bonds of a governmental unit recorded in the governmental unit's enterprise fund? Explain.

12 Discuss the similarities and differences between a governmental unit's capital projects fund and special assessment fund.

13 The accounting for a governmental unit's enterprise fund is in many respects similar to the accounting for a business entity, yet there are a number of differences between the two types of accounting. Identify at least three of the differences.

14 Accounting for nonexpendable trusts for which a governmental unit acts as custodian requires the establishment of two separate trust funds. Why is this true?

15 Is a consolidated balance sheet appropriate for all funds and account groups of a governmental unit? Explain.

EXERCISES

Ex. 16-1 Select the best answer for each of the following multiple-choice questions:

1 A credit to the Fund Balance account in a journal entry to record the budget of a governmental unit's general fund indicates that:
 a Estimated expenses exceed actual revenues
 b. Actual expenses exceed estimated expenses
 c Estimated revenues exceed appropriations
 d Appropriations exceed estimated revenues

2 Which of the following types of governmental revenues would be susceptible to accrual under the modified accrual basis of accounting?
 a State sales tax
 b County property tax
 c City income tax
 d City business licenses

3 Which governmental fund would account for plant assets in a manner similar to a business enterprise?
 a Enterprise fund
 b Capital projects fund
 c General fixed assets group of accounts
 d General fund

4 If a government entity established a data processing center to service all agencies within the entity, the data processing center should be accounted for as:
 a A capital projects fund
 b An internal (or intragovernmental) service fund
 c An agency fund
 d A trust fund

5 The Reserve for Encumbrances—Prior Year account represents amounts recorded by a governmental unit for:
 a Anticipated expenditures in the forthcoming fiscal year
 b Expenditures for which purchase orders were made in the prior fiscal year but payment will be made in the forthcoming fiscal year
 c Excess expenditures in the prior fiscal year which will be offset against amounts budgeted for the forthcoming fiscal year
 d Unanticipated expenditures of the prior fiscal year which became evident in the current fiscal year

6 Which of the following types of revenues generally would be recorded in the general fund of a government entity?
 a Receipts from a city-owned parking structure
 b Property taxes
 c Interest earned on investments held for retirement of employees
 d Revenues from internal (or intragovernmental) service funds

Ex. 16-2 The Town of Mason Enterprise Fund had the following:

Prepaid insurance paid in December, Year 6 .... $ 43,000
Depreciation expense for Year 6 129,000
Doubtful accounts expense for Year 6 14,000

Compute the amount to be included in the statement of revenues and expenses of the Town of Mason Enterprise Fund for the above items.

Ex. 16-3 On July 1, Year 4, the City of Haynes paid $115,000 out of general fund revenues for a central garage to service its vehicles, with $67,500 being applicable to the building, which has an economic life of 25 years, $14,500 to land, and $33,000 to machinery and equipment, which has an economic life of 15 years. A $12,200 cash contribution was received by the garage from the general fund on the same date.

Prepare the journal entry or entries to record the above transactions in the appropriate fund established for the central garage. Identify the fund.

Ex. 16-4 On June 30, Year 1, the Town of Warren issued $160,000 principal amount of special assessment bonds at 100 to finance in part a street improvement project estimated to cost $215,000. The project is to be paid by a $15,000 contribution from the Town of Warren General Fund and by a $200,000 special assessment against property owners (payable in five equal annual installments beginning July 1, Year 1).

Prepare the journal entry or entries to record the above transactions in the appropriate fund established for the street improvement project. Identify the fund.

Ex. 16-5 On July 1, Year 7, the County of Pinecrest issued $400,000 in 30-year, 8% general obligation term bonds of the same date at 100 to finance the construction of a public health center.

Prepare the journal entry or entries to record the above transaction in all funds or account groups affected. Identify the funds or account groups.

Ex. 16-6 The city council of Haliburton adopted a budget for the general operations of the city government during the fiscal year ending June 30, Year 5. Revenues were estimated at $695,000. Legal authorizations for budgeted expenditures were $650,000. In addition, taxes of $160,000 were levied and billed for the special revenue fund of Haliburton, of which 1% was estimated to be uncollectible.

Prepare the journal entry or entries to record the above transactions in the appropriate funds. Identify the funds.

Ex. 16-7 On July 25, Year 3, office supplies estimated to cost $2,390 were ordered from a vendor for delivery to the office of the city manager at Gaskill. The City of Gaskill, which operates on the calendar year, maintains a perpetual inventory system for such supplies. The supplies ordered July 25 were received on August 9, Year 3, accompanied by an invoice for $2,500.

Prepare the journal entries to record the above transactions in the appropriate fund. Identify the fund.

Ex. 16-8 Agatha Morris, a citizen of Roark City, donated common stock valued at $22,000 to the city under a trust indenture dated July 1, Year 6. Under the terms of the indenture, the principal amount is to be kept intact; use of revenue from the stock is restricted to financing academic scholarships for needy college students. On December 14, Year 6, dividends of $1,100 were received on the stock donated by Morris.

Prepare the journal entries to record the above transactions in the appropriate funds. Identify the funds.

SHORT CASES FOR ANALYSIS AND DECISION

Case 16-1 Bradley King, executive vice president of Passaic Company, a publicly held manufacturing company, has been elected to the city council of Megalopolis. Prior to assuming office as a city councilman, King asks you to explain the principal differences in accounting and financial reporting for a large city as compared to a large manufacturing company.

Instructions

a Describe the principal differences in the purpose of financial accounting and reporting and in the types of financial reports of a large city as compared to a large manufacturing company.

b Why are inventories often disregarded in accounting for local government entities? Explain.

c Under what circumstances should depreciation be recorded for local government entities? Explain.

Case 16-2 You have been requested to examine the financial statements of the funds and account groups of Ashburn City for the fiscal year ended June 30, Year 7. During the course of your examination you learn that on July 1, Year 6, the city issued at principal amount $1,000,000 20-year, 8% general obligation serial bonds to finance additional power-generating facilities for the Ashburn City electric utility. Principal and interest on the bonds are repayable by the Ashburn City Electric Utility Enterprise Fund. However, for the first five years of the serial maturities of the bonds—July 1, Year 7, through July 1, Year 11—a special tax levy accounted for in the Ashburn City Special Revenue Fund is to contribute to the payment of 80% of the interest and principal of the general obligation bonds. At the end of the five-year period, it is anticipated that revenue from the electric utility's new power-generating facilities will create cash flow for the Ashburn City Electric Utility Enterprise Fund sufficient to pay all the serial maturities and interest of the general obligation bonds during the period July 1, Year 12, through July 1, Year 26.

You find that the accounting records of the Ashburn City Electric Utility Enterprise Fund include the following amounts relative to the general obligation bonds at June 30, Year 7:

8% general obligation serial bonds payable ($50,000 due July 1, Year 7) $1,000,000

Interest payable (interest on the bonds is payable annually each July 1)   80,000

Interest expense   80,000

The statement of revenues and expenses for the year ended June 30, Year 7, prepared by the accountant for the Ashburn City Electric Utility Enterprise Fund shows a net loss of $20,000. You also learn that on July 1, Year 7, the Ashburn City Special Revenue Fund paid $104,000 ($130,000 × 80% = $104,000) and the Ashburn City Electric Utility Enterprise Fund paid the remaining $26,000 ($130,000 × 20% = $26,000) to the fiscal agent for the 8% general obligation serial bonds. The $130,000 was the total of the $50,000 principal and $80,000 interest due on the bonds July 1, Year 7.

Instructions Do you concur with the Ashburn City Electric Utility Enterprise Fund's accounting and reporting treatment for the 8% general obligation serial bonds? Discuss.

Case 16-3 The controller of the City of West Fork has asked your advice on the accounting for an installment contract payable by the city. The contract covers the costs of installing automatic gates, coin receptacles, and ticket dispensers for the 20 city-owned parking lots in the downtown district. Installation of the self-parking equipment resulted in a decrease in the required number of parking attendants for the city-owned parking lots and a reduction in the city's salaries and related expenditures.

The contract is payable monthly in amounts equal to 40% of the month's total parking revenue for the 20 lots. Because no legal or contractual provisions require the City of West Fork to establish an enterprise fund for the parking lots, both parking revenue and parking-lot maintenance and repairs expenditures are recorded in the City of West Fork General Fund. The parking-lot sites are carried at cost in the City of West Fork General Fixed Assets group of accounts.

The city controller describes the plans for accounting for payments on the contract as follows: Monthly payments under the contract are to be debited to the Expenditures account of the General Fund and to the Debt Service section of the expenditures subsidiary ledger. The payments also will be recorded in the General Fixed Assets group of accounts as additions to the Improvements Other than Buildings account. A footnote to the General Fund balance sheet will disclose the unpaid balance of the installment contract at the end of each fiscal year. The unpaid balance of the contract will not be included in the General Long-Term Debt group of accounts, because the contract does not represent a liability for borrowing of cash, as do the bond and other long-term debt liabilities of the City of West Fork.

Instructions What is your advice to the controller of the City of West Fork? Explain.

Case 16-4 Wallace and Brenda Stuart, residents of James City, have donated their historic mansion, "Greystone," in trust to James City to serve as a tourist attraction. For a nominal charge, tourists will be guided through Greystone to observe the paintings, sculptures, antiques, and other art objects collected by the Stuarts, as well as the mansion's unique architecture.

The trust indenture executed by the Stuarts provides that the admissions charges to Greystone (which was appraised at $5,000,000 as of the date of the trust indenture) are to cover the operating expenditures associated with the tours, as well as maintenance and repairs costs for Greystone. Any excess of admissions revenues over the above costs are to be donated to James University for scholarships to art and architecture students.

Instructions Discuss the fund accounting issues, and related accounting matters such as depreciation, which should be considered by officials of James City with respect to the Stuart Trust.

PROBLEMS

16-5 Your examination of the financial statements of the Town of Arlington for the year ended June 30, Year 6, disclosed that the Town's inexperienced accountant was uninformed regarding governmental accounting and recorded all transactions in the General Fund. The following Town of Arlington General Fund trial balance was prepared by the accountant:

TOWN OF ARLINGTON GENERAL FUND

Trial Balance

June 30, Year 6

	Debit	Credit
Cash	$ 12,900	
Accounts receivable	1,200	
Taxes receivable—current	8,000	
Vouchers payable		$ 15,000
Appropriations		350,000
Expenditures	344,000	
Estimated revenues	290,000	
Revenues		320,000
Town property	16,100	
Bonds payable	36,000	
Fund balance		23,200
Totals	$708,200	$708,200

Your audit disclosed the following:

(1) The accounts receivable balance was due from the Town's water utility for the sale of scrap iron. Accounts for the water utility operated by the Town are maintained in an enterprise fund.

(2) The total tax levy for the year was $270,000. The Town's tax collection experience in recent years indicates an average loss of 3% of the net tax levy for uncollectible taxes.

(3) On June 30, Year 6, the Town retired at principal amount 4% general obligation serial bonds totaling $30,000. The bonds were issued on July 1, Year 4, in the total amount of $150,000. Interest paid during the year also was recorded in the Bonds Payable account.

(4) On July 1, Year 5, to service various departments the town council authorized a supply room with an inventory not to exceed $10,000. During the year supplies totaling $12,300 were purchased and debited to Expenditures. The physical inventory taken at June 30, Year 6, disclosed that supplies totaling $8,400 were used.

(5) Expenditures for Year 6 included $2,600 applicable to purchase orders issued in the prior year. Outstanding purchase orders at June 30, Year 6, not entered in the accounting records amounted to $4,100.

(6) The amount of $8,200, due from the state during Fiscal Year 6 for the Town's share of state gasoline taxes, was not entered in the accounting records, because the state was late in remitting the $8,200.

(7) Equipment costing $7,500, which had been purchased by the General Fund, was removed from service and sold for $900 during the year, and new equipment costing $17,000 was purchased. These transactions were recorded in the Town Property account. The Town does not record depreciation in the General Fixed Assets group of accounts.

Instructions

a Prepare adjusting and closing entries for the Town of Arlington General Fund at June 30, Year 6.

b Prepare adjusting entries for any other funds or groups of accounts. (The Town's accountant had recorded all the above transactions in the General Fund.)

16-6 The trial balance of the Webster School District General Fund is presented below:

WEBSTER SCHOOL DISTRICT GENERAL FUND
Trial Balance
December 31, Year 5

	Debit	Credit
Cash	$ 47,250	
Short-term investments	11,300	
Taxes receivable—delinquent	30,000	
Inventory of supplies	11,450	
Vouchers payable		$ 20,200
Payable to Internal Service Fund		950
Reserve for encumbrances		2,800
Reserve for inventory of supplies		11,450
Fund balance		66,400
Estimated revenues	1,007,000	

(cont.)

WEBSTER SCHOOL DISTRICT GENERAL FUND
Trial Balance
December 31, Year 5 (concluded)

	Debit	Credit
Appropriations...		$1,000,000
Revenues		1,008,200
Expenditures	$1,000,200	
Encumbrances	2,800	
Totals	$2,110,000	$2,110,000

Details of the Fund Balance account for Year 5 were as follows:

Fund Balance

Date	Explanations	Debit	Credit	Balance
12/31/4	Balance forward			63,400 cr
1/2/5	Record budget for Year 5		7,000	70,400 cr
12/31/5	Increase inventory reserve	4,000		66,400 cr

Instructions
a Prepare closing entries for the Webster School District General Fund.
b Prepare the following financial statements for the Webster School District General Fund for the year ended December 31, Year 5:
   (1) Statement of revenues, expenditures, and encumbrances
   (2) Statement of changes in fund balance
   (3) Balance sheet

16-7 The following summary of transactions was taken from the accounting records of the Carswell School District General Fund before the accounting records had been closed for the year ended June 30, Year 5:

CARSWELL SCHOOL DISTRICT GENERAL FUND
Summary of Transactions
For Year Ended June 30, Year 5

	After-closing balances, June 30, Year 4	Before-closing balances, June 30, Year 5
Accounts with debit balances:		
Cash...	$400,000	$ 700,000
Taxes receivable.................................	150,000	170,000
Estimated revenues...............................	-0-	3,000,000
Expenditures	-0-	2,842,000
Expenditures—prior year..........................	-0-	-0-
Encumbrances	-0-	91,000
Totals	$550,000	$6,803,000

(cont.)

CARSWELL SCHOOL DISTRICT GENERAL FUND
Summary of Transactions
For Year Ended June 30, Year 5 (concluded)

	After-closing balances, June 30, Year 4	Before-closing balances, June 30, Year 5
Accounts with credit balances:		
Estimated uncollectible taxes	$ 40,000	$ 70,000
Vouchers payable	80,000	408,000
Payable to other funds	210,000	142,000
Reserve for encumbrances	60,000	91,000
Fund balance	160,000	182,000
Revenues from taxes	-0-	2,800,000
Other revenues	-0-	130,000
Appropriations	-0-	2,980,000
Totals	$550,000	$6,803,000

Additional information:
(1) The estimated taxes receivable for the year ended June 30, Year 5, were $2,870,000, and taxes collected during the year totaled $2,810,000.
(2) An analysis of the transactions in the Vouchers Payable account for the year ended June 30, Year 5, follows:

	Debit (credit)
Current expenditures (all subject to encumbrances)	$(2,700,000)
Expenditures for prior year	(58,000)
Vouchers for payments to other funds	(210,000)
Cash payments during year	2,640,000
Net change during year	$ (328,000)

(3) During Year 5 the General Fund was billed $142,000 for services furnished by other funds of the Carswell School District.
(4) On May 2, Year 5, purchase orders were issued for new textbooks at an estimated cost of $91,000.

Instructions Based on the data presented above, reconstruct the original journal entries to record all transactions of the Carswell School District General Fund for the year ended June 30, Year 5, including the recording of the budget for the year. Do not prepare closing entries at June 30, Year 5, other than for expenditures for the prior year.

16-8 Because the controller of the City of Broadcreek resigned, the deputy controller attempted to compute the cash required to be derived from property taxes for the General Fund for the year ending June 30, Year 7. The computation was made as of January 1, Year 6, to serve as a basis for establishing the property tax rate for the fiscal year ending June 30, Year 7. The mayor of Broadcreek has requested you to review the deputy controller's computations and obtain other necessary information to prepare for the City of Broadcreek General Fund a formal statement of the cash required to be derived from property taxes for the fiscal year ending June 30, Year 7. Following are the computations prepared by the deputy controller:

City resources other than proposed property tax levy:

Estimated General Fund cash balance, Jan. 1, Year 6	$ 352,000
Estimated receipts from property taxes, Jan. 1 to June 30, Year 6	2,222,000
Estimated revenues from investments, Jan. 1, Year 6, to June 30, Year 7 .	442,000
Estimated proceeds from issuance of general obligation bonds in August,	
Year 6	3,000,000
Total City resources	$6,016,000

General Fund requirements:

Estimated expenditures, Jan. 1 to June 30, Year 6	$1,900,000
Proposed appropriations, July 1, Year 6, to June 30, Year 7	4,300,000
Total General Fund requirements	$6,200,000

Additional information:
(1) The General Fund cash balance required for July 1, Year 7, is $175,000.
(2) Property tax collections are due in March and September of each year. You note that during February, Year 6, estimated expenditures will exceed available cash by $200,000. Pending collection of property taxes in March, Year 6, this deficiency will have to be met by the issuance of 30-day tax-anticipation notes of $200,000 at an estimated interest rate of 9% per year.
(3) The proposed general obligation bonds will be issued by the City of Broadcreek Water Enterprise Fund to finance the construction of a new water pumping station.

Instructions Prepare a statement as of January 1, Year 6, to compute the property tax levy required for the City of Broadcreek General Fund for the fiscal year ending June 30, Year 7.

16-9 The following data were taken from the accounting records of the Town of Touton General Fund after the accounts had been closed for the fiscal year ended June 30, Year 3:

TOWN OF TOUTON GENERAL FUND
Data from Accounting Records
For Year Ended June 30, Year 3

	Balances July 1, Year 2	Fiscal Year 3 Changes		Balances June 30, Year 3
		Debit	Credit	
Assets				
Cash	$180,000	$ 955,000	$ 880,000	$255,000
Taxes receivable	20,000	809,000	781,000	48,000
Estimated uncollectible taxes	(4,000)	6,000	9,000	(7,000)
Total assets	$196,000			$296,000
Liabilities, Reserve, & Fund Balance				
Vouchers payable	$ 44,000	880,000	889,000	$ 53,000
Payable to Internal Service Fund ...	2,000	7,000	10,000	5,000
Payable to Debt Service Fund	10,000	60,000	100,000	50,000
Reserve for encumbrances	40,000	40,000	47,000	47,000
Fund balance	100,000	20,000	61,000	141,000
Total liabilities, reserve, & fund balance	$196,000	$2,777,000	$2,777,000	$296,000

Additional data:
(1) The budget for Fiscal Year 3 provided for estimated revenues of $1,000,000 and appropriations of $965,000.
(2) Expenditures totaling $895,000, in addition to those chargeable against Reserve for Encumbrances, were made.
(3) The actual expenditure chargeable against the July 1, Year 2, Reserve for Encumbrances was $37,000.

Instructions Reconstruct the journal entries for the Town of Touton General Fund indicated by the above data for the year ended June 30, Year 3. Do not attempt to differentiate between current and delinquent taxes receivable, or between reserves for encumbrances for Year 2 and Year 3.

16-10 You were engaged as independent auditor of the City of Engle as of June 30, Year 2. You found the following accounts, among others, in the accounting records of the General Fund for the fiscal year ended June 30, Year 2:

Special Cash

Date		Reference	Debit	Credit	Balance
Year 1					
Aug. 1		CR 58	301,000		301,000 dr
Sept. 1		CR 60	80,000		381,000 dr
Dec. 1		CD 41		185,000	196,000 dr
Year 2					
Feb. 1		CD 45		4,500	191,500 dr
June 1		CR 64	50,500		242,000 dr
June 30		CD 65		167,000	75,000 dr

Construction in Progress—Main Street Sewer

Date		Reference	Debit	Credit	Balance
Year 1					
Dec. 1		CD 41	185,000		185,000 dr
Year 2					
June 30		CD 65	167,000		352,000 dr

Bonds Payable

Date		Reference	Debit	Credit	Balance
Year 1					
Aug. 1		CR 58		300,000	300,000 cr
Year 2					
June 1		CR 64		50,000	350,000 cr

Premium on Bonds

Date		Reference	Debit	Credit	Balance
Year 1					
Aug. 1		CR 58		1,000	1,000 cr

Assessment Revenue

Date		Reference	Debit	Credit	Balance
Year 1					
Sept. 1		CR 60		80,000	80,000 cr

Interest Expense

Date		Reference	Debit	Credit	Balance
Year 2					
Feb. 1		CD 45	4,500		4,500 dr
June 1		CR 64		500	4,000 dr

The accounts resulted from the project described below:

The city council authorized the Main Street Sewer Project and a 5-year, 3% bond issue of $350,000 dated August 1, Year 1, to permit deferral of assessment payments. According to the terms of the authorization, the property owners were to be assessed 80% of the estimated cost of construction; the balance was to be made available by the City of Engle General Fund on October 1, Year 1. On September 1, Year 1, the first of five equal annual assessment installments was collected from the property owners, and a contract for construction of the sewer was signed. The deferred assessments were to bear interest at 5⅝% from September 1, Year 1. The project was expected to be completed by October 31, Year 2.

Instructions

a Prepare the journal entries which should have been made in the City of Engle Special Assessment Fund for the year ended June 30, Year 2. Amortize the bond premium by the straight-line method.

b Prepare the journal entries at June 30, Year 2, for City of Engle funds, other than the Special Assessment Fund, to record properly the results of transactions of the Main Street Sewer Project.

16-11 The following deficit budget was proposed for Year 3 for the Eastside School District General Fund:

EASTSIDE SCHOOL DISTRICT GENERAL FUND
Budget
For Year Ending December 31, Year 3

Fund balance, Jan. 1, Year 3	$128,000
Revenues:	
Property taxes	112,000
Investment interest	4,000
Total	$244,000
Expenditures:	
Operating	$120,000
County treasurer's fees	1,120
Bond interest	50,000
Fund balance, Dec. 31, Year 3	72,880
Total	$244,000

A general obligation bond issue of the School District was proposed in Year 2. The proceeds were to be used for a new school. There are no other outstanding bond issues. Information about the bond issue follows:

Principal amount $1,000,000
Interest rate   5%
Bonds dated   Jan. 1, Year 3
Coupons mature   Jan. 1 and July 1, beginning July 1, Year 3
Bonds mature serially at the rate of $100,000 per year, starting Jan. 1, Year 5.

The School District uses a separate bank account for each fund. The General Fund trial balance at December 31, Year 2, follows:

EASTSIDE SCHOOL DISTRICT GENERAL FUND
Trial Balance
December 31, Year 2

	Debit	Credit
Cash	$ 28,000	
Temporary investments—U. S. Treasury 4% bonds, interest payable on May 1 and Nov. 1	100,000	
Fund balance		$128,000
Totals	$128,000	$128,000

The county treasurer collects the property taxes and withholds a fee of 1% on all collections. The transactions for Year 3 were as follows:

Jan. 1   The proposed budget was adopted, the general obligation bond issue was authorized, and the property taxes were levied.
Feb. 28 Property tax receipts from county treasurer, $49,500, were deposited.
Apr. 1   General obligation bonds were issued at 101 plus accrued interest. It was directed that the premium be used for payment of interest.
Apr. 2   The School District disbursed $47,000 for the new school site.
Apr. 3   A contract for $950,000 for the new school was approved.
May 1   Interest was received on temporary investments.
July 1   Interest was paid on bonds.
Aug. 31 Property tax receipts from county treasurer, $59,400, were deposited.
Nov. 1   Payment on new school construction contract, $200,000, was made.
Nov. 1   Interest was received on temporary investments.
Dec. 31 Operating expenditures during the year were $115,000.

Instructions Prepare journal entries to record the foregoing Year 3 transactions in the following funds or groups of accounts. (Closing entries are not required.)
a General Fund
b Capital Projects Fund
c General Fixed Assets group of accounts
d General Long-Term Debt group of accounts
Eastside School District does not use a Debt Service Fund.

16-12 The City of Cochrane City Hall Capital Projects Fund was established on July 1, Year 2, to account for the construction of a new city hall financed by the sale of bonds. The building was to be constructed on a site owned by the City.
The building construction was financed by the issuance on July 1, Year 2, of $1,000,000 principal amount of 4%, 10-year term bonds.

The only funds in which the transactions pertaining to the new city hall were recorded were the City of Cochrane Capital Projects Fund and General Fund. The Capital Projects Fund's trial balance at June 30, Year 3, follows:

CITY OF COCHRANE CITY HALL CAPITAL PROJECTS FUND
Trial Balance
June 30, Year 3

	Debit	Credit
Cash	$ 893,000	
Vouchers payable		$ 11,000
Reserve for encumbrances		723,000
Appropriations...		1,015,000
Expenditures	140,500	
Encumbrances	715,500	
Totals	$1,749,000	$1,749,000

An analysis of the Reserve for Encumbrances account follows:

	Debit (Credit)
Contract with General Construction Company	$(750,000)
Purchase orders placed for materials and supplies.......................	(55,000)
Receipt of and payment for materials and supplies	14,500
Payment of General Construction Company invoice, less 10% retention	67,500
Balance in Reserve for Encumbrances account	$(723,000)

An analysis of the Appropriations account follows:

	Debit (Credit)
Principal amount of bonds..	$(1,000,000)
Premium on bonds	(15,000)
Balance in Appropriations account	$(1,015,000)

An analysis of the Expenditures account follows:

	Debit (Credit)
Progress billing invoice from General Construction Company (with which the City contracted for the construction of the new city hall for $750,000; other contracts will be let for heating, air conditioning, etc.) showing 10% of the work completed	$ 75,000
Charge from the General Fund for clearing the building site	11,000
Payments to suppliers for building materials and supplies purchased	14,500
Payment of interest on bonds outstanding	40,000
Balance in Expenditures account..	$140,500

Instructions
a Prepare a working paper for the City of Cochrane City Hall Capital Projects Fund at June 30, Year 3, showing:
(1) Preliminary trial balance.
(2) Adjustments. (Formal adjusting entries are not required; however, explain adjustments at bottom of working paper.)
(3) Adjusted trial balance.
b Prepare the required adjusting or closing entries at June 30, Year 3, for the following:
(1) Debt Service Fund
(2) General Fixed Assets group of accounts
(3) General Long-Term Debt group of accounts

16-13 The accounting records of the City of Winslow were maintained by an inexperienced accountant during the year ended December 31, Year 5. The following trial balance of the General Fund was available when you began your examination:

CITY OF WINSLOW GENERAL FUND
Trial Balance
December 31, Year 5

	Debit	Credit
Cash	$ 75,600	
Taxes receivable—current	29,000	
Estimated uncollectible current taxes		$ 9,000
Taxes receivable—delinquent	4,000	
Estimated uncollectible delinquent taxes		5,100
Building addition constructed	25,000	
Special assessment bonds payable		50,000
Serial bonds paid	8,000	
Vouchers payable		13,000
Fund balance		33,500
Estimated revenues	180,000	
Appropriations		174,000
Revenues		177,000
Expenditures	140,000	
Totals	$461,600	$461,600

Your examination disclosed the following:
(1) The estimate of losses of $9,000 for current taxes receivable was found to be a reasonable estimate.
(2) The Building Addition Constructed account balance is the cost of an addition to the City Building. The addition was constructed during Year 5 and payment was made from the General Fund as authorized.
(3) The Serial Bonds Paid account reports the annual retirement of general obligation bonds issued to finance the construction of the City Building. Interest payments of $3,800 for this bond issue are included in Expenditures.
(4) A physical inventory of the current operating supplies at December 31, Year 5, revealed an inventory of $6,500. The decision was made to record the inventory in the accounting records; expenditures are to be recorded on the basis of usage rather than purchases.

(5) Operating supplies ordered in Year 4 and chargeable to Year 4 appropriations were received, recorded, and used in January, Year 5. The outstanding purchase orders for these supplies, which were not recorded in the accounting records at December 31, Year 4, amounted to $4,400. The vendors' invoices for these supplies totaled $4,700.

(6) Outstanding purchase orders at December 31, Year 5 for operating supplies totaled $5,300. These purchase orders were not recorded in the accounting records.

(7) The special assessment bonds were issued December 31, Year 5, to finance a street paving project. No contracts have been signed for this project and no expenditures have been made.

(8) The balance in the Revenues account includes credits for $10,000 for a note issued to a bank to obtain cash in anticipation of tax collections to pay current expenses and for $900 for the sale of scrap iron from the city's water utility. The note was still outstanding at year-end. The operations of the water utility are accounted for in an enterprise fund.

Instructions

a Prepare adjusting and closing entries for the City of Winslow General Fund at December 31, Year 5.

b The foregoing information disclosed by your examination was recorded only in the General Fund, even though other funds or account groups were involved. Prepare adjusting entries for any other funds or account groups involved.

16-14 The City of Loring has engaged you to examine its financial statements for the year ended December 31, Year 1. The City was incorporated as a municipality and began operations on January 1, Year 1. You find that a budget was approved by the city council and was recorded in an "Operating Fund," and that all transactions have been recorded on the cash basis in the Operating Fund. The City's accountant has provided the Operating Fund's trial balance at December 31, Year 1, as follows:

CITY OF LORING OPERATING FUND
Trial Balance
December 31, Year 1

	Debit	Credit
Cash	$238,900	
Bonds payable		$200,000
Premium on bonds payable		3,000
Fund balance		12,100
Estimated revenues	114,100	
Appropriations		102,000
Revenues		108,400
Expenditures	72,500	
Totals	$425,500	$425,500

Additional information is given below:

(1) Your examination of the expenditures subsidiary ledger revealed the following information:

	Budgeted	Actual
Personal services	$ 45,000	$38,500
Supplies	19,000	11,000
Equipment	38,000	23,000
Totals	$102,000	$72,500

(2) Supplies and equipment in the amount of $4,000 and $10,000, respectively, had been received, but the vouchers had not been paid at December 31, Year 1.

(3) At December 31, Year 1, outstanding purchase orders for supplies and equipment not yet received were $1,200 and $3,800, respectively.

(4) The inventory of supplies on December 31, Year 1, was $1,700 by physical count. A city ordinance requires that the expenditures for supplies are to be based on usage, not on purchases.

(5) Your examination of the revenues subsidiary ledger revealed the following information:

	Budgeted	Actual
Property taxes	$102,600	$ 96,000
Licenses	7,400	7,900
Fines	4,100	4,500
Totals	$114,100	$108,400

It was estimated that 5% of the property taxes would not be collected. Accordingly, property taxes were levied in an amount so that collections would yield the budgeted amount of $102,600.

(6) On November 1, Year 1, the City of Loring issued 8% general obligation term bonds with $200,000 principal amount for a premium of $3,000. Interest is payable each May 1 and November 1 until the maturity date of November 1, Year 15. The city council ordered that the cash from the bond premium be set aside and restricted for the eventual retirement of the debt principal. The bonds were issued to finance the construction of a city hall, but no contracts had been signed as of December 31, Year 1.

Instructions Prepare a working paper for the City of Loring Operating Fund at December 31, Year 1, showing adjustments and distributions to the proper funds or groups of accounts. Formal adjusting entries are not required; however, explain each adjustment at the bottom of the working paper. The following column headings are suggested:
Operating Fund Trial Balance
Adjustments
Adjusted Operating Fund Trial Balance
General Fund
Debt Service Fund
Capital Projects Fund
General Fixed Assets Group of Accounts
General Long-Term Debt Group of Accounts

17

ACCOUNTING FOR NONPROFIT ORGANIZATIONS

A *nonprofit organization* is a legal and accounting entity which is operated for the benefit of society as a whole, rather than for the benefit of an individual proprietor or a group of partners or shareholders. Thus, the concept of *net income* is not meaningful for a nonprofit organization. Instead, like the internal service fund described in Chapter 16, a nonprofit organization strives only to obtain revenue sufficient to cover its expenses.

Nonprofit organizations comprise a significant segment of the United States economy. Colleges and universities, voluntary health and welfare organizations such as United Way, most hospitals, philanthropic foundations such as the Ford Foundation and the Rockefeller Foundation, professional societies such as the AICPA, and civic organizations such as Kiwanis are familiar examples of nonprofit organizations.

Until recent years, the accounting standards and practices which constitute generally accepted accounting principles were not considered to be entirely applicable to nonprofit organizations. The following quotation, which appeared in various auditing publications of the AICPA until 1976, outlines this situation:[1]

> ... the statements ... of a not-for-profit organization ... may reflect accounting practices differing in some respects from those followed by enterprises

[1] *Statement on Auditing Standards No. 1,* "Codification of Auditing Standards and Procedures," AICPA (New York: 1973), p. 136.

organized for profit. In some cases generally accepted accounting principles applicable to not-for-profit organizations have not been clearly defined. In those areas where the independent auditor believes generally accepted accounting principles have been clearly defined, he may state his opinion as to the conformity of the financial statements either with *generally accepted accounting principles* or (less desirably) with *accounting practices* for not-for-profit organizations in the particular field, and in such circumstances he may refer to financial position and results of operations. In those areas where he believes generally accepted accounting principles have not been clearly defined, the provisions covering special reports as discussed under cash basis and modified accrual basis statements are applicable.

In the period 1972 to 1974, the unsettled state of accounting for nonprofit organizations was improved by the AICPA's issuance of three *Industry Audit Guides:* "Hospital Audit Guide" (1972), "Audits of Colleges and Universities" (1973), and "Audits of Voluntary Health and Welfare Organizations" (1974).[2] The status of an *Industry Audit Guide* is set forth in a "Notice to Readers" in each *Guide;* the following language in the "Hospital Audit Guide" is typical:[3]

> This audit guide is published for the guidance of members of the Institute in examining and reporting on financial statements of hospitals. It represents the considered opinion of the Committee on Health Care Institutions and as such contains the best thought of the profession as to the best practices in this area of reporting. Members should be aware that they may be called upon to justify departures from the Committee's recommendations.

The accounting concepts included in an *Industry Audit Guide* have the **substantial authoritative support** required for all generally accepted accounting principles.

The three *Industry Audit Guides* referred to above cover only three types of nonprofit organizations. Thus, in 1978, the AICPA issued an exposure draft of a proposed *Statement of Position* entitled "Accounting Principles and Reporting Practices for Nonprofit Organizations Not Covered by Existing AICPA Audit Guides." The proposed *Statement of Position* applies to at least 21 types of nonprofit organizations, ranging from cemetery societies to zoological and botanical societies.[4] If issued in final form, the *Statement of Position* would be applicable to the subject nonprofit organizations for fiscal years beginning after December 31, 1979.[5]

We shall discuss in some detail the hospital, college, and health and welfare *Industry Audit Guides* in subsequent sections of this chapter. First,

[2] "Audits of Colleges and Universities" was amended in 1974 by the AICPA in *Statement of Position 74–8,* "Financial Accounting and Reporting by Colleges and Universities." "Hospital Audit Guide" was amended in 1978 by the AICPA in a *Statement of Position* entitled "Clarification of Accounting, Auditing, and Reporting Practices Relating to Hospital Malpractice Loss Contingencies."

[3] "Hospital Audit Guide," AICPA (New York: 1972).

[4] Exposure Draft: *Proposed Statement of Position on Accounting Principles and Reporting Practices for Nonprofit Organizations Not Covered by Existing AICPA Audit Guides,* AICPA (New York: 1978), p. 5.

[5] Ibid., p. 17.

however, we shall describe the characteristics of nonprofit organizations which have a bearing on their accounting principles and practices.

Characteristics of nonprofit organizations

Nonprofit organizations are in certain respects *hybrid.* These organizations have some characteristics comparable to those of government entities, and other characteristics similar to those of business enterprises.

Characteristics Comparable to Those of Government Entities Among the features of nonprofit organizations which resemble characteristics of government entities are the following:

1 *Service to society.* Nonprofit organizations render services to society as a whole. The members of this society may range from a limited number of citizens of a community to almost the entire population of a city, state, or nation. Like the services rendered by government units, the services of nonprofit organizations are of benefit to the many rather than the few.

2 *No profit motivation.* As previously stated, nonprofit organizations do not operate with the objective of earning a profit. Consequently, nonprofit organizations usually are exempt from federal and state income taxes. Government units, except for enterprise funds, have the same characteristics. (As pointed out in Chapter 16, enterprise funds sometimes are assessed an amount in lieu of taxes by the legislative branch of government.)

3 *Financing by the citizenry.* Like government units, most nonprofit organizations depend on the general population for a substantial portion of their revenue, because charges for their services are not designed to cover all their operating costs. Exceptions are professional societies and the philanthropic foundations established by wealthy individuals or families. Whereas the citizenry's contributions to government revenue are mostly **involuntary** taxes, their contributions to nonprofit organizations are **voluntary** donations.

4 *Stewardship for resources.* Because a substantial portion of the resources of a nonprofit organization are donated, the organization must account for the resources on a stewardship basis similar to that of government entities. The stewardship requirement makes **fund accounting** appropriate for most nonprofit organizations as well as for government entities.

5 *Importance of budget.* The four preceding characteristics of nonprofit organizations cause their **operating budget** to be as important as for government entities. Nonprofit organizations may employ a **traditional budget,** a **program budget,** a **performance budget,** or a **planning, programming, budgeting system.** These types of operating budgets are described in Chapter 16.

Characteristics Comparable to Those of Business Enterprises Among the characteristics of nonprofit organizations which resemble those of business enterprises are the following:

1 *Governance by board of directors.* Like a business corporation, a nonprofit corporation is governed by elected or appointed directors, trustees, or governors. In contrast, the legislative and executive branches of a government unit share the responsibilities of its governance.

2 *Measurement of cost expirations.* Governance by a board of directors means

that a nonprofit organization does not answer to a lawmaking body as does a government unit. One consequence is that **cost expirations,** or **expenses,** rather than **expenditures,** usually are reported in the operations statement of a nonprofit organization. Allocation of expenses (including depreciation) and revenue to the appropriate accounting period thus is a common characteristic of nonprofit organizations and business enterprises.

3 *Use of accrual basis of accounting.* Nonprofit organizations employ the same accrual accounting techniques used by business enterprises. The modified accrual basis of accounting used by some government entity funds is inappropriate for nonprofit organizations.

ACCOUNTING FOR NONPROFIT ORGANIZATIONS

The basic accounting unit for most nonprofit organizations is the *fund,* which is defined in Chapter 16 (see page 615). Separate funds are necessary to distinguish between assets which may be used as authorized by the board of directors and assets whose use is restricted by donors. Funds commonly used by nonprofit organizations include the following:

Unrestricted fund (sometimes called **unrestricted current fund** or **current unrestricted fund**)

Restricted fund (sometimes called **restricted current fund** or **current restricted fund**)

Endowment fund

Agency fund (sometimes called **custodian fund**)

Annuity and life income funds

Loan fund

Plant fund (sometimes called **land, building, and equipment fund**)

Unrestricted fund

In many respects, the **unrestricted fund** of a nonprofit organization is similar to the **general fund** of a government unit. The unrestricted fund includes all the assets of a nonprofit organization which are available for use as authorized by the board of directors and which are not restricted for specific purposes. Thus, like the general fund of a government unit, the unrestricted fund of a nonprofit organization is **residual** in nature.

Designated Fund Balance of Unrestricted Fund The board of directors of a nonprofit organization may designate a portion of an unrestricted fund's assets for a specific purpose. The earmarked portion should be accounted for as a segregation of the unrestricted fund balance, rather than as a separate restricted fund. For example, if the board of directors of the Civic Welfare Organization earmarked $5,000 of the unrestricted fund's assets for the purchase of new office equipment, the following journal entry would be prepared for the Civic Welfare Organization Unrestricted Fund:

Journal entry for designation of portion of fund balance of unrestricted fund

Undesignated Fund Balance....................................	5,000	
Designated Fund Balance—Equipment..................		5,000
To record designation of portion of fund balance for purchase of office equipment.		

The Designated Fund Balance—Equipment account is similar to a retained earnings appropriation account of a business enterprise and is reported in the Civic Welfare Organization's balance sheet as a portion of the Unrestricted Fund balance.

Revenue of Unrestricted Fund The revenue of the unrestricted fund of a nonprofit organization is derived from a number of sources. For example, a hospital derives unrestricted fund revenue from patient services, educational programs, research and other grants, unrestricted gifts, unrestricted income from endowment funds, and miscellaneous sources such as donated merchandise and services. A university's sources of unrestricted fund revenue include student tuition and fees; governmental grants and contracts; gifts and private grants; unrestricted income from endowment funds; and revenue from auxiliary enterprises such as student residences, food services, and intercollegiate athletics. The principal revenue sources of voluntary health and welfare organizations' unrestricted funds (and all other funds) are cash donations and pledges from the citizenry. Other revenue may include membership dues, interest, dividends, and gains on the sale of investments.

Revenue for Services A hospital's patient service revenue and a university's tuition and fee revenue are accrued at full rates, even though part or all of the revenue is to be waived or otherwise adjusted. Suppose, for example, that Community Hospital's patient service revenue records for June, Year 3, included the following amounts:

Patient service revenue components of a hospital

Gross patient service revenue (before recognition of charity allowances and contractual adjustments)	$100,000
Charity allowances for indigent patients	8,000
Amount to be received from Civic Welfare Organization for indigent patients	3,000
Contractual adjustment allowed to Blue Cross	16,000

The journal entries below would be appropriate for the Community Hospital Unrestricted Fund at June 30, Year 3:

Accounts Receivable	100,000	
Patient Service Revenue		100,000
To record gross patient service revenue for month of June at full rates.		
Accounts Receivable	3,000	
Charity Allowances	5,000	
Allowances and Doubtful Accounts		8,000
To record gross charity allowances for June ($8,000), less amount receivable from Civic Welfare Organization ($3,000).		
Contractual Adjustments	16,000	
Allowances and Doubtful Accounts		16,000
To record contractual adjustments allowed to Blue Cross for June.		

The contractual adjustments recorded in the third journal entry above illustrate a unique feature of a hospital's operations. Many hospital receivables are collectible from a **third-party payer,** rather than from the patient receiving services. Among third-party payers are the U.S. government (Medicare and Medicaid programs), state programs such as Medical in California, Blue Cross, and private medical insurance carriers. The hospital's contractual agreements with third-party payers usually provide for payments by the third parties at less than full billing rates.

In the statement of revenue and expenses of Community Hospital for June, Year 3, the Charity Allowances and Contractual Adjustments accounts, together with a provision for estimated uncollectible accounts for the month, would be deducted from the Patient Service Revenue account to provide net patient service revenue for the month. The Allowances and Doubtful Accounts ledger account would be treated as an offset to the Accounts Receivable account in the balance sheet, as in accounting for business enterprises. The write-off of an account receivable would be accomplished in the customary fashion. For example, the accounts of indigent patients would be written off by Community Hospital by the following journal entry in the Unrestricted Fund at June 30, Year 3:

Journal entry to write off uncollectible accounts of a hospital	*Allowances and Doubtful Accounts* 8,000	
	Accounts Receivable	8,000
	To write off uncollectible balances of indigent patients as follows:	
	J. R. English *$1,500*	
	R. L. Knight *4,000*	
	S. O. Newman *2,500*	
	Total *$8,000*	

Donated Merchandise and Services In addition to cash contributions, nonprofit organizations receive donations of merchandise and services from the public. For example, a hospital may receive free drugs, or a "thrift store" may receive donated articles of clothing. The donated merchandise should be recorded in the Inventories account at its current fair value, with a credit to a revenue account in the unrestricted fund.

Donated services should be recorded in the unrestricted fund as salaries expense, with an offset to a revenue account, if the services are rendered to the nonprofit organization in an employee-employer relationship. The value assigned to the services should be the going salary rate for comparable salaried employees of the entity, less any meals or other living costs absorbed for the donor of the services by the nonprofit organization.

Pledges A *pledge* is a commitment by a prospective donor to contribute a specific amount of cash to a nonprofit organization at a future date or in installments. Because the pledge is in writing and signed by the pledgor, it resembles in form the *promissory note* used in business. However, pledges generally are not enforceable contracts.

Under the accrual basis of accounting, unrestricted pledges are recorded as receivables and revenue in the unrestricted fund of a nonprofit organization, with appropriate provision for doubtful accounts. Recording of revenue from pledges in this fashion is specifically mandated by the *Industry Audit Guides* "Hospital Audit Guide" and "Audits of Voluntary Health and Welfare Organizations."[6] However, the "Audits of Colleges and Universities" *Industry Audit Guide* makes the recording of pledges optional, as indicated in the following passage:[7]

> Pledges of gifts ... should be disclosed in the notes unless they are reported in the financial statements. The notes to the financial statements should disclose the gross amounts by time periods over which the pledges are to be collected. ...
> If the pledges are reported in the financial statements, they should be

---

[6] "Hospital Audit Guide," p. 10; "Audits of Voluntary Health and Welfare Organizations," AICPA (New York: 1974), p. 14.

[7] "Audits of Colleges and Universities," AICPA (New York: 1973), p. 8.

accounted for at their estimated net realizable value in the same manner as gifts received. . . .

The reason for the inconsistent treatment of pledges in the three *Industry Audit Guides* is not apparent. The "Audits of Colleges and Universities" *Guide* apparently sanctions use of notes to financial statements to correct an error in the application of accounting principles—the omission of receivables and revenue—in the financial statements themselves. The authors believe this to be an improper use of footnotes.

Revenue from Pooled Investments Many of the funds of nonprofit organizations have cash available for investments in securities and other money-market instruments. To provide greater efficiency and flexibility in investment programs, the investment resources of all funds of a single nonprofit organization may be pooled for investment by a single portfolio manager. The pooling technique requires a careful allocation of investment revenue, including gains and losses, to each participating fund of the nonprofit organization.

To illustrate the pooling of investments, assume that on January 2, Year 5, the four funds of Civic Welfare, Inc., a nonprofit organization, pooled their individual investments, as follows:

Pooling of investments by nonprofit organization		At Jan. 2, Year 5	
	Cost	Current fair value	Original equity, %
Unrestricted Fund	$ 20,000	$ 18,000	15.00
Restricted Fund	15,000	22,000	18.33
Plant Fund	10,000	20,000	16.67
Wilson Endowment Fund	55,000	60,000	50.00
Totals	$100,000	$120,000	100.00

The original equity percentages in the above tabulation are based on *current fair value,* not on *cost.* The current fair values of the pooled investments at January 2, Year 5, represent a common "measuring rod" not available in the cost amounts, which represent current fair values at various dates the investments were purchased.

Realized gains and losses, interest revenue, and dividend revenue of the pooled investments during Year 5 would be allocated to the four funds in the ratio of the original equity percentages. For example, if $18,000 realized gains of the investment pool during Year 5 were reinvested, and if interest of $5,000 and dividends of $4,000 were earned by the pool during Year 5, these amounts would be allocated as follows:

Allocation of revenue from pooled investments to respective funds	Original equity, %	Realized gains	Interest and dividends
Unrestricted Fund	15.00	$ 2,700	$1,350
Restricted Fund	18.33	3,300	1,650
Plant Fund	16.67	3,000	1,500
Wilson Endowment Fund	50.00	9,000	4,500
Totals	100.00	$18,000	$9,000

Each of the funds participating in the investment pool would debit Investments and credit Gains on Sale of Investments for its share of the $18,000. Each fund also would debit Cash (or Receivable from Unrestricted Fund) and credit Interest and Dividend Revenue for its share of the $9,000 earned from interest and dividends.

If another fund of Civic Welfare, Inc., entered the investment pool at December 31, Year 5, the original equity percentages would have to be revised, based on the December 31, Year 5, current fair values of the investment portfolio. For example, if the Harris Endowment Fund entered the Civic Welfare, Inc., investment pool at December 31, Year 5, with investments having a cost of $32,000 and a current fair value of $36,000 at that date, the equity percentages would be revised as illustrated below:

Revision of fund equities in pooled investments	At Dec. 31, Year 5		
	Cost*	Current fair value†	Revised equity, %
Unrestricted Fund	$ 22,700	$ 21,600	12.00
Restricted Fund	18,300	26,400	14.67
Plant Fund	13,000	24,000	13.33
Wilson Endowment Fund	64,000	72,000	40.00
Subtotals	$118,000	$144,000	
Harris Endowment Fund	32,000	36,000	20.00
Totals	$150,000	$180,000	100.00

* Cost for four original pool member funds includes $18,000 realized gains of Year 5.
† Current fair value of original pooled investments totaling $144,000 at December 31, Year 5, allocated to original pool member funds based on original equity percentages computed on page 676.

Realized gains and losses, interest revenue, and dividend revenue for periods subsequent to December 31, Year 5, would be allocated in the revised equity percentages. The revised equity percentages would be maintained until the membership of the investment pool changed once again.

Expenses of Unrestricted Fund   The expenses of unrestricted funds are similar in many respects to those of a business enterprise—salaries and wages, supplies, maintenance, research, and the like. The question of whether depreciation should be recorded as an expense by a nonprofit organization has not been answered uniformly by the AICPA. The "Hospital Audit Guide," "Audits of Voluntary Health and Welfare Organizations," and the *Proposed Statement of Position* specify that depreciation should be recorded as an expense of each accounting period.[8] However, "Audits of Colleges and Universities" takes a position that is contrary:[9]

> Current funds expenditures ... comprise ... all expenses incurred, determined in accordance with the generally accepted accrual method of accounting, except for the omission of depreciation. ...

> Depreciation expense related to depreciable assets comprising the physical plant is reported neither in the statement of current funds revenues, expenditures, and other changes nor in the statement of changes in unrestricted current funds balance. The reason for this treatment is that these statements present expenditures and transfers of current funds rather than operating expenses in conformity with the reporting objectives of accounting for resources received and used rather than the determination of net income. Depreciation allowances, however, may be reported in the balance sheet and the provision for depreciation reported in the statement of changes in the balance of the investment-in-plant fund subsection of the plant funds group.

In the opinion of the authors, the financial reporting requirements of colleges and universities do not differ sufficiently from those of other nonprofit organizations as to make the recognition of depreciation expense inappropriate.

Assets and Liabilities of Unrestricted Fund   The balance sheet of a nonprofit organization typically presents the assets, liabilities, and fund balance for each fund either one below another or in adjacent horizontal columns. Most assets and liabilities of a nonprofit organization's unrestricted fund are similar to the current assets and liabilities of a business enterprise. Cash, investments, accounts receivable, receivables from other funds, inventories, and short-term prepayments are typical assets of an unrestricted fund.

The "Audits of Colleges and Universities" and "Audits of Voluntary Health and Welfare Organizations" *Industry Audit Guides* segregate plant assets into a separate fund. In contrast, the "Hospital Audit Guide" includes the following quotation:[10]

[8] "Hospital Audit Guide," p. 4; "Audits of Voluntary Health and Welfare Organizations," p. 12; *Proposed Statement of Position,* p. 16.
[9] "Audits of Colleges and Universities," pp. 26, 9–10.
[10] "Hospital Audit Guide," p. 4.

Property, plant and equipment and related liabilities should be accounted for as a part of unrestricted funds, since segregation in a separate fund would imply the existence of restrictions on asset use.

In the opinion of the authors, segregation of plant assets in a separate fund is logical accounting practice for any nonprofit organization.

The liabilities of an unrestricted fund include payables, accruals, and deferred revenue comparable to those of a business enterprise, as well as Payable to Other Funds accounts.

Restricted fund

Nonprofit organizations establish *restricted funds* to account for assets available for current use but expendable only as authorized by the donor of the assets. Thus, a restricted fund of a nonprofit organization resembles the special revenue fund of a government unit, because the assets of both types of funds may be expended only for specified purposes.

The AICPA's "Hospital Audit Guide" includes in the restricted funds category a broad spectrum of restricted resources:[11]

Funds for specific operating purposes
Funds for additions to property, plant, and equipment
Endowment funds

In contrast, "Audits of Colleges and Universities" and "Audits of Voluntary Health and Welfare Organizations" limit the restricted fund category to resources for specific operating purposes.[12] Thus, we once again find contradictory treatment of like items in the three AICPA *Industry Audit Guides.*

The assets of restricted funds are not derived from the operations of the nonprofit organization. Instead, the assets are obtained from restricted gifts or grants of individuals or government units; revenue from restricted fund investments; gains on sales of investments of the restricted fund; and restricted income from endowment funds. These assets are transferred to the unrestricted fund as revenue of that fund at the time the designated expenditure is made.

To illustrate, assume that on July 1, Year 4, Robert King donated $50,000 to Community Hospital, a nonprofit organization, for the purchase of beds for a new wing of the hospital. On August 1, Year 4, Community Hospital expended $51,250 for the beds. These activities would be recorded in the accounting records of Community Hospital as follows:

[11] Ibid., p. 9.
[12] "Audits of Colleges and Universities," p. 16; "Audits of Voluntary Health and Welfare Organizations," p. 2.

Journal
entries for
restricted
donation to
nonprofit
organization

In Robert King Restricted Fund:

Year 4

July 1 Cash 50,000

   Fund Balance 50,000
   To record receipt of gift from Robert King for beds for
   new wing.

Aug. 1 *Fund Balance* 50,000

   Payable to Unrestricted Fund 50,000
   To record obligation to Unrestricted Fund for amount
   expended in accordance with Robert King's gift.

In Unrestricted Fund:

Year 4

Aug. 1 *Plant Assets* 51,250

   Cash 51,250
   To record purchase of beds for new wing.

   1 *Receivable from Robert King Restricted Fund* 50,000

   Other Operating Revenue 50,000
   To record receivable from Robert King Restricted Fund
   for beds purchased.

Endowment fund

An *endowment fund* of a nonprofit organization is comparable to a *non-expendable trust fund* of a government unit, described in Chapter 16. A *pure endowment fund* is one for which the principal must be held indefinitely in revenue-producing investments. Only the income from the pure endowment fund's investments may be expended by the nonprofit organization. In contrast, the principal of a *term endowment fund* may be expended by the nonprofit organization after the passage of a period of time or the occurrence of an event stipulated by the donor of the endowment principal. A *quasi-endowment fund* is established by the board of directors of a nonprofit organization, rather than by an outside donor. At the option of the board, the principal of a quasi-endowment fund later may be expended by the entity which established the fund.

The income of endowment funds is handled in accordance with the instructions of the donor or the board of directors. If there are no restrictions on the use of endowment fund income, it is transferred to the nonprofit organization's unrestricted fund. Otherwise, the endowment fund income is transferred to an appropriate restricted fund.

Agency fund

An *agency fund* of a nonprofit organization is identical to its counterpart in a government unit. An agency fund is used to account for assets held by a nonprofit organization as a custodian. The assets are disbursed only as instructed by their owner.

For example, a university may act as custodian of cash of a student organization. The university would disburse the cash as directed by the appropriate officers of the student organization. The net assets of the student organization would appear as a *liability* of the university's agency fund, rather than as *fund balance,* because the university has no equity in the fund.

Annuity and life income funds

Annuity Fund Assets may be contributed to a nonprofit organization with the stipulation that the organization pay specified amounts period- ically to designated recipients, for a specified time period. An *annuity fund* is established by the nonprofit organization to account for this arrangement. At the end of the specified time period for the periodic payments, the unexpended assets of the annuity fund are transferred to the unrestricted fund, or to a restricted fund or endowment fund speci- fied by the donor.

The following journal entries illustrate the accounting for the Ruth Collins Annuity Fund of Ridgedale College, a nonprofit organization, for the fund's first fiscal year ending June 30, Year 2:

Journal entries for annuity fund of nonprofit organization	Year 1	
	July 1 Cash 50,000	
	Annuity Payable	35,000
	Fund Balance	15,000
	To record receipt of cash from Andrea Collins for an annuity of $6,000 per year each June 30 to Ruth Collins for her lifetime. Liability is recorded at the actuarially determined present value of the annuity, based on Ruth Collins's life expectancy.	
	1 Investments 45,000	
	Cash	45,000
	To record purchase of interest in Ridgedale College's investment pool.	

```
Year 2
June 30  Cash ...........................................   1,500
           Investments ...................................   2,000
               Annuity Payable ...........................            3,500
           To record share of revenue and gains of Ridgedale
           College investment pool.


      30  Annuity Payable ................................   6,000
               Cash ......................................            6,000
           To record payment of current year's annuity to Ruth
           Collins.


      30  Fund Balance ...................................   1,000
               Annuity Payable ...........................            1,000
           To record actuarial loss based on revised life expect-
           ancy actuarial valuation of Ruth Collins's annuity.
```

Note that, in the first of the preceding journal entries, the revenue and gains on the annuity fund's share of the investment pool are credited to the Annuity Payable account. This is necessary because the actuarial valuation of the annuity at the date of establishment of the annuity fund valued the annuity liability at its then present value.

Life Income Fund   A *life income fund,* like an annuity fund, is used to account for stipulated payments to a named beneficiary (or beneficiaries) during the beneficiary's lifetime. The payments from an annuity fund are made directly from the *principal* of the fund, but in a life income fund only the *income* is paid to the beneficiary. Thus, payments to a life income fund's beneficiary vary from one accounting period to the next. In contrast, payments from an annuity fund are fixed in amount.

Loan fund

A *loan fund* may be established by any nonprofit organization, but loan funds most frequently are included in the accounting records of colleges and universities. Student loan funds usually are *revolving;* that is, as old loans are repaid, new loans are made from the receipts. Loans receivable are carried in the loan fund at estimated realizable value; provisions for doubtful loans are debited directly to the Fund Balance account, not to an expense account. Interest on loans is credited to the Fund Balance account, ordinarily on the cash basis of accounting.

Plant fund

We have already noted (pages 678–679) the inconsistent accounting treatment for plant assets of hospitals as compared to colleges and universities and voluntary health and welfare organizations. There are also inconsistencies in the contents of the *plant funds* of the three types of nonprofit organizations, as follows:

1 A *plant replacement and expansion fund* is a subdivision of the *restricted fund* category of a hospital. In the hospital's plant replacement and expansion fund are recorded the cash, investments, and receivables earmarked by donors for expenditure for plant assets.[13]

2 The following excerpt describes the accounting for the plant fund of a voluntary health and welfare organization:[14]

> *Land, building and equipment fund* (often referred to as plant fund) is often used to accumulate the net investment in fixed assets and to account for the unexpended resources contributed specifically for the purpose of acquiring or replacing land, buildings, or equipment for use in the operations of the organization. Mortgages or other liabilities relating to these assets are also included in this fund. When additions to land, buildings, or equipment used in carrying out the organization's program and supporting services are acquired with unrestricted fund resources, the amount expended for such assets should be transferred from the unrestricted fund to the plant fund and should be accounted for as a direct addition to the plant fund balance. Gains or losses on the sale of fixed assets should be reflected as income items in the plant fund accounts. The proceeds from the sale of fixed assets should be transferred to the unrestricted fund; such transfers should be reflected as direct reductions and additions to the respective fund balances.

3 In contrast to the two preceding types of plant funds, "Audits of Colleges and Universities" provides for the following:[15]

> The plant funds group consists of (1) funds to be used for the acquisition of physical properties for institutional purposes but unexpended at the date of reporting; (2) funds set aside for the renewal and replacement of institutional properties; (3) funds set aside for debt service charges and for the retirement of indebtedness on institutional properties; and (4) funds expended for and thus invested in institutional properties.
>
> Some institutions combine the assets and liabilities of the four subfund groups for reporting purposes; however, separate fund balances should be maintained. Resources restricted by donors or outside agencies for additions to plant should be recorded directly in the particular fund subgroup, generally unexpended plant funds.

Thus, in the three AICPA *Industry Audit Guides* for nonprofit organizations, we find wide variations in the composition and accounting for plant funds. The differences in the plant funds of the three types of nonprofit organizations are not supported by any theoretical differences in their accounting objectives.

[13] "Hospital Audit Guide," pp. 9, 41.
[14] "Audits of Voluntary Health and Welfare Organizations," pp. 2–3.
[15] "Audits of Colleges and Universities," p. 44.

Financial statements for nonprofit organizations

All nonprofit organizations issue a balance sheet incorporating all funds of the organization. The assets, liabilities, and fund balances for each fund are listed in horizontal or vertical sequence in the single balance sheet. This type of balance sheet presentation emphasizes the unitary nature of the nonprofit organization, despite its use of separate funds for accountability purposes.

Because a nonprofit organization does not operate for gain, an income statement is inappropriate. Instead, a statement of revenue and expenses is issued, with the final amount labeled "Excess of revenue over expenses" or a similar caption. Changes in fund balances may be summarized in a separate statement or may be annexed to the statement of revenue and expenses.

The AICPA's "Hospital Audit Guide" recommends a statement of changes in financial position for the unrestricted fund.[16] However, "Audits of Voluntary Health and Welfare Organizations" and "Audits of Colleges and Universities" specifically waive a statement of changes in financial position, because the information is available in the other financial statements.[17] The *Proposed Statement of Position* issued by the AICPA requires nonprofit organizations which it covers to present a statement of changes in financial position, unless the information contained in that statement is included elsewhere in the financial statements or notes.[18]

Illustrative Financial Statements of Nonprofit Organizations Many of the matters discussed in this chapter are illustrated in the financial statements and notes of the Financial Accounting Foundation in the Appendix to this chapter starting on page 686.

FASB interest in accounting for nonprofit organizations

In 1978, the FASB placed on its agenda the accounting for nonprofit organizations and government entities. A research study authorized by the FASB, *Financial Accounting in Nonbusiness Organizations,* identified 16 issues in accounting and reporting for nonprofit organizations (and government entities). Among these issues were the following:[19]

1 Do users (of financial reports of nonprofit organizations) need a report of operating flows that is separate from a report of capital flows?

2 Do users need an operating statement?

3 How should endowment earnings be measured?

[16] "Hospital Audit Guide," p. 38.
[17] "Audits of Voluntary Health and Welfare Organizations," p. 33; "Audits of Colleges and Universities," p. 55.
[18] *Proposed Statement of Position,* p. 8.
[19] Robert N. Anthony, *Financial Accounting in Nonbusiness Organizations,* FASB (Stamford: 1978), pp. xi–xii.

4 Should a single set of concepts apply to all types of nonbusiness organizations, or should there be one set for governmental organizations and one or more additional sets for nongovernmental, nonbusiness organizations?

The FASB's interest in accounting for nonprofit organizations indicates that significant changes in this area of accounting may be expected in the near future.

Appendix: Financial Statements and Notes of Financial Accounting Foundation

STATEMENT OF FINANCIAL POSITION	December 31	
	1977	1976
Current Assets:		
Cash	$ 368,494	$ 97,377
Time and certificates of deposit	1,914,223	1,614,198
Subscription, publication and royalty receivables, less allowance for uncollectible accounts of $15,000 and $10,000 at December 31, 1977 and 1976, respectively	604,906	560,254
Contributions receivable (Note 1)	6,565	48,400
Prepaid expenses and other current assets	151,997	92,453
Total current assets	3,046,185	2,412,682
Current Liabilities:		
Accounts payable	429,248	414,325
Withheld and accrued employee benefits	265,174	168,892
Other current liabilities and accrued expenses	152,934	195,482
Deferred subscriptions (Note 1)	447,216	373,144
Total current liabilities	1,294,572	1,151,843
Working Capital	1,751,613	1,260,839
U.S. Treasury Notes, at amortized cost which approximates market (Note 3)	5,003,455	4,040,812
Furniture, equipment and leasehold improvements, at cost less accumulated depreciation and amortization (Note 4)	416,700	401,657
General Fund Balance	$7,171,768	$5,703,308

STATEMENT OF CHANGES IN FINANCIAL POSITION	Year Ended December 31	
	1977	1976
Source of Working Capital:		
Excess of revenue over expenses	$1,468,460	$1,265,637
Charges not requiring current outlay of working capital:		
Depreciation and amortization of furniture, equipment and leasehold improvements	62,688	59,426
Amortization of premium on purchase of U.S. Treasury Notes	25,795	26,563
Total from operations	1,556,943	1,351,626
Redemption of U.S. Treasury Notes	1,000,000	—
Total source of working capital	2,556,943	1,351,626
Use of Working Capital:		
Purchase of U.S. Treasury Notes	1,988,438	2,011,188
Expenditures for furniture, equipment and leasehold improvements	77,731	22,073
Total use of working capital	2,066,169	2,033,261
Increase (Decrease) in Working Capital	490,774	(681,635)
Working Capital at Beginning of Year	1,260,839	1,942,474
Working Capital at End of Year	$1,751,613	$1,260,839
Increases (Decreases) in Working Capital are Summarized by Components Below:		
Cash and time and certificates of deposit	$ 571,142	$ (494,381)
Subscription, publication and royalty receivables	44,652	61,782
Contributions receivable	(41,835)	(53,250)
Prepaid expenses and other current assets	59,544	40,536
Accounts and other payables	(68,657)	(292,032)
Deferred contributions	—	200,000
Deferred subscriptions	(74,072)	(144,290)
	$ 490,774	$ (681,635)

The accompanying Notes to Financial Statements are an integral part of these statements.

STATEMENT OF REVENUE, EXPENSES AND CHANGES IN GENERAL FUND BALANCE

	Year Ended December 31	
	1977	**1976**
Revenue:		
Contributions (Note 1)	$4,077,723	$3,772,327
Interest income	424,924	331,798
Royalties from publishers	569,704	517,953
	5,072,351	4,622,078
Subscription and publication sales (Note 1)	2,015,978	1,508,700
Less: Direct cost of sales	703,881	666,245
	1,312,097	842,455
Total	6,384,448	5,464,533
Expenses:		
Financial Accounting Standards Board:		
Salaries and related expenses:		
Salaries and wages	2,604,533	2,398,037
Employee benefits and employment costs	355,536	362,341
	2,960,069	2,760,378
Occupancy and equipment expenses:		
Rental of office space and equipment (Note 8)	308,494	309,241
Telephone, electricity and maintenance	122,237	104,764
Depreciation and amortization (Note 1)	62,688	59,426
	493,419	473,431
Other operating expenses:		
Professional fees (Note 5)	282,168	223,095
Printing and distribution costs related to discussion memoranda and exposure drafts provided at no charge	97,691	211,708
Office supplies and photocopies	107,248	98,118
Travel and meetings	97,257	85,636
Research material and systems	23,096	28,502
Postage, parcel and wire service	28,152	19,958
Insurance	32,283	16,047
Other	96,847	53,830
	764,742	736,894
Total Standards Board	4,218,230	3,970,703
Financial Accounting Foundation:		
Salaries and benefits	51,377	46,918
Legal fees	317,070	103,350
Other	329,311	77,925
Total Foundation	697,758	228,193
Total	4,915,988	4,198,896
Excess of Revenue Over Expenses	1,468,460	1,265,637
General Fund Balance at Beginning of Year	5,703,308	4,437,671
General Fund Balance at End of Year	$7,171,768	$5,703,308

The accompanying Notes to Financial Statements are an integral part of this statement.

NOTES TO FINANCIAL STATEMENTS

Donated Services. A substantial number of people have donated significant amounts of time to the activities of the Foundation and the Standards Board. No value has been reflected in the statements for these donated services because there is no clearly measurable basis to determine the amount.

1. Accounting Policies

Significant accounting policies followed in preparing the accompanying financial statements are summarized below.

Presentation. The financial statements include the activities of the Financial Accounting Standards Board and the Financial Accounting Standards Advisory Council. The Statement of Revenue, Expenses and Changes in General Fund Balance sets forth separately the expenses of the Foundation and the Standards Board (including the Advisory Council), thereby giving recognition to their separate responsibilities as described in the Certificate of Incorporation and By-Laws of the Foundation.

Basis of Accounting. The financial statements have been prepared on the accrual basis of accounting.

Contributions. Contributions received in the current period but specified as support for a subsequent period are deferred. Commitments for support of future periods are not recorded. Commitments for contributions made currently for support of the current year's activities are accrued at year-end to the extent that future collectibility is reasonably certain.

Subscriptions. Revenues from publication subscriptions are taken into income on a pro rata basis over the twelve-month subscription period. Costs of subscription fulfillment are recorded when incurred.

Depreciation and Amortization. Depreciation and amortization of furniture, equipment and leasehold improvements is provided on a straight-line basis over their estimated useful lives or the remaining term of the lease, whichever is appropriate.

Pensions. The Foundation has a funded, non-contributory pension plan covering all staff personnel and a funded, non-contributory retirement income plan covering members of the Standards Board. The annual pension provision for the staff plan is determined based on actuarial cost methods and includes provision for past service cost. The annual retirement income plan provision for the members of the Standards Board is equal to 10% of their annual compensation and is used to purchase annuities.

2. Organization and Tax Status

The Foundation is incorporated under the Delaware General Corporation Law to operate exclusively for charitable, educational, scientific and literary purposes within the meaning of Section 501(c)(3) of the Internal Revenue Code of 1954.

3. U.S. Treasury Notes

At December 31, 1977, the following U.S. Treasury Notes were held by the Foundation:

Amortized Cost	Rate	Maturity
$1,002,138	7⅞%	May 15, 1978
1,009,900	8¾	August 15, 1978
997,708	6	March 31, 1979
801,036	7½	December 31, 1979
992,673	6½	February 15, 1980
200,000	8	February 15, 1983
$5,003,455		

4. Furniture, Equipment and Leasehold Improvements

	December 31	
	1977	1976
Furniture and equipment	$370,788	$311,989
Leasehold improvements	296,045	281,989
	666,833	593,978
Accumulated depreciation and amortization	(250,133)	(192,321)
	$416,700	$401,657

5. Professional Fees—Standards Board

	Year Ended December 31	
	1977	1976
Legal	$128,309	$119,205
Research	107,714	70,676
Audit and Other	46,145	33,214
	$282,168	$223,095

6. Standards Board, Advisory Council and Foundation Expenses by Function and Activity

The format of functional expense information which follows has been revised from that of prior years to reflect the activities of the Standards Board, Advisory Council and Foundation in a more meaningful manner. Amounts for 1976 have been restated to conform to the 1977 format.

	Year Ended December 31	
	1977	1976
Financial Accounting Standards Board:		
Board & Research	$3,678,845	$3,550,008
Administrative and General	529,767	411,153
Financial Accounting Standards Advisory Council	9,618	9,542
Financial Accounting Foundation:		
Fund Raising	107,301	103,620
Direct expenses relating to the Statement of Position to the Senate Subcommittee on Reports, Accounting, and Management	374,976	—
Structure Review Committee	62,510	—
Other (Primarily Legal)	152,971	124,573
Total Expenses	$4,915,988	$4,198,896

7. Pension and Retirement Income Plans

Pension expense was $143,000 in 1977 and $137,000 in 1976. At December 31, 1977 and 1976, assets of the funds exceeded vested benefits. The Foundation's policy is to fund plans currently.

8. Lease Commitment

The Foundation occupies office space under a ten-year lease expiring July 1983. The lease provides for annual rental payments of approximately $280,000, plus escalation for the Foundation's pro rata share ($3,000 in 1977 and $1,000 in 1976) of the landlord's increased operating expenses and real estate taxes.

9. Commitment from the Accounting Research Association, Inc.

As of December 31, 1977, the Accounting Research Association, Inc. (ARA), an organization created by the American Institute of Certified Public Accountants, has fulfilled its commitment to use its best efforts to raise sufficient funds from sources within the accounting profession to ensure that the Foundation received in each of the five years ending December 31, 1977, at least $2,000,000 from these sources. As of December 31, 1977, the ARA held funds in excess of its commitment which were raised in this connection of approximately $2,300,000, which have not been reflected in the accounts of the Foundation.

Report of Ernst & Ernst, Independent Auditors

Board of Trustees
Financial Accounting Foundation

We have examined the statements of financial position of the Financial Accounting Foundation as of December 31, 1977 and 1976, and the related statements of revenue, expenses and changes in general fund balance, and of changes in financial position for the years then ended. Our examinations were made in accordance with generally accepted auditing standards and, accordingly, included such tests of the accounting records and such other auditing procedures as we considered necessary in the circumstances.

In our opinion, the financial statements referred to above present fairly the financial position of the Financial Accounting Foundation at December 31, 1977 and 1976, and the results of its operations and the changes in its financial position for the years then ended, in conformity with generally accepted accounting principles applied on a consistent basis.

Ernst & Ernst

E&E

New York, New York
February 17, 1978

REVIEW QUESTIONS

1 What is a *nonprofit organization?*

2 List at least four types of nonprofit organizations in the United States.

3 What role do the AICPA's *Industry Audit Guides* play in the determination of accounting principles for nonprofit organizations? Explain.

4 What are the three characteristics of nonprofit organizations which resemble those of government entities?

5 What characteristics of nonprofit organizations resemble those of business enterprises?

6 Define the following terms applicable to nonprofit organizations:
a Designated Fund Balance
b Third-party payer
c Pledge
d Pooled investments
e Term endowment fund

7 Differentiate between an *annuity fund* and a *life income fund* of a nonprofit organization.

8 There are several inconsistencies in the accounting principles for like items set forth in the AICPA's *Industry Audit Guides* for nonprofit organizations. Identify at least three of these inconsistencies.

9 Hospitals and universities often "rebate" or otherwise reduce their basic revenue charges to patients and students, respectively. How are these reductions reflected in the revenue accounting for the two types of nonprofit organizations? Explain.

10 a Should a nonprofit organization record donated merchandise in its accounting records? Explain.
b Should a nonprofit organization record donated services in its accounting records? Explain.

11 Identify the financial statements which are issued by a hospital.

EXERCISES

Ex. 17-1 Select the best answer for each of the following multiple-choice questions:
1 Assets available for current use by a nonprofit organization but expendable only as authorized by the donor are accounted for in:
a An agency fund
b A term endowment fund
c A life income fund
d A restricted fund

2 Interest on a nonprofit organization's loans receivable is credited to:
a Interest Revenue in the unrestricted fund
b Fund Balance in the loan fund
c Annuity Payable in the annuity fund
d Interest Revenue in the loan fund

3 A preferable caption for the final amount of a nonprofit organization's statement of revenue and expenses is:
   a Increase (decrease) in fund balance
   b Net income (loss)
   c Net results of operations
   d None of the above

4 A Designated Fund Balance account appears in a nonprofit organization's:
   a Unrestricted fund
   b Restricted fund
   c Endowment fund
   d Loan fund

5 The current fair value of merchandise donated to a nonprofit organization should:
   a Not be recorded in the accounting records
   b Be credited to the Fund Balance account of the unrestricted fund
   c Be credited to a revenue account of the unrestricted fund
   d Be credited to the Fund Balance account of a restricted fund

6 A Fund Balance account should not appear in the accounting records of a nonprofit organization's:
   a Restricted fund
   b Endowment fund
   c Agency fund
   d Annuity fund

Ex. 17-2 For the month of September, Year 6, Redwood Hospital's patient service revenue records included the following:

Amount to be received from United Way for indigent patients	$ 6,500
Charity allowances for indigent patients	12,000
Contractual adjustment allowed for Medicare patients	8,500
Gross patient service revenue (before recognition of charity allowances and contractual adjustments)	125,000

    Prepare the September 30, Year 6, journal entries to reflect the above in the accounting records of Redwood Hospital.

Ex. 17-3 On July 1, Year 5, three funds of Wilmington College pooled their individual investments, as follows:

	At July 1, Year 5	
	Cost	Current fair value
Restricted Fund	$ 80,000	$ 90,000
Quasi-Endowment Fund	120,000	126,000
Annuity Fund	150,000	144,000
Totals	$350,000	$360,000

    During the year ended June 30, Year 6, the Wilmington College investment pool reinvested realized gains of $10,000 and received dividends and interest totaling $18,000.
    Prepare journal entries at June 30, Year 6, for each of the three Wilmington College funds to reflect the results of the investment pool's operations during Fiscal Year 6.

Ex. 17-4 In your examination of the financial statements of Local Health Center, a non-profit organization, you find the following journal entries in the Restricted Fund:

Receivable from Unrestricted Fund	10,000	
Fund Balance		10,000

To record board of directors' authorization of resources to be expended for clinic equipment.

Clinic Equipment	9,500	
Accounts Payable		9,500

To record receipt of invoice for clinic equipment.

No related journal entries had been made in any other fund.

Prepare necessary adjusting journal entries at December 31, Year 1, for all affected funds of Local Health Center.

Ex. 17-5 The "Summary of Significant Accounting Policies" note to the unaudited financial statements prepared by the controller of Wabash Hospital for the year ended June 30, Year 3, includes the following sentence: "Pledges for contributions are recorded when the cash is received." Another note reads as follows:

Pledges   Unrestricted pledges receivable, received and collected during the year ended June 30, Year 3, were as follows:

Pledges receivable at July 1, Year 2 (10% doubtful)	$ 50,000
New pledges received during year	300,000
Pledges receivable at July 1, Year 2, determined to be uncollectible during year	(15,000)
Pledges collected in cash during year	(275,000)
Pledges receivable at June 30, Year 3 (12% doubtful)	$ 60,000

All pledges are due six months from the date of the pledge. Pledge revenue is recorded in the Unrestricted Fund.

Assume that you are engaged in the examination of the financial statements of Wabash Hospital for the year ended June 30, Year 3, and are satisfied with the propriety of the amounts recorded in the hospital's "Pledges" note. Prepare the necessary adjusting entry or entries for the Unrestricted Fund of Wabash Hospital at June 30, Year 3.

SHORT CASES FOR ANALYSIS AND DECISION

Case 17-1 The characteristics of voluntary health and welfare organizations differ in certain respects from the characteristics of state or local government units. As an example, voluntary health and welfare organizations derive their revenue primarily from voluntary contributions from the general public, but government units derive their revenues from taxes and services provided to their jurisdictions.

Instructions
a Describe **fund accounting** and discuss whether its use is consistent with the concept that an accounting entity is an economic unit which has control over resources, accepts responsibilities for making and carrying out commitments, and conducts economic activity.
b Distinguish between the accrual basis of accounting and the modified accrual basis of accounting and indicate which method should be used for a voluntary health and welfare organization.

c Discuss how methods used to account for plant assets differ between voluntary health and welfare organizations and government units.

Case 17-2 During the June 20, Year 10, meeting of the board of directors of Roakdale Nursing Home, a nonprofit organization, the following discussion transpired:

Chair. "We shall now hear the report from the controller."

Controller. "Our unrestricted contributions are at an all-time high. I projected an Unrestricted Fund excess of revenue over expenses of $100,000 for the year ended June 30."

Chair. "That's too high a figure for us to have a successful fund-raising drive next year. I'll entertain a motion that $80,000 of unrestricted contributions be recorded in the Restricted Fund."

Director Walker. "So moved."

Director Hastings. "Second."

Chair. "All those in favor say 'aye'."

All Directors. "Aye."

Chair. "The chair directs the controller to prepare the necessary journal entries for the Unrestricted Fund and the Restricted Fund."

Instructions Do you concur with the action taken by the board of directors of Roakdale Nursing Home? Explain.

Case 17-3 The board of trustees of Toledo Day Care Center, a nonprofit organization, has asked you, as independent CPA for the Center, to attend the current meeting of the board to participate in the discussion of a proposal to create one or more endowment funds. At the meeting, the board members ask you several questions regarding the required operating and accounting treatment of endowment funds. Among the questions posed by trustees were the following:

1 Is only the *income* of an endowment fund expendable for current operations?

2 Under what circumstances, if any, may endowment fund *principal* be expended as decided by the board?

3 Must a separate set of accounting records be established for each endowment fund, or may all endowment fund operations be accounted for in the Restricted Fund?

Instructions Prepare a reply for each of the trustees' questions. Number your replies to correspond with the question numbers.

Case 17-4 The controller of Lakeland Hospital, a nonprofit organization, proposes to present the Provision for Doubtful Accounts Receivable account as an expense in the statement of revenue and expenses of Lakeland Hospital Unrestricted Fund. As the hospital's independent CPA you oppose this treatment. You point out that the AICPA's "Hospital Audit Guide" requires the provision for doubtful accounts to be offset against gross patient service revenue in the statement of revenue and expenses of a hospital's unrestricted fund. The controller's rejoinder is that there are so many contradictions among the AICPA's three *Industry Audit Guides* for nonprofit organizations that there should be some latitude for managers of nonprofit organizations to report operating results on the same basis as a business enterprise.

Instructions How would you respond to the statement of the controller of Lakeland Hospital? Support your reply by sound accounting theory for nonprofit organizations.

PROBLEMS

17-5 On July 1, Year 6, the four funds of City Welfare Services, a nonprofit organization, formed an investment pool. On that date, cost and current fair values of the four funds' investments were as follows:

	At July 1, Year 6	
	Cost	Current fair value
Unrestricted Fund	$ 50,000	$ 60,000
Restricted Fund	20,000	15,000
Plant Fund	80,000	90,000
Arnold Life Income Fund	100,000	105,000
Totals	$250,000	$270,000

During the six months ended December 31, Year 6, the investment pool re-invested realized gains totaling $15,000 and received dividends and interest totaling $25,000. On December 31, Year 6, the Restricted Fund withdrew from the pool and was awarded securities in the amount of its share of the pool's aggregate December 31, Year 6, current fair value of $300,000. On January 2, Year 7, the Edwards Endowment Fund entered the City Welfare Services investment pool with investments having a cost of $70,000 and a current fair value of $75,000. During the six months ended June 30, Year 7, the investment pool re-invested realized gains totaling $40,000 and received dividends and interest totaling $60,000.

Instructions
a Prepare a working paper for the City Welfare Services investment pool, computing the following (round all percentages to two decimal places):
(1) Original equity percentages at July 1, Year 6
(2) Revised equity percentages at January 2, Year 7
b Prepare journal entries to record the operations of the City Welfare Services investment pool in the accounting records of the participating Unrestricted Fund.

17-6 Among the transactions of the Unrestricted Fund of Alta Hospital, a nonprofit organization, for the month of October, Year 8, were the following:
(1) Gross patient service revenue of $80,000 was billed to patients. Provision was made for indigent patient charity allowances of $4,000; amounts receivable from Bovard Welfare Organization for indigent patients of $2,500; contractual adjustments allowed to Medicaid of $6,000; and doubtful accounts of $8,000.
(2) Donated services approximating $10,000 at going salary rates were received from volunteer nurses. Meals costing $200 were served to the volunteer nurses at no charge by the Alta Hospital cafeteria.
(3) New pledges, due in three months, totaling $5,000 were received from various donors. Collections on pledges amounted to $3,500, and the provision for doubtful pledges for October, Year 8, was $800.
(4) Paid the $500 monthly annuity established for Arline E. Walters by a contribution by Walters to Alta Hospital three years ago.
(5) Received and expended $3,000 from Charles Watson Restricted Fund for new surgical equipment, as authorized by the donor.

Instructions
a Prepare the journal entries for the above October, Year 8, transactions of the Alta Hospital Unrestricted Fund. Number each group of entries to correspond to the number of each transactions group.
b Prepare journal entries required for other funds of Alta Hospital as indicated by the transactions of the Unrestricted Fund.

17-7 A newly elected board of directors of Dupar Hospital, a nonprofit organization, decided that effective January 1, Year 98:

(a) The existing ledger account balances are to be properly adjusted and three separate funds (Unrestricted Fund, James Dupar Endowment Fund, and Plant Replacement Fund) are to be established.
(b) The fund balance of the James Dupar Endowment Fund and an amount equal to the Accumulated Depreciation account of the Unrestricted Fund are to be invested in securities.
(c) All accounts are to be maintained in accordance with the AICPA's "Hospital Audit Guide."

The board engaged you to determine the proper account balances for each of the funds. The trial balance of the ledger at January 1, Year 98, follows:

DUPAR HOSPITAL
Trial Balance
January 1, Year 98

	Debit	Credit
Cash	$ 50,000	
Investment in U.S. Treasury bills	105,000	
Investment in common stocks	417,000	
Interest receivable	4,000	
Accounts receivable	40,000	
Inventories	25,000	
Land	407,000	
Building	245,000	
Equipment	283,000	
Accumulated depreciation		$ 376,000
Accounts payable		70,000
Bank loan payable		150,000
James Dupar Endowment Fund		119,500
Surplus		860,500
Totals	$1,576,000	$1,576,000

The following additional information is available:
(1) Under the terms of the will of James Dupar, founder of the hospital, "the principal of the bequest is to be fully invested in trust forevermore in mortgages secured by productive real estate in Webster City and/or in U.S. government securities . . . and the income therefrom is to be used to defray current expenses."
(2) The James Dupar Endowment Fund account balance consists of the following:

Cash received in Year 1 by bequest from James Dupar	$ 81,500
Net gains realized from Year 56 through Year 89 from the sale of real estate acquired in mortgage foreclosures	23,500
Revenue received from Year 90 through Year 97 from investment in U.S. Treasury bills	14,500
Balance per ledger, Jan. 1, Year 98	$119,500

(3) The Land account balance was composed of the following:

Year 20 appraisal of land at $10,000 and building at $5,000 received by
  donation at that time. (The building was demolished in Year 40.) . . . . $ 15,000
Appraisal increase based on insured value in land title policies issued in
  Year 57 380,000
Landscaping costs for trees planted 12,000
Balance per ledger, Jan. 1, Year 98 . . . . $407,000

(4) The Building account balance was composed of the following:

Cost of present hospital building completed in January, Year 57, when the
  hospital began operations $300,000
Adjustment to record appraised value of building in Year 67 . . . . (100,000)
Cost of elevator installed in January, Year 83 45,000
Balance per ledger, Jan. 1, Year 98 . . . . $245,000

The economic lives of the hospital building and the elevator when new
were 50 years and 20 years, respectively.
(5) The hospital's equipment was inventoried on January 1, Year 98. The total
of the inventory agreed with the Equipment account balance in the ledger.
The Accumulated Depreciation account at January 1, Year 98, included
$158,250 applicable to equipment, and that amount was approved by the
board of directors as being accurate. All depreciation is computed on a
straight-line basis, with no residual value.
(6) A bank loan was obtained to finance the cost of new operating room
equipment purchased in Year 94. Interest on the loan was paid to December 31, Year 97.

Instructions Prepare a working paper to present the adjustments necessary
to restate the ledger account balances and to distribute the adjusted balances
to establish the required fund accounts. Formal journal entires are not re-
quired; however, explain each adjustment (including supporting computa-
tions) at the bottom of the working paper. The following column headings are
suggested:
  Unadjusted trial balance
  Adjustments
  Adjusted trial balance
  Unrestricted Fund
  James Dupar Endowment Fund
  Plant Replacement Fund

17-8 The accountant for Kaplan Vocational School, a nonprofit organization, resigned on March 1, Year 8, after having prepared the following trial balance
and analysis of cash as of February 28, Year 8:

KAPLAN VOCATIONAL SCHOOL
Trial Balance
February 28, Year 8

Debits

Cash for general current operations $258,000
Cash for restricted current uses 30,900
Common stock donated by L. M. Nash 11,000
Bonds donated by O. P. Quinn 150,000

(cont.)

KAPLAN VOCATIONAL SCHOOL
Trial Balance
February 28, Year 8 (concluded)

Debits

Land	$ 22,000
Building	33,000
General current operating expenses	38,000
Faculty recruitment expenses	4,100
Total	$547,000

Credits

Mortgage note payable on plant assets	$ 30,000
Revenue from gifts for general operations	210,000
Revenue from gifts for restricted uses	196,000
Student fees	31,000
Surplus	80,000
Total	$547,000

KAPLAN VOCATIONAL SCHOOL
Analysis of Cash
For Six Months Ended February 28, Year 8

Cash for general current operations:			
Balance, Sept. 1, Year 7		$ 80,000	
Add: Student fees	$ 31,000		
Gift of H. I. Johnson	210,000	241,000	
Subtotal		$321,000	
Less: General current operating expenses	$ 38,000		
Payment for land and building	25,000	63,000	$258,000
Cash for restricted current uses:			
Gift of H. I. Johnson for faculty recruitment		$ 35,000	
Less: Faculty recruitment expenses		4,100	30,900
Checking account balance, Feb. 28, Year 8			$288,900

    You were engaged to determine the proper account balances for the school as of August 31, Year 8, the close of the school's first fiscal year. Your examination disclosed the following information:
(1) In September, Year 7, L. M. Nash donated 100 shares of Wilder, Inc., common stock with a current fair value of $110 per share at the date of donation. The terms of the gift provide that the stock and any dividend revenue are to be retained intact. At any date designated by the board of directors, the assets are to be liquidated and the proceeds used to assist the school's director in acquiring a personal residence. The school will not retain any financial interest in the residence.
(2) O. P. Quinn donated 6% bonds in September, Year 7, with a principal amount and current fair value of $150,000 at the date of donation. Annual payments

of $3,500 are to be made to the donor during the donor's lifetime. Upon the donor's death the fund is to be used to construct a school cafeteria. The actuarial valuation of the O. P. Quinn annuity at August 31, Year 8, was $122,143.

(3) No transactions have been recorded in the school's accounting records since February 28, Year 8. An employee of the school prepared the following analysis of the checking account for the period from March 1 through August 31, Year 8:

Balance, Mar. 1, Year 8			$288,900
Less: General current operating expenses	$14,000		
Purchase of equipment	47,000	$61,000	
Less: Student fees		8,000	
Net expenses		$53,000	
Payment for director's residence	$11,200		
Less: Sale of 100 shares of Wilder, Inc., common stock	10,600	600	53,600
Total			$235,300
Add: Interest on 6% bonds		$ 9,000	
Less: Payment to O. P. Quinn		3,500	5,500
Balance, Aug. 31, Year 8			$240,800

Instructions Prepare a working paper presenting the trial balance at February 28, Year 8, adjusting entries, transaction entries from March 1 through August 31, Year 8, and distributions to the proper funds. The following column headings are recommended:

Unadjusted trial balance, Feb. 28, Year 8
Adjustments and transactions—Debit
Adjustments and transactions—Credit
Adjusted trial balance, Aug. 31, Year 8
Unrestricted Current Fund
Restricted Current Fund
O. P. Quinn Annuity Fund
Plant Fund—Investment in Plant

Formal journal entries are not required; however, explain each adjustment and transaction (including supporting computations) at the bottom of the working paper. Disregard accrued interest on mortgage note payable.

17-9 Presented below is the balance sheet of Restful Hospital at December 31, Year 6:

RESTFUL HOSPITAL
Balance Sheet
December 31, Year 6

Unrestricted Fund

Assets			Liabilities & Fund Balances		
Current assets			Current liabilities		
Cash	$	20,000	Accounts payable	$	16,000
Accounts receivable	$	37,000	Accrued expenses payable		6,000
Less: Allowances and			Total current liabilities	$	22,000
doubtful accounts		7,000			
Net accounts receivable	$	30,000	Mortgage bonds payable	$	150,000

(cont.)

RESTFUL HOSPITAL
Balance Sheet
December 31, Year 6 (concluded)

Assets		Liabilities & Fund Balances	
Inventory of supplies	$ 14,000	Fund balances	
Total current assets . .	$ 64,000	Investment in plant	$2,116,000
		Undesignated	12,000
Plant assets		Total fund balances	$2,128,000
Land	$ 370,000		
Buildings	$1,750,000		
Less: Accumulated			
depreciation	430,000		
Net buildings	$1,320,000		
Equipment	$ 680,000		
Less: Accumulated			
depreciation	134,000		
Net equipment	$ 546,000		
Total plant assets	$2,236,000	Total liabilities &	
Total assets	$2,300,000	fund balances	$2,300,000

Restricted Funds

Plant Replacement and Expansion Fund
Assets

Cash	$ 53,800		
Investments	71,200		
Total assets	$125,000	Fund balance	$125,000

Endowment Fund
Assets

Cash	$ 6,000		
Investments	260,000		
Total assets	$266,000	Fund balance	$266,000

During Year 7 the following transactions were completed:

(1) Gross debits to Accounts Receivable for hospital services were as follows:

Room and board	$ 780,000
Debits for other professional services	321,000
Total debits to Accounts Receivable	$1,101,000

(2) Deductions from gross revenue were as follows:

Provision for doubtful accounts $30,000

Charity allowances 15,000

    Total deductions from gross revenue $45,000

(3) The Unrestricted Fund paid $18,000 to retire mortgage bonds payable with an equivalent face amount.

(4) During the year the Unrestricted Fund received general contributions of $50,000 and income from Endowment Fund investments of $6,500. The Unrestricted Fund has been designated to receive the income earned on Endowment Fund investments.

(5) New equipment costing $26,000 was acquired. An x-ray machine which originally cost $24,000 and which had a carrying amount of $2,400 was sold for $500.

(6) Vouchers totaling $1,191,000 were issued for the following items:

Administrative services expense .... $ 120,000

Fiscal services expense 95,000

General services expense 225,000

Nursing services expense 520,000

Other professional services expense 165,000

Supplies 60,000

Expenses accrued at Dec. 31, Year 6 6,000

    Total vouchers issued $1,191,000

(7) Collections on accounts receivable totaled $985,000. Accounts written off as uncollectible amounted to $11,000.

(8) Cash payments on vouchers payable during the year were $825,000.

(9) Supplies of $37,000 were issued for nursing services.

(10) On December 31, Year 7, accrued interest earned on Plant Replacement and Expansion Fund investments was $800.

(11) Depreciation of buildings and equipment was as follows:

Buildings .... $ 44,000

Equipment 73,000

    Total depreciation $117,000

(12) On December 31, Year 7, an accrual of $6,100 was made for fiscal service expense on the mortgage bonds.

Instructions For the period January 1, Year 7, through December 31, Year 7, prepare journal entries to record the transactions described above for the following funds of Restful Hospital:

  Unrestricted Fund

  Plant Replacement and Expansion Fund

  Endowment Fund

Each journal entry should be numbered to correspond with the transactions described above. Your working paper should be organized as follows:

Trans. No.	Accounts	Unrestricted fund		Plant replacement and expansion fund		Endowment fund	
		Debit	Credit	Debit	Credit	Debit	Credit

In addition to the ledger accounts included in the December 31, Year 6, balance sheet of Restful Hospital, the following ledger accounts are pertinent:

Unrestricted Fund
    Administrative Services Expense
    Charity Allowances
    Depreciation Expense
    Fiscal Services Expense
    General Services Expense
    Loss on Disposal of Plant Assets
    Nursing Services Expense
    Other Professional Services Expense
    Patient Service Revenue
    Provision for Doubtful Accounts
    Unrestricted Gifts and Bequests Revenue
    Unrestricted Revenue from Endowment Fund

Plant Replacement and Expansion Fund
    Interest Receivable

18

ACCOUNTING AND REPORTING FOR THE SEC

The Securities and Exchange Commission (SEC) is an agency of the United States government created in 1934 to oversee the interstate issuances and trading of securities. Since its creation, the SEC's functions have expanded to include administration of the following United States statutes:

Securities Act of 1933, governing interstate issuances of securities to the public

Securities Exchange Act of 1934, governing trading of securities on national securities exchanges and over the counter

Public Utility Holding Company Act of 1935, governing interstate public utility holding company systems for electricity and gas

Trust Indenture Act of 1939, governing the issuance of bonds, debentures, and similar debt securities under an indenture meeting the requirements of the Act

Investment Company Act of 1940 and *Investment Advisers Act of 1940,* governing operations of investment companies and investment advisers

In this chapter, we shall concentrate on the SEC's administration of the Securities Act of 1933 (the 1933 Act) and the Securities Exchange Act of 1934 (the 1934 Act).

In addition, as pointed out in Chapter 14, the SEC assists United States district courts in the administration of corporate reorganizations under Chapter 10 of the Bankruptcy Act.

From its inception, the SEC has assumed an aggressive role in fulfilling its mission as "watchdog of Wall Street." In that role, the SEC has had a significant influence on the body of generally accepted accounting principles, especially with respect to financial statements presentation and disclosure by publicly owned corporations.

Organization and scope of the SEC

The SEC is administered by five commissioners appointed for five-year terms by the President and confirmed by the Senate of the United States. No more than three commissioners can be members of the same political party.

On June 30, 1976, the staff of the SEC, exclusive of the commissioners, totaled 1,918, with 1,217 headquartered in Washington, D.C., and 701 in the seventeen regional branches and offices.[1] The organization and scope of the SEC is presented in the organization chart on page 704.

Role of the SEC in establishment of accounting principles

Both the 1933 Act and the 1934 Act empower the SEC to establish rules for the accounting principles underlying financial statements and schedules included in reports filed with the SEC. The SEC rarely has used this authority directly. Instead, it usually has endorsed actions on accounting principles by organizations in the private sector (currently the Financial Accounting Standards Board), while reserving the right to issue its own pronouncements when necessary. This posture of the SEC has been described as follows:[2]

> In Accounting Series Release No. 4 (1938) the Commission stated its policy that financial statements prepared in accordance with accounting practices for which there was no substantial authoritative support were presumed to be misleading and that footnote or other disclosure would not avoid this presumption. It also stated that, where there was a difference of opinion between the Commission and a registrant as to the proper accounting to be followed in a particular case, disclosure would be accepted in lieu of correction of the financial statements themselves only if substantial authoritative support existed for the accounting practices followed by the registrant and the position of the Commission had not been expressed in rules, regulations or other official releases. For purposes of this policy, principles, standards and practices promulgated by the FASB in its Statements and Interpretations will be considered by the Commission as having substantial authoritative support, and those contrary to such FASB promulgations will be considered to have no such support.
>
> ... Information in addition to that included in financial statements conforming to generally accepted accounting principles is also necessary. Such additional disclosures are required to be made in various fashions, such as in

---

[1] 42d Annual Report of the SEC for the Fiscal Year Ended June 30, 1976 (Washington: 1977), p. 169.
[2] Accounting Series Release No. 150, SEC (Washington: 1973).

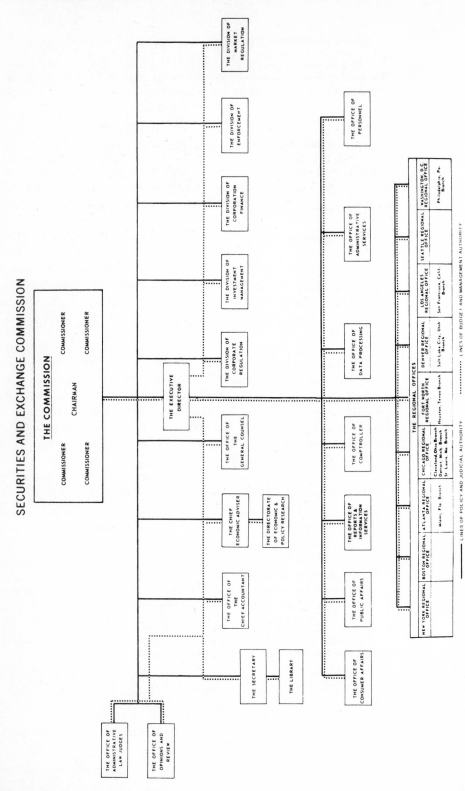

SECURITIES AND EXCHANGE COMMISSION

Source: 42d Annual Report of the SEC for the Fiscal Year Ended June 30, 1976 (Washington: 1977), p. iv.

> financial statements and schedules reported on by independent public accountants or as textual statements required by items in the applicable forms and reports filed with the Commission. The Commission will continue to identify areas where investor information needs exist and will determine the appropriate methods of disclosure to meet these needs.

Thus, the SEC differentiated between *generally accepted accounting principles* and *disclosures* in financial statements and schedules, and expressed an intention to concentrate on pronouncements on disclosures. The principal devices used by the SEC to communicate its requirements for accounting principles and disclosures have been *Accounting Series Releases, Regulation S-X,* and *Staff Accounting Bulletins.*

Accounting Series Releases (ASRs) In 1937 the SEC initiated a program of pronouncements by the chief accountant of the Commission designed to contribute to the development of uniform standards and practice in major accounting questions. As of the end of 1978, over 250 *ASRs* have been issued, with approximately half of them published after 1972. However, fewer than half of the *ASRs* dealt solely with accounting principles and disclosures; the remainder covered auditing standards, independence of auditors, and administrative proceedings of the SEC involving accountants.

Among the *ASRs* dealing with accounting principles and disclosures are the following:

ASR No. 142, "Reporting Cash Flow and Other Related Data." In this Release, the SEC concluded that financial reports should not present *cash flow* (net income adjusted for noncash expenses and revenue) per share and other comparable per-share computations, other than those based on net income, dividends, or net assets.

ASR No. 148, " . . . Disclosure of Compensating Balances and Short-Term Borrowing Arrangements." This Release defined a *compensating balance* as the portion of a checking account, savings account, or certificate of deposit in a lending institution which is support for existing borrowing arrangements with the lender. Compensating balances which are *legally restricted* under the terms of the borrowing arrangement must be segregated and classified as current or noncurrent assets, depending on the classification of the related loan. Other compensating balances not legally restricted are disclosed in footnotes. In addition, the Release requires disclosure of the average interest rate and general terms of current borrowings on bank loans and commercial paper.

The following note to the financial statements of Avco Financial Services, Inc., filed with the SEC, illustrate the application of *ASR No. 148:*

Note 5—Short-Term Debt, Compensating Balances, etc.

Bank borrowings are arranged under short-term lines of credit. These borrowings are either on a demand basis or provide for maturities ranging up to 90 days. Interest is generally at the prime current lending rate. Commercial paper is issued with maturities up to 270 days with interest at prevailing market rates. The weighted average interest rates on short-term debt outstanding at November 30, 1976 and 1977, without giving effect to the costs of maintaining the lines of credit, were 10.1% and 8.4%, respectively, for bank borrowings (primarily consisting of borrowings in Australia and the United Kingdom) and 5.7% and 7.0%, respectively, for commercial paper.

The maximum aggregate short-term debt outstanding at any month end during the years ended November 30, 1976 and 1977 was $443,018,000 and $438,842,000, respectively. The average aggregate amount of such short-term debt outstanding during the years ended November 30, 1976 and 1977 was $414,550,000 and $388,319,000, respectively, and the related weighted average interest rate was 6.6% and 6.3%, respectively. The weighted average interest rate is determined primarily by reference to daily outstanding principal amounts and excludes the cost of maintaining the lines of credit.

At November 30, 1976 and 1977 the Company had lines of credit with various banks amounting to $814,596,000 and $818,401,000, respectively, of which $244,050,000 and $303,932,000, respectively, related to long-term loans. The unused portion of these lines amounted to $543,053,000 and $513,996,000, respectively, of which $1,616,000 and $10,167,000, respectively, related to long-term loans. In support of these lines the Company maintains compensating balances with the majority of its lending banks. For short-term borrowings the Company generally maintains compensating balances of 10% of the lines of credit plus an additional 10% of the amounts actually borrowed. For certain long-term borrowings the Company maintains compensating balances equal to 10% or 15% of the amounts borrowed under the lines of credit.

Compensating balances, which are based on collected bank ledger balances, are not legally restricted and are subject to withdrawal without sanction.

ASR No. 149, ''. . . Improved Disclosure of Income Tax Expense.'' In this Release, the SEC mandated several disclosures concerning income taxes which are illustrated in the following note to financial statements of Computer Network Corporation filed with the SEC:

(7) Income Taxes

The provisions for income taxes in the statements of income (loss) include provisions for state income taxes of $15,000, $27,000, $2,678, $177,546 and $86,103 for the years ended March 31, 1973 through March 31, 1977, respectively, and $33,360 and $93,158 for the six months ended September 30, 1976 and 1977, respectively, and provisions for deferred income taxes, arising primarily from use of the cash basis of accounting for Federal income tax return purposes, of $21,268 and $11,513 for the years ended March 31, 1976 and March 31, 1977, and $37,420 and $(41,868) for the six-month periods ended September 30, 1976 and 1977, respectively.

The provisions for income taxes for 1976 and 1977 vary from the amounts of income taxes determined by applying the Federal income tax rate of 48% to income before taxes for the reasons reflected in the following table.

| | Percent of pre-tax income | | | |
| | Year ended March 31 | | Six months ended September 30 | |
	1976	1977	1976	1977
Computed "expected" tax expense	48.0%	48.0%	48.0%	48.0%
States income taxes, net of Federal income tax benefit	5.2	5.2	5.2	5.2
Utilization of investment tax credit	—	(19.1)	(12.8)	(22.1)
Other	1.1	1.7	(.9)	(1.3)
Actual tax expense	54.3%	35.8%	39.5%	29.8%

Operating loss carry-forwards have been utilized to offset the provision for Federal income taxes, and resultant benefits of $104,000, $171,000, $8,000, $641,780, and $79,018 for the years ended March 31, 1973 through 1977, respectively, and $74,946 for the six months ended September 30, 1976, have been classified as extraordinary items.

The Company has no remaining operating loss carry-forwards. The Company had investment tax credit carry-forwards of approximately $500,000 at September 30, 1977.

ASR No. 190, " . . . Disclosure of Certain Replacement Cost Data." This controversial Release required certain companies regulated by the SEC to disclose in an unaudited note or separate section of the financial statements the current replacement cost of inventories, cost of goods sold, productive capacity (essentially a measure of plant assets), and depreciation and amortization. The following note to financial statements of Pennsylvania Power & Light Company filed with the SEC illustrates the requirements of **ASR No. 190:**

17. Replacement Cost Data (Unaudited)

In compliance with the rules of the SEC, the Company has estimated certain replacement cost information for utility plant in service and depreciation. The Company has not included replacement cost data for materials and supplies inventory since the amount of the inventory is not significant. Replacement cost data relating to fuel inventories have not been included since changes in cost levels are recovered through the operation of fuel adjustment clauses.

Although the replacement cost data disclosed herein have, in the Company's opinion, been reasonably estimated in accordance with rules and interpretations of such rules published by the SEC, the Company believes that investors should be aware of the imprecision and limitations of this information and of the many subjective judgments required in the replacement cost estimation.

The replacement cost of utility plant is based on the hypothetical assumption that the Company would replace its entire productive capacity as of December 31, 1977, whether or not the funds to do so were available or such "instant" replacement were physically or legally possible. This assumption requires that the Company contemplate actions as of December 31, 1977 that ordinarily would not be addressed all at one time.

Accordingly, the information should not be interpreted to indicate that the Company actually has present plans to replace its productive capacity or that actual replacement would or could take place in the manner assumed in estimating the information. In the normal course of business, the Company will replace its productive capacity over an extended period of time. Decisions concerning replacement will be made in light of the economics, availability of funds, fuel availability, equipment availability, customer demand and regulatory requirements existing when such determinations are made and could differ substantially from the assumptions on which the data included herein are based.

The replacement cost data presented are not necessarily representative of the "current market value" of existing facilities or of the "fair value" of utility plant as that term is used in rate proceedings before the PUC.

The replacement cost information presented does not reflect all of the effects of inflation on the Company's current costs of operating the business. The Company has not attempted to quantify the total impact of inflation, environmental and other governmental regulations (except as set forth below) and changes in other economic factors on the business because of the many unresolved conceptual problems and rate-making considerations involved in doing so. Accordingly, it is the Company's view that the replacement cost data presented herein cannot be used alone to determine the total effect of inflation on reported net income.

The computed replacement cost of the Company's utility plant in service and related accumulated depreciation with comparative historical cost data are as follows (millions of dollars):

	Historical cost	Computed replacement cost
Utility plant in service at December 31, 1977		
Subject to replacement cost determination	$2,216	$5,045
Land, plant held for future use and intangibles at original cost	116	116
Total plant in service	2,332	5,161
Less accumulated depreciation	509	1,197
Net plant in service........................	$1,823	$3,964

Regulation S-X The SEC issued **Regulation S-X** to provide guidance for the form and content of financial statements and schedules required to be filed with the SEC under the various laws which it administers. Since the adoption of **Regulation S-X** in 1940, the SEC has amended the document extensively through the issuance of **ASRs**, including those identified in the preceding section of this chapter.

Regulation S-X consists of numerous rules subdivided into 18 articles. Among the most significant articles of **Regulation S-X** for accountants preparing financial statements and schedules for filing with the SEC are the following:

Article 3 Rules of General Application
 4 Consolidated and Combined Financial Statements
 5 Commercial and Industrial Companies
 11 Contents of Statements of Other Stockholders' Equity
 11A Statement of Source and Application of Funds
 12 Form and Content of Schedules

Article 12 of **Regulation S-X** describes and illustrates a number of supporting schedules which may be required in a filing of financial statements with the SEC. Among these schedules are the following:

Schedule I Marketable Securities—Other Security Investments
 V Property, Plant and Equipment
 VI Accumulated Depreciation, Depletion and Amortization of Property, Plant and Equipment
 IX Bonds, Mortgages and Similar Debt
 XVI Supplementary Income Statement Information

Rule 5-04(b) of **Regulation S-X** permits the combining or omission of schedules, as follows:

> When information is required in schedules for both the registrant and the registrant and its subsidiaries consolidated it may be presented in the form of a single schedule, provided that items pertaining to the registrant are separately shown and that such single schedule affords a properly summarized

presentation of the facts. If the information required by any schedule (including the notes thereto) may be shown in the related financial statement or in a note thereto without making such statement unclear or confusing, that procedure may be followed and the schedule omitted.

An illustration of Schedule V included in a filing with the SEC by The Signal Companies, Inc., appears below:

THE SIGNAL COMPANIES, INC. AND SUBSIDIARY COMPANIES
Schedule V—Property
For the Year Ended December 31, 1976
(Dollars in thousands)

	Balance December 31, 1975	Additions at cost	Retirements	Other	Balance December 31, 1976
Company (1)	$ 5,755	$ 256	$ (405)		$ 5,606
Consolidated:					
Land and improvements .	$ 58,562	$ 2,345	$ (2,862)		$ 58,045
Buildings and improvements	241,792	11,611	(8,705)	$ (2,741) (4)	241,957
Machinery and equipment	325,829	39,791	(11,264)	—	354,356
Motor vehicles leased to customers	17,344		(5,817)	545 (3)	12,072
Total	$643,527	$53,747	$(28,648)	$ (2,196)	$666,430

For the Year Ended December 31, 1975
(Dollars in thousands)

	Balance December 31, 1974	Additions at cost	Retirements	Other	Balance December 31, 1975
Company (1)	$ 5,821	$ 321	$ (387)	—	$ 5,755
Consolidated:					
Land and improvements .	$ 42,885	$ 4,047	$ (1,085)	$ 12,715 (2)	$ 58,562
Buildings and improvements	136,730	13,592	(1,279)	92,749 (2)	241,792
Machinery and equipment	191,766	57,602	(7,516)	83,977 (2)	325,829
Motor vehicles leased to customers	29,739	—	(14,528)	2,133 (3)	17,344
Total	$401,120	$75,241	$(24,408)	$191,574	$643,527

(1) Properties of the Company are comprised primarily of land and buildings and improvements thereto.

(2) Properties of acquired company at date of acquisition.

(3) Cost of leased manufactured trucks transferred from inventory.

(4) Adjustment to properties of acquired company.

Staff Accounting Bulletins The following excerpt from **ASR No. 180** describes the **Staff Accounting Bulletins** issued by the SEC:

> The Securities and Exchange Commission today announced the institution of a series of Staff Accounting Bulletins intended to achieve a wider dissemination of the administrative interpretations and practices utilized by the Commission's staff in reviewing financial statements. The Division of Corporation Finance and the Office of the Chief Accountant began the series today with the publication of Bulletin No. 1. . . . The statements in the Bulletin are not rules or interpretations of the Commission nor are they published as bearing the Commission's official approval; they represent interpretations and practices followed by the Division and the Chief Accountant in administering the disclosure requirements of the federal securities laws.

The following example from **Staff Accounting Bulletin No. 1** illustrates the contents of a typical Bulletin:

> *Facts:* Company E proposes to include in its registration statement a balance sheet showing its subordinate debt as a portion of stockholders' equity.
>
> *Question:* Is this presentation appropriate?
>
> *Interpretive Response:* Subordinated debt may not be included in the stockholders' equity section of the balance sheet. Any presentation describing such debt as a component of stockholders' equity must be eliminated. Furthermore, any caption representing the combination of stockholders' equity and only subordinated debt must be deleted.

Role of the SEC in initial offerings of securities

We have pointed out that the SEC administers the 1933 Act, which regulates the interstate issuance of securities to the public. The term **security** has the following definition in Section 2(1) of the 1933 Act:

> The term "security" means any note, stock, treasury stock, bond, debenture, evidence of indebtedness, certificate of interest or participation in any profit-sharing agreement, collateral-trust certificate, preorganization certificate or subscription, transferable share, investment contract, voting-trust certificate, certificate of deposit for a security, fractional undivided interest in oil, gas, or other mineral rights, or, in general, any interest or instrument commonly known as a "security," or any certificate of interest or participation in, temporary or interim certificate for, receipt for, guarantee of, or warrant or right to subscribe to or purchase, any of the foregoing.

The Registration Statement Unless securities to be issued interstate to the public are exempted under Section 3 of the 1933 Act, or unless the transactions under which securities are to be issued are exempted under Section 4 of the 1933 Act, a **registration statement** for the securities must be filed with the SEC. The purpose of the registration statement is to provide "full and fair" disclosure of all information required by prospective purchasers of the securities registered. Until the registration statement becomes effective (a minimum of 20 days after its filing), the registered securities cannot be sold. The filing of an amendment to the original registration statement prior to its effective date starts the 20-day period anew, unless the SEC had consented to the filing of the amendment.

The SEC reviews the registration statement for form and content in a variety of ways. Often, the SEC issues a letter of comments ("deficiency letter") suggesting desirable modifications in the registration statement. These modifications usually are made by the registrant and incorporated in one or more *amendments* to the registration statement.

It is important to stress that *the SEC does not approve or disapprove registration statements.* To emphasize this fact, Rule 425 of Regulation C under the Securities Act of 1933 requires the following in bold type on the face of every prospectus (the first section of a registration statement):

"THESE SECURITIES HAVE NOT BEEN APPROVED OR DISAPPROVED BY THE SECURITIES AND EXCHANGE COMMISSION NOR HAS THE COMMISSION PASSED UPON THE ACCURACY OR ADEQUACY OF THIS PROSPECTUS. ANY REPRESENTATION TO THE CONTRARY IS A CRIMINAL OFFENSE."

Schedules A and B of the 1933 Act list basic requirements for registration statements. However, the SEC has prescribed a series *of Forms* (actually formats) for registration statements under the 1933 Act. Among these are the following:

Form S-1, for all issuers of securities other than foreign governments and issuers which can use another Form

Form S-7, for issuers of securities who have an extensive history of reporting to the SEC under the 1934 Act

Form S-8, for certain issuers of securities offered to employees under an employee benefit plan

Form S-14, for issuers of securities in a business combination

Form S-16, a "short form" for selected issuers of securities similar to the registrants who can use Form S-7

Because *Form S-1* essentially may be used by any United States company registering securities with the SEC, it will be discussed below in some detail.

Form S-1 The *Form S-1* registration statement is divided into two parts. Part I, "Information Required in Prospectus," includes 21 items of information which as of the effective date of the *Form S-1* registration statement will be included in a *prospectus* provided to purchasers and others interested in the registered securities. Part II, "Information Not Required in the Prospectus," includes 10 items of information.

Many of the 31 total items required in a *Form S-1* registration statement are written descriptions dealing with the registered securities; the registrant company, its business, and its properties; and the directors and officers of the registrant company, their remuneration, and their ownership of securities of the registrant company. However, the following items of a *Form S-1* registration statement require accounting presentations:

Item 5, Capital Structure The requirements of this item are illustrated by the excerpt below and on page 714 from a preliminary (incomplete) prospectus for convertible subordinated debentures filed with the SEC by Tipperary Corporation.

CAPITALIZATION

The following table sets forth the capitalization of the Company as of September 30, 1977, and as adjusted to reflect the sale of the Debentures and the application of a portion of the net proceeds as described.

	Outstanding	As adjusted
Short-term debt:		
Current maturities of long-term debt	$ 943,000	$ 857,000
Long-term debt(1)		
Unsecured note payable to institutional lender(2)	$20,000,000	$20,000,000
Unsecured note payable to banks(3)	5,000,000	—
Secured note payable to bank(4)................	3,014,000	—
Other	2,513,000	2,513,000
Total notes payable	$30,527,000	$22,513,000
__% convertible subordinated debentures due 1998		$15,000,000
Shareholders' equity:		
Common stock, $.50 par value; authorized 10,000,000 shares; issued and outstanding 4,652,044 shares(5)	$ 2,326,000	$ 2,326,000
Capital in excess of par value	13,704,000	13,704,000
Retained earnings	1,342,000	1,342,000
Total shareholders' equity	$17,372,000	$17,372,000

(1) See Notes 3 and 7 of Notes to the Consolidated Financial Statements for further information with respect to long-term debt and contingencies.

(2) The principal of this note is payable in installments of $770,000 on January 15, and July 15 beginning January 15, 1979 with interest at 10½%. For additional information with respect to the restrictions placed on the Company as a result of this loan agreement, see Note 3 of Notes to the Consolidated Financial Statements.

(3) This is an unsecured note payable to banks which is due December 31, 1978. Interest is charged at the greater of the prime rate of either the Midland National Bank or the Chase Manhattan Bank plus 1¾%. This debt represents a $5,000,000 line of credit.

(4) This secured note payable to a bank is due in 35 monthly installments equal to 90% of net income (as defined) of various subsidiaries beginning October 31, 1977 with the balance due September 30, 1980 with interest at the prime rate of either the Midland National Bank or the Chase Manhattan Bank plus 1¾% payable monthly. The note is secured by the outstanding stock of the subsidiaries and accounts receivable and certain properties of the subsidiaries.

(5) At September 30, 1977, 555,684 shares of Common Stock were reserved for issuance upon exercise of stock options granted or to be granted under employee stock option plans. _____ shares of Common Stock will be reserved for issuance upon conversion of the Debentures offered hereby.

Item 6, Summary of Operations   Essentially, the Summary of Operations is a set of comparative income statements for the last five fiscal years of the registrant, together with appropriate *stub period* income statements for interim periods between the two most recent fiscal years and the dates of comparative balance sheets presented as part of Item 21 (see below) of the *Form S-1* registration statement. Extensive footnotes are required for various items in the Summary of Operations.

Item 21, Financial Statements   The basic financial statements included in a *Form S-1* registration statement are the following:

1 A consolidated balance sheet of the registrant and its subsidiaries at a date within 90 days prior to the date of filing the *Form S-1* registration statement, except that certain large registrants with a history of filings with the SEC under the 1934 Act may include a balance sheet at a date within six months prior to the filing. If the balance sheet described above is not audited, it must be accompanied by an audited balance sheet, in most cases at a date within one year of the date of filing the registration statement.

2 Consolidated income statements of the registrant and its subsidiaries for each of the three fiscal years preceding the date of the most recent balance sheet filed, and for any stub period. The income statements for the complete fiscal years must be audited. Typically, the income statements required by Item 21 are presented in Item 6, Summary of Operations.

3 Consolidated statements of retained earnings and other stockholders' equity for the same periods for which consolidated income statements are presented.

4 Consolidated statements of changes in financial position for the same periods for which consolidated income statements are presented.

In addition to the above, some registrants having subsidiaries must file unconsolidated financial statements for the same periods as the consolidated financial statements described above, and separate financial statements of subsidiaries not consolidated and investees accounted for by the equity method.

The principal schedule required by Item 21 of *Form S-1* registration statement is Schedule XVI, Supplementary Income Statement Information. Often, as permitted by *Regulation S-X,* Schedule XVI is filed as a note to the registrant's income statement. This technique is illustrated in the following note to financial statements filed with the SEC by Federal Express Corporation (amounts are in thousands):

11. Supplementary Income Statement Information

The following amounts were charged to costs and expenses:

	Year ended May 31			Six months ended November 30	
	1975	1976	1977	1976	1977
Maintenance and repairs	$6,402	$9,200	$13,563	$6,401	$7,119
Depreciation and amortization of property and equipment ..	4,603	4,996	5,411	2,695	2,940
Amortization of intangible assets	973	639	600	300	275
Taxes other than income taxes:					
Payroll	1,122	1,602	2,328	867	1,187
Other	532	429	616	370	410
Rents, including cost of leased aircraft	3,315	7,952	13,021	5,902	9,216
Advertising costs	1,055	1,452	2,734	1,689	2,460
Provision for bad debts	938	614	1,087	707	988

The provision for bad debts in the preceding note is not required by the instructions for Schedule XVI included in *Regulation S-X.* All other items presented in the note are required by *Regulation S-X* when the amounts exceed 1% of total revenue.

Items 5, 6, and 21 of the *Form S-1* registration statement are included in Part I, Information Required in Prospectus. Among the accounting presentations in Part II, Information Not Required in Prospectus, are the following:

1 Schedules, other than Schedule XVI, required by the applicable rule of *Regulation S-X.*
2 Historical financial information for a seven-year period, if the registrant does not have a history of filings with the SEC. Included in this requirement is information about revaluations of plant assets or intangible assets, restatements of the Capital Stock account, and write-offs of debt discount or issue costs.

The preceding discussion indicates that the filing of a registration statement with the SEC under the 1933 Act is a complex matter. In addition to provisions of the 1933 Act, *Regulation S-X, Staff Accounting Bulletins,* and *Form S-1,* the following SEC materials should be considered by accountants in a registration of securities:

1933 Act Release No. 4936 (as amended), "Guides for Preparation and Filing of Registration Statements"
General Rules and Regulations under the Securities Act of 1933
Regulation C under the Securities Act of 1933

Reporting to the SEC by publicly owned companies

Under the provisions of the 1934 Act, companies whose securities are listed on national securities exchanges must register the securities with the SEC and must make periodic reports to the SEC. Also subject to the registration and reporting requirements of the 1934 Act are companies with total assets over $1 million and 750 or more shareholders whose stock is traded interstate over the counter, and companies having 300 or more shareholders which registered securities under the 1933 Act, if they were not in the other two categories of companies subject to the 1934 Act. The purpose of the registration and reporting requirements of the 1934 Act is to keep the SEC, and thus the public, informed as to the current affairs of companies whose securities are bought and sold by the public.

Registration of Securities under the 1934 Act   The principal form for registration of securities listed on national securities exchanges or traded over the counter is *Form 10,* which closely resembles the *Form S-1* registration statement under the 1933 Act. A Summary of Operations (Item 2), financial statements and schedules (Item 18), and historical financial information are required by *Form 10* in a format similar to *Form S-1.*

Form 10-K Annual Report   A *Form 10-K* must be filed with the SEC within 90 days after the close of each fiscal year by companies subject to the periodic reporting requirements of the 1934 Act. Accounting data required in *Form 10-K* include a Summary of Operations (Item 2) and audited financial statements and schedules (Item 13) similar to those required for a *Form S-1* registration statement, but for the *last two fiscal years only.*

Form 10-Q Quarterly Report   As stated in Chapter 12, companies subject to the reporting requirements of the 1934 Act must file a *Form 10-Q* with the SEC 45 days after the end of each of the *first three quarters* of each fiscal year. Condensed, *unaudited* financial statements are presented in *Form 10-Q* as follows:

1 Balance sheets at the end of the current quarter and the comparable quarter of the preceding year
2 Income statements for the current quarter, for the fiscal year to date, and for the cumulative twelve-month period to date, for both the current year and the preceding year

3 Statements of changes in financial position for the current fiscal year to date, and for the comparable period of the preceding fiscal year

Detailed footnotes and schedules required by *Regulation S-X* do not apply to the unaudited financial statements included in *Form 10-Q.*

Form 8-K **Current Report**   Companies subject to the reporting requirements of the 1934 Act must file a *Form 8-K* with the SEC within 15 days of the occurrence of events such as the following:

1 Change in control of the reporting company
2 Acquisition or disposal of assets by the reporting company, including business combinations
3 Bankruptcy or receivership of the reporting company
4 Change of independent auditors for the reporting company

In addition, a company may choose to report to the SEC on *Form 8-K* any other event which it considers important to shareholders, within 10 days after the close of the month in which the event occurs.

If a business combination is reported on *Form 8-K,* financial statements of the combinee must be included, as follows:

1 A balance sheet at a date reasonably close to the date of the business combination. If that balance sheet is unaudited, an audited balance sheet at the close of the preceding fiscal year also is required
2 Audited income statements, statements of other stockholders' equity, and statements of changes in financial position for the past three fiscal years, and unaudited financial statements for the stub period

The financial statements of the combinee must meet the requirements of *Regulation S-X,* except that no schedules are filed.

Like the requirements for a *Form S-1* registration statement under the 1933 Act, the requirements for *Form 10, Form 10-K, Form 10-Q,* and *Form 8-K* are complex. In addition to the provisions of the 1934 Act, *Regulation S-X, Staff Accounting Bulletins,* and the respective *Forms,* accountants should consider the General Rules and Regulations under the Securities Exchange Act of 1934 issued by the SEC.

Rules for proxies and tender offers

Under provisions of the 1934 Act, the SEC has issued Regulation 14A to govern the solicitation of proxies from shareholders of companies subject to the 1934 Act, and Regulation 14D-1 to govern the making of *tender offers* (see Chapter 5, page 189) to shareholders of companies subject to the 1934 Act.

Regulation 14A   Before a proxy solicitation may be undertaken, a proxy statement must be furnished to the solicited shareholders, preceded or accompanied by an annual report if the solicitation is by management of the company. A *preliminary* proxy statement must be filed with the SEC for review and comment prior to distribution of the *definitive* proxy statement to the shareholders.

Information required in the proxy statement is described in Schedule 14A of Regulation 14A. Essentially, Schedule 14A requires "full and fair" disclosure of all matters to be voted on at the forthcoming meeting of shareholders whose proxies are solicited. If the shareholders are to vote on authorization or issuances of securities, modification or exchanges of securities, or business combinations, the proxy statement must include the same financial statements of the company which are required in a *Form 10* registration statement, and Schedule XVI. In addition, for proxy statements including a proposed business combination, comparable financial statements of the proposed combinee company must be included. The SEC may waive the requirement for financial statements "in appropriate circumstances."

Regulation 14D-1 Anyone (a person, group of persons, or corporation) making a tender offer to a company's shareholders for more than 5% of the company's outstanding shares of stock must file a statement with the SEC describing the tender offer. Information required in the statement is set forth in Schedule 14D of Regulation 14D-1. If the tender offer is made by a business enterprise, financial statements of the enterprise which would be required for a *Form 10* registration statement must be included in the tender offer statement or incorporated by reference to another SEC filing by the enterprise.

Recent developments in accounting and reporting for the SEC

A number of developments affecting SEC accounting and reporting have occurred recently. Committees of the United States Senate and House of Representatives have considered proposing legislation which would require the SEC to assume sole responsibility for the promulgation of generally accepted accounting principles. The SEC has initiated a series of public hearings to determine the extent, if any, to which its voluminous and complex reporting requirements have limited the ability of business enterprises, especially small companies, to issue securities to the public. The SEC has proposed a simplified *Form S-18* registration statement for public issuances of securities not exceeding $3 million.

Another significant recent development was the issuance late in 1977 of the *Report of the Advisory Committee on Corporate Disclosure.* This Committee was established by the SEC to consider the effectiveness of the United States corporate disclosure system and to make recommendations for improvement of the system. One of the recommendations of the Committee was that the SEC should establish a single disclosure form, *Form C-D,* to prescribe the content of registration statements, periodic reports, and proxy statements and tender-offer statements. Another recommendation was for the revision of *Regulation S-X* to eliminate requirements which differ from generally accepted accounting principles. Other recommendations of the Committee, such as encouragement of inclusion of financial forecasts and other "soft data" in filings with the SEC, have been acted upon by the Commission. Thus, significant changes in accounting and reporting for the SEC may be expected in future years.

REVIEW QUESTIONS

1 Identify the six United States statutes administered by the SEC.

2 What position did the SEC announce in *ASR No. 150* regarding its role in the establishment of accounting principles?

3 What are *Accounting Series Releases?*

4 Describe the requirements of *ASR No. 148,* " . . . Disclosure of Compensating Balances and Short-Term Borrowing Arrangements."

5 What information regarding replacement costs is required to be reported by *ASR No. 190,* ". . . Disclosure of Certain Replacement Cost Data"?

6 How do accountants use *Regulation S-X* in filings with the SEC?

7 Identify three *Forms* used in registering with the SEC securities to be issued under the provisions of the Securities Act of 1933.

8 "If the SEC permits a registration statement under the Securities Act of 1933 to become effective, the SEC has approved the issuance of the securities." Do you agree? Explain.

9 Define the term *stub period* in a Summary of Operations included in a *Form S-1* registration statement.

10 Is historical financial information required in every *Form S-1* registration statement filed with the SEC? Explain.

11 Identify the three classes of companies which are subject to the periodic reporting requirements of the Securities Exchange Act of 1934.

12 Differentiate between *Form 10-K* and *Form 8-K* filed with the SEC under the Securities Exchange Act of 1934.

13 Under what circumstances must financial statements of a company be included in a proxy statement issued to the company's shareholders under the provisions of the Securities Exchange Act of 1934?

14 What *tender offers* are regulated by the Securities Exchange Act of 1934?

15 What was the recommendation concerning *Regulation S-X* included in the *Report of the Advisory Committee on Corporate Disclosure* to the SEC?

EXERCISES

Ex. 18-1 Select the best answer for each of the following multiple-choice questions:

1 One of the major purposes of federal regulation of securities is to:

a Establish the qualifications for accountants who are members of the public accounting profession

b Eliminate incompetent attorneys and accountants who participate in the registration of securities to be offered to the public

c Provide a set of uniform standards and tests for accountants, attorneys, and others who practice before the SEC

d Provide sufficient information to investors who purchase securities

2 Under the Securities Act of 1933, subject to some exceptions and limitations, it is unlawful to use the mails or instruments of interstate commerce to sell or offer to sell a security to the public unless:

a A surety bond sufficient to cover potential liability to investors is obtained and filed with the SEC

b The offer is made through underwriters qualified to sell the securities on a nationwide basis

c A registration statement has been filed with the SEC and is in effect

d The SEC approves the financial merits of the offering

3 Under which of the following circumstances is a public offering of securities exempt from the registration requirements of the Securities Act of 1933?

a There was a prior registration within the past year

b The issuing corporation is a public utility subject to regulation by the Federal Power Commission

c The issuing corporation was closely held prior to the offering

d The issuing corporation and all prospective purchasers of the securities are located within one state, and the entire offering, sale, and distribution is made within that state

4 A company planning to register its securities for trading on a national securities exchange usually would file with the SEC a:

a *Form S-1* **b** *Form 10* **c** *Form 8-K* **d** Schedule 14A

5 In what filing with the SEC is it unnecessary to include supporting schedules required by *Regulation S-X?*

a *Form 10-Q* **b** *Form S-1* **c** *Form 10-K* **d** *Form 10*

6 The portion of a *Form S-1* registration statement which subsequently is provided to prospective purchasers of the registered securities is:

a Part II **b** The trust indenture **c** The prospectus **d** Some other portion

Ex. 18-2 During the year ended May 31, Year 6, Cargill Company had the following bank loans, none of which required compensating balances:

Date of note	Date due	Interest rate	Principal amount	Interest expense
June 16, Year 5	Sept. 14, Year 5	10%	$50,000	$1,250
Aug. 25, Year 5	Oct. 24, Year 5	10½%	30,000	525
Nov. 18, Year 5	Feb. 16, Year 6	11%	80,000	2,200
Jan. 6, Year 6	Apr. 6, Year 6	10¾%	40,000	1,075
Mar. 12, Year 6	June 10, Year 6	11¼%	50,000	1,250

There were no borrowings on commercial paper by Cargill.

Compute the following (as required by *ASR No. 148*) for a note to the May 31, Year 6, financial statements of Cargill Company filed with the SEC in *Form 10-K:*

a Weighted-average interest rate on short-term debt outstanding at May 31, Year 6.

b Maximum aggregate short-term debt outstanding at any month-end during the year ended May 31, Year 6.

c Average aggregate amount of short-term debt outstanding during the year ended May 31, Year 6, rounded to the nearest dollar.

d Weighted-average interest rate on short-term debt outstanding during the year ended May 31, Year 6, rounded to the nearest tenth.

Ex. 18-3 Randolph Company's journal entry for income taxes at September 30, Year 4, the end of its fiscal year, was as follows:

Income Taxes Expense ($37,312 + $12,100)	49,412	
Income Taxes Payable		49,412

To provide for income taxes for the year as follows:

	Federal	State
Pretax accounting income	$100,000	$100,000
Less: Nontaxable municipal bond interest	(10,000)	(10,000)
Add: Nondeductible goodwill amortization	4,000	4,000
Taxable income, state		$ 94,000
State tax at 15%		$ 14,100
Less: Investment tax credit		(2,000)
State income tax	(12,100)	$ 12,100
Taxable income, federal	$ 81,900	
Federal tax at 48%	$ 39,312	
Less: Investment tax credit	(2,000)	
Federal income tax........................	$ 37,312	

Prepare a reconciliation, in percentages rounded to the nearest tenth, between the statutory federal income tax rate (48%) and Randolph Company's effective income tax rate (49.4%, computed as $49,412 ÷ $100,000), required by **ASR No. 149** for a note to Randolph's September 30, Year 4, financial statements filed with the SEC in **Form 10-K**. Combine any reconciling items that individually are less than 5% of the statutory federal income tax rate. Use the format on page 707.

Ex. 18-4 The ledger accounts for plant assets of Mohawk Company had the following balances at the beginning and end of Year 5:

	Jan. 1, Year 5	Dec. 31, Year 5
Land	$150,000	$200,000
Building	800,000	800,000
Machinery and equipment	325,000	400,000

During Year 5, Mohawk purchased for $50,000 cash a parcel of real property adjoining its present land to provide space for constructing an addition to its building during Year 6. The net increase of $75,000 in the Machinery and Equipment account during Year 5 was composed of the following:

Additions at cost (none in excess of 2% of total assets)	$125,000
Retirements at cost	(20,000)
Write-down of idle machinery to net realizable value	(30,000)
Net increase in Machinery and Equipment account during Year 5.........	$ 75,000

Prepare a Schedule V, entitled Plant Assets, for Mohawk Company to include in its *Form 10-K* filed with the SEC for Year 5. Use the format on page 710.

Ex. 18-5 Included among the expense accounts of Unger Company for the year ended March 31, Year 2, were the following:

Advertising expense	$ 40,000
Amortization expense: goodwill	20,000
Amortization expense: leasehold improvements	25,000
Amortization expense: patents	15,000
Depreciation expense: buildings	40,000
Depreciation expense: machinery and equipment	30,000
Income taxes expense	125,000
Maintenance and repairs expense	45,000
Payroll taxes expense	50,000
Property taxes expense	40,000
Rent expense	65,000

Unger's total sales revenue for the year ended March 31, Year 2, was $1,400,000.

Prepare a Supplementary Income Statement Information note, in lieu of Schedule XVI, for Unger's March 31, Year 2, financial statements included in its *Form 10-K* filed with the SEC. Use the format on page 715.

SHORT CASES FOR ANALYSIS AND DECISION

Case 18-1 Edgewater Company, a land developer, purchased a large tract of land on which to construct a high-rise apartment complex. To finance the construction, Edgewater plans to offer for sale 100,000 shares of its common stock to about 1,000 prospective investors located throughout the United States at $50 per share.

Instructions
a Discuss the implications of the Securities Act of 1933 for Edgewater's offer to sell shares of its common stock.
b The Securities Act of 1933 is considered a disclosure statute. Describe the means provided and the principal types of information required to accomplish this objective of disclosure.

Case 18-2 Wasatch Company, a closely held corporation which has been your audit client for many years, is considering "going public" by offering 150,000 shares of its common stock for interstate sale to the public at $10 per share. After the public offering, Wasatch expects to have between 350 and 450 shareholders. The company has no present plans to register its securities for trading on a national securities exchange. Harry Wasatch, the president of Wasatch Company, asks you to write a memorandum describing the company's responsibilities for reporting to the SEC if it decides to complete the public offering of its common stock.

Instructions Write the memorandum requested by the president of Wasatch Company.

Case 18-3 Among the recommendations to the SEC made by the *Advisory Committee on Corporate Disclosure* were the following:
(1) The SEC should develop disclosure guides for specific industries to encourage uniform textual and financial statement disclosures of material items which are unique to a particular industry.

(2) The SEC should develop on an industry basis the most effective product-line breakdown for displaying sales information.

Instructions   Assume that you are a member of the SEC staff. Write a response to the two recommendations made by the *Advisory Committee on Corporate Disclosure.*

APPENDIX

COMPOUND INTEREST TABLES

	Page
Table 1: Future Amount of $1, $a_{\overline{n}|i} = (1 + i)^n$	726
Table 2: Present Value of $1, $p_{\overline{n}|i} = \dfrac{1}{(1 + i)^n}$	729
Table 3: Future Amount of an Ordinary Annuity of $1, $A_{\overline{n}|i} = \dfrac{(1 + i)^n - 1}{i}$	732
Table 4: Present Value of an Ordinary Annuity of $1, $P_{\overline{n}|i} = \dfrac{1 - \dfrac{1}{(1 + i)^n}}{i}$	735

Table 1 Future Amount of $1 at Compound Interest Due in n Periods: $a_{\overline{n}|i} = (1 + i)^n$

n	$\frac{1}{2}\%$	1%	$1\frac{1}{2}\%$	2%	$2\frac{1}{2}\%$	3%
1	1.005000	1.010000	1.015000	1.020000	1.025000	1.030000
2	1.010025	1.020100	1.030225	1.040400	1.050625	1.060900
3	1.015075	1.030301	1.045678	1.061208	1.076891	1.092727
4	1.020151	1.040604	1.061364	1.082432	1.103813	1.125509
5	1.025251	1.051010	1.077284	1.104081	1.131408	1.159274
6	1.030378	1.061520	1.093443	1.126162	1.159693	1.194052
7	1.035529	1.072135	1.109845	1.148686	1.188686	1.229874
8	1.040707	1.082857	1.126493	1.171659	1.218403	1.266770
9	1.045911	1.093685	1.143390	1.195093	1.248863	1.304773
10	1.051140	1.104622	1.160541	1.218994	1.280085	1.343916
11	1.056396	1.115668	1.177949	1.243374	1.312087	1.384234
12	1.061678	1.126825	1.195618	1.268242	1.344889	1.425761
13	1.066986	1.138093	1.213552	1.293607	1.378511	1.468534
14	1.072321	1.149474	1.231756	1.319479	1.412974	1.512590
15	1.077683	1.160969	1.250232	1.345868	1.448298	1.557967
16	1.083071	1.172579	1.268986	1.372786	1.484506	1.604706
17	1.088487	1.184304	1.288020	1.400241	1.521618	1.652848
18	1.093929	1.196147	1.307341	1.428246	1.559659	1.702433
19	1.099399	1.208109	1.326951	1.456811	1.598650	1.753506
20	1.104896	1.220190	1.346855	1.485947	1.638616	1.806111
21	1.110420	1.232392	1.367058	1.515666	1.679582	1.860295
22	1.115972	1.244716	1.387564	1.545980	1.721571	1.916103
23	1.121552	1.257163	1.408377	1.576899	1.764611	1.973587
24	1.127160	1.269735	1.429503	1.608437	1.808726	2.032794
25	1.132796	1.282432	1.450945	1.640606	1.853944	2.093778
26	1.138460	1.295256	1.472710	1.673418	1.900293	2.156591
27	1.144152	1.308209	1.494800	1.706886	1.947800	2.221289
28	1.149873	1.321291	1.517222	1.741024	1.996495	2.287928
29	1.155622	1.334504	1.539981	1.775845	2.046407	2.356566
30	1.161400	1.347849	1.563080	1.811362	2.097568	2.427262
31	1.167207	1.361327	1.586526	1.847589	2.150007	2.500080
32	1.173043	1.374941	1.610324	1.884541	2.203757	2.575083
33	1.178908	1.388690	1.634477	1.922231	2.258851	2.652335
34	1.184803	1.402577	1.658996	1.960676	2.315322	2.731905
35	1.190727	1.416603	1.683881	1.999890	2.373205	2.813862
36	1.196681	1.430769	1.709140	2.039887	2.432535	2.898278
37	1.202664	1.445076	1.734777	2.080685	2.493349	2.985227
38	1.208677	1.459527	1.760798	2.122299	2.555682	3.074783
39	1.214721	1.474123	1.787210	2.164745	2.619574	3.167027
40	1.220794	1.488864	1.814018	2.208040	2.685064	3.262038
41	1.226898	1.503752	1.841229	2.252200	2.752190	3.359899
42	1.233033	1.518790	1.868847	2.297244	2.820995	3.460696
43	1.239198	1.533978	1.896880	2.343189	2.891520	3.564517
44	1.245394	1.549318	1.925333	2.390053	2.963808	3.671452
45	1.251621	1.564811	1.954213	2.437854	3.037903	3.781596
46	1.257879	1.580459	1.983526	2.486611	3.113851	3.895044
47	1.264168	1.596263	2.013279	2.536344	3.191697	4.011895
48	1.270489	1.612226	2.043478	2.587070	3.271490	4.132252
49	1.276842	1.628348	2.074130	2.638812	3.353277	4.256219
50	1.283226	1.644632	2.105242	2.691588	3.437109	4.383906

TABLE 1 727

Table 1 Future Amount of $1 (*continued*)

n \ i	3½%	4%	4½%	5%	5½%	6%
1	1.035000	1.040000	1.045000	1.050000	1.055000	1.060000
2	1.071225	1.081600	1.092025	1.102500	1.113025	1.123600
3	1.108718	1.124864	1.141166	1.157625	1.174241	1.191016
4	1.147523	1.169859	1.192519	1.215506	1.238825	1.262477
5	1.187686	1.216653	1.246182	1.276282	1.306960	1.338226
6	1.229255	1.265319	1.302260	1.340096	1.378843	1.418519
7	1.272279	1.315932	1.360862	1.407100	1.454679	1.503630
8	1.316809	1.368569	1.422101	1.477455	1.534687	1.593848
9	1.362897	1.423312	1.486095	1.551328	1.619094	1.689479
10	1.410599	1.480244	1.552969	1.628895	1.708144	1.790848
11	1.459970	1.539454	1.622853	1.710339	1.802092	1.898299
12	1.511069	1.601032	1.695881	1.795856	1.901207	2.012196
13	1.563956	1.665074	1.772196	1.885649	2.005774	2.132928
14	1.618695	1.731676	1.851945	1.979932	2.116091	2.260904
15	1.675349	1.800944	1.935282	2.078928	2.232476	2.396558
16	1.733986	1.872981	2.022370	2.182875	2.355263	2.540352
17	1.794676	1.947901	2.113377	2.292018	2.484802	2.692773
18	1.857489	2.025817	2.208479	2.406619	2.621466	2.854339
19	1.922501	2.106849	2.307860	2.526950	2.765647	3.025600
20	1.989789	2.191123	2.411714	2.653298	2.917757	3.207135
21	2.059431	2.278768	2.520241	2.785963	3.078234	3.399564
22	2.131512	2.369919	2.633652	2.925261	3.247537	3.603537
23	2.206114	2.464716	2.752166	3.071524	3.426152	3.819750
24	2.283328	2.563304	2.876014	3.225100	3.614590	4.048935
25	2.363245	2.665836	3.005434	3.386355	3.813392	4.291871
26	2.445959	2.772470	3.140679	3.555673	4.023129	4.549383
27	2.531567	2.883369	3.282010	3.733456	4.244401	4.822346
28	2.620172	2.998703	3.429700	3.920129	4.477843	5.111687
29	2.711878	3.118651	3.584036	4.116136	4.724124	5.418388
30	2.806794	3.243398	3.745318	4.321942	4.983951	5.743491
31	2.905031	3.373133	3.913857	4.538039	5.258069	6.088101
32	3.006708	3.508059	4.089981	4.764941	5.547262	6.453387
33	3.111942	3.648381	4.274030	5.003189	5.852362	6.840590
34	3.220860	3.794316	4.466362	5.253348	6.174242	7.251025
35	3.333590	3.946089	4.667348	5.516015	6.513825	7.686087
36	3.450266	4.103933	4.877378	5.791816	6.872085	8.147252
37	3.571025	4.268090	5.096860	6.081407	7.250050	8.636087
38	3.696011	4.438813	5.326219	6.385477	7.648803	9.154252
39	3.825372	4.616366	5.565899	6.704751	8.069487	9.703507
40	3.959260	4.801021	5.816365	7.039989	8.513309	10.285718
41	4.097834	4.993061	6.078101	7.391988	8.981541	10.902861
42	4.241258	5.192784	6.351615	7.761588	9.475526	11.557033
43	4.389702	5.400495	6.637438	8.149667	9.996679	12.250455
44	4.543342	5.616515	6.936123	8.557150	10.546497	12.985482
45	4.702359	5.841176	7.248248	8.985008	11.126554	13.764611
46	4.866941	6.074823	7.574420	9.434258	11.738515	14.590487
47	5.037284	6.317816	7.915268	9.905971	12.384133	15.465917
48	5.213589	6.570528	8.271456	10.401270	13.065260	16.393872
49	5.396065	6.833349	8.643671	10.921333	13.783849	17.377504
50	5.584927	7.106683	9.032636	11.467400	14.541961	18.420154

Table 1 Future Amount of $1 (*continued*)

n \ i	7%	8%	9%	10%	12%	15%
1	1.070000	1.080000	1.090000	1.100000	1.120000	1.150000
2	1.144900	1.166400	1.188100	1.210000	1.254400	1.322500
3	1.225043	1.259712	1.295029	1.331000	1.404928	1.520875
4	1.310796	1.360489	1.411582	1.464100	1.573519	1.749006
5	1.402552	1.469328	1.538624	1.610510	1.762342	2.011357
6	1.500730	1.586874	1.677100	1.771561	1.973823	2.313061
7	1.605781	1.713824	1.828039	1.948717	2.210681	2.660020
8	1.718186	1.850930	1.992563	2.143589	2.475963	3.059023
9	1.838459	1.999005	2.171893	2.357948	2.773079	3.517876
10	1.967151	2.158925	2.367364	2.593742	3.105848	4.045558
11	2.104852	2.331639	2.580426	2.853117	3.478550	4.652391
12	2.252192	2.518170	2.812665	3.138428	3.895976	5.350250
13	2.409845	2.719624	3.065805	3.452271	4.363493	6.152788
14	2.578534	2.937194	3.341727	3.797498	4.887112	7.075706
15	2.759032	3.172169	3.642482	4.177248	5.473566	8.137062
16	2.952164	3.425943	3.970306	4.594973	6.130394	9.357621
17	3.158815	3.700018	4.327633	5.054470	6.866041	10.761264
18	3.379932	3.996019	4.717120	5.559917	7.689966	12.375454
19	3.616528	4.315701	5.141661	6.115909	8.612762	14.231772
20	3.869684	4.660957	5.604411	6.727500	9.646293	16.366537
21	4.140562	5.033834	6.108808	7.400250	10.803848	18.821518
22	4.430402	5.436540	6.658600	8.140275	12.100310	21.644746
23	4.740530	5.871464	7.257874	8.954302	13.552347	24.891458
24	5.072367	6.341181	7.911083	9.849733	15.178629	28.625176
25	5.427433	6.848475	8.623081	10.834706	17.000064	32.918953
26	5.807353	7.396353	9.399158	11.918177	19.040072	37.856796
27	6.213868	7.988061	10.245082	13.109994	21.324881	43.535315
28	6.648838	8.627106	11.167140	14.420994	23.883866	50.065612
29	7.114257	9.317275	12.172182	15.863093	26.749930	57.575454
30	7.612255	10.062657	13.267678	17.449402	29.959922	66.211772
31	8.145113	10.867669	14.461770	19.194342	33.555113	76.143538
32	8.715271	11.737083	15.763329	21.113777	37.581726	87.565068
33	9.325340	12.676050	17.182028	23.225154	42.091533	100.699829
34	9.978114	13.690134	18.728411	25.547670	47.142517	115.804803
35	10.676581	14.785344	20.413968	28.102437	52.799620	133.175523
36	11.423942	15.968172	22.251225	30.912681	59.135574	153.151852
37	12.223618	17.245626	24.253835	34.003949	66.231843	176.124630
38	13.079271	18.625276	26.436680	37.404343	74.179664	202.543324
39	13.994820	20.115298	28.815982	41.144778	83.081224	232.924823
40	14.974458	21.724521	31.409420	45.259256	93.050970	267.863546
41	16.022670	23.462483	34.236268	49.785181	104.217087	308.043078
42	17.144257	25.339482	37.317532	54.763699	116.723137	354.249540
43	18.344355	27.366640	40.676110	60.240069	130.729914	407.386971
44	19.628460	29.555972	44.336960	66.264076	146.417503	468.495017
45	21.002452	31.920449	48.327286	72.890484	163.987604	538.769269
46	22.472623	34.474085	52.676742	80.179532	183.666116	619.584659
47	24.045707	37.232012	57.417649	88.197485	205.706050	712.522358
48	25.728907	40.210573	62.585237	97.017234	230.390776	819.400712
49	27.529930	43.427419	68.217908	106.718957	258.037669	942.310819
50	29.457025	46.901613	74.357520	117.390853	289.002190	1083.657442

TABLE 2   729

Table 2   Present Value of \$1 at Compound Interest Due in _n_ Periods: $p_{\overline{n}|i} = \dfrac{1}{(1 + i)^n}$

n \ i	½%	1%	1½%	2%	2½%	3%
1	0.995025	0.990099	0.985222	0.980392	0.975610	0.970874
2	0.990075	0.980296	0.970662	0.961169	0.951814	0.942596
3	0.985149	0.970590	0.956317	0.942322	0.928599	0.915142
4	0.980248	0.960980	0.942184	0.923845	0.905951	0.888487
5	0.975371	0.951466	0.928260	0.905731	0.883854	0.862609
6	0.970518	0.942045	0.914542	0.887971	0.862297	0.837484
7	0.965690	0.932718	0.901027	0.870560	0.841265	0.813092
8	0.960885	0.923483	0.887711	0.853490	0.820747	0.789409
9	0.956105	0.914340	0.874592	0.836755	0.800728	0.766417
10	0.951348	0.905287	0.861667	0.820348	0.781198	0.744094
11	0.946615	0.896324	0.848933	0.804263	0.762145	0.722421
12	0.941905	0.887449	0.836387	0.788493	0.743556	0.701380
13	0.937219	0.878663	0.824027	0.773033	0.725420	0.680951
14	0.932556	0.869963	0.811849	0.757875	0.707727	0.661118
15	0.927917	0.861349	0.799852	0.743015	0.690466	0.641862
16	0.923300	0.852821	0.788031	0.728446	0.673625	0.623167
17	0.918707	0.844377	0.776385	0.714163	0.657195	0.605016
18	0.914136	0.836017	0.764912	0.700159	0.641166	0.587395
19	0.909588	0.827740	0.753607	0.686431	0.625528	0.570286
20	0.905063	0.819544	0.742470	0.672971	0.610271	0.553676
21	0.900560	0.811430	0.731498	0.659776	0.595386	0.537549
22	0.896080	0.803396	0.720688	0.646839	0.580865	0.521893
23	0.891622	0.795442	0.710037	0.634156	0.566697	0.506692
24	0.887186	0.787566	0.699544	0.621721	0.552875	0.491934
25	0.882772	0.779768	0.689206	0.609531	0.539391	0.477606
26	0.878380	0.772048	0.679021	0.597579	0.526235	0.463695
27	0.874010	0.764404	0.668986	0.585862	0.513400	0.450189
28	0.869662	0.756836	0.659099	0.574375	0.500878	0.437077
29	0.865335	0.749342	0.649359	0.563112	0.488661	0.424346
30	0.861030	0.741923	0.639762	0.552071	0.476743	0.411987
31	0.856746	0.734577	0.630308	0.541246	0.465115	0.399987
32	0.852484	0.727304	0.620993	0.530633	0.453771	0.388337
33	0.848242	0.720103	0.611816	0.520229	0.442703	0.377026
34	0.844022	0.712973	0.602774	0.510028	0.431905	0.366045
35	0.839823	0.705914	0.593866	0.500028	0.421371	0.355383
36	0.835645	0.698925	0.585090	0.490223	0.411094	0.345032
37	0.831487	0.692005	0.576443	0.480611	0.401067	0.334983
38	0.827351	0.685153	0.567924	0.471187	0.391285	0.325226
39	0.823235	0.678370	0.559531	0.461948	0.381741	0.315754
40	0.819139	0.671653	0.551262	0.452890	0.372431	0.306557
41	0.815064	0.665003	0.543116	0.444010	0.363347	0.297628
42	0.811009	0.658419	0.535089	0.435304	0.354485	0.288959
43	0.806974	0.651900	0.527182	0.426769	0.345839	0.280543
44	0.802959	0.645445	0.519391	0.418401	0.337404	0.272372
45	0.798964	0.639055	0.511715	0.410197	0.329174	0.264439
46	0.794989	0.632728	0.504153	0.402154	0.321146	0.256737
47	0.791034	0.626463	0.496702	0.394268	0.313313	0.249259
48	0.787098	0.620260	0.489362	0.386538	0.305671	0.241999
49	0.783183	0.614119	0.482130	0.378958	0.298216	0.234950
50	0.779286	0.608039	0.475005	0.371528	0.290942	0.228107

Table 2 Present Value of $1 (_continued_)

n \ i	3½%	4%	4½%	5%	5½%	6%
1	0.966184	0.961538	0.956938	0.952381	0.947867	0.943396
2	0.933511	0.924556	0.915730	0.907029	0.898452	0.889996
3	0.901943	0.888996	0.876297	0.863838	0.851614	0.839619
4	0.871442	0.854804	0.838561	0.822702	0.807217	0.792094
5	0.841973	0.821927	0.802451	0.783526	0.765134	0.747258
6	0.813501	0.790315	0.767896	0.746215	0.725246	0.704961
7	0.785991	0.759918	0.734828	0.710681	0.687437	0.665057
8	0.759412	0.730690	0.703185	0.676839	0.651599	0.627412
9	0.733731	0.702587	0.672904	0.644609	0.617629	0.591898
10	0.708919	0.675564	0.643928	0.613913	0.585431	0.558395
11	0.684946	0.649581	0.616199	0.584679	0.554911	0.526788
12	0.661783	0.624597	0.589664	0.556837	0.525982	0.496969
13	0.639404	0.600574	0.564272	0.530321	0.498561	0.468839
14	0.617782	0.577475	0.539973	0.505068	0.472569	0.442301
15	0.596891	0.555265	0.516720	0.481017	0.447933	0.417265
16	0.576706	0.533908	0.494469	0.458112	0.424581	0.393646
17	0.557204	0.513373	0.473176	0.436297	0.402447	0.371364
18	0.538361	0.493628	0.452800	0.415521	0.381466	0.350344
19	0.520156	0.474642	0.433302	0.395734	0.361579	0.330513
20	0.502566	0.456387	0.414643	0.376889	0.342729	0.311805
21	0.485571	0.438834	0.396787	0.358942	0.324862	0.294155
22	0.469151	0.421955	0.379701	0.341850	0.307926	0.277505
23	0.453286	0.405726	0.363350	0.325571	0.291873	0.261797
24	0.437957	0.390121	0.347703	0.310068	0.276657	0.246979
25	0.423147	0.375117	0.332731	0.295303	0.262234	0.232999
26	0.408838	0.360689	0.318402	0.281241	0.248563	0.219810
27	0.395012	0.346817	0.304691	0.267848	0.235605	0.207368
28	0.381654	0.333477	0.291571	0.255094	0.223322	0.195630
29	0.368748	0.320651	0.279015	0.242946	0.211679	0.184557
30	0.356278	0.308319	0.267000	0.231377	0.200644	0.174110
31	0.344230	0.296460	0.255502	0.220359	0.190184	0.164255
32	0.332590	0.285058	0.244500	0.209866	0.180269	0.154957
33	0.321343	0.274094	0.233971	0.199873	0.170871	0.146186
34	0.310476	0.263552	0.223896	0.190355	0.161963	0.137912
35	0.299977	0.253415	0.214254	0.181290	0.153520	0.130105
36	0.289833	0.243669	0.205028	0.172657	0.145516	0.122741
37	0.280032	0.234297	0.196199	0.164436	0.137930	0.115793
38	0.270562	0.225285	0.187750	0.156605	0.130739	0.109239
39	0.261413	0.216621	0.179665	0.149148	0.123924	0.103056
40	0.252572	0.208289	0.171929	0.142046	0.117463	0.097222
41	0.244031	0.200278	0.164525	0.135282	0.111339	0.091719
42	0.235779	0.192575	0.157440	0.128840	0.105535	0.086527
43	0.227806	0.185168	0.150661	0.122704	0.100033	0.081630
44	0.220102	0.178046	0.144173	0.116861	0.094818	0.077009
45	0.212659	0.171198	0.137964	0.111297	0.089875	0.072650
46	0.205468	0.164614	0.132023	0.105997	0.085190	0.068538
47	0.198520	0.158283	0.126338	0.100949	0.080748	0.064658
48	0.191806	0.152195	0.120898	0.096142	0.076539	0.060998
49	0.185320	0.146341	0.115692	0.091564	0.072549	0.057546
50	0.179053	0.140713	0.110710	0.087204	0.068767	0.054288

TABLE 2 731

Table 2 Present Value of $1 (*continued*)

n \ i	7%	8%	9%	10%	12%	15%
1	0.934580	0.925926	0.917431	0.909091	0.892857	0.869565
2	0.873439	0.857339	0.841680	0.826446	0.797194	0.756144
3	0.816298	0.793832	0.772183	0.751315	0.711780	0.657516
4	0.762895	0.735030	0.708425	0.683013	0.635518	0.571753
5	0.712986	0.680583	0.649931	0.620921	0.567427	0.497177
6	0.666342	0.630170	0.596267	0.564474	0.506631	0.432328
7	0.622750	0.583490	0.547034	0.513158	0.452349	0.375937
8	0.582009	0.540269	0.501866	0.466507	0.403883	0.326902
9	0.543934	0.500249	0.460428	0.424098	0.360610	0.284262
10	0.508349	0.463193	0.422411	0.385543	0.321973	0.247185
11	0.475093	0.428883	0.387533	0.350494	0.287476	0.214943
12	0.444012	0.397114	0.355535	0.318631	0.256675	0.186907
13	0.414964	0.367698	0.326179	0.289664	0.229174	0.162528
14	0.387817	0.340461	0.299246	0.263331	0.204620	0.141329
15	0.362446	0.315242	0.274538	0.239392	0.182696	0.122894
16	0.338735	0.291890	0.251870	0.217629	0.163122	0.106865
17	0.316574	0.270269	0.231073	0.197845	0.145644	0.092926
18	0.295864	0.250249	0.211994	0.179859	0.130040	0.080805
19	0.276508	0.231712	0.194490	0.163508	0.116107	0.070265
20	0.258419	0.214548	0.178431	0.148644	0.103667	0.061100
21	0.241513	0.198656	0.163698	0.135131	0.092560	0.053131
22	0.225713	0.183941	0.150182	0.122846	0.082643	0.046201
23	0.210947	0.170315	0.137781	0.111678	0.073788	0.040174
24	0.197147	0.157699	0.126405	0.101526	0.065882	0.034934
25	0.184249	0.146018	0.115968	0.092296	0.058823	0.030378
26	0.172195	0.135202	0.106393	0.083905	0.052521	0.026415
27	0.160930	0.125187	0.097608	0.076278	0.046894	0.022970
28	0.150402	0.115914	0.089548	0.069343	0.041869	0.019974
29	0.140563	0.107328	0.082155	0.063039	0.037383	0.017369
30	0.131367	0.099377	0.075371	0.057309	0.033378	0.015103
31	0.122773	0.092016	0.069148	0.052099	0.029802	0.013133
32	0.114741	0.085200	0.063438	0.047362	0.026609	0.011420
33	0.107235	0.078889	0.058200	0.043057	0.023758	0.009931
34	0.100219	0.073045	0.053395	0.039143	0.021212	0.008635
35	0.093663	0.067635	0.048986	0.035584	0.018940	0.007509
36	0.087535	0.062625	0.044941	0.032349	0.016910	0.006529
37	0.081809	0.057986	0.041231	0.029408	0.015098	0.005678
38	0.076457	0.053690	0.037826	0.026735	0.013481	0.004937
39	0.071455	0.049713	0.034703	0.024304	0.012036	0.004293
40	0.066780	0.046031	0.031838	0.022095	0.010747	0.003733
41	0.062412	0.042621	0.029209	0.020086	0.009595	0.003246
42	0.058329	0.039464	0.026797	0.018260	0.008567	0.002823
43	0.054513	0.036541	0.024584	0.016600	0.007649	0.002455
44	0.050946	0.033834	0.022555	0.015091	0.006830	0.002134
45	0.047613	0.031328	0.020692	0.013719	0.006098	0.001856
46	0.044499	0.029007	0.018984	0.012472	0.005445	0.001614
47	0.041587	0.026859	0.017416	0.011338	0.004861	0.001403
48	0.038867	0.024869	0.015978	0.010307	0.004340	0.001220
49	0.036324	0.023027	0.014659	0.009370	0.003875	0.001061
50	0.033948	0.021321	0.013449	0.008519	0.003460	0.000923

Table 3 Future Amount of an Ordinary Annuity of \$1 per Period: $A_{\overline{n}|i} = \dfrac{(1 + i)^n - 1}{i}$

n \ i	$\frac{1}{2}$%	1%	$1\frac{1}{2}$%	2%	$2\frac{1}{2}$%	3%
1	1.000000	1.000000	1.000000	1.000000	1.000000	1.000000
2	2.005000	2.010000	2.015000	2.020000	2.025000	2.030000
3	3.015025	3.030100	3.045225	3.060400	3.075625	3.090900
4	4.030100	4.060401	4.090903	4.121608	4.152516	4.183627
5	5.050251	5.101005	5.152267	5.204040	5.256329	5.309136
6	6.075502	6.152015	6.229551	6.308121	6.387737	6.468410
7	7.105879	7.213535	7.322994	7.434283	7.547430	7.662462
8	8.141409	8.285671	8.432839	8.582969	8.736116	8.892336
9	9.182116	9.368527	9.559332	9.754628	9.954519	10.159106
10	10.228026	10.462213	10.702722	10.949721	11.203382	11.463879
11	11.279167	11.566835	11.863262	12.168715	12.483466	12.807796
12	12.335562	12.682503	13.041211	13.412090	13.795553	14.192030
13	13.397240	13.809328	14.236830	14.680332	15.140442	15.617790
14	14.464226	14.947421	15.450382	15.973938	16.518953	17.086324
15	15.536548	16.096896	16.682138	17.293417	17.931927	18.598914
16	16.614230	17.257864	17.932370	18.639285	19.380225	20.156881
17	17.697301	18.430443	19.201355	20.012071	20.864730	21.761588
18	18.785788	19.614748	20.489376	21.412312	22.386349	23.414435
19	19.879717	20.810895	21.796716	22.840559	23.946007	25.116868
20	20.979115	22.019004	23.123667	24.297370	25.544658	26.870374
21	22.084011	23.239194	24.470522	25.783317	27.183274	28.676486
22	23.194431	24.471586	25.837580	27.298984	28.862856	30.536780
23	24.310403	25.716302	27.225144	28.844963	30.584427	32.452884
24	25.431955	26.973465	28.633521	30.421862	32.349038	34.426470
25	26.559115	28.243200	30.063024	32.030300	34.157764	36.459264
26	27.691911	29.525632	31.513969	33.670906	36.011708	38.553042
27	28.830370	30.820888	32.986679	35.344324	37.912001	40.709634
28	29.974522	32.129097	34.481479	37.051210	39.859801	42.930923
29	31.124395	33.450388	35.998701	38.792235	41.856296	45.218850
30	32.280017	34.784892	37.538681	40.568079	43.902703	47.575416
31	33.441417	36.132740	39.101762	42.379441	46.000271	50.002678
32	34.608624	37.494068	40.688288	44.227030	48.150278	52.502759
33	35.781667	38.869009	42.298612	46.111570	50.354034	55.077841
34	36.960575	40.257699	43.933092	48.033802	52.612885	57.730177
35	38.145378	41.660276	45.592088	49.994478	54.928207	60.462082
36	39.336105	43.076878	47.275969	51.994367	57.301413	63.275944
37	40.532785	44.507647	48.985109	54.034255	59.733948	66.174223
38	41.735449	45.952724	50.719885	56.114940	62.227297	69.159449
39	42.944127	47.412251	52.480684	58.237238	64.782979	72.234233
40	44.158847	48.886373	54.267894	60.401983	67.402554	75.401260
41	45.379642	50.375237	56.081912	62.610023	70.087617	78.663298
42	46.606540	51.878989	57.923141	64.862223	72.839808	82.023196
43	47.839572	53.397779	59.791988	67.159468	75.660803	85.483892
44	49.078770	54.931757	61.688868	69.502657	78.552323	89.048409
45	50.324164	56.481075	63.614201	71.892710	81.516131	92.719861
46	51.575785	58.045885	65.568414	74.330564	84.554034	96.501457
47	52.833664	59.626344	67.551940	76.817176	87.667885	100.396501
48	54.097832	61.222608	69.565219	79.353519	90.859582	104.408396
49	55.368321	62.834834	71.608698	81.940590	94.131072	108.540648
50	56.645163	64.463182	73.682828	84.579401	97.484349	112.796867

TABLE 3 733

Table 3 Future Amount of an Ordinary Annuity of $1 (*continued*)

n \ i	3½%	4%	4½%	5%	5½%	6%
1	1.000000	1.000000	1.000000	1.000000	1.000000	1.000000
2	2.035000	2.040000	2.045000	2.050000	2.055000	2.060000
3	3.106225	3.121600	3.137025	3.152500	3.168025	3.183600
4	4.214943	4.246464	4.278191	4.310125	4.342266	4.374616
5	5.362466	5.416323	5.470710	5.525631	5.581091	5.637093
6	6.550152	6.632975	6.716892	6.801913	6.888051	6.975319
7	7.779408	7.898294	8.019152	8.142008	8.266894	8.393838
8	9.051687	9.214226	9.380014	9.549109	9.721573	9.897468
9	10.368496	10.582795	10.802114	11.026564	11.256260	11.491316
10	11.731393	12.006107	12.288209	12.577893	12.875354	13.180795
11	13.141992	13.486351	13.841179	14.206787	14.583498	14.971643
12	14.601962	15.025805	15.464032	15.917127	16.385591	16.869941
13	16.113030	16.626838	17.159913	17.712983	18.286798	18.882138
14	17.676986	18.291911	18.932109	19.598632	20.292572	21.015066
15	19.295681	20.023588	20.784054	21.578564	22.408664	23.275970
16	20.971030	21.824531	22.719337	23.657492	24.641140	25.672528
17	22.705016	23.697512	24.741707	25.840366	26.996403	28.212880
18	24.499691	25.645413	26.855084	28.132385	29.481205	30.905653
19	26.357181	27.671229	29.063562	30.539004	32.102671	33.759992
20	28.279682	29.778079	31.371423	33.065954	34.868318	36.785591
21	30.269471	31.969202	33.783137	35.719252	37.786076	39.992727
22	32.328902	34.247970	36.303378	38.505214	40.864310	43.392290
23	34.460414	36.617889	38.937030	41.430475	44.111847	46.995828
24	36.666528	39.082604	41.689196	44.501999	47.537998	50.815577
25	38.949857	41.645908	44.565210	47.727099	51.152588	54.864512
26	41.313102	44.311745	47.570645	51.113454	54.965981	59.156383
27	43.759060	47.084214	50.711324	54.669126	58.989109	63.705766
28	46.290627	49.967583	53.993333	58.402583	63.233510	68.528112
29	48.910799	52.966286	57.423033	62.322712	67.711354	73.629798
30	51.622677	56.084938	61.007070	66.438848	72.435478	79.058186
31	54.429471	59.328335	64.752388	70.760790	77.419429	84.801677
32	57.334502	62.701469	68.666245	75.298829	82.677498	90.889778
33	60.341210	66.209527	72.756226	80.063771	88.224760	97.343165
34	63.453152	69.857909	77.030256	85.066959	94.077122	104.183755
35	66.674013	73.652225	81.496618	90.320307	100.251364	111.434780
36	70.007603	77.598314	86.163966	95.836323	106.765189	119.120867
37	73.457869	81.702246	91.041344	101.628139	113.637274	127.268119
38	77.028895	85.970336	96.138205	107.709546	120.887324	135.904206
39	80.724906	90.409150	101.464424	114.095023	128.536127	145.058458
40	84.550278	95.025516	107.030323	120.799774	136.605614	154.761966
41	88.509537	99.826536	112.846688	127.839763	145.118923	165.047684
42	92.607371	104.819598	118.924789	135.231751	154.100464	175.950545
43	96.848629	110.012382	125.276404	142.993339	163.575989	187.507577
44	101.238331	115.412877	131.913842	151.143006	173.572669	199.758032
45	105.781673	121.029392	138.849965	159.700156	184.119165	212.743514
46	110.484031	126.870568	146.098214	168.685164	195.245719	226.508125
47	115.350973	132.945390	153.672633	178.119422	206.984234	241.098612
48	120.388257	139.263206	161.587902	188.025393	219.368367	256.564529
49	125.601846	145.833734	169.859357	198.426663	232.433627	272.958401
50	130.997910	152.667084	178.503028	209.347996	246.217476	290.335905

Table 3 Future Amount of an Ordinary Annuity of $1 (*continued*)

n \ i	7%	8%	9%	10%	12%	15%
1	1.000000	1.000000	1.000000	1.000000	1.000000	1.000000
2	2.070000	2.080000	2.090000	2.100000	2.120000	2.150000
3	3.214900	3.246400	3.278100	3.310000	3.374400	3.472500
4	4.439943	4.506112	4.573129	4.641000	4.779328	4.993375
5	5.750740	5.866601	5.984711	6.105100	6.352847	6.742381
6	7.153291	7.335929	7.523335	7.715610	8.115189	8.753738
7	8.654021	8.922803	9.200435	9.487171	10.089012	11.066799
8	10.259803	10.636628	11.028474	11.435888	12.299693	13.726819
9	11.977989	12.487558	13.021036	13.579477	14.775656	16.785842
10	13.816448	14.486562	15.192930	15.937425	17.548735	20.303718
11	15.783599	16.645487	17.560293	18.531167	20.654583	24.349276
12	17.888451	18.977126	20.140720	21.384284	24.133133	29.001667
13	20.140643	21.495297	22.953385	24.522712	28.029109	34.351917
14	22.550488	24.214920	26.019189	27.974983	32.392602	40.504705
15	25.129022	27.152114	29.360916	31.772482	37.279715	47.580411
16	27.888054	30.324283	33.003399	35.949730	42.753280	55.717472
17	30.840217	33.750226	36.973705	40.544703	48.883674	65.075093
18	33.999033	37.450244	41.301338	45.599173	55.749715	75.836357
19	37.378965	41.446263	46.018458	51.159090	63.439681	88.211811
20	40.995492	45.761964	51.160120	57.274999	72.052442	102.443583
21	44.865177	50.422921	56.764530	64.002499	81.698736	118.810120
22	49.005739	55.456755	62.873338	71.402749	92.502584	137.631638
23	53.436141	60.893296	69.531939	79.543024	104.602894	159.276384
24	58.176671	66.764759	76.789813	88.497327	118.155241	184.167841
25	63.249038	73.105940	84.700896	98.347059	133.333870	212.793017
26	68.676470	79.954415	93.323977	109.181765	150.333934	245.711970
27	74.483823	87.350768	102.723135	121.099942	169.374007	283.568766
28	80.697691	95.338830	112.968217	134.209936	190.698887	327.104080
29	87.346529	103.965936	124.135356	148.630930	214.582754	377.169693
30	94.460786	113.283211	136.307539	164.494023	241.332684	434.745146
31	102.073041	123.345868	149.575217	181.943425	271.292606	500.956918
32	110.218154	134.213537	164.036987	201.137767	304.847719	577.100456
33	118.933425	145.950620	179.800315	222.251544	342.429446	644.665525
34	128.258765	158.626670	196.982344	245.476699	384.520979	765.365353
35	138.236878	172.316804	215.710755	271.024368	431.663496	881.170156
36	148.913460	187.102148	236.124723	299.126805	484.463116	1014.345680
37	160.337402	203.070320	258.375948	330.039486	543.598690	1167.497532
38	172.561020	220.315945	282.629783	364.043434	609.830533	1343.622161
39	185.640292	238.941221	309.066463	401.447778	684.010197	1546.165485
40	199.635112	259.056519	337.882445	442.592556	767.091420	1779.090308
41	214.609570	280.781040	369.291865	487.851811	860.142391	2046.953854
42	230.632240	304.243523	403.528133	537.636992	964.359478	2354.996933
43	247.776497	329.583005	440.845665	592.400692	1081.082615	2709.246473
44	266.120851	356.949646	481.521775	652.640761	1211.812529	3116.633443
45	285.749311	386.505617	525.858734	718.904837	1358.230032	3585.128460
46	306.751763	418.426067	574.186021	791.795321	1522.217636	4123.897729
47	329.224386	452.070320	626.862762	871.974853	1705.883752	4743.482388
48	353.270093	490.132164	684.280411	960.172338	1911.589803	5466.004746
49	378.999000	530.342737	746.865648	1057.189572	2141.980579	6275.405458
50	406.528929	573.770156	815.083556	1163.908529	2400.018249	7217.716277

TABLE 4 735

Table 4   Present Value of an Ordinary Annuity of $1 per Period: $P_{\overline{n}|i} = \dfrac{1 - \dfrac{1}{(1 + i)^n}}{i}$

n	$\frac{1}{2}$%	1%	$1\frac{1}{2}$%	2%	$2\frac{1}{2}$%	3%
1	0.995025	0.990099	0.985222	0.980392	0.975610	0.970874
2	1.985099	1.970395	1.955883	1.941561	1.927424	1.913470
3	2.970248	2.940985	2.912200	2.883883	2.856024	2.828611
4	3.950496	3.901966	3.854385	3.807729	3.761974	3.717098
5	4.925866	4.853431	4.782645	4.713460	4.645829	4.579707
6	5.896384	5.795476	5.697187	5.601431	5.508125	5.417191
7	6.862074	6.728195	6.598214	6.471991	6.349391	6.230283
8	7.822959	7.651678	7.485925	7.325481	7.170137	7.019692
9	8.779064	8.566018	8.360517	8.162237	7.970866	7.786109
10	9.730412	9.471305	9.222185	8.982585	8.752064	8.530203
11	10.677027	10.367628	10.071118	9.786848	9.514209	9.252624
12	11.618932	11.255077	10.907505	10.575341	10.257765	9.954004
13	12.556151	12.133740	11.731532	11.348374	10.983185	10.634955
14	13.488708	13.003703	12.543382	12.106249	11.690912	11.296073
15	14.416625	13.865053	13.343233	12.849264	12.381378	11.937935
16	15.339925	14.717874	14.131264	13.577709	13.055003	12.561102
17	16.258632	15.562251	14.907649	14.291872	13.712198	13.166118
18	17.172768	16.398269	15.672561	14.992031	14.353364	13.753513
19	18.082356	17.226009	16.426168	15.678462	14.978891	14.323799
20	18.987419	18.045553	17.168639	16.351433	15.589162	14.877475
21	19.887979	18.856983	17.900137	17.011209	16.184549	15.415024
22	20.784059	19.660379	18.620824	17.658048	16.765413	15.936917
23	21.675681	20.455821	19.330861	18.292204	17.332110	16.443608
24	22.562866	21.243387	20.030405	18.913926	17.884986	16.935542
25	23.445638	22.023156	20.719611	19.523456	18.424376	17.413148
26	24.324018	22.795204	21.398632	20.121036	18.950611	17.876842
27	25.198028	23.559608	22.067617	20.706898	19.464011	18.327031
28	26.067689	24.316443	22.726717	21.281272	19.964889	18.764108
29	26.933024	25.065785	23.376076	21.844385	20.453550	19.188455
30	27.794054	25.807708	24.015838	22.396456	20.930293	19.600441
31	28.650800	26.542285	24.646146	22.937702	21.395407	20.000428
32	29.503284	27.269589	25.267139	23.468335	21.849178	20.388766
33	30.351526	27.989693	25.878954	23.988564	22.291881	20.765792
34	31.195548	28.702666	26.481728	24.498592	22.723786	21.131837
35	32.035371	29.408580	27.075595	24.998619	23.145157	21.487220
36	32.871016	30.107505	27.660684	25.488842	23.556251	21.832253
37	33.702504	30.799510	28.237127	25.969453	23.957318	22.167235
38	34.529854	31.484663	28.805052	26.440641	24.348603	22.492462
39	35.353089	32.163033	29.364583	26.902589	24.730344	22.808215
40	36.172228	32.834686	29.915845	27.355479	25.102775	23.114772
41	36.987291	33.499689	30.458961	27.799489	25.466122	23.412400
42	37.798300	34.158108	30.994050	28.234794	25.820607	23.701359
43	38.605274	34.810008	31.521232	28.661562	26.166446	23.981902
44	39.408232	35.455454	32.040622	29.079963	26.503849	24.254274
45	40.207196	36.094508	32.552337	29.490160	26.833024	24.518713
46	41.002185	36.727236	33.056490	29.892314	27.154170	24.775449
47	41.793219	37.353699	33.553192	30.286582	27.467483	25.024708
48	42.580318	37.973959	34.042554	30.673120	27.773154	25.266707
49	43.363500	38.588079	34.524683	31.052078	28.071369	25.501657
50	44.142786	39.196118	34.999688	31.423606	28.362312	25.729764

Table 4   Present Value of an Ordinary Annuity of $1 (continued)

n \ i	3½%	4%	4½%	5%	5½%	6%
1	0.966184	0.961538	0.956938	0.952381	0.947867	0.943396
2	1.899694	1.886095	1.872668	1.859410	1.846320	1.833393
3	2.801637	2.775091	2.748964	2.723248	2.697933	2.673012
4	3.673079	3.629895	3.587526	3.545951	3.505150	3.465106
5	4.515052	4.451822	4.389977	4.329477	4.270284	4.212364
6	5.328553	5.242137	5.157872	5.075692	4.995530	4.917324
7	6.114544	6.002055	5.892701	5.786373	5.682967	5.582381
8	6.873956	6.732745	6.595886	6.463213	6.334566	6.209794
9	7.607687	7.435332	7.268791	7.107822	6.952195	6.801692
10	8.316605	8.110896	7.912718	7.721735	7.537626	7.360087
11	9.001551	8.760477	8.528917	8.306414	8.092536	7.886875
12	9.663334	9.385074	9.118581	8.863252	8.618518	8.383844
13	10.302738	9.985648	9.682852	9.393573	9.117079	8.852683
14	10.920520	10.563123	10.222825	9.898641	9.589648	9.294984
15	11.517411	11.118387	10.739546	10.379658	10.037581	9.712249
16	12.094117	11.652296	11.234015	10.837770	10.462162	10.105895
17	12.651321	12.165669	11.707191	11.274066	10.864609	10.477260
18	13.189682	12.659297	12.159992	11.689587	11.246074	10.827603
19	13.709837	13.133939	12.593294	12.085321	11.607654	11.158116
20	14.212403	13.590326	13.007936	12.462210	11.950382	11.469921
21	14.697974	14.029160	13.404724	12.821153	12.275244	11.764077
22	15.167125	14.451115	13.784425	13.163003	12.583170	12.041582
23	15.620410	14.856842	14.147775	13.488574	12.875042	12.303379
24	16.058368	15.246963	14.495478	13.798642	13.151699	12.550358
25	16.481515	15.622080	14.828209	14.093945	13.413933	12.783356
26	16.890352	15.982769	15.146611	14.375185	13.662495	13.003166
27	17.285365	16.329586	15.451303	14.643034	13.898100	13.210534
28	17.667019	16.663063	15.742874	14.898127	14.121422	13.406164
29	18.035767	16.983715	16.021889	15.141074	14.333101	13.590721
30	18.392045	17.292033	16.288889	15.372451	14.533745	13.764831
31	18.736276	17.588494	16.544391	15.592811	14.723929	13.929086
32	19.068865	17.873552	16.788891	15.802677	14.904198	14.084043
33	19.390208	18.147646	17.022862	16.002549	15.075069	14.230230
34	19.700684	18.411198	17.246758	16.192904	15.237033	14.368141
35	20.000661	18.664613	17.461012	16.374194	15.390552	14.498246
36	20.290494	18.908282	17.666041	16.546852	15.536068	14.620987
37	20.570525	19.142579	17.862240	16.711287	15.673999	14.736780
38	20.841087	19.367864	18.049990	16.867893	15.804738	14.846019
39	21.102500	19.584485	18.229656	17.017041	15.928662	14.949075
40	21.355072	19.792774	18.401584	17.159086	16.046125	15.046297
41	21.599104	19.993052	18.566109	17.294368	16.157464	15.138016
42	21.834883	20.185627	18.723550	17.423208	16.262999	15.224543
43	22.062689	20.370795	18.874210	17.545912	16.363032	15.306173
44	22.282791	20.548841	19.018383	17.662773	16.457851	15.383182
45	22.495450	20.720040	19.156347	17.774070	16.547726	15.455832
46	22.700918	20.884654	19.288371	17.880067	16.632915	15.524370
47	22.899438	21.042936	19.414709	17.981016	16.713664	15.589028
48	23.091244	21.195131	19.535607	18.077158	16.790203	15.650027
49	23.276565	21.341472	19.651298	18.168722	16.862751	15.707572
50	23.455618	21.482185	19.762008	18.255925	16.931518	15.761861

TABLE 4 737

Table 4   Present Value of an Ordinary Annuity of $1 (*continued*)

n \ i	7%	8%	9%	10%	12%	15%
1	0.934579	0.925926	0.917431	0.909091	0.892857	0.869565
2	1.808018	1.783265	1.759111	1.735537	1.690051	1.625709
3	2.624316	2.577097	2.531295	2.486852	2.401831	2.283225
4	3.387211	3.312127	3.239720	3.169865	3.037349	2.854978
5	4.100197	3.992710	3.889651	3.790787	3.604776	3.352155
6	4.766540	4.622880	4.485919	4.355261	4.111407	3.784483
7	5.389289	5.206370	5.032953	4.868419	4.563757	4.160420
8	5.971299	5.746639	5.534819	5.334926	4.967640	4.487322
9	6.515232	6.246888	5.995247	5.759024	5.328250	4.771584
10	7.023582	6.710081	6.417658	6.144567	5.650223	5.018769
11	7.498674	7.138964	6.805191	6.495061	5.937699	5.233712
12	7.942686	7.536078	7.160725	6.813692	6.194374	5.420619
13	8.357651	7.903776	7.486904	7.103356	6.423548	5.583147
14	8.745468	8.244237	7.786150	7.366687	6.628168	5.724476
15	9.107914	8.559479	8.060688	7.606080	6.810864	5.847370
16	9.446649	8.851369	8.312558	7.823709	6.973986	5.954235
17	9.763223	9.121638	8.543631	8.021553	7.119630	6.047161
18	10.059087	9.371887	8.755625	8.201412	7.249670	6.127966
19	10.335595	9.603599	8.950115	8.364920	7.365777	6.198231
20	10.594014	9.818147	9.128546	8.513564	7.469444	6.259331
21	10.835527	10.016803	9.292244	8.648694	7.562003	6.312462
22	11.061241	10.200744	9.442425	8.771540	7.644646	6.358663
23	11.272187	10.371059	9.580207	8.883218	7.718434	6.398837
24	11.469334	10.528758	9.706612	8.984744	7.784316	6.433771
25	11.653583	10.674776	9.822580	9.077040	7.843139	6.464149
26	11.825779	10.809978	9.928972	9.160945	7.895660	6.490564
27	11.986709	10.935165	10.026580	9.237223	7.942554	6.513534
28	12.137111	11.051078	10.116128	9.306567	7.984423	6.533508
29	12.277674	11.158406	10.198283	9.369606	8.021806	6.550877
30	12.409041	11.257783	10.273654	9.426914	8.055184	6.565980
31	12.531814	11.349799	10.342802	9.479013	8.084986	6.579113
32	12.646555	11.434999	10.406240	9.526376	8.111594	6.590533
33	12.753790	11.513888	10.464441	9.569432	8.135352	6.600463
34	12.854009	11.586934	10.517835	9.608575	8.156564	6.609099
35	12.947672	11.654568	10.566821	9.644159	8.175504	6.616607
36	13.035208	11.717193	10.611763	9.676508	8.192414	6.623137
37	13.117017	11.775179	10.652993	9.705917	8.207513	6.628815
38	13.193473	11.828869	10.690820	9.732651	8.220993	6.633752
39	13.264928	11.878582	10.725523	9.756956	8.233030	6.638045
40	13.331709	11.924613	10.757360	9.779051	8.243777	6.641778
41	13.394120	11.967235	10.786569	9.799137	8.253372	6.645025
42	13.452449	12.006699	10.813366	9.817397	8.261939	6.647848
43	13.506962	12.043240	10.837950	9.833998	8.269589	6.650302
44	13.557908	12.077074	10.860505	9.849089	8.276418	6.652437
45	13.605522	12.108402	10.881197	9.862808	8.282516	6.654293
46	13.650020	12.137409	10.900181	9.875280	8.287961	6.655907
47	13.691608	12.164267	10.917597	9.886618	8.292822	6.657310
48	13.730474	12.189136	10.933575	9.896926	8.297163	6.658531
49	13.766799	12.212163	10.948234	9.906296	8.301038	6.659592
50	13.800746	12.233485	10.961683	9.914814	8.304498	6.660515

INDEX

AAA (American Accounting Association), 99, 417
Account sales (see Consignments)
Accountability technique of accounting:
  bankruptcy, 554–556
  estates, 585, 591–592
  trusts, 598–600
Accountants International Study Group, 279,
  408–409, 501
Accounting changes, 270, 475
Accounting Principles Board (AICPA):
  Opinion No. 10, 100
  Opinion No. 16, 191, 192, 203–204, 210, 212,
    419
  Opinion No. 18, 71, 235, 314, 399
  Opinion No. 19, 431
  Opinion No. 20, 270
  Opinion No. 22, 253
  Opinion No. 23, 420–421
  Opinion No. 26, 367
  Opinion No. 28, 469–476
  Opinion No. 30, 405, 467–468
  Statement No. 4, 620–621
Accounting Research Bulletin (AICPA):
  No. 40, 196–197
  No. 48, 197, 200
  No. 51, 234, 355–356, 415, 417, 423
Accounting Research Study (AIPCA):
  No. 3, 99–100
  No. 5, 210
  No. 10, 210
Accounting Standards Executive Committee
  (AICPA):
  Proposed Statement of Position on Accounting
    Principles and Reporting Practices for
    Nonprofit Organizations Not Covered by
    Existing AICPA Auditing Guides, 670, 678,
    684
  Statement of Position 75-4, 477–479
AICPA (see American Institute of Certified Public
  Accountants)
American Accounting Association (AAA), 99, 417
American Institute of Certified Public Accountants
  (AICPA):
  "Accounting for Retail Land Sales," 111–113
  Accounting Trends & Techniques, 234
  action regarding business combinations, 203
  "Audits of Colleges and Universities," 670,
    675–676, 678, 679, 683, 684
  "Audits of State and Local Governmental
    Units," 613–614, 616–617, 619, 638, 640,
    641
  "Audits of Voluntary Health and Welfare
    Organizations," 670, 675, 678, 679, 683,
    684
  "Hospital Audit Guide," 670, 675, 678, 679, 683,
    684
  Statement on Auditing Standards No. 1, 669,
    670

Andersen, Arthur, & Co.:
  Accounting Standards for Business Enterprises
    throughout the World, 501
  annual report, 87–94
Arrangements (see Bankruptcy)

Bankruptcy:
  accounting: for arrangement, 558–560
    for corporate reorganization, 563
  accounting and reporting for receiver or trustee,
    554–556
  acts of bankruptcy, 546
  adjudication, 547
  appraisal of bankrupt's estate, 547
  arrangements, 556–561
  composition of Bankruptcy Act, 544–545
  confirmation of arrangement, 558
  corporate reorganization, 561–564
  creditors having priority, 545–546
  creditors' role, 546–548, 557–558
  discharge of bankrupt, 548–549
  dividends to creditors, 548
  footnote disclosure: of arrangement, 560–561
    of corporate reorganization, 563–564
  Form 8-K, 717
  insolvency, defined, 544
  involuntary petition, 546
  ordinary, 545–556
  petition: for arrangement, 557
    for reorganization, 561–562
  plan of reorganization, 562–563
  preference, 546, 548
  property claimed as exempt, 546
  proposed change in bankruptcy law, 564–565
  receiver, 547, 554–557
  reorganization compared to agreement, 564
  role of accountant, 549–554, 558–560, 563
  role of court, 547
  rules, 545
  statement of affairs (financial statement),
    549–554
  statement of affairs (legal document), 545
  statement of realization and liquidation, 555–556
  trustee, 548, 554–556, 562
  voluntary petition, 545
Bankruptcy Act, 544–545, 547–549, 556, 558
Branches and divisions:
  accounting system, 143–145
  alternative methods of billing merchandise
    shipments, 146–147, 155–165
  combined financial statements with home office,
    148, 154–155
  expenses incurred by home office, 146
  foreign, 520–523
  periodic inventory system, 162–165
  perpetual inventory system, 159–161
  reciprocal accounts, 145–146, 165, 168–170
  sales agency contrasted, 143
  segments of a business enterprise, 142–143
  separate financial statements, 147–148

Branches and divisions:
  start-up costs of new branches, 172
  transactions between, 170-172
  working paper for combined financial
    statements, 151-153, 160-161, 166-167
Business combinations:
  acquisition: of assets, 190
    of capital stock, 189-190
  allocation of cost of combinee, 192
  antitrust considerations, 188-189
  appraisal of accounting standards, 209-211
  bargain purchase, 192,209
  consolidated financial statements at date of
    combination, 233-254, 266-278
  contingent consideration, 192
  defined, 187
  determination of cost of combinee, 191-192
  establishing price for, 190
  exchange ratio, 190-191
  Form 8-K, 717
  Form S-14, 712
  goodwill, 192, 209, 242, 249, 251-253, 304,
    409-410
  income taxes of purchased subsidiary, 419-420
  methods of accounting, 191-196
  methods for arranging, 189-190
  "negative goodwill," 192, 209
  out-of-pocket costs, 191-192, 203, 269, 275
  pooling-of-interests accounting, 196-202, 210
  presentation and disclosure in financial
    statements, 206-209
  proxy statements, 718
  purchase accounting, 191-195, 202, 209-210
  reasons for, 188
  statutory consolidations, 198
  statutory mergers, 189
  tender offer, 189, 717,718
  working paper for postmerger income statement,
    207

CASB (*see* Cost Accounting Standards Board)
Clayton Act, 188
Compensating balances, 705-706
Consignments:
  account sales, 116-117
  accounting methods: for consignee, 117-120
    for consignor, 120-128
  defined, 114
  distinguished from sales, 115
  nature of Consignment In account, 119-120
  nature of Consignment Out account, 125, 128
  return of unsold goods by consignee, 124-125
  rights and duties of consignee, 115-116
  separate determination of gross profits, 120
Consolidated financial statements:
  advantages and shortcomings, 254, 299-300
  changes in parent company ownership interest
    in subsidiary, 404-409

Consolidated financial statements:
  choosing between equity method and cost
    method, 292-293
  consolidating financial statements working
    papers, 240, 242-243, 250-251, 269-272,
    275-277, 296-298, 304-308, 310-313,
    327-328, 331-333, 349, 351, 352, 355, 357,
    358, 361-364, 367, 370-373, 375-380,
    402-403, 408, 410-411, 413, 416, 418,
    423-426
  consolidation policy, 234, 253
  controlling financial interest, 235
  cost method of accounting for subsidiaries,
    291-293, 301, 309-314, 414
  date of business combination, 233-251,
    266-278
  developing consolidation elimination, 241-242,
    248-249
  discounting intercompany notes, 337-338
  entity theory, 278-280, 355
  equity method of accounting for subsidiaries,
    235-236, 291-309, 314, 325-334
  foreign subsidiaries, 234, 524
  income taxes, 339, 418-426
  indirect shareholdings, 416
  installment acquisition of parent company's
    controlling interest in subsidiary, 398-404
  intercompany leases, 338-339
  intercompany loans, 335-338
  intercompany management fees, 339
  intercompany profit: in depreciable assets,
    359-364, 425-426
    in intangible assets, 364
    in inventories, 349-356, 423-424
    in land, 357-359, 424-425
  intercompany profits and losses, 347-373,
    423-426
  intercompany sales: of merchandise, 348-356
    of plant assets and intangible assets, 356-364
  intercompany transactions not involving profit or
    loss, 334-339
  minority interest, 244, 248, 249, 251-253,
    278-280, 309, 333, 355-356, 362, 367, 381,
    404, 407-414, 416, 424-427
  nature of, 233-234
  parent company acquisition of minority interest,
    404
  parent company sale of portion of subsidiary
    stockholdings, 405
  parent company stock owned by subsidiary,
    417-418
  parent company theory, 278-280, 355
  partially owned pooled subsidiary, 273-278,
    330-334
  partially owned purchased subsidiary, 244-251,
    301-314
  purchase of affiliate's bonds, 364-373, 426
  reciprocal shareholdings, 416-417
  special problems, 398-432
  statement of changes in financial position,
    427-432

Consolidated financial statements:
  stock dividends of subsidiary, 414–415
  subsequent to date of business combination, 291–314, 325–334
  subsidiary with preferred stock, 409–414
  subsidiary issuance of additional shares to outsiders, 405–409
  treasury stock transactions of subsidiary, 415–416
  unconsolidated subsidiary, 235–236
  wholly owned pooled subsidiary, 267–273, 325–330
  wholly owned purchased subsidiary, 236–244, 293–301
Corporate reorganization (see Bankruptcy)
Cost Accounting Standard 403, 464–466
Cost Accounting Standards Board (CASB), 464
Cost method of accounting for subsidiaries, 291–293, 301, 309–314, 414

Depreciation:
  estates and trusts, 584, 591
  government entities, 617, 637, 640
  nonprofit organizations, 672, 678

Entity theory of consolidated financial statements, 278–280, 355
Equity method of accounting for subsidiaries, 235–236, 291–309, 314, 325–334
Estates and trusts:
  accounting: for estates, 585–593
    for trusts, 598–601
  charge and discharge statements, 593–596, 600
  claims of creditors against estates, 583
  closing entry for trust, 600–601
  closing estates, 584, 596
  distributions to devisees, 583
  estate and inheritance taxes, 583–584
  estates, defined, 581
  exempt property and allowances, 582–583
  legal and accounting aspects: of estates, 580–597
    of trusts, 597–601
  personal representative of decedent, 581–582
  probate of wills, 581
  Revised Uniform Principal and Income Act, 584–585, 598
  Uniform Probate Code, 580–584, 591, 597
  wills, 581

FASB (see Financial Accounting Standards Board)
Financial Accounting Standards Board (FASB):
  Discussion memorandum: "An Analysis of Issues Related to Accounting for Business Combinations and Purchased Intangibles," 187, 210–211, 253

Financial Accounting Standards Board (FASB):
  Discussion Memorandum: "An Analysis of Issues Related to Financial Reporting for Segments of a Business Enterprise, 459–460, 462–464
    "An Analysis of Issues Related to Interim Financial Accounting and Reporting," 476
  Financial Accounting in Nonbusiness Organizations, 684–685
  interest in accounting for nonprofit organizations, 684–685
  Interpretation No. 18, 475
  Statement of Financial Accounting Standards:
    No. 3, 475
    No. 4, 367
    No. 8, 504–507, 510, 518–520, 524–526
    No. 14, 458, 459, 461–464, 466, 467
    No. 18, 459
    No. 20, 507, 510
    No. 21, 459
"Financial Disclosure Practices of American Cities: A Public Report," 641
Financial forecasts:
  AICPA pronouncement, 478–479
  arguments: in opposition, 477
    in support, 477
  defined, 477
  illustration, 479–480
  importance of assumptions, 479
  SEC's position, 476, 719
  standards, 345–346
Financial statements:
  charge and discharge statement, 593–596, 600
  combined, 148, 154–155
  consolidated, 244, 253, 270, 273, 278, 427–432
  disclosure: of arrangements, 560–561
    of corporate reorganizations, 563–564
    of foreign currency matters, 524–525
  filings with the SEC, 714, 716, 717
  government entities, 628–629, 632–641, 643–652
  installment sales presentation, 112–114
  interim, 468–476
  nonprofit organizations, 684–689
  partnership, 16–17
  postmerger income statement, 207
  presentation and disclosure of business combinations, 206–209
  statement of affairs, 549–554
  statement of realization and liquidation, 50, 52, 53, 56, 57, 59, 60, 66–67, 555–556
Foreign currencies (see Multinational companies)

Goodwill:
  in business combination, 192, 209, 242, 249, 251–253, 304, 409–411
  "negative," 192, 209
  in partnership accounting, 23–27, 29
Government entities:
  accounting: for capital projects funds, 630–633

Government entities:
  accounting: for debt service funds, 633–635
    for enterprise funds, 636–638
    for general fund, 620–630
    for internal (intragovernmental) service funds,
      638–639
    for special assessment funds, 635–636
    for special revenue funds, 630
    for trust and agency funds, 639–640
  accounting entity, 615–616
  checklist for accounting, 642
  criticism of accounting, 641, 643
  encumbrance accounting technique, 617–618,
    624, 625, 632, 636, 637
  financial statements, 628–629, 632–641,
    643–652
  funds, defined, 615
  general fixed assets and general long-term debt
    groups of accounts, 640
  general obligation bonds, 630, 631, 633, 637,
    638, 640
  modified accrual basis of accounting, 616, 617
  nature of, 613–614
  performance budget, 619
  planning, programming, budgeting system
    (PPBS), 619
  program budget, 619
  prototype consolidated financial statements of
    U.S. government, 643–652
  recording budget, 618–621
  recording expenditures, 617
  recording purchase orders, 617–618
  revenue bonds, 633, 637
  special assessment bonds, 633, 635, 636
  theory of accounting, 614–621
  traditional budget, 619
  types of operating budgets, 619

Income taxes:
  exchange gains and losses, 520
  forward exchange contract, 511
  installment method, 110–111
  intercompany transactions, 339
  interim financial statements, 473–475
  out-of-pocket costs of business combination,
    196, 203, 269, 275
  paid on intercompany profits, 423–426
  purchased subsidiary, 419–420
  SEC requirements, 706–707
  undistributed earnings of subsidiary, 421–422
Installment method of accounting (see Installment
  sales)
Installment sales:
  accounting for retail land sales, 111–112
  cost recovery method of accounting, 98
  defaults and repossessions, 107–108
  financial statement presentation, 112–114
  installment method: of accounting, 98–108
    for income tax purposes, 110–111

Installment sales:
  interest on installment contracts, 109–110
  methods for recognition of profits, 97–98
  recognition of gross profit at time of sale, 97–98
  sales of merchandise on installment plan by
    dealer, 102–108
  single sale of real estate on installment basis,
    100–102
  special characteristics, 96–97
  trade-ins, 108–109
Interim financial statements:
  costs associated with revenue, 470–472
  costs and expenses other than those associated
    with revenue, 472
  disclosure, 475–476
  income tax provisions, 473–475
  misleading statements, 469–470
  problems, 469
  revenue, 470
Internal control:
  cash transactions at branches, 142
  expenses of branches, 145, 146
  inventories of branches, 147
International accounting standards (see
  Multinational companies)
International Accounting Standards Committee,
  501–502
International Federation of Accountants, 502
Investment Advisers Act of 1940, 702
Investment Company Act of 1940, 702

Joint ventures:
  accounting, 71–73
  corporate, 70–71
  defined, 70

Line of business reporting (see Segment reporting)

Mattel, Inc., 469–470
Minority interest (see Consolidated financial
  statements)
Multinational companies:
  accounting: for forward exchange contracts,
    507–516, 524
    for transactions involving foreign currencies,
      502–515
  actions to narrow differences in international
    accounting standards, 501–502
  consolidated or combined financial statements,
    515–525
  criticism of FASB Statement No. 8, 525–526
  current/noncurrent method of foreign currency
    financial statements translation, 517
  current rate method of foreign currency financial
    statements translation, 517–518
  defined, 500
  exchange gain or loss, 505–511, 513–515, 520,
    525
  exchange rates, 502–503
  financial statement disclosures, 524–525

Multinational companies:
  forward exchange contracts: for foreign
      currency exposed positions, 524
    to hedge foreign currency commitments in
        general, 507–510
    to hedge identifiable foreign currency
        commitment, 510–512
    for speculation, 512–515
  monetary/nonmonetary method of foreign
      currency financial statements translation,
      517
  standards for translation established by FASB,
      518–520
  temporal method of foreign currency financial
      statements translation, 516
  transactions involving foreign currencies,
      504–505
  translation of financial statements of foreign
      subsidiaries, 524
  two- and one-transaction perspectives, 506
  variations in international accounting standards,
      500–502

National Council on Governmental Accounting:
  Exposure Draft: GAAFR Restatement Principles,
      615–616, 643
  *Governmental Accounting, Auditing and
      Financial Reporting,* 621, 630, 638, 643
Nonprofit organizations:
  accounting for, 672–685
  agency fund, 681
  annuity fund, 681–682
  assets and liabilities of unrestricted fund,
      678–679
  characteristics, 671–672
  defined, 669
  depreciation, 678
  designated fund balance of unrestricted fund,
      672–673
  donated merchandise and services, 675
  endowment fund, 680
  expenses of unrestricted fund, 678
  financial statements, 684–689
  interest of FASB in accounting, 684–685
  life income fund, 682
  loan fund, 682
  plant fund, 678, 683
  pledges, 675–676
  restricted fund, 679–680
  revenue: from pooled investments, 676–678
    for services, 673–675
    of unrestricted fund, 673–678
  third-party payer, 674
  unrestricted fund, 672–679

Parent company (*see* Consolidated financial
    statements)

Parent company theory, 278–280, 355
Partnerships:
  adjustment of prior years' net income, 17–18
  admission of new partner, 20–27
  advance planning for installment payments to
      partners, 62–67
  bonus: to continuing partners, 30
    to managing partner, 15–16
    to new partner, 26–27
    to old partners, 23–26
    to retiring partner, 29
  capital accounts, 5–6
  changes in personnel, 19–30
  characteristics of, 2
  death of partner, 30
  defined, 1
  dissolution, defined, 19
  distribution of cash in liquidation, 48
  distribution of loss or gain from realization, 47,
      49
  division of net income or loss, 7–16
  drawing accounts, 5, 14
  equity in assets vs. share in earnings, 7
  goodwill: to new partner, 27
    to old partners, 23–26
    to retiring partner, 29
  income-sharing arrangements, 7–16
  income statement, 16–17
  incorporation, 69
  installment payments to partners in liquidation,
      60–69
  interest on partners' capitals, 11–13, 16
  limited partnerships, 2
  liquidation, 46–69
  loans to and from partners, 6
  marshalling of assets, 57–58
  organization, 2–6
  owners' equity accounts, 5–6
  partnership contract, 4–5
  retirement of partner, 28–30
  right of offset, 48
  salary allowances to partners, 13–16
  separate entity, 3–4
  statement of partner's capitals, 17
  statement of realization and liquidation, 50, 52,
      53, 56, 57, 59, 60, 66–67
  Uniform Partnership Act, 1, 7, 48
  valuation of partners' investments, 6, 25–26
Pooling-of-interests accounting (*see* Business
    combinations; Consolidated financial
    statements)
Prior period adjustments, 18, 272–273
Professional corporations, 1
Public Utility Holding Company Act of 1935, 702
Purchase accounting (*see* Business combinations;
    Consolidated financial statements)

Related party transactions, 6, 334–339, 347–373
*Report of the Advisory Commitee on Corporate
    Disclosure,* 718–719

Retail land sales (*see* Installment sales)
Revised Uniform Principal and Income Act,
   584–585, 598
Right of offset, 48, 119–120

Sales agencies (*see* Branches and divisions)
SEC (*see* Securities and Exchange Commission)
Securities Act of 1933, 702, 703, 711, 712, 716
Securities Exchange Act of 1934, 702, 703, 716,
   717
Securities and Exchange Commission (SEC):
   accounting and reporting, 702–719
   Accounting Series Releases (*ASRs*): defined,
      705
      No. 142, 705
      No. 148, 705–706
      No. 149, 706–707
      No. 150, 703, 705
      No. 180, 711
      No. 190, 707–709
   corporate reorganizations, 562, 564, 702
   financial forecasts, 478, 719
   Form C-D, 718
   Form 8-K, 717
   Form 10, 716, 718
   Form 10-K, 716
   Form 10-Q, 468–469, 716–717
   Form S-1, 712–716
   Form S-7, 712
   Form S-8, 712
   Form S-14, 712
   Form S-16, 712
   Form S-18, 718
   General Rules and Regulations under the
      Securities Exchange Act of 1934, 717
   interim financial statements, 468–470, 716–717
   organization and scope, 703, 704
   prospectus, 712
   recent developments in accounting and
      reporting, 718–719
   registration of securities under the 1934 Act,
      716
   registration statement under the 1933 Act,
      711–716
   Regulation C under the Securities Act of 1933,
      712
   Regulation 14A, 717–718
   Regulation 14D-1, 717, 718
   Regulation S-K, 467
   Regulation S-X, 705, 709–710, 715, 717, 719
   reporting by publicly owned companies,
      716–719
   requirements for segment information, 467
   role in establishment of accounting principles,
      703, 705
   role in initial offerings of securities, 711–176
   rules for proxies and tender offers, 717–718
   Securities Act Release No. 33-4936, 716
   Securities Act Release No. 33-5699, 478
   security, defined, 711

Securities and Exchange Commission (SEC):
   Staff Accounting Bulletins, 705, 711, 715, 717
   subsidiary issuance of additional shares to
      outsiders, 409
   supporting schedules, 709–710, 714–715, 717,
      718
Segment reporting:
   allocation of nontraceable expenses, 464–466
   background, 459
   definition of industry segment, 458
   disclosure of identifiable assets and other
      information, 466–467
   dominant segment, 461
   effects of disposal of segment, 467–468
   illustrations, 481–483
   intersegment sales or transfers, 462–463
   major customers, 462
   major issues, 459–460
   measure of segment income, 463–466
   operations: in different industries, 461
      in foreign areas and export sales, 462
   presentation of segment information, 467
   profitibility, 464
   reportable segments, 461
   revenue, 463
   SEC requirements, 467
   segment of business enterprise, defined,
      142–143
   segment contribution approach, 464
   segment operating results to be reported,
      462–467
   segment sales, 462–463
   significant segment, 461
   specification of segments, 460–462
   traceable expenses, 464
Subsidiary (*see* Consolidated financial statements)

Tender offer, 189, 717, 718
Transnational corporation (*see* Multinational
   companies)
Trust Indenture Act of 1939, 702
Trusts (*see* Estates and trusts)

Uniform Partnership Act, 1, 7, 48
Uniform Probate Code, 580–584, 591, 597

Westec Corporation scandal, 202
Working papers:
   combined financial statements for home office
      and branches, 151–153, 160–161, 166–167
   consolidating financial statements, 240,
      242–243, 250–251, 269–272, 275–277,
      296–298, 304–308, 310–313, 327–328,
      331–333, 349, 351, 352, 355, 357, 358,
      361–364, 367, 370–373, 375–380, 402–403,
      408, 410–411, 413, 416, 418, 423–426
   postmerger income statement, 207
   translation of foreign branch trial balance, 523